D1452410

Claude Bernard and
Animal Chemistry

This volume is published as part of a long-standing cooperative program between the Harvard University Press and the Commonwealth Fund, a philanthropic foundation, to encourage the publication of significant and scholarly books in medicine and health.

Claude Bernard and Animal Chemistry

The Emergence of a Scientist

Frederic Lawrence Holmes

A Commonwealth Fund Book
Harvard University Press
Cambridge, Massachusetts
1974

© *Copyright 1974 by the President and fellows of Harvard College*
All rights reserved
Library of Congress Catalog Card Number 73-88497
SBN 674-13485-0
Printed in the United States of America

To the memory of my father and mother:
Frederic Everett Holmes (1899–1972)
and Florence Jauch Holmes (1899–1969)

Contents

Illustrations

Foreword
Joseph S. Fruton

Claude Bernard achieved lasting fame as a physiologist and as a sage. The experimental achievement came first, through his discovery of the glycogenic function of the liver in 1848; his reputation as a philosopher grew steadily after the publication of his *Introduction to the Study of Experimental Medicine* in 1865. The adulation accorded the sage has tended to obscure the travail of the experimenter. In tracing Bernard's research during the 1840's, Professor Holmes has redressed the balance, and has shown the scientist at work in the laboratory. And hard work it was: the daily entries in Bernard's notebooks attest to his total immersion in the problems he examined, his readiness to expend intense effort and to repeat experiments many times, and his critical attitude toward his own results. In reading his notes, one senses that Bernard was under pressure to prove himself as a scientist; he was already in his thirties, and had not yet established himself in the highly competitive academic society he sought to enter. One also senses that although he had acquired masterly skill in experimental surgery, his command of chemical techniques was less certain, and that he was struggling to catch up with his younger contemporaries. The Claude Bernard of the 1840's who emerges from his research notes is altogether more convincing and interesting than the one depicted in the *Introduction* some twenty years later.

Professor Holmes has helped us to appreciate the limitations of a great scientist's later recollections of the events surrounding a discovery that made him famous. One readily understands the impulse to depict the achievement as a step-by-step use of sound reason and controlled experiment, rather than as a stumbling and assiduous testing of hunches suggested by the work of others. Unfortunately, such reminiscences often distort the historical record and nourish romantic illusions about the "scientific method" and how "breakthroughs" are made in science. By clarifying the record, the historian of science does not diminish the experimental genius of his subject; if, in the pages of this important book, Bernard's stature as a sage appears somewhat less, his qualities as a scientist and as a human being are greatly enhanced, and we see more clearly why he became the leading physiologist of the nineteenth century.

Preface

This book is principally the story of six important years in the scientific life of Claude Bernard. They are not the years usually stressed in biographical accounts of his career. The discoveries and writings which formed the base of his influence were concentrated between 1848 and 1865, and this period of his scientific "maturity" has received most attention. Much less has been written about the years between 1842 and 1848, during which the medical student and assistant to François Magendie evolved into an independent, creative investigator. Accounts of how Bernard acquired his mastery of physiological experimentation sometimes have an aura of mystery. Some writers have credited him with a prescient understanding from the beginning; they see in his earliest publications the mature methodology which resulted in his later discoveries.[1] Others, noting that the conclusions he presented in his first memoirs proved erroneous, have tried to define some later point at which he suddenly hit his stride. Thus Jean Louis Faure contends that when Bernard failed in a competition for a post in the Faculty of Medicine in 1844, this "healthy check cast him back completely to the life for which he was created." At that point he entered a period of "extraordinary fruitfulness," in which he "put to work his great power as an experimenter."[2] Bernard's best-known biographer, J. M. D. Olmsted, was less romantic, but he too saw a dramatic transition. "The beginning of Bernard's really effective and original scientific work, culminating in his first important discovery, followed closely on his marriage" in 1845. Olmsted guessed that the resulting release from his immediate financial anxieties might have removed a source of distraction, and that the new responsibility may have overcome a certain indolence in his temperament.[3]

Such interpretations were in part attempts to fill the vacuum left by the apparent paucity of information concerning Bernard's early activities. The few scientific articles he published before 1848 did not provide a broad enough picture of his research to indicate how he spent those years. Meanwhile a store of manuscript materials capable of providing a more realistic account remained largely unused. Brought together eventually at the Collège de France, where Bernard had done much of his experimentation and teaching, these documents were classified and catalogued between 1962 and 1965 by Professor Mirko Drazen Grmek.[4] Afterward Grmek used some of the laboratory notebooks in this collection to illuminate the background of a number of Bernard's most important discoveries.[5]

Bernard's laboratory notebooks enable one to follow his path month by month, sometimes from day to day. Fortunately they cover quite fully the period from 1842 to 1848. Although they do not include every experiment he performed during that time, they appear to be complete enough so that the whole pattern of his research can be reconstructed. From them one can depict not only the connections between his scattered publications, but the general process of the formation of an experimental scientist. The notebooks demonstrate that there is no need to invoke a psychological explanation for a change in Bernard's pace, because he worked almost unremittingly at his experiments throughout the period; nor was there any sudden change discernible in the quality of his work. This record makes clear that the germs of many of the concerns and ideas on which he concentrated in his later years were present very early. But these first years should not be seen as a mere preparation for the productive years ahead. They formed a distinct epoch in Bernard's life, within which he either solved or gave up some of the central problems with which he began. The resulting portrait of a talented but not fully proven man, aspiring toward goals which might well elude him, would be meaningful even if the later, more famous stage of his career had not followed.

Bernard's notebooks show that the papers he published in this period were only superficial markers of the trail he was following. He pursued certain problems with remarkable tenacity and limited success, while his most visible achievements came largely out of subsidiary investigations. His early research efforts were indissolubly linked with his later discoveries, yet he did not carry them out with a special foreknowledge of the road ahead, as some historical discussions of them have implied. A comparison of his investigations with those of his contemporaries discloses that although he sought to follow a highly individual course, and saw himself from the beginning as a reformer, he was nevertheless constrained to take into account advances by his colleagues and to adjust his directions according to the leads they provided. His early contributions were received with interest, but were not generally superior to the efforts of other men working on the problems with which he dealt. He was entering a vigorous field of activity, and it required six years of strenuous research for him to reach its forefront.

Bernard is revealed in his early notebooks as an extraordinarily complex man, whose scientific approach is not easily summarized. It was richer and more capricious than the idealized version he made famous in his *Introduction to the Study of Experimental Medicine*. Sometimes he was cautious and reflective, at other times boldly speculative. Sometimes he pursued new clues with inspiration, at other times he tenaciously clung to approaches which seemed to be getting him nowhere. His reasoning was often incisive, but occasionally vague, just as his experimental procedures were in some respects unusually rigorous but in other respects below the best standards of his time. Once in a while he hastily published results which he had not firmly established, though at other times he very carefully checked his findings before committing himself to them. Sometimes he was alert to exploit conclusions made public by his colleagues, but he also missed the significance of some of the most important initiatives in his field.

The examination of Bernard's investigations gives substance to one of his most revealing comments about himself. Late in his life he wrote:

For more than two years, at the beginning of my career, I wasted my time pursuing theories and chimeras. It is a remarkable fact, that one imagines that the truth is in himself, and I insisted on repeating experiments which insisted on responding to me always in the same way, contrary to my views. It was not until after a long deception that I ended by reflecting and thinking that the struggle was not equal and that my will could not change the laws of nature and that I could do no better than to follow the indications of natural phenomena, using theories as torches intended to illuminate the path and needing to be replaced as they were consumed.[6]

The record does not, however, support the notion that here at last is the explanation of that supposed sudden change in Bernard which separated inauspicious beginnings from his later successful investigations. For there appears to have been no such sharp transition as he remembered long afterward. He carried on that "unequal struggle" through almost all of the period which culminated in two of his greatest discoveries.

Although I have tried to portray in close detail the research Bernard carried on betweeen 1842 and 1848, I have not attempted to include all aspects of it. Of the several lines which he pursued I have focused entirely on his studies of digestion, nutrition, and related problems. He was at the same time deeply involved in experiments on the nervous system and the effects of poisons, and he participated in other shorter investigations. Each area, however, involved a separate set of issues, even though Bernard drew important connections between them. To describe fully the background for each field and yet preserve the continuity of Bernard's own research in a single narrative would make the story extraordinarily cumbersome. The fact that he himself kept these different facets of his research in separate notebooks seems a reasonable endorsement for treating them as distinct activities. Of these I believe that his investigations of digestion and nutrition shed the most light on his general scientific development. The complexity of the background is greatest because for these problems he was less able to rely on Magendie's experience than in the cases of the nervous system and of poisons. Very soon he had to begin to find his own way through a variety of other influences. This field also raised for him the most difficult problems for the definition of physiology itself, because of the intimate dependence of the subject upon chemistry. Finally, this research led in the relatively compact period of six years to an important resolution of one of the major issues through which Bernard tried to delineate his own distinctive approach to experimental physiology.

Limiting the central narrative to those few years, I have tried to follow the individual events comprising it as closely as the remaining record allows. The resulting length may appear excessive, but is essential to my purpose. It would be easy to select only the most interesting or crucial highlights; but to depict only the peaks in a terrain full of valleys and lower slopes would be to represent as discrete, neatly demarcated investigations, episodes which were actually linked in a single but multidirectional progression. Furthermore, to eliminate the steps which are not logically essential to explain that progression in retrospect would be to exaggerate the rationality, foresight, and singleness of purpose with which he pursued his path. It is important to see, for example, that at a point in which he had just found some clue germinal to an important later development, Bernard may with good reason have been equally interested in another aspect of the investigation which ultimately left no mark. Finally, the richness and fullness of Bernard's laboratory notebooks provide such an exceptional opportunity to follow the daily ventures of a gifted scientist that I felt the opportunity should be exploited as fully as possible. I found that each of the many episodes composing his research in these years had a particular interest and a distinctive pattern, usually with a few surprises. Bernard was too imaginative ever to allow his research to become routine. Those ideas which did not work out were often as fascinating as those which did. Each episode reveals something about the quality of Bernard's mind and work. I am only too aware that I have not always been able to convey the sense of excitement which lies hidden in the notebooks themselves, and that my exposition of details necessary to comprehend the moments of insight may sometimes grow tedious. Tedium is itself an essential side of scientific research, however, and it is difficult to sense the quickening pace at climactic moments if one has not felt the slowness of movement during the interludes between them.

Though the story centers on Claude Bernard, it is not oriented entirely in his direction. To portray his involvement in questions which transcended his particular point of view, it is necessary to understand from their own vantage points the roles of other men who took up the questions. I have devoted considerable space to such men. A substantial portion of the book narrates the ventures into animal chemistry of two organic chemists, Justus Liebig and Jean-Baptiste Dumas, and their respective supporters. Ever since Bernard treated their approach to the subject as an example of the wrong relationship between chemistry and physiology, historians have characterized the efforts of these men to deal with physiological phenomena mostly by their shortcomings.[7] I have tried to modify this perspective by following the development of this school independently of Bernard's attitude toward it. Then it becomes evident that despite the weaknesses he saw, the vision of the significance of the chemical phenomena of life that these chemists provided was highly important. Even those who, like Bernard, opposed their methods, were moved to view the phenomena differently from the physiologists who came before. Much of Bernard's early work and thought reflected his need to respond to them. The juxtaposition of detailed accounts of their story and his in the same book not only enables the reader to evaluate these interactions from both sides; it also highlights the striking contrast in the style with which these well-established chemists moved into a new area, and the way in which the fledgling physiologist set out to claim the same area for his own future activity.

The purpose of a book evolves as it is written. When I began I was examining Bernard's early years chiefly to find the sources of the opinions he maintained in his later writings, and the roots of his later successes. Only when I was well along did I begin to perceive him in those years as a person whose eventual success was not yet inevitable. His talents and determination gave the promise of future achievement, but he could easily have gone the way of many other bright young scientists in Paris, playing a minor part, gradually losing his drive for creative investigation, or finding insufficient support to continue. His strengths were tied to some serious limitations, and his avenue toward greatness was at first a narrow one. There was no guarantee that his will, insights, and technical skill would lead him to the heights of his field. It is best to imagine Bernard during the 1840's, therefore, not as a person advancing toward his position of the 1850's and 1860's, but as one whose fate was uncertain. During most of the period with which this book deals, the prospect of returning to Villefranche as a village doctor was as real for Claude Bernard as the prospect of ascent to the Académie des Sciences, the Académie Française, and the adulation of his peers.

This project would not have been possible without the generous help which Dr. Grmek has given me. He first drew my attention to the collection of Bernard's manuscripts at the Collège de France in 1963, while he was cataloguing them. When I arrived in Paris two years later his guidance rescued me from the bewilderment that the huge collection at first produced. His published catalogue, which appeared soon afterward, has been a valuable research tool, and his articles about Bernard have demonstrated the importance of the laboratory notebooks. I am grateful also to the administrator of the Collège de France, M. Etienne Wolff, for making the resources of that institution available in order to provide me with microfilms of a large number of items from the manuscript collection. Mlle. Oswald, the archivist of the Collège de France, was especially helpful in enabling me to see in a limited time the documents I needed. The archivist of the Académie des Sciences, Mme. Pierre Gauja, and her staff made my visits to that institution as pleasant as they were profitable, and supplied me with copies of many relevant materials. Dr. Geneviève Nicole-Genty, librarian of the Académie de Médecine, very kindly had made for me copies of two of Bernard's notebooks preserved there. Herr W. Leist, librarian of the University Library in Giessen, and Herr Hans Steil, director of the Liebig Museum there, devoted a great deal of time and effort not only to showing me the collections of manuscripts relating to Liebig, but to making my two days in Giessen a memorable experience. The efficient staffs of the Bayerische Staatsbibliothek and the Deutsches Museum in Munich enabled me to benefit greatly from the short time I was able to spend in those institutions.

Most of this book I wrote while a member of the Department of the History of Science and Medicine at Yale University. The support of the university, which granted me two leaves of absence for research, the encouragement of my colleagues, and the stimulating discussions with extraordinarily talented students, all helped overcome my natural tendencies to flag in the midst of a project which proved more extensive than I had foreseen. The convenience and pleasure of working in the Medical Historical Library of the Yale Medical Center more than compensated for my unsystematic habits. Having immediate access to published literature I needed made the writing immeasurably simpler than it otherwise would have been. The generous financial support made possible by NSF research grants GS-1988 and GS-3086, and USPHS training grant 5-TO1-LM-00103 gave me the opportunity both to conceive and to complete my plan. A grant from the Commonwealth fund has enabled the manuscript to be published without condensation.

Although I began my investigation of this topic prior to the publication of Joseph Schiller's important book *Claude Bernard et les problèmes scientifiques de son temps*, his study has helped me to clarify some aspects of my thoughts in ways that I may not have been able fully to account for in individual footnotes. I have profited even more from several stimulating discussions with him concerning our mutual interests in Claude Bernard. The hospitality of M. Jean Théodoridès has made my research visits to Paris more enjoyable, and his knowledge of Bernard has helped my own efforts. Four years ago I had the privilege of participating in a course on the history of biochemistry given at Yale by Dr. Joseph S. Fruton, a distinguished biochemist whose knowledge of nineteenth century science is as deep as that of most historians of science. His insights concerning the development of a field closely related to the present story have provided an important part of my education. His reading and careful criticisms of this manuscript have saved me from many inaccuracies. Professor Donald Fleming of Harvard read the manuscript and gave very valuable advice, including the suggestion to compare Bernard's conception of the relationship between chemistry and physiology with Auguste Comte's hierarchy of the sciences. Professor Fleming also provided strong encouragement at a time when it was most needed.

Miss Ulrike Rainer, who typed the manuscript, Miss Christine Tattersall, who did the later revisions, and Mrs. Janis Corrigall and Mrs. Elaine Osborne, who finished the work that remained after I came to the University of Western Ontario, contributed through their care, effectiveness, and good cheer, much more than those pages alone.

The editors with whom I worked at the Harvard University Press, Mr. Murray Chastain, Mrs. Ann Louise McLaughlin, and Miss M. Kathleen Ahern, made the publishing of the book a heartening and pleasant experience for me.

In the twilight of his life my father dutifully read the portion of this manuscript that was then finished, and seemed to derive enjoyment from it. I am grateful for those last times in which we were able to talk about it, for the book represents my effort to fulfill in my own way values I believe he demonstrated during his life.

For a long time my wife Harriet has shared my hopes for this book and has sustained my interest in it by never losing confidence that it would be finished and be worth the problems it created. Her unerring eye for a clumsy sentence has rid the final draft of a number of egregious examples. I am glad finally to be able to give a favorable report to the girls, Catherine, Susan, and Rebecca, who frequently renewed my effort by asking, "Daddy, how is your book coming?"

F.L.H.

Claude Bernard and
Animal Chemistry

Every one follows his own path. Some have been trained for a long time and proceed by following the track which had been marked out. I myself have reached the scientific arena by indirect ways and I have been freed from rules by running forth cross country, which others perhaps would not have dared to do. But I believe that in physiology that has not been bad, because it has led me to new views.

Claude Bernard, *Cahier de notes*, ed. M. D. Grmek (Paris: Gallimard, 1965), pp. 128–129.

I

Chemists, Physiologists, and the Problem of Nutrition

None of the many scientific articles and volumes of lectures that Claude Bernard produced has attained such renown as his *Introduction to the Study of Experimental Medicine*,* a book he wrote while illness kept him from his customary research and teaching. A major reason for its lasting appeal is that in it Bernard extracted from numerous particular experiences what he considered to be their most general consequences. Although he referred to his own past work for illustrations, he avoided getting so involved in the details of these background events as to distract from his focus on broad principles. While this approach gave the treatise its timeless quality, and the penetrating lucidity and simplicity which characterizes much of it, the resulting clarity is in some key passages more apparent than real. On close examination some of the central positions he took seem cryptic or ambivalent. What he really meant can sometimes be understood only by returning to the earlier experiences from which he had reached these conclusions. The point of view he expressed concerning one of the fundamental issues in biology, the relation between physics and chemistry and the investigation of living organisms, illustrates this problem.

At the beginning of his discussion defining the differences between "experimental practice with living beings" and that on inorganic bodies, Bernard wrote that physiologists make use of "instruments and

---

* *Introduction à l'étude de la médecine expérimentale.* All translations from references cited by German or French titles in the footnotes are my own. Ordinarily I have translated these titles in the text.

procedures borrowed from physics and chemistry in order to study and measure the diverse vital phenomena whose laws they seek to discover." But, confusion had frequently occurred, he added, because one has seen and often still sees chemists and physicists who, in place of limiting themselves to asking that the phenomena of living bodies furnish them with means or arguments appropriate to establish the principles of their science, try besides to absorb physiology and to reduce it to simple physico-chemical phenomena. They give explanations or systems of life which are sometimes beguiling by their misleading simplicity, but which in every case injure the biological science by introducing into it a false direction and errors which afterward require a long time to dispel. In short, biology has its special problem and its fixed point of view: it only borrows from the other sciences their aid and their methods, but not their theories.[1]

It is not easy to tell precisely what Bernard was saying in this and similar statements. One might infer that he was denying that vital phenomena are fundamentally physical-chemical processes; that he was maintaining, as he did elsewhere, that the manifestations of vital phenomena are determined by physical and chemical conditions but that they follow laws of a different order. Here, however, he was not defining ultimate modes of explanation, but methods of experimental practice. To take a stand that would not permit physiological phenomena to be treated as composed of physical-chemical ones would seem paradoxical for someone who had been one of the first to reduce a key physiological process to a reaction describable in chemical terms and reproducible in the laboratory with reagents extracted from the organism; or for one who at another time taught that in all physiological investigations "the grand principle is not to stop until one has reached, for the phenomena one is studying, the physico-chemical explanation suitable to them." [2] Clearly, in the above passage from his *Introduction* Bernard must not have meant to condemn all efforts to explain biology in terms of physical and chemical theories, but was complaining about the activities of certain chemists and physicists of his own time whose methods he could not sanction. Although physical theories such as those of Emil Du Bois-Reymond sometimes evoked this reaction from Bernard, his attitude was shaped principally by the activities of the chemists whom we shall discuss in the following chapters.

When Bernard began his first animal experiments in 1840 and 1841 under the guidance of François Magendie, he entered into the midst of a confrontation between chemistry and physiology. The rapid development of methods for identifying and analyzing organic compounds had made it essential to investigate such vital phenomena as respiration, digestion, and nutrition in the light of the new chemical knowledge. There were, however, divergent opinions concerning the most fruitful way to bring about this association. Those who were trained primarily as chemists often sought to treat biological problems by extensions of the methods they had found successful in their own fields, whereas those who were accustomed to dealing with organisms by anatomical studies or vivisection tried to absorb the principal results of the chemists' discoveries into views of physiological processes they had evolved from their own experience.

The chemical school was defined most distinctively in the efforts of followers of Antoine Lavoisier to extend the theory of respiration he had propounded near the end of the eighteenth century. Lavoisier had concluded that respiration is a form of combustion in which carbon and hydrogen are oxidized to carbonic acid and water, releasing caloric which accounts for the heat produced in warm-blooded animals. In principle he had demonstrated the equivalence of the processes by calorimetric measurements as well as by collecting and analyzing the gases exchanged in breathing. In practice, however, he left serious difficulties which occupied experimentalists throughout the next half-century. Prominently engaged in attacking these problems were the Parisian chemists of the early nineteenth century who carried on the chemical approach of Lavoisier, especially those of the circle around Claude Louis Berthollet and Pierre Simon de la Place in the Société d'Arcueil.[3] These two men, as well as Pierre Dulong, Cezar Despretz, Alexander von Humboldt, and François De la Roche took part in or encouraged respiration experiments with improved versions of Lavoisier's calorimeters, pneumatic chambers, gazometers, and analytical techniques. They attempted to determine more accurately whether the heat actually produced by an animal matches that due theoretically to the chemical reactions of respiration; to ascertain whether the site of the reactions is in the lungs or throughout the body; to measure the proportion between the oxygen inspired and the carbonic acid exhaled; and to detect if nitrogen is absorbed or released. Typically, in these experiments, the investigator placed an intact animal in a chamber arranged so that he could measure the net results of its chemical exchanges with the surrounding atmosphere, without delving into the complications of what happened within the organism.

While a few chemists struggled to produce conclusive empirical evidence for their conviction that combustion reactions must be the source of animal heat, the two outstanding physiologists of the time doubted the adequacy of the theory. In Germany, Johannes Müller weighed with skeptical detachment the evidence for and against the "chemical theory of heat," even though he recognized that most chemists accepted it. He acknowledged that the recent investigations of Dulong and of Despretz had shown that about seven tenths of the heat produced is accountable by the formation of carbonic acid; but chemists had acquiesced too readily, he believed, in Lavoisier's "bold hypothesis" that the inspired oxygen not accounted for in the exhaled carbonic acid must combine with hydrogen to form water, and that this supposed reaction is the source of the extra heat needed, according to Lavoisier's own experiments, to account for all of the observed animal heat. From Müller's viewpoint there was no proof that such a reaction takes place. Water vapor is found in the exhaled air, but this is more likely to be the result of simple evaporation from the warm moist surfaces of the pulmonary passages than of the oxidation of hydrogen. This unsubstantial hypothesis, invented, he claimed, simply to prop up the combustion theory of Lavoisier and Laplace, could for a long time be acceptable only to chemists, not to physiologists.[4]

Everett Mendelsohn has recently argued that those physiologists who cast doubt on the chemical theory of respiration were "often suspicious of chemical and physical analyses applied to the organism and more anxious to establish separate 'biological' laws to explain living things." Describing the objections of Benjamin Brodie as representative of many "life-oriented biologists," he concluded that they questioned not only the adequacy of a given chemical process to account for animal heat, but the acceptability of any chemical explanation of biological phenomena.[5] Such a generalization, however true it may have been for some men, cannot easily be applied to Müller, even though he was one of the most influential proponents of a special vital or organizing principle. Müller did not deny that chemical combustion is the source of a portion of the measured heat that he felt had been demonstrated experimentally to derive from it, and he encouraged further extension of chemical methods of investigation of the process. But as a physiologist he was concerned about aspects of the situation which were unimportant to chemists who regarded an animal primarily as the site of a combustion process. The variations in local heat production in different parts of an animal due to alterations in physiological conditions, for example, were to him important factors unaccountable by the simple chemical theory. Not being a chemist, on the other hand, he did not feel as firmly as they did that chemical processes are the only conceivable source of heat. That portion of

Claude Bernard in 1849

the animal heat for which chemists had not established to his satisfaction a chemical source he was willing to attribute to "organical processes" of unspecified nature and even to the unassailable activities of a vital principle.[6]

In France, also, the most eminent experimental physiologist of the early nineteenth century entertained some doubts about the chemical theory of respiration. As shown in a manuscript recently published by Jean Theódorides, François Magendie wondered whether, in spite of the great influence Lavoisier's conclusions had acquired, the similarity between combustion and respiration might not be less complete than generally supposed. Subjecting the ideas to a "severe logic," he thought, would show that though the deduction was natural and persuasive, it had not yet received the indispensable experimental proof.[7]

When Claude Bernard began his physiological training he was quickly exposed to both the prominence of and the doubts concerning the chemical theory of respiration. A notebook begun by Bernard in 1839, while he was still a medical intern, reflects these concerns. Following several topical sentences which summarized Lavoisier's theory of respiration, Bernard listed objections both to Lavoisier's view that combustion occurs in the lungs and to the alternative theory that it takes place in the blood. He then wrote (referring to a currently popular corollary of the chemical theory which ascribed the final conversion of nutrients into blood, a process known as hematosis, to the chemical effects of respiration during the passage of the nutrient fluids through the lungs): "Have the chemists not given an adventurous theory and is hematosis not a vital action." [8] It is not clear whether this was Bernard's own idea or a question raised by a lecturer to whom he was listening, but in either case the query reveals a germinal and skeptical influence on him regarding "the chemists."

Just as Bernard was undertaking his first experimental researches on physiological phenomena related to chemical processes, several dramatic developments focused intensified attention on these problems. The emergence of a new phase in their investigation is symbolized by three events which occurred in rapid succession in the summer of 1841. On July 5 and 26, and August 2, Magendie presented before the French Academy of Sciences a lengthy report of studies which had been carried on for ten years by a commission appointed originally to adjudicate claims for the nutritive value of gelatin. On August 20 Jean-Baptiste Dumas closed his course at the School of Medicine with a boldly conceived lecture entitled *Essai de statique chimique des êtres organisés*. In the same month Justus Liebig published in his *Annalen der Chemie und Pharmacie* the first results of investigations of the chemistry of animal nutrition which he had begun during the previous year. In the aftermath there followed research, theories, and debates that were critical to the founding of the field of animal nutrition. The participants, however, came into sharp conflict and revealed starkly the incompatibility of the respective assumptions, methods, and criteria of verification which the chemists and physiologists involved brought to the problem. The issues they raised posed challenges which Bernard had to take up as he searched for his own way to resolve the same general questions.

The results which Magendie announced on behalf of the Gelatin Commission had been long awaited. For nearly fifty years scientists, physicians, administrators, and public benefactors in France had been concerned about the nutritive qualities of gelatin. During the eighteenth century, before chemical criteria for distinguishing different types of substances extractible from animal matter had been established, gelatin had often been regarded as the basic nutrient substance from which the tissues of the body are formed. [9] The fervor for relieving the plight of the poor during the period following the French Revolution led many people to advocate making bouillon with gelatin extracted from bones. Besides forming a cheap nutrient, they believed, it would utilize for the public good a resource previously wasted. A government directive even proclaimed it a national objective to encourage the use of gelatin bouillon. Among the enthusiasts for gelatin was the chemist Jean D'Arcet, who thought that the public resistance to eating gelatin extracted from bones would disappear if the naturally insipid taste and odor of the substance were overcome by adding the proper seasoning. When D'Arcet died in 1801, his son Joseph dedicated himself to fulfilling his father's hopes. In 1812 the young D'Arcet developed a new method to extract gelatin cheaply on a large scale, using hydrochloric acid to dissolve the calcium phosphate out of the bones. He then invited the Philanthropic Society to use gelatin made by his process in the bouillon and soup which that organization distributed to convalescents and poor people. The Society in turn asked the Faculty of Medicine for an opinion concerning the nutritive value and salubrity of D'Arcet's gelatin. Five commissioners appointed by the Faculty to respond to the question reported back in 1814 that everyday experience, as well as the opinions of many authors who had written on the topic, left no doubt that gelatin was the most nutritive constituent of animal matter. To make certain that D'Arcet's gelatin was healthful, the commissioners fed forty patients in the internal clinic of the Faculty of Medicine a special bouillon containing it. Using one fourth of the meat normally used in the preparation of beef bouillon, they replaced the remainder with gelatin and vegetables. The other three fourths of the meat they served as roasts. After three months of this diet they observed no ill-effects, and they expressed enthusiasm in their report for the dietary improvement that could be achieved at such low cost by using gelatin in this way.[10]

D'Arcet was greatly encouraged by this support, and his confidence was further increased by a memoir which Magendie published in 1816. Magendie had fed several dogs diets respectively of pure sugar, olive oil, gum, and butter. The dogs all died within a little more than thirty days, from which Magendie concluded that animals must have a source of nitrogen in their food.[11] These experiments have been considered the beginning of the scientific investigation of nutrition; for the first time animals were submitted over an extended period of time to a diet "whose chemical composition would be rigorously controlled."[12] To D'Arcet the outcome of Magendie's research simply confirmed that he himself had been on the right track. The diet of the indigent, based largely on vegetable matters, was poor in nitrogen. The addition of gelatin, a nitrogenous substance, supplied the nitrogen necessary to "render the aliment complete." [13] Determined now to persevere until he had made gelatin available for widespread use, D'Arcet patented in 1817 another process for extracting the substance by passing steam continuously under low pressure through a chamber containing crushed bones. During the next decade he perfected the apparatus until the operation could be carried out inexpensively on a large scale. By 1828 several hospitals in Paris were beginning to set up the equipment and supply gelatin bouillon to their patients.[14] The director of the royal medallion mint, M. A. de Puymaurin, established a system for serving free gelatin soup to his workers to help them conserve their wages. He suggested similar installations for naval ships and armies in the field, estimating in elaborate detail the savings to be realized by substituting gelatin bouillon for ordinary bouillon.[15]

These activities soon evoked skeptical reactions. Alfred Donné, the chief of the clinic at the Charité, the first hospital to adopt the system for supplying gelatin, was a zealous supporter of the plan until he began to hear complaints from the other physicians. Forming his own doubts then, Donné decided to test the nutritive properties of gelatin on himself and on two dogs. For six days he replaced what he ordinarily ate between eight in the morning and six in the evening with gelatin and a small amount of bread, while maintaining his customary dinner. During that time he felt faint and hungry, and he lost two pounds. The dogs refused to eat gelatin at all, even after he had given them nothing else for several days. Consequently, Donné read a memoir to the Academy of Sciences in June 1831 in which he questioned the current use of gelatin.[16] His action brought other criticisms to the surface. D'Arcet countered by obtaining letters from supervisors at the Saint-Louis Hospital who declared that his process had functioned well there for two years. It delivered a clear bouillon which had caused no complaints and had produced a "sensible improvement" in the nutrition of the patients.[17] Already, however, there were rumors that the bouillon made at the Hôtel-Dieu, one of Paris's most important hospitals, was less satisfactory. In November, thirteen physicians, surgeons, and pharmacists of that hospital reported that the gelatin had a nauseous odor and putrified rapidly in warm weather. The bouillon made with it was turbid, and its unappetizing aroma made it repugnant to many of the patients. There was no proof, they asserted, that gelatin possessed any nutritive value. A medical student had subsisted for four days on gelatin and bread and had experienced a variety of digestive disorders. The economic benefits were, they claimed, minimal, and often cancelled out by the need to throw away the gelatin that spoiled. They recommended the immediate suppression of the program, and the Hôtel-Dieu soon afterward discontinued it. Among those who signed the recommendation was Magendie.[18] Meanwhile, a chemist and pharmacist, who now managed a glue factory, was stimulated by Donné's memoir to undertake further experiments with gelatin. Jean-Nicholas Gannal fed himself, his family, and a group of medical students gelatin for several weeks, at the end of which they had acquired such a violent distaste for the substance that they were forced to discontinue the investigation. On gelatin alone they suffered violent headaches and other disturbances. Gelatin mixed with considerable bread provided a sufficient nourishment, but no better, they thought, than the same quantity of bread together with pure water. Gannal concluded that gelatin was not only useless, but harmful, and he began a campaign to force the hospitals to stop serving it.[19]

The Academy of Sciences appointed a commission, chaired by Louis-Jacques Thenard, to evaluate Donné's memoir. Magendie and Michel Eugène Chevreul were also members, and Dumas joined the commission soon after he entered the Academy in 1832. In 1834 D'Arcet himself was nominated to the commission, a position he accepted with some misgiving.[20] The task of the commission, soon known as the Gelatin Commission, expanded rapidly beyond the bounds of Donné's work. Testimonials began to come from institutions in various parts of France where D'Arcet's process had been used and considered highly valuable;[21] other institutions reported that they had given up the use of gelatin. D'Arcet defended his efforts tenaciously, arguing that where the gelatin had been found wanting it was because administrators or workers had failed to carry out the process according to his instructions.[22] He sought to arrange a large-scale test by having an army expedition supplied with biscuits containing gelatin.[23] The controversy entered the public press, where the *Gazette médicale* expressed particularly hostile opinions concerning gelatin.[24] While the debate continued it became clearer, as Donné pointed out in 1835, that several distinct issues were involved. On one level was the question whether there was chemical justification for defining gelatin as a nutrient material. It was quite a different matter, however, to determine experimentally whether gelatin had real nutritive value, and still another matter to establish whether the substance could be served economically and beneficially in public institutions.[25] For none of these questions was there sufficient evidence to give a clear answer, yet the stakes for social policies were high enough to demand some sort of authoritative decision. Gannal added a further dilemma by condemning the public morality of "experimenting" on involuntary subjects by continuing to feed patients gelatin in the hospitals before the Gelatin Commission had pronounced on the issue.[26]

Faced with all these pressures, the Gelatin Commission gathered reports, inspected institutions which served gelatin, and made simple chemical analyses of the bouillon produced by D'Arcet's procedure; but year after year it remained officially silent. Those people directly involved in the question grew increasingly impatient. Gannal repeatedly asked the Academy to take action.[27] D'Arcet found himself in a very unpleasant position. As a member of the commission he felt he could not speak out publicly until it finished its investigation, but in the meantime a cloud of uncertainty hung over his life work.[28] In 1836 Magendie finally began to carry out for the commission a series of feeding experiments on dogs. When François Arago expressed dissatisfaction with the length of time the commission had taken, during a meeting of the Academy in December 1838, Magendie claimed that the body was pursuing its work zealously and would soon present its report.[29] Eighteen more months passed, however, and in June 1840 the Minister of the Interior called upon the Academy to hasten the work of the commission. Thenard then announced that the experiments were completed, and Magendie, who was writing the report, added that he was nearly ready to communicate it;[30] but it took him another year to make good on his promise.

The first portion of Magendie's report was a historical survey of the gelatin question, the remainder an account of the experiments the commission had carried out. They had fed dogs gelatin in pure form, seasoned, and mixed in different proportions with bread, with meat, or with both. They compared diets of bread and the gelatin bouillon produced at the Saint-Louis, the hospital which had achieved the most favorable results with D'Arcet's process, to diets of bread and an equivalent amount of good meat bouillon. Many unforeseen difficulties interfered with their results. The dogs would not eat pure gelatin at all, and even some of the mixtures they turned down after the first few days. The commission decided, however, that either the refusal of a substance or loss of weight during the period in which an animal subsisted on it was evidence that it was an "insufficient nutrient." They concluded that gelatin itself was not an adequate nutrient, but that it could be added to other nutrients within certain limited proportions without harmful effects. In order to make their results more meaningful, however, the members of the commission had decided that they should compare them with similar experiments using other "immediate principles" analogous to gelatin. In this way, as Magendie explained, their work underwent "an immense extension" until it became "a veritable study of alimentation in general." [31]

The investigators first tried feeding the dogs albumin in the form of egg-white. The dogs would not eat it, even mixed with bread. The result was surprising, for unlike gelatin, whose preparation involved an alteration of the matter contained in bones, the albumin was used in its natural form. Furthermore, as a characteristic constituent of blood as well as of eggs, albumin had long been regarded as a principal source of the substance of the animal body. Even more unsettling was the case of blood fibrin.[32] Since 1785, when Antoine Fourcroy showed that the properties of blood fibrin appeared identical to those of muscle fiber,[33] fibrin had been considered, as Magendie put it, "the nutritive substance *par excellence*," needing only to coagulate and become organized in order to form the principal element of animal tissue. The dogs learned to eat pure fibrin extracted from beef blood, but they nevertheless gradually lost weight, and one died of starvation after two months. Because Magendie had found in his earlier work that single "immediate principles" do not provide adequate nourishment, he tried various mixtures of albumin, fibrin, and gelatin, but even then the dogs developed all the signs of inanition. This result seemed paradoxical to him, for he considered meat, which is a complete, excellent nutrient, to be merely a natural mixture of the same principles he had mixed artificially. Just as puzzling was the fact that gluten, a substance derived from vegetables, was alone of those he tried able to sustain the dogs indefinitely.[34]

Faced with all of these unpredictable results, Magendie was understandably cautious in the conclusions he drew on behalf of the commission. He only summarized the results so far obtained, suggested areas for continued research, and added, "Have we not above all made it evident that science is still in its first steps in every aspect of the theory of nutrition?" [35] Similarly, while describing the unforeseen result with fibrin, he said that it "shows how much we have to do before we shall have even an approximate theory of nutrition." [36]

The report of the Gelatin Commission substantiated the claim that its members had earlier made to explain their delays; the task they were charged with was "immense," and had forced them to "undertake a multitude of minute, delicate, and very tedious experiments." [37] The great variety of alimentary conditions they needed to consider required them to make hundreds of experiments, and in order to make the effects of a given aliment evident they had to prolong many of these tests for as long as three or four months. They found no clear standards to guide them in determining what an adequate nutrient is, either quantitatively or qualitatively. Before they could ascertain, for example, whether any particular diets were any better than no food at all, they had to starve twenty-two dogs to death to determine for how long a time dogs of different ages can survive without nourishment.[38] Nevertheless, the technical obstacles they encountered cannot account for all the time the commission took to deliver its first report. Much of it must be ascribed to the political influences confronting them, to deep divisions of opinion among the members of the commission itself, and perhaps to a reluctance to handle a problem which must have appeared overwhelming.

Under such circumstances, it is hardly surprising that Magendie's report satisfied almost no one. He had read the historical introduction, at the session of July 5, while D'Arcet was away from Paris. When D'Arcet returned, he was upset that after waiting so long the commission had suddenly acted in his absence; and he complained that Magendie had given a biased account, passing over all documents favorable to gelatin and dwelling at length on those which aroused prejudice against it or even ridiculed it.[39] Suspecting that the introduction was a prelude to a condemnation of gelatin, D'Arcet demanded that the commission reach a definitive agreed position before Magendie continued his report.[40] As a result, its further presentation was delayed for two weeks,[41] and it may well have been in part because of D'Arcet's action that in the end the document made no general pronouncement about the policy of using gelatin as a food. That omission, however, brought the commission trouble from other quarters. When Magendie had finished reading his report, the Academy discussed whether or not to accept it. Ducrotay de Blainville objected that the commission had not judged Donné's memoir as it had been instructed, but had presented instead independent research by its own members. The majority of the assembly, including Magendie, accepted this view, so that the report did not receive the official sanction of the Academy. When de Blainville asked Magendie what the commission thought about the original question, whether gelatin mixed with other nutrients could be usefully employed as a dietary supplement, Magendie admitted that they had reached no answer. This outcome annoyed many who had waited ten years for a verdict on the continued use of gelatin in public institutions.[42] Gannal was so discontented that he published an open letter to Thenard, for whom he had once served as a chemical assistant, calling on Thenard as president of the commission to demand the suppression of gelatin in the hospitals. Since the commission had found gelatin not to be a "good aliment," in fact none at all, Gannal considered it indefensible of Magendie and of the Academy to condone its further use.[43] As we shall see, chemists such as Liebig and Boussingault, who were concerned with animal nutrition, were dissatisfied with the Gelatin Commission for other reasons. Holding quite different criteria for the judgment of nutritive value, they considered Magendie's experiments ill-conceived and his conclusions unjustified. The Gelatin Commission was suffering the fate which all too often befalls scientists when science is invoked to solve problems dictated by social needs, rather than problems predicted by the state of the science of the time to be solvable. There were simply not sufficient conceptual or technical means available to answer the questions put to the commission, so that its efforts to respond were doomed to appear inadequate. Its immediate embarrassment obscured the fact that the practical demand had stimulated Magendie and his colleagues to undertake a study of great significance for the longer-range development of the science of nutrition. Compared to the rather cursory feeding experiments of Donné, Gannal, and others, those carried out by the commission set entirely new standards of thoroughness. If the commissioners did not obtain any conclusive answers, they at least revealed more than anyone had known about the degree of effort which would be required even to pursue the questions.

The activities of the Gelatin Commission served to initiate Claude Bernard into the experimental investigation of animal nutrition. In 1840 and 1841, the first years in which Bernard worked extensively in the laboratory of the Collège de France under the direction of Magendie, he was mostly involved with research on the nervous system.[44] He also carried out for Magendie, however, a number of extended feeding experiments forming part of Magendie's program of research for the commission. On January 16, 1841, Bernard began comparative feedings of boiled and raw bones to two dogs. The dog on the former diet lost weight until it died on the fifty-ninth day, while that on the latter remained healthy and gained weight. On March 23 he began feeding the second dog exclusively beef tendons. After seventeen days the dog refused to eat any more until it was given raw bones. Bernard fed another dog mutton bones, the phosphates of which had been removed with hydrochloric acid, for two weeks, then switched it to gelatin derived from similar bones by digesting them in warm water. As soon as the dog started on the second diet it began to grow thin and lose its vivacity, and it died on the thirteenth day. Another dog treated similarly was dead on the eighteenth day.[45] These results were incorporated into the report of the commission as evidence that the parenchyma of the bones from which gelatin is made comprises a complete nutrient, but that the conversion of that substance to gelatin destroys some of its nutrient properties.[46]

At the meeting following the completion of Magendie's report, the Academy voted to ask the commission to "continue the work which it has begun." [47] Bernard again participated in its investigations. In July 1842 he began a series of experiments in cooperation with D'Arcet, in which he gave four dogs a daily ration of soup containing white bread, water, and lard. After a week each animal had gained weight, and Bernard reduced the portions during the following week. That change caused the dogs to lose weight, so he began feeding them daily portions intermediate between those of the first and the second week. Over the next month the dogs sometimes lost and sometimes gained weight. Apparently Bernard was trying to establish a barely adequate or slightly insufficient diet in order to test whether or not adding gelatin to it would improve it. Having settled on a soup containing 145 grams of bread and 15 grams of lard, he began in September to add to each ration ten grams of gelatin sent to him by D'Arcet, mixing it with the soup according to D'Arcet's instructions. At first some of the dogs gained and some lost weight, but over the next month they gradually stopped eating the soup and grew thinner and weaker until Bernard halted the experiment. On November 6 he began a second series of experiments. He fed three dogs on the previously established quantity of ordinary soup and three on the same soup with twenty grams of gelatin added. This time he seasoned both soups with a mixture of salts. Over a period of a month all the dogs but one continued to eat the soups. The dogs on each type of diet lost weight, but all remained healthy.[48] When Bernard sent the records of the first twenty days of the experiment to D'Arcet, the latter was convinced that they vindicated his belief in the value of adding gelatin, for the dogs that had eaten the gelatinous soup had "lost the least weight." [49] This was clearly a partisan evaluation of the outcome. At the time D'Arcet gave his opinion the figures were:

Dogs on ordinary soup	*Dogs on gelatin soup*
1. lost 275 grams	4. lost 330 grams
2. gained 20 grams	5. lost 300 grams
3. lost 925 grams	6. lost 55 grams

By the end of the experiment the numbers were somewhat more favorable to gelatin:

Dogs on ordinary soup	*Dogs on gelatin soup*
1. lost 325 grams	4. lost 940 grams
2. lost 1790 grams	5. lost 175 grams
3. lost 630 grams	6. lost 340 grams [50]

Yet the results hardly comprised an unequivocal demonstration that such a supplement of gelatin could turn the soup into a complete nutrient.

There is no record of what significance Bernard attributed to his results. Most likely he was mainly impressed with the complexity of the phenomena of nutrition, and he must have acquired the conviction of his mentor, Magendie, that only rigorous experiments on live animals, such as those the commission was performing, could offer hope of eventual solutions. But Bernard came into contact with other influences as well through this research. For chemical analyses of the nutrient substances he and Magendie relied on the talents of other scientists. Thus Bernard sent samples of mutton and beef bone to Dumas for a comparative analysis. When he found an insoluble substance in another bone he sent it to Apollinaire Bouchardat, the chief pharmacist of the Hôtel-Dieu and professor of hygiene of the Faculté de Médecine, to determine its nature. Edmond Frémy, one of the most accomplished of the younger chemists in France, analyzed for Bernard the excretory materials of the dogs in one of the experiments.[51] Thus Bernard's involvement in an investigation of great interest to the scientific and medical community of Paris helped him to become acquainted with some of its leading figures. These men were also deeply interested in questions related to nutrition, but approached them in ways different from Magendie's approach. Their views too became important for Bernard's own scientific course.

When Jean-Baptiste Dumas delivered his lecture on the "chemical statics" of plants and animals in August 1841, he appeared to be making a sudden move into a new field. For nearly two decades Dumas had been known mainly for his analyses and interpretations of the composition of organic compounds. Besides characterizing such substances as the plant alkaloids, oxamide and methyl alcohol and its related compounds, Dumas had proposed and vigorously defended a general theory of the composition of ethers. In 1840 he was pressing for the acceptance of his "law of substitutions" and his "theory of

Jean-Baptiste Dumas

types," two conceptions with which he hoped to revise current views concerning the classification and structure of organic molecules.[52] None of these activities was immediately related to the nutritional processes of living organisms. Yet from the beginning of his career Dumas had been more concerned with such questions than the printed record of his research up until 1841 would indicate. As a young man in Geneva he had undertaken with the physician J. L. Prévost a series of impressive investigations in a wide variety of biological problems. Among these was a study of digestion in which he participated with Prévost and a pharmacist named Le Royer.[53] When Dumas decided in 1822, after a visit from Alexander von Humboldt, to come to Paris, he chose to focus his efforts on chemistry. Fourteen years later his interest in physiological phenomena was revived through the work of Jean-Baptiste Boussingault.

Boussingault had returned to France in 1832 after a colorful ten-year career in South America, where he had alternated scientific expeditions with military adventures in the service of the *Libertador* of the continent, Simón Bolívar. A year later Boussingault acquired through his marriage a large farm at Bechelbronn in Alsace. There he set up a laboratory and began a long series of experiments in agricultural chemistry. Just before leaving South America he had noticed with fascination that the very sterile soil of coastal Peru was rendered highly fertile by applying guano, a substance composed mostly of ammoniacal salts. With that in mind, he undertook on his farm an investigation of the source of nitrogen in plants. In 1836 he completed analyses of the proportions of nitrogen in various crops; he proposed to use the nitrogen content as a measure of their nutritive value, justifying his choice by Magendie's experimental demonstration of the necessity for nitrogen in animal diets.[54] Next he carried out a set of highly ingenious experiments in order to determine whether plants can absorb nitrogen from the atmosphere. He caused seeds of clover and of wheat to germinate in sterile soil, so that they could draw materials only from distilled water and from carefully filtered air. He then compared the quantities of carbon, hydrogen, oxygen, and nitrogen in the seeds to the quantities of the same elements in the germinated seedlings. The surprising outcome was that the nitrogen content of the clover increased, whereas that of the wheat remained the same. Some plants, therefore, could obtain their nitrogen from the air, whereas others required a source of nitrogen in the soil. Both types gained carbon, hydrogen, and oxygen, confirming the accepted view that plants draw these elements from the water and the carbon dioxide of the air.[55] Boussingault applied the same principles on a practical scale by measuring the yields of the four elements from crops grown in the field. Determining the total quantity of these elements accumulated by the plants on a given acreage during a complete cycle of crop rotation, and subtracting from this the amounts supplied to the field in the fertilizer, he found the net gain which each of several rotation systems could provide over that which the soil must furnish to them.[56]

Boussingault became associated with Dumas just as these investigations were beginning to look impressive. In 1836 Dumas replaced Thenard in the latter's organic chemistry course at the Sorbonne, and asked Boussingault in turn to substitute for him at the École polytechnique for the academic year 1836–37.[57] During the next four years Dumas followed with growing enthusiasm the progress of Boussingault's investigations. When Boussingault submitted two memoirs on the topic to the Academy of Sciences in 1838 and 1839, Dumas was among the referees appointed to examine them, and in both cases he wrote the reports. Praising the work highly, Dumas emphasized that its significance was less in the specific results Boussingault had obtained than in the method he had created. By applying to the problem of plant growth the combustion method of elementary analysis developed for the investigation of organic compounds, and by extending his experiments over long time periods, Boussingault had made possible the investigation of processes which some scientists had thought to be beyond the reach of analysis.[58] Boussingault had, according to Dumas, "introduced the use of the balance in the study of questions of general physiology."[59] Since the balance symbolized for chemists of the period the basis on which their science had been built since Lavoisier had introduced quantitative methods, Dumas meant, in effect, that Boussingault was bringing the rigor of modern chemistry to a field which had not previously enjoyed comparable certainty or precision.

Although the experiments of Boussingault which Dumas discussed before the Academy concerned only plants, Dumas depicted their significance in the broader terms of the material balances between the organisms living on the surface of the globe. By their respiration, he pointed out, animals render to the air the water and carbon dioxide which plants absorb and from which they again supply animals with carbon and hydrogen in their food. The great merit of Boussingault's research, Dumas added, was that it showed a similar exchange takes place for nitrogen. Plants derive from the air the nitrogen which herbivorous animals acquire from the substance of the plants.[60] In his second report Dumas wrote, in January 1839, that Boussingault's experiments, "encompassing the action of plants on the water, on the air, and on fertilizers, that of animals on the aliments and on the air itself, lead toward the foundation, through accurate analyses, of the true statics of animals and plants."[61]

While Boussingault's work was drawing Dumas's attention to the role of plants in the balance of nature, a change in his own teaching responsibilities caused Dumas to review the chemical processes that occur in animals. In 1838 he obtained the chair of pharmacy and organic chemistry at the École de Médecine. There he continued his usual lectures on organic chemistry, but in keeping with the interests of his new audience he began to insert topics more directly related to the composition and functions of the animal body. In that year, for example, he discussed the chemistry of urine, blood, milk, and other body fluids. He devoted one lecture to digestion, and another to "the chemical phenomena of respiration," a topic which especially interested him because of his admiration for Lavoisier. Dumas summarized the well-known debate over whether the combustion process occurs in the lungs or during the passage of the blood through the circulation.

He focused on a theory of respiration he ascribed to Eilhard Mitscherlich, according to which oxygen absorbed through the lungs converts organic constituents of the blood to lactic acid. The latter is then supposed to react with sodium carbonate contained in the blood, forming sodium lactate and releasing the carbonic acid to be exhaled. Sodium lactate is in turn decomposed to form more sodium carbonate.[62] The theory Dumas described was actually a slight modification of one proposed jointly by Mitscherlich, Leopold Gmelin, and Friedrich Tiedemann in 1833. While Mitscherlich was visiting Heidelberg in 1831, the three scientists had attempted to extract carbonic acid gas from venous and arterial blood by means of a vacuum pump. They failed to detect any; but when they first acidified the blood with acetic acid they were able to extract a considerable quantity of carbonic acid. To explain this result they assumed that normal alkaline blood contains, not free carbonic acid, but that substance bound in the form of alkali carbonates. Since, they said, after exposure to the air most organic fluids, including blood, contain acetic or lactic acid, they theorized that the oxygen absorbed into the circulation produces the same substances there. These acids in turn release the carbonic acid from its alkali base.[63] Dumas was simplifying this theory by eliminating acetic acid from consideration, a choice he probably made because lactic acid had been found widely distributed in animal matter, in muscles as well as in blood and urine.[64] He also made the theory more elegant by deriving the sodium carbonate of the blood from the sodium lactate, for the original authors had imagined that the lactic or acetic acid was eventually excreted.[65] Dumas supported his interpretation by referring to some older experiments of Friedrich Wöhler concerning the effects on the urine caused by feeding various compounds to dogs. Sodium or potassium salts of acetic and other "vegetable" acids produced carbonates in the urine, and Wöhler assumed that the carbonates were formed by the decomposition of the vegetable acids.[66] Dumas mentioned that Gustav Magnus had recently succeeded in extracting carbonic acid and oxygen from blood by displacing these gases with hydrogen gas. When Dumas himself sought to demonstrate to his class the extraction of gases from the blood of a sheep, he was unsuccessful.[67] There is no indication that he took note of the fact that Magnus's classic investigation had removed the experimental basis on which the respiration theory of Mitscherlich rested.

Since the time of Lavoisier many experiments had been made to measure the rate at which animals exhale carbonic acid. Dumas added his own attempt. Designing a simple apparatus into which he exhaled, he measured the amount of carbonic acid which he expired in a single normal breath, and from that he calculated that in one day a man would burn 170 grams of carbon.[68]

In 1839 Dumas repeated many of the same themes in his course, but it was apparent that on the second time around he had had a chance to reflect more extensively on some aspects of animal chemistry, and that he was being influenced by certain current developments. He discussed at length, for example, the question of whether fibrin and albumin were chemically identical. On the basis of their properties and his own opinion that one of these substances contained more nitrogen than the other, he believed they were not. But he reported to his class that new analyses by the Dutch chemist Gerardus Mulder gave identical proportions of carbon, hydrogen, oxygen, and nitrogen in the two substances, as well as in casein.[69] The prominence he gave to Mulder's analyses suggests that Dumas sensed that these results and Mulder's conclusion that fibrin, albumin, and casein contain a common "proteine" radical, would have an important impact on animal chemistry.

During his 1839 lectures Dumas also placed the chemical phenomena of animal respiration within the context of the broad consequences he had recently drawn from Boussingault's experiments. After describing the apparatus with which Boussingault had proved that plants decompose carbonic acid and water, Dumas stressed that the action of plants on the atmosphere counterbalances the effects of animal respiration. The mode of action of plants, he asserted, "is entirely inverse to that which one observes in animals: in plants [there are] reduction apparatuses: in animals, combustion apparatuses."[70] That general relationship of plants and animals had long been evident. In the late eighteenth century Joseph Priestley had discovered that plants "restore" air vitiated by animal respiration, and the chemical interpretation of these reciprocal actions was inherent in Lavoisier's theories of respiration and of vegetation.[71] For Dumas, however, the statement took on a more pervasive meaning than it had for his predecessors; he saw the inverse relation of plants and animals not merely as a summation of their interactions with each other and the atmosphere, but as a definition of the sense of all of their internal chemical processes as well. Moreover, that definition posed for him "the most remarkable problem which organic chemistry has to solve," the elucidation of the chemical transformations within animals. Because he believed that these reactions were essentially combustion processes, taking place chiefly in the blood, the problem to solve was what action oxygen has on blood; this question could in turn be elucidated by knowledge of the general modes of action of oxygen on organic compounds. The old conception of Lavoisier, that respiration was a simple, direct burning of carbon and hydrogen, no longer sufficed, for it was clear to Dumas that there must be a complex series of gradual transformations. That was no reason to give up hope of understanding them, he felt, for chemists were now discovering and describing complex partial oxidation reactions of organic compounds.[72] Up until the past decade the combustion of organic compounds had ordinarily resulted either in their complete decomposition to carbonic acid and water, or in a mélange of so many products that the reactions were impossible to interpret. Now, however, chemists were learning to control the reaction conditions closely enough to produce limited conversions of one compound into another of a higher oxidation state.[73] In his lecture Dumas illustrated various modes of action of oxygen on organic materials. One of them was "true oxidation comparable to the oxidation of lead," such as occurs in the conversion of oil of bitter almonds to benzoic acid:

$$C^{28}H^{12}O^2 + O^2 = C^{28}H^{12}O^4 = C^{28}H^{10}O^3, H^2O$$

and in the similar conversion of aldehyde to acetic acid:

$$C^8H^8O^2 + O^2 = C^8H^6O^3, H^2O.[74]$$

Another mode of action of oxygen was characterized by the loss of hydrogen, as in the conversion of indigo blue to "indigo white" by means of oxygen. Salicine reacted with sulfuric acid and potassium chromate to give oil of spiraea, which could be further oxidized to other products. Such reactions demonstrated, Dumas emphasized, that it is not enough to determine the final result of a decomposition, for by moderating the oxidizing action carefully one can obtain very interesting intermediate compounds. These enabled one to imagine how in living organisms the oxidations take place by steps.[75]

Dumas's discussion typified the approach he and a number of other organic chemists relied on as they took up the question of the chemical manifestations of vital processes. He did not think of investigating the phenomena directly with experiments on living animals, but believed he could explain the processes by reference to similar reactions he could carry out on organic materials in the chemical laboratory. That he should view the problem in this manner was a natural consequence of his position. Dumas had not been involved in experiments on the chemical processes of living animals for so long that he was not fully aware of the hidden surprises likely to upset inferences derived from a knowledge of the chemical properties of substances alone. When basing his theories on the oxidation reactions of organic compounds, on the other hand, he could draw on a wealth of intimate knowledge, for he had been engaged in the study of such processes for many years. Several of the illustrations he used in his lecture derived, in fact, from his own discoveries. Dumas came to a new set of problems with the confidence born of his eminent success in the field which he brought to bear on them, and perhaps with too little sense of the limitations imposed by his lack of direct experience with the problems themselves.

The very accessibility of the problems of animal chemistry to solutions drawn from organic chemistry depended, for Dumas, on his conviction that the essential phenomena in animal chemistry were oxidation reactions; for that was the type which organic chemists were learning to control. The consequence was a double standard, in which the internal chemistry of plants became correspondingly inaccessible. The reduction reactions which plants are able to carry out, Dumas told his listeners, were of a sort "which chemistry is not able to reproduce," and they were therefore "still mysterious." [76]

During the next two years Dumas continued to discuss these topics in his organic chemistry lectures. Meanwhile, in April 1840 there appeared in French a treatise on organic chemistry, by Justus Liebig, with a long introduction on the applications of that science to agriculture and physiology. One of Liebig's principal themes was the source of the elements assimilated by plants. Unlike Boussingault, Liebig had not himself performed experiments on plant growth, but relied on past investigations, logical arguments, and general calculations to make his case. He noted, for example, that the experiments of Priestley, Senebier, and De Saussure had long ago established that the carbon is derived from the atmosphere; only the ignorance of chemistry by physiologists had permitted the opinion to persist that the carbon came from organic matter in the soil. To overwhelm this reactionary position, Liebig added simple calculations showing that the quantity of carbon represented in the plants grown in a field or forest far exceeded what the soil could have contained. His clinching proof was that in spite of the fact that animals are continually absorbing oxygen and emitting carbonic acid, the quantity of oxygen in the atmosphere remains constant and the very small percentage of carbonic acid does not increase. There must, therefore, be a cause which removes the carbonic acid and one which replaces the oxygen, and "both these causes are united in the process of vegetation." For the case of nitrogen Liebig made the novel suggestion that ammonia arising from the decay of animal matter diffused into the atmosphere and dissolved in rain water, which carried it into the soil. Although the ammonia could not be detected in the air, Liebig supported his contention by distilling several hundred pounds of rain water and finding ammonia in it.[77] In 1841 Dumas and Boussingault took up experimentally the question of whether the proportion of oxygen in the air is actually invariable. Using a new method to weigh directly the quantities of oxygen and of nitrogen, they determined that the proportions of the two gases were constant to at least one part in a thousand, and by comparing their results with earlier measurements they inferred that these proportions did not measurably change in different localities, altitudes, seasons, or years. They too argued that the constancy was to be expected because of the harmonious balance between the actions of plants and animals, and also because the reservoir of the air was so vast compared to the rate of gaseous exchanges produced by living organisms. Dumas and Boussingault made no mention of Liebig's recent discussion of the same question.[78]

At the close of his course at the École de Médecine for 1841, Dumas gave a lecture summarizing his ideas concerning the role of material exchanges in the phenomena of organized beings. He did this, he afterward asserted, because several students had asked for a more coherent overview of the topics which had come up during the course, and because he and Boussingault felt for the first time sufficient confidence in their general point of view to regard it as a feasible guide for more detailed studies and for practical applications. He had worked out these ideas in such close cooperation with Boussingault, he said, that it was no longer possible to identify which of them was the originator of the various facets of their system. Dumas presented his "tableau" also as the logical extension of the pathway which Lavoisier had marked out for organic chemistry.[79]

Dumas gave a highly schematic, yet vivid picture of the interactions linking plants, animals, and the atmosphere. He now stated in the starkest terms the contrasting nature of plants and animals. "The vegetable kingdom," he affirmed, "constitutes an immense reduction apparatus"; whereas animals "constitute, from the chemical point of view, combustion apparatuses." Thus what he had once described simply as attributes of plants and animals had now become, for his purposes at least, their respective defining characteristics.[80] These contrasting actions of plants and animals, the fate of animal matter after death, and the properties of the atmosphere, he said, "close the mysterious circle of organic life on the surface of the globe." To a description of the material exchanges similar to what he had presented in earlier years, Dumas now added considerations about the chemical "force" involved. The unique power of plants to separate carbon and hydrogen from carbonic acid and water and to incorporate these elements, as well as nitrogen, into complex organic compounds, did not emanate from the plants alone; for they absorbed in some extraordinary way, from the inexhaustible source of the sun, the chemical force necessary to decompose the stable combinations of these elements with oxygen. In consuming the products supplied by plants, animals in turn produced heat and the force which they convert to motion. Plants, therefore, comprised a "storehouse" of combustible material for animals, just as the plants of the past had produced the combustible deposits of coal which formed the source of the chemical force released in steam engines. "That poetic comparison of the railroad locomotive to an animal," he declared, "rests on more substantial foundations than was perhaps believed." [81] Dumas's description of the overall cycle of exchanges of matter and force between organisms and their environment was a brilliant synthesis of the thought and research of the preceding half-century, and a clear anticipation of relationships soon afterward formalized in the law of the conservation of energy. Though Lavoisier had perceived the same basic relationship long before, Dumas was able to portray it more convincingly and comprehensively, both because of the emergence in the meantime of ideas about conversions of force in nature [82] and the growth in knowledge of organic compounds.

Only a small portion of Dumas's lecture actually dealt with the chemical phenomena he supposed to occur within animals; succinct as his description was, however, he delineated it as sharply as he did his view of the place of animals within the general cycle of exchanges. Probably the link which connected together into a single system for him all of the ideas he had previously been treating, was the realization that each of the major classes of animal substances was represented in plant matter by chemically equivalent substances. He had by then accepted that albumin, fibrin, and casein were of the same composition and that plants contained nitrogenous substances chemically identical to them. Plants also produced fats and sugars corresponding to those obtainable from animals. These correspondences enabled Dumas to assert with confidence that animals "do not create veritable organic materials," but only destroy what plants furnish to them. He reiterated his earlier view that a series of new compounds forms during the gradual process of respiratory oxidations, but emphasized that the new compounds were always "simpler, approaching more closely the elementary state than those which [the animals] . . . receive." The end products were always the ordinary inorganic compounds—water, carbonic acid, and ammonia. Urea he regarded as merely a special modification of the latter, formed in order to avoid the deleterious action of ammonia itself on animal tissues. After being excreted it was converted by a fermentation into ammonia. Dumas divided the three classes of nutrients into "assimilable products" and "combustible products." The former, including albumin, fibrin, casein, and fats, were assimilated "almost intact" to serve for the growth and renovation of organs; the latter, including sugars and fats, were consumed in respiration.[83]

The physiological aspects of Dumas's system became very influential during the years following its appearance. One reason for its popularity was that physiologists had previously been unable to explain, or even give a persuasive coherent description of, the incessant exchanges of matter which form so prominent a feature of animal life.[84] Dumas not only portrayed the processes of nutrition and respiration as an integral series of events, but gave them a clear significance for the life of the animal and for its part in processes on an even grander scale. The outlines of the picture he sketched have remained basic to our understanding of the meaning of the chemical processes of living organisms. Yet his picture represented these processes to be as simple and clear within the organism as were their net results. Although he gave his lecture just a few days after Magendie had finished reporting for the Gelatin Commission that animal nutrition was so complicated that almost nothing was yet known about it, Dumas presented his views as though the major problems were all resolved. "All these phenomena of life so complicated in appearance," he maintained, "are connected in their essential features to a general formula so simple that in a few words one has, as it were, enunciated all, recalled all to mind, foreseen all." [85] His attitude was remarkably unaffected by the fact that as a member of the Gelatin Commission Dumas had been aware for years of the insurmountable difficulties that body had encountered in attempting to define the value of a nutrient. His serene assurance, in spite of all that, that no processes need be assumed in the animal except those necessary to fill in his general scheme, is well illustrated by his treatment of digestion. While discussing that process in 1838 he had expressed the belief that "the gastric juice contains some special principle capable of producing remarkable transformations." [86] Afterward, however, the demonstration of the identity of plant and animal substances seemed to make such a conception superfluous. "As soon as it was proven to us," he said in his lecture of 1841, "that an animal does not create any organic material; that it is limited to assimilating it to itself or to expending it in burning it, it was no longer necessary to search for all those mysteries in digestion that one was not sure to find there at all." Digestion in his new view was simply a process of absorption, in which materials were put into a state of division, if they were not already so, in which they could pass into the circulation. [87] By presenting this view Dumas was, in effect, dismissing the efforts of physiologists who, after decades of investigations, had finally established the first clear indications that gastric digestion involved distinct chemical transformations. [88]

As the preceding account has shown, and as other historians have also recently stressed, [89] Dumas treated the chemistry of the animal body in a manner conditioned by his view that the problem fell within the domain of organic chemistry. That factor was crucial, yet not by itself sufficient to explain why he delineated the processes within animals as such simple, easily fathomable phenomena. If Dumas's general experience as a chemist oriented his approach, more peculiar features of his individual scientific personality helped to shape it. Dumas had displayed in organic chemistry itself much of the same theoretical boldness that he applied to the study of living organisms. Repeatedly he had derived broad, simple generalizations from a few striking discoveries concerning the composition of certain strategic organic compounds. From some ingenious experiments and a subtle chain of inferences he created in 1828 a theory of the composition of ethers by which he tried to explain the relations between the composition of many of the most important organic compounds. He defended his theory with determination against strong criticisms, confident that the facts it could interpret justified using it in spite of other contradictory phenomena his adversaries brought to bear on it. With his substitution theory and his theory of types, he similarly claimed that the consequences he had drawn from a few striking reactions were applicable to the whole range of organic compounds. His constant aim was to discern the simple ideas which could reduce the bewildering complexity of empirical observations to logical order. Satish Kapoor has cogently pointed out that Dumas held a sophisticated view of the status of theories in science. He considered them not permanent truths, but temporary devices used to direct the further research which ultimately would replace them with better ones. Dumas's position, as Kapoor puts it, was "that a theory was essentially an imaginative construction, elaborated by a scientist in much the same way as an inventor made a new object." [90] Sometimes, however, Dumas used this conception to justify proposing theories with a facility that to his contemporaries appeared insouciant. Moreover, in practice Dumas could not always maintain the detachment from the fate of his theories which he professed in principle. He tended to become their zealous champion, proclaiming them to have withstood the tests of criticism which others saw as sufficient to reject them. [91]

As Dumas ventured into another field, his faith in the power of his theoretical generalizations was probably only enhanced by the superficiality of his knowledge of physiology. Not foreseeing the pitfalls in his path, he strode rapidly, overlooking difficulties which would have been obvious to one deeply engaged in physiological problems. Yet his overconfidence in this respect probably came as much from his youthful introduction to physiological research as from his subsequent position in organic chemistry. Because of that exposure he must have supposed that he was better qualified than most organic chemists to deal with physiological questions. Being out of touch with the recent development of that field, however, he seemed not to appreciate that it had become a more complicated subject than the physiology he had known in 1824.

The nature and scope of the problems Dumas presented were conducive to the merging of the internal processes of animals with the outward manifestations of these processes. Dumas was less interested in animal functions for their own sake than in the place of animals within the material cycles on the surface of the earth. He therefore tended to let the boundaries where physiological processes interact with the external world define the nature of the steps in between.

The foregoing may seem more than ample to explain the way in which Dumas summarized animal chemistry in his lecture. There was, however, another equally important condition, the fact that he had developed these views mainly for his course. Dumas made a sharp distinction between the way he presented scientific questions at the Academy of Sciences and the way he dealt with them in his teaching. At the Academy he was cautious, at least in his own eyes, not to set forth views which might cause his colleagues to lose confidence in him if he should prove mistaken. He tried, he believed, to give as many striking facts as he could, while subordinating his ideas. In his lectures to students, on the other hand, he felt that it was necessary to display "the poetry of science." There he treated the "highest questions" boldly and without embarrassment before the judgments of others. There, ideas came first and facts afterward. Ideas inspired ardent young audiences, he thought, and established a mutual rapport between him and them.[92] Dumas was, in fact, an outstanding orator. Gifted with an eloquent, facile style of speech adorned by rich imagery, he was well known in Paris for his ability to excite his listeners with "grand theories which open new horizons." [93] Clearly the "sublime simplicity" [94] of the laws of plants and animals which he sought to convey in his famous closing lecture of 1841 was partly rhetorical, an expression of the enthusiasm of a man who delighted in resolving the great mysteries of nature for his admiring audiences.

On the same day that Dumas delivered his lecture it was published in the daily newspaper *Journal des débats*, in a column ordinarily devoted to reports of the meetings of the Academy of Sciences. The editor of that column, Alfred Donné, commented that he was printing it because its author was able to express with great clarity and elegance the general principles governing the life of plants, animals, and men. Readers would not mind, Donné added, if the picture given "is sometimes poetic." [95] Thus Dumas's ideas appeared fittingly in the form of an essay addressed to the general public. If it had remained there, it would have raised few problems. Not content with that format, however, Dumas had the lecture reprinted in the fall in a specialized scientific journal with which he was associated, the *Annales des sciences naturelles;* [96] in December it came out again in a separate "second edition," which Dumas hoped would furnish a basis for studies of chemical phenomena in general physiology, medicine, and agriculture.[97] Thus Dumas was blurring his own distinction between his two scientific "theaters" by utilizing an essay conceived in the free style of his lectures as a serious scientific memoir. His motive may be discernible in another remark by Donné, that the problem treated in the lecture was "entirely the order of the day in the present state of the science: it occupies scientists of the first-rank in France and especially in Germany." [98] Dumas must have been anxious to establish a claim to the ideas he had formulated before it was too late. The cause of that anxiety was undoubtedly the activities of his German counterpart, Justus Liebig.

Liebig's scientific path was in many ways strikingly similar to that of Dumas. He was, like Dumas, involved during the 1830's principally in investigations of the composition and reactions of organic compounds. The two men emerged as leaders of their field over the same

Justus Liebig

period. Repeatedly they took up the same questions, and nearly as frequently they disagreed over the answers. Liebig proposed his own theory of the constitution of ethers and supported it resourcefully in opposition to Dumas's theory. Liebig perfected the general method for the combustion analysis of organic compounds, and he was at least a match for Dumas in identifying new compounds. At the end of the decade Liebig too turned his attention rather abruptly to applications of chemistry to plant and animal physiology. His concern with plants was utilitarian; he wished to bring the illumination of chemistry to bear on the improvement of agriculture, an interest which appears to have originated when he attended the meeting of the British Association for the Advancement of Science in 1837. He was stimulated to take up animal chemistry by several events. A beautiful investigation of the properties of uric acid and its derivatives, completed by Liebig and Wöhler in 1838, seemed more than any of Liebig's earlier research to open up a new way toward an understanding of the "metamorphoses" within animals through which their nitrogenous constituents are transformed into excretory products.[99] Another development which influenced Liebig even more than it did Dumas was the work of G. J. Mulder.

Mulder was, in 1837, a busy physician in Rotterdam who performed chemical experiments in his spare time. During that year he applied Liebig's method of combustion analysis to determine the elementary compositions of albumin and fibrin. Within the range of expected accuracy, the proportions of carbon, hydrogen, nitrogen, and oxygen in the two substances turned out to be identical. As he continued his investigation, Mulder began in 1838 to correspond with Liebig, sending detailed accounts of his progress in return for Liebig's encouragement and suggestions. By then Mulder had discovered in wheat an albumin with the same composition, and he believed he had confirmed that "the principal substance of animals is directly furnished by the vegetable kingdom." Fibrin and albumin differed only with respect to the very small amounts of sulfur and phosphorus both contained, and when heated with caustic potash both yielded a substance free of these two elements. Mulder gave the product the formula $C^{40}H^{62}N^{10}O^{12}$ and decided that fibrin and albumin were combinations of ten atoms of this radical with an atom of phosphorus and, respectively, one and two atoms of sulfur.[100] At Jöns Berzelius's suggestion, Mulder shortly afterward named the radical "proteine." [101] By October he informed Liebig that he had found casein to have essentially the same composition, differing only in that its ten proteine atoms were joined to a single atom of sulfur.[102] During the next year Mulder investigated salts and decomposition products of these substances, interpreting them all to fit his formula for proteine.[103]

Liebig was skeptical about Mulder's theoretical interpretations, but highly impressed with his analyses. Liebig suggested to Julius Vogel, a young physician studying in his laboratory, the project of confirming them. Vogel obtained results very close to those of Mulder and agreed with him that albumin, fibrin, and casein have the same elementary composition. He showed also that the three substances resembled each other in important chemical properties. When coagulated and heated with an excess of concentrated hydrochloric acid, each produced the same distinctive violet color. Undoubtedly reflecting Liebig's views, Vogel called it premature to calculate a formula for these substances. With numbers as high as Mulder was proposing, even the best of analyses could easily leave an error amounting to many atoms.[104]

During the next two years Liebig and his students extended further the investigations and ideas suggested to them by Mulder's work. By August 1841, Liebig was able to report that they had isolated from plant materials nitrogenous substances identical with each of the three animal substances. The likenesses, he emphasized, were not limited to their elementary compositions; it was not merely a matter of numerical proportions. For he showed by means of an imposing series of reactions that what he called plant albumin, plant fibrin, and plant casein were scarcely distinguishable from their animal counterparts. Both kinds of fibrin were insoluble in water. Albumin from both sources was soluble in cold water and acetic acid, but coagulated when the water was heated. Plant casein dissolved in both hot and cold water but precipitated in acetic acid, just as did casein from milk. Besides demonstrating agreement in these defining characteristics, Liebig established the equivalence of the respective plant and animal substances through numerous reactions with acids, alkalis, and salts. From the consistency of his results he might well have felt justified in taking literally his partially metaphorical conclusion that "herbivorous animals receive the chief components of blood, its albumin and fibrin perfectly constituted, even if not in the same form: . . . they nourish themselves with flesh, blood, and cheese which plants create." [105]

If that generalization was an embellished version of Mulder's conclusion, the further physiological deductions Liebig drew from it resembled in outline those Dumas was making public at almost the same time. Liebig too maintained that since plants produce the principal constituents of animal substances, only a change in their form, not their composition, is needed for their assimilation to the animal body. Like Dumas, he stated that the nitrogenous plant substances form the organized parts of the animal body, whereas the nitrogen-free nutrients are consumed in respiration. Liebig elaborated these ideas, however, in a quite different manner, reflecting the different circumstances under which he had become involved in animal chemistry. Liebig had, to be sure, first expressed his ideas on the topic in his own lecture course during the winter of 1840–41, where he had stated his physiological conclusions in the form of general propositions. [106] It was, however, the investigations carried out in his laboratory in response to Mulder which formed the occasion for his first published discussion, and he consequently presented his views in the form of closely reasoned scientific arguments rather than a sweeping didactic lecture. Having dealt previously with the role of plants and animals in the larger cycles of matter, Liebig was now focusing his attention on animal nutrition itself. This definition of his subject induced him to reason from his conceptions about the nature of processes within animals rather than from the conditions of their role in the balance of nature. Thus he based his arguments about the role of nitrogenous and non-nitrogenous aliments on the proportions of the elements in these compounds and the assumption that the compounds would be used in the animal in such a way as to require the least amount of exchanges of the elements from one compound to another. Since all organized parts of an animal are composed of nitrogenous materials, he said, and since the nitrogenous substances obtained by the animal in its food, whether that food be vegetable or animal, contains precisely the proportions of elements necessary to constitute the animal substances, then the non-nitrogenous substances which an animal eats cannot contribute any portion of their elements to the formation of the animal material. Consequently, such substances, in particular starch, sugar, and fats, must serve some other purpose in the animal. That purpose, he claimed, was to protect the organized parts of the body from the constant threat of decomposition by oxidation. By supplying carbon to convert the oxygen breathed in to carbonic acid, the fat and sugar an animal ate enabled it to withstand the effects on it of the surrounding atmosphere without wasting the substance of its organs. This process served also for the production of animal heat, a subject on which Liebig promised to say more at a later time.[107]

There were also significant substantive differences between Liebig's physiological generalizations and those of Dumas. According to Liebig only those animal tissues which carry on "vegetative" functions, such as nutrition and reproduction, are composed of compounds completely fashioned by plants. The substances of nerves and brain, which possess feeling, will, and motion, must have a higher level of organization than vegetative substances, so that there must be in animals special apparatuses capable of forming them.[108] Furthermore, Liebig noted that domestic herbivores often contain large quantities of fat which must come from the non-nitrogenous starch, sugar, or gum in their diets. Such a transformation could easily take place, he maintained, for elementary analyses showed that the proportion of hydrogen to carbon in starch and some sugars is the same as in fats. Therefore the fat could be produced from the sugar in these animals merely by a removal of oxygen.[109]

Although Liebig, like Dumas, considered animals to be unable to produce those constituents of their bodies which plants furnish them, he did not characterize animals as pure "consumers" of organic compounds capable only of oxidations which reduce the complexity of the materials they receive. Liebig thought that, beginning from the ready-made constituents of their blood, animals can perform some transformations which are synthetic, and some which involve reduction rather than oxidation. Both of these functions Dumas ascribed exclusively to plants. Liebig's view of the relationship of plants and animals was on the whole less influenced by the desire to depict a grand symmetrical system, and seemingly based on more specific empirical evidence. Liebig's physiological conclusions in fact must have appeared to him to follow immediately from the chemical identities he had carefully established. Yet he, no less than Dumas, was engaged in speculating about the processes supposed to go on inside animals with no direct knowledge of them.

II

Paris and Giessen at Odds

Following the publications of August 1841 a three-sided contest emerged around the positions they represented. In the ensuing mixture of research and debate, scientific issues became inseparably entangled with priority issues, personal and national rivalries, bitter feelings, and the competition between chemists and physiologists to define the grounds upon which the problems of nutrition were to be worked out. At first the chemists appeared to dominate the situation. Liebig and Dumas, who had already been rivals in organic chemistry, now seemed to be transferring their competition to an alluring new arena for applied chemistry. Their individual relations were exacerbated by the feeling each had for the shifting scientific balance between Germany and France. Having personally made Germany the leading center for chemical training in Europe, Liebig was determined that the French acknowledge the equality, if not the superiority, of German science. The French chemists, trained in an era when Paris was considered the scientific capital of the world, were loath to accept the evidence of their relative decline and sometimes pretended not to notice the progress being made elsewhere. At the same time both groups of chemists seemed somewhat resentful toward the activities of the Gelatin Commission. Underlying this attitude was probably a sense that the authority of Magendie, the principal champion of experimental physiology, constituted a threat to their own initiatives.

These feelings, which affected the way in which the people involved subsequently dealt with the substantive scientific disagreements among them, were mirrored by Liebig in an exchange of letters with his closest friend among the Parisian chemists, Théophile-Jules

Pelouze. On October 28 Liebig wrote Pelouze complaining that his book on agricultural chemistry was being ignored in France, even though it had been enthusiastically received in England and Germany. He had designed his work, he said, to persuade agriculturalists that agriculture cannot progress without a knowledge of chemistry, yet a French professor of agriculture admitted without shame that he knew nothing about chemistry. "What a strange state of affairs," he remarked, "in a country which continually calls itself the best educated in Europe." Meanwhile, he claimed, certain eminent French chemists were starting to incorporate his ideas into their own writings without acknowledging the source. A recent article by Boussingault and Anselme Payen, he said, had expressed opinions on the role of humus and the general nature of fertilizers which no one had understood until he himself had written about them.[1]

A few days later Liebig received a letter from Pelouze dealing with "the eternal gelatin question." Pelouze himself had been peripherally involved in the question the previous June, when he had analyzed a sample of pure gelatin D'Arcet had given him and found it to have the same elementary composition Liebig was finding for albumin, fibrin, and casein.[2] Now he reported that in the aftermath of the commission report D'Arcet was "more preoccupied and tormented about gelatin than ever," and was preparing a volume in defense of his position. At D'Arcet's request Pelouze asked Liebig for permission to quote from an old letter Liebig had sent D'Arcet. In it Liebig had praised D'Arcet's service to humanity and characterized the opposition to his views as born of passion and personal interests. Although Pelouze wrote that he feared D'Arcet "exaggerates the nutritive property as much as his antagonists belittle it," he believed there was no reason not to think that gelatin was as nourishing "as many other things which people eat everywhere continuously."[3] Although showing his usual caution about theoretical questions, Pelouze thus seemed to doubt the decisiveness of Magendie's experiments, probably because its chemical composition appeared to qualify gelatin in the class of nutrients.

Liebig answered Pelouze on November 1 with far less restraint:

But what ideas they have in Paris about nutrition!! If one had proven that the faeces or the urine of persons nourished by gelatin contained gelatin, I would not say anything, but to conclude from the facts which one has observed that gelatin cannot serve for something in the organism is an absurdity. It cannot replace or be changed into blood, nor make fat, but it can serve for the reproduction of membranes and of the substance of cells, and it does serve for that. Please say to Mr. D'arcet that I am busy with a large work on nutrition, in which I shall treat everything which pertains to gelatin; a first memoir has appeared in the August issue of my *Annalen*, and you will make me grateful if you would get it into the *Annales de chimie*. Mr. D'arcet can make of my letter whatever seems advantageous to him. It is a disgrace for the physiologists that experiments so poorly made can have value in their eyes. Without having a clear idea about assimilation can one be proud of such experiments [?]. One recommends chocolate, arrowroot, and such things as nourishing, which do not produce a drop of blood, which cannot replace in any way that which the organs have lost. Have my memoir translated, my dear Pelouze, and do not be afraid of compromising me. Each word in my memoir has been discussed and re-discussed with the most able physiologists of Germany, and it is only after having convinced them of the correctness of my views that I have decided to print them. There is a great reform coming in physiology, and that reform is based on organic chemistry. It is a triumph over empiricism and over the hollow theories which they have imagined. It makes no difference to me if the French physiologists adopt my views, but they will not dare to reject my experiments and my analyses, and certainly in recognizing them as true, they will be forced to come to the same conclusions . . . You will conclude, my dear Pelouze, that I am angry, and that it is resentment which makes me talk so. You do not deceive yourself. The French physiologists will have to pay some attention to me. It was not for chemistry, but for physiology and for agriculture that I have sacrificed a year of my life, and I do not like to have someone insult my child, which has been raised with much care and pain.[4]

Tactfully Pelouze wrote back to Liebig on December 10 that he "had read with infinite pleasure" Liebig's memoir on nutrition, and that it would appear within a few weeks in the *Annales de chimie*. He added,

One is beginning to pay great attention to your physiological ideas and work and the reprint [of the introduction to your volume on organic chemistry] which M. Masson has made has been immensely successful . . . Millon, who is a physician and a good physiologist, has adopted all of your views and is teaching them in his course of chemistry at the Val de Grâce. Frémy is enthusiastic about them, as I have already told you.

I have been taking a fine anatomy lesson each week for a month, and I intend, indeed, when I have learned it, to devote myself ardently to physiological chemistry. Then I shall at least be able to talk about it with you with some knowledge.[5]

This report that his views had acquired a following in Paris did not allay Liebig's fear that Dumas and Boussingault were exploiting his ideas. On November 6 he had written his English disciple, Lyon Playfair, that in the lecture published in the *Journal des débats* Dumas had "in a shameless way taken my theory of the growth of plants, of crop rotations, of fertilizers, etc. as his own." He did not then feel that it was worth the trouble to do anything about it, but Playfair's answer may have helped him to change his mind. Playfair wrote that Dumas's lecture, which had been reprinted in the *Philosophical Magazine*,

> is the most disgraceful piracy in the annals of science. Dumas's most bitter enemy could not wish him a greater evil than the publication of that lecture; it will expose him to the just contempt of all right thinking men. I have heard several speak of it—*not chemists*, but they had all detected the plagiarism.[6]

Whether or not Liebig needed that goad to his own suspicions, he used his concern as a justification for putting quickly into print more of his physiological conceptions. In the December issue of his *Annalen* he published "The vital processes in animals and the atmosphere." He had had to write this article hastily, he said in an introductory note, instead of preparing more leisurely the book he planned on the subject, so that he would not have to see what he had been teaching in his courses appear in print first under other authorship. The lecture printed in the *Journal des débats*, he complained, had utilized the "truths" established in his *Agricultural Chemistry*, "naturally without mentioning that I or anyone else had ever occupied himself with these subjects."[7] Dumas had, in fact, not been very generous in his essay in the credit he gave to Liebig's contributions to those portions involving plant chemistry; but Liebig's claim was, at the least, an exaggeration, for Dumas did mention Liebig there as among those who had "fixed attention on the role of ammoniac in nitrogenous fertilizers."[8]

In his second paper on animal chemistry Liebig approached the subject in a manner quite different from that of his first article. He adduced no new analyses of organic substances and elaborated very little on specific chemical features of nutritional processes. He attempted instead to establish general principles upon which the meaning of the concept of the *Stoffwechsel* in animals must depend. Similarly to Dumas, his central idea was an affirmation of Lavoisier's conclusion that the combustion of carbon and hydrogen to carbonic acid and water is the source of animal heat. But Liebig developed from that conclusion some important implications not commonly appreciated until then, by which he made clearer than ever before how widely embracing these phenomena were. All vital actions, Liebig claimed, arise out of transformations of chemical force obtained from the interaction of the carbon and hydrogen of the nutrients with oxygen. No matter what intermediate forms the nutrients take within the body, or under what conditions these steps take place, the end result will still be carbonic acid and water,[9] and for a given amount of hydrogen and carbon consumed the same quantity of heat must be produced as would result from their direct combustion. Thus, whatever the details of unknown physiological processes might turn out to be, their general consequences will be the same. Therefore, strict proportionalities must prevail in animals between the amount of nutrients eaten, the quantity of air respired, and the total of heat produced. These conclusions Liebig drew from his comprehension of the nature of physical and chemical processes and his conviction that they must take place in organisms according to the same principles as elsewhere. Most of the items of common-sense information with which he tried to demonstrate his views were not rigorous. The most significant experimental data he discussed, those of Despretz, he had to explain away, since the results did not unequivocally support his belief in the chemical theory of animal heat.[10]

Three months later, in March 1842, Liebig added a third installment in his *Annalen*, "Nutrition, blood and fat formation in the animal body." Much of this article was a restatement of the results described the previous August, but presented with less chemical detail and more extensive development of the physiological inferences. Here he went well beyond Dumas in his willingness to deduce the details of processes supposed to take place in the animal from comparisons of the composition of body substances and of nutrients. Most notably he enlarged on the distinction between nitrogenous or *plastic* nutrients capable of assimilation to the organized body, and the non-nitrogenous, or respiratory, nutrients. In an elaborate comparison of the nutrition of carnivorous and herbivorous animals he tried to demonstrate that the flesh consumed by the carnivores provides both the material incorporated into tissue and the carbon and hydrogen whose combustion sustains the heat of the animal. In herbivores, however, the nitrogenous constituents are decomposed too slowly to furnish the requisite carbon, and this is supplied instead by carbon from the starch, sugars, or gums included in vegetable diets. Liebig also presumed to describe the anatomical pathways within the body along which the nutritional transformations took place. Concerning gelatin, he stated more fully the view mentioned in his letter to Pelouze, without directly saying, as he had in private, that he was countering the report of the Gelatin Commission. He also developed further his previously published theory that fat is formed in animals by the removal of oxygen from starch and similar nutrients. Whether these substances or the nitrogenous nutrients are the source of fat, he pointed out, the conversion must in any case involve the separation of oxygen, for all of these nutrients contain a larger proportion of that element than fats do. From this argument he drew a number of physiological corollaries, such as that fat forms in an animal when too little oxygen is inspired in proportion to the food eaten, the oxygen released in the reaction helping to make up the deficit.[11]

In his discussion of the formation of blood from nitrogenous nutrients Liebig restated a former position in a way that brings out more emphatically how his general conception of the transformation which animals can produce differed from the conception Dumas held:

One can say, that the animal organism produces its blood only in respect to the form, that it lacks the capacity to create it out of other substances that are not identical with its chief constituents. To be sure, it cannot be maintained that the animal lacks the ability to create other compounds; we know, on the contrary, that its organization generates a large series of other compounds differing in composition from the constituents of the blood, but the starting point of the series, this it cannot form.[12]

These products were not limited to compounds simpler than the nutrients, but included many at a more complex level of chemical organization than plants can reach.

During these same months Dumas too was promising to develop further the principles he had outlined in August. In time, he said, he would apply them to the discussion of details; but he seemed to be making less progress than Liebig. The successive editions of his essay merely added to the original lecture an appendix supposedly giving the facts upon which his conclusions were based. These included determinations of the compositions of carbonic acid, water, and ammonia; extracts from previously published papers of Boussingault demonstrating that carbon, hydrogen, and in some cases nitrogen, are absorbed from the air by plants; and analyses by Anselme Payen showing that starch and sugar can be represented as a series of compounds of carbon and various proportions of water. He reported that:

Since the first edition of this essay appeared, M. Liebig has published skillful researches on the composition of fibrin, albumin, and casein taken from animals and from plants. He has found these bodies identical in their composition, whatever their origin, as we have admitted ourselves. Thus, this point cannot any longer be questioned, the researches of Liebig having extended, moreover, over a great variety of products.[13]

Liebig's results suggested, Dumas added, that he himself might have given a somewhat too high proportion of hydrogen in these compounds, but that further research was needed to decide which formu-

lae were more accurate. Thus while giving some recognition to Liebig's work Dumas cleverly tried to make it appear as a confirmation of
his own views, without divulging the evidence from which his own
were derived. Among the documents in the appendix were two items
dealing directly with physiological observations; he put in some measurements of his own respired air and calculations of the daily consumption of carbon like those he had used in his course for the past
three years, and he gave reasons similar to those Liebig was giving just
at that time for discounting the difficulties for the theory of animal
heat raised by the experiments of Dulong and Despretz. Altogether
the data Dumas presented only loosely supported his general essay.
The expanded treatise seemed rather like a holding action until he
could get around to the further elaboration he claimed to be forthcoming.[14]

Dumas returned to the subject in February 1842, still not to develop his ideas further, but to refute the charge that he and Boussingault had copied from the lectures and publications of Liebig. In an
article bearing the same title as his original lecture Dumas sought to
prove that he had expressed each of the major points earlier than 1840,
when Liebig began teaching "an analogous system of ideas." Although
the sources of the elements which plants incorporate into organic
matter were known in part since early in the century, Dumas contended, the decisive proofs rested upon the statical methods Boussingault had recently applied to the problem. Dumas recalled that he
himself had already reported to the Academy of Sciences in 1839 on
the significance of this work and had at that time contrasted the "reducing" role of plants with the "combustion" role of animals. The
opinion that animals digest their nutriments without substantially altering them, he said, was based on the experiments published in 1824
by Prévost and Leroyer showing that the chyle of herbivores contains
the same nutritive elements as their aliments, including vegetable albumin. Dumas was able to cite theses submitted to the Faculty of
Medicine in 1839 which verified that he was teaching, a year before
Liebig did, that respiration occurs in successive stages in the blood
rather than in a single step in the lungs. He pointed out that his course
had already followed for three years the general pattern of thought
outlined in the published lecture.[15]

Dumas thus had no trouble disproving Liebig's complaint that he
had not even been interested in these topics until Liebig himself took
them up. On one point, however, Dumas was sufficiently vague to
lend some credibility to Liebig's charge that he had profited more than

he acknowledged from the analyses of nitrogenous animal and vegetable substances made at Giessen. According to Dumas, he had confirmed that animal chyle is made up of plant nutrients: "By making
the analyses of several vegetable aliments ourselves, we have completed this idea." [16] He gave no further details, however, of any such
analyses. Liebig afterward pounced heavily on this lack of substantiating data to allege that Dumas had clandestinely borrowed his own
results. In defending the originality of his ideas Dumas summarized
them again but added little new; he did make a few statements clearer
than before. For example, he made a more complete distinction between the physiological roles of the three classes of nutrients: 1. nitrogenous aliments which are destined for assimilation and enter
through the lacteal vessels; 2. fats, which can be placed in reserve for
the requirements of respiration, and 3. soluble non-nitrogenous aliments which are directly absorbed by the veins and burned consecu-
tively in the blood. These were distinctions about which, according to
Dumas, Liebig had not spoken. (The third memoir of Liebig discussed above appeared a few weeks after Dumas's statement). [17]

Dumas's explanations hardly mollified Liebig, especially since the
French chemists managed just then to add insult to the injury he
believed he had already received. In the same issue of the *Annales de
chimie* the French translation he had asked Pelouze to make of his first
memoir on animal chemistry appeared, but with two critical editorial
footnotes. The first, referring to Liebig's statement that the nitrogenous principles of animals derive from plants, said, "It is scarcely
necessary to remark that this theory with all of its developments was
announced and published by MM. Dumas and Boussingault several
months before the publication of the memoir of M. Liebig." [18] Aside
from its offensive tone the note was unfair, since Liebig's memoir had
originally appeared almost simultaneously with Dumas's lecture. Far
more influential for future events was the second note. After commenting that Liebig and Dumas and Boussingault held similar views
concerning nitrogenous nutrients, it added:

But M. Liebig thinks that herbivorous animals *make* fat with sugar or
starch, whereas MM. Dumas and Boussingault assert as a general rule that
animals, of whatever kind, *do not make* fat or any other organic alimentary
material, and that they borrow all of their aliments, whether they are sugar,
starch, fat or nitrogenous substances, from the vegetable kingdom.

If the assertion of M. Liebig were well-founded, the general formula stated
by MM. Dumas and Boussingault as a summary of the *chemical statics* of the
two kingdoms would be false.

But the Gelatin Commission has placed beyond doubt that animals which eat fat are the only ones where one finds that fats accumulate in the tissues.[19]

The author of the note was twisting the work of the Gelatin Commission to his own purposes. The commission had reported experiments in which animals fed for prolonged periods on fat alone were found to have abnormally large quantities of fat infiltrated throughout their tissues. Magendie had drawn no conclusion, however, such as the one implied here that these results supported the view that animals cannot convert other substances to fat.[20]

Whatever may have been the intent of this note, for Liebig it meant the throwing down of a gauntlet which he could not hesitate to seize. As he saw the situation, "Through this note the investigation of the origins of fatty materials in the animal body suddenly became a controversial issue [*Streitfrage*]."[21]

The issue arose under circumstances of intensifying hostility between Liebig and the French chemists. Boussingault revealed something of the depth of feeling in a letter to Dumas from his farm, after reading Dumas's response to Liebig's complaint that they had used his ideas. It began, "You have placed your finger firmly in M. Liebig's throat."[22] Further on, Boussingault expressed some of the underlying causes of resentment toward Liebig. Having heard that Dumas had become dean of the Faculty of Sciences, he commented,

Now it is essential to organize great resources for research at the faculty, people have produced enough hot air [*limonade gazeuse*] over it. It is truly shameful for France, and I am never so good a Frenchman as when I am along the banks of the Rhine, it is truly shameful that an evil hole like Giessen is a focal point of science, a place where all of the chemical world of Europe meet, and that one would only come to Paris to see our scientists as one comes there to see the zoo of the botanical gardens, purely for curiosity.[23]

Boussingault went on to praise Dumas for his efforts to preserve the predominant place in science which France had inherited from their predecessors.

Feelings were also running high in Giessen. In January Liebig had written his former student Charles Gerhardt, that "everything Dumas says in his 'Essai' on *respiration and animal heat* is taken from my course, as well as everything relative to the identity of the nitrogenous nutrients." During the winter semester of 1840–41, Liebig explained, he had given a course in animal physiology covering these topics, "which were absolutely unknown except to me and my listeners." Among the latter was Charles Marignac, a student recommended to him by Dumas, who had returned to Paris in the spring. In this way, Liebig suggested, Dumas must have got word of the ideas which he appropriated for his lecture of the following summer. "All of the wretched tricks that Dumas uses to exhalt himself in the eyes of the ignorant, at the expense of others, will be of little use to him," Liebig added, for everyone will see "that his ideas are born of my work." Gerhardt's reply further strengthened Liebig's belief that Dumas was systematically abusing his rights. Having translated Liebig's treatise on organic chemistry into French, Gerhardt felt well qualified to say that "the famous lecture on the chemical statics of organized beings is nothing but a copy" of the introduction to that treatise. "Unfortunately we care too much for form in France, and that explains the success of that lecture." Gerhardt, who had become the professor of chemistry at Montepellier in southern France the previous spring, went on to complain that Dumas had arranged that appointment to get him away from Paris. There existed in French science, he claimed, an inquisition against those who dared speak the truth about the intrigues of the bigwigs, and he had been relegated to Montpellier because he was too independent to play the role of a courtesan.[24] Such a characterization of Dumas only reinforced the opinion Liebig had long held; more than once he had publicly accused Dumas of suppressing opinions in Paris contrary to his own. Dumas's article defending his originality therefore only further offended Liebig, moving him to publish in his *Annalen* an "Answer to Herr Dumas's justification with regard to a plagiarism." There he made public his allegation that Marignac had transmitted his ideas to Dumas. Liebig argued that Dumas *must* have got from him the basic conception that animals obtain their nitrogenous constituents from plant matter, because the elementary analyses made in his laboratory were the only proof available of the chemical identity of these animal and vegetable substances. The formulas Dumas cited, he claimed, could only have derived from his own calculations. The reasons Dumas gave for holding similar ideas earlier Liebig dismissed as unsubstantiated opinion. Thus, not even entertaining the possibility that Dumas might have drawn certain inferences without having what he himself considered adequate evidence, Liebig treated the fact of Dumas's having drawn the conclusion as sufficient demonstration that Dumas had had access to his unpublished results.[25]

Informed of the contents of Liebig's article even before it appeared, Dumas quickly wrote him expressing indignation that Liebig should try to implicate a young chemist in his strange accusations. Since his own ideas on respiration and animal heat were only slight modifications of those of Lavoisier, Dumas saw no reason either to claim them for himself or to restore the rights of anyone else to them. If Liebig's contributions had not been adequately credited in the lecture, Dumas said, the oversight was due only to "my absolute ignorance of claims you might have to the discovery of ideas on which I have relied." [26] At Dumas's request Marignac sent a public letter to the *Annales de chimie*, and a private one to Liebig, explaining that when he had heard Liebig's lectures he did not know enough about organic chemistry to recognize their novelty. Consequently, when back in Paris he did not think of mentioning anything about them to Dumas until after he saw Dumas's published lecture and noticed the "great similarity between the views of the two scientists." [27]

On May 2 Dumas gave over one of his course lectures at the École de Médecine to the "painful duty" of answering Liebig's charges. He found himself placed in a position vis-à-vis Liebig which he had not sought, Dumas said, but the situation had reached a point that required explanations. Briefly recapitulating the history of the affair, Dumas then showed that each of the ideas Liebig claimed to have come from him had been stated earlier. Adolphe Brongniart had argued in 1828 that plants must obtain carbon from the atmosphere; Boussingault had established the source of their hydrogen. The proof of the importance of ammonia derived from a report on the use of ammonium sulphate as a fertilizer, given in 1835 by a manufacturer named Schattemann, as well as from the experiments of Boussingault. Liebig's discovery of ammonia in rain water was interesting, but only confirmed what had been predictable ever since the experiments of de Saussure. With respect to the crucial question of the evidence for the identity of plant albumin, fibrin, and casein with those of animals, Dumas cited a series of observations preceding Liebig's analyses. They included the studies of digestion by Prévost, Leroyer, and himself, a discovery of a casein-like material in legumes by Henri Braconnot, and finally the research of Mulder. Liebig had therefore not added anything fundamentally new on the subject. Taking the offensive, Dumas commented that in some of these questions Liebig had failed to mention those who preceded him. As for the general views expressed in his own lecture, Dumas repeated that he had been stating them since 1838 in the Academy and in his course. In his recent article Liebig had dismissed such statements by Dumas as "unmotivated opinions" lacking experimental background. To that Dumas retorted that all of the memoirs by Boussingault on which he had based his views could not possibly have been performed by chance, without a scientific goal.[28]

In private Liebig was even more upset than in public. To Pelouze he confessed in a letter written on April 27 that he regretted having been too harsh in his refutation of Dumas's justifications, but he "had been very irritated." The two editorial comments attached to his translated paper had also got him into further trouble. Because there was a letter (R) beneath them, he supposed that Victor Regnault had written them, and wrote an indignant letter to Regnault only to find out that he had been mistaken and had only angered another colleague unnecessarily.[29] The "R" stood for *Redacteur*, who had in this case, at least so Liebig later assumed, been Dumas himself.[30] On July 2 Liebig wrote Pelouze again, apparently in a state of great agitation centering around Dumas. "In the Dumas affair," he lamented,

I have offended the whole membership of the gelatin commission.[31] If M. Dumas wishes to have a war, he will be sorry for it, but what profit will come of all these discussions for science. None, I am sure; we exchange unkind sentences, we make each other swallow bile . . . we disturb the tranquillity necessary for our daily work, all of that I admit, but can I allow to pass in silence the behavior of a highway robber!?[32]

In such a calm atmosphere Liebig's famous *Animal Chemistry* appeared.[33] Based on an extension of the ideas he had stated in the previously mentioned journal articles, his book had such an impact that it became very difficult for anyone intending to treat problems of digestion, nutrition, or respiration to avoid contending with his chemical approach to physiology.

As far as can be told from the remaining record, Liebig was mistaken in his belief that Dumas and Boussingault had deliberately or surreptitiously appropriated his ideas. In his mind a chain of unlikely coincidences fitted together to give an apparently irrefutable circumstantial case. His judgment was deeply colored, however, by his long distrust of Dumas; by 1841 he was all too ready to suspect the worst of him whenever their paths crossed. It was in part because he had become disgusted with the debates over Dumas's substitution theory, which he had come to feel Dumas was using as a vehicle for personal ambitions, that Liebig had withdrawn from theoretical organic chemistry in 1840 and had concentrated his efforts on agricultural and physiological chemistry.[34] In May 1841, Liebig had roundly criticized Dumas, asserting in his *Annalen* that Dumas's spirit summed up the faults of French chemistry. Dumas was, according to Liebig, wasting his energy on the substitution theory, dealing with chlorinated compounds that were no longer organic and of no practical significance. Meanwhile, too few chemists were following the ex-

ample of Mulder. Almost nothing was known about the most important compounds in plant and animal chemistry. Dumas's theoretical
speculations "in no way make our insights into the character of natural
phenomena clearer, do not help us at all, if we are to explain something in the organism of plants or animals."[35] Not knowing that
Dumas himself had been treating such topics in his course, and overrating the power of his own opinions over his colleagues, Liebig fancied that his remarks had caused Dumas to realize belatedly that he
had been on the wrong track. When Dumas came out with his lecture
three months later, Liebig was sure that Dumas was now trying to
"seize" the new territory that Liebig and his students were opening
up.[36] The opinions of Playfair and Gerhardt undoubtedly assured
Liebig that his perception of the situation was true and would find
general support. Neither of these men, however, was an objective observer, for both were former students and admirers of Liebig. Playfair
was not in a position to know about Dumas's recent activities. Gerhardt was aware of what Dumas had been teaching, for he had studied
with him and assisted him over the preceding three years; but Gerhardt was himself at such odds with Dumas by then that he was as
ready as Liebig to find fault with his conduct.[37] Thus, most of the
pieces fell into a pattern for Liebig, except that there was no obvious
way that Dumas could have got hold of Liebig's unpublished views on
animal chemistry. He had only to persuade himself that a subterranean channel from Giessen to Paris existed, and when he thought of
Marignac's connections the circle seemed closed. Liebig was undoubtedly deeply convinced of the justness of his grievance, yet it was
largely a product of his lively imagination.[38]

It should be said, however, that Dumas and Boussingault created
part of the difficulty by not acknowledging more fully the contributions Liebig's writings on agricultural chemistry had made to the
questions they were now pursuing. Even though they had been interested in the subject for several years, and the views they were expressing in 1841 can be accounted for largely as extensions of their own
prior investigations, the resemblances between their discussions and
those of Liebig could not have been entirely coincidental. On the
other hand, the harsh, repeated criticisms Liebig had made of Dumas's work and character must have made it unpleasant for Dumas to
give Liebig credit even where he knew it was due. The whole affair is
best viewed as another episode in the long, often bitter rivalry into
which these two distinguished chemists had become inextricably enmeshed.[39]

From Pelouze Liebig learned that he had been elected a foreign member of the French Academy of Sciences.[40] The honor, which he had coveted, seemed to placate him, as possibly it had been intended to do, and the most acrimonious aspects of his debate with the French chemists subsided. During the preceding months emotions had largely overshadowed substantive issues. The history of the clashes of these men may seem at first glance inconsequential for an understanding of the scientific state of animal chemistry; yet the feelings evoked and the personal characteristics displayed help to explain the ensuing course of research. Originally, Dumas and Boussingault may or may not have had strong convictions behind their statements about the sources of animal fat. Afterward, however, their theory of its exclusively vegetable origin had emerged as one of the decisive points of difference between their views and those of Liebig. Feelings conspired with reason to magnify the importance of the divergence. Accused of copying his ideas from Liebig, Dumas seized upon this disagreement as one way of emphasizing the independence of his own views. In his discussion of Liebig's claims during his course, Dumas declared that for the case of non-nitrogenous aliments:

There is no dispute possible on the subject of priority, but here the opinions of M. Liebig are in complete disagreement, and I would even say that the opinions of M. Liebig on this subject are in such contradiction with the principles which we have posed and which we admit with all their consequences, that this alone seems to prove that his opinions, taken from the most general point of view, differ essentially from ours.[41]

After Dumas and Boussingault had made such a stand, the desire to vindicate themselves in the face of their rivals probably helped spur the French scientists on to pursue the exceedingly painstaking experiments they carried out in the following years to garner support for their contention. Personal animosities thus may have had a positive influence upon an important series of researches. On the other hand the same involvements led the French chemists to concentrate so fixedly on surmounting the criticisms Liebig directed at the work they produced that they did not respond to more fundamental criticisms of their methods aimed at them from other directions.

III

The Debate over the Source of Animal Fat

In the spring of 1842 Dumas oriented his course at the École de Médecine around his controversial ideas about plants and animals. Whereas he had pulled the general picture together only in his closing lecture the previous year, he now felt in a position to use that synthesis as an introduction and guide to the whole subject of organic chemistry. He began on April 11 with a new version of his lecture on "The statics of organized beings." The basic ideas were still the same, but he presented them from a different perspective. The grand cycle of nature was still the underlying assumption, but it was now muted, and Dumas now appeared to be chiefly concerned with the problem of human and animal nutrition. Thus he devoted the first half of his talk to the nature of the alimentary substances of animals, and then showed that plants contained precisely these kinds of material. Afterward he discussed the sources of the elements from which plants composed these substances, but instead of focusing on the movements of materials between animals, plants, and the atmosphere, he stressed the practical question of how best to supplement the nitrogen in the soil of a given locale so as to increase the productivity of the land. The key issue was to provide an inexpensive source of ammonia. He directed his eloquence this time toward utilitarian objectives. "To produce ammonia cheaply," he declared, is to "augment the population; in a word, to produce humans." [1]

In support of this practical emphasis, Dumas stressed the quantitative aspect of nutrition. From the results of his old measurements of the rate of exhalation of carbonic acid and from some recent measurements by Louis Lecanu of the amount of urea secreted daily by hu-

48

mans, Dumas estimated that a person requires fifteen grams of nitrogen and three hundred grams of carbon each day to replace the quantities of these elements lost. He then calculated the carbon and nitrogen contents of the ordinary ration of a French military officer and concluded that they were sufficient to fulfill the requirements for good nutrition. All too often, however, the general population was not adequately nourished, and such calculations, Dumas maintained, demonstrated that chemistry is an essential guide for legislators wishing to relieve human suffering.[2]

Dumas also used a different way to demonstrate his earlier contention that plants provide all of the nutrient materials animals require. The most common food of herbivorous animals, he pointed out, was grain. If one separates the constituents of wheat by mixing flour with water, the insoluble portion is gluten, a complex material. By further extractions in ether and alcohol, gluten yields a material similar to casein, "gluten proper," which resembles gelatin, and a residue of vegetable fibrin. The water-soluble fraction deposits starch; when heated it produces coagulated albumin, and by evaporation it yields sugar. Thus by eating grain, herbivores obtain all the essential materials that carnivores assimilate from other animals. This result, he pointed out, was in harmony with the experiments of the Gelatin Commission showing that gluten is the substance best suited to sustain the life of dogs when given alone. The fact that wheat grain contained starch instead of the fat that carnivores eat did not bother Dumas, because neither substance had to be assimilated, and either could be consumed equally well in respiration.[3]

It is evident that the new elements Dumas added to his lecture must have been inspired by the articles Liebig had published on the topic since Dumas had last treated it. To show that a single plant source contains all of the constituents of an animal diet was perhaps to illustrate in an original and dramatic way the general principle involved; but his demonstration that plant materials contain the constituents he enumerated bears enough resemblance to Liebig's memoir of the previous August to make it likely that Dumas profited from Liebig's discussion.[4] Similarly, though based on different data, Dumas's calculations of the quantitative nutritional requirements were in the same spirit as those Liebig had given in his second memoir.[5] Dumas extended Liebig's approach by including nitrogen, whereas Liebig had considered only carbon. It is probable that Liebig's example had influenced Dumas to shift his emphasis from the balance of nature to the requirements of animal nutrition, and particularly to pose the issue in terms of the equivalence between a carnivorous and a herbivorous diet. To adopt the latest ideas in the field in his teaching was entirely reasonable, but the notes of Dumas's lecture do not suggest that he acknowledged he was drawing on Liebig's work.[6]

During his next three lectures Dumas discussed methods of organic analysis, the composition of the air, and plant nutrition as investigated by Boussingault and his predecessors.[7] Treating "the phenomena of combustion in organized beings" in the fifth lesson, he made a major exception to the contrasts he had previously drawn between plants and animals. Normally, the green parts of plants in the sunlight decompose carbonic acid and water and disengage oxygen, he maintained, but during germination, flowering, and fertilization, a plant burns carbon and hydrogen, producing carbonic acid and water. At such times "it has completely changed roles, and functions, with respect to the air, as an animal would." To confirm this view Dumas cited observations by a number of scientists of carbonic acid evolved by large flowers and of situations in which the temperature of parts of plants was slightly above that of the air, so that they must be producing some heat. One could admit that combustion occurs in plants, Dumas asserted, "without any repugnance, even while fully adopting the views I profess." The general phenomenon was still the reducing role of plants. On the surface Dumas's position might appear to have become absurd, since he had nearly defined plants and animals by their opposed roles: he was even led to say that "a plant sometimes becomes an animal." [8] It was not unprecedented, however, to make a distinction between "animal" and "plant" properties which did not entirely coincide with the division of organisms into the plant and animal kingdoms. During the eighteenth century, chemists had begun to extract from plant materials substances with the properties by which they had formerly characterized animal matter. For a long time they regarded such substances as "animal" matter in spite of their source, a habit which was still traceable in the designations "plant albumin," "plant fibrin," and "plant casein." Dumas's discussion again revealed his double standard, however, for he did not admit that animals might in turn exhibit plant-like reduction processes. The inconsistency was still rooted in the way Dumas hoped to investigate the processes. To admit that combustions occur in plants raised no methodological problems, for he had already admitted that chemistry was incapable of reproducing all of the phenomena of the life of plants.[9] To accept the inverse, however, would have threatened his goal of reproducing the phenomena of the life of animals by means of organic chemistry.

The way in which Dumas intended to pursue that quest became clearer in his lecture on fats. Of the three classes of organic substances considered important in nutritional processes, fats were chemically the most adequately described. The masterful research of Michel Eugène Chevreul, completed in 1825 after more than ten years' work, had shown that these endlessly variable substances could be analyzed into a few specific chemical compounds of fixed elementary composition, combined in definite proportions. Besides proving that fats are composed of glycerol joined to one or more of a few similar acids, Chevreul provided analyses of the elementary composition of these constituents which were, for their time, models of precision. Chevreul set standards that influenced all investigations of organic compounds over the following decades; for fats themselves his results were so thorough and impressive that most chemists thought they could hardly improve on them.[10] Nevertheless Chevreul's *Recherches chimiques sus les corps gras* (Chemical researches on fatty bodies) contained numerous leads for further studies. He reported, for example, that the distillation of stearic acid gave rise to a different substance, and that the reaction of the same acid with nitric acid gave a distinct new acid, but he did not identify these products.[11] In 1825 Antoine Bussy and Louis Lecanu began distilling different fats in order to characterize more fully the resulting compounds. The latter included in most cases margaric acid, a compound so similar to stearic acid that Chevreul had not differentiated them until after he observed that the melting point of the acid which was derived from human, pig, jaguar, and goose fat was lower than that obtained from mutton and beef fat. Later Chevreul had shown that one acid contained one sixth less oxygen than the other.[12]

According to Chevreul, the formula for hydrated stearic acid was $C_{70}H_{135}O_5$, that for margaric acid $C_{34}H_{65}O_3$. Berzelius suggested, however, that if one made slight, reasonable corrections in these formulas, both acids could be considered to contain the same radical, $R = C_{35}H_{67}$. Margaric acid would then be $R + 3O$ and stearic acid $2R + 5O$. The two acids would then be related as were hyposulfuric and sulfuric acid, or chloric and oxychloric acid; that is, they would represent two degrees of oxidation of the radical.[13]

In 1838 Liebig decided that it was time to reassess Chevreul's investigations in the light of the important advances in analytical methods which had been made since 1825. The task was so large that he assigned six outstanding young chemists in his laboratory to work on it. The question he particularly wished to resolve was, what was the source of the margaric acid that Bussy and Lecanu had obtained from fats that had not previously contained it? Since these fats were largely comprised of stearic acid, the problem became "How and in what way can margaric acid originate from stearic acid?" [14] Franz Varrentrap investigated margaric acid, while Joseph Redtenbacher concentrated on stearic acid. From the results of combustion analyses differing somewhat from those of Chevreul, they modified his formulas respectively to $C_{34}H_{66}O_3$ and $C_{72}H_{132}O_5$. The changes fit nicely with Berzelius's interpretation of their composition. In addition, Redtenbacher was able to produce margaric acid by distilling pure stearic acid. In other words, he said, "out of the stearic acid of cattle comes the acid of human fat." Because there were a number of other products as well, his interpretation of the reaction was complicated and hypothetical, but in accordance with Berzelius's view of the constitution of the two acids, Redtenbacher regarded the conversion as an oxidative decomposition. [15]

As Dumas reviewed the cumulative results of these investigations with his usual sharp eye for generalizations, he concluded that the composition of fatty acids would lead to "an exposition of the transformations which fats undergo in animals." Noting that stearic acid predominated in the fat of herbivorous animals and margaric acid in carnivores, and adopting a conception of the transformation of one acid to the other similar to that established by Bussy and Redtenbacher, Dumas inferred that the fats containing stearic acid represented the original state in which animals assimilated them from plants. By the time the fats have passed from herbivores into carnivores, they have already undergone "a beginning of combustion, and in oxidizing, stearic acid decomposes and gives margaric acid." [16] Margaric acid was known, moreover, to be oxidizable to suberic acid and finally to succinic acid. Examining the formulas for the known fatty acids, Dumas grouped them into the following series:

$$C^{34}H^{34}O^4 \quad \text{margaric acid}$$
$$C^{32}H^{32}O^4 \quad \text{palmitic acid}$$
$$C^{30}H^{30}O^4 \quad \text{unknown}$$
$$C^{28}H^{28}O^4 \quad \text{myristic acid}$$
$$C^{26}H^{26}O^4 \quad \text{cocinic acid}$$
$$C^{24}H^{24}O^4 \quad \text{lauric acid}$$
$$C^{22}H^{22}O^4 \quad \text{unknown}$$
$$C^{20}H^{20}O^4 \quad \text{unknown}$$
$$C^{18}H^{18}O^4 \quad \text{capric acid}$$

$C^{16}H^{16}O^4$ unknown
$C^{14}H^{14}O^4$ enanthic acid
$C^{12}H^{12}O^4$ caproic acid
$C^{10}H^{10}O^4$ valeric acid
$C^8 H^8 O^4$ butyric acid
$C^6 H^6 O^4$ unknown
$C^4 H^4 O^4$ acetic acid
$C^2 H^2 O^4$ formic acid

Each acid could be derived from the previous one by removing two "molecules" of carbon and two of hydrogen.[17] The identification of this sequence, one of several efforts by Dumas to establish classifications of related organic compounds, was an important contribution to the conception that Gerhardt shortly afterward generalized as "homologous series."[18] For Dumas, however, the idea served also as a means to reduce the phenomena in the animal economy involving fats "to the greatest simplicity"; for after passing into the blood in a state of emulsion, he believed, fats underwent just such a sequence of successive decompositions, until they either became volatile acids which were excreted in perspiration or reached the final state of carbonic acid and water. Calculating the amount of heat that the combustion of the carbon and hydrogen in 200 grams of fat could provide, Dumas asserted that it would be sufficient to account for the heat produced by a man in one day.[19]

Dumas's new elaboration of his physiological views revealed, more fully than had his well-publicized lecture, the assumptions on which he based them. The development he gave them shows also the close connection between his physiological thought and the dynamic growth of organic chemistry itself. In 1838 he had only enumerated general modes of oxidation reactions of organic compounds which might be analogous to the processes of respiration. In 1842, largely because of new studies of the relations and reactions of fatty acids, he was able to propose a specified sequence of transformations he thought actually occurred in the blood. This advance did not make his theory any less speculative, but did make it more concrete. He had now at least provided some details of the processes that might occur if his general principles were correct. The principles themselves were still very simple, but the phenomena deduced from them were beginning to appear more intricate than Dumas's earlier descriptions had suggested. Dumas also relied on a criterion of proof for his theories that soon came to characterize the physiological efforts of the

organic chemists; his central argument for inferring that a class of reactions takes place in animals was that such a reaction had been produced outside of them. The recent demonstration of the conversion of
stearic acid to margaric acid became the justification for believing that
not only that reaction, but others of the same general type, occur
physiologically. Another assumption implied in his discussion was
that one needed to show that the conditions where one supposed a reaction to occur within the animal were conducive to that reaction.
Dumas asserted, for example, that the alkalinity of the blood and the
emulsification of the fats within it both favored the combustion of the
fats, just as a cloth impregnated with a fat or oil dissolved in alkali
would spontaneously heat up until it reached the combustion point.
Both the cloth and the emulsion caused the fat to be in a finely divided
condition in which it was easily combustible.[20] The conditions
Dumas considered, therefore, were limited to the chemical properties
of blood itself. That the blood happened to be moving within the circulatory vessels of the organism did not differentiate the situation in
his mind from the condition of blood in an ordinary chemical vessel.
Even within that restricted definition, he was obviously satisfied with
a much cruder definition of conditions than he would have accepted
within organic chemistry itself as a statement of the circumstances
under which a given reaction would take place. Theories are often
most easily constructed for phenomena about which the fewest data
are available.

While Dumas expounded his physiological views at the École de
Médecine, scientists outside of Paris still knew them only from the
briefer, doctrinaire statements in his well-known lecture. Finally, in
the fall of 1842, he began to present the "experimental development"
of his theories that he had long promised. At the Academy of Sciences
he read a paper in November on the "neutral nitrogenous materials of
organisms." "The exact demonstration of the laws which we have
stated," he said, "required a great number of very delicate analyses." [21] These analyses seemed intended to fill in the most glaring gap
in his earlier argument, the fact that independently of Liebig's research he had no specific data to demonstrate the chemical identity of
the crucial animal and vegetable substances. With the assistance of
two younger chemists, Auguste Cahours and Saint-Eve, he improved
the precision of measurement of the constituent elements by taking
extraordinary care to analyze completely dry materials, by working
with large enough quantities of nitrogen gas so that he could detect
slight differences in volume, and by other refinements. Among the

analyses Liebig had reported the previous year, the carbon and nitrogen determinations in different trials with the same substance generally varied by 1 percent or more. Dumas, by comparison, usually achieved for the same kind of substance from different animal and vegetable sources results consistent to several tenths of a percent. Instead of treating his own investigation as a further development of Liebig's, however, Dumas conspicuously avoided any reference to the work of his counterpart except to correct him on certain special points.[22] Whether from stubborn pride in his independent path, or resentment over past grievances, or as Liebig would have put it, because of personal ambition, Dumas seemed unable to acknowledge even the most evident contributions of Liebig to the problem. Liebig, of course, could do little more for Dumas.

The most significant outcome of the higher order of precision which Dumas achieved in his analyses was to show that the elementary compositions of the recognized types of nitrogenous substances were not all alike as Mulder and Liebig had supposed. Fibrin contained a greater proportion of nitrogen than did casein or albumin, which were identical in composition. (His values for fibrin ranged from 16.41 to 16.72%, those for albumin from 15.66 to 15.82%). He found also that, contrary to Liebig's opinion, "legumine," a substance discovered by Braconnot in peas and beans, differed in composition from casein, and he showed that its properties were also different. It was, therefore, "a distinct compound" which must play an important role in the nutrition of some animals. From a study of the reactions of fibrin and legumin he came to suspect that each might be composed of casein or albumin and of some other constituent containing more nitrogen.[23]

From such results one might expect Dumas to have been led to suspect that the interactions of these substances in the animal body must be more complex than previously supposed and to involve transformations more substantial than the "slight changes in form" which both he and Liebig had postulated as sufficient to convert nutrients to tissue substances. There was, however, a curious dichotomy between the finer discriminations he sought in the chemical foundations for his physiological theories and the continued simplicity of the theories themselves. Thus he maintained as unqualifiedly as ever that "plants alone have the privilege of fabricating these products, which animals secure from them, either to assimilate them or destroy them." He drew up, in fact, a little table to dramatize the opposed features of processes in plants and animals.[24] Evidently the real basis of his theory was still a schematic conception of the symmetry of nature.

Dumas's *a priori* commitment to the scheme was transparent from the very procedure by which he set out to give experimental proofs after he had "established it in principle."

In their memoir Dumas and Cahours published the argument Dumas had previously given in his course, that cereal grain, the principal food of herbivores, was capable of supplying each of the classes of nutrient that animals need.[25] He tried also to justify more fully the inclusion of the processes which nitrogenous substances undergo within the body in the category of destructive oxidations to which he thought all chemical changes in animals were limited. All of the nitrogen which a man eats in his food reappears as urea in the urine. The sole end result, therefore, of the absorption of nitrogenous substances is the production from them of urea. As the researches of Wöhler showed, urea can be considered to be a combination of the oxides of cyanogen and of ammonia. Consequently, "the nitrogenous matter is converted into urea by a veritable combustion." From a hypothetical equation showing that albumin can be represented as decomposable into urea, carbonic acid, and water, he calculated the quantity of heat which ought to be released in the reaction. He computed from this quantity and the rate of production of urea in an animal that the combustion would not produce sufficient heat to cover the heat lost by the animal. The non-nitrogenous nutrients were thus needed to supply the difference, he concluded,[26] strengthening his earlier contention that they were "respiratory aliments." The argument was a somewhat more sophisticated version of one Liebig had made in his *Animal Chemistry.*[27] Though even his new evidence for his physiological theories was at best circumstantial, Dumas asserted that it amounted to a nearly irrefutable demonstration.

Meanwhile, Dumas and Liebig were drifting into an extended confrontation over the principal issue between them, the source of animal fat. Liebig's original reasons for maintaining that animals convert starch and sugar to fats were rather slim. As we have seen, they consisted of the common knowledge that domestic animals are fattened by feeding them grains and the speculation that the chemical reaction would require only the removal of oxygen from the sugar molecules.[28] These arguments he repeated in his *Animal Chemistry*, but as an afterthought, probably in reaction to the editorial note Dumas had attached to his earlier article, he added two more persuasive items of evidence. In an appendix he reprinted portions of a recent book by F.W. Gundlach in which the author showed that bees can produce wax when kept on a diet of pure honey, or even on sugar alone. Gundlach had measured the amount of honey consumed and of wax produced and calculated that twenty pounds of honey are required to form one pound of wax.[29] In the preface of *Animal Chemistry* Liebig wrote:

How clear are now to us the relations of the different articles of food to the objects which they serve in the body, since organic chemistry has applied to the investigation her *quantitative method* of research!

When a lean goose, weighing 4 lbs., gains, in thirty-six days, during which it has been fed with 24 lbs. of maize, 5 lbs. in weight, and yields 3½ lbs. of pure fat, this fat cannot have been contained in the food, ready formed, because maize does not contain the thousandth part of its weight of fat, or of any substance resembling fat.[30]

Liebig then referred to the experiments of Gundlach as proof of the "formation of fat from sugar in the animal body." In spite of the grand allusions to a new quantitative method, the example of the goose Liebig adduced was not a particularly impressive sample of the advantages that he contended the rigor of chemistry could confer upon physiology. As he later explained, while he was writing his preface a friend had informed him of the results of fattening a goose. He had then simply looked up in the chemical literature two different analyses of maize which made no mention that it contained any fats or oils. Without making a special investigation himself, he inserted his conclusion into his introductory discussion of methods, too hastily apparently to revise the main treatment of the topic in his book.[31] Nevertheless, his statement became the germinal point for researches which were as laborious as his had been casual.

Dumas was probably unaware of the sources of Liebig's information when, "after searching for a considerable time" for a way to explain observations backed by Liebig's "great authority," he and his colleague Anselme Payen were ready to challenge Liebig's case. On October 24 he reported briefly to the Academy that they had "by precise experiments" ascertained that maize contains about nine percent of a yellow oil. From Liebig's figures they calculated that the food could therefore have supplied 1.25 of the 1.75 kilograms of fat the goose yielded. The rest they presumed the goose already contained prior to the feeding. They would soon show in addition, they said, that cattle and milk cows always furnish the same amount or less of fatty material than they can obtain in their food.[32]

The French chemists had apparently won an easy round, but Liebig was too formidable not to mount an effective counterattack when caught off guard. In December he published a reply which implicitly conceded that he had not prepared his position as carefully as he might have done, because he had considered it nearly self-evident that starches and sugars produce animal fat. Now he made up for his lack by putting together a combination of data and reasoning which seemed to make the assumptions of Dumas and his colleagues untenable. He drew crucial evidence from their own camp by utilizing the experiments of Boussingault himself. In 1839 Boussingault had measured the total intake of food and the urine, excrements, and milk produced by a cow over a period of several days. His object had been to see whether the food supplied sufficient amounts of the elements, in particular of nitrogen, to balance the losses of the animal.[33] Liebig, however, used the same figures in a different way. The diet had consisted of potatoes and hay. Making his own analyses of the percentage of fats contained in these foods, he calculated the total amount of fat which the cow could have ingested and found it to be less than one fourth of the quantity of butter produced in the milk. Because of Dumas and Payen's report Liebig analyzed maize himself by two different methods and found no more than 4.67 percent of oil instead of the nine percent they reported. The proportion of fatty material thus varied so greatly in different varieties of the feed, he said, that no arguments one way or the other could be drawn from the data on the goose which he once had used as proof of his own view. He could cite other figures on the raising of pigs, however, in which the dietary source of fat seemed clearly inadequate to account for the fat obtained when they were slaughtered. Thus from purely quantitative considerations Liebig was able to adduce counter-instances which appeared to refute the French theory. He went beyond this, however, to criticize more basically the foundations for Dumas's views. All substances extractable from organic matter in ether were customarily regarded as fatty substances, he pointed out, and had been treated so in the foregoing calculations. Yet the ether-soluble constituents of plant matters such as hay were quite different in properties and composition from butter or other animal fats. They consisted of chlorophyll or waxy compounds, and did not contain either margaric or stearic acids, the chief constituents of animal fat. Thus even if these substances were the source of the fat they would have to be considerably altered in the animal. But nearly all of the waxy matter contained in the food of a cow, Liebig showed, could be recovered in its faeces, and therefore could not contribute to the formation of fat.[34]

Dumas's opinion, Liebig asserted, was derived from the "purely hypothetical principle that animal organisms cannot create any nutritional material." That the animal does not create them [*erzeugt*] Liebig agreed, but it does transform them [*verwandelt*], he contended, so that it can produce fat so long as it is presented with a substance "from which it can arise through a conversion [*Umwandlung*]." He had already suggested, he recalled, how such a conversion from sugar or starch was possible on chemical grounds, and there was every reason to believe it occurred in animals. Although he emphasized his agreement with Dumas that animals cannot produce the nitrogenous substances essential to their organization, he ended by expressing a general point of view in striking contrast to the symmetrical opposition Dumas saw between the processes of animals and of vegetables. "It can scarcely be doubted," he said, "that with respect to the formation of many of their constituents, similar processes can take place in animals as do in plants." [35]

Even after this consolidation of his position, Liebig was more vulnerable than either the plausibility of his reasoning or a retrospective judgment of the issue might indicate. His adversaries held important tactical advantages which they utilized effectively, as they joined forces to support the position they had come to agree on. Boussingault provided their most important asset, in his unique experience and facilities for carrying out the lengthy, rigorous feeding experiments upon which the question seemed most directly to turn. He had come to concentrate on the source of animal fat while carrying out experiments on his farm in the fall of 1842 to ascertain the most effective and economical foods for raising livestock. Testing diets composed entirely of roots, he found that cows did not do as well as they did when their usual hay and wheat were added. This result led him to undertake a special investigation of the "role of the fatty or waxy principles" contained in these forage constituents. Not until he had arrived at that question independently in this way did Boussingault learn that in Paris Dumas and Payen were also becoming increasingly involved in the fat question. [36] If Dumas was concerned primarily to defend the general principles of his system, Payen joined the enterprise, like Boussingault, chiefly out of his interest in the practical agricultural implications. For many years Payen had sought to bring chemical knowledge to the aid of industrial and agricultural practices. After studying chemistry for two years in the laboratories of Chevreul and Louis Nicholas Vauquelin, Payen began in 1814 to direct a sugar beet factory owned by his father. During the next two decades he worked to improve the cultivation and refining of sugar beets, and investigated the use of plant and animal materials for fertilizer. During the 1830's he carried out a series of important experiments on the properties and reactions of starch. These interests led him to examine the constituents of plant tissues and to discover that very young plants, as well as the buds and other growing parts of older ones, contained much larger proportions of nitrogenous substances than did plant material in general. Extending his analyses of plant tissue, Payen found that plant "membranes" all consisted of cellulose, a material which was, when purified, always identical in its composition.[37]

In 1835 Payen took Dumas's place in a course on "chemistry applied to the arts and agriculture" at the École Centrale, and with Dumas's support Payen obtained a permanent position in that school. During the next few years the two men consulted each other on various scientific questions and apparently became good friends.[38] Payen enthusiastically supported Dumas during the controversy over the substitution theory. In 1838 Payen competed with Boussingault for a position in the Academy of Sciences, but Boussingault won. At about the same time Payen established two experimental farms in order to expand his investigations of ways to ameliorate crop production. Although he was already well-respected for both his scientific and his applied research, Payen only began what he considered a full-time career in science in 1839, at the age of forty-four. Appointed at that time as a professor at the Conservatoire Royal des Arts et Métiers, he gave up his commercial enterprises in order to devote all of his attention to research and teaching. As mentioned earlier, Payen and Boussingault examined together in 1841 the nitrogenous content of fertilizers, an investigation representing a natural convergence of their interests. On his second try Payen was elected, in January 1842, to the Academy of Sciences.[39]

Payen was highly impressed with the physiological system of Dumas and Boussingault. He was particularly interested in the point that they attributed to plants the special action of forming all of the fatty bodies essential to animals, for he had found during his many analyses of plant substances, that fatty materials were universally distributed within the vegetable kingdom. Even substances which appeared poor in fats yielded them on analysis. After carefully examining the theories of Dumas and Boussingault in the light of his own experience, Payen decided to be "the first to rally to views, the great value of which no one appreciates better than I." [40] Payen was sympathetic on doctrinal grounds to Dumas's contrasts between plants and animals, for he too had tried to establish a distinctive characteristic to

Jean-Baptiste Boussingault

Anselme Payen

separate them. His discovery of the cellulose membrane common to all plant material differentiated plants clearly, he thought, from animals, whose membranes contained "quaternary" nitrogenous substances instead.[41] Yet just as his scientific objectives had always grown out of his utilitarian concerns, Payen was interested in the fat question mainly because the choice of foods to fatten livestock depended on the outcome of the debate. His studies had prepared him, he said, to foresee the role that these views would play in the destiny of French agriculture. As a person who had recently and relatively late in his career attained his place in the scientific establishment, Payen must also have been pleased and flattered to become a partner in the defense of the ideas of his prestigious friend Dumas, now at the apex of that establishment. Believing that the common research effort of the three chemists revived the original spirit of scientific cooperation for which the Academy of Sciences had been founded, Payen hoped that they would attract other members to join with them. The scope of the problem made it necessary, he maintained, to invoke the cooperation of "the methods of practical chemistry and the illumination of animal or plant physiology, two sciences represented with such distinction in the Academy." [42] It turned out, as will be seen, that the chemists were not prepared to incorporate the opinions their efforts evoked from physiologists.

Payen realized that if the widespread presence of fats in plants made plausible the view that they supply fats to animals, it remained to be proved that plants supplied sufficient quantities to account for all the fats animals produced. He therefore applied himself to gathering data on that question. In addition to determining the percentage of fatty matter in food crops, he used his agricultural contacts to obtain information on the feeding of farm animals. At his request some farmers tested the effects of changes in the daily rations of their horses, cattle, pigs, or geese. Their reports, Payen thought, were "in accord with our ideas and our results." [43] Meanwhile Boussingault was providing stronger support for the same conclusion by means of carefully controlled feeding experiments. By January 1843 the three chemists believed they had enough evidence to present a new defense of their theory.

On January 23 Payen began to read in the Academy a memoir by the three chemists summarizing the case they had assembled. Apparently the press of other business during the next three sessions prevented him from continuing, so that on February 13 the authors submitted their manuscript for publication in the *Compte rendu* without finishing its presentation.[44] The most critical data they had were the quantitative comparisons of the nutritive supply of fats and the amounts produced by the animal. By determining the amount of fatty material in foods such as hay, commonly held to contain very little of it, he and Dumas found that the butter which a cow ordinarily supplies can be provided by the fatty substances in their normal food. Their data derived from general agricultural experience and analyses of the average fat contents of food and milk. More decisive were the experiments Boussingault had been carrying out expressly to resolve the question, in which he recorded the exact amounts of food eaten and milk produced, and analyzed samples of the same materials for their fat content. From large-scale experiments on seven cows which furnished a total of 17,976 liters of milk, Boussingault could show that they had eaten 689 kilograms of fatty substances and given only 673 kilograms of butter. This most impressive case Payen supplemented with the records he had obtained from other scientifically oriented agriculturalists, all leading to the same conclusion: "A cow extracts from its aliments nearly all of the fatty material which they contain and converts this fatty matter into butter." [45]

Payen also gave further details of the analyses he and Dumas had already announced in refutation of Liebig's original statement that maize contains no fatty substances. Then he dealt with the problem of the wax bees produced when fed only sugar. Such observations do not prove that the bees have converted sugar to wax, he contended, for they may well be forming the wax from fat stored in their own bodies, and probably would be able for some time to go on producing it when fed nothing at all. In experiments performed by Huber sixty years before, the wax from bees fed sugar exclusively became more easily fusible, which meant, according to Payen, that animal fats probably were being incorporated into the wax.[46]

To his quantitative arguments Payen added a few bits of qualitative evidence that dietary fat is assimilated into an animal while retaining its original properties. Magendie and other physiologists had observed fat globules in the chyle and even in the blood of animals which had eaten large amounts of fat. There "they persist for a long time unaltered and remain at the service of the animal." No such substances were visible or extractable from the same fluids of animals on nonfat diets. Furthermore, by changing the quality of the fatty materials in the diets of cows one can alter the quality of and the proportions of different fatty acids contained in their butter.[47]

In spite of these latter arguments the French chemists were soften-

ing the rigid statements of Dumas's "Chemical statics of organized beings." Instead of saying that animals absorb and assimilate fats "almost intact" as the plants have formed them, they were now
maintaining that "the fatty matter passes in its natural state into the
animal which it nourishes, and it becomes fixed there more or less
modified." [48] What they insisted on was only that "fatty substances
cannot be entirely formed [*se former de toutes pièces*] in the animal." [49]
This change was undoubtedly due to the fact that they too had realized that the waxy materials in green plants they counted as fats were
chemically distinct from animal fat. They retained their basic point of
view that all transformations in animals are oxidative decompositions,
however, by extending the scheme Dumas had discussed in his course
in 1842. After passing into the blood of herbivorous animals waxes
were, they claimed, converted by a "commencement" of oxidation
into stearic or oleic acid. The transformation of these acids into
margaric acid and the subsequent steps proceeded as Dumas had already described them. [50] Thus their general statements seemed to be
moving toward Liebig's view that conversions, if not the creation, of
nutritive materials take place in animals, but substantively they still
opposed his position by admitting only one class of conversions.

When Liebig saw the memoir of Payen, Dumas, and Boussingault
it was obvious to him that they were still refuting the statements in his
Animal Chemistry without taking into account his more recent article
on the formation of fat. Therefore he sent to the Academy a letter
which reemphasized his chief objections to the French view, and he
mailed Payen a copy of his article. [51] The letter, read at the session of
March 6, repeated his calculations based on Boussingault's older feeding experiments and his own analyses, but asserted more definitely
that he himself had found "to his great surprise" that the excrements
contain nearly all of the waxes ingested by a cow in its food. He said
also that it is difficult to conceive how wax, "a substance which is not
saponifiable, and whose melting point is higher than the temperature
of an animal, can pass into its blood to undergo there oxidation and
transformation into stearic acid." [52]

Liebig's letter provoked in the French Academy a lively debate,
during which Payen, Dumas, Boussingault, and Magendie all played
prominent parts. Payen replied by repeating the arguments for the
French chemists' claim that maize contains nine percent fatty matter.
If Liebig had been unable to extract as much, Payen said, it was probably because he had used rancid maize. [53] This was no longer a critical
point, however, for both sides had gone beyond Liebig's original ac-

count of the fattening of a goose, which had depended on the figure for fat in maize, to better developed cases. Afterward, Dumas spoke and more adroitly attacked the central support for Liebig's present position. "It is not rational," he asserted, "to conclude from experiments on one cow to those on another," because the quantity of fats extractable from nutrients varies according to the procedures used. Dumas indicated that he would formulate his response more precisely at another meeting. He wrote out his reply and read it on March 13.[54] For the conclusion drawn from Boussingault's experiments, he pointed out, Liebig had taken figures for the consumption of food and the production of milk and excrements from two different investigations made at Bechelbronn, combining them as if they represented a single case. Then from analyses of similar foodstuffs and of milk made at Giessen he had computed the quantities of fats he supposed to have been involved in Boussingault's results. The proportions of fat vary so widely both in the food and milk, however, Dumas asserted, that such a procedure can have no value. Liebig had composed "a fictitious experiment" by joining together real but heterogenous results. His conclusion was based on "animals too chimerical" to be taken seriously. The French chemists, on the other hand, were preparing to prove their case on the basis of actual and strictly controlled experiments which would show Liebig "how much care and precaution a truly serious discussion of such facts requires." [55]

Less telling actually, but typical of the deft debating which often seemed as important to both the French chemists and Liebig as did the scientific question itself, was a criticism Dumas made of Liebig's doubt that wax can be transformed into fat in the animal body. According to Dumas, Liebig "does not understand how it [wax] can be converted into fat or butter." But, Dumas noted, Liebig was able to imagine perfectly well how fibrin, sugar, and other related substances may be converted into fat in animals and how sugar can become wax in bees. If so, how can it be unreasonable to suppose that wax, "by an almost isomeric metamorphosis," changes into fatty acids. This argument shrewdly made Liebig appear inconsistent, but did not address the question whether the conversions either chemists envisioned were objectively supportable. Furthermore, whether by misunderstanding or design, Dumas was somewhat misrepresenting Liebig's statements when he portrayed him as not understanding the process on chemical grounds alone, for Liebig's skepticism included the difficulty of conceiving the physiological absorption of wax into the blood.[56]

After three weeks, during which the Academy was distracted by the election of new members,[57] the same contestants returned at the session of April 3 to the question of fat nutrition. The occasion was another letter from Liebig responding to the published answers of the French chemists to his first. In the new exchange the tide seemed to be running more strongly against Liebig, who could add little new evidence for his views. He indicated some interesting contradictions in the French position, but they were based on subtle reasoning and couched in ironic statements which could readily be overlooked. The French chemists, in contrast, were ready to make public new observations admirably suited to their purposes.

Liebig asserted in his letter that Dumas had no basis for calling his experiment fictitious, for he had measured the amounts of food and excrements of a real cow in Giessen. The quantity of milk it gave just turned out to be the same as that rendered by a cow in Boussingault's experiments which had eaten the same kind and amount of food.[58] Dumas was able to show in reply, however, that the figures Liebig had given in his earlier account of this investigation were exact duplicates of those recorded by Boussingault, so that it was not credible that they could have derived from an independent experiment.[59] If Liebig really did perform the experiment as he claimed, his result nearly justified his conclusion that "the fatty matters contained in the potatoes and the hay contribute nothing to the formation of butter, since they are excreted in the faeces"; [60] but he mixed his own data so casually and indistinguishably with figures from Boussingault's work, that Dumas seems not to have been unreasonable in discounting the results in the form in which Liebig presented them. If Liebig had as solid a case as he purported to have it is hard to see why he did not publish a more formal and precise description of his research.

In their response to the new letter the French chemists were able to bring to bear detailed descriptions of investigations highly favorable to their cause. Dumas rose first and addressed himself chiefly to the question of the chemical conversion of wax to animal fat. He was now armed with more than the rhetorical argument he had used last time. By a timely coincidence he could report that in his laboratory a M. Lewy of Copenhagen had just demonstrated that, contrary to Liebig's opinion, wax can be saponified. When treated with boiling potash, beeswax yielded a soluble soap. Beeswax purified by boiling water and cold alcohol contained two "immediate principles," cerine and myricine, each of which was acidic. From their elementary analyses Lewy found that each is composed of proportions of carbon, hydrogen, and oxygen representable by the formula $C^{68}H^{68}O^4$. When heated with an oxide of potassium the cerine yielded hydrogen gas and another acid. The latter had exactly the same melting point as stearic acid, and its elementary analysis was compatible with the formula $C^{68}H^{68}O^7$, which Liebig accepted as that of hydrated stearic acid. Lewy's results thus served as an ideal chemical foundation for Dumas's contention that waxes are more closely related to the constituents of animal fat than Liebig believed, and for his theory that in the animal body waxes may be converted to fatty acids by a small degree of oxidation. Liebig's chemical objection was thus obviated, Dumas concluded, and the crucial issue revolved once again around the results of quantitative feeding experiments.[61]

When Boussingault spoke following Dumas, it appeared that if such experiments were indeed the deciding factor, the French case was growing steadily stronger. After noting that deductions drawn from his older memoirs were useless for the question of fats because he had designed them for other purposes and made no effort to determine the uniformity of the fat content of food or milk, Boussingault exhibited an illustrative set of results from his recent experiments performed "especially and directly" to resolve the problem at issue. These included a daily record of the milk produced by one of the cows over a period of thirty days, the total of each of four kinds of food the animal had eaten in that time, the weight of the excrements, and determinations of the percentages of fatty matters contained in representative samples of each of these materials. On a balance sheet drawn up from these figures he showed that 1614 grams of fatty matters had been supplied altogether in the food. The total in the milk and excrements was 1413 grams.[62] When such extended, carefully controlled experiments were consistently yielding results favorable to them, it is not surprising that Dumas and his colleagues felt Liebig's vague report of a comparatively cursory investigation to be no more than a nuisance to dispose of, even, as Dumas put it, "if the experiment of M. Liebig is real."[63]

Payen became ill during the meeting and could not take his turn to answer Liebig's letter until two weeks later. Then he focused on a passage in which the latter declared, "I have denied and I deny still the presence of fats (combinations of fatty acid with glycerine) in the nutrients of cattle . . . I deny the presence of bile (or rather the materials soluble in ether contained in bile) in the same nutrients; I deny the presence of fish oil and spermaceti in sea plants";[64] and Liebig did not believe that the plants cows eat contain butter. This was not a valid objection to their views, according to Payen, for the French chemists did not claim a literal identity between nutrient fats and those of the animal itself. They had been aware without Liebig's mention of it that plant waxes differ from animal fat. "We have always said, that these substances become fixed in the tissues of animals more or less modified." Under the general denomination of *fatty materials*, he declared, they had always included fixed oils, fats, waxes, and other substances "because of the evident analogy which exists in their elementary composition. It is always these materials, according to us, to which the role falls which M. Liebig attributes to starch and to sugars." [65]

He emphasized this point, Payen said, so that the issue would not drift away from the original one without Liebig realizing it, or become lost in details. In spite of this protestation the issue was in fact drifting. Although, as we have seen, the French chemists had already adopted in their joint memoir the phrase about the modification of nutrient fats, they had not always spoken in this way; Dumas's original generalizations had suggested an interpretation quite like that which Liebig was parodying. Moreover, when Payen asserted that his statement equating the role they ascribed to fatty materials with the role Liebig ascribed to sugars expressed the "fundamental distinction between our conclusions," [66] the nature of the debate was shifting even further. Instead of two opposed views of the general type of processes which can occur in animals, out of which the question of the source of fat emerged as a special case, their differences were now posed as a more limited question—from what substances can an animal form fat? Even as they denied it, the French chemists were being prodded by Liebig to clarify specific aspects of their scheme at the expense of its overall simplicity.

Although the three chemists generally exuded confidence during these debates that they were firmly consolidating their position, there were occasional hints that they sensed its underlying fragility. In the joint memoir Payen mentioned that Dumas had already "given the Academy a glimpse" of a possible alternative explanation of the source of animal fat. Sugars, he had said, can be represented as composed of carbon monoxide, water, and olefiant gas (ethylene). Since olefiant gas can be converted into various alcohols which yield fatty acids upon oxidation, there is, "chemically speaking, nothing to oppose" the possibility that in digestion sugar gives rise to oils which take part in the formation of fat. [67] Later, while summarizing his refutation of Liebig's first letter, Dumas declared, "Ready to give up our opinion if there is reason to, we regard for the moment the supposition that all fats are formed in the food as a sufficient explanation and in the best accord with the facts." [68] Among the three men themselves there was probably greater uncertainty than these public expressions revealed. In a memorandum commenting on Liebig's article of the previous December, Boussingault indicated some of the arguments that he and his associates used against it, but he also remarked that if the experiments of Huber on bees were correct, "it is evident that our opinion is not well-founded." While summarizing the reasons for discounting Liebig's use of his own earlier experiments, Boussingault added, "Nevertheless in discussing my experiment on the cow . . . I recognize that it is not favorable to the opinion that we support." By his own estimate the cow, fed on hay and potatoes, had produced 180 more grams of fat in its milk than it had received in its food. Boussingault had to fall back on the surmise that hay contained more than the accepted value of fat and on the possibility that ether might not extract all of the fat from potatoes. [69] The French chemists were probably aware that the nature of the issue was such that in order to prevail they had to prove that the outcome of every reliable test of the sufficiency of dietary fat was favorable to them; whereas Liebig needed only one well-authenticated contrary result to overturn them. It is not surprising, then, that even as they publicly pressed the present evidence which they believed strongly supported them, they were preparing themselves for future setbacks.

In the debates of the spring of 1843 some of the general assumptions with which these chemists approached physiological problems emerged more distinctly than they had in the original descriptions of animal nutrition by Dumas and Liebig. When both sides were forced to defend statements under attack they revealed more clearly what criteria they recognized for judging the validity of their conceptions of the chemical processes in animals. The criteria were not themselves under question, however, for generally the adversaries shared them and differed only in their application. One has therefore to detect them from the kinds of arguments brought to bear on disputed points. One such assumption was that that theory was to be preferred which required the least complicated chemical transformations to be envisioned in the animal. Liebig considered his explanation of the conversion of sugar to fat convincing because it involved only a removal of oxygen. He questioned the conversion of wax to fat at least partially on the grounds that wax was chemically quite different from fat and the conversion consequently would have to be complex. Dumas, on the other hand, argued in favor of the transformation of wax to fat that it required a less extensive chemical alteration than the changes one would have to imagine if sugars, starches, and other substances served as sources. The French chemists used, as a reason for advocating the nutritive source of all animal fat rather than an alternative theory, the argument that "it is the simplest way to explain it." [70] So long as nutritive fat was shown to provide an adequate supply, they said, "nothing authorizes [us] to regard the animal as capable of producing" fat. [71]

Simplicity, however, was only a provisional standard by which to choose between competing theories. Liebig and his French rivals expected in common that when someone supposed a transformation of substances to occur in the animal he should be able to explain it on the basis of the chemical compositions of the substances involved, reduced if possible to an equation. A fully satisfactory verification for them seemed to require, in addition, the imitation of the proposed reactions in the chemical laboratory. Thus, when Liebig challenged the plausibility of the conversion of wax in animals to fat, Dumas responded with the demonstration that waxes could be oxidized to stearic acid and that a reaction could be stated consistent with these results and the elementary analyses of the substances involved: [72]

$$C^{68}H^{68}O^4 + H^3O^3 = C^{68}H^{68}O^7 + H^3$$
cerine   stearic acid

Liebig for the time being had to be content without such a demonstration of the conversion of sugars to fat to complete his arguments based on the similar proportions of hydrogen to carbon in the two classes of compound. He invoked, however, the nearest thing to such a reaction that he could find. The syrup left over in the preparation of beet sugar, he pointed out, yields a large quantity of fusel oil. Furthermore, by distilling volatile oils, he had obtained materials which solidified to tallow-like materials containing some margaric acid. Such observations seemed to him to make it not improbable that the conversion of sugars to fats takes place in animals. [73] Liebig was less consistent than the French chemists in limiting the reactions supposed to take place in animals to those demonstrable in such ways, for, as we have seen, he acknowledged that many unknown synthetic transformations occur. Both, however, utilized such arguments over the conversions which were in dispute. Neither seemed bothered by the fact that they accepted that plants somehow can perform all of the synthetic reactions which were then beyond any possibility of artificial duplication.

Dumas and his colleagues sometimes acted as though they were less concerned to resolve the scientific problems than to maintain the debate between themselves and Liebig. As the outlines of the original confrontation over whether animals can or cannot form substances lacking in their nutrients became blurred in the details of the specific case of the source of fat, they instinctively sought new definitions of their differences which would preserve the sense of contest. That is what Payen seemed to be doing when he posed the issue as whether sugar or fatty materials play a certain role in the formation of animal fat. It became clear also that when Dumas sketched his "alternative" theory of the formation of fatty acids from sugar he was preparing a way so that if he had to concede that sugars are a source of animal fat he could still oppose Liebig's theory of the manner in which the conversion occurs. In the issue of the *Annales des sciences naturelles* for June 1843 the joint memoir of Dumas, Boussingault, and Payen was reprinted. Appended to the original text was a comparative summary of the positions of Liebig and of the three French chemists which seems to have been designed subtly to shift the grounds of the controversy if the need should arise. Although the authors reiterated all of the arguments in favor of their view that the source of animal fat is nutrient fatty matters, they added:

> M. Liebig would consider starch and sugar as capable of being transformed into a *neutral fat* by a simple elimination of oxygen. We cannot share that opinion, and if sugar takes part in the formation of fats, that can only be, in our view, as the source of *fatty acids*.[74]

They contended that if there were such a conversion, it must take place during digestion, before the separation of the chyle; whereas Liebig envisioned a process occurring after the chyle has passed into the blood and caused by inadequate respiration producing insufficient oxidation of the substances in the blood. "Such is, in short," they concluded, "the true expression of the two systems: the future will judge them."[75] The "system" of the French chemists described here was not the one with which they had entered the fray, but it would suffice for a new banner if they were forced to abandon the old.

The combination of the habitual rivalry of Dumas and his associates with Liebig and of their predilection for pursuing the problem of animal nutrition under ground rules which both sides accepted resulted in fixing the attention of the French chemists firmly on their disputes with their German counterpart. These same tendencies made them relatively impervious to demands that they satisfy not only their own criteria of verification but also those presented by physiologists. Their myopic view of the limits of the problem is best exemplified by what happened when Magendie entered the discussions at the Academy. As he raised questions within the bounds the chemists themselves had set for the debate they hastened to answer him, but the more fundamental doubts which he expressed they ignored. Magendie had become indirectly involved in the kind of nutritional investigation the chemists were carrying on by his appointment a year earlier as chairman of an Admiralty commission which included Boussingault and Payen. The commission was charged with examining the nutrition of military horses. Boussingault was away and did not participate in the experiments of the commission, most of which seemed to be carried out by a young chemist in Payen's laboratory. Liebig's first letter to the Academy stating that the waxes ingested by an animal are excreted in its faeces so impressed Magendie that he picked up some tables prepared from the experiments of the commission and made a quick calculation which he believed confirmed Liebig's position. The waxy matters contained in the excretions of the horses, according to his figures, exceeded that which they had eaten. As soon as Liebig's letter had been read to the assembled Academicians Magendie asked for the floor to announce his support of it. Payen, obviously alarmed lest "inferences contrary to the observations should get around and be credited," [76] rose immediately afterward to disarm Magendie's claim by suggesting that there must be flaws in his reasoning. [77] At the following meeting Payen produced detailed documents in support of his reply. Contrary to Magendie's "memory," he said, the investigators on the commission had taken into account the quantity of fatty materials in the excretions and had found that the dietary sources still exceeded those consumed by the animals. Magendie had simply not assessed correctly all of the results available. Magendie had to admit that the fuller presentation of data, which had not been available to him before, refuted his conclusion. [78] A week later he had to report sheepishly that he had in addition made a simple arithmetical error in his calculations. [79] Consequently he withdrew his disagreement with the immediate conclusions of his colleagues. While criticizing their results within the field of investigation defined by them, Magendie was clearly at a disadvantage by being less familiar with the details of the methods and data. During his remarks, however, he admonished them that whatever the outcome of this type of experiment, it would not go very far toward resolving the general questions of animal nutrition. "It is very fortunate for physiology," he said,

that chemists as able as MM. Liebig, Dumas, Boussingault and Payen are undertaking such research, from it can only result great advantages for that science: but one must not attempt to go too fast. It is undoubtedly important to know that vegetables contain materials which are analogous, indeed even similar to the organic elements of animals: but from there demonstrate that it is these vegetable materials exclusively which form the tissues of animals there is a great distance, which cannot be crossed except by numerous direct experiments. I do not doubt that the learned chemists I have just named will execute them successfully; but the experiments do not exist at all today, and consequently the question of the nutrition of animals remains still what it has been for a long time, one of the most obscure questions in science.[80]

Dumas quickly responded that he "did not believe that it was necessary at that moment to defend the opinions concerning general physiology which M. Magendie had just attacked." [81] Then he brought the discussion back to the questions raised by Liebig, which he treated in detail. Obviously he wished to limit the issue to terrain with which he was familiar and not to be drawn out into physiological considerations where Magendie's experience was superior to his own. Payen did remark that he hoped that Magendie would discuss more fully sometime the applicability of scientific research to the phenomena of digestion; but his general reaction to Magendie's intervention was that he "is one of the founders of experimental physiology, to whom his own successes have given the right to be a little difficult." [82]

Magendie's criticism was tactful and mild compared to that which another observer of these discussions directed at Dumas, Payen, and Boussingault. Alfred Donné, who was still covering the meetings of the Academy of Sciences for the *Journal des débats*, was a staunch defender of the priority of physiological factors over chemical and physical analyses of organic phenomena.[83] As a physician he may also have been somewhat conservative scientifically; but he himself had made some important studies of the chemical composition of animal and nutrient substances in addition to the investigation of the nutritive value of gelatin, which had led to the formation of the Gelatin Commission, and he had pioneered in microscopic observations of blood, chyle, and other fluids.[84] Already during October, when Dumas and Payen reported their analysis of maize to undermine Liebig's position, Donné had expressed skepticism about the "grand and simple" system of Dumas, but remarked that he would wait for "the development of these ideas in the work which M. Dumas promises us," before deciding whether to risk attacking them or be persuaded by his evidence.[85] By the time he had sat through the debates in the spring, Donné had apparently heard enough. Like Magendie, he asserted that to show an analogy between certain vegetable aliments and products of nutrition in animals gave the chemists no right to claim that these are entirely equivalent. Donné, however, objected more severely to the whole enterprise of Dumas, whom he described as "the head of the new school," constructing upon the work of his associates "a monument of chemical physiology." [86]

Ignoring the recent clarifications of the extent to which the French chemists considered nutrients to be modified in the animal, Donné portrayed Dumas's system in its starkest form. He summarized Dumas's view of animal nutrition as nothing but "the transport into the interior of animals of principles entirely formed in plants," the animals contributing nothing to their formation. "In the minds of physiologists [*Dans l'esprit des physiologistes*]," however, animals receive from their nutrients only the elements of the substances they need:

They rejoin these elements, associate them, combine them, to make from them first the blood, and later, by a marvelous workmanship of the organism, by a series of elaborations and of transformations, fibrin, fat, albumin, and finally flesh, bones, nervous tissue, seminal fluid, bile, milk, urine, etc. One is, in short, as far as possible away from that physiology of the Middle Ages, to which M. Dumas seems to want us to return, and according to which one should imagine that serpents have venom because they eat venomous substances.

Have you, Donné asked Dumas rhetorically,

followed the organic molecule from its entrance into the digestive organs until the end of its course, to be able to affirm that it is indeed the same fat, the same fibrin, the same albumin, separated by you from plants in your laboratory, which you encounter later in the milk of animals, in their muscles and in their various tissues? . . . You have seen the entrance and the exit from the labyrinth, but you have not penetrated into the interior. [87]

Donné sympathized with Liebig's objections, since they favored the destruction of Dumas's scheme, but he recognized that both chemists were playing similar games. How can physiologists choose between the conclusions of these two concerning the most complicated phenomena of nature, he complained, when they themselves cannot even agree on the analysis of a grain of cereal? The researches of Dumas, Boussingault, Payen, and Liebig on organic composition had all contributed powerfully to the progress of chemistry; but, Donné said:

we fear that, after having rashly dragged physiology into the laboratory of the chemist and reduced the phenomena of nutrition to the proportions of an analysis or the procedures of filtration, one will deprive it for a long time of the more real, even though more limited assistance which it can receive from the application of the physical sciences.[88]

Donné expressed here the principal objections that Claude Bernard later maintained against the procedures of the chemists, stated in even more forceful, uncompromising terms. For Dumas and his colleagues this criticism must have appeared, however, even more than that of Magendie, to be merely harassment from the outside. At any rate, when Dumas opened his course again at the École de Médecine, he repeated most of the lectures he had given the year before, betraying no loss of confidence in his approach to physiological questions. To his previous discussion of the role of fats in the animal economy he added only a reaffirmation of his position in his debate with Liebig.[89] Undeterred by the charge that he had not penetrated into the interior of animals, he developed further his conception of the combustion of nutrient substances in the blood. During a lecture on the "mineral matters in organized beings," on May 20, he elaborated on his earlier statements that the alkalis in the blood play a key role in respiration. The presence of soda in the blood, he said, "modifies the processes of combustion there in a very notable fashion." To illustrate the effects, he demonstrated that a solution of gallic acid could be passed through oxygen gas without change; but after he converted the acid to barium gallate by mixing it with baryta, the solution absorbed oxygen and turned blue. The acid was destroyed by a "true combustion," he told his audience, and one could say that "gallic acid is respiring." Some human maladies might be attributable to incomplete combustion caused by insufficient alkali, he thought, and could be cured by administering alkaline drinks.[90] On June 10 Dumas took up the chemistry of glucose and stressed the crucial role of that substance in animal nutrition. Starch and dextrine, he said, are converted to glucose in the stomach. Entering the blood, the glucose undergoes a slow combustion under the influence of the alkalis in the blood. To demonstrate the ease with which glucose is oxidized in the presence of alkali, he showed that indigo blue, mixed with glucose, caustic potash, and water, was converted to indigo white. In the process, he inferred, the water decomposed, its oxygen going to the glucose while its hydrogen reduced the indigo. Dumas admitted, however, that it was not certain whether glucose itself passed into the blood or whether it was first transformed to lactic acid.[91] His indecision reflected, as we shall later see, a debate then occurring among people who were investigating digestion more directly. His discussion shows that he was paying somewhat closer attention to the results of recent physiological experiments than when he had belittled the search for special conversion processes in digestion. Nevertheless, he was still pushing ahead with the same basic conviction that the main requirement for nutritional theories was a knowledge of the chemical transformations of the substances involved. The first shock to his position came not from his physiological critics, but from a new chemical discovery concerning a crucial organic reaction.

IV

The French Chemists on the Defensive

In June 1843 Jules Pelouze reported to the Academy of Sciences some important research on fermentation, which also placed him in the center of the controversy over animal nutrition. Up until then, Donné remarked in the *Journal des débats*, Pelouze had taken remarkably little part in the "great question presently agitating chemistry." [1] Pelouze had had, in fact, every reason to stay out of those debates. His career had for ten years been closely involved with that of Dumas. Both had been at the same time research assistants at the École Polytechnique, where they had undertaken in 1833 a joint investigation on the volatile oil of mustard. Pelouze had substituted for Dumas in some of his courses, and later replaced him as professor of chemistry at the École Polytechnique. [2] Pelouze had, however, become allied with Liebig and Berzelius during the controversies between them and Dumas over the composition of organic compounds. In 1836 Pelouze had become a kind of unofficial representative in Paris of Liebig's chemical school. In 1837 Pelouze accused Dumas of appropriating some of his experiments for a paper Dumas published with Liebig during a brief period in which Liebig and Dumas tried to work together. The acrimonious dispute that followed threatened at one point to destroy Pelouze's friendship with Liebig, and left Pelouze feeling that Dumas was an insidious, crafty schemer who covered his ignoble deeds with polished pronouncements made in bad faith. [3] Two years later Pelouze was convinced that Dumas was using the theory of substitutions as a device to elevate himself to the position of *"Chef de l'École"* of the new organic chemistry, and to denigrate the contributions of other chemists. Pelouze described Dumas's actions then as charlatanism. He took

77

it upon himself to challenge the value of the substitution theory at a meeting of the Academy, and urged Liebig to oppose the theory publicly.[4] This affair led to more unpleasant incidents, and Pelouze resolved afterward not to engage in any further public discussions whatsoever with Dumas.[5] It is not surprising, therefore, that when Dumas and Liebig began a new feud over physiological theories, Pelouze remained discreetly silent. His letters to Liebig, however, leave little doubt about where his sympathies lay. In May 1842, when Liebig's anger over Dumas's supposed plagiarism was at a peak and Liebig wrote that he had decided to do battle over the matter, Pelouze advised him to go ahead with his own work, undisturbed by what others might be doing or saying "about the same questions that you have already taken up several years ago."[6] In December he reported to Liebig that Dumas and Payen had been busy for several months analyzing hay. It seemed to Pelouze that in Paris people were in too much haste "to give the solution to so many complicated problems concerning the role of aliments." The many analyses and new results must contain numerous errors, he thought, in spite of the "appearance of certitude" with which they were being announced. Having heard that Liebig had discovered in the fatty material of maize a peculiar acid distinguishing it from animal fat, Pelouze commented, "There now, M. D[umas's] goose is cooked!!" In Paris, he added, one was not permitted to doubt the identity of the fat in maize with that in the goose which eats it. Pelouze toyed with the idea of an experiment in which he would put a few weevils in a jar of wheat. Pelouze was sure that after they had multiplied for a time, the weevils would contain far more fat than had been in the grain.[7] By April 1843 Pelouze believed that further experiments such as those Liebig had communicated to the Academy would soon resolve the issue. He could not see what the conversion of wax to stearic acid that Dumas had adduced in favor of his theory had to do with the formation of fat in animals. He seemed surprised that Boussingault, who had talked to him recently about the origin of fat, "persists in believing that the fats are absorbed by animals from plants and only modified by them."[8]

   If Pelouze was unimpressed by the efforts of Dumas and his colleagues, he felt quite differently about the endeavors of Liebig. "No one in the world is as able as you," he wrote Liebig, "to illuminate the great questions of physiological chemistry." He longed to spend his next vacation at Giessen in order to take up the subject seriously with his old friend.[9] Before he could do that, however, his own research suddenly put him in a position to lend Liebig unexpected support.

Théophile Jules Pelouze

During the preceding years the subject of fermentation had been expanding rapidly. Once referring primarily to the conversion of the sugar into alcohol or acetic acid under the influence of yeast, it was now coming to mean a whole class of reactions, the specific products of which depended not only upon the substance fermented, but also on the organic matter, or "ferment," placed in contact with it. In 1841 Edmond Frémy, one of Pelouze's first students and very close friends, who had succeeded him as assistant in chemistry at the École Polytechnique,[10] discovered that although sugar fermented with animal matter usually forms a mixture of products, under carefully controlled conditions it is completely transformed into pure lactic acid.[11] Pelouze repeated Frémy's experiments. He soon found that under different conditions he could obtain another product resembling butyric acid, a substance which Chevreul had isolated nearly thirty years before during his investigations of fats. With his younger collaborator, Amédée Gélis, Pelouze then embarked on an extensive investigation to establish whether the fermentation product was truly identical with the butyric acid derived from butter. The melting points and other physical properties, the salts formed with alkalies, alkaline earths, and metals proved to be exactly the same for the substances derived from both sources. By repeated elementary analyses under varied circumstances they revised the formula for butyric acid and proposed as the equation of the fermentation reaction:

$$\overbrace{C^{12}H^{28}O^{14}}^{\text{glucose}} = \overbrace{C^8H^{14}O,H^2O}^{\text{butyric acid}} + 4(CO^2) + 8H + 2(H^2O).$$

They also explored previously unknown chemical properties of the acid such as its reactions with ethyl and methyl alcohols to form esters; the conditions of these reactions, they pointed out, were of special interest for theories of organic composition. Pelouze and Gélis were even able to synthesize from butyric acid and glycerine a pale yellow oil which they identified tentatively as butyrine, a fatty material Chevreul had discovered in butter.[12] This result provided the starting point from which Pelouze's student, Marcellin Berthelot, later devised generalized methods for synthesizing fats and laid important foundations for synthetic organic chemistry.[13]

Although Pelouze's paper was therefore highly significant for the development of organic chemistry itself, he made clear in his presentation that he thought it would also play a role in the current question of nutrition. As he put it:

This observation will inevitably occupy an important place in the present discussion of the formation of fats in animals. Without wishing in any way to judge in advance the methods which Nature employs in the numerous modifications which she causes aliments to undergo, we cannot refrain from remarking that the transformation of sugar into butyric acid is carried out without the intermediary of any large increase of temperature and without the application of any of those energetic reagents which would be apt to destroy the equilibrium and the vitality of the animal economy; but that on the contrary the transformation takes place under very simple conditions and with materials which organic nature itself makes available.[14]

He added that ordinary fatty acids might have a similar relation to sugars, and to starches as well.

Pelouze thus made his intervention into the debate with as much reserve as possible. His statement was guarded, almost cryptic, and the consequences to be drawn from it were merely implied. Nevertheless, nearly everyone present must have seen at once what his results meant for Dumas and his associates.[15] The process Pelouze was describing fulfilled precisely the conditions for what they themselves regarded as the most convincing kind of demonstration that a reaction can be considered to occur in animals. Chemically the proof of the transformation was impeccable. Pelouze had demonstrated it far more soundly than Lewy had demonstrated the supposed conversion of wax to stearic acid. Furthermore, that the proof happened to involve the formation from sugar of a characteristic constituent of butter was extraordinarily strategic, since the supporters of Dumas relied heavily on measurements of the amount of butter produced by cows as the most convenient indicator of the fats formed in an animal. Donné reported the event as an unexpected new blow delivered against the theories of Dumas.[16]

Payen did his best to regroup in the face of this blow. Commenting on Pelouze's presentation, he appeared to waver between two courses. The first would be to concede the main issue and fall back on the consolation of claiming that the "alternate" theory suggested by Dumas had already predicted such transformations; the second would be to hold out, denying that the conversion of sugar to butyric acid implied the conversion of sugar to fats. He hinted at the first direction by saying, "The production of butyric acid . . . turns out to be included in a hypothesis which MM. Dumas, Boussingault and Payen have themselves presented" in their joint memoir. His hope for the second alternative was contained in his remark that butyric acid is far from the major constituent of butter, forming only a small percentage of it. Therefore, he concluded, "the production of that acid at the expense of sugar would be entirely inadequate to provide the key to the formation of the fat of the cream in the milk of cows." [17]

Payen's resistance was not so forlorn as it appeared to some other observers at the time, and as it would seem afterward when Pelouze's discovery was regarded as the early stage of a trend which continued to run counter to the views of Dumas's group. Payen was correct that the case against them was not proved; for the impact of Pelouze's work on the question was less in the reaction actually discovered than in the potential future discoveries of analogous reactions it suggested, as Pelouze himself was aware. On the other hand they had in the past accepted the demonstration of one representative reaction as evidence that a general class of reactions involving related compounds may occur in animals. Dumas himself had theorized that organic acids from acetic acid to the higher fatty acids form a series of compounds with related properties and compositions,[18] so that it was reasonable to expect, as Pelouze did, that other members of the series could also sometime be derived from sugars. Payen must, then, have had at least some foreboding that he was falling back to a position which was vulnerable to further erosion. What reaction Dumas had is not known. Although present and probably presiding over the meeting, he took no part in the discussion so relevant to his views.[19]

Donné was delighted at the turn of events. It was evident to him that if sugar can be converted to a fatty product by the chemistry of the laboratory alone, there was even more reason to believe that the much more powerful agents of the living organism can achieve such transformations. Everyone will understand, he wrote, what the consequences are for "the grand structure" of Dumas. The "ingenious" effort of Payen to attenuate the reaction to Pelouze's presentation he discounted as ineffectual. Dumas he taunted for his silence:

Perhaps he is already thinking of preparing for himself an honorable retreat, leaving his collaborators to continue the fight; perhaps there will no longer be any talk of the new physiological theory, just as there is no longer any talk of the theory of substitutions and of so many others. We would be sorry, for in truth the victory would have been carried too easily over such a brilliant and productive adversary.[20]

If Donné was smug, Liebig was jubilant. To a German correspondent he wrote a few weeks later, "In [the question of] the formation of fat I have carried off a glorious victory. Pelouze has found that sugar in contact with putrifying and fermenting matter decomposes into butyric acid and hydrogen gas."[21] The scent of victory was premature, however, for though serious, the blow was not fatal. Aside from Payen's response there was still the standard of simplicity to invoke; so long as the French chemists could show that dietary fatty matter is *sufficient* to account for the fatty products of animals, they could still justify assuming that it is not formed in them. Neither had Dumas withdrawn from the question, for during the summer months he was engaged in research crucial to just this argument.

In February, when Dumas, Payen, and Boussingault explained away the production of wax by bees fed only sugar, they had announced that Henri Milne Edwards, an eminent zoologist of the Academy who had been a close friend of Dumas ever since the latter arrived in Paris,[22] was undertaking research to support their reasoning that the bees probably formed the wax from fatty materials previously stored in their bodies.[23] Dumas then joined the investigation, performing the chemical analyses while Milne Edwards undoubtedly handled the bees. During July and August they carried out a classic balance experiment, closing the loopholes in the work of Huber and Gundlach which had enabled them to claim those earlier results to be inconclusive. They confined a swarm of 2005 bees in a hive with access only to honey for food. Separating out 117 individuals, they dried and pulverized these and extracted all of the fatty contents of their bodies with alcohol and ether. From this result they calculated the total of fatty matter contained in the remainder of the swarm at the beginning of the trial and the average for each bee. They determined also the amount of wax which the bees could derive from the small proportion present in the honey. On August 8, the end of the experiment, they measured the total amount of wax which the bees had formed in their combs, in particles scattered on the floor, and in the bodies of larvae which they had produced in the meantime. From a second sample of the bees they ascertained the average quantity of fatty materials remaining in their bodies at the end of the period.[24]

It must have been a dramatic moment in the Academy of Sciences when Milne Edwards stood up on September 18 to present the results of this research, even though Dumas was away in England and Boussingault in Alsace. In the joint memoir which he read he sustained the suspense almost until the end. First he explained why the older naturalists had assumed that the waxes are supplied to bees by plants and what the investigations of Huber and of Gundlach left to be desired. Then he reported a preliminary experiment of their own "unfavorable to the theory of Huber." Bees fed only pure sugar ceased to produce wax after a few days. When he reached the point of summarizing the data of the definitive experiment, however, he had to say at last that they showed unequivocally that the fatty materials contained in the bees at the beginning and those received nutritively were together quite insufficient to account for what the insects had produced. The former totaled on the average 0.0022 grams for each bee, while the latter amounted to 0.0106 grams. Moreover, the bees had not even lost fatty substances, for their bodies contained more at the end than at the beginning. Milne Edwards and Dumas had no choice but to conclude that the bees "actually *produce* wax." As Milne Edwards neared the end of the memoir the long controversy appeared to be over: "The production of wax constitutes therefore a true animal secretion, and in that regard the opinion of older naturalists and of some modern chemists, among whom one of us believed he must place himself, must be rejected." [25]

They put the best light they could on the outcome by calling themselves "fortunate to have been the first to dispel the doubts" left by the experiments of Huber; and they expressed an optimistic view of the future contributions of similar studies:

At a moment in which chemistry is penetrating further and further into the domain of physiology, all opinions must be submitted to the test of the balance, which will separate truth from error, and will teach us in what cases there is a simple passage of alimentary materials into the humors, and in which cases these products, on the contrary, are modified or transformed under the influence of the organism.[26]

If these statements really represent the common opinion of Milne Edwards and Dumas, then the latter had learned over the past few months considerably more caution than he had once had about presupposing what processes occur in animals. At the same time he was asserting that the way to proceed to establish more information was through the method pioneered by Boussingault and exemplified here: that is, by deductions drawn from comparative measurements of the substances consumed by and produced by an animal.

If there really are "crucial experiments" in science which settle a disputed question with one clean stroke, this should have been one. Liebig had raised the phenomenon under study as a critical argument for his view. Dumas and his associates had not denied the cogency of the argument, only the soundness of the evidence for it. Both sides implicitly acknowledged in advance that a demonstration satisfactory to everyone that bees do produce wax from sugar would be decisive for the general issue between them. The experimental result that Dumas and Milne Edwards themselves delivered obviously fulfilled this condition, and their conclusions suggest that they did indeed accept its verdict.

Real scientists, however, often do not react as logic would have it. In the discussion that followed it became evident that instead of giving up the issue the partisans of the French theories were once more going to redefine it. In the absence of his colleagues the task again fell to Payen. He had had a few minutes to think out his response, for Milne Edwards had shown him the results just before the meeting began. Gamely, Payen suggested that the experiment was not entirely conclusive and ought to be repeated on a larger scale, because the fat content of the bees and of the honey may not have been uniform, or the bees might have obtained some fatty substances from the wood or other materials of the cage. This kind of argument, used effectively against less rigorous investigations earlier, was implausible here, and Payen himself recognized that it was not likely to carry conviction. More interesting was his assertion that the nutritional issue which had been absorbing the attention of the Academy consisted actually of three fundamentally distinct problems. The first two, whether vegetable materials contain fatty substances and whether these are assimilated to animals, he claimed had been fully resolved in favor of the

French group, and were "perhaps the most important of our studies." [27]

The third problem, as Payen now saw it, was what other substances can form fat in animals, and this was again divisible into two
separate questions. One concerned "the transformation of albumin,
fibrin, and gelatin into fat, transformations which we do not
admit." [28] Here, true to form, Payen was seeking to build up another
point of confrontation with Liebig in place of that which might be losing its force. Already the previous spring, in the summary added to
the later published version of their joint memoir, Payen, Dumas,
and Boussingault had asserted that Liebig had believed herbivores
could form fat from fibrin, albumin, casein, and other constituents of
the blood. Then, however, they had added, "we believe that he has
given up this opinion." [29] Liebig had, in fact, discussed in his *Animal
Chemistry* the possibility of such conversions, not, however to claim
that they necessarily take place, but only that if they did, his argument about the loss of oxygen involved would still hold. Up until
now, therefore, neither side had regarded this as a question at issue.

Though Payen might try to subordinate it, he could not avoid that
"last point," "the transformation in the animal economy of sugars into
fatty matters." By deftly recasting former statements he made it
sound as though he, Dumas, and Boussingault had all along been
"urging the possibility" of such processes and had only cautioned earlier that there was then insufficient evidence to prove them. Still, not
overlooking any routes that might promise an escape from the admission that he and his colleagues had lost the issue over which they had
contended, Payen hoped at the same time to deny the generality of
what he had just indicated that they had been saying. He asked Milne
Edwards, therefore, if he thought "that there is a true equivalence between that special secretion [of wax by bees] and the general distribution, the accumulation of fat in the adipose tissue of animals." He
himself believed there was not, and cited several examples from practical investigations showing that foods containing fat enabled animals
to fatten, whereas nonfat foods nourished without fattening. Among
these cases was a result he had just received from Boussingault which
demonstrated that a diet of pure potatoes is not suitable to produce fat
in pigs. [30]

Payen's remarks constituted clever maneuvering, but it is hard to
see how he could have got by with it in anything but a sympathetic
audience. Clearly he was portraying the "great question of animal nutrition" in a way that he himself had not viewed it a few months ear-

lier. What he now delineated as distinct problems he and his colleagues had previously treated as pieces of evidence for the one generalization that animals obtain all of their fats from fatty substances in their nutrients. If he was disingenuous with respect to the history of the affair, however, he was not foolish in redefining the several aspects of the question as separate problems, for each could stand independently. What suffered was merely the grand system of Dumas, and Dumas was not present to comment on its demise.

After Payen, other commentators kept the discussion going for a long time. Louis-Jacques Thenard remarked that animals do not obtain the materials necessary for their constitution "completely formed in plants," but obviously form them by modifying the nutrients. Still he thought that they probably assimilated to each of their constituent substances the nutrient materials most closely resembling them. The evidence favored the formation of fats from sugars, he believed, but experiments made up until then were inadequate to determine what other transformations take place. The physiologist Pierre Flourens reported that he had maintained two bears for two years on a diet of pure bread, and that in that time they had grown quite fat.[31]

During the discussion Milne Edwards himself appeared to retract the impression left by the conclusion of his memoir that he and Dumas considered their investigation to have settled the general issue of the source of animal fat. In answer to Payen's query he said that he did not by any means think that the secretion of wax by a few kinds of insects provided with a special gland necessarily indicated that the fats which accumulate in almost all parts of most animals have the same mode of origin. He agreed with Payen that foods containing fats were more effective for fattening livestock than were nonfat foods, and would continue to be so even if it were eventually proven that all animals have the power to convert sugar to fats.[32] This practical consolation was one that grew more important to the French group as their theoretical position grew more difficult.

Milne Edwards, however, also volunteered his own appraisal of what the general theoretical issue over animal nutrition had become. As Thenard had just stated, he said, no one can deny that animals are capable of modifying nutrients and forming new products from them.

The question, in my view, consists therefore in the limits of that modifying faculty and in the nature of its tendencies. Thus, according to some, the animal organism would possess the power to perform the greatest transformations, to make fibrin, albumin, or gelatin, for example, at the expense of a non-nitrogenous aliment, or to make from fibrin fat as easily as muscle fiber;

according to others, on the contrary, that faculty would be very limited, and would operate only under the influence of inspired oxygen. That is, if I am not deceived, the basis of the theory of M. Dumas, and it is very nearly the opinion which seems to me to bring together in its favor the most positive arguments. It appears to me that the constituent materials of the body of the animal must be envisioned as forming a certain number of natural and quite distinct families, of which the various species can have a common origin, but do not arise from the source or the products of another group. Thus, nothing in science seems to me to authorize one to believe, with M. Liebig, that fibrin can become fat: but it seems to me easy to admit that albumin can become fibrin or gelatin; that the oil of the almond can become animal fat. Each aliment thus serves only for the creation of a certain order of products, and consequently the aliments of different families cannot replace each other in their physiological roles. Envisioned from that point of view, the discussion which the Academy has witnessed for the last several months will only be secondarily influenced by the question raised in our note.[33]

The equivocations in Milne Edwards's statement reflect his difficulty in simultaneously supporting his comrades in the Academy and adapting their views to the realities of the changing situation. In the process of softening Dumas's theories he was diminishing the distance which had originally separated them from the ideas of Liebig. Whether he sensed this or not, he attempted to restore the distance by setting up a hypothetical rival position which he then vaguely associated with Liebig by means of the purported opinions of the latter about the conversion of fibrin to fat. Finally, Milne Edwards's statement that the production of wax by bees did not seriously affect the general view he was expressing makes sense only if he was prepared to regard waxes and sugar as species of one "family." Such a broad interpretation would make his view that the modifying faculty of the animal is "very limited" nearly meaningless. In spite of his different perspective as a zoologist, therefore, Milne Edwards could not maintain a view of the situation detached from his scientific association with Dumas and the other chemists. His representation of the position of the three chemists was clearer than any they had given themselves after they qualified the original statements that the animal absorbs its constituents totally formed; so that his statement suggests that out of the debates in the Academy was at least emerging gradually a more distinct perception of what the various views of the chemical processes in animals meant. Unfortunately, the clarification Milne Edwards provided of these aspects of the general theories of his colleagues came just as the generalizations were becoming untenable.

Donné naturally saw in the results of Dumas and Milne Edwards precisely that broad import which Milne Edwards was denying them. He rejected Payen's arguments based on the unsuitability of certain nonfat diets. These could be explained physiologically by difficulties in digestion rather than chemically, he remarked, and he pointed out that in the meeting Thenard had cited molasses as an example of a diet mostly of sugar which did fatten cattle. The structure of Dumas's system had been severely shaken, he felt. Again he chided Dumas, this time for seeming to abandon his theories in the memoir with Milne Edwards while still having his collaborator Payen defend them. Donné was suspicious that Dumas was biding his time, protecting himself so that whatever way the issue might ultimately be decided, he could "find himself in accord with one or the other of his allies." [34]

"As for M. Payen," Donné ended his report of the discussion, "we urge him to moderate his zeal for upholding the ideas of his leader. He could one day well find himself alone in supporting the burden of a hypothesis which he did not invent and for which he is not responsible." [35] Donné was partly right, for Dumas apparently did gradually disengage himself from the questions which he had presumed so daringly to solve two years before. Payen was not left alone, however, for with him still was his staunchly committed and resourceful colleague Boussingault.

In October two more observations unfavorable to Dumas's views were reported. They were less substantial than those already discussed, but perhaps indicate how the presence of the debate itself was drawing out minor observations which could be made relevant to it. Charles Chossat, a physician from Geneva well known for his studies of starvation in animals, presented to the Academy some experiments made several years before on the effects of a diet of sugar. It was "the lively interest excited recently" by the question of the source of fat, he said, which led him to bring up this old work. He had found that animals fed nothing but sugar until they died contained nearly normal amounts of fat deposits, whereas those which died after complete involuntary abstinence contained almost none. From this Chossat inferred "that sugar favors the production of fat." [36] Meanwhile in Munich a Dr. Vogel found that beer contains only a very small quantity of fatty matter. In view of the generally attested fattening effects of beer, he said, the work "furnishes a new proof in favor of the theory of the formation of fat established by professor Liebig." [37]

Since spring Liebig himself had been publicly silent about the continuing debates over the source of animal fat. One reason may have been that he was not actively gathering new evidence for his theory and therefore had little more to add. Yet one can sympathize with his own explanation. Further communications sent to the Academy, he felt, would only cause his adversaries wilfully to misrepresent his statements again before their colleagues, and he could not appear in person to prevent such actions. What he thought they had done to him in the meeting of September 18, however, was too much to bear in silence. To Milne Edwards he sent a private letter disavowing that he had said that nitrogenous substances such as fibrin are converted to fat in animals. He cited passages in his *Animal Chemistry* in which he had stated that nitrogenous nutrients produce the nitrogenous constituents of animals and non-nitrogenous nutrients are the source of the non-nitrogenous constituents. Those passages which might seem to indicate otherwise, he asserted, were included merely to establish that even if one believed, contrary to his own views, that nitrogenous nutrients are converted to fat, it would still be necessary to assume that oxygen is removed, because the nitrogenous compounds as well as sugars contain a higher proportion of oxygen than do fats. Liebig complained to Milne Edwards also about the juvenile arguments Payen had been using to "pour ridicule on my views," but declared that he firmly intended to avoid further public discussions which were only dragging a scientific question of the highest interest into the mud. Milne Edwards replied warmly, apologizing for his own error and regretting too that the discussion of the question had taken on such a sharp tone as to detract from the dignity of science. He promptly communicated Liebig's rebuttal to the meeting of the Academy of October 20, but along with portions of Liebig's letter he presented statements from Liebig's *Animal Chemistry* which had led him "necessarily to believe that Liebig admitted the possibility of the formation of fat by the deoxidation of fibrin as well as by the analogous modifications effected in the constitution of starch or sugar." Milne Edwards had at first intended to finish by saying, "That scientist assures me that he has never held that opinion, and I can consequently only express regret that I, have misunderstood his thought." He must have looked at the passages again, however, and decided that he had been justified in his initial reading of them, for he crossed out the last sentence and wrote instead, "I would own that even today I do not know how else to interpret them." By making that alteration in his note Milne Edwards may well have assured the continuation of the controversy. It is not clear whether he intended to insist still that Liebig had actually meant what Liebig himself denied, or whether, as he claimed, he merely wished to show that he had not previously been frivolous in assuming that these were Liebig's views. The response nevertheless further aroused Liebig's ire, so that he forgot his resolve to end public discussion of the matter. In his view the French zoologist was playing the "common dialectical trick," of twisting his opinions into erroneous statements which could then easily be disproved. Consequently Liebig published the full contents of his letter in his *Annalen* and spelled out in further detail how he believed the scientists of the Academy were misusing him. His most telling point was that although when challenged Milne Edwards said only that Liebig "admitted the possibility" of the conversion, he and also Payen had in their earlier statements represented him as asserting a definite theory that the conversion takes place. Undoubtedly they were trying to make the most of Liebig's remarks in order to portray him as differing with them on a question where they assumed he could not be right. By reacting so sharply he probably prevented them, if they so intended, from maneuvering him into a new confrontation. On the other hand, his statements concerning the conversion of nitrogenous substances to fat were equivocal enough, and his *Animal Chemistry* generally separated hypothetical ideas from purported statements of fact so indistinctly that the French chemists could easily have got the impression that he was in this case more positive than he intended to be. Moreover, a strategic typographical error reinforced the misunderstanding. At one point where Liebig had originally written, "when animals form fat at the expense of non-nitrogenous aliments," the French translation omitted the "non," so that the phrase appeared as a definite statement of what the French scientist claimed to be his opinion.[38]

This new skirmish between Liebig and his rivals would seem merely to illustrate how unproductive their squabbles could become, except that it also symbolizes well the obstacles to full communication which exist inevitably among people even when they happen to be scientists. It is impossible to debate without summarizing the views of others with whom one is contending, and a summary always to some degree represents inadequately the full statement. When in addition there is a desire to put statements of an adversary in a disadvantageous light, the chances of intentional or unintentional distortion are greatly enhanced, as are the chances that one whose statements are involved will see the other's version as inaccurate. Often it becomes nearly impossible for the participants, and difficult for historians afterward, to distinguish between interpretations unanticipated by the author but within the limits of the ambiguity inherent in the statement itself; misunderstanding of the statement; and deliberate misrepresentation. Moreover the author when challenged may easily see in his own statement, clearer indications of his views than are evident to others, especially if he has since writing it become more certain of them. Thus in his article Liebig summarized his earlier statements as though they left no doubt that the conversion of nitrogenous substances to fat which he described there was not his *own* view. The original statements are subject to that interpretation, but need not necessarily be interpreted that way; yet to him, in retrospect at least, that must have been what he meant. There is, then, no sharp line between clarification and altering the record of one's past position. Such problems frequently vexed the relations between the two camps involved in the fat controversy.

It was because he needed to defend his earlier position rather than because he himself had made any further progress that Liebig had returned to the question of fat formation. Naturally, however, he took the opportunity to remark on the recent events which had so greatly strengthened his views. He duly noted the importance of the experiments of Pelouze and of Dumas and Milne Edwards. He stripped one more layer from the defenses of Dumas's theory by reporting that both Gerhardt in France and Ronalds in his own laboratory had disproved the conversion of wax to stearic acid which Lewy had described. He also had new troubles for the French chemists concerning that facet of the problem on which they still hoped to prevail, the measurement of the adequacy of fat in the diets of domestic animals. Lyon Playfair had, according to Liebig, proved by numerous experiments that cows produced a quantity of butter equal to more than ten times the total of the ether-soluble constituents they received in their food. For good measure Liebig quoted a letter written to him in June by a sugar beet manufacturer in Lille who had substituted molasses for linseed-oil cakes in the diets of eight milk cows and fifty cattle. He had found no decrease in the butterfat produced by the former, and the latter fattened with unusual rapidity. In closing, Liebig taunted Payen for trying to separate the question of beeswax from that of general fat formation. "All exclusive principles," he said, "such as those which depend on the different classes of animals having unequal powers for forming substances, lose all their value as generalizations." [39]

Strenuously though Liebig denied having maintained that nitrogenous substances are converted to fat in animals, he pointed out in his letter to Milne Edwards that there was now evidence that this process probably does take place; for "Dr. Wurz, an outstanding young chemist in Strasburg," had just found that putrifying fibrin decomposes into various products, including butyric acid.[40] The chemist was Adolph Würtz, a former student of Liebig, who later became one of the most influential scientists in Paris. The observations Liebig referred to were not published until June 1844, in the *Annales de chimie*. Würtz there described how he isolated the butyric acid and identified it by tests similar to those Pelouze had used. He took precautions to counter the possible objection that the butyric acid derived from fat combined with the fibrin. After describing the research itself, Würtz drew a conclusion of a type now becoming familiar. If fibrin can be transformed into butyric acid, he said, one may imagine that it can also under certain conditions form neutral fat. "Even though one might not have succeeded in bringing about that transformation artificially, one understands at least that in certain circumstances it can take place in the organism."[41] Clearly the chemists' own expanding control of organic reactions was challenging the order they had sought to impose on the organic reactions they envisoned in nature.

When Liebig invoked in his article the experiments of Lyon Playfair, he was surprisingly late in bringing this evidence to bear in his favor; for Playfair had read these results to the Chemical Society of London in January 1843, and the memoirs of the society including it were probably published by the middle of that year. Moreover, Playfair kept in close enough touch with Liebig so that one would expect that the latter would be informed quickly of what Playfair was doing. Liebig could well have used Playfair's results when he was engaged in debate with the French chemists during that spring. Although Liebig exaggerated the difference between the butter produced and dietary fat in his report of the work, the results as Playfair himself had announced them still seemed on the surface to be more impressive support than what Liebig used then for his case. Playfair had already presented them as a conclusive demonstration of the correctness of Liebig's theories against those of Dumas.[42]

Playfair undertook his investigation as part of his program to bring science to the aid of agriculture in England, and he reported it in an article aimed at showing farmers how by choice of diet and living conditions they could influence favorably the output of milk from their cows. On each of five consecutive days he gave a different diet to a cow, and measured the amount of milk it gave the same day and the proportions of the constituents of the milk. The first day the cow ate "after-grass," the second day hay and oatmeal. On the third day he fed it hay, oatmeal, and bean-flour. It consumed only potatoes during the fourth and fifth days. To estimate the amounts of fatty and waxy substances in the food for each day he utilized analyses of similar foods by Liebig and other chemists. The quantity of butter produced varied considerably, depending, Playfair thought, on the food, the exercise the cow underwent, and the temperature of its surroundings on that day; but in each case the butter ranged from two to four times the amount of the fatty bodies eaten on the same day. He concluded that the butter "could not have arisen solely from the fat contained in the food. Hence it must have been produced by a separation of oxygen from the elements of the unazotised ingredients of the food of the animal, in the manner pointed out by Liebig." [43]

As we have already seen, and as this passage itself suggests, Playfair was far from a dispassionate observer of the respective theories of Liebig and Dumas. In his autobiography he later described himself as Liebig's "favorite pupil." After studying in Liebig's laboratory he returned to England, where he translated Liebig's *Agricultural Chemistry* and became a general advocate of the views it contained. In 1841 he had offered to use sixty acres of farmland to put Liebig's agricultural theories "to experiment on a large scale," and he enlisted the support of several other experimental farms for the same purpose. [44] He undoubtedly undertook the experiments on fat production in a similar spirit. His naïve conviction about the status of Liebig's nutritional theories is best expressed in a footnote to the foregoing report of his experiments: "In this paper we take for granted that the leading features of Liebig's 'Animal Physiology' are acknowledged as true." [45] Throughout the paper he applied these theories in a very direct and simple way to explain the effects of differing conditions on the output of milk.

Partisanship need not by itself imply, however, that the results were invalid, much as the author may have desired them in advance to come out in favor of his mentor. Playfair was considered an able experimenter, and undoubtedly performed and reported his analyses accurately. Yet inherent in the investigation was a weakness which he himself acknowledged:

The value of these experiments is certainly very much diminished by not being extended over a series of days on each kind of food. But in England, where the price of aether is so exorbitantly high, the expense of such experiments is a serious consideration for a private individual. As they were conducted under the same conditions with respect to temperature and exercise, an indication of the effects produced by the various foods has been obtained, although the final effects have escaped detection. [46]

That in spite of this partial disclaimer Playfair still described the result as conclusive proof of Liebig's theory is probably more a measure of his devoted confidence in Liebig than in his own work. As the paragraph reveals, the English scientist did not have the financial resources to carry out an investigation of the scope which Boussingault was used to applying to such problems, and was therefore vulnerable to criticism from the French chemists. The heaviest blow to them came not from Liebig or his supporters, but from a fellow French scientist.

On February 12, 1844, one day less than a year after Payen, Dumas, and Boussingault confidently presented to the Academy their case for the dietary source of all animal fat, their cause met in that same assembly the most devastating setback it had yet suffered. The bearer of the bad news was Jean François Persoz, a chemist trained under Thenard who had, ten years earlier, participated with Payen in the discovery of diastase. In 1835 Persoz had published a general theory of chemical composition which met little favor in Paris.[47] By 1837 he was professor of chemistry at the University of Strassbourg. He was at first restless and dissatisfied, but he had a large, well-equipped laboratory,[48] and he stayed there permanently. Persoz followed the discussions of the fat question in the Academy with special interest, because he had long before made an observation which seemed to him in disagreement with the results of the feeding experiments Payen and Boussingault were reporting. In 1838 he had fattened two geese according to the procedures customarily followed in Alsace, and found that they gained more fat than their total increase in weight. He suspected, therefore, that some of the other substances of the geese's own bodies had taken part in the formation of fat. After the experiments of Pelouze and of Dumas and Milne Edwards had shaken the theory of the alimentary source of fat, Persoz decided to repeat and extend his own earlier experiments.[49] He was in a sense returning to the original case that Liebig had adduced in his *Animal Chemistry* in support of his theory of fat formation. In place of the simple calculation Liebig had made, however, Persoz set out to procure a detailed set of reliable data. Beginning late in November with ten geese of similar size and weight, he deprived them of nourishment for twelve hours. Then he sacrificed one of them and determined the weight of its blood, its liver, the fat surrounding its intestines, and the fat in subcutaneous tissues and other regions of the body. The remaining animals he fed maize and weighed daily so long as they continued to gain rapidly. After periods ranging from nineteen to twenty-four days he killed each one and determined the weight of the above constituents of each of their bodies. From the differences between the weights estimated for each goose before fattening, assuming that the proportions were the same as in the one killed at that time, and the measured weights of the fattened animals, Persoz established how much each animal had gained of total weight and of fat. He ascertained also the weight of fatty materials each had obtained from the maize. Various approximations were necessary, which he discussed in the memoir he sent to the Academy. Though he drew a number of subsidiary conclusions, the one which stood out above all was that the fat formed was in most cases more than double the amount available in the maize. The results, he said, "prove to us peremptorily that a large proportion of fat must have formed at the expense of the sugar and of the starch in the maize." The goose, in fact, could "be considered as a veritable laboratory where fat is manufactured." Fittingly, the three referees who examined Persoz's memoir and communicated it to the Academy were Magendie, Dumas, and Boussingault.[50]

V

The Persistence of Jean-Baptiste Boussingault

In the face of the bad news which had beset the nutritional theories of the French chemists repeatedly during the preceding eight months, Jean-Baptiste Boussingault stubbornly set out in the spring of 1844 on a massive effort to establish their view of the source of animal fat. The investigations which he carried out involved so many extended feeding trials and analyses that they took him more than a year to complete. Why he persisted so doggedly in spite of the evidence which already appeared to indicate that he had little chance of succeeding is at first sight very puzzling. There were, however, several scientific and personal factors which may have concurred to reinforce his determination not to give in. First, he was setting up rigorous standards for nutritional experiments of the general type involved, and he probably felt he had to continue until he was satisfied that he had judged this case by the same standards. Second, he believed that there had been too much discussion of the question by others and too little experimentation.[1] He undoubtedly expected that the results he could obtain would surpass and supersede all of what had been done before. His own previous experiments had all come out consistent with his views, and he must have trusted his own work more than that of anyone else on the topic. Such an attitude would not have been wholly unjustified. Finally, he still had a passionate desire not to allow the supporters of Liebig to triumph. He so deeply distrusted the scientists at Giessen that he suspected them of spying on his research in Bechelbronn so that they could pounce on his results as fast as he reached them to use them for their own purposes.[2]

This explanation, however, has one crucial flaw; for none of it applies to the investigation of Persoz. If even one sound contrary result was sufficient to decide in favor of the formation of fat from other nutrients, how could Boussingault avoid conceding the issue in the spring of 1844? Certain of his statements suggest that he followed a thoroughly human, if scientifically illogical, course. Rather than confront first the situation in which he stood the greatest chance of encountering a definitive decision against him, he took up weaker links in the chain of evidence being posed in support of Liebig's views. Although aware that sooner or later he would have to refute or confirm Persoz's results, he hastened first to attack those of Playfair and of Chossat where he must have felt more confident that he would prevail. He also continued with other feeding experiments similar to those which had already turned out satisfactorily for him. Whether he sensed that he was only in a position to win a few last battles in a war that was doomed, or whether he was hopeful of ultimate success during that year, can only be guessed at from his published papers and feelings he expressed in letters to Dumas.

Among the experiments in which Boussingault was engaged during the spring was one to see if the fat eaten by young pigs was sufficient to account for the quantity of fat formed in their bodies as they grew to maturity. To Dumas he wrote on May 26: "You will soon have news about my pigs, but I have so little curiosity that even though I have all of the data, I do not yet know if the result is for or against us. In practical terms the question has been judged in our favor; there still remains the physiological question." [3] Here Boussingault seemed to be merely carrying on dutifully to the end, resigned to the likelihood of an outcome he was in no hurry to reach, and consoling himself with the consideration that foods containing fat would remain the most practical fattening agents even if it were to turn out that other aliments are convertible to fat. If he was discouraged about the theoretical issue, however, he was only showing it privately. In 1844 he permitted the republication of the physiological sections of his treatise, *Rural Economy*, in which he had maintained uncompromisingly "this fundamental principle, *that animals find their own substance in the aliments which nourish them.*" [4] In February of the same year a third edition of Dumas and Boussingault's *Chemical Statics of Living Organisms* appeared, to which Boussingault had added a preface assuring the readers that they had not yet "changed their minds about any point," in spite of those people who had contradicted them about some "principles of detail." [5]

During the same spring Boussingault found a new source of encour-

agement in an investigation which he had probably sponsored. Félix
Letellier, a physician working at least part of the time in Boussingault's laboratory, made a critical study of the experiments from
which Charles Chossat had announced in the previous autumn that
sugar stimulates the production of fat in pigeons. Chossat's investigation was inadequate to establish his inference, Letellier decided, because the pigeons fed exclusively sugar died so soon that the presence
of fat in their bodies afterward could not prove that it derived from
this aliment. Letellier considered it more likely that the sugar had only
served to spare fat previously in reserve by supplying some of the
requirement of the animals for respiratory aliments. Moreover, Chossat's methods for measuring the fat at autopsy were neither uniform
nor accurate. Repeating the experiments with greater precision and
making certain that the turtle doves he used obtained water with the
sugar so that they lived longer, Letellier found that when they did die
they generally contained less fat than the average for normal birds of
the same species. Dietary sugar, he therefore concluded, does not
favor the production of fat in the animals.[6] Although Chossat's result
had never figured among the most decisive factors in the fat question,
this refutation of it was the first reversal of the trend which had gone
progressively against the theories of the French chemists for nearly a
year.

During the summer Boussingault's own feeding experiments were
going so well that he again felt that he might be on the way to resolving the issue in favor of the "opinion which MM. Dumas, Payen, and
I profess concerning the formation of fat."[7] Still, he could not quite
believe that everything would work out as he hoped, and he knew that
he was procrastinating about the problem of Persoz's work. In August
he wrote a long letter to Dumas describing his progress. The letter
portrays so vividly his research and its unusual problems, Boussingault's blend of buoyant good humor and fatigue, of optimism,
caution, and apprehensive premonition, and his openly partisan feelings, that it is worth quoting in full the relevant portion:

Bechelbronn August 14, 1844

Here is the work which I promised you on nourishment with sugar beets and
with potatoes. If you have decided to begin the war again, present it at the
Academy, and in any case have it printed in our *Annales*. Perhaps at the
Academy you could deliver a few lines of introduction and especially a few
lines at the end.

I have made a copy of a first experiment on the pigs, and the results are so much in favor of direct assimilation that I will not make them public, I shall wait for a second which is being finished at the moment, then for a third. If this first experiment had been contrary to our ideas, I should have published it as hurriedly as you did in the affair of the bees; one is always welcomed by the public when one entertains them with a disappointment, even while doing it with all possible gravity. For the cows on potatoes one can proceed with complete assurance; I present facts first, and I believe them to be perfectly confirmed. I have spared no effort or expense to observe well; then I explain the facts in my own way, or rather in our way, perhaps it would even be [good] if in the conclusion your name and that of Payen would appear: you look into it.

Here is the result of the first experiment. Two twin brothers, 7 months old have paid the price of the observation. One of them, no. 1, which weighed 60.55 kgm. in life was bled. Its brother, no. 2 was put on potatoes and fresh water, it was deprived of its litter, a circumstance which must not be neglected, for a pig on potatoes eats up its litter. That pig weighed 9.5 kgm. In 205 days, after the death of its brother, it has eaten 1500 kil. of potatoes; it then weighed 34.5 kgm. It had gained 24 to 25 kgm. I had it killed and dissected by the same artist who had done the anatomy of the other.

Pig no. 1 weighing 60.5 kgm.			no. 2 weighing 84 kgm.	
with bristles and ears	5.01		7.96	
boiled and dried	3.83		9.00	
bones and fats adhering to the bones	0.87		0.90	
bacon fat (without the skin)	9.47	Fat 15.48 kgm.	10.00	Fat 17.39 kgm.
lard	2.30		3.50	
fat adhering to the interior	2.84		2.99	
red meat	23.20		34.25	
blood	2.17		2.60	
intestines	10.86		13.25	
excretions	0.15			
	60.55		84.05	

In the yellow potato as in the red potato I find by means of a good method, 0.002 of fine fat. The nourishment therefore has furnished 3 kgm. of *anhydrous* fat, which would make more than the fat found in excess. But in making a reduction for the fat of the excrement which has been measured very accurately and analyzed, it becomes evident that pig no. 2 contains only the fat which it ought to have according to our ideas of direct assimilation. You will understand that one could not publish a result so favorable, our friends would say that it is a novel [*un roman*]. After all, the experiment has been conducted with very special care, and notice that the infractions of the instructions which the swine-herd might have committed, would have to be unfavorable to us. If one does not permit himself to publish these results, one could talk about them with his true friends. Perhaps you could even tell the Academy of the situation as it is, that is that the result is so satisfactory that we do not dare to publish it before seeing it confirmed by other experiments. You may talk about it anyway, although a moment of pleasure for our *friends* will arrive later.

Now comes a question which has deeply engrossed me. I had at first judged the preceding result to be of only very slight value; here is the reason. Pig no. 2, nourished during 205 days with potatoes, gained only an insignificant quantity of fat, that is very well and it is understandable; but what one can less easily understand is how pig no. 1 could have acquired before its death, in seven months, which was its age, 15 to 16 kilog. of fat. It is true that while it nursed and during the two months which followed that, the basis of its nourishment was milk, or coagulated milk; but afterward the pig had no more than 5 or 6 kgm. of potatoes mixed with slops. Therefore the question came up, what is slops and how much of it does a pig consume each day. You will understand, my dear friend, that for a member of the Academy of Sciences who has been one of the illustrious staff-officers of the *libertador*, it is humiliating enough to analyse dish-water. I have nevertheless gone through with it, and it is quite painful I can assure you, I have lost my appetite as a result of the deep disgust which the odor of the kitchen impressed on me. Don't become too alarmed, however: I still weigh 100 kgm. The source of the slops given to the pigs each day was 1° all of the whey, 2° all of the butter-milk; 3° the wastes from the table and the dish-water which derives from the 32 people who are fed at Bechelbronn. The dish-water (you must play your part in it) does not go into the slops whole, one allows it to settle in a trough; and it is only the upper part, the deposit which forms there, which goes to the swinery, the intermediate layer is thrown out. Here is an analysis of slops: 1 litre of slops evaporated in the *bain marie* left a brown, crystallin residue weighing 47.3 gr. In 1/ . . . of that material, rich in milk sugar, [extraction by] ether indicated, after taking all precautions, 0.091 of a very good fat. Consequently the litre of slops contains 4.34 gr. of fat.

Two series of experiments have shown me that each pig receives per day, with the potatoes, in 2 meals, 9 to 10 litres of slops, in which there are 36 to 43 grams of *anhydrous* fat. Which, added to 12 gr. of fat from the potatoes, and to that of the solid debris, amounts certainly to 60 grams of fat per day, which augmented by $^1/_5$ makes 72 to 80 gr. per day of hydrated fat. You understand that it is impossible to give an exact number, but it is evident to me that a pig receives each day, in its slops, a much greater quantity of fat than is commonly supposed. I have prepared my cages for Persoz's geese, but I do not feel any more that I have the courage to undertake the work; I have had enough and I need to lie fallow; I will become stupid if I persist so stubbornly in these questions and I have indeed decided to let them take their chances.

Boussingault [8]

Whether it was weariness or misgivings about the possible outcome that made Boussingault hesitate to continue with his repetition of the experiments of Persoz, he was ready soon afterward to challenge the results of Playfair. In October he published his own investigations on the nourishment of cows. The recent observations of Playfair on the subject, he began, "seem conclusive at first glance," but are unsuitable to support his conclusions. In the first place, Playfair had used a figure for the fat content of hay which was only half of the more recently accepted value. After corrections were made for this, the dietary fat would cover the butter formed for the two days in which Playfair had fed his cow hay. In the remaining cases the contrary results were still invalid, because the experiment did not last long enough to draw any inferences about the source of the butter in the milk. Boussingault had no doubt that for such short periods cows would continue to deliver butter even if they did not eat at all, which would hardly justify the conclusion that the butter is created from nothing. The butter produced on the days that Playfair's cow ate only potatoes was formed, Boussingault believed, at the expense of the reserve fat of the cow itself. To prove this he carried out the long-term experiments which Playfair himself had admitted would be more satisfactory but which the English scientist could not afford. Boussingault maintained two cows for seventeen days on a diet of sugar beets, weighing the animals daily and making the usual determinations of the fatty matters contained in the food, the excretions, and the milk. Both cows produced butter weighing more than the fats they received in their food, but over the period they lost considerably more weight than the weight of the butter. They therefore could have been consuming their own reserve substances to make up the deficit. By then they were in poor condition, so he switched them to a diet of hay. After fifteen days they had regained much of their original weight, and the food had supplied an excess of fat over that produced in the milk and excrements. Boussingault went through a similar cycle using potatoes in place of sugar beets and obtained analogous results. [9]

The diets of sugar beets and of potatoes obviously could not sustain the health of the cows, but Boussingault wished to show that the inadequacy lay entirely in the insufficient supply of fat. Therefore he considered what other nutritional requirements of an animal must be met. These were, he assumed, that there be enough nitrogenous substances in the aliments to replace the losses of these substances in the excrements of the animal; a supply of carbon adequate to replace the quantity of that element consumed in respiration; and sufficient salts, particularly phosphates, to compensate for the continual expulsion of those substances. The sugar beets and the potatoes, he was able to show, provided ample amounts of each of these constituents. The best explanation, then, of the deterioration of the cows, he believed, was that the aliments did not contain enough of those materials analogous to fats which are necessary to "form the fats of the tissues and the various secretions such as milk and bile." [10]

Once again Boussingault had maintained his position successfully by performing more exacting experiments than his competitors could. But he also reflected in his reasoning about the requirements of nutrition the fact that he still saw that problem through the limited perspective of the chemists, without paying much heed to the lessons in the work of the Gelatin Commission.

Finally, Boussingault had to come to terms with the results of Persoz. During the winter he carried out experiments on geese similar to those the chemist from Strasbourg had done a year previously. On January 13, 1845, as he was preparing to leave Bechelbronn, he wrote to Dumas an interim account of the outcome:

I have positively finished all of the experiments which I had begun. I shall discuss all of that in Paris; I am conscious of having achieved a fine study, but it could well pronounce against us. The geese have behaved themselves in an unworthy manner. If one takes into account only the yellow oil of maize soluble in ether (0.070) the geese have made fat and a great deal of fat; if one accepts everything in the maize which is soluble in ether and alcohol and *insoluble in water*, the geese have not made fat; for there is nearly 0.12 soluble in ether and in alcohol.

The ducks on [a diet of] peas have behaved well.

The ducks on rice have shown themselves to be partisans of our ideas, in the first series. I have just slaughtered the second series and I find considerable fat; I shall not know the final result until tomorrow morning, when the boiled fats have solidified.

I believe that the truth is in the whole of my experiments, the question now is to draw it out of them.

It might well turn out that one would be obliged to invoke a new fat forming [*graissogène*] agent. On the back I shall set out my results very simply, each person will infer from them the consequences which please him.

Rice is the aliment which must resolve the question.

My ducks on nonfat rice have made prodigious amounts of fat, there is one which is as fat as Rayer.[11] Another which has had nothing but butter for nourishment is as fat as Mr. Sylvestre, just as Letellier has established with turtle doves.

It was time for all that to end, I am tired of killing, of hacking, of skinning, of boiling; the blood was flowing in torrents, for two months Bechelbronn resembled a modern Spain . . .

Whatever may be the outcome of my work you will be satisfied, for I have taken every precaution to be exact, and from it will emerge many interesting facts. We shall never be completely wrong, for nothing fattens either so well or so quickly as fat.[12]

Another five months went by before Boussingault was ready to state publicly the outcome he already suspected privately in this letter. Having apparently returned again to Bechelbronn in the meantime, he wrote finally to François Arago a brief summary of the results of his long effort. The letter was read to the Academy on June 16. His research had established, he said:

1. that pigs eight months old, raised on the normal diet of the piggery, contain much more fat than they have received in their aliments; 2. that pigs nourished for six months with potatoes do not produce more fat than the potatoes contain; 3. that in the fattening of pigs (I operated on *nine* individuals) there is much more fat assimilated than is found in their rations; 4. that aliments which, given alone, do not have the faculty of developing fatty matters, acquire that faculty in a surprising manner as soon as one adds fat to them, even though fat alone produces starvation; 5. that the rations which are capable of fattening but contain only a minimal quantity of fat are always rich in nitrogenous principles.

I have fattened geese, and as M. Persoz first observed, I recognized that the fat produced exceeds considerably the oil contained in the maize. Thus, on that point my experiments fully confirm those which M. Persoz has communicated to the Academy.[13]

At last the central issue was undeniably settled. Not only Persoz's geese, but also Boussingault's pigs had behaved unworthily; and the French chemist had proved beyond doubt that, in spite of his own views, animals form fat from other classes of food. The only question now left for the partisans of the theory of Dumas, Payen, and Boussingault was what interpretation they might try to place on its demise. The comments of Milne Edwards and of Payen, as well as Boussingault's letter, suggest that their first reaction was to dwell on the role French scientists had played in demonstrating that a conversion takes place, without admitting that in the terms by which they had originally defined their differences with Liebig, the demonstration was a clear verdict in favor of his position. Boussingault emphasized his agreement with Persoz and did not mention Liebig. Milne Edwards stood up to say that the results were in accord with the earlier research he had done with Dumas on bees, and showed that the situation in mammals was like that in insects. He noted that in both instances they had found that there must be some fatty matters in the diet to promote the conversion of the nonfatty matters into fat. Payen picked up the latter point and turned it into another argument that the "practical" aspects of the opinions of the three French chemists had been verified. He even managed to assert that the result proved, contrary to "the opinion of a learned foreign chemist," that potatoes and similar aliments are not as suitable for fattening animals as are grains rich in fats.[14]

"As for the purely scientific question," Payen concluded, "it seems to be solved, especially by restoring to a middle state that which might have been too exclusive in the two divergent opinions, and in that regard all of the investigations would have contributed to the definitive solution." [15] Thus Payen upheld to the end the claims of the French chemists to have come out with a victory on one front and at least a draw on the other. In what way, however, he considered the outcome of the physiological issue to have been a compromise between Liebig's position and their own he did not specify. Undoubtedly, yet another redefinition of what the issue had been was involved, but perhaps the vagueness of his statement is its own best comment.

Liebig was naturally not disposed to see the outcome of the dispute as a compromise, nor even to allow that the French scientists had contributed significantly to that outcome. Without waiting even for the full disclosure of the details of Boussingault's research he pronounced in his *Annalen* his own post mortem on the affair, which he described as the unambiguous opposition of views it once had been:

> The three-year controversy over the question, whether the animal organism is capable of creating fat, has finally reached a decision without further appeal. The two defenders of the view that all fat in the animal body derives as such from the plant have definitively abandoned it. Mr. Boussingault and Payen have, each in his own way, been persuaded that their previous view must be rejected.[16]

In victory Liebig was notably uncharitable. Although he admitted that he could not fully appreciate Boussingault's conclusions until a fuller report was available, he felt no need to wait until then to declare that "none of the results announced by Mr. B. is new or adds the slightest amount to the facts already known about the formation of fat." All of his conclusions were already common knowledge from agricultural practice. Liebig took the occasion to judge experiments like those of Letellier worthless because animals under starvation conditions could not be expected to store up fat. He rebuked Milne Edwards for certain comments he had made following Boussingault's letter. But he was, as usual, most scornful toward Payen. Referring to Payen's statement that all of the investigations had contributed, Liebig retorted that, aside from an analysis of maize nine years before, the only contributions Payen had made were his "views seized out of the air," such as the explanation that bees formed wax from their own fat. Just in case Payen had meant him by that "foreign chemist," Liebig denied that he had ever claimed that potatoes were as good for fattening as were grains. With typical superficiality, Liebig asserted, Payen was now acting in the Academy as though his former views had never existed, and that he had held "for all of his life" the opinion that fat is formed in the animal.[17]

Though harsh, the rebukes Liebig aimed at Payen were what the latter might have expected for consistently interpreting the events of the controversy as favorably as possible to the French chemists at Liebig's expense. But the statement that Boussingault had contributed nothing new was, in light of the fact that Liebig knew well his customary thoroughness and had often utilized his results, a display of arrogance. It was also hasty, for when the full memoir appeared a few weeks later it became evident that Boussingault was providing by far the most comprehensive data yet available to establish the formation of fat in animals. His report occupied sixty pages in the *Annales de chimie*, and included more than two dozen tables testifying to the labor involved. For the two pigs raised on potatoes and slops he kept daily records of the food, excrements, and weight increases for 93 and 205 days respectively. He made similar measurements for more than 300 days on three pigs maintained on potatoes alone, and for 98 days on nine pigs being fattened on regular diets. In repeating Persoz's investigation he made the same observations during 31 days on 11 geese and on ducks. He repeated the experiment with ducks on rice. In each case he made careful analyses of the quantities of fat and other constituents of samples of the food and excrements, taking precautions to obtain reasonable average values for the huge quantities of these substances involved in the experiments. He also had to dissect each animal in order to weigh its constituent parts and extract its various

stores of fat. The published memoir confirmed in data what the live-
lier descriptions in Boussingault's letters had suggested of the scope
of the work.[18]

Moreover, Boussingault did not limit himself to the thorough demonstration that animals in several different dietary situations produced
fat which must have had an origin different from the fatty matters
included in their nourishment; for he took some steps toward ascertaining more definitively what may be the nutrient source of this fat.
The observation alluded to briefly in his letter to Arago, that when
used alone, starch foods containing very little fat do not enable animals to fatten, might be taken to indicate, Boussingault said, that
starch or sugar cannot be transformed into fat in the animal. Another
explanation, however, was that the nutrients were inadequate for different reasons. To test this alternative for the two diets in question,
potatoes and rice, he determined by elementary analysis the carbon
and nitrogen in the food and excrements, and estimated the quantities
of these elements which the animals would normally assimilate during
growth on a regular diet. Then from the difference between the total
amount of each element absorbed and excreted and the quantities
which the animals would obtain from their *normal* diets he calculated
indirectly what they normally consumed in respiration.[19] Comparing
the total requirement for carbon thus obtained with the carbon received in the nonfat diets, he found in the case of rice that there was
barely enough of that element to cover the needs of respiration and
very little surplus in the case of potatoes. Consequently, there was
probably too little left to form fat and the result still permitted one to
believe that starch is capable of being transformed into fat.[20]

His experiments and discussion left undecided, Boussingault acknowledged, whether the fat formed in the animal from other matters
derived from starch and sugars, from proteins [*matières protéiques*],[21] or
from a joining of substances of these two classes. The fact that those
nonfat diets which were effective in fattening contained relatively
large proportions of nitrogenous principles "tempted" him to attribute
the origin of fat to the latter. In support of this alternative, which he
presented "with reservations," he mentioned Würtz's discovery of the
conversion of albumin to butyric acid; and he reported that he himself
had since then obtained an analogous reaction from "gladiatine," a nitrogenous substance extracted from maize.[22]

In the introduction to his paper Boussingault reviewed the positions
which had been taken concerning the formation of fat. These were the
"two extreme opinions," that it is entirely formed in the ailments, or

that it is elaborated in the blood; the "moderate" view that it is produced during digestion by a fermentation; and the view that nitrogenous principles contribute to that formation. He himself, he declared, had "executed these researches disengaged from any preconceived idea," and now limited himself to presenting the data as he had observed them.[23] His claim to have lived up to this scientific ideal was true only in a special sense, for the objectivity he professed was not what he had sought, but what had been forced on him by that data. He gave a more candid and relaxed glimpse of his feelings after the controversy had come to an end, in a note he sent a few weeks later to Dumas:

Saturday December 27, 1845

Dear friend. Come then to dine at 8 Rue du pas de la mule on Tuesday the 30th. You will have to pass judgment on the worth of a paté of fatty liver, prepared with livers fattened by a new method, necessarily contrary to our theoretical ideas.

Sincerely yours,
Boussingault
r.s.v.p.[24]

Now that the issue was resolved, who had really won and who had lost? In an ideal science it would be improper to ask the question. Everyone gains when research leads closer to the truth, and one's individual contribution is not what counts so much as participating in the movement. But the participants themselves in this case obviously regarded a victory and a defeat as at stake in their actions, and so did many contemporaries. Liebig acted like a winner, and the French chemists by their very reluctance to acknowledge when Liebig was proved right showed that they construed doing so as an admission that they were losing. Some of Liebig's followers later saw in his triumph during these debates the source of much of his influence on animal chemistry in the ensuing decades.[25] The view of the situation which the participants held, furthermore, did much to determine what the situation actually became. Because they saw it as a contest, they carried on a contest. Had the French chemists not been emotionally involved in the desire to best Liebig, they probably would not have pursued their investigations in the way they did, and might not have attained the results which resolved the issue. If, then, it is legitimate to ask the question, it is less clear what the answer is. One might say that by their researches the supporters of Dumas's views only destroyed the facets of their theory step-by-step until they finally showed simply that Liebig had been right all along. One might just as well say, on the other hand, that it was they, not Liebig, who demonstrated that bees can convert wax to sugar, and that geese and pigs can transform other nutrient substances to fat, and who provided the first circumstantial evidence that the process involves the conversion of sugar to fatty acids rather than directly to fats. These were not very impressive achievements to Liebig, for with the exception of the last point he considered them to be common knowledge already. But then much of science consists of proving more rigorously or precisely what is already believed by some to be true. Liebig's ideas could, in fact, be considered as no more than the catalyst spurring the French chemists on to their experiments. Nevertheless, historians need not entirely accept the attitude of scientific communities themselves that credits should be allotted to each scientist as a measure of his stature. The most realistic view of the situation is that neither side would have done what it did without the stimulus of the other, so that the outcome was a product of their indissoluble web of interactions.

The significance of the affair was not limited to the bare establishment of the phenomena mentioned in the preceding paragraph; it was a broader test of the whole approach to the chemical phenomena of life inherent in the conceptions of Liebig and of Dumas. Both men had been able to envision the general significance and nature of such phenomena in some ways more clearly than physiologists had up until then, but in their self-confidence they had at first seen no distinct boundaries on the range of inferences they could attach to their knowledge of chemical composition and reactions. The contest which emerged between them revealed to each something of their lack of caution and forced them to seek firmer supports. The supports they found were based on their own characteristic chemical criteria: refinements in the knowledge of chemical composition; chemical reactions achieved in the laboratory to establish the possibility of their natural occurrence; and comparisons of the composition of the materials entering an animal with those which leave or accumulate in it. If they were not very receptive to the criticism that the criteria themselves were not enough, the participants nevertheless learned between 1841 and 1845 that it was more difficult to prove what happens in the animal than they had initially assumed.[26] At the same time they justified their assertion that their views of animal nutrition comprised a suitable framework within which to pose and answer more specific questions. They showed that their own methods of investigation could provide a critique of their hypotheses and contribute to further elucidation of the problems. In his memoir of 1845 which ended the controversy, Boussingault affirmed forcefully his faith in the future of the chemical approach: "People have not yet been generally persuaded to envision animals as simple combustion systems whose raisers must at each moment, in order to obtain profitable results, calculate with precision the quantity of carbon and of hydrogen which they can consume. One must not seek to force his convictions on them: but the more I am occupied with nutrition, the more I find that analogy sound." There was, he added, a crucial distinction between firing a furnace and nourishing an animal; for, besides the combustible, one needs in the latter case to supply material for the maintenance and growth of the apparatus. "Perhaps the day is not far off when science will be able to indicate with accuracy the proportion which exists between the aliments which are consumed and the aliments which become flesh or fat." [27]

Superficially, Boussingault may seem to have been merely reciting the simplistic ideas of the original lecture of Dumas, but the context gave it an important difference in meaning. He was not so much imposing narrow limits on the internal processes imaginable in animals as he was seeking a means for measuring the overall rates of reactions whose details he did not know. His comments referred especially to the calculations, previously mentioned,[28] by which he compared the carbon exhaled in respiration with the amounts of that element in the diet. This approach, which he utilized on other occasions as well, provided a model for similar modes of research which his successors later pursued with increasing refinement. Liebig's *Animal Chemistry*, especially the third edition which he published in 1846, supplied further suggestions for carrying out such investigations, and, in the work which followed, the influence of Liebig was more visible than that of the French chemists. Nevertheless, the controversy in which both played their part, and in which Boussingault made the most extensive empirical contributions, did much to legitimize the features common to the conceptions of both groups. From the level of widely read treatises the contest brought these ideas into the center of the experimental arena.

Physiologists such as Donné, who asserted that innumerable chemical transformations take place in the animal body, seem retrospectively to have been more realistic than the chemists who conceived them as relatively few and simple. The latter had not been merely capricious, however, in preferring to consider the faculty of the organism for performing such changes to be very limited, as Milne

Edwards put it.[29] Physiologists were sometimes content to describe the processes as so complex that they only appeared obscure and mysterious, largely beyond analysis. The chemists, because they could see farther in certain directions than the physiologists, perceived the possibility, and even the ultimate necessity of expressing physiological processes in terms of specific chemical reactions. They could only portray this possibility concretely, however, by means of the kinds of reactions with which they had had experience in dealing with the substances derived from organisms. Despite the now celebrated synthesis of urea by Wöhler, the reactions which they knew about in 1841 involving what were regarded as the chief chemical constituents of animal matter consisted mostly of partial or complete oxidative decompositions, and it was these reactions which they projected into the organism. Even Liebig, who saw the necessity of acknowledging that animals perform synthetic chemical transformations, could give no account of them at all to make them less elusive. For the decomposition of the nitrogenous and non-nitrogenous constituents of the body into excretory products, on the other hand, he could propose hypothetical equations supported in some cases by reactions he had produced artificially.

When they proposed hypothetical chemical reactions within animals, Liebig and Dumas were also extrapolating an approach they had already been using in their own field. In the 1830's both men had been engaged in efforts to reconstruct the mechanism and the steps in organic reactions from their analyses of the initial reagents and the end products. Often they postulated intermediary compounds, some of which they afterward discovered, others of which remained theoretical. They had sufficient reason to believe, however, that speculations concerning these intermediates stimulated and directed the search for the compounds themselves. When they transferred that mode of reasoning to physiological reactions, they were undoubtedly not aware of how much more vast the unknown region between the beginning and final steps was. Yet here too the conviction that there were intermediary compounds analogous to those they were tracing in their laboratory reactions helped initiate the long search for them.

The most striking recent development in physiological chemistry in 1841 was the generalization that there were three general categories of substances present in most organic matter, and that for each type the species were more alike in composition than had hitherto been suspected. The inference that fewer changes of composition than previously believed were required to assimilate the nutrient material provided by one organism to the organized substance of another was a natural first assumption to make. Therefore, when Dumas and Liebig sought to reformulate physiological problems by means of chemistry, the form of their conceptions reflected this particular juncture in the history of chemistry. Already, however, a new area of physiological chemistry was beginning to emerge which could modify their vision. The butyric acid fermentations which Pelouze and Würtz discovered in 1843 were examples of a type of phenomena to which more attention was being given each year. The chemistry of "ferments" was beginning to enable chemists to produce more selective transformations of physiologically important substances than had been possible before. The above two cases were particularly notable for involving transitions from one of the three major classes of organic substance to another. Such reactions, therefore, promised not only finer control, but a broader range of demonstrable reactions. By means of small but reproducible variations in conditions, chemists could obtain different and specific products from the same organic substance. They therefore were coming to have evidence, persuasive to them, that many reactions might occur in nature with discriminating selectivity. By 1845 the prospects for physiological insights based on these processes were considerably more prominent than they had been in 1841. Thus, when Boussingault finally proved to the satisfaction of the French chemists that starch is converted to fat, Milne Edwards suggested that the next step would be to locate the ferment responsible.[30] In 1846 Magendie commented that the catalytic transformations with organic ferments which chemists had been studying for several years were "of great interest for physiology, for they are of such a nature that they can clarify the theory of digestion which is still so obscure, and the even obscurer theory of nutrition." [31] Gradually it became easier to imagine a broader "power" of transformation in animals without placing this power beyond the reach of chemical investigation, although the continued influence of the original treatises of Liebig and of Dumas sustained also for a long time the image of a rather simple, straightforward series of oxidations.

After the close of the debate over the origin of animal fat the three men who had most actively defended the vanquished position responded in quite different ways. Payen retreated to the practical level which had always been his primary concern, and there he stood his ground, collecting new evidence that herbivorous farm animals can best be fattened on plants containing the most fatty materials.[32]

Dumas found another question on which he could revive his view that the products animals form depend on their alimentation. Comparing the milk produced by female dogs on meat diets with that produced by the same animals when fed bread, Dumas found milk sugar (lactose) only in the latter cases. "The presence of milk sugar," he asserted, "appeared tied to the presence of bread in the aliments of the animal." [33] He seemed to avoid the question, however, of what such a finding would prove, even if true, about the general capacity of animals to form substances, in view of the proof of their ability to produce fats. Only Boussingault faced the logical question raised by the outcome of the fat controversy—where and from what other nutrient is the fat created in animals?

The new investigations Boussingault took up showed a strong continuity with his previous research, but the changed situation also imparted new trends to his approach. There was a more marked physiological dimension necessitated by the fact that he now had to try to locate a process within the animal body. Moreover, when the period of intense competition with Liebig had passed, Boussingault became more concerned with the attitudes of the physiologists, personified especially by Magendie. Armed with his own criteria for judging the adequacy of a nutrient substance, Boussingault set out partly to explain, partly to challenge, the results which the Gelatin Commission had reported on that subject five years before. In spite of his more physiological turn Boussingault retained much of the characteristically chemical technique of his past work. The very title of the memoir he published on his research of 1846, "Statical experiments on digestion," indicates that he was still attempting to extend to nutrition that application of the chemical balance sheet which he had pioneered.

During his earlier experiments with ducks he had noticed once that rice removed from a gizzard contained more fat than uneaten rice did. Inconclusive though the observation was, it suggested to him that perhaps the starch or albumin in rice is converted into fat in the digestive cavity. Then he found that the chyme in the small intestine of a duck fed on rice was richer in fat than the food. He decided therefore to probe the possibility further. The prospect of finding such a process must have been attractive to the old partisan in the campaign against Liebig. In 1843 the position that he, Dumas, and Payen were preparing to fall back on, if they needed to, was that starches are converted into fatty acids in digestion rather than directly into fats in the blood as Liebig maintained. [34] In his 1845 paper Boussingault had referred to this view as the "moderate opinion." He had even rationalized that it merged "from a physiological point of view" with the theory of the pre-existence of fat in the nutrients, because the transformation would take place in the stomach, "a cavity where the aliments are still outside the animal organism." [35] Boussingault had not advocated that position in his paper at that time, but his new chance observations must have tempted him to contemplate retrieving once again a semblance of the old general scheme he had formerly espoused.

Though in principle digestion may occur outside the organism, in practice Boussingault had to penetrate inside the animals to investigate the problem. The way he went about it resembled in some respects what physiologists had been doing for a long time. In each of twenty-three experiments he fed the animal a particular nutrient substance, then after a certain period he killed it, opened its intestinal tract, collected and analyzed the contents to determine whether or not any fat had been formed. He was, in short, searching for some of those mysteries in digestion which Dumas had once said could never be found there; [36] and he was taking a short step into the interior of the "labyrinth" that Donné had criticized the chemists for not entering. [37]

The method Boussingault used was to compare the total quantity of dry matter and the fat content of the food ingested with the corresponding amounts found in the digestive tract and excretions. He discovered first, however, that even a duck which has not eaten for 36 hours has in its digestive cavity a certain amount of matter, including 0.17 gram of fat. In each experiment, therefore, he subtracted this amount from the amount found after feeding to ascertain how much had derived from the food itself. The net amount of fat he compared with what the food would have contained originally. Since some of the nutrients were absorbed into the circulation before he killed the animal, a small excess of fat in the food over that in the digestive system would not prove that no fat had been formed during digestion, but the reverse, he thought, would demonstrate unequivocally that it had been. In the first tests with complex nutrients—rice, cheese, and cocoa—there was less intestinal fat than supplied in the food. When he fed a duck lard he found that much of it was directly excreted, no more being absorbed than was absorbed of the smaller proportions of fats in the other foods. This apparent limit on the rate at which the animal can absorb fat made him think that if he gave it pure starch or sugar, and if a conversion of these substances to fat occurred, then more fat should be formed than could be absorbed, and the excess should be left in the digestive tract. Consequently, if no excess were found, there would be very good reason to believe that fat is not formed from starch during digestion. The result verified this conclusion. From albumin and from casein, on the other hand, he obtained an excess of fat in the digestive tract over that in the state of abstinence, even though the nutrients he had prepared seemed to contain no fat. Although he did not say so, this result must have furnished satisfying support for the view he had already favored in 1845—that nitrogenous principles are the source of the fats formed in animals.[38]

The question of the formation of fat apparently started Boussingault on this research, but in the outcome another nutritional problem became at least as prominent. From the difference between the total of dry constituents of the food ingested and that excreted or left in the digestive system, he deduced how much must have been absorbed in the hours between the feeding and killing of the duck. Assuming that the nitrogenous and non-nitrogenous nutrients were absorbed in the same proportions in which they existed in the food, he calculated how much carbon this absorption represented. He divided by the time since the feeding to obtain an hourly rate and compared this rate with what he had computed from other experiments to be the rate at which a duck consumes carbon in respiration. As in previous investigations he then judged an aliment to be inadequate if it supplied too little carbon to meet the needs of the animal for producing heat. He had advanced on his earlier view by adding the physiological criterion that the element not only needed to be supplied in the food, but absorbed into the bloodstream to be considered available for the nutritional requirements of the animal. Yet the assumptions he made as a basis for his calculations showed that he still treated an organism as a rather simple chemical system. Setting the proportions of the absorbed constituents equal to those in the food; considering the intestinal contents of an unfed duck to be a constant amount which could be subtracted in each experiment from the actual contents; treating the indirectly calculated rate of absorption as immediately connected with the respiratory exchange over the same time, as though the carbon must be consumed as fast as it enters the blood; applying a figure for the respiratory consumption also calculated indirectly on another animal—all these procedures took little account of the complexities and variations of physiological phenomena. If any one of the approximations was seriously in error the entire computation would be invalidated. To consider such calculations dependable it was necessary to regard the animal, as we have seen Boussingault did, as essentially an apparatus for combustion. He reiterated this conception in his conclusion, reminding readers of the "elevated views of Dumas," who had first made the distinction between respiratory aliments which support combustion and those which are assimilated.[39]

Among the substances that Boussingault found did not provide enough carbon was gelatin. Because of the report made "in the name of a commission and by the agency of Magendie," he said, he had believed that gelatin was not a nutrient, and therefore that all of it which is eaten must be directly excreted. His experiments showed, on the contrary, that much of it is absorbed. Moreover, the uric acid excreted during the period was 3.40 grams, compared to 0.09 grams during a similar period of abstinence, so that the gelatin must have undergone further transformations similar to those which other nitrogenous nutrients undergo. Like albumin and casein, however, it did not provide an adequate rate of absorption of carbon. Consequently, he asserted, gelatin cannot be "absolutely deprived of a nutritive faculty," but like other nitrogenous substances it was an "incomplete aliment." Boussingault showed similarly that fibrin and other nutrients on which Magendie had reported supplied insufficient carbon. This property must be a primary cause of their inadequacy for nourishment, he concluded, because the continuous demand of the animal for respiratory carbon is more imperative than its need for a continuous supply of materials to be assimilated.[40] Thus Boussingault felt he was explaining in more fundamental terms why the Gelatin Commission had found that these substances, when fed alone to animals, were unsuitable for nutrition. In spite of a certain convergence between the means Boussingault was using to investigate nutrition and those of the physiologists, their standards of judgment were still far apart. For Boussingault there was a clear and simple quantitative chemical criterion of nutritional sufficiency; for Magendie there was only the less explanatory but also less fallible criterion of whether the nutrient can sustain indefinitely the health of the animal.

Boussingault sent his completed memoir to Dumas on August 29, for presentation to the Academy. His accompanying letter shows that he felt more strongly about the role of Magendie than the article which was to be published reveals. Boussingault asked Dumas especially to "lay stress on that part which concerns the experiments made with that substance [gelatin]." His remarks about the Gelatin Commission seemed reasonable, he said, "but if Magendie makes trouble [*si Magendie fait le méchant*]," he was prepared to reply with a ten-page statement

showing that the observations of the Gelatin Commission had proved
only that the dogs did not like gelatin and that they often died "from
grief" when confined in a basement for three months. "I am performing an act of justice," he wrote,

rather than an act of friendship in emphasizing the grandeur of the views
which you have expressed in digestion. The principal merit of my study is to
justify completely your ideas on the aliments which you have named respiratory. An animal which receives only a pure albuminoid [41] burns its own substance and ends by dying of starvation, because that albuminoid is not able to
furnish enough carbon. Do not object if I have recalled your conceptions
with some warmth; it is because I have been provoked by all these petty
works of physiologists who are coming to say to us in 1846 that sugar enters
the blood in order to be burned. [42]

The work to which Boussingault alluded was undoubtedly a short
note that Magendie had presented to the Academy one month earlier.
In it he showed, among other things, that if starch is injected into the
bloodstream of an animal it is gradually transformed there into sugar.
Ten minutes after the injection the first trace of sugar became detectable. "From that time on the blood was analyzed from hour to hour,
and we were thus able to assure ourselves that the quantity of glucose
in it increased for five hours; after which that quantity gradually
diminished, and ended by disappearing completely." The experiment
demonstrated, he said, that "the blood can create and probably destroy glucose." To see if the same phenomenon occurs when the
starch is introduced by the "regular phenomena of life," he then fed a
dog large amounts of starch for several days and found that under
these circumstances he could consistently recognize sugar in the
blood. [43] His experiment is now regarded as an important contribution
to the history of physiology, because it contained direct evidence that
sugar can be present in the blood of normal animals, not only of diabetics. [44] Boussingault, however, saw it merely as the purported discovery of what Dumas had long before established in principle by his
theory that sugar is one of the nutrients consumed in the blood to support animal heat. Aside from the question that can be raised of
whether Dumas had had sufficient reason to assume that this process
takes place, Boussingault might at least have regarded Magendie's
work as welcome confirmation. That it only annoyed him suggests
that even though the contrast in methods between his investigations
and those of the physiologists was less sharp than before, there was
still such a deep gulf in point of view between the chemists and physi-

ologists that one school could not easily appreciate the value of what the other was doing.

In 1848 Boussingault edged a little further into the labyrinth of the animal organism in his pursuit of the question of animal fat. One of the arguments he and his colleagues had earlier used to justify the direct assimilation of all fat from nutrients was the observation that fat globules are visible in the blood of animals fed large quantities of fat.[45] Having found in his experiments of 1846, however, that there seemed to be a limit on the rate at which animals can absorb fat, he came to doubt the significance of this older observation. Furthermore, Sandras and Bouchardat had shown in the meantime that variations in diet do not apparently change the quantity of fat in the blood of a dog. Boussingault therefore compared the blood of pigeons fed respectively starch, egg white, and nothing. Those which had received no fat, he found, maintained about the same proportion of it in their blood as those who had been nourished abundantly with it. The result, he said, was "an evident proof that the immediate origin of the fat of the blood is not always nutrient fat."[46] Thus he found new ways to disprove what he had once supported. These ways were becoming more and more like what physiologists themselves were doing. His new study of animal nutrition, however, was soon overshadowed by the achievements of the emerging master of this type of research, Claude Bernard.[47] Ironically, Bernard shortly afterward utilized a discovery based on an investigation quite similar to that of Boussingault, but involving sugar in the blood rather than fat, to illustrate the shortcomings of the kind of chemical physiology with which Boussingault had been identified.

VI

Origins of Claude Bernard's Research
in Animal Chemistry

"Twenty-five years ago," Bernard wrote in his *Introduction to the Study of Experimental Medicine*, "at the beginning of my physiological career, I tried, and I believe I was one of the first, to carry experimentation into the internal environment of the organism, in order to follow step by step and experimentally all of those transformations of materials which the chemists were explaining theoretically." [1] The context of his remark shows that it was theoretical explanations based on the "chemical statics" typified in Boussingault's earlier research, [2] on measurements of the balance between aliments and excretions, which Bernard recollected he had set out to put to the test by a new approach. Looking back, however, Bernard saw the issue more clearly and simply than he could have at the beginning, for his later accomplishments dominated his memory of the earlier events. In the sentences following the above statement Bernard recounted that he had "instituted experiments at that time [*alors*]," to ascertain how sugar is destroyed in the organism and found instead that it is produced there. These were not actually his first experiments, but were ones he carried out several years afterward, when he had developed a physiological approach characteristically his own. When he began he was not one of the first to carry experimentation into the interior of the organism (his concept of the "internal environment of the organism" was not even formulated then); his first investigations of the phenomena of nutrition and more generally of the chemical transformations which occur in animals were very much like what his mentor and other predecessors had already been doing. What he *was*, perhaps

118

one of the first to do was to utilize these methods in sustained conscious response to the new theories of the chemists; for it is evident that from the start of his career he was deeply concerned with their views.

The impact which the treatises of Liebig and of Dumas made in 1841 would have made it difficult for Bernard not to have felt their influence as he sought his first footholds in experimental physiology at just that time. A suggestion of his direct contact with the ideas of the former can be obtained from an early notebook Bernard kept, containing what appear to be notes taken down from lectures he heard or from his reading. Filling two pages in it is a summary of a section of Liebig's *Animal Chemistry*, entitled "Theory of respiration," and there are other statements also reflecting Liebig's views. Following a résumé of a discussion by Liebig of the amount of oxygen which enters the blood every minute, Bernard's notes paraphrase a general conclusion which was fundamental to Liebig's conception of animal chemistry:

> What happens to that enormous quantity of oxygen drawn out of the air by a single individual?
> It comes out again in the form of a hydrogenated compound and a carbonated one, having combined with the carbon and the hydrogen of the individual or of the aliments which it takes in.

Further on, under the heading *"nutrition,"* Bernard recorded an even broader claim:

> All vital actions are the result of the reciprocal action of the air and of the principles of the aliments. The movements of the organism are nothing else but these combinations (Liebig).[3]

Clearly a person just taking up the investigation of animal nutrition and related phenomena could not easily escape coming to terms with such basic propositions.

Bernard was exposed in a very direct manner to the ideas of Dumas. In April 1843, just as he was starting to focus on problems of animal nutrition in his own research, Bernard began attending Dumas's lectures at the École de Médecine. He heard the eminent chemist discuss Boussingault's investigations of vegetation, and their joint experiments on the composition of the air. He listened while Dumas summarized earlier debates on respiration and animal heat, and while Dumas presented his own controversial views on those subjects. Bernard took down in his notes a brief account of Dumas's own description of the differences between his position and that of Liebig concerning the source of animal fat, at almost the same time that Dumas and his colleagues were defending their theory in the Academy of Sciences. From Dumas's course Bernard learned about the chemistry of blood and of sugar, and along with these topics Dumas's emphasis on the role of the blood alkalis in respiration. During July Bernard followed Dumas's descriptions of the nature and digestive role of saliva, gastric juice, bile and chyle. "Digestion," Bernard quoted Dumas as saying, "is the function most accessible to chemistry." These lectures must have particularly interested Bernard because, as we shall see, he was at this very time becoming deeply involved in the investigation of digestion.[4]

Dumas's treatment of animal chemistry thus impinged forcefully on Bernard just when Bernard was setting out to establish his own scientific orientation toward the same questions. The excitement created in the scientific world of Paris by the debates over animal fat must also have made the ideas of Dumas and of Liebig lively sources of conversation in the laboratories where Bernard worked. Yet despite the fact that he sometimes depicted himself in later years as having assumed Dumas's theories without question at the beginning of his career, Bernard was actually in little danger of being overwhelmed by them, even when he heard them with all the eloquence and persuasiveness of Dumas's oratorical power; for he spent most of his time in those years in two places where Dumas's approach was viewed with misgivings. From 1841 until 1844 Bernard was *préparateur* to Magendie at the Collège de France, and in casual conversations about the approach of the chemists to physiological questions, he must have heard from his mentor reservations at least as strong as those Magendie had stated publicly. Long afterward Bernard wrote, "Yet I remember that at that time, in spite of the illustrious names who were supporting that theory [of Dumas, Payen, and Boussingault], Magendie and other scientists could not comprehend that all of the butter that the milk of a cow furnishes could be derived from the grass on which it grazed."[5] Magendie never lost an opportunity to impart through word and deed his creed concerning the care with which "one must distinguish, in physiology, between that which is probable and that which has been proven by experiment."[6] As we have seen, Magendie admonished the chemists themselves that their theories did not meet the latter standard. He expressed a more sarcastic private opinion, uncovered recently in a manuscript fragment, in which he referred to "Mr. Dumas who sums up the animal as a locomotive and Mr. Liebig who regards a good coat as the equivalent of a good meal." The prestige of the "great discoveries of the new chemistry," he added, "has fascinated the best spirits and closed the door to doubt."[7]

If Magendie's opinion encouraged his student to open the door to doubts about the approach of Dumas and Liebig, the other major influence on Bernard's research must have induced in him a special skepticism toward the theories of the French chemist; for Bernard worked frequently during these years in the laboratory of Jules Pelouze.[8] The distrust Pelouze harbored for Dumas's whole manner of proposing and using scientific theories, his private opinion of Dumas and Boussingault's nutritional ideas, and the contribution he himself made to the question of animal fat, make it highly probable that Pelouze would have urged Bernard to be on his guard concerning what he had heard in Dumas's lectures. In view of Bernard's close personal contact with men intimately involved in the controversies aroused by Dumas's theories, it is no wonder that the issues in question so deeply impressed him that they preoccupied him long after the events themselves were over. Neither is it surprising that, far from accepting the terms on which the chemists were discussing the topic, Bernard was predisposed from the beginning to challenge their assumptions.

Although the views of Dumas, of Magendie, and of Pelouze surrounded Bernard most pervasively as he took up the problems of animal nutrition, he encountered in the richly diverse scientific milieu of Paris other approaches to the same problems. He attended, for example, the course of Pierre Honoré Bérard, the professor of physiology in the Faculty of Medicine. There Bernard heard a more traditional physiological description of digestion. Bérard discussed the chemistry and actions of the digestive juices, but he devoted most of his time to such topics as the anatomy of the digestive tract and glands, and the physical actions of digestion, the latter including mastication, swallowing, the contractions of the stomach, and the mechanism of vomiting. Bérard dealt also with such questions as the conditions under which gastric juice is secreted and the alterations brought about in digestion by pathological changes. He often referred to the experiments of the American physician William Beaumont, particularly to Beaumont's observations concerning digestive movements, the effects of various pathological conditions, and the digestibility of different aliments. Bérard reviewed the long-debated question of the nervous control of digestion, especially of the role of the pneumogastric nerves.[9] Some of the themes on which Bérard dwelt were similar to those Claude Bernard himself later stressed and accused the chemists of neglecting.

Up until 1842, when he completed his two-year internship, Bernard was still spending most of his time in medical training. In the environment of the hospitals, where he served under several physicians in addition to Magendie, he found physiological phenomena treated chiefly in their relation to illnesses. Bernard was particularly attracted to Pierre-François Rayer, whose service he followed at the *Charité* in 1840. With Rayer he had the opportunity to observe closely many cases of diabetes, a disease then considered to be connected with abnormalities in nutrition.[10] Bernard must have been impressed also by Rayer's special interest in the relation between diseases and abnormalities in the anatomy and functions of the kidneys.[11]

One of Bernard's earliest areas of interest has received little attention from historians. Soon after entering medical school in 1834, he and two of his fellow students had helped to support themselves by teaching in a school for girls. Bernard gave a course in natural history.[12] Where he himself learned the subject is unclear, but he must have been influenced by the activities at the Museum d'Histoire Naturelle of the followers of the great Georges Cuvier, who had died only two years before. Continuing his interest in the subject, Bernard followed in 1840 the famous lectures of the outstanding comparative anatomist Ducrotay de Blainville at the Sorbonne and the Jardin des Plantes. Here Bernard heard the former student and later rival of Cuvier describe animal functions from the standpoint of comparative anatomy. De Blainville stressed that the goal of comparative anatomy is to determine the function of each organ in relation to its form. He also emphasized the need to consider all functions over the whole animal series, tracing their progressive degradation from their most perfect state in humans down to their rudiments in such simple creatures as sponges. De Blainville's views were a blend of those of Cuvier, Lamarck, and Xavier Bichat, with many original twists of his own.[13] Though Bernard later reacted against the conception of a physiology dependent on anatomy, de Blainville's lectures left such a strong imprint on his mind that he remembered and cited them many years afterward.[14] De Blainville expressed a number of general ideas which may have formed germinal points for Bernard's own thought. These included the importance of the relation between an organism and its milieu, and the conception that nutritive processes are comprised of closely linked "successive, alternative movements of composition and decomposition." [15] The latter idea, which was the basis for a central theme in Bernard's later writings, was in sharp contrast with the theories of Dumas.

During the period in which he was making his transition from medicine to physiological research, Bernard thus came into contact with widely diverse approaches to the same general biological problems.

These viewpoints represented such disparate fields of activity as the dominant laboratory science of the era, organic chemistry, the fledgling experimental physiology pursued by Magendie and a few others, the well-established zoology of the Museum of Natural History, and the powerful Parisian medical establishment. Their divergent perspectives did not make Bernard an eclectic, for he was always more concerned to mark out his own distinctive mode of investigation than to assimilate the views of others who dealt with the same questions. The breadth of the influences to which he was exposed did help, however, to give him a certain independence from any single conventional pattern. He drew something from each of the traditions he encountered, rejected some aspects of each, and mixed their elements in his own way. Nevertheless, his own approach soon became tied more closely to that of Magendie than to any other individual or school. If he acquired important ideas by listening to the others, he imbibed Magendie's views and methods more deeply by working directly for him. Bernard's early physiological investigations were so tightly intertwined with the experiments he carried out to assist Magendie, that his own work only gradually emerged as a separate endeavor.

That Magendie's manner of investigation was a principal source of Bernard's attitude concerning the proper way to study the chemical phenomena of life is forcefully supported by Bernard's record of a set of experiments the two men performed together for Magendie's course at the Collège de France in 1842 and 1843. Dealing mostly with animal heat and respiration, these experiments seem clearly to have represented Magendie's response to some of the questions Liebig and Dumas were raising. The first series was entitled "Research on the causes which produce and sustain animal heat." Magendie and Bernard began by inserting thermometers through the jugular vein and carotid artery of a dog into the right and left chambers of its heart, in order to determine whether the temperature of arterial and venous blood differed. They were unable to detect any difference, but thought the temperature might not be the same in blood vessels more distant from the heart. These measurements were probably an unsuccessful first attempt to find out where the animal heat was produced, by locating where the temperature of the blood increased.[16] In later years Bernard refined and extended the same basic experiment until his methods were delicate enough to map out the variations in temperature through the major arterial and venous trunks of the body.[17] For now, however, he and Magendie turned to other means to try to characterize respiratory combustion. They withdrew 200 grams of blood from a dog, heated it to 48° C and replaced it, to see if the animal heat would be increased; but they found that the temperature of the animal dropped instead. Next they asked whether "the subtraction of a great quantity of blood has an effect on the temperature of the animal?" Their objective here seems to have been a direct test of the doctrine that respiration is a slow combustion caused by the interaction of inspired oxygen with combustible substances in the blood; for, if that were so, one would expect that with less blood present there would be less combustible material available and proportionately less heat produced. Bleeding a dog, however, did not change its temperature until they had removed so much as to cause it to faint.[18]

Attacking the problem from the other direction, Bernard and Magendie tried to introduce gases into the animal by ways other than the lungs, to see if the animal heat would be affected. The injection of carbonic acid and of oxygen into the subcutaneous tissue of a rabbit lowered its temperature, whereas hydrogen and nitrogen produced no change. They noticed that the temperature seemed to drop whenever the breathing accelerated, an effect which they also obtained when they caused the animals to respire in the different gases.[19] They tried various ways of bringing oxygen directly into contact with blood. They mixed the gas with arterial and venous blood in flasks maintained at a constant temperature; they injected oxygen into the peritoneal cavity of a dog and then opened the portal vein so that blood also entered the cavity; and they injected oxygen into the jugular vein of a dog. "In all these experiments, which have been varied as much as possible in order to avoid error," they concluded, "there has constantly been a lowering of the temperature by the mixture of the oxygen with the blood." That result was plainly contradictory to the doctrine that respiration is a combustion caused by the contact of oxygen with the blood. They tested the same doctrine in another way. "If the chemical phenomenon of respiration is a combustion which sustains the temperature of the animal, it is evident," they concluded, "that by causing very combustible materials to enter through the lungs, one will develop a greater quantity of heat." When they injected a solution containing phosphorus and oil, however, they found no variation in the temperature.[20]

By placing frogs and dogs in an atmosphere of hydrogen, Magendie and Bernard discovered, as Lazzaro Spallanzani had shown long before, that animals can evolve carbonic acid even when they are not inspiring oxygen, and they inferred from this that oxygen is not essential to the formation of carbonic acid. Then they queried whether it was the exhalation of carbonic acid through the lungs which maintained animal heat. To answer this they hoped to determine whether the temperature of an animal was proportional to the quantity of carbonic acid exhaled. Their efforts to determine the normal quantity of carbonic acid breathed out by a rabbit did not, however, give "excessively rigorous figures." Finally, they tried to find out if the injection of water into the veins would change the quantity of carbonic acid exhaled.[21]

Assuming that Bernard's summary of these experiments was reasonably complete, they were tentative, inconclusive explorations, most of them, as he noted, needing to be repeated. He did not record that he or his teacher derived from them any general conception of the nature of respiration, although Magendie may well have had more to say about that in his lectures. At any rate, the purpose of their investigations seems clear. They were subjecting the theories of respiration of the chemists to the "severe logic" of direct experiment that Magendie believed they required. The results, if not sufficient to disprove the chemical theories, must at least have encouraged the skepticism of the two physiologists. The contrast between their approach and that of Dumas to the same problem is striking. He had based his theory on knowledge of the oxidation reactions of specific organic compounds, whose existence in the blood under suitable conditions he simply deduced from the general requirements of the situation. Magendie and Bernard barely treated the chemical reactions of respiration; instead, they tried to ascertain the source of animal heat by intervening in its production in the animal itself, in such a way that from the nature of the agent used, the site of its action, and the alterations it produced in the process they might elucidate the nature of the latter. Like the chemists, they underestimated the complexity of the organism, and their "direct" experiments led them little closer than did the theoretical deductions of the chemists, to the internal mechanism from which the animal heat emanated. Nevertheless, Bernard acquired from this and similar experiences the conviction that this approach was the only reliable way to probe the chemical and physical processes of life. Repeatedly he returned in his own teaching more than a decade later to experiments related to these. More important still, he retained in his work throughout his career some of the general features of the experimental approach embodied in this investigation.

Bernard's first independent effort to deal with the chemical theories about physiological processes came out of a line of investigations which seemed superficially to have little to do with the controversies prevailing at the time. He hoped to establish a foundation for animal chemistry by experiments in which he would inject various chemical reagents into the circulation—or certain organs or tissues—of animals, and then trace by vivisection or by autopsies how and where they had reacted within the body. The source of his methods was research which Magendie and earlier students of Magendie had carried out over many years concerning the phenomenon of absorption. These studies began in 1809 when Magendie isolated a section of the intestine of a dog so that it communicated with the rest of the body only by a single artery and vein. When he injected the poison called "upas" into the intestinal segment, the animal was poisoned just as if the normal connections had been intact. He obtained a similar result by injecting a leg detached except for its crural artery and vein. In 1820 he showed that a poison can be absorbed directly through the walls of a vein. Freeing a section of the jugular vein of a dog from its attachments, and isolating the vessel by slipping a card under it, he then dripped nux vomica (an extract of a seed containing strychnine) on the vein and found that the animal was quickly poisoned. From these and many similar experiments Magendie believed he had proved the falsity of the popular doctrine that only the endings of the lymphatic vessels can absorb substances into the body and that these exert a selective "vital action" so that only those materials needed by the organism can enter. The process takes place through all tissues, he claimed, and is purely physical. The latter view he substantiated by showing repeatedly that it occurs as readily through dead tissues as through the corresponding ones in living animals. Extending his methods, he and his students found that the rate of absorption varies greatly, depending on the site and on the nature of the substance absorbed. Highly vascular areas, such as the lungs and connective tissues, absorb very rapidly; the stomach lining absorbs less rapidly because of its protective mucus layer; and the skin absorbs very slowly.[22] The general result of his research, he believed, was "that every liquid and every solid capable of dissolving in our humours is imbibed across [all of] our different tissues."[23]

Most often Magendie used powerful poisons such as upas, nux vomica, and hydrocyanic acid (known also as prussic acid) to demonstrate absorption, for the immediately recognizable effect on the animal was a reliable indicator that the substance had penetrated into the general circulation. Sometimes, however, he utilized a chemical reaction with a visible product to show that a particular substance had reached a given location. At one time, for example, he injected a mixture of phosphorus and oil into the circulation of a dog. Soon afterward the animal exhaled white fumes from its nose. Magendie explained that so long as the phosphorated oil was "in contact with the blood," no reaction occurred, but as soon as it passed through the surface membrane of the lungs and came into contact with the air a combustion took place.[24] In 1823 one of his students, Michael Fodéra, made very effective use of a reaction with an easily detectable product in order to trace the absorption of fluids through various tissues. His procedures were similar to those Bernard utilized twenty years later.

At the time Fodéra began his research with Magendie the experiments of the latter had dealt primarily with absorption from the tissues into the circulation. Fodéra wished to demonstrate that the process takes place in the same way in other directions. For this purpose poisons were less useful than a substance whose presence could be traced in local regions. Fodéra used various reagents, but the most effective was based on a well-known chemical reaction which produced the strikingly colored substance known as Prussian blue. Hydrocyanate of potassium (or prussiate of potassium, as it was also called), reacted with a salt of iron (Fodéra used sulfate of iron), to form cyanate (prussiate) of iron, which was deposited as a bright blue dye.[25] Fodéra used this marker in a number of ingenious ways. He injected prussiate of potassium into a loop of intestine which was itself immersed in a solution of iron sulfate. The appearance of a blue color after about an hour demonstrated that the two salts had migrated together through the intestinal walls. He was able to follow the stages in the further absorption. The walls of the intestine gradually deepened in color, then in turn the fluids of the lymphatic vessels and veins became colored. Similarly, he traced the course of prussiate of potassium injected into subcutaneous tissues. Finally, to determine whether substances absorbed from the stomach can enter the kidneys by another route quicker than the circulation, as some people thought, he injected the same salt into the stomach of an animal and collected specimens of urine at frequent intervals, testing each sample with a drop of iron sulfate. As soon as a blue coloration revealed that the potassium salt had reached the urine, Fodéra opened the animal and found that the serum of blood drawn from several portions of the circulatory system also contained the salt. There was therefore no need to assume a second channel between the stomach and kidneys. Fodéra's experiments were described by the person who reported them to the Academy as "a fine supplement to the work of Magendie on absorption." [26]

Although the crucial research on absorption was finished long before Bernard came into contact with Magendie, the latter continued to
emphasize his conception of the process and to demonstrate the experiments in his later teaching. The topic formed, for example, a major
portion of his lectures at the Collège de France in 1836. Undoubtedly
Bernard learned directly from Magendie of the importance of investigating these phenomena. If any further emphasis was necessary for
the younger man, however, he might have received it in a timely manner from the publication of the above lectures in 1842.[27]

During his first year as Magendie's formal assistant Bernard was,
aside from his participation in the work of the Gelatin Commission,
occupied primarily with investigations of the nervous system.[28] In the
fall of 1842, however, he began to take up other projects as well. One
of these was to help Jean L. M. Poiseuille with his research on the dy-
namics of the circulation.[29] Another began with the following entry in
his laboratory notebook:

September 20, 1842
Project of experiments with Mr. [Jean-Baptiste-Rozier] Coze to verify experimentally the following therapeutical propositions, which agree moreover
well enough with the generally known facts of the action of medicaments.
   1. Medicaments (or poisons or aliments) cannot act unless they have previously been absorbed. The experiments of M. Magendie and of many other
physiologists have sufficiently demonstrated that proposition.

Furthermore it is useful to know by what pathways they must be
absorbed. Such substances cannot be introduced directly into the vessels, the note continued, but must pass through the capillaries. There
must also be means of eliminating such substances from the blood.
Bernard theorized that medicaments are selectively excreted from
those organs which normally secrete analogous products.[30]
In developing these ideas Bernard was influenced by Coze, who had
at about that time formulated several theoretical propositions to explain the actions of certain classes of medicinal substances. Among
them was the statement "that the substances which contain principles
identical to those which normally comprise part of a secretion are
eliminated by the organs which preside over that secretion." Coze,
who was then dean of the Faculty of Medicine at Strasbourg, was in
Paris during September and October. The research which he and Bernard undertook together consisted of a series of injections of substances such as ether, alcohol, and various essential oils into different
animals, followed by autopsies to determine how these had affected

the animals. Coze returned to Strasbourg soon afterward, but Bernard continued to follow the lines of thought and investigation stimulated by this brief collaboration.[31] In November he performed several experiments in which he injected prussiate of potassium, poisoned the animal a few minutes later, and then examined where in the meantime the salt had penetrated. In December he made several tests of the effects of injections of sulfate of quinine.[32] These experiments were evidently inspired by the combined influence of Coze and of Magendie. They were so similar to those carried out in earlier years in Magendie's laboratory, that it seems likely that the teacher had put his young assistant onto them for training, and perhaps to refine certain aspects of what had already been done. The professor himself was close at hand to advise Bernard when Bernard encountered technical difficulties.[33]

During the course of this work, however, a new question which entered first only as a subsidiary technical problem emerged to become a primary object of the investigation itself. On December 26 Bernard injected tartar emetic into the jugular vein of a dog. To induce vomiting he afterward introduced acidified sulfate of quinine into its esophagus. He also cut the pneumogastric nerves of the animal. Unexpectedly the dog died, and Bernard could find no visible cause. In his notebook he listed the possible reasons he could think of. One of these was that the death might have resulted from a combination between the two substances introduced, even though one had entered the stomach, the other the veins. This possibility led him to consider new experiments to determine if chemical combinations can occur between substances introduced either together or by separate pathways into the blood.[34] At about this time he referred in his notebook to Coze's ideas as a general "chemical theory" of the action of medicaments on organs of the body.[35] The pages in which he may have discussed that theory itself have been removed from the notebook, so that it is difficult to assess the direct impact of Coze's views upon a set of theoretical propositions which Bernard wrote down shortly afterward. Bernard's statements seem to have been inferences he himself drew concerning normal physiological processes, but to have been in the same spirit as Coze's statements concerning the actions of drugs. Bernard's views were entitled "On the physiology of the blood, necessary before pathology." They began:

No chemical combination is produced in the blood.
The blood transports all substances in a state of mixture and combinations

take place only in the organs of secretion and excretion, from which the chemical composition of secretions and excretions arises.

Combinations, compositions or decompositions, form also in the stomach before absorption.

Consequently there are only two places chosen for [*lieux d'élection pour*] combinations. In the stomach for absorption. In the glands for the secretions. The blood is only the intermediary or vehicle between the two systems.

But before arriving at their second place of combination, [the glands], all liquids pass through the lungs—or through the lungs and the liver. What action can these two organs exert on them?

. . . .

Is there no chemical combination produced in the blood?

Inject dilute solutions of prussiate of potassium and of persulfate of iron [ferric sulfate].

Cause the two substances to be absorbed by the stomach, one after the other.

See if the serum will be colored by the reaction or if the reaction will only take place in the glands? in the secretions.

Do decompositions take place [in the stomach] before absorption?

For example, will prussiate of potassium be transformed into lactate of potassium: [36] the reaction will indicate that for us.[37]

The entry continued with several other related queries, including a question about what action the oxygen introduced into the blood might have. These passages show that Bernard was speculating rather boldly for a person who was just becoming acquainted at first hand with the study of chemical phenomena in organisms. He seemed to be posing his hypotheses with little regard for prevailing ideas. It was the common view, for example, not only in the schools of Dumas and Liebig, but among the prominent teachers of physiology in Paris at the time, that the blood is the focal point of the principal chemical transformations of the body.[38] Evidently wavering between his theory that chemical combinations cannot take place in the blood and the suggestion that, if they do, certain experimental observations might be explainable, Bernard was here proposing to test the question by means of the procedures he had learned by repeating Magendie's absorption experiments. But if he could continue to utilize the same techniques, such as the Prussian blue reaction, which his predecessors had developed, his purpose implied a novel interpretation of the results obtained. Previously the blue coloration had been regarded simply as an indicator of the presence in the same place of the two salts which produced it, it being assumed that wherever they came together they would react. Bernard was now questioning that assumption with his suggestion that perhaps no chemical combinations take place in the blood. In his interpretation the two salts might under some conditions be in contact and yet not interact. A blue coloration would indicate not merely the simultaneous presence of the two salts in a given region, but that they had reached a place in the body where chemical combinations occur. The problem to be elucidated by the method was no longer where do substances penetrate in the body, but where are they transformed? [39]

On January 20, 1843, Bernard undertook the first experiments which seem to have been based on these ideas. He injected prussiate of potassium into the jugular vein of a puppy, and four minutes afterward injected perchloride of iron [ferric chloride]. Ten minutes later he withdrew some blood, and in twenty minutes the animal died. Bernard found no coloration in the organs of the body, but by testing with the two reagents he discovered that the prussiate had entered the urine and the iron had got into the lungs. His conclusion was that "the two salts have not combined in the blood." On the same day he tried another set of reagents, copper sulfate and ammonia, whose reaction had the advantage that it produced a "coloration rather than a precipitate." In another experiment he injected sugar into the circulation and could find no traces of it in four samples withdrawn in succession. He was uncertain whether this result indicated the proportion was too small to detect or the sugar had combined with the tissues. [40]

Bernard must have been highly encouraged by these first attempts to implement his ideas experimentally, for in his "reflections" on the work of the day he wrote:

It is perhaps in experiments of this kind that one must find the true laws of animal chemistry and perhaps the foundations of a classification of that part of science—for between the chemistry of the living animal and that which occurs in the crucibles there is analogy but not identity.

Before explaining certain phenomena of life by chemistry, it is therefore important to know up to what point these chemical reactions can take place. These researches are necessary today when one is talking a great deal about the pathological state of the blood and when one is trying to apply chemistry to the explanation of vital phenomena.

New research on the simultaneous administration of several substances in order to know if one would be right to employ complex formulas—see the experiments with tartar emetic and sulfate of quinine. [41]

Thus Bernard imagined in these experiments the beginnings of a whole new approach to animal chemistry, one which could provide more dependable knowledge than the explanations others were espousing. The passage does not make explicit, however, whether Bernard was hoping to subject the explanations of any particular individuals to the kind of experimental critique he envisioned. He undoubtedly was not responding to the theories of Liebig and of Dumas alone. His allusion to pathological states of the blood refers to other contemporary efforts to relate diseases to alterations in the proportions of fibrin, albumin, red cells, and salts in that fluid.[42] He may in addition have been comparing his proposed researches with studies which Louis Mialhe, a pharmacist associated with the Faculty of Medicine, had published during the previous eighteen months. Mialhe showed that when a mercuric or mercurous salt reacts with alkali chlorides, such as sal ammoniac and common salt, corrosive sublimate (mercuric chloride) is produced. Mialhe investigated these reactions very thoroughly from a chemical standpoint. He tried a large number of compounds of mercury, and observed the effects of changing various conditions upon the amount of sublimate produced and the rate of the reaction. From these results he drew the immediate conclusion that the same process occurs in the human body when calomel or other mercurial substances are used therapeutically. "Since the different liquids contained in the organs of man include common salt and sal ammoniac, sometimes accompanied by hydrochloric acid and other acids which can further facilitate their action," he said, "it follows that all of the phenomena which I have just reported take place in the human body, when one introduces into it any mercurial preparations."[43]

Bernard was probably familiar with Mialhe's work: his teacher Magendie had served as a commissioner, along with Dumas and Pelouze, to report it to the Academy in August 1841. The analogy between the phenomena with which Bernard was dealing and those which Mialhe had treated makes it plausible that Bernard would have perceived a connection between their respective efforts. Each was concerned with certain clearly defined chemical reactions of salts, which he could readily produce outside the organism, which did not comprise processes occurring as part of normal physiological functions, but which could be envisioned as able to take place within the body if the reagents were introduced into it. If Bernard did have Mialhe in mind, he would be implying that in studying only the chemical nature of the reactions Mialhe had not gone far enough to justify his conclusion; to show that the process can actually take place in the body he would have to utilize methods of directly observing its results in the body, as Bernard himself was attempting to do.

The connection between Bernard's experiments and the issues which Dumas and Liebig were debating may seem by comparison rather remote. Superficially there is little in common between the reaction of iron with prussiate of potassium in the body and the question of the nutrient source of fat or the claim that plants create the nitrogenous constituents of animals. Yet, in view of the impact their chemical explanations of the phenomena of life were creating at the time Bernard wrote down his thoughts, there seems little doubt that the views of these two chemists must have been a major source of the stimulus he felt to seek an alternate approach. Bernard's own later recollection that he had begun his research under the influence of their theories strengthens such an inference. It was characteristic of Bernard to reflect on the broadest possible implications of the specific phenomena he was investigating. It is not unlikely, therefore, that he was meditating that if he could succeed by his procedures in tracking certain reactions within the body, the method could somehow be extended to treat many other reactions which take place there, including those central to the current questions of nutrition. Perhaps he conceived by himself the idea that artificial but easily traceable reactions could lead to an understanding of the natural ones, but he may also have been aided by an essay written a few years earlier by Michel Eugène Chevreul, the distinguished discoverer of the composition of fats. Chevreul had observed during his studies of dyeing that Prussian blue, when fixed on cotton and exposed to sunlight in a vacuum, is bleached, as a portion of the cyanogen is removed and the ferric salt is reduced to a ferrous salt. On exposure to oxygen the blue color is restored. This reversible process, Chevreul maintained, can help to explain by analogy the kind of phenomena which occur in living organisms as the blood cyclically changes color in its vessels, first absorbing, then losing oxygen. If one had knowledge of the species of compounds involved in the vital processes as one did in the Prussian blue analogue, Chevreul believed, one could give a chemical explanation of the respiratory phenomenon.[44]

Although Bernard's program for extending his research did not lead as systematically as he had envisioned to new foundations for animal chemistry, he was disposed throughout his career to probe physiological problems of a chemical nature by methods analogous to those to which Magendie's investigations of absorption had introduced him; that is, by injecting certain substances into the body, either directly or through the digestive system, and subsequently tracing their fate inside the organism or their effects on particular parts of the body.

Although Bernard could leap ahead mentally in January 1843 to envision himself laying new foundations for animal chemistry, his approach was still more a hope than an achievement. He could not begin to challenge the chemical explanations of his day until he could find ways to prove that his own methods would work. He needed still to determine what chemical reagents were suitable to his objectives, to learn what physiological situations would enable their reactions to illuminate the questions he was asking, and to cope with complications which would interfere with the results he was seeking. He needed also to reduce the very general questions he had posed to more specific ones susceptible to specific answers. With all these problems he struggled during the spring.

Among the reactions he attempted to utilize was that between lactic acid and bicarbonate of soda. He reasoned that if he injected them into the blood and they reacted there to form carbonic acid, he could detect the product as an increase in the rate of the respiratory exhalation of that gas. The experiments, however, were inconclusive.[45] He used also cyanide of mercury in some experiments. When decomposed he expected it would produce cyanic acid, which would poison the animal, or at least be detectable by its odor.[46] At one point he thought of "giving calomel to an animal in the blood of which one will have introduced a certain quantity of sodium chloride."[47] The remark suggests that Bernard may have considered testing directly whether the reactions take place which Mialhe claimed to occur in animals. Apparently, however, he did not follow up his idea.

Most of his effort Bernard devoted to developing the basic method with which he had begun, using the Prussian blue reaction. He repeated his first experiments, varying them by injecting the reagents in different places or changing other conditions, and he obtained variable results. To ascertain how far the Prussian blue might spread in the body after it had formed, he injected the dye itself into the jugular vein along with an excess of lactate of iron. All of the blue collected in the lungs, indicating to him that the product of his test reaction would not itself dissolve in the blood or pass into the general tissues.[48] In another case he injected lactate of iron[49] into the stomach of a young rabbit and prussiate of potassium in the rectum. The prussiate passed into the urine, he found, but the iron only entered the blood and remained there. The result was very interesting to him, but enigmatic enough so that he felt it needed to be repeated "with great care."[50] In a variation on this experiment he injected prussiate into the stomach of one rabbit, lactate of iron into the stomach of a second animal. Then he collected urine from both and mixed them. No reaction occurred. The prussiate had reached the urine, but again the iron had only reached the blood.[51] Bernard also encountered some setbacks, finding that he had been misled by phenomena which interfered with the interpretation of the reactions. In March, for example, he realized that prussiate mixed with an acid gives a greenish color which he had been regarding erroneously as the blue resulting from a reaction with iron. Certain experiments in which he had concluded that there was iron in the urine had therefore to be redone.[52] In April he wrote down: "All of the experiments made up until now with the cyanides have been badly interpreted." The tests from which he had inferred that reactions do not occur in the blood and that salts of iron do not pass into the urine he had now to reject because the absence of Prussian blue could be explained as well by the presence of the carbonate.[53]

While he contended with these technical problems Bernard was also gradually coming to focus his attention on one aspect of the set of physiological queries and propositions he had formulated a few weeks earlier. This was his idea that the stomach is one of a restricted number of places in which chemical combinations are formed within the body. In his early experiments this view was subordinated to his effort to substantiate his hypothesis that no combinations occur in the blood, a notion which he believed his first results supported. During February he sought to strengthen that conclusion. After several more experiments similar to the first trials he felt that he had demonstrated fairly well that substances do not combine in the blood, whether they are introduced together or absorbed separately into the stomach and the veins. Some uncertainty remained, which he thought he could clear up by further variations of procedure such as injecting the substances respectively into two different animals, withdrawing a sample of blood from each and mixing them together. Presumably this maneuver would further test whether blood itself is an environment permitting reactions between two chemical reagents. As he felt himself nearing a resolution of this question, however, the question of where such reactions do take place grew more prominent. After the preceding discussion in his notebook Bernard wrote "Do combinations take place in the stomach? Inject prussiate and lactate into the stomach of a dog? will those substances combine there?" [54] Although he had now formulated the proposition as a specific experimental question, the next investigations he carried out were not yet fully directed to it. On March 5 he injected one substance into the stomach, the other into a vein, still looking primarily for the effects in the blood, urine, and general tissues. The question of the stomach, however, was recurring to him with mounting insistence and elaboration. After the conclusion of his experiments on that day he wrote down five suggestions for future investigations. The topic which he developed most was:

5. Inject lactate into the stomach, then prussiate in the veins—will there be prussian blue in the stomach? for it would seem according to the preceding experiments that combinations no longer take place between two bodies introduced into animal fluids (serum, urine, etc.). It is necessary that one of the bodies be in a free state. Now in the stomach bodies are dissolved in liquids which although secreted are mixed with foreign liquids which permit combination—perhaps prussiate emitted from the surface of the stomach will combine with the prussiate [sic—probably intended "iron"] in the stomach. Then the combination not being soluble, it will be eliminated through the bowels. Would it be in the stomach that all combinations would take place? [55]

Thus the passage suggests that Bernard was now finding reason to expect reactions in the stomach in their very absence elsewhere, and that he was beginning already to formulate a hypothesis to explain why they should occur particularly in that organ. Shortly afterward, perhaps on the same day, he tried on a young rabbit the experiment outlined here. At the autopsy of the animal he observed "traces of prussian blue" on the mucous lining of the stomach. The result was encouraging. "Nevertheless," he remarked, "the phenomenon would have to be more distinct to be incontestable." [56] On March 12 he introduced iron filings mixed with distilled water into the stomach of another rabbit and then injected prussiate into its jugular vein. Opening the stomach, he saw "evident blue spots" on the stomach lining. When he injected more prussiate, more blue spots appeared in the stomach where the iron filings were. Although he cautioned himself that the demonstration "was not yet complete" and required further research, Bernard now believed that he could definitely conclude that the iron and prussiate had combined in the stomach. [57]

Bernard's success stimulated him to put down a series of "reflections" on the consequences of these results. "It appears," he wrote, "that the stomach is the point of combination of all of the substances of the blood, and that because of the acid contained in the stomach." Thus Bernard was not only growing more confident of his conclusion, but had adopted a different explanation for it from the one he had been considering a week earlier. He now thought he could prove that the acidity of the stomach is the cause of the reactions which occur there, by opening the intestinal tract of a dead rabbit and sprinkling iron filings along it. When he then added a solution of prussiate, he expected he would obtain a blue reaction in the stomach but not in the intestines; an acid indicator would show that the former was acidic, the latter not. A hint of a new direction which these ideas were beginning to give to his thought was that he wrote "the acid has reacted on [the iron]" and then by adding a word above the line changed it to "the gastric acid has reacted on it." Further in his discussion he outlined a scheme according to which there are three locations in the body where combinations can form: "1. the stomach, combinations of liquids; 2. lungs, combination of gas; 3. tissue, combination of solids." [58]

On the third page of these reflections Bernard made what seems to be a significant shift in the perspective from which he viewed the phenomena he had been investigating. "In nutrition," he wrote,

the stomach acts by its acid on the aliments, forming from them products capable of entering into the combinations of the tissues. These compounds would need to be defined, for organic analysis does not give them in reality, because it decomposes them and undoubtedly forms new products, other than those which actually exist in the living economy.

According to the preceding experiments and those which will follow, it would seem that the products of the *alkaline* blood come into the stomach, to act or react with the *acid* products of the stomach. And that afterward these new compounds would thus be absorbed in turn in order to form all of the constituents of our organs. There would therefore be in the stomach 1. absorption of a principle modified by the acid. 2. arrival of that same product in the stomach, new combination and reabsorption, then further separation (do research on that subject). [59]

Until now Bernard had been considering the stomach (insofar as it related to his own investigations), only as a place in which, by contrast to other parts of the body, chemical reactions would take place. Having established that point, he felt that he was now seeing the result in a new light as the basis for a theory of nutrition. Here he was discussing not the reactions of the special reagents which he had actually utilized, but the transformations which he thought normal nutrient substances might undergo. Since his experiments thus far had not dealt with nutrient materials, [60] he was clearly making another mental leap from the specific phenomena he was studying to what he saw as a very general implication. This was a transition point in his research: for by perceiving a rather different problem from what he had been working on, he subtly shifted the emphasis in his future experiments until eventually they came to be about that problem too.

Bernard seemed to be following an independent path in his investigation, reaching the problem of nutrition as his own steps led him in that direction. The reference to the inability of organic analysis to describe nutrient compounds as they are in the living animal, however, shows that he was continuing to compare the merits of his approach with those of more chemically oriented investigations. Another passage in his remarks gives more pointed evidence of the same concern:

> In nutrition it does not appear reasonable to admit that fat or other immediate principles are absorbed in their natural state. They are changed by the acids of the stomach into margarates, oleates particular to the nature of the animal—if one introduces them into the blood the transformation would equally take place as they arrived by another way in the stomach.[61]

The most prominent supporters of the view which Bernard here termed unreasonable were, of course, Dumas, Payen, and Boussingault. The passage suggests that even as he pursued his own way, Bernard had their theories very much in mind. That would not be surprising, since he wrote these reflections six days after the first major debate between these chemists and Liebig in the Academy, where Magendie participated. His statements show also that Bernard's own ideas were tending toward a theory quite opposite to Dumas's theory that digestion is merely a dissolution of aliments. He therefore had already found an area in which he might be able to confront those chemical explanations of vital phenomena.

Despite these new ideas, Bernard did not make a sharp break from either the objectives or the procedures of his preceding investigations. During the next four months he continued experiments designed to elucidate his more general earlier question of where in the body reactions can take place. More and more, however, his emphasis turned toward the problems of nutrition or digestion outlined in his reflections of March 12. Perhaps this shift was hastened by a disappointment regarding what he had earlier treated as the most pressing question. His discovery in April that solutions of carbonate of iron do not react with prussiate of potassium he felt had invalidated the indications he had thought he had that combinations do not form in the blood. "Now one cannot support the same opinion any longer," he recognized, for it was based on "a false interpretation of the reactions of cyanides."[62]

Before he could develop his conception of the combinations which he believed to occur in the stomach, Bernard needed to confirm by more decisive results what he had already found there. The next time he injected iron filings into that organ and prussiate in a vein he was able to produce "a superb blue coloration" in the stomach. In the intestines he found less blue, and evidence of iron oxide reduced, leading him to wonder if combinations formed in the stomach and carried into the intestines might be decomposed there by the action of bile. In a similar experiment he observed that the blue in the stomach was more intense in certain regions than in others.[63] A little later he performed some experiments which were somewhat more of a departure for him and which tended to merge his own previous techniques with methods which other physiologists were already applying to the specific problem of digestion. He made a preparation of iron filings and "pepsin," the latter a term used by Theodor Schwann to define the organic constituent of gastric juice responsible for the specific digestive action of the stomach. Bernard procured the acidic pepsin by soaking the stomach lining of a calf for twelve hours in warm water. He then digested the iron filings in the pepsin for the same length of time. The preparation reacted with prussiate to give a "fine blue coloration." Evidently he was trying to determine more concretely what conditions in the stomach enabled such reactions to occur. Afterward he injected the "compound" of iron and pepsin into the jugular vein of a rabbit and prussiate into the other jugular vein. No reaction occurred in the blood, but the prussiate which infiltrated directly into the connective tissue of the blood colored those tissues strongly blue.[64] Bernard made no comment in his notebook on the general aim of this experiment, and subsequent similar trials did not give the same result. Nevertheless, the indication that the iron prepared with pepsin had passed into the tissues and there reacted with prussiate probably was the germinal observation from which he developed a few months later a general nutritional theory; that is, that the action of gastric juice upon aliments is an essential precondition for the further transformations in the organism by which the nutrients are assimilated.

Bernard also began carrying out in April some more conventional investigations of digestion. He nourished dogs with pure starch, then by means of potassium iodide, the standard indicator for starch, he tested the contents of the stomach and intestine, and the chyle of a dog to ascertain where the nutrient is transformed into sugar or dextrin. While interested in the properties of chyle he noticed that prussiate injected into the blood of an animal could be found in the former fluid. This result increased his confidence in the theory that substances present in the blood enter the stomach to undergo chemical change;

for the prussiate must have passed from the blood through the stomach to reach the chyle.[65] In June he carried out a series of experiments to elucidate this process; they consisted of the usual injections, followed by a tracing of the blue coloration through the stomach, intestines, and into the lacteal vessels. The color extended, he found, only as far as the mesenteric ganglions through which the latter pass. At the conclusion of this research he felt it was "quite clear that substances introduced directly into the blood (prussiate) enter the stomach and combine there with the gastric juice." Bernard's attention, which had been drawn progressively from the general question of where chemical reactions occur in the body, to the stomach as a site of such reactions, and then to the acid of the stomach as a condition of those reactions, was now coming to a narrower but sharper focus on the question of the action of gastric juice upon materials introduced into the stomach. Gastric juice he was beginning to see as the agent of the chemical changes he had been studying, and he started about this time to speculate about how that special fluid may be produced.[66]

In July Bernard apparently broke off his experiments and did not take them up again until October. In six months he had moved by small steps from the problem of tracing absorption to a nascent theory of the action of gastric juice upon nutrient materials. The trend of his interests took him from a type of investigation which his teacher had originated toward a problem in which Magendie had not specialized but which other contemporary physiologists were pursuing vigorously. The investigation of gastric digestion already had a long history. Before following Bernard further on his course, therefore, it is essential to make a lengthy digression in order to discuss some of the highlights of the experimental tradition upon which he had increasingly to draw.

VII

The Investigation of Digestion,
1750–1830

The general approaches to the investigation of the digestive action of the stomach upon which physiologists relied during the 1840's can be traced back to experiments performed nearly one hundred years before by the versatile French scientist René Antoine Ferchault de Réaumur. Réaumur had taken up a question debated for a long time previously, whether digestion consists of a mechanical grinding of food into small particles or a special solvent action. His own work demonstrated that neither theory was exclusively correct, for both processes occur. He showed that the muscular stomachs of birds with gizzards could exert such force as to crush strong metal cylinders. The thin-walled stomachs of other types of birds, however, could not produce such effects. They contained, on the other hand, a very active solvent, a conclusion he established using his well-known buzzard, a bird which swallows all parts of its prey and afterward regurgitates the indigestible components. Réaumur suspended pieces of meat on a thread running through a metal tube, which he then wrapped with more thread so that only fluids might penetrate to the food. He then forced the bird to swallow the tube. A day or so later, when the bird had thrown the tube up, Réaumur found the meat reduced to a fraction of its original size and weight. It no longer resembled meat in color or consistency, but was soft and grayish, and felt unctuous. Even bone, which he similarly fed to the animal, was softened and lost a considerable part of its weight. Grains and other vegetable foods which are not part of the buzzard's ordinary diet were, however, little altered.[1]

With these experiments Réaumur had resolved the issue which had led him to his study. Digestion was, in some animals at least, "Uniquely the work of a solvent, whose existence is fully demonstrated." [2] Réaumur wished also, however, to learn "what is the nature of that liquor." To do so he placed in the little tubes pieces of sponge, which soaked up enough gastric juice in the stomach before they were regurgitated so that he could perform a few preliminary tests on the liquid. It was somewhat opaque and turbid, and its taste was more salt than bitter. (The classification of the taste was an important part of eighteenth-century chemical analyses.) He moistened "blue paper" with the juice, which it reddened. The liquid was therefore acidic. The most important test of the properties of the liquor, he thought, was to see if it would dissolve meat in a vessel, as he assumed it does in the stomach. He therefore placed a piece of meat in a tube with the juice; so that the latter could act under normal conditions, he maintained the tube at near body temperature, and for a basis of comparison he kept alongside it a piece of meat in ordinary water. Réaumur did not succeed in producing an artificial digestion, a failure which he attributed to an inadequate amount of gastric juice. He did notice that the meat in the juice became less spoiled than that in the water. From this and analogous observations he rejected an idea common at the time that digestion is itself a kind of putrefaction. [3]

Réaumur was not in a position to ascertain the chemical nature of gastric digestion. He could only describe the physical changes which the food underwent; he sought to characterize the solvent action of the gastric juice by analogy to the action of acids on metals. Its selective action, exerted on some foods but not on others, he felt was somehow similar to the way in which *aqua regia* dissolves gold but not silver. [4]

More significant than the particular results he obtained was the problem Réaumur defined and the ways in which he set out to solve it. He himself urged others to extend his methods in order to reach a more satisfactory conclusion than he had had the time or means to attain. [5] He had originated three general procedures. First, he found methods to retrieve and examine food which had undergone a natural process of digestion. Although his buzzard experiment was most famous and successful, he realized the need to extend the method to other animals with which he could not take advantage of the habit of regurgitation. When he used dogs and sheep, for example, he had to sacrifice the animals and search in their digestive tracts for the tubes enclosing the digested food. His second method was to seek to remove the supposed active agent from the stomach and to duplicate digestion outside the animal, where the physical or chemical nature of the process could be more directly followed. The third aspect was the examination of the chemical properties of pure gastric juice. These three approaches, nascent in the memoirs Réaumur presented to the Academy of Sciences in 1752, provided a framework for the experiments on digestion of several generations of physiologists, including important parts of the work of Claude Bernard.

What Réaumur began Lazzaro Spallanzani finished. Following very closely the plan of research set out in Réaumur's two articles, the skillful Italian experimentalist applied his predecessor's approach so thoroughly, between 1777 and 1780, that he succeeded in demonstrating the dissolving power of gastric juice in numerous types of birds and mammals, and in humans. He too enclosed the food to be swallowed in perforated containers, whose design he improved in order to make the food more accessible to the fluids in the stomach. Like Réaumur, he obtained with sponges gastric juice to use for artificial digestion. Spallanzani, however, succeeded repeatedly in dissolving pieces of food outside the stomach with this fluid, perhaps because he procured larger quantities of it, perhaps because he explored systematically the effects upon the process of varying the conditions. He tried maintaining the vials in which it was taking place at different temperatures, finding that gastric juice was no more effective than water at low temperatures, but that at the temperature of the body its action on foods was similar to that of the stomach itself. To provide a steady body temperature he sometimes carried the vials around in his armpit. For each trial he carefully provided a control containing water in place of gastric juice, and took care "that all circumstances should be alike" except for the difference in the fluids. He strengthened Réaumur's conclusion that the process is quite unlike putrefaction, and showed also that it has no particular resemblance to ordinary fermentation.[6]

With less success Spallanzani tried to characterize gastric juice chemically. He tested each sample by reacting it with a strong alkali (deliquescent salt of tartar) and with mineral acids, but observed no color change or effervescence. Moreover, gastric juice did not dissolve coral as acids do. Consequently he considered the juice to be "neither acid nor alkaline, but neutral." Yet the stomach had long been considered acidic, and he himself confirmed its property, and the property of gastric juice itself, of curdling milk. Some chemists would consider this result alone a proof of the existence of a "latent acid," he acknowledged. In the face of such difficulties, Spallanzani wavered. He admitted "the presence of an acid principle in the stomachs of some animals, and man himself. It is, however, not perpetual, but depends on the quality of the food." He "very willingly" left his readers "to adopt what opinion they shall think most probable" concerning the latent acid of the gastric juice. For a more comprehensive analysis of that juice he sent samples to his colleague at the University of Padua, Giovanni Antonio Scopoli, professor of chemistry and natural history. Scopoli subjected the material to a distillation analysis of the type which had been applied routinely to organic substances for over a century; he reported the taste and smell of the several liquids which passed into the receiver. In the residue Scopoli found a neutral salt which emitted sal ammoniac when reacted with a fixed alkali. From this result and the fact that gastric juice precipitated silver from solution, Scopoli inferred that it contains marine acid combined into a neutral salt.[7] Spallanzani found that the quantity and properties of gastric juice varied according to the conditions under which he obtained it. That derived from fasting animals seemed "purer" and more transparent than that from a stomach containing food, so whenever possible he procured the former. The juice found in the stomach cavity differed, he thought, from that discharged from the lining of the esophagus or a particular portion of the stomach. He regarded the active solvent, therefore, as a mixture of these and of bile regurgitated from the small intestine.[8]

Despite the comprehensiveness of Spallanzani's demonstration of the digestive action of gastric juice, doubts and disagreements with his conclusions were common during the next fifty years. Some people continued to defend the theory of fermentation, contending that a mere process of solution was inadequate to account for the conversion of the widely diverse foods animals eat into the uniform, bland end product of digestion known as chyle. Others debated over whether gastric juice was neutral or acid, and if it were the latter, what the nature of the acid was. Some questioned more basically the whole theory that gastric juice is the agent of digestion. Experiments which A. Jenin de Montegre reported to the French Institute in 1812 enhanced such skepticism. Using his own gastric juice, obtained by vomiting, Montegre found that it acted just like saliva, having no special solvent properties corresponding to those of the stomach itself. These results encouraged a growing school of vitalists in France who denied that digestion is a chemical process at all.[9]

Meanwhile, methods for isolating and identifying organic substances had been undergoing a gradual but fundamental change. This development had now reached the point at which a new kind of investigation of the chemical aspects of biological phenomena was becoming possible. The tests which Scopoli did for Spallanzani represented the traditional basis for analyzing animal or vegetable matter. Since the sixteenth century, herbalists and chemists had customarily sought to separate these materials into their constituent substances by operations oriented around distillations of the gross matter. The limitations of these methods became increasingly evident during the seventeenth century, however, and several generations of analysts sought for ways to avoid the disruptions of the substances thought to be due to the fire. By the early eighteenth century they were turning increasingly to extraction by means of the solvents water and alcohol in order to separate constituents which had not lost their distinctive properties. The first person to portray this approach as a new general "order of analysis" was the popular French teacher of chemistry, Guillaume-François Rouelle. By avoiding the destructive agent fire, Rouelle claimed, one could attain by these methods "a true idea of the composition of plants." Typically, he applied a double extraction procedure. First he would digest pieces of the plant in alcohol, then evaporate the alcohol to leave whatever had dissolved in it as a residue, or precipitate substances by adding water to the alcoholic solution. The materials soluble in alcohol but insoluble in water he called resin. Then he extracted from the remaining plant material the substances soluble in water and called them "extractive matter." He discovered a third type of substance soluble in both alcohol and water, which he named "extracto-resinous." Thus Rouelle defined the categories of plant constituents on the basis of their solubility properties. With such methods he was able to isolate the "green matter" from plants, by extraction in alcohol.[10]

Rouelle's method did not dominate the analysis of vegetable matter in the same way that distillation formerly had, because chemical investigation was becoming too progressive for any simple orthodox set of operations to remain unaltered. In mineral chemistry, the application of methods for separating and identifying acids and bases by forming soluble and insoluble salts was expanding rapidly. Carl Wilhelm Scheele introduced these methods into the study of vegetable acids with such spectacular success as to overshadow the achievements made with Rouelle's extraction procedure. Nevertheless, Rouelle's approach strongly influenced his successors. The solvent method was soon broadened by the addition of ether, a liquid whose preparation and properties were just becoming known. Antoine

Baumé found that ether "dissolves all essential and fatty oils in all proportions." [11]

In 1728 Iacopo Bartolomea Beccari had separated two constituents from wheat flour by kneading it in water. The portion soluble in water was starch, a typical plant substance. The insoluble portion, however, which he named gluten, was more like a typical "animal substance." It putrefied instead of fermenting, and when distilled yielded volatile alkali. [12] Rouelle's younger brother, Hilaire Marin Rouelle, investigated these substances further. In 1772 he announced that he had extracted the gluten from other plants. He obtained it by expressing the juice of green plants and extracting what was soluble in alcohol and in water. The insoluble residue was the gluten. Since it was apparently a general constituent of plants, he renamed it "vegeto-animal" matter. He showed that in its distillation products and its insolubility in water it resembled the "caseous" matter of milk. [13] This identification of a substance widespread in plants and present in animal constituents as well was a crucial development, simple though the criteria were by which Rouelle characterized it. The result not only helped to undermine the traditional belief that plant matter was unlike animal matter, but to define a type of substance of fundamental importance to both kingdoms.

Scheele and Claude Louis Berthollet began to apply to materials thought to contain such substances some of the tests which had proved so powerful in the identification of acids, bases, and salts; that is, they reacted them with the known alkalis, alkaline earths, metals, and acids. Both chemists found further properties common to gluten and materials derived from such sources as wool, liver, and flesh, defining them more distinctly as members of a closely related group of substances. [14] The question soon arose whether there were properties which might differentiate specific substances within this group. In 1785 Antoine Fourcroy took up that problem in order to determine whether muscle fiber, the supposed physical substrate for the property of irritability, according to Albrecht von Haller, was chemically unique. He compared it with three other materials—gelatin, albumin from blood and from eggs, and the matter which solidified when blood coagulated, which he called gluten and his successors called fibrin. He used all of the kinds of analyses available in order to characterize them: distillation products, solubilities, and the reactions with acids and alkalis. He found several distinguishing qualities. Gelatin dissolved completely in water, fermented before putrefying, and gave relatively little volatile alkali. Albumin dissolved in water also, but remained viscous. It coagulated when heated and when placed in acids or alcohol, did not ferment, and dissolved in alkali. It gave more volatile alkali. Gluten was insoluble in water, alcohol and alkalis, but dissolved in acids, and it gave the most volatile alkali. Muscle fiber he found almost identical in properties to the gluten.[15]

The criteria by which Fourcroy was able to differentiate these substances were not adequate to identify unequivocally all the other animal substances which he and others investigated. From this time on there were continuous difficulties in that substances which agreed in certain essential characteristics would differ in others, raising doubts about the validity of the categories. The boundaries were indefinite; there were frequent cases of apparently intermediate substances. Nevertheless, his distinctions served as a fruitful basis for further development. By the beginning of the nineteenth century a number of chemists were occupied with such investigations, including Fourcroy himself, Louis Nicolas Vauquelin, and Louis Jacques Thenard in France; Alexander Marcet and John Bostock in England; and Berzelius in Sweden.

Bostock searched particularly for chemical tests which would discriminate more sharply between what he considered to be the three generally distributed "animal fluids," albumin, gelatin, and mucus. He thought that such terms were being used quite vaguely. Using the purest sources of the substances he knew, he tried on each of them a series of reagents, including oxymuriate of mercury, nitromuriate of tin, tannin, acetate of lead, nitrate of silver, nitromuriate of gold, and alum. Oxymuriate of mercury precipitated only albumin; nitromuriate of gold precipitated both albumin and gelatin; lead acetate precipitated albumin and mucus. Thus by combinations of such tests Bostock could distinguish the three types with increased precision. He still regarded the defining characteristic of albumin, however, to be its property of being coagulated by heat; that of gelatin to solidify when cold and liquefy with gentle heat; and that of mucus the negative property of not coagulating under either condition.[16]

Jöns Berzelius began studying animal chemistry in 1806 and published a treatise on the subject in 1808 in Swedish. French and German translations began to appear in 1813. As in other areas of chemistry, Berzelius became the most important influence in this field, largely because he applied a higher degree of critical rigor to problems which others had first undertaken. Berzelius investigated the constituents of the various fluids contained in animals. He began with blood, then analyzed such secreted fluids as bile, saliva, mucus membranes, serous fluids, and the humor of the eye. Finally, he dealt with three excretions, perspiration, urine, and milk. At the same time he examined more fully than his predecessors the chemical properties of the different "animal matters" contained in these liquids.[17]

Analyzing beef and human blood, Berzelius compared the fibrin, albumin, and coloring matter separable from it. Fibrin was insoluble in water. Alcohol and ether both produced some decomposition, so that they were unsuitable to use in analyzing the substance. He reacted fibrin with dilute and concentrated acetic, muriatic, sulfuric, and nitric acid. It formed an insoluble compound with each of the concentrated acids but dissolved in the weaker acids. Nitric acid caused fibrin in addition to "undergo a sort of decomposition" which produced malic acid and a yellow substance. Caustic alkali dissolved the fibrin, acid reprecipitated it, although the original material had been altered. The coloring matter of the blood contained iron, was distinct in color from fibrin, and did not spontaneously coagulate like the latter, yet it reacted in the same way to all of these tests, so that Berzelius inferred that it "has the same chemical properties, and consequently the same chemical composition as fibrin." Albumin also produced the same reactions with acids and alkalis, its sole difference from fibrin being that it "does not coagulate spontaneously, but requires a higher temperature for that." "Fibrin, albumin, and the coloring matter, he concluded, resemble one another so intimately, that they can be considered as modifications of one and the same substance." He called them collectively "albuminous matters." [18]

In each of the secretions Berzelius found a particular "albuminous" matter which he thought gave the fluid its distinctive character, the rest of the constituents being identical to the non-albuminous substances in blood. He separated the constituents of each secretion into portions soluble in alcohol and in water; usually each of these extracts contained an "animal matter." The distinctive matter in the bile created some difficulty for his general view, because it resembled albuminous matters in some properties, but lacked the most characteristic element in their composition, nitrogen. From saliva Berzelius obtained a "particular matter" soluble in water but not in alcohol, as well as a mucus insoluble in both. Mucus, as Bostock's discussion suggests, was considered by some people to be a substance generally distributed in animal materials. Berzelius showed, however, that nasal mucus, that from the trachea, the intestines, and the urinary conduits had somewhat different properties, though all shared the insolubility properties and inability to be coagulated by heat. Mucus could, furthermore, be clearly distinguished from albumin, because the latter was soluble in acetic acid, whereas the former precipitated in it. He thought that in each mucus there was an identical "animal matter," the variations in different sources deriving from different admixtures.[19]

Berzelius' identification of "albuminous matter" and of mucus illustrates well the nature of the problems involved in defining these substances. Complete identity of properties in material derived from different sources was seldom obtained, so that there was always some uncertainty over whether the observed differences between substances meant they were distinct, were modifications of a single substance, combinations of substances, or impure substances. Nevertheless, the types Berzelius delineated proved workable categories during the following decades, and the scope of the general analytical procedure steadily expanded. Gradually, standard sequences of operations were established for identifying the "animal matter," or "albuminous matter," of animal and plant fluids and tissues. The simple "order of analysis" of Rouelle had grown into a highly complex and powerful mode of investigation.

By the 1820's this progress in methods of organic analysis suggested that the time was ripe for new investigations of the chemical phenomena of digestion. Such reasoning motivated the French Academy to propose in 1823 a prize for whoever could determine "by a series of chemical and physiological experiments what are the phenomena which follow one another in the digestive organs, during the act of digestion." Competitors were to examine first the changes which simple "immediate principles," such as "gelatin, albumin, sugar, etc." undergo, then to deal with the more complex ordinary foods in which these are combined.[20] The ability of the Academy to pose the problem in these terms was itself an outcome of the recent developments in chemistry which had made it possible to consider individually some of the immediate principles comprising alimentary matter.

Two memoirs were submitted for the prize. One was by the Frenchmen François Leuret and Louis Lassaigne. The other came from two German colleagues at the University of Heidelberg, the physiologist Friedrich Tiedemann, and the chemist Leopold Gmelin. The Academy did not award the prize to either, but offered to each a portion of the prize money as an encouragement to further effort. Of the two memoirs, however, that of Tiedemann and Gmelin was more complete and more significant in its influence on further developments.

Unlike some contemporaries, Tiedemann and Gmelin did not ques-

tion Spallanzani's general assertion that gastric juice produces digestion in the stomach. They sought rather to extend his conclusion by a
more specific chemical description of the process. They retained the
three basic approaches which had emerged from Réaumur's memoirs:
that is, they fed animals aliments and examined their condition in the
digestive system a few hours afterward; they duplicated digestion
with gastric juice outside of the stomach; and they analyzed gastric
juice chemically. They did not limit their concern to the stomach, but
extended some of the same procedures to the events in the small intestines associated with the secretion of bile, pancreatic juice, and the
glands of the intestinal wall. They also investigated salivation, the
changes which occur lower in the intestines, and absorption of aliments into the lacteal vessels and the blood.

Of these approaches, that to which they gave least attention was artificial digestion. They devoted only two pages to it out of a report to-
taling nearly seven hundred, and concluded merely that they had
"confirmed" Spallanzani's assertion.[21] They expended, on the other
hand, far more effort to analyze the digestive juices. One of the principal obstacles they saw to a determination of the changes which individual alimentary materials undergo was the uncertainty over whether
the substances they found along the digestive tract derived from the
aliment or from the digestive fluids. Consequently, they analyzed the
latter in meticulous detail, hoping that by comparing these results
with the contents of the stomach or intestines during digestion they
could ascertain what part of those contents had come from each
source.[22]

To collect each digestive juice in a pure state was a difficult problem
in itself. For gastric juice, pancreatic juice, and the intestinal secretions they had to "devise and carry out new ways of proceeding."
When they opened the stomach of a fasting dog, for example, they
found only a small amount of a salty fluid, which was almost entirely
neutral in its reaction with litmus. After forcing another animal to
swallow quartz stones, however, they obtained a "copious" and
strongly acidic fluid. The stomach therefore must only secrete gastric
juice, they inferred, when it is mechanically or chemically stimulated.
They had not only a procedure for procuring gastric juice, but an
explanation for the divergence of opinion among their predecessors
over whether it is acid.[23] According to Johannes Müller, it was this
work which "finally settled the question." [24] Tiedemann and Gmelin
similarly observed during their investigations that pancreatic juice,
bile, and intestinal mucus seemed to be secreted in response to excita-
tion by the chyme entering the small intestine.[25]

The principal mode of analysis which they applied to the digestive juices as well as to the contents of the digestive tract after feeding was to separate the constituents by solvents. Usually they would first evaporate the fluid to dryness, then put the residue into boiling alcohol. Whatever portion dissolved in the alcohol they tried to separate further. Sometimes a substance would crystallize as the alcohol cooled; in other cases they had to evaporate the solvent until something precipitated. The separated material they would then treat with water, sometimes dissolving part or all of it. The portion which had been insoluble in the initial extraction with alcohol they also separated into portions soluble and insoluble in water, each of which they often subjected to further similar operations. Matter soluble neither in water nor alcohol they sometimes tried to dissolve in acetic acid. At various points in the analysis they also utilized ether to separate certain constituents. When they had separated the components of the fluid as far as feasible by such methods, they tested the respective portions with a standard sequence of reagents. Among these were chlorine, hydrochloric and other mineral acids; metallic salts such as chloride of tin, lead acetate, copper sulfate, mercurous nitrate and silver nitrate; tincture of gall-nuts, and litmus. Some of the precipitates and color reactions which resulted identified inorganic salts present. Others, considered in conjunction with the solubility properties which determined the solvent portion in which they occurred, revealed the probable existence in the fluid of such "animal matters" as albumin, fibrin, gelatin, gluten, casein, "salivary matter," mucus, or osmazome. The formation of a precipitate with the gall-nut preparation was especially characteristic of several of the animal matters.[26] Tiedemann and Gmelin thus exploited thoroughly the chemical procedures developed over the previous decades for identifying such substances.

By such means Tiedemann and Gmelin ascertained that the gastric juice of dogs and horses contained no albumin. It did yield osmazome, a substance soluble in alcohol, and "salivary matter," insoluble in alcohol but soluble in water. Having settled that there is a free acid in gastric juice, they attempted to determine its nature. By distilling the juice from a horse they found one acidic fraction which produced a precipitate with silver nitrate, so that they inferred that the juice contained hydrochloric acid. They confirmed its existence in the stomach by feeding a dog calcareous stones. Afterward they observed large quantities of calcium chloride, which they attributed to a neutralization reaction between the ingested calcium carbonate and hydrochloric acid in the digestive fluid. In some samples of gastric juice, however, they were unable to detect the acid by distillation. They found evidence that acetic acid and, in horses, butyric acid were also present.[27] William Prout had already announced in 1823 that "the acid in question is the *muriatic acid* [hydrochloric acid]." Prout had determined the amount of muriate [chloride] originally combined with alkaline bases by evaporating the juice, burning the residue, dissolving the remaining matter, and reacting it with silver nitrate. He had then neutralized a second portion of gastric juice with alkali. Treating it in a similar manner, he determined the total amount of muriate. Subtracting the first result from the second gave him the amount of the free acid which had been present. Unlike Tiedemann and Gmelin, Prout had concluded, from certain other tests, that there were no other free acids.[28]

After analyzing the gastric juice itself, Tiedemann and Gmelin were ready to try to follow the changes which various aliments undergo along the digestive tract. Using dogs, they waited in each case for a certain time after feeding, then killed the animal, opened up its stomach and intestines, and analyzed the materials they found in the different portions. They utilized in turn, as "simple" aliments, liquid albumin, coagulated albumin, fibrin, gelatin, butter, cheese (casein), starch, and gluten. They then tried "composed" nutrients, including milk, raw meat, cooked meat, meat and bread, bones, and other combinations.[29] After completing these experiments on dogs they repeated some of them for comparison on cats, horses, cows, and sheep. They also did similar experiments with birds, reptiles, and fish. From all of these painstaking efforts Tiedemann and Gmelin seem at first sight to have derived relatively sparse general conclusions about the chemical nature of digestion. They themselves pointed out that the task set by the French Academy was so enormous that they might be excused if they could often reach "only conjectures in place of definite conclusions, and had in some cases abstained even from the former."[30] In the case of the complex nutrients they could do little more than describe the visible changes during the stages of digestion.

For some of the simple "animal substances" they found evidence that one type may be transformed into another in digestion, though they could not be certain what the resulting substances were. The characteristic properties of fibrin disappeared in the stomach, and in its place was a substance with properties like albumin. Since they had not detected any albumin in gastric juice itself, they thought that a part of the fibrin may have been transformed into it. Gelatin also seemed to turn into something else, but the product did not have exactly the same properties as albumin. Casein lost its characteristic features, but their tests showed that it could not have been changed into either albumin or gelatin. Gluten was "only little changed" in the stomach, but since the resulting stomach fluid showed some coagulation when boiled, they thought the nutrient might have become "similar to albumin." [31] Transformations were even more difficult to prove in the small intestine, they reported, because the digestive juices secreted into it contained albumin. Therefore when they found that substance after feeding gluten or other animal matters, they could not tell if a conversion had occurred there.[32] Even if the obscurity of these results had applied to every one of the aliments they tried, Tiedemann and Gmelin's research would still have been a significant attack on the general problem, helping to define more specific problems for others to probe further. In one crucial case, however, they were able to establish more precisely the chemical nature of the transformation involved. Starch was the only simple aliment they used for which there was a distinctive identification test, applicable even when the material was mixed with a variety of other organic substances. When reacted with iodine it produced a characteristic blue or violet color not easily confused with any effect which a constituent of the digestive juices might cause.

After they had fed a dog starch for several days and opened its intestinal tract about three hours after its last meal, they found starch in the stomach and intestine, but not in the chyle, blood, or urine. Somewhere during digestion, they inferred, starch disappears.[33] They knew immediately what to look for in its place, for one of the few chemical transformations of an important organic nutrient substance into another which had at this time been clearly demonstrated was the conversion of starch to sugar. Gottlieb Sigismund Kirchhoff, the director of the imperial apothecary in St. Petersburg, Russia, had shown in 1812 that such a change can be produced by means of sulfuric acid. In 1816 he proved that the reaction can also take place when only materials from the plant matter containing the starch are used. If he separated the gluten in grain from its starch, the latter afterward underwent no changes; but when he mixed the ground gluten and starch together again and kept them in warm water for six hours, they formed sugar. The sugar produced was in proportion to the starch used, and only a small proportion of gluten was necessary, so the starch was evidently the source of the sugar and the gluten an agent favoring the transformation. The result provided also a definitive test for the presence of sugar, its ability to undergo alcoholic fermentation. Kirchhoff could show that when starch appears to ferment it is only because it has first produced sugar. Fermentation thus became a specific test for sugar.[34]

With this knowledge available to them in 1823, it is not surprising that after their first experiment, in which starch appeared not to be absorbed in its original state, Tiedemann and Gmelin undertook another one "in order to ascertain if the starch was transformed into sugar or into 'starchgum' (dextrin)." [35] This time they waited five hours after feeding before killing the animal, and then they found that the starch had disappeared even from the stomach. Next they undertook a "search for sugar." They evaporated to dryness portions of the fluid contents of the stomach and of the intestines, chyle, urine, blood from the portal vein and from the vena cava. The residues they extracted with alcohol, in which any sugar present should dissolve. After evaporating these solutions they placed the remaining solid matter from each fluid in a pneumatic flask over mercury, added yeast, and observed substantial fermentation from each. Therefore, they concluded, "as soon as starch dissolves in the digestive juices, it loses its property of turning iodine blue and is transformed, at least in part, into sugar." [36]

This discovery by Tiedemann and Gmelin was a special landmark in the history of animal chemistry. It must have been one of the first occasions on which anyone had produced direct evidence that a substance had undergone within the animal body a specific chemical transformation which had also been demonstrated in the laboratory with the same substance isolated from any organism. When Claude Bernard set out twenty years later to follow inside the animal the reactions which chemists inferred theoretically to occur there, he had at least one clear precedent to guide him.

After recounting their experiments, Tiedemann and Gmelin presented a "theory of digestion" based on them. The most persuasive and general conclusion to be drawn, they felt, was that "simple as well as composed aliments are undeniably dissolved and converted to chyme by the gastric juice." [37] Unlike many earlier physiologists, however, they did not envision all manner of foods being reduced somehow to a single uniform chyme or chyle; they noted carefully the variations in these fluids corresponding with the digestion of different nutrients, implying that the composition of the former depends upon the nature of the particular types of nutrient which are dissolved to form it. They wished also to go beyond what those before them had done by asking what the constituent of the gastric juice is that dissolves nutrients. For this they could only speculate, but here again they displayed the significance of distinguishing between the processes which might occur with different alimentary substances. They did not assume that there was one universal agent, but sought explanations based on the solubility properties of the various "immediate principles." Since uncoagulated albumin, gelatin, osmazome, sugar, gum, and cooked starch were soluble in water, the water content of gastric juice might suffice for these. Coagulated albumin, fibrin, coagulated casein, gluten, and similar substances, on the other hand, were insoluble in water but soluble in acid. It was natural to suppose, therefore, that the acid whose presence they had established in gastric juice was the solvent for them. To test the latter theory they placed some of the materials in this category in acetic acid and hydrochloric acid, but the results were not satisfactory and they did not comment on them.[38] Afterward Johannes Müller did similar experiments with several acids, none of which dissolved meat or albumin. Consequently he had to conclude that "we do not know the active principle." [39] Tiedemann and Gmelin believed that besides solution a "special decomposition" occurred in the stomach, for other substances probably underwent transformations similar to that of starch. They conjectured that the organic constituents of gastric juice, "salivary matter" or osmazome, might contribute to such conversions, since (as Kirchhoff had shown), gluten exerts such an action on starch.[40] Inconclusive though Tiedemann and Gmelin's theories of digestion were, they were searching and suggestive.

Tiedemann and Gmelin were as interested in the changes which aliments undergo after they leave the stomach as they were in gastric digestion. They regularly followed the changes in the physical and chemical properties of the intestinal contents through to the end of that tract. To ascertain the role of bile in digestion they performed vivisection experiments in which they blocked its duct. Finding that the secretion of bile was not, as Prout and others supposed, essential for the formation of chyle, they decided that the fluid separated from the liver served chiefly for the excretion of waste products. While analyzing the contents of the digestive cavities they frequently treated in the same manner the chyle in the lacteal vessels which, in accordance with the view still common despite Magendie's experiments, they regarded as the pathway by which nutrients are assimilated into the blood. They sometimes analyzed the blood itself. They did not reach any general conclusions about the chemical changes attending the absorption of the nutrients into these vessels. They were able to show, however, that after an animal was fed a diet of butter for four days, its chyle contained much more fat than usual, and there was fat in its urine. They found fat also in its blood, which they could not "directly prove" had come from the digested butter, but because of the excess of fat in the chyle they thought that it probably had. In the experiments with starch they found sugar in the chyle and blood. Their aim was thus considerably broader than the study of digestion; for they were seeking to trace the course of nutrient substances as far as possible into the animal on the way toward their eventual assimilation or excretion. [41]

Tiedemann and Gmelin were after a chemical explanation of nutritional phenomena, and their work contributed substantially toward that goal. Gastric juice, they said, owes its action to its chemical composition, and "its effect upon aliments is a chemical one." Nevertheless, they maintained, "digestion is a vital process, an event conditioned by the life of the animal." For it to operate, the stomach must be in such a condition that it can respond to stimuli by secreting gastric juice; it must be able to separate an acid fluid from alkaline blood, and it must dispatch digested material from the stomach into the intestine so that undigested portions can be exposed to the chemical action of gastric juice. These functions can only take place through the connection and interactions of the stomach with the entire living organism. Since antiquity, they noted, it had been clear that the pneumogastric nerves influence digestion, and recent experiments had indicated many ways in which disruption of the nervous system affected digestion. The sectioning of the pneumogastric nerves was thought to slow it down primarily by stopping the motions of the stomach. By their own vivisection experiments on dogs Tiedemann and Gmelin found that after these nerves are severed the stomach no longer becomes acidic, even when the animal has swallowed food. They believed, therefore, that the secretion of gastric juice also is under the influence of nervous action. [42]

In his general treatise on human physiology Tiedemann supported a rather mild form of vitalism. [43] When he and Gmelin insisted upon the vital aspects of digestion in the foregoing situation, however, they were not invoking an ultimate philosophical principle; they were espousing the importance of dealing experimentally with events which involve a higher level of organization in the animal than chemical means of analysis alone can treat. Their position was like that which Claude Bernard later defended.

The highly ambitious objective imposed upon Tiedemann and

Gmelin by the terms of the prize competition caused their specific discoveries and observations to be overshadowed by the bulk of their attempt to reveal the general nature of the digestive process. This may have been one reason why some people were disappointed in their results, feeling that they had failed to clinch the disputed gastric juice theory of digestion. As Jerome Bylebyl has described, William Beaumont dramatically achieved the latter end a few years later when he utilized the opportunity of an accidental stomach fistula in his patient to show more decisively than anyone before him that artificial digestion with gastric juice outside the stomach has essentially the same outcome as digestion in that organ.[44] Such a demonstration, however, was not a major goal of Tiedemann and Gmelin, for they had already accepted the conclusion. When Beaumont ended an era of doubt about the gastric theory of digestion, Tiedemann and Gmelin had already helped to open an era of extensive investigation of its chemical nature. Their monumental study was important less for its definitive solutions for a few problems than for the promise it held of means to deal further with the general question.[45]

Tiedemann himself later gave up experimental physiology and returned to comparative anatomy. Another physiologist who took a similar turn, Daniel Frederik Eschricht, afterward related to Claude Bernard that it was the lack of reliable foundations for physiology, and the conflicting claims of chemical, physical, and vitalistic explanations which had discouraged Tiedemann, as well as Johannes Müller and himself, from pursuing the science further.[46] The work on digestion which Tiedemann had produced with Gmelin remained, however, a potent influence on the next generation of physiologists. Accessible to French scientists in translation, the treatise was among the most important sources of information for Bernard himself, and one he often cited. The way of applying chemistry to vital phenomena with which Bernard has been identified was clearly discernible in their work. They too used chemistry as a tool to study these processes rather than as a source of theoretical explanations.[47] Bernard, in fact, regarded their work as a model of the proper relationship between biology and chemistry—the biologist "governing," in the sense of posing the problems, and the chemist giving aid. That relationship was expressed, he wrote in the draft of his unpublished "Principles of Experimental Medicine," in the placement of Tiedemann's name before that of Gmelin on their memoir. This order of priorities he contrasted directly with the less satisfactory situation when "a chemist does physiology[;] he makes it too simple and tries to absorb physiology into chemistry." His examples of the latter practice were Lavoisier and, of course, Liebig and Dumas.[48]

The tradition that Bernard was the founder of experimental physiology has made it difficult to appreciate fully the continuity between his investigations and those which came before. It is not necessary to maintain that he created that approach by himself in order to protect his stature as the most successful practitioner and most articulate spokesman in his time for the relation between chemistry and physiology which he professed. If he argued repeatedly that physiological considerations must control chemical considerations in the study of vital phenomena, the reason was not that he was the first to grasp this relationship. Rather he emphasized it again and again because the impact of the theories of Liebig, Dumas, and their followers threatened to upset this balance just as its potential was becoming evident.

The researches on digestion which Leuret and Lassaigne entered for the prize offered by the Academy covered some of the same ground that Tiedemann and Gmelin examined. The two Frenchmen also traced the events of digestion from the mouth to the chyle and blood; they too devised methods to collect bile and pancreatic juice and they distinguished as well the acidic gastric juice secreted when the stomach is stimulated, from the fluids present in the stomach at other times. But Leuret and Lassaigne's treatise was far less meticulous, less comprehensive, and less incisive. It was a useful contribution, whereas that of Tiedemann and Gmelin was a brilliant one. Much of Leuret and Lassaigne's investigation consisted of variations of experiments their predecessors had already tried, and most of their conclusions were reassessments of issues previously raised. Thus they repeated Spallanzani's artificial digestion experiments using gastric juice retrieved from the stomach in sponges, and reaffirmed his theory that gastric juice digests aliments, at a time when the theory had come into question. The new departure which the Academy had called for, to trace the changes which different nutrient substances undergo, they attempted, but they did not focus on it with the persistence that Tiedemann and Gmelin did. They asserted that they had performed numerous experiments of this sort, and they listed in a table at the end of their treatise the substances they had found in the chyle, stomach, intestines, and excretions of dogs fed respectively fibrin, gum, sugar, bread, and grain. They discussed these results only nominally, however, and they drew no conclusions about the chemical changes which take place. They felt, in fact, that the procedures for chemical analysis of the time were incapable of ascertaining what changes are involved in the conversion of food to chyle, and they resorted instead to a microscopic search for globules common to the chyme, the chyle, and the blood. Finding them, as they thought, they believed they had proved that digestion consists of the formation of these globules by the "infinite division" of alimentary substances. Unlike Tiedemann and Gmelin, they retained the older, conventional view that, except for fats, the chyle remains the same no matter what foods go into its formation.[49] Although it may be asking for prophetic judgment to expect the Academicians who evaluated the two entries to foresee that it would be the German treatise which would be the central influence on the next stage in the study of digestion, one can nevertheless hardly avoid agreeing with the complaint of Tiedemann and Gmelin that, in awarding equal honorable mention to both works, the Academy had grossly favored its countrymen at the expense of their foreign competition.[50] Berzelius wrote in his authoritative *Annual Report on the Progress in the Physical Sciences*, for 1828, that the judgment of the French Academy had been hasty, superficial, and unfair to Tiedemann and Gmelin. The work of Leuret and Lassaigne, he thought, was not worth even "modest claims," and revealed that the authors were inexperienced chemists. The German contribution, by two men of whom "each was among the most outstanding investigators of our time in his own field," would persuade anyone who read it of its superior value. Berzelius summarized Tiedemann and Gmelin's investigation at great length, because it was, he said, "in my opinion one of the most important that animal chemistry has received in a great many years." He looked forward with interest to the continuation of research which he undoubtedly regarded as a very appropriate application to direct physiological experiments of the chemical methods which he himself had helped to develop.[51]

VIII

The Pepsin Theory

Among the men whom Tiedemann and Gmelin inspired to undertake further research on digestion was Erhard Friedrich Leuchs, of Nürnberg. In 1831 Leuchs examined the question of what in the gastric juice causes the transformation of starch to sugar that Tiedemann and Gmelin had detected. One possibility was the acid; but since Leuchs thought that saliva "can in part replace gastric juice," he tested the action of the former secretion. Mixed with cooked potato starch and warmed, saliva dissolved the material within two hours, producing a sweetish solution. With uncooked starch, saliva converted to sugar only that portion which the heat dissolved. Even when made alkaline, saliva could still produce the transformation, so that Leuchs concluded that the gastric acids are not essential to the process.[1]

Another relatively unknown person, Johann N. Eberle of Würzburg, pursued the question of digestion in a more comprehensive way. He had taken up the problem, he said, because of the numerous contradictory observations which had been reported. Such disagreements between Tiedemann and Gmelin, and Leuret and Lassaigne, as whether hydrochloric acid is the only acid in gastric juice, and whether pancreatic juice is the same as or different from saliva, particularly concerned him. Obviously, however, he valued the work of Tiedemann and Gmelin more highly than that of any of those with whom they differed. To them, Eberle wrote, "we are indebted for nearly all of the solid knowledge which we have about this highly important subject."[2] Eberle modeled his own lengthy treatise, published in 1834, on the plan of their memoir, utilizing many of their results as well their procedures. He too tried to deal with the changes which foods undergo from the mouth all the way until they are absorbed into the blood. He focused especially, however, on the question of what the agents in the gastric juice are that produce chymification, and on this question he achieved a crucial advance. After confirming the view of Tiedemann and Gmelin that acetic acid and sometimes butyric acid exists in gastric juice, even though hydrochloric acid always predominates, Eberle carried out a more comprehensive series of experiments than theirs to establish whether or not any of these acids can produce with various types of aliments the effects which occur in normal digestion. In some cases the aliments did dissolve, but often they became hard, and the properties of the products were generally not similar to chyme produced in the stomach from the corresponding aliments.[3]

Two years before, while investigating the function of the spleen in living animals, Eberle had noticed that during digestion the contents of their stomachs were covered with mucus. In one rabbit the pieces of food were surrounded by membranes so cohesive that he thought at first they consisted of pieces of the mucous membrane which had separated from the stomach walls. After closer inspection, however, he concluded that the material was a solid mucus secreted from the mucous membrane. He therefore devoted his "entire attention to this mucus formation" and found it in all animals while they were digesting, most prominently when the stomach contained solid pieces of aliments. The mucus was markedly acid, and when he tried to digest fibrin, coagulated albumin, and casein artificially with it, he saw "with an indescribable joy" that they were "completely chymified." In normal digestion, he believed, the mucus and the acids of the gastric juice are secreted together. Mucus derived from other organs, or from the stomachs of fasting animals, was incapable of "chymifying" aliments by itself, but acquired that ability when he added to it hydrochloric or acetic acid. Eberle had therefore discovered a new means of "artificial digestion," which meant now digestion not only outside of the stomach but also with artificial gastric juice. He prepared the latter from the dried mucous membrane of the stomach of a calf. Whenever he wished to use the gastric juice, he took a portion of the dried membrane, which he cut into pieces, put into a test tube with water until it softened, then added ten or twelve drops of hydrochloric acid (or a larger amount of acetic acid). The preparation, when somewhat diluted, was of the same consistency, color, and taste as natural gastric juice. He could obtain similar results whether he used the membrane itself or mucus secreted by the membrane.[4]

To test the action of his artificial gastric juice, Eberle made simultaneous comparative studies of the digestion of various aliments in it, and of the changes which the same nutrients underwent in natural digestion investigated in the manner of Tiedemann and Gmelin. The aliments he utilized included coagulated egg albumin, casein, milk, fibrin, gluten, raw meat and liver, bread and lettuce, milk and biscuits, and cabbage and potatoes. In each case he tested the resulting substances, diluted by water, with most of the same reagents that Tiedemann and Gmelin had used. Then he extracted with alcohol and with water as they had done and tested these portions similarly with the reagents. He did not always carry the analyses to the point of identifying the constituent substances, for in order to decide whether the products of a particular aliment digested artificially possessed the same properties as that aliment digested naturally did, he needed only to ascertain whether their respective reactions with each of the usual reagents were identical. In most cases there were only slight differences or none at all. The divergences which did appear were most marked when vegetable nutrients had been included.[5]

Eberle analyzed natural and artificial gastric juice and found that both contained osmazome, salivary matter, and pure mucus, as well as the free acids and soluble neutral salts. Only the acids, the salts, and the water of the gastric juice secreted in the stomach derive directly from the blood, he believed; the mucus, salivary matter, and osmazome he thought are produced by the mucus membrane, the surface of which the acids dissolve off.[6]

Further emulating Tiedemann and Gmelin, Eberle gave a "theory of digestion" following his description of the experiments. He considered gastric digestion, as they did, to be above all the dissolution or liquefaction of the nutrient substances, but like them he believed that there were chemical changes involved, caused by some unknown special chemical affinity between nutrient substances and the mucus. He accepted their conclusion that starch is converted to sugar, but the changes for which he himself found evidence were different from what they had found. Fibrin, which they had suspected to be partially changed into albumin, he thought was more probably only dissolved, and he saw no evidence that anything more occurred to gluten. Albumin, on the other hand, which Tiedemann and Gmelin had observed only to be dissolved, Eberle found to be destroyed and converted into something else. Two hours after he had fed coagulated albumin to a cat the contents of its stomach failed to give the reactions characteristic of albumin. They did not coagulate when boiled, nor did they react with potassium ferrocyanide, and they produced only a very slight reaction with nitric acid and with sublimate. The product of artificial digestion behaved similarly. From the residue of the filtrates produced by alcohol and water he obtained osmazome and salivary matter, so he inferred that albumin is converted to these substances in chymification. Although gastric juice itself already contained osmazome and salivary matter, he was convinced that the amounts in the chyme derived from albumin were unmistakably greater. Even though this was his most definite instance of an apparent chemical change, Eberle drew a general conclusion about digestion in the stomach which seems inconsistent with it. Simple nutrients, he maintained, were only dissolved in the stomach, whereas more complex mixed foods underwent chemical changes by the interaction of the various substances dissolved together. To support the latter view he could adduce an experiment using milk and biscuits, in which the chyme yielded gelatin, a substance not present in these foods. Yet in the end Eberle spoke of all of the chemical changes in the stomach as secondary. The purposeful transformations which make aliments more similar to the constituents of the animal and thus prepare them for assimilation, he thought, began in the intestine.[7]

Eberle was well aware that his artificial digestion had a potential significance beyond the immediate results. Its success persuaded one, he wrote, "that chymification is a purely chemical act, which is merely modified through vital actions." The outcome supported the belief that the other life processes could similarly be understood.[8] Yet, as the confusion in his conclusions suggests, this lone scientist, improvising resourcefully with little equipment or backing,[9] was apparently not fully able to perceive the implications of his achievement. Eberle died prematurely, in the same year that he presented his treatise.[10] No man was in a better position to comprehend the value of his contribution than Johannes Müller, whose large view of the whole field of physiology few notable discoveries escaped. Müller must have seen immediately the importance of Eberle's memoir, for in the winter of 1834–35, the same year as its publication, he was undertaking experiments to test Eberle's results. With his acute instinct for the heart of a question Müller did not try to repeat the numerous experiments with different aliments, but concentrated on the crucial case of coagulated albumin, recognizing that the chemical transformation which Eberle had reported held a major clue to the nature of the digestive process. At first somewhat skeptical of Eberle's results, Müller quickly found that his own confirmed them.[11] The next fall he continued the investigation, joined by his gifted young assistant, Theodor Schwann, and in 1836 they published their conclusions in a joint memoir. Schwann wrote the article, but because Müller had begun the project and his name appears first, it is difficult to separate the thought of the professor from that of the assistant.

Müller and Schwann called Eberle's conclusion that the active "principle" of digestion inheres in acidified mucus a "brilliant discovery, one of the most important in animal chemistry." [12] Like Eberle himself, they felt that the meaning of his experiments extended beyond the subject of gastric digestion, for his observation that in his artificial digestions albumin is converted to something else was "the first knowledge about the action of animal substances on one another." [13] This statement embodied more insight than its rather cryptic form reveals at first sight, for it connected the phenomenon with a class of chemical reactions whose distinctive features were just beginning to be recognized. As we have seen already, Kirchhoff had shown in 1816 that gluten from plant material in contact with starch caused the latter to become sugar. Following his discovery, other chemists sought to characterize this reaction more fully. In 1833 two of the chemists who ten years later were to play prominent parts in the fat controversy, Anselme Payen and Jean Persoz, together isolated from germinating grain seedlings and from other plant materials a substance which seemed responsible for the action on starch. When they mixed a solution of the substance with starch at a moderately warm temperature, the starch rapidly separated into three components, which Payen and Persoz described as varieties of dextrin. One was identical with the interior of a starch granule; it was soluble in hot water, insoluble in cold water, and colored iodine blue. The second was soluble in cold water but did not color iodine; it appeared analogous to gum. The third product was a fermentable sugar. If the action were prolonged, all of these products were converted gradually to sugar. The most significant aspect of their discovery was that the purified substance which produced the action had "so much energy that one part by weight suffices to render the interior substance of two thousand parts of dry starch soluble in warm water, and to bring about afterward the conversion of the dextrin into sugar." Because of its separating action they named the substance *diastase*. [14]

A process involving such unequal quantities could not readily be understood as an ordinary chemical reaction. According to current conceptions, one substance could cause another to decompose when one of its own constituents possessed a stronger affinity for a constituent of the second substance than did the other constituents of that substance. The constituents with the stronger affinities combined, displacing the other portions from their original compounds. The small amount of diastase required, however, made it improbable that it could act in such a way, and its discovery consequently focused the attention of chemists on processes which did not seem to be explainable by affinities.[15] At about the same time, Eilhard Mitscherlich examined another process for which the conventional explanation by affinities seemed insufficient. The reaction of alcohol and sulfuric acid, producing ether, had been interpreted as a decomposition brought about by the attraction of the acid for elements of water contained in the alcohol. By means of a carefully controlled distillation, however, Mitscherlich was able to collect the ether and water together, while the sulfuric acid remained in the distillation flask. Furthermore, he could convert as much alcohol to ether as he wished, without consuming a significant amount of the acid. Alcohol therefore simply decomposed, he inferred, when it came into contact with sulfuric acid under certain conditions. There are, Mitscherlich said, many reactions which come about in this way, and he named them "decomposition and combination through contact." Other examples he mentioned were the decomposition of hydrogen peroxide in the presence of small amounts of a metal; the conversion of sugar to alcohol or acetic acid and the decomposition of urea, in each of which the contact substance was a very small quantity of a ferment; and the transformation of starch to sugar with sulfuric acid.[16]

In his *Annual Report* for 1835 Berzelius elaborated on Mitscherlich's view and related it to the action of diastase. Berzelius named the general phenomenon *catalysis*. Its unknown cause, or "catalytic force," he said, "seems actually to consist in the fact that bodies are able, through their mere presence, not through their affinities, to arouse affinities [in another substance] which at the given temperature lie dormant." These bodies therefore can cause decompositions which would otherwise only occur at higher temperatures, their effect being analogous to that of heat itself. Berzelius wondered whether different degrees of catalytic force might produce different products, just as different temperatures do. He considered it probable, though not yet demonstrated, that each catalytic body acted only on certain "composed bodies." The body which transforms sugar to alcohol, called a ferment, was such an agent.[17]

"If we apply this idea to the chemical processes of living nature," Berzelius added, "it can provide us with a wholly new light." Diastase, for example, was distributed in potatoes only in those regions where it could produce, like a "secretory organ," from insoluble starch a soluble substance for the formation of sap in the growing seeds. He predicted that diastase was only the first of many such agents which would be found. There must be, he claimed, "thousands of catalytic processes occurring between the tissues and fluids of living plants and animals." This catalytic force could account for the formation of the many distinct substances out of the common raw material, blood or sap, a phenomenon for which previously no cause had been found. [18]

Johannes Müller too had been thinking that other actions in organisms must be produced by means similar to diastase. From the results of William Beaumont's artificial digestion experiments, Müller had suspected that gastric juice acted on aliments "in the same way" that diastase acted on starch. [19] Eberle's discovery of the role of mucus now appeared to fulfill that expectation. The process was "fully parallel" to the conversion of starch to sugar in plants, Müller and Schwann wrote, and was the first example in animals of "chemical action by contact." Their use of the term "contact" suggests that Müller and Schwann were influenced particularly by Mitscherlich, who was one of their eminent colleagues at the University of Berlin. Whether they had seen Berzelius's treatment of the general question when they wrote their article is less certain, [20] but they utilized the example of diastase and portrayed future possibilities very much as did the Swedish chemist. "One could imagine," they wrote, "how by such a simple means, namely, through the contact of an organic material, so many transformations of substances are carried out in the animal body." [21]

Although Müller and Schwann confirmed Eberle's basic conclusions, they did not carry out their experiments in exactly the same manner. They used coagulated albumin for most of their studies, not because of the importance of its transformation alone, but also because they could cut it into uniform cubes, making it easier to recognize the nature and degree of the alterations which it underwent, and consequently helping them to make more reliable comparisons of the effects of various conditions on digestion. The process generally was slower in their investigations than in those of Eberle, but otherwise they observed the same phenomena he had described. They found, as he had, that digestion is "no mere solution, but a chemical conversion as well," whereby albumin is decomposed into osmazome, salivary matter, and a third peculiar "animal matter" which Schwann detected. In only two respects did their results differ substantially from his. They could not verify his assertion that acidified mucus from organs other than the stomach has digestive power, and they discovered that it was not necessary to have mucus itself in the gastric juice; an extract made by treating the mucous membrane with dilute acid was as active as the entire acidified mucous layer. They did not believe that this extract could be mucus in solution, because mucus was nearly insoluble in acids.[22]

On the basis of their investigation Müller and Schwann reopened at a new level the old question of whether digestion is a kind of fermentation. By the original meaning of alcoholic fermentation, it clearly was not, for the products were different, the active material was different, and as they showed in a special set of experiments, the digestion of albumin produced no carbonic acid or any other gas. Neither was the digestive principle the same as diastase, for they established that diastase does not dissolve albumin.[23] Thus the question of what the digestive principle is, and how it acts, was still open, and the younger of the two collaborators now took up this question on his own.

The resulting paper by Theodor Schwann, "Concerning the nature of the digestive process," was easily the most sophisticated treatment of that subject during his time, and if measured against the background of contemporary concepts and methods available, one of the most penetrating of any time. By an interlocked sequence of incisive questions and carefully controlled experiments Schwann systematically narrowed down the many possibilities one could imagine concerning the nature and action of the "digestive principle" to those alternatives which were compatible with empirical evidence. When he finished he had not only achieved a discovery later regarded as a landmark, but had reformulated the whole problem of what digestion may be.[24]

Schwann proceeded by dividing the question of the nature of digestion into component questions, posing alternative answers between which he could choose by comparing the results of artificial digestions when he had varied one factor while keeping the others constant. The first question was: what are the active materials in digestion? The discoveries of Eberle and his own work with Müller had already made clear that there were two factors, an acid and something derived from mucus. Taking up first the role of the acid, Schwann asserted that there were five possible ways in which it could act during the digestive process. First, it might be a mere solvent for the second digestive material. To test this view he partially neutralized a portion of artificial gastric juice. Nothing precipitated, the fluid remained acidic, yet it was no longer capable of digesting. The hypothesis was therefore eliminated. The second possibility was that the acid formed with the other principle a chemical combination which comprised the active agent. If this were true the gastric juice ought to be most active when for a given amount of the digestive principle there was some fixed proportion of acid. He therefore compared the effects of digesting identical pieces of albumin for the same period of time in several portions of artificial gastric juice which were identical except for the fact that various quantities of acid had been added, or had been removed by partial neutralization. A significant change in either direction from the normal proportion of acid he found did diminish the activity of the gastric juice. Further experiments revealed, however, that the activity depended not upon the ratio between the quantities of acid and of digestive material, but between the former and the amount of water in which both were dissolved. Digestion thus depended critically on the general "degree of dilution" of the acid, but the necessity of a definite compound between it and the digestive principle was ruled out. A third possibility, that the acid is necessary in order to dissolve the products of digestion, he also eliminated by these experiments, because digestion ceased when the acid was diluted, even though the products of digestion were themselves soluble in equally dilute acid. A fourth possibility was that the acid combines with the products of digestion. Schwann determined, however, that the amount of alkali necessary to neutralize the acid in artificial gastric juice was the same after digestion as before, so this hypothesis too was untenable; acid was not used up in the process. The only possibility left, Schwann concluded, was that "the acid contributes to the decomposition of the organic substances in digestion through its presence, without becoming changed itself"; or, as he expressed it in another place, it "predisposes the digestive substances by its contact to decompose." [25]

Having settled his first query, Schwann turned to the question "how does the other . . . digestive principle work?" The two possibilities here also were ordinary chemical combination or contact action, the latter of which he clearly was seeking to demonstrate. There were two criteria for judging whether the process was comparable to other known contact processes, he stated: (1) the quantity of the agent must be very small and not proportional to the amount of the product; and (2) the agent should not be decomposed itself, or at least should not enter into combination with the product. Turning to the first criterion, Schwann prepared a series of artificial gastric juices diluted to .08, .04, .01, .005, and .0025 of normal strength. Their digestive activities not only were not proportional to the proportion of "digestive principle," but the 1 and 4 per cent solutions actually digested more rapidly than the normal. The 4 per cent solution he calculated to contain only one part of dry weight to 100 parts of dried albumin digested. Therefore, according to both aspects of the first standard, the action seemed to be, like fermentation, a contact phenomenon. To assess the second criterion, whether the digestive principle remains unchanged, he used the gastric juice from the preceding experiments over again and found that by comparison with fresh preparations they had "lost a part of their digestive force." He could not answer the question whether the loss represented a combination of the principle with the digestive products. Therefore he remained uncertain whether digestion met both requirements of a true contact process, but he noted that the other known organic processes, alcoholic and acetic fermentation, which met the first qualification, were similarly uncertain with respect to the second.[26]

With systematic thoroughness Schwann went over the question of whether digestion and fermentation shared enough additional characteristics to be considered the same type of process. Among several important differences he pointed out between them was that fermentation occurred only to sugars, whereas digestion decomposed animal substances as well. By experiments in an atmosphere free of oxygen he proved that digestion, unlike alcoholic fermentation, required none of that gas even to initiate the process; digestion required acid, on the other hand, and fermentation did not. Balancing off such divergences, however, were significant similarities in the conditions accompanying both phenomena. Both took place only when there was sufficient water present. Both required a warm temperature. Schwann found, for example, that digestion at 10–12° Réaumur took four times as long to produce a given effect as it did at 32°. When heated for a few minutes to boiling, the digestive juice was "completely and forever destroyed," a property which was similar to, though even more absolute than that of the alcoholic ferment. One difference which Müller and he had observed, that digestion does not produce carbonic acid or other gas, Schwann did not regard as basic, for it meant merely that the products of digestion happen not to be gaseous. Whether the parallels were strong enough to include digestion within the concept of fermentation or whether there ought to be a new term to include them both, Schwann considered a "mere dispute over words." He preferred to extend the familiar concept of fermentation, because it had in common with digestion the crucial characteristic of being "a spontaneous decomposition of organic materials, brought about through a substance acting (through contact?) in a very small quantity."[27]

Schwann had now reached the critical question, what is this "active digestive principle analogous to a ferment?" The first aspect of this question to answer was whether the principle consists of mucus itself dissolved in the digestive fluid, of some decomposition product engendered from the mucus, or of another substance present already with the mucus. If it were the first, he argued, then in any preparation containing some undissolved mucus the fluid ought to be saturated with the principle. He showed experimentally that this condition was not met, so that according to either of the remaining alternatives the principle must be something distinct from mucus.[28] Schwann therefore set out to determine its chemical properties. He could not apply the usual methods of solvent extraction to separate it, however, because alcohol destroyed the digestive power of gastric juice; even if he did procure the active principle that way he would not be able to recognize it. He resorted instead to a procedure which was as novel and potent as his conception of the gastric ferment itself.

The idea was to determine the behavior with respect to certain reagents of the digestive principle in the gastric juice itself, without isolating the substance, merely by observing whether the digestive force accompanied the precipitate caused by these reagents or remained in the fluid.[29]

The digestive principle would not be active, of course, in the form of a precipitate itself. To prove that a given reagent had removed it from solution he had to wash the precipitate thoroughly, then react it with another reagent intended to release the principle from the insoluble compound it had formed by forming an even less soluble salt with a component of the first reagent. Then he had to show that the filtrate in which the second reaction had taken place was active and consequently had received the digestive principle.

The first reagent he tried was potassium carbonate, to neutralize the acid. A precipitate formed, but when washed and acidified it did not digest albumin. The original filtrate, however, regained its activity when he added acid. This result established that the principle is soluble in neutral water. Then he utilized several of the reagents ordinarily used to identify the various "animal matters." Lead acetate partially precipitated the principle from an acid solution and completely from a neutral solution. Potassium ferrocyanide did not precipitate it; sublimate precipitated it, and tincture of gall-nuts destroyed it, probably Schwann thought, by forming a permanent compound with it. Boiling coagulated it. Together these tests showed that in the combination of its reactions the digestive principle differed from any of the known substances such as mucus, albumin, casein, osmazome, or salivary matter. On the basis of these properties Schwann tried to develop a procedure for isolating the digestive principle. Using a sequence of the same precipitation reactions, he was able to separate salivary matter and obtain an active fluid which he thought contained the digestive principle and osmazome. Hoping that further research would lead to complete isolation, he meanwhile felt confident that he had demonstrated at least that the digestive principle is "a peculiar substance." [30]

Before his article was printed, Schwann added an appendix to it. He had assumed, he said, that the digestive principle which he had studied on the basis of its effects upon albumin would operate in a similar manner with all nutrients. Reflecting afterward, however, that, unlike albumin, some aliments undergo with diluted acids alone the same changes that artificial gastric juice produces, he now believed that his conclusions as he had originally presented them should be restricted to the digestion of coagulated albumin. In order to extend their applicability he performed new experiments in which he compared the results of digesting various aliments in diluted acid with the results when he added a small amount of gastric juice to the same solution. The digestive agent was clearly essential for the digestion of fibrin and muscle fiber; the former also, he showed, was chemically transformed as albumin was, yielding osmazome, salivary matter, and a substance similar to albumin. Since he could now say that the digestive principle "causes the digestion of the most important animal nutrients," he gave it the name *pepsin*. Some substances, however, including gelatin, gluten, and coagulated casein, dissolved as easily in dilute acid as in gastric juice, and gave products with most of the same properties that Tiedemann and Gmelin had reported as the outcome of natural digestion in the stomach. Schwann could not claim, therefore, that pepsin was an essential agent for the digestion of all animal matters. He hoped that further research could clarify the situation. [31]

Starch posed the opposite problem, for Schwann observed that neither dilute acid nor dilute acid together with artificial gastric juice could duplicate the conversion of starch into sugar which Tiedemann and Gmelin had found to occur in digestion. Schwann sought a solution for this difficulty in Leuchs's observation that saliva is capable of changing starch into sugar. Schwann repeatedly confirmed this reaction, showing that it could also occur when a small amount of acid, equivalent to that in the stomach, was added. "These changes of starch," Schwann ended, "agree therefore with those which Tiedemann and Gmelin observed and, if natural gastric juice is perhaps also incapable of producing this transformation, the digestion of starch will find an adequate explanation in the effect of saliva swallowed with it." [32]

Whatever standard one applies to Schwann's memoir, whether one judges it by the degree to which it surpassed previous knowledge and conceptions of the digestive process or by its conformity to modern descriptions, his achievement was outstanding. The logic of his thought was precise and thorough, his methods were ingenious, and his vision was broad. He redefined the mode of action of the digestive agent and characterized the agent as a chemical substance. He demonstrated its operation on a major class of aliments, but saw beyond the prevalent idea that a single agent is responsible for the digestion of every type of food material. He contributed strong support for the view that digestion involves chemical changes as well as solution. He perceived that the action of the digestive principle comprised one instance of a whole new class of chemical processes peculiarly characteristic of organisms, and he provided a model for the experimental investigation of such processes. The first simple efforts of Réaumur to dissolve pieces of meat in a juice collected from the cavity of a stomach had over eighty years developed into a highly sophisticated area of research.

In Germany physiologists regarded the collective efforts of Eberle, Müller, and Schwann as the beginning of a new phase in the investigation of digestion. Others began carrying out further researches based on their methods for preparing artificial gastric juice. Among those who followed up Eberle's studies was the eminent Czech professor of physiology at the University of Breslau, Jan E. Purkyně. During the summer of the year Schwann's paper appeared, Purkyně and two of his pupils, Gabriel G. Valentin and S. Pappenheim, investigated the properties of juices prepared from the gastric mucus of humans, various vertebrates, and crustaceans. With their preparations they were able to digest "almost all parts of animals." Having discovered numerous simple, microscopic glands in the mucous lining of stomachs, they assumed that the organic digestive principle originates in them. Valentin examined Schwann's pepsin and found a strong resemblance between it and liquid albumin. In 1838 Purkyně and Pappenheim attempted to form artificial gastric juice in new ways which might provide insight into the manner in which the stomach normally produces it. By means of galvanic electricity they tried to separate free acid in various materials which could conceivably serve as its natural source; these included saliva, blood serum, and the mucous lining it-

self ground up and mixed with distilled water. In each instance hydrochloric acid appeared at the oxygen electrode of the solution. After
such treatment the fluid containing mucus lining was able to digest
cubes of albumin. The result suggested to them that the acid in gastric
juice may derive from the same source as the organic digestive agent,
probably from the same glands. Utilizing an analogy commonly made
at the time between nervous action and a galvanic current, they speculated that nervous actions on these glands may release hydrochloric
acid without requiring a special secretory process.[33]

In 1839 Franz Simon, a *Privatdocent* at the University of Berlin,
digested casein obtained from coagulated milk in artificial gastric
juice. From comparative tests of the digested casein and of casein
merely dissolved in water with the usual reagents, he found that the
former differed in three properties from the latter. It was precipitated
by sublimate, and coagulated by heat and by alcohol. Consequently
Simon concluded that during digestion casein is converted to albumin.[34] During the same year Adolph Wasmann submitted an inaugural dissertation in Berlin which extended Schwann's experiments
with pepsin. By microscopic studies he observed that certain areas of
the stomach lining contain special glandular cells.[35] Small pieces of
this glandular membrane [*Drüsenhaut*] in acidulated water could digest
in one and a half hours as much as ordinary artificial gastric juice did
in six to eight hours. Wasmann claimed, therefore, that these glands
are the principal source of pepsin. He also obtained pepsin mixed with
less other organic material, he believed, by extracting from this glandular material in water instead of acid. He performed on the extract
additional precipitation reactions of the type Schwann had used, and
obtained a preparation which he thought contained little else besides
the pepsin itself. Observing that albumin and other aliments dissolve
in very dilute, boiling acid, Wasmann decided that acid must be
regarded as having "digestive power," and that the role of pepsin is
merely to make the process occur more rapidly at the temperature of
the body.[36]

Schwann's investigation of digestion drew another response from
an unexpected quarter. Justus Liebig had not yet become involved in
animal chemistry in 1836, but he reprinted an extract of Schwann's
paper in his *Annalen der Pharmacie*. In an editorial footnote Liebig
remarked that "Schwann's observations must lead to remarkable and
interesting results," but they could only be interpreted from the "correct viewpoint" when the active organic material had been isolated
and when the changes that albumin and other digestible substances

underwent had been examined by elementary analysis. "The name *pepsin*," he contended, "is for the present only the representation of an idea," and the supposed products of gastric digestion were merely designations for certain properties. The latter substances would "only begin to exist in reality for us when elementary analysis protects us from mistakes." Furthermore, according to Liebig, the term *catalysis*, which Schwann applied in this paper to the action of pepsin, actually explained nothing.[37] The task of defining the reaction by determining the elementary composition of the substances involved was not easy, Liebig thought, but it should be pursued, and whoever solved it would be the "true discoverer." [38] Liebig's reservations were not unreasonable; as we have seen, Schwann himself regarded the isolation of pepsin as the desired goal. Yet Liebig underrated the importance of what Schwann had already done, in part at least because he judged the question in the light of his own experience in a different area of research. Over the preceding eight years he had helped establish the standard that in order to determine the nature of an organic compound one must isolate it in pure form and ascertain accurately its elementary composition. He assumed, therefore, that pepsin must be treated in the same way, not perceiving that Schwann had developed an incisive new means to characterize a substance present in such small amounts that it could not readily be handled by the customary techniques, yet whose crucial property, its special activity, provided at least a convenient interim indicator of its identity. Similarly, in his claim that only elementary analysis could establish that real changes occurred in the composition of the substances digested, Liebig was demanding that standards appropriate to his own field be applied to a problem for which they had not yet proved adaptable. He was implicitly refusing to acknowledge the adequacy of the criteria upon which those interested in physiological chemistry had come to rely for the identification of "animal matters," their solubilities and characteristic reactions. At the time, however, the latter criteria were, for these complex substances, more discriminating than was their identification by elementary composition.

When he learned of Mulder's analyses of albumin, fibrin, and casein, Liebig probably felt that the time had come to attempt to carry out the task he had delineated in his note. At any rate, the student in his laboratory who verified Mulder's results in 1839, Julius Vogel,[39] applied the same analytical procedures shortly afterward to the question of what chemical changes albumin and fibrin undergo when they are digested. Following the artificial digestion procedures of Eberle and Schwann, Vogel confirmed their observation that albumin loses its special property of coagulating with heat, and that organic substances appear, soluble respectively in water and in alcohol and water. But he considered their identification of these substances as osmazome and salivary matter inadequate, because these were vague terms which different chemists applied to quite different materials. He therefore attempted to specify the nature of the digestive change further, by giving a fuller account of the reactions of the product with acids, alkalis, and salts, and by determining its elementary composition. For the latter purpose he isolated the insoluble salt which it formed with copper. His combustion analysis showed that the ratio of carbon to nitrogen in the digested albumin was the same as in undigested. Therefore he concluded that "albumin is not substantially changed in its elementary composition through artificial chymification, although it loses its capacity to coagulate through heat and to be coagulated through alcohol." Similarly, he found that fibrin underwent no change in its elementary proportions even though it lost the property of clotting in aequous solutions. Thus, while Vogel upheld the view that chemical transformations occur in digestion, his own contribution was a negative one in the sense that it revealed no discernible changes in the material constitution by which organic chemists ordinarily specified definite compounds. Perhaps that is why he remarked that his investigations of digestion would be more interesting to physiologists than to chemists.[40]

Vogel's work was potentially of broader interest than he thought, for he was attempting to bring together the latest results of the long physiological tradition of investigating digestion with the new methods the chemists were using to comprehend organic reactions through knowledge of the composition of the compounds involved. If Liebig himself had fully appreciated the value of the nascent synthesis which had occurred under his own supervision, the disparity between the approaches of the chemists and the physiologists might have been less severe than it became; but he was only equipped to view the situation from one side. He could see that there was no solid evidence for a chemical transformation by the criteria of ordinary organic chemistry. He was not in close enough touch with the trend of experiments in the field of digestive physiology to share the sense of those engaged in it that there were growing indications of some special kind of transformations, even though these were still difficult to specify. Moreover, when he incorporated into his *Animal Chemistry* in 1841 the most general discoveries derived from the investigations connecting Eberle with Vogel, Liebig treated them not as a research opening to be pursued further, but as simple observations to be fitted into his broader theoretical structure. He no longer needed to seek the further evidence for chemical transformations for which he had called in 1836, because his more recent belief that the constituents of blood are formed in plants fit best with the view that digestion did not produce such changes. Probably drawing on Vogel's conclusion that certain properties of albumin and fibrin changed but that their elementary compositions did not, Liebig argued that gastric juice merely renders the constituents of food soluble "in virtue of a new grouping of their atoms." As he also put it, "the food undergoes a change in its state of cohesion, becoming fluid without any other change of properties." [41] Thus, although Liebig paid more attention to the recent efforts of physiologists than Dumas had done by then, both chemists discounted in their general formulations the physiologists' own search for indications of changes of chemical composition in digestion, because both began with the premise, based on elementary analyses of the substances involved, that food required no such changes.

Liebig subordinated the results of the experiments on digestion in a second way to his doctrinal requirements, for he used the discovery that the mucus lining of the stomach produces an artificial gastric juice chiefly as evidence that the digestive action of gastric juice was a form of fermentation, by the terms of his own definition of fermentation. Two years earlier he had asserted that ferments were spontaneously decomposing animal materials, whose particles were set into motion during the process. This motion, communicated to the particles of other substances in contact with the ferments, caused them in turn to undergo changes. The fact that the mucus lining membrane of the stomach was especially active after being dried and exposed to air indicated for him that the gastric juice, too, owed its digestive properties to its state of progressive decomposition. [42] On the whole Liebig's interpretation of digestion consisted of rather loosely connected, not entirely consistent ideas, befitting his cursory acquaintance with the problems the subject presented. Paradoxically, Claude Bernard, who rejected Liebig's method of treating biological phenomena, maintained a little later a conception of the action of digestive ferments which had more in common with that of Liebig than with the conclusions of Schwann's remarkable investigation.

Those German physiologists who had fixed their attention more closely on pepsin [43] had shown by 1840 that the pathway entered by Eberle, Müller, and Schwann could lead to continuing progress and further insights. At the same time it was evident, however, that considerable confusion and obscurity still surrounded the topic of digestion. Both aspects of the situation were well portrayed in a lengthy review of the subject which C. F. Burdach wrote in the ninth volume of his influential *Treatise of Physiology*. Recent observations had made it clear, Burdach believed, that digestion cannot be considered a mere dissolution, but involves the transformation of certain substances to others. Although the general nature of such changes was not yet understood, "a great step" had been taken by the discovery of Tiedemann and Gmelin of the conversion of starch to sugar, a discovery which had "opened the way," and by the discovery by Eberle that coagulated albumin is transformed to osmazome and ptyalin [salivary matter]. Burdach described the artificial digestions of the immediately preceding years and Schwann's view that digestion is a catalytic action. It was a type of process, Burdach maintained, which is "placed at the extreme limits of our chemistry, and takes place almost exclusively with respect to organic products." [44]

In spite of the successful investigations of chemical changes, Burdach maintained, "the chemical theory of digestion does not completely suffice." Among the difficulties he enumerated were that:

the so-called artificial digestion is only analogous to digestion in the stomach; artificial gastric juice acts less upon fibrin than upon albumin, and exercises no action upon vegetable substances. And, furthermore, what is digestion in the stomach itself, considered from the chemical point of view? If it is only a simple liquefaction of aliments, we can dispense with it when we take the latter in a liquid form. But if starch is converted into sugar, and vegetable albumin into gelatin, what benefit do we obtain from that? What becomes of the sugar and the gelatin? And why is fibrin, which the blood requires, nevertheless converted into albumin, which although produced in digestion, is in turn transformed into osmazome and ptyalin? [45]

Burdach was objecting perceptively that although the evidence of the occurrence of individual chemical changes in digestion was important, the changes so far claimed to occur fell into no meaningful overall pattern. He himself conjectured that digestion probably reduced all aliments to some identical product which was not albumin or any other constituent of the blood, but "a rudiment of these diverse substances, a sort of neutral material, at the expense of which all of them might originate." [46]

Burdach's views were not wholly based on the chemical evidence, for he, like Johannes Müller, felt that chemistry supplied a necessary but insufficient explanation of vital processes. His rejection of the idea that digestion merely dissolves aliments derived partly from the observed chemical changes, but more emphatically from his conviction that the animal organism must in some purposeful manner create from nutrients the special materials of its own body; otherwise it could not maintain its own chemical composition in spite of the diversity of foods it eats. In that respect, he said, the animal body "shows itself to a certain degree independent of its aliments." Digestion he considered to be only a preparation for the elaboration which takes place further on, but "like life" it maintains itself by adapting itself actively to changing circumstances. The digestive process, for example, is more energetic when it must contend with food which is more abundant or more difficult to digest. The dependence between the vital process and the chemical ones was, however, reciprocal. "Even though digestion is accomplished by life . . . it is only possible by means of certain chemical conditions introduced by vital action." [47] Burdach's attitude was probably rooted in his earlier association with *Naturphilosophie* and his own primary interest in embryological, developmental phenomena, both factors foreign to the immediate scientific milieu Claude Bernard entered. Yet Burdach's treatise was a valuable source of information about all aspects of physiology. It was cited prominently by French physiologists,[48] and there is evidence that Bernard was familiar with it from an early period of his career.[49] The resemblances between some of Burdach's general views and those Bernard later expressed suggest that the attitude of the German biologist toward the relation of chemistry and vital processes fitted into the background from which Bernard drew his own opinions.

IX

French Investigations of Digestion

The volume of Burdach's treatise discussed in the preceding chapter appeared in French translation in 1841, during the same year that Bernard undertook his first experiments. A German view of the recent history of the problem of digestion was thus readily accessible to French scientists by then, if not before. Yet apparently even after this time French physiologists took relatively little notice of the investigations with artificial gastric juice and the pepsin theory which were so widely engaging their German counterparts. Before 1840 the French apparently did not produce any major new studies of digestion. Between 1840 and 1842, however, two significant investigations were undertaken. Both of these took as their principal starting point the treatises of Tiedemann and Gmelin rather than the more recent studies of Eberle, Müller, Schwann, or their followers. In 1842 Bouchardat and Sandras began the report of their work with a brief historical introduction, recalling the prize the Academy had offered in 1825. "Since the works of MM. Leuret and Lassaigne, of MM. Tiedemann and Gmelin," they added, "the history of the digestion of aliments has been enriched by the fine experiments presented in the first report of the so-called Gelatin Commission or in the courses of M. Dumas and of M. Liebig." The editor of the journal in which their article appeared, being somewhat better informed, added a footnote to draw the attention of readers to "the interesting works of MM Eberl[e], Schwann and Muller on the same subject." [1] The next major French author of a study of digestion, Nicolas Blondlot, did devote some attention to the results of the three Germans, but Blondlot too followed more closely in the course opened up by Tiedemann and Gmelin (as well as by the methods of William Beaumont, as will be described later). Moreover, in the relatively minor portion of his work summarizing his own efforts to produce an artificial gastric juice, Blondlot claimed that he had made "a great many experiments on that subject, before knowing about the works published in Germany." [2]

The existence of such a situation helps to illustrate some of the subtleties involved in describing or explaining the nature of "national" scientific traditions. Over a period of at least five years there existed a sharp difference in the knowledge or attitudes of corresponding scientists in two neighboring and leading scientific nations with regard to the state of an important field of research. What were for those in one of these countries exciting new developments were hardly visible to those in the other. How to account for the gap is less clear. A minor factor may have been the language barrier. Neither the treatises of Eberle nor those of Schwann were available in French, and some French scientists were prone to be unaware of what was written in other languages. Yet inaccessibility of the literature cannot be an adequate reason, for, as the history of the fat controversy exemplifies, when French scientists were interested in what was happening in Germany they found out about it very quickly. There were ample means for translating and printing in French journals what they considered important. If those French scientists who knew of the German investigations of artificial digestion thought them unimportant, there is a possible explanation for their attitude. According to an account given later by Payen, Gabriel Valentin, one of the first to follow up Schwann's work on pepsin in Germany, had come to Paris and offered to repeat for Magendie the artificial digestion experiments demonstrating the action of pepsin. At the Collège de France, in the presence of Magendie, Poiseuille, Payen, and several others, Valentin attempted to digest fibrin and coagulated albumin by Schwann's methods. The experiments failed, however—an outcome which Valentin attributed to the weakness of the acid employed. [3] Perhaps the French physiologists consequently dismissed the pepsin theory as experimentally unsound. If they did, however, they must have been predisposed not to take it seriously. Anyone who had read Schwann's memoir carefully would not have been able to write it off on the basis of one unsuccessful effort to repeat it, particularly in view of the stress Schwann placed on the effects of different concentrations of the acid.

Why then did French physiologists take the pepsin theory and related investigations so much less seriously than did the Germans? Undoubtedly feelings of national rivalry such as we have noted on other occasions would tempt them to discount to some extent achievements occurring in the other country. Yet it was not even truly self-serving to ignore new lines of investigation for such reasons when the consequence could only be for them to put themselves at a disadvantage in pursuing the same general problem. The French scientists must not fully have understood the significance of the work. Since they were no less able or intelligent, this suggests that even though there was no tight barrier to communication between the scientific communities of France and of Germany, there was a definite tendency for results emanating from beyond the fringes of the French scientific circle to loom less large to its members than work arising within that circle. Such a filtering process was irregular and capricious, for when it became clear to some people within the French community that a given work from outside it had to be reckoned with, its impact could be very significant.[4] Thus, even while failing to appreciate the latest innovations in the study of digestion in Germany, French physiologists looked for guidance to the older achievements, not of the last Frenchmen who had worked on the problem, but of the two German scientists Tiedemann and Gmelin.[5] Even a scientific community strongly prejudiced in favor of its own people [6] can maintain only a very limited degree of arbitrary autonomy from what others are doing.

The lag in recognition of the work of Eberle, Müller, and Schwann in France may make it more understandable how Dumas could maintain in 1841 in his lecture on *chemical statics* that digestion is "a simple function of absorption," by which soluble aliments pass into the blood and insoluble materials are divided finely enough to enter the lacteal vessels.[7] The strongest evidence that digestion produces chemical transformations lay in those recent German publications. Even if he were not familiar with these, however, Dumas would have had to pass over the observations of Tiedemann and Gmelin and others indicating some chemical changes. These observations were still equivocal enough so that Dumas could have tried to explain them away. That he merely dismissed such efforts with the cavalier statement that they represented a search for mysteries which were not there suggests that his great success in his own field of organic chemistry had given Dumas such self-assurance that he would make pronouncements concerning other fields without bothering about what the people in those fields had been doing.

Apollinaire Bouchardat, the senior author of the "Researches on digestion" presented to the Academy of Sciences in May 1842, was at

Apollinaire Bouchardat

the time a well-known hospital pharmacist, a member of a group who helped to maintain some contact between chemistry and medicine at a time when most Parisian physicians were paying little attention to scientific research.[8] Bouchardat had combined chemical investigations and medical practice especially in his studies of diabetes. He took up the problem of digestion in a new effort to fulfill the objectives of the prize offered seventeen years before. Like Tiedemann and Gmelin, their predecessors in that attempt, Bouchardat and his collaborator Sandras proceeded by feeding different kinds of simple nutrients to dogs and comparing the contents of the digestive tract a few hours afterward with the contents in a fasting animal. They believed, however, that from these same methods they had reached sufficiently novel results to present a theory of digestion different from those then prevailing. After feeding fibrin, gluten, uncoagulated albumin, and casein, they observed that the stomach contained in each case the same substance in a dissolved state. Outside the stomach they found that very dilute hydrochloric acid was also able to dissolve these nutrients.

Previous authors had not realized that the latter process could occur, they claimed, because they had not suspected that an acid which in high concentration dissolves the aliments but precipitates them when present in moderate proportion, would dissolve them when it was extremely dilute. They were evidently not aware that Valentin, Wasmann, and Vogel, among the German physiologists, had been making analogous observations. At any rate, Bouchardat and Sandras concluded that hydrochloric acid is the "agent of dissolution" of these substances in digestion. They acknowledged that coagulated albumin and fibrin did not dissolve in the acid alone, and consequently that "the simultaneous presence of some particular material produced in the stomach of living animals is necessary to dissolve these substances." There was no hint, however, that specific investigations of the properties of this material had been carried out in Germany.[9]

Concerning the digestion of starch, Bouchardat and Sandras challenged directly what had been Tiedemann and Gmelin's most impressive discovery. After feeding that aliment to a dog they could find no trace of sugar or of dextrin in the digestive tract. Tiedemann and Gmelin, they felt, might have observed fermentations produced by the action of yeast on "extractive materials." Their negative result Bouchardat and Sandras based on what they considered a more precise test for sugar, its property of rotating polarized light. They did find, however, that the residue of the stomach fluids contained lactic acid, which they separated from the alcoholic extract as insoluble calcium lactate, and identified by forming from the latter the characteristic salt zinc lactate. In view of the discovery of lactic acid fermentation by Frémy the previous year, one might think that their finding was open to the same objection which they were making to Tiedemann and Gmelin's conclusion that starch produces sugar. Bouchardat and Sandras were nevertheless confident that their own result superseded the older one. "We regard as confirmed," they said, "the transformation [of starch] into lactic acid." [10]

They found, as others had before them, that fats pass unaltered through the digestive tract into the chyle, except, as they thought, for being emulsified by the action of bile and pancreatic juice. Unlike many other physiologists, however, they did not believe that those nutrients which the digestive agent dissolves enter the chyle. When they dyed fibrin or gluten with saffron, that color did not appear in the chyle. After feeding starch they could find no trace of it in the chyle. Chyle, they concluded, was not a general, homogenous product of the digestive elaboration of food, but the route by which certain aliments, especially fats, which do not dissolve in digestion, are absorbed into the circulation. The nutrients which do dissolve they believed to be absorbed directly from the stomach into the veins.[11]

Although Bouchardat and Sandras's investigation was related most directly to the problems and methods raised by Tiedemann and Gmelin, the work they presented in the spring of 1842 reflected also the impact of those events of the preceding summer with which the present narrative opens. The special attention they gave to gluten in their memoir they connected with the great interest in the nutritive properties of that substance revealed by the experiments of the Gelatin Commission. The section on starch they introduced by noting that it is the most important of "that class which M. Dumas proposes to call respiratory aliments." [12] Thus, even when not essential to the particular problem under study, the work of the Gelatin Commission and the ideas of Dumas seemed to form for French scientists a part of the background for any treatment of nutritional phenomena.

The views of Dumas may have influenced Bouchardat and Sandras more deeply than their explicit reference to him would indicate. Though their results included the claim to the discovery of a chemical transformation, they always described digestion in general terms as a dissolution, even in the case of starch, and their principal conclusion with respect to nitrogenous aliments was that they are dissolved in the stomach. Perhaps, not being in touch with the newer German research, they were merely reaffirming what had been for Tiedemann and Gmelin and others still the predominant characteristic of digestion. On the other hand, there is indirect evidence that Dumas's portrayal of digestion may have strengthened their inclination in this direction. After they submitted their memoir to the Academy, a committee composed of Dumas, Magendie, Flourens, Milne Edwards, and Payen was appointed to evaluate their work. As it happened, Dumas himself delivered the report of this committee, in January 1843. Dumas was able to summarize the objective of the investigation of Bouchardat and Sandras as the determination of the means by which nature manages "to render certain aliments soluble, or else to divide them up to a degree suitable to render them proper to pass into the chyliferous vessels." [13] This statement was, as can readily be seen, only a slight adaptation of the description of digestion Dumas himself had already given in his well-known essay. Perhaps he was not representing their ideas as accurately as his own, yet their own summary statements so easily lend themselves to Dumas's interpretation as to suggest that they may have been viewing the question partly through his conception of it.[14]

The members of the commission were at least more aware than Bouchardat and Sandras that one could not entirely ignore the German artificial digestion experiments. "The authors have gone too far," Dumas reported, "in considering hydrochloric acid as the sole agent of dissolution of nitrogenous substances." One must also take into account the "animal material which one has designated under the names of *pepsin* or of [c] *hymosine*, which probably functions in the manner of diastase, and which MM. Schwan and Deschamps have pointed out in the stomach." [15] This passage suggests how grudgingly the French scientists acknowledged the significance of Schwann's achievement, for the investigation of Michel Deschamps, which they were trying to present here as of equal weight with that of Schwann, was actually a relatively minor contribution, made four years after the publication of Schwann's memoir. Deschamps, a pharmacist in Avalon, had tried by means of preparations made from the mucus lining of the stomach, similar to those which the German physiologists had been using, to identify the agent which causes milk to coagulate in the stomach. From this special problem (with which Schwann had also dealt), Deschamps tried to make general deductions about the nature of digestion and also tried unsuccessfully to substitute his term chymosine for pepsin. [16]

The commission concluded that the opinions Bouchardat and Sandras expressed in their memoir appeared sound, "but the physiological experiments on which they rested, reproduced under its eyes, have not given results as clear as it would have liked." The commission therefore decided only to encourage the authors to pursue further this important but difficult problem. [17]

A German review of Bouchardat and Sandras's article was less charitable. Carl Lehmann, who was himself engaged in research on digestion, wrote that their investigation, "although not uninteresting in itself, will nevertheless offer little new to German physiologists and chemists . . . The authors seem to have been completely unfamiliar" with investigations of properties of dissolved protein materials by Valentin and others as well as with the research of Schwann, Pappenheim, and Wasmann concerning the digestive properties of hydrochloric acid. Although Lehmann agreed with the two French scientists that lactic acid sometimes appears in the digestion of starch, he thought that the evidence that he and others had found that sugar too is formed could not be denied. Their contention that substances dissolved in the stomach are directly absorbed from that organ contradicted some investigations by German physiologists, and their assertion that chyle does not contain all of the dissolved nutrients had long been agreed upon and taught by such leading German physiologists as E. H. Weber, Johannes Müller, and Valentin. It seemed only a diplomatic gesture when Lehmann finished his remarks by saying that he did not intend his comparison of results reached in different lands to detract from the "excellent investigations and genuinely ingenious conclusions" of the authors.[18] Having conceived their investigation from a local point of view, Bouchardat and Sandras had produced a result of only local significance. They resolved no general questions about the nature of digestion. The effect of their work was only to throw doubt upon certain previous conclusions within the scientific community of Paris, and to make the problem of digestion a topic of more immediate concern there. Their memoir, however, represented only the first stage of research which afterward led the two men to results of broader interest.

At the time that the commission of the Academy reported on Bouchardat and Sandras's memoir, Claude Bernard had just embarked on the series of investigations of chemical reactions within animals which, as we have seen, drew him during the following months toward the question of gastric digestion.[19] A comparison between his course of research and the experimental tradition extending from Réaumur to his own day reveals quite clearly the autonomous pathway by which he reached this problem. Neither the questions he was asking nor the procedures he was using seem based directly on what his predecessors and contemporaries had done in the study of digestion. The explanation, of course, is not that Bernard was able deliberately to take up the problem with a totally fresh perspective, but that he drifted into that subject in an unusual direction from the experiments on absorption with which he had begun. Two of the experiments he performed late in the spring, however, were digressions from the smooth progression of most of his investigation, and they suggest that he was by then beginning to try to bring his research into some kind of connection with contemporary work on digestion. One of these was his effort to trace the course of starch through the digestive tract, an experiment obviously patterned after the observations of Tiedemann and Gmelin and possibly stimulated by the uncertainty Bouchardat and Sandras had raised about the alteration of that aliment. The other was the experiment involving pepsin and iron filings, in which Bernard seemed to be adapting the outcome of Schwann's work to his own plan of investigation.[20] Here Bernard appeared more open to newer German research than some of his colleagues were, although it became apparent a little later that his understanding of the pepsin theory was quite superficial.

It may well have been because he was becoming involved in problems for which he felt he needed to acquire more background knowledge, that Bernard decided to attend Dumas's lectures during the spring and summer of 1843. The description of digestion he heard from Dumas reflected the recent developments in Paris. Dumas favored the interpretations of Bouchardat and Sandras and followed their opinions in most respects. As he had done in his report to the Academy, however, he noted that their theory that dilute gastric acid dissolves aliments did not explain everything. The other factor involved was pepsin, or chymosine, whose general properties he summarized. If Bernard's notes are indicative, however, he did not get from Dumas a deep understanding of Schwann's approach to the nature of pepsin.[21] Probably more important for Bernard was what Dumas taught concerning the properties and reactions of specific organic substances, and about practical methods for identifying the constituents of such fluids as blood, chyle, bile, and urine. These became of central importance for Bernard's later investigations. To detect albumin in the urine, for example, Bernard usually relied on the precipitation reactions with nitric acid or corrosive sublimate which Dumas described.[22] Dumas also summarized the method of determining urea by forming its nitrate, which Bernard frequently applied afterward.[23] Bernard learned much about the properties of starch, its conversion to sugar, and the role of diastase in that process. Most significant of all, he heard about a new test for glucose: "Salt of copper with an alkali (copper tartrate with potash) character for recognizing grape sugar or glucose—procedure pointed out by M. Fromerz and perfected by Baresville." [24] The fact that he so badly misspelled Barreswil's name suggests that Bernard was not yet acquainted with the chemist who became so important to him a few months later.

In the interlude between Bernard's research during the first half of 1843 and his return to the problem in the fall, interest in digestion became more intense in Paris as a result of the appearance of the *Analytical Treatise on Digestion* of Nicolas Blondlot. Although formerly an intern and surgeon in Paris hospitals, he was now serving as a surgeon and professor of chemistry at the medical school of Nancy, in northeastern France. The importance of his contribution lay chiefly in a dramatic technical innovation. The "precious results" which William Beaumont had achieved by exploiting the accidental fortune of caring for a patient with a gastric fistula suggested to Blondlot that he could imitate that situation by creating an artificial fistula in the stomach of an animal.[25] Cutting through the abdominal wall of a dog, he drew its stomach up to the opening, made two short incisions through the

coats of that organ, and maintained the edges of the cuts in contact
with the edges of the outer wound with ligatures until they had grown
together. This left a small opening directly into the interior of the
stomach. The hole tended to close up again, but by inserting a short
silver tube with a flange on each end he was able to maintain a permanent entrance into the stomach. Most of the time he kept the tube
closed with a stopper. By simply removing the latter he could withdraw fluid from the stomach whenever he wished. Blondlot's method
had an even broader effect upon the investigation of digestion than the
experiments of Beaumont which inspired it, for others who treated
the problem of digestion afterward could easily duplicate it and develop variations of it adapted to related problems. His technique enabled Blondlot himself to recapitulate with a new facility the general
plan of research which Tiedemann and Gmelin had pursued. The
much improved opportunity for obtaining large supplies of gastric
juice under better controlled conditions brought renewed emphasis on
the analysis of the fluid and the investigation with it of digestion outside of the stomach. Experiments on natural digestion also became
much simpler. No longer was it necessary to slaughter an enormous
number of animals. Blondlot used only two for his numerous experiments, and one of them remained healthy for more than two years. In
addition he was able to sample the contents of the stomach repeatedly
during the course of a given feeding experiment.[26]

The first of the old problems to which Blondlot addressed his new
method was the nature of gastric juice itself. Before analyzing it, he
believed, one had to obtain it under proper conditions. When his dog
swallowed solid food he could collect immediately afterward a large
amount of pure gastric juice through the fistula. Mechanical stimulation of the stomach wall caused a direct flow, he asserted, but only if
the stomach was already in a turgid condition in response to the presence of aliments. Thus, he claimed, when Tiedemann and Gmelin
had collected gastric juice from the stomach after the purely mechanical stimulus of causing a dog to swallow stones, they had not really
obtained pure gastric juice, but only a feeble proportion mixed with
mucus. "Alimentary materials," Blondlot concluded, constitute "the
special stimulant under the influence of which the stomach pours out
its chymifying juice."[27]

With gastric juice obtained in this way, Blondlot reassessed the
diverse opinions which other people had expressed concerning the nature of its free acid. Previous authors had variously claimed it to be
hydrochloric, acetic, lactic, or phosphoric acid, or a combination of

some of these; but the evidence, he thought, was not convincing for any one of these. The observation of hydrochloric acid by Tiedemann and Gmelin was particularly shaky, according to Blondlot, because it was based on only a few "exceptional" cases in which by distilling the fluid they had obtained a distillate that "slightly" reddened litmus and formed a precipitate with silver nitrate. In "numerous cases," however, Blondlot asserted that Tiedemann and Gmelin had received no acidic distillate from this procedure, even though hydrochloric acid, as well as acetic acid, are volatile enough so that if either were present it should have passed into the receiver. Such cases they had ascribed, he said, "quite simply" to the free acid's having been retained in solution by an animal matter.[28] Here, as in a number of other cases, Blondlot was somewhat misrepresenting statements of his predecessors by repeating them incompletely, so that their case seemed worse than it did in the original accounts. According to Tiedemann and Gmelin's own description of one of the "exceptional" cases to which Blondlot referred, the "weak" reddening of litmus applied only to the first portion of the distillate. The second portion reddened it "strongly." It was true that in "most cases" they did not receive an acid, but they pointed out, as Blondlot did not, that these involved fasting animals. They attributed those results to there being "too small a quantity" of acid, or else to the retention of the acid by animal matter; but Blondlot repeated only the second, weaker explanation. Thus, although the evidence of hydrochloric acid Tiedemann and Gmelin had obtained was preliminary, their positive instance was more definite than Blondlot depicted it, and it was not merely aberrant, as he implied, because they could explain the negative cases by differences in the digestive conditions.[29] At any rate, having weakened Tiedemann and Gmelin's case in his recounting of it, Blondlot disposed of it by repeating the distillation and finding the fluid in the receiver completely neutral. The fluid left in the retort, however, remained acidic. This outcome, he was confident, narrowed the alternatives down to the two nonvolatile acids, lactic and phosphoric. In an effort to decide between them, he tried to neutralize gastric juice with calcium carbonate. To his surprise the fluid did not effervesce or become less acidic. This result, he claimed, "is by itself more significant than all of the analytical labors undertaken up until now to elucidate the question." If any free acid had been present, there must have occurred an effervescence as it displaced carbonic acid from the carbonate, and the solution should have been neutralized. The only way to account for the result, he asserted, was to assume that the acidic reaction of gastric juice resulted not from a free acid but from acid phosphate of lime. This soluble acidic salt does not effervesce with carbonate and is not neutralized by it. To support his contention he showed that when he added various acids to gastric juice insoluble calcium salts formed, demonstrating the presence of lime in the juice. Its presence was further proof of the impossibility that free lactic or hydrochloric acid could exist in the fluid, he said, for neither could remain in solution together with calcium. Blondlot's analyses of the organic constituents of gastric juice yielded less idiosyncratic conclusions. He merely reported that in addition to mucus there was a particular organic material, so far not isolated. He thought the latter might be a soluble portion of mucus or a closely related substance, and regarded it as perhaps the source of the specific properties of the fluid.[30]

Following the pattern by now customary, Blondlot examined next the effects of gastric digestion on the usual series of simple and complex aliments. In each case he compared the result of digestion in the stomach with digestion of the same material outside of it by means of gastric juice collected from the fistula. With each of the nitrogenous substances, fibrin, fluid and coagulated albumin, gluten, and casein, he observed a very similar result. The material softened and then liquified, but when he looked at the resulting fluid through a microscope he saw tiny individual particles of what he took to be the alimentary material in the same solid form in which it had been originally. The ordinary chemical tests he applied seemed also to show that the original substance remained essentially unaltered. The action of gastric juice on these aliments, he concluded, was not to transform them chemically, but only to dissolve a small proportion of each and to soften the rest so that the very small particles of it could be detached from one another. Since non-nitrogenous aliments were either soluble in water or sufficiently fluid to be absorbed into the chyle vessels, he suspected that they would undergo no special action of gastric juice. This view he confirmed by showing that digestion does not appear to change fats, gum, or sugar.[31]

Even starch Blondlot found to remain unchanged in digestion. Injecting starch granules mixed with water directly into the stomach through the fistula and removing a sample of the stomach contents after an hour, he observed after the latter had stood twelve more hours at body temperature that the material had not undergone "the least change." The result, he concluded, "demonstrates in the most peremptory manner that starch is not at all converted into sugar in the stomach as MM. Tiedemann and Gmelin had accepted." This instance suggests clearly the degree to which Blondlot shaped his observations through his expectations, for his experiment was set up so as to make it least likely that the starch would be converted. He himself remarked that starch dissolves in water only after the tegument enclosing each granule is broken, and that only then can it be transformed into sugar. Yet by placing unbroken granules directly into the stomach he avoided the action of mastication which could have crushed the granules. Through the microscope he recognized the grains still unbroken after digestion. Furthermore, he was either consciously or unknowingly ignoring Schwann's observation that gastric juice does not digest starch but that the saliva mixed with starch before it is swallowed may continue to act on it in the stomach. Completing his case for the absence of any conversion of starch, Blondlot found no evidence of the lactic acid which Bouchardat and Sandras had recently claimed to be the outcome of its digestion.[32]

From his investigation of all of these aliments, and of compounded foods as well, Blondlot concluded that neither of the previous general theories of digestion was correct. The process did not consist of chemical metamorphoses, nor was it an ordinary complete dissolution of the aliments. The action of gastric juice, he asserted, is "an action *sui generis*," imparting a "diminution in the consistency" of the aliments so that they may become divided into fine particles.[33]

As the preceding summary has already indicated, Blondlot was not content simply to contribute a potent new method for the study of digestive phenomena. He set himself the far more difficult task of reformulating the entire subject. "We would not accept any of the contested facts" [stated by anyone else], he announced, "without submitting them first to a scrupulous verification." After having separated the truths from all of the intermingled errors and controlled them by his own experiments, he wished to "be able to form a systematic whole" from them.[34] Thus Blondlot imagined that he could resolve the whole problem of digestion, which he described as in a thoroughly confused state up until then. With his new operative procedure he took a valuable step toward that goal; yet in his ambition to reach it in one leap he crossed the line between independent critical thought and iconoclasm. His treatise reveals a strong tendency to rectify and pass definitive judgments on the efforts of those who came before him, a practice which often caused him to belittle their achievements. In the process he sometimes distorted their views as well, and he seemed not to appreciate the progressive nature of research. When he was able to

penetrate further than those who had come before, he did not generally see his contribution as a further development from foundations
they had laid but as proof of their inadequacies (with the notable exception of Beaumont). He was "astonished," for example, at the uncertainties left by Tiedemann and Gmelin's analyses of gastric juice.
"It is easy to see that they far from justify the importance which is
generally accorded to them." [35] Their real importance was not that
they were beyond criticism by later investigators such as Blondlot,
but that as pioneer efforts they set a precedent on which others like
himself could improve. Blondlot found it similarly "surprising" that
Tiedemann and Gmelin said they had obtained "copious" gastric juice
from the dog which swallowed stones, and he characterized their
procedure as a "vain" attempt.[36] The method of Tiedemann and
Gmelin did become obsolete after Beaumont and Blondlot developed
a better one, but this did not make it a less important advance for its
own time. "The theory put forth by Doctor Eberle relative to the formation of artificial gastric juice is completely false," Blondlot wrote,
since mucus from places other than the stomach is inactive.[37] Johannes Müller, too, had taken exception to Eberle's views on the last
point, but having a more realistic conception of the nature of scientific
development than Blondlot did, Müller regarded his correction as a
relatively minor revision of an important discovery rather than a repu-
diation of Eberle's views.[38] Perhaps Blondlot's most seriously erroneous estimate of a contribution of his predecessors was his dismissal of
Schwann's pepsin as "a false discovery, having no value except for
those people to whom chemical knowledge is foreign," on the grounds
that Schwann had not actually isolated pepsin as he "thought" he
had.[39] Blondlot thus missed the whole point of Schwann's reasoning,
which was that the properties of pepsin could be elucidated even if
one could not yet completely isolate the substance itself. Having written off the views about artificial gastric juice "adopted . . . by the majority of the German physiologists," Blondlot presented in their stead
some analogous but less developed experiments of his own which he
claimed to have worked out independently.[40] In his general conclusion Blondlot ruled out all evidences of chemical changes occurring in
digestion as "chemical transformations which have never existed except in the imaginations of the authors." [41]

Blondlot did not uniformly reject the findings of others. In many
cases he judged that his own observations confirmed those of his predecessors. On the whole, however, he seemed predisposed to portray
the current state of the problem of digestion as unsatisfactory in order

to demonstrate the need for the synthesis he was providing. His high aim seems also to have affected his view of his own results. Both his theory that the source of gastric acidity is acid phosphate of lime and that gastric digestion is a special action distinct from either a chemical transformation or an ordinary dissolution seem to reflect a desire to wipe the slate clean of old misconceptions and fill it in anew. His "difficult task" led Blondlot in his own thought as well as in his judgment of others to throw out of balance an otherwise acute insight into the problems of digestion. He pressed his results to yield not only reasonable inductions but speculative generalizations. His characterization of the changes which nutrients undergo in digestion appear to be based on empirical tests which he could perform under better conditions than anyone before him because of his technical innovation; but as one reads through them the impression grows that the results were conforming to a predetermined pattern. That pattern is perhaps most transparent in the section on starch. A similar situation was his treatment of coagulated albumin, upon which Eberle, Müller, and Schwann had principally based their arguments for a chemical conversion. Blondlot reported that when this nutrient matter was digested it separated into microscopic particles of albumin. He reported tests with nitric acid, sublimate, and infusion of gall-nuts which he considered to confirm the presence of albumin, but he made no mention of a key test which had led the other physiologists to infer that the substance disappears in digestion: that it no longer coagulated when boiled.[42] In many subsidiary questions Blondlot also exhibited a fondness for systematic and symmetrical generalizations.

The speculative bent of Blondlot's physiological ideas differed in a basic way from the speculations of the chemical schools of Liebig and of Dumas. He was not, like them, deducing the nature of processes in the organism from a knowledge of organic chemical composition and reactions or of the net exchanges between the organisms and their environments. His method was clearly to trace the actual changes which substances undergo in the animal, and he contributed to that goal. Neither did he view the problem of nutrition in wholly chemical terms. Though the digestive process itself he considered to be completely subordinate to the "general laws of chemistry," because the stomach cavity is outside of the organism, he thought that the later stages in the formation of chyle are vital processes, "submitted to the special laws of the living economy."[43] Observing that the amount of gastric juice secreted varied according to the amount and kind of aliment entering the stomach, he described the latter as having "a particular sensibility, a veritable chemical intuition which . . . permits it to judge the nutritive nature of substances placed in contact with its walls." [44] After noticing that the preliminary operations of chewing and swallowing stimulate the flow of gastric juice even before aliments reach the stomach, he emphasized the "admirable unity" of the animal economy, in which each part supports the others in intimate recipro- cal relationships. [45] Clearly Blondlot maintained a physiological orien- tation contrasting with the more exclusively chemical basis of Du- mas's conceptions. Nevertheless, Blondlot shared with Dumas the tendency to fit what he observed into a vision of simple, uniform processes occurring in animals. The manner in which Blondlot ap- proached the problem of digestion illustrates, I believe, the difficulty in separating all of those who dealt with nutritional phenomena into distinct categories of chemical theorist and experimental physiologist.

That Blondlot appeared to stand on a diffuse boundary between two schools is made more evident by the fact that the kinship between his ideas and those of Dumas turned out to be more than a general style of reasoning. Throughout the historical introduction and most of the body of his treatise, Blondlot represented his work as a continua- tion of the physiological tradition from Réaumur to Beaumont. Only on page 254 did the first fairly obvious clue appear that conceptions from elsewhere might also be guiding him. There he wrote, "Consid- ered from a general point of view there is thus a tight connection be- tween plants and animals; what the first produce, the second destroy, and from their remains the first reconstitute the composed elements to which we give the name of aliments." [46] Not until the final conclusion of his section on natural digestion, however, did he come completely out in the open. After presenting his own arguments that digestion is a division or partial dissolution without chemical transformation, he remarked that the recent discoveries of chemists have supported the view, previously opposed persistently, that all of the immediate prin- ciples of animals are found in plants, and that digestion consequently changes only their form without altering their nature. "One can espe- cially consult on that point," he said, "the brilliant Essay on the chem- ical statics of organized bodies published by Dumas." Reciting Du- mas's view that in digestion soluble materials pass into the blood while insoluble materials are divided finely enough to enter the lacteal ves- sels, Blondlot then added:

That theory, so simple, to which the author has been led by important philo- sophical considerations, is precisely that at which I have arrived myself by the route of experiment: and I confess that it is not without some satisfaction that I have seen the result of my research confirm in this way the fortunate suggestions of so distinguished a scientist.[47]

One may raise the question whether in fact Blondlot had converged independently upon Dumas's position, or whether it had influenced him from the beginning. It is not certain when he began his research, but a statement that one of the dogs he used had lived for two years [48] makes it possible that he started about the time that Dumas's essay appeared. The evidence in favor of chemical changes occurring in digestion was, of course, still questionable enough so that one would not necessarily have had to be persuaded in advance that they did not exist in order not to find them. Nevertheless, Blondlot's unqualified praise of Dumas's ideas contrasted strikingly with his critical assessment of others who had studied digestion. It would probably be futile to speculate further on the genesis and motivation of Blondlot's thought. Ironically his treatise confirming Dumas's views came out almost at the same time as Dumas himself was being forced by the outcome of his investigation with Milne Edwards to retreat into silence about them.

In the Academy of Sciences Blondlot's work aroused a lively response. On September 11, Pierre Flourens, the permanent secretary, announced the publication of the book and summarized its principal conclusions.[49] On October 2 he displayed to the assembly the results of artificial digestions performed in his own laboratory with gastric juice obtained according to the procedure of Blondlot. Flourens praised Blondlot for his service to physiologists in giving them a method for procuring abundant gastric juice at will. At the same session Payen declared that he also had repeated Blondlot's experiments, using gastric juice that the latter had furnished him. With this ample supply of juice Payen also was able to isolate from it its active principle, an objective in which he related he had failed several years before with Schwann's methods, following the visit of Valentin. The substance, which he had obtained by methods he did not describe, was so active that it could digest three hundred times its weight of beef and reacted more rapidly than gastric juice itself. He refused to call it pepsin, because, he said, it is secreted not only when the animal is fasting, but "at the moment when the aliment has stimulated the stomach." Therefore he named it *gasterase*.[50] This reason seems so unconvincing that Payen's motive for dissociating his substance from the investigations of Schwann can best be ascribed to a carry-over of the same national fervor which he was displaying at that time in the controversy with Liebig. Since this was also a period in which things were going badly for the French chemists in that debate, the scientists in the Academy must have taken some satisfaction in the belief that the work of Blondlot seemed to have returned the initiative in the investigation of digestion to France.

X

Bernard's First Theory of
Gastric Digestion

Claude Bernard was probably not in Paris when Blondlot's treatise first appeared. According to Olmsted, he went home to St. Julien during September and October, as he did almost every year, to help oversee the vintage.[1] He must have resumed his research on digestion as soon as he returned, for the first entry in his new series of experiments was dated October 1843 (the second page more specifically October 25).[2] He took up that subject again, therefore, in the wake of the interest Blondlot's experiments had created among scientists in Paris. Neither in his notes nor in his publications did Bernard state that he was moved to pursue these investigations or to modify the direction of his previous efforts because of this circumstance. The timing and nature of the new phase of his research, however, afford strong circumstantial evidence that Blondlot's book, as well as earlier investigations of digestion along the line Blondlot was continuing, had impinged significantly on Bernard's plans. His most direct response was to begin about this time to utilize the gastric fistula operation. In his M.D. thesis, presented in December, Bernard wrote that he had been able to confirm Blondlot's observations concerning the changes in the stomach lining and the collection there of drops of gastric juice at the moment aliments enter the stomach, using "dogs prepared for that purpose in the laboratory of Magendie." [3] Although he did not, during this period, describe in his notebook the preparation of a gastric fistula, he referred once to removing materials from the stomach and once to inserting a reagent into that organ through a fistula during the course of the experiments that he probably performed in October or

November. In an entry dated December 10, 1843, he mentioned utilizing a dog with a "large gastric fistula . . . 2 months old." [4] These remarks suggest, therefore, that he probably began exploiting the technique quite promptly after he heard of Blondlot's work. In these experiments he regularly used gastric juice whose source he did not record, but which most likely he obtained from such fistulas. Evidence of a further immediate influence of Blondlot is that, when describing the properties of gastric juice in his thesis, Bernard dealt with its chemical composition by simply inserting Blondlot's analysis. [5]

That Bernard was not only adopting current procedures but directing the aim of his research more closely at those problems with which Blondlot and his predecessors had been concerned is evident from the nature of the new factors which entered his investigation at this time. Several of the experiments of this period he entitled in his notebook "experiments on gastric juice." By the end of the previous spring he had already approached the idea that gastric juice was the agent of the chemical changes he had been following, but he had not yet made that fluid itself the central topic of his investigation. To do so now was in part, therefore, simply a culmination of the trend of his own work, but the way he did it implies as well a closer contact with that contemporary research which was so strongly oriented to the same topic. Bernard apparently began in the fall, for example, his first experiments using artificial digestion with gastric juice removed from the stomach. Most of his research of the past spring had involved primarily the special reagents whose products he could easily identify, whereas the new line he now began featured two of the simple alimentary substances, albumin and sugar, to which his predecessors had already given so much attention. If these changes seem to reveal that Bernard's research interests were converging toward what others were doing, he nevertheless did not simply drop his own peculiar approach or pick up the problem of digestion wholly in the manner of his contemporaries. The procedures of his new experiments retained a strong resemblance to his previous investigations. As was his habit, he modified his approach gradually rather than abruptly, adapting it to questions of the day which he seemed to have increasingly in view. It was another transition point in the pathway he followed: a compromise between the tendency, already evident, to go his own way and a growing need to absorb the efforts of others on similar problems.

Bernard's notebook indicates that in the block of experiments begun in October he worked out several problems whose results formed an important part of his medical thesis in early December. His records

leave uncertain, however, whether at the start he already had in mind
the view which he demonstrated in his thesis by means of these experiments or whether the outcome of the initial experiments may have
suggested this view.[6] His first "experiment on gastric juice" did not
literally involve that fluid at all. Bernard simply injected albumin into
the jugular vein of a rabbit; an hour and forty-five minutes later he
found, by means of nitric acid, "a fine precipitate of albumin" in the
urine. By the same test the urine of a normal rabbit showed no trace of
albumin. In parentheses Bernard added to his record of the experiment "(it would be necessary to inject albumin into the stomach of
another animal to see if the urine will contain it)." [7] Clearly, Bernard
was following a procedural plan derived from his former experiments
on the pathways along which substances are absorbed into and pass
through or out of the body. Yet the title of the experiment, as well as
subsequent events, indicates that he was already, at least to some extent, posing a different question; that by injecting an aliment directly
into the bloodstream he was seeking indirectly to ascertain the role of
digestion by seeing what would happen to a nutrient if it bypassed
that process on the way into the organism. If it did, the parenthetical
remark would mean not that Bernard was thinking only that he ought
to compare the result of injection by another route, as he had often
done before, but that he should check his finding that an undigested
nutrient is excreted from the circulation by means of a counterproof
comparing the behavior of the same nutrient digested normally. If he
expected to show that digested albumin did not pass out of the blood
in the same manner that the undigested substance did, the first experiment he undertook to that end must have been a disappointment to
him. When he injected albumin mixed with the gastric juice of a dog
into the jugular vein of a rabbit, he found fifteen minutes later a "great
quantity" of albumin in its urine. He tried again the next day, however, this time injecting albumin digested first in a stomach (possibly
then removed through the gastric fistula, though few details of this
particular experiment are recorded), and found no albumin in the
urine.[8] Then Bernard undertook a series of similar experiments apparently intended to find conditions under which he could inject
digested albumin into the blood and not have it appear in the urine.
That he sought such a situation persistently despite repeated instances
in which the outcome was the opposite or else equivocal is a good clue
that he knew from the start what he wished to prove by these experiments, and that he was determined that they fulfill his expectations.
One of his early successes resulted from mixing the albumin digested

in the stomach of a dog with bile and soda to neutralize it, before injecting the resulting solution into a rabbit. After two hours the urine contained no trace of albumin, whereas the same quantity of liquid albumin when injected directly into the vein caused albumin to appear in the excretion.[9] This result evidently led Bernard to do further comparative experiments to determine which of the conditions had rendered the albumin capable of remaining within the organism. Repeating the preceding procedure together with one in which he did everything the same except that he omitted the soda, so that the injected solution remained acidic, he found in the former case no albumin in the urine and in the latter a small amount. Since he had also recently observed that acidic gastric juice injected by itself into an animal made it very sick, he concluded that it must be the acidity of the digested albumin not neutralized by soda which "produces accidents and perhaps allows a little albumin to pass." Again he digested blood in the stomach of a dog, removed it through the fistula, neutralized it with bile and soda, and injected it; and again no trace of albumin appeared in the urine. Bernard regarded it as confirmed, therefore, that an essential condition for the latter result was that the liquid must be alkaline when injected.[10] The action of bile also appeared necessary, however, for when he performed the experiment omitting that fluid the urine contained "much albumin." He wrote, "Conclusion: the gastric juice thus does not suffice to dissolve the albumin. Also necessary is bile, which probably separates the parts not combined with the gastric juice."[11] Additional experiments of the same kind supported his opinion. Bernard appeared to be contemplating a theory of digestion which would involve bile as an agent essential to help prepare albumin for its assimilation into the blood. In the experiments previously noted, bile had usually precipitated some material from the digested nutrient. Now he turned to study that phenomenon in more detail, comparing the reactions of bile with pure gastric juice, gastric juice mixed with liquid albumin, pure liquid albumin, serum, and slightly acidified albumin. The observation that bile seemed to precipitate all of the albumin from the acid solution, whereas "if there had been an action of the stomach, not everything would be precipitated," strengthened his opinion that bile may precipitate from a mixture of aliment and gastric juice everything which has not combined with the latter.[12] Incorporated in these conjectures was a conception he had already expressed during his spring research, that the essential action of gastric juice is to combine directly with substances in the stomach. This was a conception quite different from that of the followers of Schwann.

Apparently Bernard did not follow the direction in which these observations and ideas would seem to be leading him—that is, to consider that bile plays an indispensable role in the digestive process or to investigate its action further. Instead he must have inferred that the problem was to produce a complete reaction between the aliment and the gastric juice so that nothing would remain to be either precipitated by the bile or excreted in the urine. If so, his response was probably conditioned by the persistence of his earlier belief that the stomach is the principal site of the chemical reactions of the body. If this interpretation is valid it would explain the fact that in his next experiments he prepared albumin by artificial digestion in gastric juice, emphasizing more than previously the proportions of aliment and juice, the time and the temperature at which he carried it out; and that he then injected the resulting material without first subjecting it to the further operations with bile or alkali which he had previously been investigating. By such means he began to attain results more favorable to his views; in several trials the albumin digested in such a way did not appear in the urine, whereas that substance treated comparably in distilled water did.[13] His records show that even then the results occasionally came out contrary to what he was seeking, and the incompleteness of the notes at this point leaves in doubt how Bernard finally came to satisfy himself of the conclusion he stated at the end of this series:

> Coagulated albumin dissolved in gastric juice does not pass into the urine.
> Uncooked albumin dissolved in distilled water in the same quantity passes into the urine.[14]

Bernard seems to have gone to a great deal of trouble to create conditions under which the distinction he wished to make could be verified.

So far, the investigation had centered on the physiological consequences of gastric digestion. Along the way, however, Bernard observed a few clues concerning the chemical nature of the process itself. He noticed, for example, that albumin dissolved in gastric juice lost the property of being coagulated by heat, but retained that of being precipitated by nitric acid. Since he relied mostly on the latter reaction as the test for albumin, he did not define this alteration, as some chemists might have, as a conversion of albumin to something else. A little later he noticed that gastric juice could become saturated with a substance so that it would not dissolve anything more.[15] This observation undoubtedly encouraged him in his view that a chemical combination occurs between the juice and the aliment. A novel way of investigating the combining properties of gastric juice was inherent in

an observation he had already made eight months before. After placing iron filings in the stomach for a reaction he expected between the
iron and potassium ferrocyanide, he had noticed that the acid of the
stomach itself acted upon the metal.[16] Soon after returning to his
research in October, he had introduced copper filings and iron chromate into the stomach of a dog and after opening that organ noticed
that some of the copper had been dissolved, whereas some metallic
iron was present. The purpose of this experiment, which he combined
with injection of albumin into the blood, is not clear from Bernard's
notes. Perhaps he wished to ascertain whether copper would displace
iron from a salt in the presence of gastric juice.[17] Somewhat later,
however, he drew from such scattered observations of the behavior of
metals in the stomach a plan for studying more deliberately the reactions of gastric juice itself. He placed portions of the juice in contact
respectively with lead, copper, and potassium ferrocyanide, then
maintained the tubes containing each under the conditions of an ordinary artificial digestion. With the lead, gastric juice apparently
formed some soluble salt, for the acid was partially neutralized and he
afterward separated lead from the solution by means of potassium
chromate. Copper also dissolved, the gastric juice combining completely with it, he thought, because the resulting solution was neutral.
Treated with potassium ferrocyanide, this solution changed color but
did not form a precipitate, as copper combined with an ordinary mineral acid would. "Therefore," Bernard remarked, "the salts of gastric
juice, the gastrates, are salts which behave differently" from the salts
of mineral acids. Thus he tended to think of the products of gastric action as a distinctive class of definite compounds. The gastric juice
reacted with ferrocyanide produced hydrocyanic acid, apparently by
displacing the latter from its base. Afterward he carried out similar experiments with platinum, iron, and silver. From such reactions Bernard concluded that gastric juice exerts an extraordinarily intense
chemical action and that it is a peculiar acid, dissolving everything,
more powerful than sulfuric acid.[18] Because of his particular opinion
that gastric juice forms combinations with aliments in digestion Bernard probably felt that there was a closer parallel between these reactions which form salts and the ordinary physiological action of the
juice than most of his contemporaries would have thought. Such an
analogy, for example, did not fit into the conceptions of Schwann, or
even of Blondlot, who also considered the active principle of gastric
juice to operate by contact rather than by entering an ordinary chemical combination with aliments.

Meanwhile, Bernard continued with his investigation of the comparative effects of injecting digested and undigested aliments into the circulation. The general procedures he had worked out for albumin he now applied to sugar, aided for the first time, so far as the record shows, by the chemist Charles-Louis Barreswil. Bernard did not rely on the usual test for sugar of observing whether a solution would ferment. He used the much more convenient method Barreswil had recently devised, in which sugar, if present, reduces cupric tartrate to the insoluble cuprous oxide. (If the sugar were cane sugar—that is, sucrose—it had first to be converted to glucose, or grape sugar, by adding a small amount of sulfuric acid.) This collaboration with the man who had been serving as the chief assistant to Pelouze does not firmly establish that Bernard was already doing his research on nutritional problems in Pelouze's laboratory, because, as Schiller has pointed out, Barreswil became a *préparateur* for Magendie at just about this time.[19]

After injecting a solution saturated with grape sugar into the circulation of a dog, Bernard found sugar in the urine. The following day he injected into another dog sugar digested first for six hours in gastric juice. The record in his notebook does not show whether in this attempt he obtained the result which he ultimately attained, that digested sugar did not pass into the urine whereas undigested sugar did.[20] There is some evidence that in a subsequent experiment he ran into the same sort of inconsistencies that he had encountered with albumin. Having injected one gram of sugar in fifteen cc. of water into a large rabbit and found sugar in the urine afterward, he repeated the experiment the next day, except that he added five decigrams of sodium carbonate to the solution which he injected. The second time the urine did "not show the least trace of sugar." Bernard remarked only that "this experiment is curious." Two days later he injected a solution of grape sugar into the subcutaneous connective tissue of the same rabbit, a procedure apparently intended to permit the substance to enter the blood gradually, and again found none in the urine.[21] Somehow in later experiments he must have manipulated the conditions, as he did with albumin, until he reached the outcome he sought, but these efforts have not been preserved in his notebook.

The experiment involving subcutaneous injection stimulated Bernard to consider the possibility of studying a deeper aspect of nutrition than the question on which he was engaged. He had repeated the procedure using cane sugar instead of grape sugar, but the animal died accidentally. "That last experiment should be redone," he remarked.

"It will be a means to cause cane sugar and grape sugar to reach the blood little by little in order to observe their transformation if that really takes place for the two sugars or only for cane sugar. It is known that cane sugar . . . makes lactic acid." [22] Bernard was already thinking about ways in which he might begin to trace the changes nutrients undergo within the organism after they have entered the blood.

On December 7, 1843, Bernard presented his thesis for the Doctorate in Medicine to the Faculty of Medicine of Paris. He probably had not carried out a major research effort especially for this requirement, but picked out what he could knit together around a particular subject from the work that he had been doing over the preceding year. He had been assigned to study the mucous membranes of animals at different ages of life, but he submitted instead a dissertation on "The Gastric Juice and Its Role in Nutrition." Rather lamely he explained that after gathering material on the assigned topic for four months he had found it too broad and therefore had restricted himself to a limited aspect of that problem, the mucus of the stomach and its functions. [23] This was a real, but somewhat forced, connection between what he had done and what he was supposed to do. Olmsted has described Bernard's graduation in medicine itself as a rather casual event, since he did not intend to practice. [24] Perhaps, therefore, both parties regarded the official topic as a formality. If his thesis was in some sense a makeshift, it was nevertheless a culmination of the research and of a trend of thought which Bernard had been developing ever since he began his studies of the chemical phenomena in animals.

Although few of the experiments described in his thesis appear to be exactly the ones preserved in Bernard's laboratory notebook, most of them represent refinements of the general lines of investigation revealed in the notes. The dissertation fell into two distinct parts. The first section derived primarily from the research of the preceding spring involving potassium ferrocyanide and salts of iron, whereas the second part was based on the experiments Bernard had pursued in the last two months. The parts dealt with two distinct though related problems, which he sought to integrate through a preliminary discussion of the problem of what chymification is and what the active principle of gastric juice is. This discussion included his first public statement concerning some of the main themes we have been following:

In brief, is chymification only a simple solution of aliments, or does there also occur, through the influence of gastric juice, in the materials contained in the stomach certain molecular modifications, which are only the beginning of further mutations which they are destined to undergo in our tissues?

Almost all of the chemists have accepted simple solution. They regard the gastric juice as a dissolving agent which does nothing but separate the molecules of solid aliments, without modifying them, to enable them to pass into the absorptive pathways.

In thus equating the power of gastric juice with that of a chemical solvent whose action would begin and end in the stomach, the partisans of solution have given that fluid a completely secondary role in digestion, because its action would, so to speak, be substituted for and become useless every time the substances ingested had previously been made liquid and capable of being absorbed directly: they have, in that way, completely separated chymification from the other phenomena of nutrition.

Aligning ourselves with the opposite opinion, we think that so restricted an interpretation of chymification is inadequate for physiology.

Indeed, in spite of the efforts of the most distinguished chemists on that subject, the chymifying liquid cannot yet be replaced by any other of the solvents with which one has tried to compare it.

Pushing physiological experimentation further than has been done, we shall attempt to demonstrate that there is in chymification something more than a solution or a simple catalysis.

For that reason, occupying a different vantage point from the partisans of solution, we shall not limit ourselves to determining how the aliments are dissolved in the stomach, but we shall particularly seek to establish under what conditions they can be metamorphosed in the blood and serve for the general phenomena of nutrition.[25]

We have already seen that from the beginning both Bernard's methods and his ideas about the role of the stomach had been leading him in a different direction from the conceptions of those chemists to whom he was obviously referring here. Earlier he had followed a rather insulated course, although he was conscious all along in general terms of the difference between his way and theirs. Now he was ready to bring his views into direct confrontation with theirs over the central issue of whether digestion is a process of solution or of chemical transformation. He raised his challenge not only on this specific question, but on a more fundamental one—which scientific discipline was the proper base for solving such problems—for by identifying with chemists the theory he opposed, and by terming their theory inadequate for physiology, he was implying that the criteria of chemistry itself were insufficient to resolve a question which he was claiming to be within the province of physiology. Actually, of course, the solution theory of digestion was not supported so exclusively by chemists as Bernard indicated here, since Blondlot as well as earlier physiologists had also characterized the process as predominantly one of dissolving the aliments. Nor were all chemists partisans of the solution theory, or even involved in the question. That Bernard nevertheless described the theory as the view of "almost all of the chemists" suggests that he tended to equate the most prominent school of chemistry in Paris, that of Dumas, with chemistry itself, and that he must have felt that the influence of that school was behind current expressions of similar conceptions by physiologists.

The first and longest part of Bernard's thesis did not address itself directly to the issue he had raised in his introduction. Rather it was a series of anatomical and experimental arguments concerning the origin and "physiological nature" of gastric juice. Because he thought that there were no glands in the stomach lining except for those which produce mucus, Bernard contended that gastric juice was not a glandular secretion, but was formed by certain materials in the blood which diffused directly by "exhibition" from the capillary networks of the villae in the interior surface of the stomach. He sought to verify his deduction by showing that an afflux of blood to the stomach causes an immediate flow of juice. He opened the stomach of a dog, then isolated the coeliac artery, all of whose branches except those supplying the stomach he had tied off. Just after killing the animal he injected blood from another animal into the artery at normal arterial pressure. The mucous lining became colored and turgid, as in digestion, and an acidic fluid exuded from its surface. Unfortunately, Bernard could not collect enough of it to ascertain whether or not it had the other properties of gastric juice. For further support of his view he adduced experiments using potassium ferrocyanide and a salt of iron, taken either from his research of the past spring or from variations on those experiments carried out in the fall, now evidently adapted to settle a question different from what he had had in mind during the original investigations. By his usual procedure of injecting the ferrocyanide into a vein and finding out by means of the Prussian blue reaction where it penetrated, he could show that when an animal was in digestion the ferrocyanide passed very quickly into the stomach but not into any of the other secretions. In a fasting animal the substance did not enter the stomach. From these results Bernard could confirm that gastric juice is formed by an emanation of materials directly from the blood.[26] During one of these experiments performed in the fall, Bernard was surprised to find that the blue coloration on the surface of the mucous lining did not extend into the interior of the tissue. At first he could not understand why the salts would not combine within the tissue itself, and ascribed the situation to the state of suffering of the animal.[27] But when further experiments brought similar results he turned the observations to good account, inferring from them in his thesis that gastric juice does not become acid until the moment it has poured out onto the free surface of the mucous lining. The cause of stomach acidity he ascribed, therefore, to a separation of some elements in the blood which the mucus brings about.[28]

What were separated out of the blood, Bernard believed, were the acids contained in it. He accepted the analyses of Tiedemann and Gmelin and others as having established that gastric juice contains lactic, butyric, acetic, phosphoric, and hydrochloric acids, all of which he contended are present in the blood. He said that he had injected each of these acids into the blood and found it afterward in the stomach; he had also injected salts such as iron lactate or butyrate and found the acid in the stomach, the base in the urine. The separation of the acids from the bases with which they are combined in the blood and the passage of the acids into the stomach, he concluded, "is in fact the veritable explanation of the production, so unique, of gastric juice." [29] This point of view, fixed exclusively on the general acidity of gastric juice as its characteristic property, was a logical continuation of the trend of thought Bernard had been following all along, yet in the face of the recent work of other physiologists it was a remarkably one-sided description. He did recognize that Schwann, Müller, and others considered the active agent of digestion to reside in a special material, pepsin, but he mentioned their views merely as illustrative of the diversity of opinion existing with regard to the nature of gastric juice. Failing, like Blondlot, to appreciate the historical progression of research on the problem, Bernard balanced off their view and Payen's *gasterase* against the belief of Tiedemann and Gmelin that the solvent properties derive from gastric acids, and assumed apparently that he was free to choose among such alternatives according to his own experience.[30] Clearly, even though on one former occasion he had used pepsin in an experiment, Claude Bernard had not yet assimilated the full significance of the pepsin theory.

The limited effect which the contribution of Schwann had had on Bernard's thought up until this point may also reflect a general incompleteness in his knowledge of contemporary German research at the time. His thesis provides other evidence also of his unfamiliarity with the new German literature on digestion. In his discussion of the anatomy of the stomach lining, he wrote that, except for "mucous crypts" common to that organ and the intestines, "no one has ever been able to discover in the villous membrane of the stomach" glands which might secrete gastric juice. There were, however, he noted, some peculiar corpuscles described recently by "M. Gruby," who had shown them under the microscope to Bernard. Bernard believed that these corpuscles must play a part in the formation of gastric juice; [31] but in Germany, as mentioned previously, Purkyně and Pappenheim, and Wasmann had each discovered by microscopic observations some glands which they regarded as the probable source of gastric juice. [32] Bernard did not refute these claims, he simply seemed not to know of them. David Gruby, to whom Bernard was referring, was a Hungarian who came to Paris and opened one of the first private courses in microscopy there in 1841, and Bernard was among his students. [33] Thus it was on the work of the man with whom he had a direct, personal association that Bernard depended primarily for his knowledge of the problem. The incident illustrates an early tendency, which I believe remained characteristic of Bernard, to respond more strongly to influences from within his own circle of Parisian scientists than to those from abroad; to obtain ideas more from his own experience or from others with whom he could discuss problems directly, than from the formal scientific literature. In a letter he wrote many years later to his friend Madame Raffalovich he asserted that his habit of working was to search always to understand things first as he could perceive them for himself and only afterward to read what had been written on the same subject. [34] Although he was obviously idealizing his approach in this description, the account seems to fit the general manner in which his research proceeded. His preference was both a strength and a weakness. His reliance on his own resources and judgment, together with his willingness to reassess his course when he encountered unexpected results and his tenacious pursuit of a problem until he felt he had resolved it, accounts for much of the success and originality of his work. Yet when he avoided reading widely in the publications concerning a problem in which he was interested, he did not merely, as he believed, free himself from forming his opinions under the influence of others. [35] He also incurred the risk of ignoring contributions which made the problem different from what he imagined it to be; and since he was less protected from the opinions of others than he professed to Madame Raffalovich that this procedure made him, he allowed the influences on him to be less under his control. He was more likely to be swayed by the accidental circumstances of what people he happened to know, and of what ideas were most prominently discussed in Paris. He would have been more rather than less independent if he had absorbed more systematically the work of his colleagues, especially those in Germany. At the time he wrote his thesis, he might have been less likely to attribute to chemists in general the views of digestion which were evidently those of the French chemists around Dumas. Bernard was, of course, not entirely out of touch with German physiology. Although when he was older he asked Madame Raffalovich to translate for him certain prominent physiological treatises which he had not read because they were in German,[36] he made efforts to learn that language in his early years and carefully translated for himself some crucial German writings.[37] Nevertheless, it is evident that he shared some of that provincialism which caused French scientists at times to overlook key advances which their foreign counterparts were making. Bernard's scientific outlook as well as his personal life was almost wholly centered in Paris.

The second part of Bernard's thesis was relatively short, even though it contained the work most relevant to the general problem he had defined in his introduction. He entitled it rather grandly "The Role which Gastric Juice is Destined to Fill in Nutrition." He began with a tacit admission that his view of the way in which gastric juice acts was unproven. "It is certain," he said, "that nothing authorizes one yet to say that the chyme is a combination of gastric acids with alimentary materials." He observed that "chemistry does not concede that gastric juice exerts a chemical action," because the nature of the action could not yet be specified. Bernard admitted also that he himself could not establish the chemical nature of its action on aliments, but he wished merely to show that there is such an action and that it is different from simple solution. To do this he relied chiefly on one of the series of experiments he had carried out on the reaction of gastric juice with metals. The digestive juice attacked iron with effervescence, and among the notable effects was a neutralization, or at least a decrease in acidity. The strongest parallel which he could adduce with the action of gastric juice on aliments is that when albumin dissolves in gastric juice the acidity also decreases.[38] Bernard's conviction was stronger than his argument, for, as we have already seen, it was only an assumption, and one which was incompatible with some of the important observations of his colleagues, that the action of gastric juice on food is closely analogous to the action of the acids of that juice on metals.

To demonstrate that the action of gastric juice he had tried to characterize is essential for the further steps of nutrition, Bernard utilized his injection experiments with albumin and sugar. He described them briefly, revealing no hint that he had had to try many variations of the procedures before he could attain the perfectly consistent results he reported. In each of four dogs in which he injected undigested albumin into the jugular vein he found albumin in the urine by both the test of nitric acid and of coagulation when boiled. When each of the four animals received in its blood artificially digested albumin, whether the latter was at first liquid or coagulated, none appeared in the urine. He obtained equally favorable results on one dog using cane sugar and on two dogs with grape sugar. The action of gastric juice, he could therefore claim, was necessary to render an aliment susceptible to being "decomposed in the blood" rather than to being simply eliminated from it. This result he posed as a new definition of a nutritive substance. "Thus, in order that the gastric juice render a substance assimilable, it is not sufficient that it be dissolved by that fluid; it is necessary, in addition, that that substance disappear entirely in the blood." [39]

As a transition between the two main sections of his thesis Bernard summarized his general conception of digestion:

By placing in this way in every individual an acidifying organ, nature has given them a foyer or a source from which all organic animal combinations derive.

. . . After having abandoned their undoubtedly "spent" [*épuisées*] combinations in the blood, all of the acids which by their assemblage constitute the gastric juice come into the stomach and form new combinations there with the aliments, and it is from that condition alone that the alimentary materials introduced into the circulation become fitted to serve for the further phenomena of combustion or of decomposition which occur in the blood.[40]

This passage reveals clearly that the conclusions Bernard presented about digestion in his thesis were not entirely the consequences of the experiments he produced in support of them, but the development of preconceptions which we have seen that he had when he began his investigations. The idea that the stomach is one of two types of places in the body where chemical combinations occur was one of the terse generalizations he put down at the start.[41] As he came to focus on the properties of gastric juice he projected onto that substance the same characteristics that he had earlier attributed to the stomach. His experiments during the fall seemed to support his opinion, but the evidence was indirect and woven into a framework toward which he was predisposed.

The last clause of the above quotation indicates that, despite his effort to be independent of the chemists, Bernard's conception of the underlying nature of nutritional phenomena was still heavily influenced by them. His assumption that the further metamorphoses of aliments comprised combustion and decomposition reactions in the blood was undoubtedly a reflection of Dumas's theory of animal nutrition.

Bernard's medical thesis provides a good measure of the progress he had made during his first full year of research into the chemical phenomena of life. Obviously he had not yet mastered all of the important aspects of the problem as it existed at the time he began. Seeking to substantiate a peculiar view of digestion, he did not take into account in any profound way some of the most impressive recent advances in the state of that question. His chemical methods, with the exception of the test for sugar, were relatively uncomplicated compared to those his contemporaries were using: he relied, for example, on one or two tests to identify albumin, out of the series of reagents usually applied to distinguish the various nitrogenous "principles" from one another. The logic of his case was not tight and his evidence could probably not have led him to his conclusions without a prior belief in them. Nevertheless, Bernard had shrewdly and perceptively found a way to cut through a crucial impasse in the understanding of digestion. Observing that the issue of whether or not chemical transformations occur in digestion did not appear resolvable by the criteria of chemistry because the nature of the processes could not be sufficiently defined in chemical terms, he sought to prove by physiological criteria that chemical changes not only occur but are vital. Burdach had already pointed out that even if chemistry could demonstrate that some alimentary substances are converted to others in the stomach, that alone would not demonstrate that the changes were meaningful to the organism. Bernard's endeavor can be viewed as a means of circumventing, or perhaps justifying, Burdach's objection. Bernard wished to prove that whatever the nature of the changes might turn out to be they were essential to the organism. His approach was relevant yet unorthodox at a time when most of his contemporaries were following up previously explored modes of handling the problem. Part of his originality can be ascribed to native ingenuity and independence; part also derived from the fact that the routines he learned at first were those designed not for the study of digestion but of absorption. As he made his way from one question to the other, the techniques and point of view he brought with him enabled him to make a fresh attack on the problems he saw there.

We have seen that Bernard associated with the chemists the doctrine that digestion is solution, and presented his own view of the
problem as that of physiology. Since he contended throughout his career that his approach represented the proper relation between physiology and chemistry in the investigation of vital phenomena, it is helpful to examine what he seemed to mean by physiological experimentation on the first occasion in which he publicly took this
position. Clearly the distinction to which he alluded did not lie in the
nature of the explanation of the phenomenon, for he went beyond the
chemists themselves in his desire to establish that digestion is a chemical process. One might infer more plausibly that the crucial factor was
the means by which he investigated the phenomenon; for, unlike the
chemists, he utilized experiments in which he traced digestive actions
within living animals. Yet those experiments which impinged most directly on what he defined as the central issue, that is, those by which
he tried to demonstrate that gastric juice exerts a chemical action,
were most like the experiments chemists did. Bernard tested the properties of gastric juice isolated from animals; instead of reacting it directly with nutrient materials, he tested it with metals and then reasoned by analogy to natural processes, as chemists often did. His
assertion that he had dealt by physiological means with the question
he had posed does not therefore seem fully verified by what he had actually done. Perhaps he had in mind already an ideal which he had not
yet attained. More likely he had not himself closely analysed the general issue. His conviction that his investigations were physiological in
character was probably prior to the particular methods and conceptions he brought to bear on this problem, and arose undoubtedly in
large part from his association with other people who represented the
field of physiology. That he was following a pre-eminently physiological approach was best certified by the fact that his investigation
had grown out of experiments performed under the guidance of
Magendie, whom Bernard described in the dedication of his thesis as
"the leader of the school of experimental physiology." [42] There were
others also with whom Bernard might have identified himself. His
ideas, for example, had an interesting resemblance to those of Burdach, who stressed repeatedly the primacy of biological factors in phenomena involving chemical processes. Burdach, like Bernard, had insisted that digestion must not be considered apart from other
processes in the body, but as a preparation for the further changes
which nutrients undergo in the blood. Burdach, too, rejected the idea
of simple solution on such grounds, and Bernard could well have

derived from Burdach's treatise the argument that, if digestion were no more than that, it would be unnecessary whenever liquid aliments were used.[43]

In his thesis Bernard had publicly challenged "almost all of the chemists," a rather august group for a young scientist submitting his inaugural dissertation to take on. Undoubtedly the implied threat to their position did not seriously disturb the chemists at whom it was aimed, even though Bernard's thesis was thought important enough to be reprinted in two French journals.[44] They had not been shaken earlier in the year when the more commanding figure of Magendie directly admonished them, and they were confronted by the end of 1843 with more formidable difficulties arising from within their own terms of debate. Bernard recognized, however, that he was still at the beginning, that he had challenged himself to continue the search for interpretations of nutrition adequate to physiology. Recognizing also, perhaps, that he was running into technical chemical problems too complex to handle by himself, he asked Barreswil to join with him as he continued.[45] As Olmsted and Schiller have emphasized, he had taken his first definitive step along a pathway which eventually placed him in a position to mount far more imposing challenges.[46] The year 1843 was crucial to Bernard in the same sense that Henry Guerlac has so aptly shown 1772 to have been a crucial year for Antoine Lavoisier.[47]

XI

Bernard and Barreswil in a Busy Field

Over the next four years Bernard pursued diligently the problems he had set for himself in his thesis. During the first half of this time he made no more public criticisms of the ideas or methods of the chemists. He had proposed for himself a highly ambitious goal on the basis of a few suggestive experiments open to other interpretations than that which he gave them. Afterward, perhaps, he became more conscious of the distance he still had to go to prove that his own way was viable before he would be able to reiterate his claims for its advantages over competing ways. At first he attempted simply to extend his results, using the methods and conceptions embodied in his thesis. Inexorably, however, he was forced to modify both. One by one the ideas comprising the general scheme of digestion he had presented proved untenable and he quietly dropped them. Sometimes it was his own research which contradicted his earlier ideas, but he was also forced to move closer to the theories and approaches of his contemporaries working on the same problems. The study of digestion continued to be a focus of interest in the Academy, and in spite of his preference for working things out for himself, Bernard could not follow his own path unaffected by the developments there; instead, his investigations were increasingly interacting in a tight network of mutual influences with his colleagues. Still striving to understand the underlying general character of digestion and nutrition, he conceived of broad new theories as often as his old ones collapsed. Most of these were evanescent, for his accumulating experience was making it more difficult for him to pose generalizations which he could not disprove by further experiments. Those to which he and Barreswil were rash enough to commit themselves in print met crippling criticisms from the others in their field, who were at the same time promulgating their own similarly vulnerable theories.

Meanwhile, Bernard and Barreswil, and their colleagues as well, were making significant observations about specific aspects of digestion. The several papers which the two collaborators published in 1844, 1845, and 1846 did not place them in the forefront of this activity, for older men like Bouchardat and Sandras, Mialhe and Lassaigne, were still making studies which went closer to the central problems of digestion. Through the four years, in fact, during which Bernard focused his efforts on gastric digestion, he made no major discovery concerning that topic itself. Neither did he have, for much of that time, a stable professional position by which to support himself or assure himself a place to carry out his research. Nevertheless these were the years in which Bernard was maturing as a scientist, gradually gaining control over a problem which he had at first tried to conquer with a quick thrust at what he took to be its crucial point. As he went, the experience he gained for himself was more important than the immediate contributions he made. Repeatedly he uncovered leads suggesting related lines of work from which his well-known discoveries later unfolded. Tenaciously he laid the groundwork for the achievements which seemed to come to him so easily a few years later.

Bernard and Barreswil lost no time getting started on their program of extending the approach of Bernard's thesis to other nutrients, for they began their review of the nutritive properties of "the two classes of nitrogenous or non-nitrogenous aliments" even before he presented his thesis for his degree.[1] Echoing the ubiquitous influence of the report of the Gelatin Commission, they first applied Bernard's new definition of a nutritive substance to see whether or not gelatin was an aliment. In their first experiment Bernard himself ate 20 grams of gelatin. Two hours later he found a trace of gelatin in his urine, four and six hours afterward he detected it in abundance. Next, they injected gelatin into a dog and found the substance in its urine also. When Barreswil ate gelatin they did not at first obtain any from his urine, but by the heroic measure of dining on nothing but a liter of bouillon of beef hooves he was able to produce some effect. A third human subject more cooperatively passed copious amounts of the substance. As a check, each man dined also on pure egg albumin and found no sign of it in his urine (except for one anomalous instance caused again by the troublesome constitution of Barreswil). Meanwhile, they were consistently finding gelatin excreted when they injected it into dogs. While they were at it they repeated one of the experiments of the Gelatin Commission itself, maintaining a dog as long as possible on an exclusively gelatin diet. The animal lived forty-four days, but grew steadily thinner. Perhaps Bernard did not so completely trust his new criterion of nutritional value as to dispense entirely with Magendie's straightforward old standard. He and Barreswil also digested gelatin in the stomach of a dog with a fistula, removed the resulting substance and injected it into another dog. Presumably the latter excreted the gelatin, although the laboratory notebook does not indicate the outcome.[2]

One probable manifestation of the experience Barreswil was bringing to bear on the joint effort is that Bernard's notebook began to include experiments designed to select the most effective chemical procedures for the tests he was utilizing. To detect gelatin in urine Bernard and Barreswil relied at first on precipitating with zinc sulfate, dissolving the precipitate in hydrochloric acid, and precipitating again with tannin (tincture of gall-nuts). After comparing other procedures, however, they decided that they could attain the best results by substituting barium nitrate for zinc sulfate. However, it was necessary, they noted, always to make an immediate comparison between the urine before and after the gelatin was fed or injected in order to detect the sensible differences directly.[3]

The twenty-one experiments Bernard and Barreswil performed on the nutritive character of gelatin apparently took them from the end of November 1843 until mid-April of 1844. While they were engaged on the research, the gelatin question flared up again in the Academy of Sciences. On March 11 the members heard a report from the Royal Institute of the Netherlands. Noting that the Gelatin Commission in Paris had left in doubt whether the substance might serve as a nutritive supplement to other food, a commission appointed by the Dutch Institute had in 1842 and 1843 tested various combinations of bread and gelatin on dogs. Judging nutritional value solely by the criterion of weight changes in the animals, the commissioners found that in no case did the gelatin either augment a weight gain or diminish a loss in comparison with an identical diet without the gelatin. They concluded that gelatin has "no nourishing properties," even in combination with other substances. Reports of these results immediately appeared in the press, and caused D'Arcet to address a letter to the French Academy questioning the validity of the results. D'Arcet noted that a Dutch professor had also expressed disapproval of the investigation. He then communicated letters from the latter to the meeting of March 25, prompting Joseph Gay-Lussac to ask why the French Academy, which had first taken up the question, was leaving to other scientific institutions the responsibility to resolve it. He queried Thenard, president of the Gelatin Commission, about when that body would be able to continue its work. Thenard "explained the obstacles" which had held up the report of the commission and announced that it would meet before the next session of the Academy to decide on what measures to take in order to follow out its plan of experiments.[4]

The meeting of the commission must not have produced any agreement, for at the next gathering of the Academy Magendie submitted his resignation from the investigative body. He explained that he had long before reached the opinion that gelatin was worthless as a nutrient, the previous experiments of the commission having left no doubt in his mind. Out of regard for a colleague on the commission, however, he had felt restrained from freely expressing his view. That colleague was undoubtedly D'Arcet. Feeling now at liberty to speak, Magendie stated that the commission had proved not only that gelatin lacks all nutritive properties, but that it acts as a kind of ferment, spoiling the good bouillon into which it is mixed. "The Academy," he continued, "has already delayed too long from pronouncing its judgment on a question which affects the poor and the sick. It must no longer allow to persist a doubt by the aid of which one continues in some places in France and Europe to impose gelatin on convalescents in the hospitals in place of other truly beneficial aliments." [5] Because Thenard was absent, Magendie was persuaded to postpone his resignation, but his action apparently brought the whole matter to a halt.[6]

This episode undoubtedly spurred Bernard and Barreswil on as they continued to apply their unique approach to the gelatin question. On April 14 they were ready to perform definitive "weight-by-weight" comparative experiments between the effects of injecting gelatin dissolved in water and gelatin mixed with gastric juice. Injecting five decigrams of the material in each state respectively into two dogs of the same size, they found that the precipitate of gelatin in both cases was sensibly the same. The next day in Pelouze's laboratory they repeated Bernard's earlier experiment on the injection of cane sugar into rabbits and confirmed his previous conclusion that only the undigested aliment is excreted, in contrast to the outcome with gelatin.[7] This is apparently the earliest research Bernard explicitly recorded as having taken place in Pelouze's laboratory. By then Barreswil had returned to his position as chief assistant to Pelouze, after his short stint with Magendie. It is possible that Barreswil's move, coming just after Bernard had begun to collaborate with him at the Collège de France, helped induce Bernard to spend part of his time in Pelouze's laboratory in order to facilitate their continued efforts together. Whatever the initial occasion might have been, Bernard soon became, as a contemporary source put it, "an assiduous guest" in that establishment. As we have seen, Pelouze had recently become so interested in physiological chemistry that he hoped to take it up himself. He must therefore have welcomed the opportunity to aid with his own chemical experience and facilities a person who could bring to that subject the physiological experience he himself lacked. Pelouze was at the time maintaining a well-equipped private laboratory on the rue Guenégaud. It accommodated up to twelve students, although some of the places were ordinarily filled by people who, like Bernard, were carrying out their own independent research.[8]

Bernard and Barreswil still had not reached the final results of their investigation of gelatin at the end of the series of experiments preserved in his notebook, but they must have finished up very quickly, for they sent their conclusions to the Academy of Sciences in a brief memoir the following week. They introduced their study by repeating Bernard's definition of an aliment and his idea of using gastric digestion to test individual substances. The results they presented again seemed considerably more regular than the actual course of research had been.

They summarized only one set of comparative experiments in which they had injected into three different dogs 5 decigrams each of undigested albumin, cane sugar, and gelatin, then repeated the series with the three substances artificially digested. All of the undigested aliments appeared in the urine, whereas of the digested substances only gelatin did. Although Bernard had begun the research with a direct feeding experiment on himself, he and Barreswil presented such experiments as only confirming the results of the artificial digestions. Gelatin, their conclusion implied, was not a nutrient after all, since it alone appeared constantly in the excrements, whereas after digestion the others "disappear into the economy."[9] Whether or not the interpretations the two young assistants of Magendie made of their observations were influenced by the stand he had just taken concerning gelatin, they must have been gratified to be able to present what appeared to be unqualified support for his position.

In spite of their claim that they had found a "simple procedure, easily executed," for determining if a substance is alimentary,[10] Bernard and Barreswil seem not to have followed any further this line of investigation which Bernard had intended to extend to all aliments. The result they reported for gelatin ironically fulfilled just the condition that Liebig had admitted to Pelouze two years before would force him to concede that gelatin is not nutritive.[11] I have not seen any indication that Liebig noticed their memoir or its implications for his own thought.

Simultaneously with the experiments on gelatin Bernard carried out an investigation of the influence of the pneumogastric nerves on digestion. Since the result appeared under his name alone it was evidently not a joint project with Barreswil. Nevertheless, the notebook shows that Barreswil was cooperating with him on the chemical tests involved. Sometimes Bernard did the analyses first and then Barreswil repeated them. These entries imply that Bernard was not content to divide up such experiments into a physiological aspect which he could manage and a chemical aspect which he would leave to Barreswil, but that he was taking advantage of their collaboration to teach himself how to handle the chemistry. The notebook also suggests that in these "experiments on the pneumo-gastric," what Bernard probably hoped at first to do was to utilize his own physiological definition of digestion—that is, the preparatory action essential to enable a nutriment to disappear within the animal—as a test of whether or not severing those nerves abolishes digestion. In the first two experiments he injected cane sugar into the stomachs of dogs which had undergone such an operation and then searched for sugar in the blood and urine. In the second case he found cane sugar in the urine, but in subsequent experiments the animals did not produce enough urine to test. Whether the plan proved impractical for this or some other reason, he relied afterward on more conventional means to ascertain the effects on digestion of cutting the nerves; generally he inspected directly the alterations caused in the stomach secretions or in the changes which food underwent in that organ. Among the complications he encountered was that, after the nerves were cut, the food which the animals swallowed became blocked up in the esophagus and could not reach the stomach. Therefore he had to insert the aliments through a tube. By December 10, 1843, however, he had already tried the method which obviated this difficulty and proved most effective for his purpose—the use of a large gastric fistula through which he could introduce the food and examine the changes. As soon as he severed the nerves he found that the stomach lining became pale; it stopped producing gastric juice, and a neutral mucus formed instead.[12] When he placed in the stomach of an animal in such condition a meal consisting either of raw meat or of bread in sugared milk, the stomach remained neutral and the food was not digested. After a few hours the sugared milk developed a strong acid, which Bernard attributed to a spontaneous lactic fermentation.

On May 27, 1844, Bernard read to the Academy of Sciences a memoir summarizing his research on the pneumogastric nerves. Since it was unusual for a scientist who was not a member of that distinguished group to present his work before it in person, Bernard's results must have been considered highly interesting. In his report he concluded that the sectioning of the pneumogastric nerves causes digestion to cease, not by stopping the stomach motions alone, but also by arresting the production of gastric juice.[13] Although he did not say so, what he had done was to confirm the conclusion of Tiedemann and Gmelin [14] by observing the situation more fully through the procedure of Blondlot. Thus the progress of this investigation further reveals how, as he probed more deeply into the problems of digestion, Bernard was being induced, consciously or unconsciously, to subordinate the most distinctive features of his early approach and to adopt methods and ideas derived from his colleagues.

From his own initial strategy of tracing chemical phenomena in the body by means of special chemical reactions with easily recognizable results Bernard nevertheless continued to derive useful ways to supplement his arguments. In this case he utilized the reaction of emulsin and amygdalin, two substances known to be harmless when either was injected into an animal alone, but which would poison it by forming hydrocyanic acid when both were injected together. Using two dogs, one normal, the other with its pneumogastric nerves cut, Bernard injected emulsin into the stomach of each animal, then followed it a half-hour later with amygdalin. The normal animal was unaffected, whereas the other was poisoned. The gastric juice in the first animal, Bernard explained, had so modified the emulsin that the latter could no longer react with amygdalin, whereas there was no gastric juice in the second animal. The general deduction he made was that "in gastric digestion, one could say that aliments are submitted almost exclusively to the powerful action of the gastric juice: their natural affinities then seem in some way destroyed, and no spontaneous decomposition can take place between their elements." [15]

After delivering the papers on gelatin and the influence of the pneumogastric nerves, Bernard apparently interrupted his studies of digestion for nearly five months. During this time he undertook experi-

ments on poisons and on the nervous sytem.[16] These represent the
other two major research interests he pursued throughout his career,
and he seems, at least in these early years, to have followed a kind of
rotation in which he could concentrate on one of them at a time for a
few weeks or months and then switch to one of the others. By the time
he and Barreswil returned to digestion in late September it was to
enter into what had become a lively issue in French physiology, the
controversial theory of Blondlot that the acidity of gastric juice is due
to an acid phosphate of lime. The strong local impact of Blondlot's
ideas is reflected in the way Bernard and Barreswil presented the issue
in their memoir on the problem in December. "Two opinions prevail
today in science concerning the cause of the acidity of gastric juice: in
one, one accepts that this character is due to the presence of biphosphate of lime; in the other, one attributes it to an acid existing in the
gastric juice in a free state." [17] Although they may have overstated the
case somewhat because they were portraying the problem whose resolution they believed they had achieved, nevertheless it was probably
only in Paris that one could regard the unique opinion of Blondlot as
of equal weight with the views of nearly everyone else who had dealt
with the problem during the preceding twenty years. It is essential to
take this situation into account in assessing the contribution of Bernard and Barreswil, for otherwise they appear to have been trying
only to prove what was already obvious; historical commentators have
sometimes discussed their paper as though it dealt only with the question of what acid is present rather than with the issue of whether any
free acid can be demonstrated to exist in gastric juice.

Already Blondlot's claim had induced one of the authors of the
French study of digestion entered twenty years before in the competition sponsored by the Academy to return to that question. Jean Louis
Lassaigne had since then published profusely on a variety of chemical
topics related to biological materials, but had not followed up his first
study of digestion.[18] In January 1844, however, Lassaigne wrote that
despite Blondlot's result he had reason to believe, as he had formerly,
that free hydrochloric and lactic acid exist in gastric juice. At the risk
of appearing merely to defend his old views, he said, he wished to
question the validity of the conclusion of Blondlot, whom he felt not
to have brought always to his own experiments the same scrupulous
precision that he demanded of his predecessors. According to Lassaigne, Blondlot had constructed his theory from the single observation that calcium carbonate cannot neutralize gastric acidity, without
devising any further experiments to test whether his proposed acid

salt was actually present. But the failure of the calcium carbonate to saturate the solution did not rule out the presence of a free acid, because other constituents of the juice could influence the result. Lassaigne tried to prove that Blondlot's biphosphate of lime could not exist in gastric juice. Adding a little of that salt to gastric juice obtained from a fistula, he showed that the resulting fluid had certain chemical properties which gastric juice by itself does not have.[19]

After presenting this note Lassaigne was able to procure a larger quantity of gastric juice, with which he tried to obtain further evidence of the existence of free acids. Distilling a portion, he found the last fifth of the distillate lightly acidic. It "troubled" a solution of silver nitrate, so that he believed he had proved that there were "traces of hydrocholoric acid" present. From the residue he separated out the sulfate and chloride, leaving a very acidic, sirupy liquid which he thought resembled lactic acid. He formed zinc and barium salts with it, but did not have enough material left to establish their properties. Presenting these results in a second note,[20] Lassaigne remarked that he was continuing the project, but he published no more about it. He had thus launched an effective counterchallenge to Blondlot's claim, but had not been able to settle the question decisively. The situation invited further efforts. Among those interested was Dumas, who noticed that when gastric juice was filtered through chalk it lost its ability to digest artificially, but that a trace of hydrochloric acid added afterward restored its activity. One of Dumas's students, Louis H. F. Melsens, also examined the situation. He found fault with Blondlot's reasoning that a lack of effervescence when calcium carbonate was mixed with gastric juice implied that no reaction involving a free acid took place; for Blondlot had neglected to determine by weighing before and afterward whether any carbonate was actually driven off. Therefore Melsens reacted a solid form of calcium carbonate, Iceland spar, with gastric juice and found a distinct loss in the weight of the mineral, confirming that there was a free acid present.[21]

Melsens's research illustrates how closely knit was the scientific establishment in Paris. He used gastric juice furnished by Blondlot and by Bernard for experiments probably carried out under the supervision of Dumas. Thus, men divided over the substantive issues on which the investigation bore nevertheless cooperated closely to facilitate the experiment. Another hint of tidy arrangements is that Melsens's paper was presented to the Academy at the same meeting as was the memoir on the same subject by Bernard and Barreswil.

Bernard and Barreswil apparently began their research on the nature of the gastric acid at the end of September and, like Lassaigne and Melsens, they started with a direct test of Blondlot's theory. Their first experiment consisted of adding washed phosphate of lime to gastric juice. From the fact that the salt dissolved they concluded that "there is a free acid in the gastric juice." [22] As they afterward explained, this result was incompatible with the view that the acidic factor is biphosphate of lime, for the neutral phosphate is insoluble in the acid phosphate.[23] Turning immediately to the next question—what the free acid may be—they tested first the possibility of hydrochloric acid. Distillation of the gastric juice, however, produced nothing which would react with silver nitrate. Concluding only tentatively at this point that hydrocholoric acid was not "produced," they next ruled out acetic acid when gastric juice mixed with arsenious acid and potash failed to give off the characteristic odor of cacodyle. As a countercheck they added a small quantity of sodium acetate to the juice and then were able to obtain the reaction. A fourth experiment was designed to ascertain whether hydrocholoric acid would form during distillation if lactic acid were mixed with a chloride. Eventually they decided that gastric juice itself contained this combination, though it is not clear from Bernard's notes whether at this early stage of the research they were already thinking in that direction. At any rate they found that the distillate did not precipitate silver nitrate, but the experiment was unsatisfactory, and they left it needing to be repeated.[24]

On October 17 the two men again took up the project. Distilling pure gastric juice twice more, they obtained acid distillates, but the latter did not precipitate with either silver nitrate or barium nitrate. The acid was therefore neither hydrochloric nor sulfuric acid. Varying the conditions of the operation, however, they found that the situation was more complicated than they had thought. When they carried the distillation over an open fire to the boiling point of the gastric juice they obtained an acidic distillate which "troubled" a solution of silver nitrate; but when they interposed an asbestos column in the neck of the distilling flask to prevent splashing they received an acidic product which did not react at all with the silver salt. After repeating the last experiment many times they seemed to have substantiated the conclusion that there is no hydrochloric acid. For a counterproof, however, and to assure themselves that the column had not somehow prevented hydrochloric acid from reaching the receiver, Bernard and Barreswil distilled in the same apparatus pure water to which they had added two or three drops of hydrochloric acid. The product was neutral and did not trouble silver nitrate. It did trouble them, how-

ever. The fact that they obtained the same result without the asbestos
column was even more surprising to them and led them to the conclusion that small quantities of hydrochloric acid in solution do not pass
over in distillation. Consequently "the authors who had obtained it in
that way from gastric juice had operated badly and had allowed themselves to be imposed upon [by their conceptions]." After verifying this
assertion by adding a few drops of hydrochloric acid to gastric juice itself and finding none in the distillate, they concluded that "distillation
is a method which one must renounce for finding hydrochloric acid,
supposing that it is there." Before turning away from that method,
however, they tried once more: this time, toward the end of a distillation of a few drops of hydrochloric acid in pure water, some hydrochloric acid passed over, but when they repeated the operation with
gastric juice in place of water and distilled all the way to dryness, they
produced only an acid which did not react with silver nitrate. Now
renouncing distillation again, they tried to "apprehend directly" what
the free acid was by applying various reagents to gastric juice. Oxalic
acid formed insoluble calcium oxalate. This result they regarded as
proof that free hydrochloric acid does not exist in the juice, for the
same reagent added to a solution containing calcium chloride and a
few drops of hydrochloric acid produced no precipitate. After ex-
hausting all the reactions they knew of to test for other acids, they
found only that gastric juice "had none of the properties of the acids
indicated." Driven back once more to try distillation, they again had
to revise their opinions, for they now detected hydrochloric acid "at
the end of the distillation when the product begins to burn." [25] In
view of the oxalic acid reaction, however, they still did not conclude
that the hydrochloric acid was free in gastric juice, but that it was
combined in chlorides from which it was displaced by another acid
during the distillation. By the time they presented their results they
were convinced that this free acid itself was lactic acid. [26] How they
first reached this conclusion is not clear from the notebook; the brief
statement where it is first mentioned gives the appearance of having
been almost a simple process of elimination:

> 1. —there is a *free* acid
>   —it is not H Cl
>   —it is not acetic
>   —it is not butyric
>   Is lactic—[27]

One marginal note suggests, however, that they had already recognized the need to "search for lactic a[cid]" in the distillate of gastric juice "by ox[alate] of zinc." [28]

The next step Bernard took may account for a major shift in his outlook about gastric juice, although I can only conjecture from fragmentary evidence how the change might have occurred. Following the above statements, he put down:

> 1 inject sugar + lactic A.
> 2 albumine + lactic A.
>
> pure gastric juice
> gastric juice plus pure calcium lactate } and sugar [29]

This entry implies that Bernard wished to compare the digestive activity of lactic acid, which he now regarded as the free acid in gastric juice, with the activity of gastric juice itself. Since he had previously equated gastric activity with the properties of the gastric acids, he would probably—if he were still thinking that way at this stage—have expected comparable results from the acid and the gastric juice. The note indicates also that he intended to go back to his old way of determining whether digestion had occurred, not by examining directly the changes in the aliments, but by injecting the resulting product to see whether it was assimilated or excreted. On October 20 Bernard tried such an experiment. He injected into an adult rabbit 5 decigrams of sugar mixed with a drop of concentrated lactic acid. Two hours afterward, however, sugar was present in the urine—a manifest sign, according to his criteria, that it had not been digested. There is no comment at this point to indicate that it was this result that caused Bernard to doubt his old view that the action of gastric juice results from its acids' combining with nutrients, but since he had abandoned that view by the time he published the results of this investigation, it is plausible that this experiment may have had something to do with changing his mind. If so, the next logical assumption would be that an organic substance is essential to digestion, and the next experiment which Bernard performed on the same day was evidently intended to probe that question. Into one rabbit he injected cane sugar digested with boiled gastric juice, and into another the same aliment digested with unboiled juice in the same proportions. Contrary to his expectations, no sugar appeared in the urine in the first case, whereas it did in the second. He was so sure that this result was the opposite of what should have happened that he decided the urines had probably been mislabeled. This conviction, strong enough to set aside an inconvenient result, shows that by this time he must have believed that by boiling gastric juice he would destroy an organic agent of digestion. The next day he repeated the experiments and apparently got results more compatible with his ideas, although the notes at this point are incomplete.[30] Here the record of the research ends, but the general outline of the remaining steps can be inferred from the memoir which Bernard and Barreswil submitted soon afterward to the Academy. There they reported, "One acquires the certitude that the acidity is only one of the elements of the activity of gastric juice, for when that pure fluid is submitted to a high temperature near to boiling it loses its digestive properties," even though it remains acid.[31] Bernard and Barreswil must either have succeeded in the meantime in getting the injection experiments to come out so that aliments mixed with boiled gastric juice appeared in the urine, whereas those mixed with unboiled gastric juice did not, or else they had turned to more conventional artificial digestions to establish the difference. With good reason they introduced this idea with the ambiguous "one acquires the certitude," neither claiming to have discovered it for themselves, though it probably was their own experiments which persuaded them of it, nor quite acknowledging that others had found it out long before; for Bernard and Barreswil were belatedly catching up with a conception which had been developing ever since the work of Tiedemann and Gmelin, but which the two French scientists had perhaps been slow to appreciate because Bernard's initial preconceptions so heavily emphasized the acid.[32]

On December 9 Pelouze read two papers in succession at the Acaddmy of Sciences. The first was a report of his own investigation of the chemical properties of lactic acid, the second was Bernard and Barreswil's memoir on the cause of the acidity of gastric juice.[33] The two contributions were closely related. Bernard and Barreswil began, as they had in their experiments, by demonstrating that acid phosphate of lime could not be present. To the evidence outlined above on that issue they added an explanation of why Blondlot had found no effervescence when he mixed gastric juice with a carbonate: the acid in gastric juice was merely dilute enough so that the carbonic acid which formed escaped too slowly to be observed. By concentrating the gastric juice first, they were able to produce a reaction with a manifest effervescence. After giving their reasons for believing that neither acetic acid nor free hydrochloric acid was present, they asserted that there must be some phosphoric acid to explain the fact that calcium carbonate cannot fully neutralize the juice (a fact which Blondlot had emphasized in support of his own theory). On the other hand, the fact that they could dissolve calcium and zinc oxide in gastric juice proved that there must be another acid as well, for the phosphates of both of these bases are insoluble. That other acid, they argued, was lactic acid.[34]

By distilling a solution of lactic acid and a little sodium chloride in water, Bernard and Barreswil wrote, they had obtained products duplicating almost exactly the distillates of gastric juice itself. First, a portion of pure water came over, then an acid which did not react with silver salts, and finally hydrochloric acid in the last few drops. Furthermore, they had been able, they added, to demonstrate that the gastric acid had all of the properties "indicated by M. Pelouze for lactic acid." Bernard and Barreswil were referring to the paper which Pelouze had given just before he read their own. It is likely that he was moved to return to a subject with which he had last dealt eleven years earlier in order to assist the efforts of the two young collaborators in his laboratory. As we have seen, their first attempt to identify the acid of gastric juice by means of characteristic reactions had ended inconclusively. Among the reasons Pelouze gave for taking up the problem of lactic acid again was that its chemical properties were less well known than those of other organic materials, and that in spite of the interest the subject merited "under the double point of view of chemistry and physiology," its study had been neglected. The inadequate knowledge of these properties, he asserted, was one of the reasons that the existence of the acid in gastric juice was so frequently disputed. Although much of Pelouze's memoir treated chemical transformations which went beyond the problem of identifying the acid, he also described tests for recognizing it in the presence of other acids which only a thorough knowledge of its chemistry could reveal. Lactic acid, he found, could be distinguished from the other organic acids with which it might be confused by the fact that it was the only one whose copper salt is not completely precipitated by lime. This was among the tests Pelouze supplied Bernard and Barreswil and with which they thought they had established beyond doubt the existence of lactic acid in gastric juice. Thus Pelouze provided Bernard not only a place to improve his general knowledge of chemistry, but also the benefit of his experience in the difficult problems which the physiologist encountered in his own research. At the conclusion of his paper Pelouze remarked, "It is by supporting themselves with some of the experiments reported in this memoir and with some which are their own, that MM. Bernard and Barreswil have just resolved, in a manner which appears definitive, the question so much debated of the true cause of the acidity of gastric juice." Their solution was, of course, not definitive, but with the help of Pelouze so close at hand, the difficulty could not have arisen from a lack of chemical skill.[35]

"Lactic acid," Bernard and Barreswil concluded, "is the constant cause of the acidity of gastric juice." They did not regard the peculiar properties of lactic acid as essential to the digestive process, however, for they had confirmed an experiment of Blondlot which showed that after neutralizing gastric juice one could restore its digestive action by adding another acid such as acetic, hydrochloric, or phosphoric.[36] Another of Bernard's early ideas had nevertheless been quietly relegated to his past, for the theory of gastric juice formation he had worked out in his thesis, i.e., that the gastric acids were the aggregate of all of the acids of the blood, separated from their salts by the mucous lining of the stomach, was not compatible with the new conclusion.

In his research into the cause of gastric acidity in the fall of 1844 Bernard had had to give up much of the special conception of gastric action which he had nurtured during the first year of his research on the problem, and to move considerably closer to the views of some of his colleagues. More striking, however, than the modification of his substantive ideas had been the change in the pattern of his research. No longer was he able to pursue a detached course, seeking to work out for himself a new approach to animal chemistry. Though he might hold on to some of the distinctive methods he had developed that way, he was now immersed in the same kind of investigations which were occupying his contemporaries, responding to the same issues with which those around him were concerned. This aspect of his work became even more dominant in the following year, when more than ever he and Barreswil found the cues for their next steps in what their colleagues were doing rather than in the program they had originally set for themselves.

Some of their most important leads probably reached them from a flurry of investigations and debates which focused the attention of the Academy on the digestion of starch and sugar during the early months of 1845. On January 13 Bouchardat presented a summary of research he had done over the previous decade on the various substances which can act as ferments converting starch into dextrin and sugar, and on the chemical agents which halt or retard the process. The fact that gluten, putrefied flesh, the albumin of wheat germ, and other materials catalyzed the same process, he said, raised the question whether all contain a principle identical to the diastase Payen had isolated in 1833, or different active materials which can "play the same role as diastase in successively decreasing degrees." These phenomena, he pointed out, were intimately connected with the question of the normal digestion of starchy substances.[37]

Meanwhile, together with Sandras, Bouchardat was also continuing the studies of digestion they had begun in 1842. They had already followed up their first investigation with a special study of the digestion of fats. The results, which they had reported in August 1843, had reinforced their conclusion that the chyle derives from fats, and lent some support to Dumas's theory of the direct assimilation of nutrient fats.[38] Now, on January 20, 1845, they presented the outcome of an extensive investigation of "the digestion of starch and sugar materials, and of the role which these substances play in nutrition." They were still following principally in the path of Tiedemann and Gmelin, and of Leuret and Lassaigne, but for this particular class of nutrients their inattention to the later German research was less of a handicap than it had been for their general study. Not only had Tiedemann and Gmelin themselves provided the clearest evidence for a chemical transformation of starch, but the pepsin theory did not explain the digestion of this type of nutrient. Bouchardat and Sandras had by this time improved considerably on their original effort, which they themselves criticized. "We had had," they acknowledged, "the unfortunate idea of choosing as subjects for our experiments exclusively animals [dogs] for which starches do not constitute the normal nourishment."[39] It was that circumstance, they now realized, which had prevented them from detecting the formation of dextrin or glucose during the digestion of starch. Now they examined in addition the situation for herbivores, such as rabbits, chickens, and pigeons, and they compared the digestion of cooked starch with that of the raw substance. In some of their experiments they fed the animals for several days on the appropriate diet before killing them and analyzing the contents of their stomachs, duodenums, small intestines, large intestines, and ceca. They examined also the chyle, blood, bile, urine, and excrements. They searched for starch granules with the microscope and were able to locate the places where they began to distintegrate. They identified sugars by means of the changes in the rotation of polarized light which accompany their formation; by Frommherz's [Trommer's?] reagent, which was similar to Barreswil's; and by fermentation. They found that some starch granules passed intact through most of the alimentary canal, but that the number decreased progressively from the stomach onward. Along the way they found dissolved starch, a little glucose, some dextrin, and lactic acid. The reactions which they assumed produced these substances took place in varying degrees and locations, depending upon the type of animal and the condition in which the starch was ingested. When they injected raw starch granules through a fistula directly into the stomach of a dog, as Blondlot had done, they confirmed his observation that none of it was altered. They pointed out, however, that he had chosen a very special situation, for humans and carnivores generally eat foods in which the integuments of the granules are already broken. Herbivores, they found, can digest even raw starch granules, chiefly in the small intestine. The digestion of starch consists, they concluded, in its conversion to the soluble compounds, dextrin, glucose, and lactic acid, which are absorbed into the blood through the branches of the portal vein. Thus Bouchardat and Sandras now strengthened the evidence for the basic discovery of Tiedemann and Gmelin which they had denied three years before. In most cases they found traces of glucose, dextrin, and lactic acid in the blood, but not in the urine. They inferred that these substances are destroyed in the circulation by oxidation.[40]

Bouchardat and Sandras made a more distinctive contribution through their examination of the digestion of cane sugar. Tracing its course through the stomach and intestines as they did with starch, they were able to show that it is partially transformed there to "invert sugar." This was a well-known conversion, discovered through the reversal in the direction of rotation of a beam of polarized light passing through a solution of cane sugar when the latter is reacted with a dilute acid. The sugar which resulted was fermentable, reacted with Barreswil's or Frommherz's reagent, and was regarded at the time as very similar, if not identical, to glucose.[41] Bouchardat and Sandras found that they could follow the same change in rotation of polarized light in the liquids extracted from the stomach and intestines of the animals fed cane sugar. They detected invert sugar and lactic acid also in their blood. Traces appeared in the urine when they gave the animals "excess" cane sugar, but not when they kept the quantity moderate.[42]

To elucidate further what becomes of the cane sugar in the "animal economy," Bouchardat and Sandras utilized experiments which Claude Bernard had first performed. It was one of the first instances in which Bernard could have seen a visible influence of his research upon the work of other scientists. "We have," Bouchardat and Sandras announced, "repeated successfully the experiment of MM. Bernard and Barreswil, we injected a half-gram of cane sugar into the veins of a dog, and we recovered that sugar in the urine." [43] When they injected the same amount of glucose or of invert sugar in place of the cane sugar, however, Bouchardat and Sandras obtained a result opposite to that of Bernard, for neither substance appeared in the excretions. They were considerate enough of their younger colleagues not to remark on this divergence, but to comment only concerning those results which "were entirely in accord with those of MM. Bernard and Barreswil." [44] Nevertheless, their conflicting experience with cane sugar enabled Bouchardat and Sandras to formulate a quite different interpretation of both cases, fitted into a coherent explanation of the rest of their results. Whereas Bernard had asserted that a special but unspecified action of gastric juice on all aliments is essential to their subsequent assimilation into the blood, they concluded that invert sugar, glucose, and lactic acid are capable of being rapidly destroyed in the blood, but cane sugar is not. Glucose is "destroyed with great facility under the double influence of the oxygen and the alkalis in the blood." Cane sugar under the same conditions reacts only very slowly, so that if injected directly into the blood most of it escapes unmodified into the urine. [45]

According to Bouchardat and Sandras, "The modification which gastric juice causes cane sugar to undergo to render it suitable to be destroyed in the economy" was therefore its chemical conversion to invert sugar and lactic acid. Mixing cane sugar with gastric juice which they had drawn from a stomach fistula of a dog digesting meat, they were able to follow the process by a gradual inversion of the rotation of polarized light, duplicating the result when they reacted cane sugar with dilute acid. As Bernard had done, they injected into the vein of a dog cane sugar digested first in gastric juice and found that it then did not appear in the urine. In addition, they obtained the same result with cane sugar after it had been twelve hours in very dilute hydrochloric acid. [46] Thus they presented a cogent set of concurring evidence for their interpretation of the digestion of cane sugar and of glucose. They had benefited from the work of Bernard, and where their view differed from his, he afterward found out that he had been wrong. During the next three years he spent considerable time trying to reach some of the positions which Bouchardat and Sandras had attained in 1845. [47]

In support of their theory of the destruction of the assimilable substances in the blood, Bouchardat and Sandras drew on some experiments Michel Chevreul had performed in 1824. Chevreul had found that a number of organic materials, which are ordinarily not oxidized at body temperatures, can absorb oxygen and become altered if they are first combined with an alkali. He himself had raised the question of whether the alkalinity of the blood may be essential for the respiratory combustion of carbon and hydrogen in the blood.[48] Dumas had portrayed Chevreul's studies of these "slow combustions" as the basis for understanding the phenomena of respiration.[49] Now Bouchardat and Sandras were able to append to these suppositions a more specific chemical interpretation—that in order to be oxidized in the blood the carbon and hydrogen had to be combined in the form of invert sugar, glucose, or lactic acid. With the polarimeter they showed that cane sugar in an alkaline, sodium carbonate solution remained little changed over three months, while under the same conditions glucose disappeared during that time.[50]

The general theoretical framework Bouchardat and Sandras assumed was still that of Dumas and Boussingault's *Chemical Statics*. They did not seem to doubt that the glucose, dextrin, or lactic acid they detected in the blood derived directly from the starch or sugar which had served as nourishment. They did find glucose in the blood of three patients bled shortly after they had eaten cane sugar, and none in that of a patient who had not eaten for twenty-four hours. This contrast must have reinforced their belief that the source of sugar in the blood is alimentary, but they did not appear to regard the results as a test of that view. Rather they used these experiments as further evidence that cane sugar is converted to invert sugar during the process.[51] Their idea that the assimilable sugars are gradually oxidized in the blood probably came also from Dumas. They elaborated on it by surmising that formic acid, of which they detected traces in a few blood samples, was an intermediary product.[52] To this general framework they added an ingenious theoretical facet of their own. From their observation that sugar appeared in the urine when they fed it in "excess" amounts, and when they injected a gram or more of glucose into the circulation, they inferred that the circulating fluid can contain only a limited quantity of sugar at a time without losing some by excretion. The slowness with which starch dissolves during digestion helps, they thought, to prevent too much sugar from entering the blood at once. They asserted also that whenever an excess does reach the portal vein, it is secreted from the liver with the bile back into the intestine, to be re-absorbed later. This theory of a "limited circulation" they could support with their observation of sugar in the bile of animals which had digested starch or sugar, and their discovery in some cases that the portal vein contained more sugar and lactic acid than did the arterial blood.[53]

Of all the people engaged in digestive studies during the years when Bernard became involved in the problem, Bouchardat and Sandras probably most closely resembled him in their general approach. Although some of their specific conclusions differed from his, each adopted views originated by the other. Moreover, each combined chemical analyses with physiological experiments in the same manner, and they applied some very similar methods. Bouchardat and Sandras even used the same reagent on which Bernard frequently relied, potassium prussiate, to mark how far through the alimentary canal, and other internal paths of the organism nutrient materials had penetrated.[54] Like Bernard, they were deducing rather imaginative physiological theories, not all of which could be sustained; but like him also, they reasoned to these theories from observations of the course of nutrient materials into and through living animals.

To the meeting of the Academy following the one at which Bouchardat and Sandras presented their memoir, Louis Mialhe addressed a note protesting that he had already communicated to the Academy, in April 1844, the principal result contained in their paper. That result was, according to Mialhe, that the digestion and assimilation of sugars and starch are only possible when these substances have been acted upon by alkalis. As Mialhe pointed out, Bouchardat and Sandras had repeatedly mentioned alkalinity as one of the conditions essential for the conversion of starch to sugar.[55] At the next session they replied that since that observation had not been the major objective of their paper and they had not claimed to have said anything new about the role of alkalis in nutrition, they could not easily comprehend the basis for Mialhe's priority claim. Neither did they concede that he had a right to that discovery himself, for they considered that the role of alkalis in the respiratory oxidation of aliments had already been established by Chevreul's experiments and they asserted that neither they nor Mialhe had added any further experiments on the subject.[56] On March 31 Mialhe read to the Academy a longer, more carefully prepared memoir, in which he elaborated his claim. Chevreul had shown that a variety of organic substances are more easily oxidized under alkaline conditions, Mialhe said, but had not demonstrated specifically, as he himself had done, that glucose in the presence of an alkali oxidizes at body temperature, without air. Further on in his memoir Mialhe described a set of experiments in which he had placed glucose in water from which the air had been driven out, added a cupric salt, and shown that the latter was reduced by the glucose to cuprous oxide when potash or another alkali was in the solution. It was on the basis of these experiments that Mialhe claimed to have demonstrated the necessity of alkalis in the respiratory oxidation of sugars.[57]

Mialhe argued that Bouchardat and Sandras's new theory that starch or cane sugar must be converted to glucose in order to be assimilated was so contradictory to their entire previous position, that the only plausible explanation was that they had adopted without acknowledgement the theory he had announced in 1844, that all carbohydrates must undergo transformations to new products before they can be assimilated.[58] There is little basis for judging whether or not Mialhe had grounds for his discontent. The issue was vaguely defined, for he was lumping together the question of the role of alkalinity in the digestive process and its role in respiratory oxidation. It is hard to see how he could insist that his theory must have been the source of Bouchardat and Sandras's views concerning the latter, for, as we have seen, Dumas had already emphasized in his course in 1843 the central role in respiration of glucose and the alkalinity of the blood.[59] Mialhe must have been aware of that, for he was assisting Dumas during that time with other parts of the same course.[60] Perhaps after obtaining what he regarded as the only decisive evidence for such a theory, Mialhe was relatively unmindful of other less well substantiated statements. The additional fact that Bouchardat and Sandras, eight months after his own paper appeared, had expressed an opinion concerning the conversion of starch to sugar quite different from what they had held in their publications prior to his, seemed to Mialhe convincing evidence that his work had influenced theirs. Compared from a distance, however, Bouchardat and Sandras's ideas do not appear to resemble his so closely as to provide a *prima facie* case for his accusations. Whatever the merits of his grievance, the debate he instigated over it served to highlight the importance of alkalinity as a condition for the transformation of starch to sugar, and perhaps played a part in directing Bernard's attention a few weeks later to the same condition.

Mialhe contributed far more than his priority claim alone, for in the same memoir he announced that he had isolated from saliva another ferment which transformed starch into sugar. It was so active that one part of it was sufficient to convert two thousand parts of starch. By comparing the composition of the ferment, the conditions and the character of the reaction with that of the diastase isolated from wheat, Mialhe concluded tentatively that these ferments were chemically identical. With his customary boldness he asserted that he was convinced that in animals the conversion of starch to sugar "was effected uniquely by saliva" containing this "animal diastase." He also concluded that this result completed the demonstration that the three major groups of alimentary substances are digested by means of ferments: nitrogenous matter by pepsin, fatty matter by a ferment inherent in bile, and amylaceous matter by his newly identified diastase.[61]

During April Bouchardat and Sandras pursued their parallel investigations of normal digestion and of its relations to diabetes. On April 7 Bouchardat reported that he had found diastase in the contents vomited from the stomach of diabetic patients, whereas he could not find such a ferment in the stomachs of normal individuals or of animals.[62] At the next meeting he and Sandras presented the most significant discovery resulting from their interest in digestion. Their earlier finding that starch is converted to sugar in the small intestine led them to try to locate the organ which secretes the ferment responsible for this transformation. Although they confirmed Mialhe's discovery that a material in the saliva resembling diastase produces this reaction, they rejected as a "preconceived idea" his claim that saliva is the unique agent of this transformation. Mialhe's view, they pointed out, was incompatible with their own observation of the process in the intestine. By testing gastric juice, bile, and various membranes of the digestive canal, they were able to exclude the possibility that any of these contained the ferment. Consequently, they investigated whether or not pancreatic juice, whose action they asserted to be entirely unknown, might play a role. Collecting this juice from a chicken and a goose by sectioning their pancreatic ducts and gently pressing the glands, they mixed the secretion with starch and observed a rapid transformation of the latter into dextrin and glucose. By treating the juice with alcohol they separated a precipitate which was also active. Because they could only obtain small amounts of the juice in this way, however, they developed a new method to procure its active principle. Separating the principal blood vessels from a pancreas by dissection, they mixed the remaining fragments with starch, which quickly became liquified. From pancreatic tissue ground and suspended in water they expressed a liquid which acted upon starch in the manner of diastase. As a control they treated other organs similarly and found no corresponding activity. They concluded, therefore, that in animals which are nourished by starch the pancreas is the principal source of a liquid containing the ferment which dissolves this nutrient and permits its utilization in the living economy. They emphasized also, as they had repeatedly before, that digestion does not convert all aliments into a common chyle found in the thoracic duct, but that the different classes of aliments are transformed and absorbed along independent routes. Whereas fats are emulsified by the bile and pass into the lymphatic system, they believed that proteinaceous substances are dissolved and absorbed directly from the stomach, while starches and sugars are absorbed both there and into the intestinal branches of the portal vein.[63]

The investigations of Bouchardat and Sandras and of Mialhe stimulated Louis Lassaigne once again to do some experiments on digestion. Bouchardat and Sandras had remarked that, although they agreed with Mialhe that saliva collected from the human buccal cavity converts starch to sugar, it was not yet established whether each of the salivary glands secretes a liquid containing diastase. Lassaigne took up this question, testing whether pure saliva obtained from the parotid canal of a horse and therefore unmixed with buccal mucus would have the action of diastase. At body temperature the secretion did not affect starch granules. At 75°C the starch became mucilaginous, but was not converted to dextrin or sugar. Human saliva collected from the general cavity of the mouth did not produce a reaction at body temperature either, but did convert starch to glucose at 75°C. Lassaigne concluded that saliva at the temperature of the body "does not play the role which M. Mialhe has recently attributed to it;" it merely serves, as physiologists had long supposed, to moisten aliments and dissolve some of their constituents. Lassaigne tested in a similar fashion the reactions of the pancreatic juice which Bouchardat and Sandras had reported. On pure starch granules the conversion similarly took place only at the higher temperature, but liquified starch was transformed by an extract of pancreatic tissue at body temperature.[64]

Miahle defended himself on May 19 from Lassaigne's criticism, pointing out that Lassaigne had experimented on a horse, whereas he himself had used human saliva and had already acknowledged that the salivas of different animals vary greatly in their power of converting starch to sugars. In addition, Lassaigne's conclusions were based on tests with unbroken starch granules, although Mialhe had already shown that under such circumstances that action was very much slower than when the granules had previously been crushed. Chewing of the food would crush the granules and permit the effective action of the salivary diastase. Mialhe compromised his earlier stand considerably, however, for he admitted that in animals whose saliva was relatively inactive, diastase performing the conversion was secreted from "the abdominal salivary gland," the pancreas.[65] Lassaigne decided that Mialhe had no proof for the contention that a horse crushes the starch granules during mastication. To find out if that did happen, he isolated and cut open a section of the esophogus of a horse at the Royal Veterinary School at Alfort. After feeding the horse oats he was able to collect the chewed food mixed with saliva as the horse swallowed it. Testing the moist, alkaline alimentary bol with iodine, and observing it under the microscope, he concluded that the starch granules had remained intact. On June 2 he delivered a note to the Academy in which he argued that the conditions Mialhe had supposed did not exist. While appearing to maintain his position, however, Lassaigne too yielded some ground, for he admitted that when humans eat cooked starches, the diastase in their saliva might produce dextrin or sugar; he himself had found that human saliva produces the reaction on "disaggregated" starch at or below body temperature.[66]

Bouchardat and Sandras, Mialhe, and Lassaigne may appear to have been getting mired in the complexities and variations of the process they were investigating, and in debates which were partly rhetorical. Nevertheless, they had given to the study of digestion an important impetus. They had not only characterized two new ferment actions, but were extending the range of the chemical understanding of digestion to the processes preceding and following those which occur in the stomach. Although, as we have seen, gastric digestion was already regarded as a step in this sequence, it was heretofore the only step about whose chemical nature there was any specific information. Magendie, Tiedemann and Gmelin, and Leuret and Lassaigne had collected and examined the properties of pancreatic juice, but they had had to admit that they knew nothing about its specific digestive action. Now the pancreas had a tangible function, and in the effort to describe the chemical events of digestion the emphasis was spreading out from the stomach to the entire digestive tract. These developments, inherent in the memoirs delivered at the Academy in 1845, and even the disagreements they aroused, were well suited to attract the interest of other physiologists to the same problems.

Although it cannot be definitely proved, I think that the circumstantial evidence is strong that it was this work which inspired Bernard and Barreswil to take up the next stage of their own investigation of digestion. Several important problems or methods presented here began to appear also in their experiments for the first time. Bernard, for example, took up the question of salivary action soon afterward, and he, like Lassaigne, tried to distinguish between the properties of the secretions of individual salivary glands and the properties of the mixed fluid in the mouth. Bouchardat reported that sugar is eliminated by the kidneys when it enters the blood at a rate above a certain limit, and Bernard observed a similar result a few months later.[67] But the most striking connection is that shortly after the appearance of this series of papers Bernard and Barreswil began studying the action of pancreatic secretions, using the methods of obtaining it which Bouchardat had described. It is paradoxical that Bernard came to be credited with having extended nearly single-handedly the meaning of digestion from the activities of the stomach, which were supposed to have been almost synonymous with digestion before him, to include the processes in the intestines as well.[68] As we have seen, he was in fact preoccupied almost entirely with gastric digestion at the beginning of his career, and it was most likely the activities of his Parisian contemporaries which brought forcibly to his attention the roles of pancreatic juice and of saliva.

Further evidence that these developments had a decisive impact on Bernard is that the investigations he took up in the summer of 1845 represent a conspicuous shift from the problems and approaches that he himself had been following during the previous months. He returned with these new ideas to questions from which he had been drifting away since the publication of his memoir on the gastric acid. In December 1844 Bernard had turned in a different direction suggested by certain incidental observations. During the experiments in which he had injected sugar into the blood of dogs he had noticed that the animals often licked themselves afterward, and he guessed that the reason must be that some of the sugar had passed into their salivary secretions. He thought that it would also be found in tears and in the gastric juice. If so, he speculated, then if the blood contains urea, as the experiments of Prévost and Dumas twenty years before had indicated, urea should also appear in these secretions.[69] This hypothesis led him to a series of experiments in which he removed the kidneys of a dog, as Prévost and Dumas had done, so that urea would accumulate in the blood. After a variable interval, he examined the blood, the contents of the stomach, and sometimes other body fluids. In most cases he found urea only in the blood, but in the gastric juice and other fluids he discovered large quantities of ammoniacal salts, which he presumed to have derived from the decomposition of the urea. During January 1845 he performed the operation and analyses on six different dogs. He did another similar experiment in February and one more in March. By this time he was directing his concern primarily to the difficulty of devising dependable methods for detecting urea in the blood.[70]

Although these investigations provided a few insights into digestive processes, such as a suggestion that the gastric juice is secreted all at once when food enters the stomach rather than continuously while it is there,[71] the general trend was to carry Bernard away from the problem of digestion to that of the nature of secretory processes. The presence of urea in the blood and of ammoniacal salts in the secreted fluids appeared to him to provide an illuminating model for understanding the general relationship between the composition of blood and of the substances secreted from it. He drew up a plan for a memior on secretions for which he hoped these experiments would lay the groundwork.[72]

By late spring, however, he may have found this pathway less inviting. The phenomena were complex and variable, the analytical techniques unsure, and when he broke off in March he had not made any clear advance over what he had already reached in January. Although he had taken up the research with the hope that it would yield a memoir,[73] he was unable at the time to get a publication out of it. He did not write his article on secretions, and only two years later was he ready to publish his discovery that, when the kidneys are excised, the ammonia which they ordinarily eliminate is in part removed from the blood by other secretory routes. In April Bernard performed a few experiments on absorption, using the familiar indicator potassium prussiate. The surprising discovery that after the salt, ingested with bouillon, had passed into the intestines, it appeared in the urine without being detectable in the lymph or blood, raised the intriguing possibility that there might be some direct route from the digestive tract to the kidneys.[74] Apparently, however, he did not pursue the problem to any definite conclusion in the following months.

If, as seems plausible, Bernard's research in the spring of 1845 looked less promising to him than it had earlier, there were other reasons as well to be discouraged. Since resigning in December 1844 as assistant to Magendie he had had no regular income, and in the effort to support himself he was forced to undertake such expedients as collaborating on textbooks of anatomy and surgery and participating in the vain attempt to establish a private teaching laboratory. He was, in fact, said to have been so depressed at this time about his future prospects in experimental physiology that he contemplated returning to his native village to practice medicine. His spirits are supposed to have been revived by his marriage in June, an event which Pelouze helped arrange in order to divert Bernard from leaving Paris. In the year following this change in his status his research did indeed flourish.[75] It is possible, however, that his renewed progress reflected also that he had found in the memoirs read to the Academy by Bouchardat and Sandras, Mialhe, and Lassaigne the stimulus for a new attack on digestion at a time when his earlier program seemed to have bogged down. If so, it was another occasion on which he profited more by becoming attuned to contemporary events in his field than when he followed his own precept to chart an independent course without worrying about what others were doing.

On June 18 Bernard and Barreswil performed an "experiment on digestion," in which they placed liquified starch into four different vessels containing, respectively, a fragment of a large intestine, chopped pigeon pancreas, saliva, and nothing else. Their procedure suggests strongly that they were examining the conclusions Bouchardat and Sandras had presented slightly more than two months before. The results appear to have been inconclusive, for the starch disappeared nearly or entirely under each of the conditions. Nevertheless, Bernard and Barreswil must have felt that they were on to something important, for they pursued the investigation intently over the next five days. On June 19 they compared the effects on glucose of pancreatic juice in a solution of sodium carbonate with the effects of the solution alone. (The results were not recorded.)[76]

Two days later they carried out six sets of comparative experiments. The first showed that a piece of pancreas transforms starch less rapidly when sodium carbonate is added than when the solution is neutral. For the second they prepared a pancreatic fluid by macerating the chopped gland in water and filtering the latter. They boiled one portion of this filtrate, then compared its action on starch at 38–40° with the action of an unboiled portion. After fifteen minutes the starch had disappeared in the latter case and was undiminished in the former. This experiment duplicated almost exactly methods and observations which Bouchardat and Sandras and Lassaigne had presented.[77] Next Bernard and Barreswil compared the effects of pancreatic tissue on starch with the effects when they added a drop of lactic acid to the mixture. In the first tube the transformation took place within fifteen minutes; in the second the iodine indicator for starch still reacted intensely after an hour. Such a result was to be expected in view of Bouchardat and Sandras' report that pancreatic juice is slightly alkaline and of the discussion between them and Mialhe over the necessity of alkaline conditions for the digestion of starch. No one, however, had reported checking that conclusion by acidifying pancreatic juice, so that Bernard and Barreswil were adding a logical extension to the previous research. In their last experiment of the day they took a longer step beyond what their colleagues had already reported. They made a comparison much like the preceding one, except that in place of starch they used small pieces of meat. To avoid precipitating "animal matter" in the preparation, they put into the acid tube only a trace of lactic acid. The result was the opposite of what had occurred with starch. By the next morning the meat in the acidified tube was entirely digested and dissolved, whereas that in the unacidified tube remained unchanged. They repeated the experiment with identical results. The laboratory record does not reveal any particular surprise that they might have expressed at this event, but, as the outcome shows, it was undoubtedly this experiment which put them on the trail of what they thought to be a new theory of digestion. The next day they compared the digestive effects on meat of acidified, neutral, and alkaline pancreatic fluid.[78] On June 23 they returned to the investigation of starch. Crude starch from a potato remained unchanged for six hours while mixed with pancreatic juice acidified by adding acetic acid, but when they neutralized the solution the transformation took place almost immediately. Later that day they showed that acidified pancreatic juice can digest chicken and gluten. The following day they tested further the effects of varied acidic conditions on the reaction with starch. Trying in successive runs small and large doses of phosphoric acid, they found that in each case starch remained unconverted. By this time they must have been confident of the general conclusion that pancreatic juice digests both meats and starches, but that one process requires acidic conditions, whereas the other requires alkalinity. On June 28 they compared this situation with the conditions under which gastric juice operates. A hint of the direction of their thoughts concerning the relation of the two secretions was that they designated this investigation "Comparative experiments on artificial and natural gastric juices." They showed that even though normal gastric juice did not transform starch, the same digestive fluid when neutralized could cause the starch to disappear.[79]

By now they must have believed that they were on top of something quite exciting, which they were anxious to make public. Two days later, on July 1, they undertook what they termed a "Final repetition of the experiments on artificial digestion in the memoir," a title suggesting that they had already written up their results but sensed the need for a last check. In what must have been two days of intensive activity, they performed ten digestion experiments on meat, nine on starch, and several other diverse tests. Most of the results confirmed their original conclusions, although a few anomalies occurred. When they used old, putrefying pancreatic material, for example, usually no digestion took place, but occasionally it did, drawing from Bernard the remarks "(*C'est curieux!*)" and then "(*C'est drole!*)." [80] In one group of experiments with saliva, starch disappeared both in acidic and alkaline solutions; but since it disappeared also without any digestive fluids, Bernard discarded these results. Such experiences caused him to remind himself several times that "one must use all of these liquids exceedingly fresh," [81] a lesson which he often had to recall in later years. On July 4 the last recorded experiment was finished. [82]

Bernard and Barreswil lost no time deliberating over the outcome of their investigation. Just three days after they had completed the experiments, Pelouze presented their "Third memoir on the chemical phenomena of digestion" to the Academy of Sciences. Their conclusions were sweeping. From the result that both pancreatic juice and gastric juice, and to a less extent saliva, transformed starch into sugar when the mixture was alkaline, and digested meat when it was acidic, they inferred that "there exists one active organic principle in digestion, which is common to them [the three fluids], and that it is only the nature of the chemical reaction [the acidity or alkalinity] which causes the physiological role of each of these liquids to differ, and which determines their digestive aptitude for one or another alimentary principle." They added that one could therefore easily transform one digestive fluid into another, making artificial gastric juice by acidifying pancreatic juice, and the reverse by rendering gastric juice alkaline. [83]

The new theory of digestion was as audacious as the one Bernard had described in his M.D. thesis eighteen months before, but it was also a negation of the ideas he had held then. In 1843 he had regarded gastric juice as the unique agent producing organic combinations, and the stomach the principal site of such chemical changes. Now he considered gastric juice to be no different in underlying principle from the other digestive secretions. In his earlier view the gastric acids were the prime cause of the digestive changes all aliments undergo; now he saw that acidity as merely one condition modifying the activity of an organic principle. The new theory was unfortunately no more durable than the old. There are indications that in arriving at it Bernard and Barreswil had had to stretch their own data and hedge their statements in order to include saliva in their generalizations. They conceded, in a footnote, only that the action of saliva both on meat and on starch was "less energetic" than that of pancreatic juice. The record of their final experiments shows, however, that alkaline saliva transformed starch quickly whereas, in their efforts to digest meat, acidified saliva produced "no sensible alteration," even after a prolonged period.[84] Their view was harshly criticized in its own time. Clearly Bernard had once again grasped too eagerly a thread which he imagined might enable him quickly to unravel the problem of digestion.

On July 3, as he was finishing up his research on pancreatic juice, gastric juice, and saliva, Bernard recorded some tests of the effects on starch of the individual salivary fluids obtained respectively from the parotid, sublingual, and submaxillary glands. These he compared to the action of ordinary mixed saliva.[85] Closely related though these experiments were to those intended for his memoir on digestion, he probably did not conceive them solely with this project in mind. They were performed with infusions made from the glands of horses and probably reflected the influence on Bernard of a study of the digestion of these animals in which he was assisting Magendie. The same commission on the nutrition of military horses whose work had involved Magendie in the debates over fat in 1843 [86] had been asked in April 1844 to study the digestion of these animals and its relation to their exercise. The commission began at that time but was interrupted for some reason in August and did not resume the investigation until April 1845. The nature of the experiments which it carried out during the next months suggests that here also the memoirs of Bouchardat and Sandras, Lassaigne, and Mialhe were influential.[87]

It was on April 14 that Bouchardat and Sandras remarked in the Academy that it remained to be determined whether or not each of the individual salivary secretions contained diastase. Bernard's notebook records that on April 19 two salivary fistulas were created on a horse in order to collect the secretions from the ducts of the parotid glands.[88] On May 5 Lassaigne reported to the Academy the differences between the action on starch of parotid gland saliva and mixed saliva taken from a horse.[89] Since Lassaigne was not listed as a member of the commission, it is unclear whether he was working independently or cooperating with Magendie. The fact that the first experiments on the same problem recorded by Bernard were performed in July and August suggests that perhaps the commission was following Lassaigne's leads. In any case, there was a continued close interaction between his work and theirs. Lassaigne described to the Academy on August 11 further experiments in which he had made a transverse section of the esophagus of a horse to collect the alimentory bols composed of saliva mixed with food as the animal swallowed them.[90] Twelve days later Bernard recorded a similar experiment in his notebook.[91] In October the commission made its first report to the Academy, a summary of experiments comparing the action to starch of parotid saliva and mixed saliva of a horse. They had collected the mixed saliva by means of a sectioned esophagus.[92]

In his experiments in early July, Bernard found that the fluids from the separate salivary glands transformed starch as well as mixed saliva did. In September, however, he mixed fresh parotid saliva from a horse with starch and found the starch still present the next day, whereas mixed saliva under the same conditions caused the starch to disappear.[93] These later results concurred with the conclusions of the commission, for Magendie reported that parotid saliva had no effect upon either liquified or crude starch at 40 or 75 degrees. Mixed saliva, on the other hand, transformed liquified starch instantaneously at 40 degrees and crude starch more slowly.[94] Bernard himself apparently did not immediately pursue the problem further, but he took it up again early in 1846. In later years his investigation of the functions of individual salivary glands developed in several directions, forming a central theme in his treatment not only of digestion but of the circulation, of nervous control of glandular action, of the influence of organ functions on the blood, and other problems. Thus another major facet of his physiological research grew out of his involvement in questions which concerned both his mentor and other scientists in Paris.

One might reasonably suspect that as Bernard continued along the courses marked out by the lines of research on which he had embarked, the imposing goal he had glimpsed at the beginning, to find a new physiological basis for the "true laws of animal chemistry," [95] would fade away as general and vague aims often do in the face of more concrete problems. By the summer of 1845, when Boussingault had to acknowledge the demise of the theory of fat which he and Dumas had maintained, the need to oppose the claims of the French chemists might also appear to have diminished.[96] Yet there is a passage in Bernard's notebook, inserted between records of his experiments on pancreatic digestion, which indicates that he was still keeping very much alive his intention to seek means to challenge further the chemical approach. He had made some observations on the color changes in arterial blood when he mixed it with carbonic acid and again with air. Sometime afterward he added in pencil and less legibly even than usual, the following passage:

Cause blood to pass into a dead limb. Find out if the blood will return dark through the vein in order to learn whether it is the form of the tissue which influences the decomposition of the blood in life. The idea of Mr. Dumas would be true in likening the tissues to a sponge . . . [illegible word], and chemistry cannot perceive any more difference between arterial and venous blood than for example: between sugar dissolved in gastric juice and that which is dissolved in water, and nevertheless it is impossible to deny that there is an immense physiological difference between arterial blood and venous blood.[97]

In his reference to the chemists' view of digestion Bernard was recalling his previous area of disagreement with the school of Dumas. Now, however, he was searching for a deeper physiological level on which to confront their approach. In thought, at least, he was conceiving a fundamental demonstration of both the conceptual and methodological inadequacies of the physiology promulgated by *"la chimie."* Dumas's chemical description of respiration as an oxidation of sugars and fat in the blood took no account of the interaction between that fluid and the tissues; yet the visible manifestation of changes in the properties of the blood occurred at just those points at which the two were in most intimate contact. The chemists were not interested in the detailed investigation of the anatomical location of the nutritional processes, nor in the functional implications of such a specification.

Bernard was complaining, moreover, that chemical analysis was too imprecise to detect even chemical differences whose existence could easily be demonstrated physiologically. In the 1840's there was still a common conception among physiologists that blood undergoes in its closed path a cyclical process of depletion and restitution. As it delivers nutrients as well as oxygen to the tissues and acquires waste materials from them, the blood must lose its arterial composition.[98] Bernard, who assumed this view in the first decade of his career,[99] was therefore saying that chemistry was missing a great number of critical differences when its analyses showed arterial and venous blood to be alike in their general compositions. The implication that one could use physiological criteria to ascertain chemical changes beyond the analytical grasp of chemistry itself was already inherent in some of Bernard's research. It was a position which he defined more clearly in later years as he found ways to illustrate his conviction.

The kind of investigation which Bernard was imagining here embodied what he could later define as another crucial distinction between his physiological approach and that of the chemists. His way would penetrate into the organism, to analyze the changes involved in nutritional processes at the sites where they occurred, by examining the nutritive fluid immediately before and after the change; the chemists' way deduced these changes from the overall significance of nutrition or from analogous reactions they could produce outside the animal. The procedure sketched in this note was the germinal idea for many experiments which Bernard later pondered or carried out in which he sought to ascertain the chemical events produced in the tissues by comparing the state of the blood before and after it passed through various organs in functional activity and at rest.[100] The conception implied in the note, that the central vital processes occur at the places of interaction between blood and tissues, came to preoccupy Bernard more and more in later years. For now, however, he did not have the means to turn the vision into action. He had therefore to defer his broad challenge to the chemists while he continued to tread along paths of research which were somewhat more clearly staked out.

XII

Scientific Imagination Confronted by Experimental Complexity

By September 1845 Claude Bernard was entering his fourth year of sustained physiological research. He had by then opened up several distinct lines of investigation focused on the chemical phenomena of digestion, nutrition, and absorption. Each of these lines had yielded promising results or insights, but in none of them had he reached a definitive solution of the central problems involved. Not surprisingly, therefore, in the research which he pursued during this fall he did not embark on new ventures but returned to his earlier experiments in order to probe them more deeply. The most prominent effect of his research in these months was to weaken or qualify some of the general conclusions he had drawn before, as the phenomena he observed proved to be less simple and regular than he had previously perceived them. At the same time, however, he was uncovering a few leads which would help him eventually to reach general conclusions more lasting than those of his first three years. He appears to have been unusually busy with his experiments in this time of reexamination.

A harbinger of things to come was an apparently isolated operation Bernard performed on October 6. Cutting an incision in the abdominal wall of a young dog, he inserted his finger, located the gall bladder and followed the bile duct to its insertion in the duodenal portion of the small intestine. Then he drew this segment of the intestine up to the external wound and created a duodenal fistula analogous to the usual gastric fistulas. Four days later the dog died. At the autopsy he found that both the biliary and pancreatic ducts opened into the intestine opposite to the opening, and he concluded that it was possible to collect their secretions through such an operation, and planned to repeat it without exposing as much of the intestine. The rationale for this experiment is not hard to guess. It was difficult to procure enough pancreatic juice for digestion experiments; the method of using ground pancreatic tissue or a pancreatic extract was useful, but the resulting material was not necessarily identical with the secretion which reached the intestine. Since Bernard had often performed gastric fistula operations and had in the preceding months also created parotid gland fistulas, to attempt a duodenal fistula was an almost obvious step for him to take, although the technical obstacles proved to be much more formidable. Bernard evidently did not follow up his first effort at this point, but his conclusion that *"la chose est possible"* prepared him for future opportunities.[1]

If Bernard did not quickly follow up this possibility, it may have been because he had at this time already been drawn back into an intensive reconsideration of earlier experiments. He had on September 5 injected a large quantity of cane sugar into the connective tissue of one rabbit and a similar amount of grape sugar (glucose) into a second rabbit. Contrary to the general conclusions of his M.D. thesis, neither sugar had appeared in the urine by the next day. There are various possible explanations as to why he had returned to an investigation which he seemed to have concluded two years before; one obvious factor might have been the report of Bouchardat and Sandras that they had duplicated Bernard's observation with cane sugar but did not get the same result with glucose. Now Bernard had obtained a negative result in both cases, an outcome which evidently surprised him. He pondered that perhaps grape sugar might take a very long time to reappear, and since the rabbit which had absorbed the cane sugar died accidentally, he planned to repeat the experiment. He thought also that perhaps he could find some way to hasten the excretion of the sugar. There was some evidence from his older investigations that potassium prussiate accelerated the passage of substances through the circulation, so he considered injecting it along with the sugar.[2] Six days later he tried the experiment. Using two nearly identical rabbits, he injected into one a solution containing 5 decigrams of cane sugar, and into the other the same solution with 1 decigram of the prussiate added. In both cases the sugar appeared quickly in the urine, and the prussiate seemed not to modify the process.[3] Searching for other substances which might speed up the elimination more effectively, he injected on the next day sodium carbonate into the jugular vein of a rabbit, together with a solution containing 5 decigrams of cane sugar.

The carbonate caused the sugar to begin to appear in the urine within three minutes and the elimination to be completed in half the usual time.[4] On the following day he performed a comparative experiment, this time with grape sugar, 1 gram of which he injected with and without carbonate. The results confirmed that carbonate speeded the elimination. He noticed also, however, that only a small amount of the grape sugar injected into the vein without carbonate was expelled, and he apparently assumed that the rest was assimilated. Two days later he injected 2 grams of grape sugar in distilled water into the cellular tissue of a large rabbit and found afterward that none had passed into the urine. He remarked that in a previous experiment, similar to this one except that he had used cane sugar, the sugar had appeared in the urine.[5]

Bernard appears to have been pursuing more than one objective in these experiments. His attempts to alter the rate of elimination of sugar were related in part to an interest he had long had in measuring the rate of the circulation by injecting into it substances whose motion he could trace.[6] The course of the experiments suggests, however, that his central concern was to reevaluate his previous investigation of the injection of sugars. After obtaining a result inconsistent with his generalization that aliments which have not undergone gastric digestion cannot be assimilated into the blood, he apparently tried first to test whether the contradiction was real or a misleading effect which could be removed by a closer examination of the manner in which sugar is excreted. The results of these further efforts continued to be ambiguous, but their tendency was to differentiate the behavior of grape sugar from that of cane sugar. The difference was less complete than Bouchardat and Sandras had reported, but injected cane sugar appeared in the urine under some conditions in which little or no grape sugar did.[7] The most straightforward way to relate such an outcome to Bernard's earlier conceptions was to qualify his theory to say that most aliments, including cane sugar, require digestive alteration, but that glucose is already in the form in which sugars are retained in the blood. That was already Bouchardat and Sandras' view. If so, then the alteration which digestion produces in cane sugar ought to convert it to glucose. Such reasoning would explain Bernard's objective three weeks afterward, when as part of a new group of experiments on digestion he tested the action of artificial gastric juice on cane sugar. From his remarks he obviously expected to find the cane sugar transformed into grape sugar. After four hours, however, the reaction with cupric tartrate gave "absolutely no reduction and consequently no indication of grape sugar." After he boiled a little of the solution with a drop of sulfate the same test gave an "enormous" reduction, showing that the digested material still included large amounts of cane sugar. The situation baffled Bernard, especially since he "remembered perfectly having put gastric juice and cane sugar into the stomach of a dog and 24 hours later there was grape sugar." He grasped at the possibility that the cane sugar had not yet had time to be transformed, but after two more days of digestion there was still no trace of grape sugar. He considered that his artificial gastric juice might not act in the same way as natural gastric juice, and since he had made it with lactic acid, that perhaps he was even wrong about lactic acid being active in normal gastric juice. Since the digesting solution became highly acidic, he thought it possible that the cane sugar was being converted directly to lactic acid. Apparently to test by his old criterion of assimilation into the blood whether a digestive action had taken place, he injected part of the solution into the cellular tissue of a rabbit, but thirty minutes afterward he found an enormous quantity of cane sugar in the urine. Faced with results so unsettling to his views he could only conclude that he must "study these curious phenomena tomorrow compared with that which occurs with the gastric juice of a dog." Eliminating the possibility that the problem lay in the properties of the artificial gastric juice, however, did not eliminate the dilemma, for cane sugar digested with the natural gastric juice of a dog still produced no grape sugar and, when injected, still was eliminated in the urine.[8] On October 11 he once more injected a solution containing 5 centigrams of cane sugar under the skin of a rabbit and found again that it appeared in the urine after three quarters of an hour. Now he commented with evident feeling: "Physiologically there is thus an enormous difference between cane sugar and grape sugar!" [9] He set up another series of five artificial digestions using both artificial and natural gastric juice, in order "to confirm the action of gastric juices on cane sugar," but again after eighteen hours of digestion no grape sugar had appeared in any of the tubes. On October 12 he injected under the skin of a large rabbit twice as much grape sugar as he had injected of cane sugar on the previous day, and found no trace of the grape sugar in its urine.[10]

By now Bernard could have been certain only that there was something very wrong either with his experiments or with his theories of digestion and nutrition. His older theory that gastric action is a prerequisite for assimilation of a nutrient into the organism had become untenable in the face of the contrasting results of the injections of cane and of grape sugar. He seemed to wish to explain the difference by establishing that digestion converts one kind to the other, yet he could not produce the evidence that the conversion takes place. It must have been a sobering experience for him to see his own experiments contradicting general positions he had already asserted confidently in print.

During the following days he continued to try to digest cane sugar. Finally, in two cases he maintained the digestion for four days. No grape sugar had appeared after the first fifty hours, but at last, on October 20, he found large amounts of it in the tubes by means of Barreswil's reagent.[11] This qualified success enabled him to include in his conclusions at the end of the series of digestion experiments which he was carrying out concurrently, that "cane sugar placed with gastric juice at 40° is transformed after a long time, but before that transformation has taken place the gastric juice has acquired a great acidity. What is the cause of that?"[12] Clearly he was leaving the problem still in an unsatisfactory state.

During this same two weeks Bernard's other digestion experiments were also raising challenges to his professed conception of that process. On October 6, the same day that he attempted a duodenal fistula, Bernard undertook some experiments on artificial digestion, evidently intended to extend the theory he and Barreswil had presented to the Academy in July. In keeping with their assumption that pancreatic juice and gastric juice have a common organic principle, he prepared "gastric juice" by macerating fresh pigeon pancreas in very dilute lactic acid. Then he compared the digestive action of this "pure artificial gastric juice" on roasted pigeon muscle with the action of the same juice boiled, of the juice boiled and filtered, and of the lactic acid solution alone. After eighteen hours, only the unboiled gastric juice had digested the meat.[13] Then he performed on the material resulting from this digestion a "curious experiment," which turned his investigation onto a somewhat different course. Filtering the fluid, he found that the digested meat remained on the paper, while a lympid fluid passed through. When he boiled this fluid, it became only slightly turbid, much less so than if the same gastric juice had been boiled without having been used to digest the meat. "What, therefore, has taken place?" Bernard asked himself:

That animal material which would have become turbid before the digestion has thus been carried away by combination or otherwise with the meat divided into tiny particles (digested)—In that case has the liquid conserved its acidity? Has it lost the power to dissolve the meat [?]—I have placed meat into that filtered liquid which would scarcely become turbid any more, I shall see what will have happened by tomorrow.

This new fact gives rise to interesting reflections. It will have to serve as the starting point for new investigations concerning the nature of the organic material which gastric juice contains.

1° There are two principles in gastric juice—1° the *acid* 2° the *organic material*.

Is it so that the acid might have no part in the digestion of nitrogenous substances, whereas the organic material would have no part in the digestion of non-nitrogenous substances? [14]

Thus Bernard's fertile mind had once again extracted from a simple anomalous observation another general hypothesis concerning the nature of digestion. He went on to deduce that if this view were correct, then organic material ought to disappear from gastric juice in the digestion of meat, but the acid should not be diminished; in the digestion of starch, on the other hand, the animal matter ought to remain undiminished while the acid disappears, so that gastric juice in such circumstances would become spontaneously alkaline by the time it passed into the intestine. The new hypothesis would seem to be at odds with Bernard's previously expressed view that alkalinity is the essential condition for the digestion of starch, but it did fit in with the general trend of his thinking, to ascribe the actions of the digestive juices on the two types of nutrients to conditions other than the specific nature of the individual juices. At the same time, he posed some other loosely connected speculations, such as that the principle of the gastric juice ought to exist in blood, since starch disappears in that fluid; but it was the idea quoted above which guided his next steps. To verify the hypothesis, he saw, "it will be necessary to make comparative experiments with natural gastric juice." [15]

Bernard's faith in his new idea undoubtedly increased the next day, when he discovered that the new portion of meat he had placed in the filtered fluid from the previous digestion had only barely begun to digest after eight to ten hours. This residual action was due, he thought "to the small quantity of organic matter which remained" after the earlier digestion. He set out immediately to substantiate further the first portion of his theory, that this organic matter of gastric juice is consumed in digesting nitrogenous aliments. After a preliminary set of tests designed apparently to ascertain the conditions of acidification under which the previously prepared artificial gastric juice digested most effectively, Bernard began a second series on October 10, in which he compared the digestive action of this juice with that of natural gastric juice obtained from a dog. After eighteen hours of digestion he found that the filtrate obtained at the end from the natural juice was still acidic and that when boiled its resulting turbidity was "very noticeably less" than when another portion of the same gastric juice not used for digestion was boiled. The appearance of the cloudiness produced was also different in the two cases. The digesting artificial gastric juice had already reached a similar condition the day before—evidence, Bernard thought, that the "combination of that organic material" took place more quickly than did the combination of the equivalent material in the natural juice. He detected some differences in the appearance of the fluids obtained from the artificial and the natural juices, but attributed them to the fact that the natural juice was mixed with saliva. He did not consider that the differences might be due to fundamental differences between the natural gastric juice and his pancreatic preparation.[16]

Similar experiments performed on October 13 and 14 yielded still more definite indications of a change in the properties of the gastric fluid after digestion. Bernard heated natural gastric juice which had been digesting meat for twenty hours comparatively with a sample of the same juice which he had not used. The former produced only a slight cloudiness, which settled to the bottom when it cooled; the latter became "very abundantly" cloudy and no precipitate formed when it cooled. He confirmed the phenomenon again with two more digestions run over the next two days. In each case heating precipitated less from the fluid already used for digestion than from the unused juice.[17]

So far, things were going smoothly for Bernard's new theory, and even before the last of these experiments had ended he went on to another aspect of the question. Taking some more of the same natural gastric juice, he added one portion to a starch solution. An equal portion he made alkaline with sodium carbonate and added it to another starch solution. Only the alkaline juice caused the starch to disappear. This result was more in keeping with the view he and Barreswil had published than with his latest hypothesis that acid is consumed in the gastric digestion of starch. At any rate, he continued in this direction, running five more similar experiments on October 15. All of them came out as expected except for one case in which artificial "pancreatic" gastric juice digested the starch even though the "reaction of the liquid was always acid, rather feebly, however." A more serious difficulty turned up when he carried out a comparative experiment using his own saliva in place of the gastric juice. The alkaline juice immediately transformed the starch. Then he took the same quantity of saliva mixed with a trace of lactic acid. It caused the starch to disappear within twenty minutes. "Yet the reaction is very plainly acid," Bernard added with mild surprise.[18]

The next day Bernard ran into still deeper trouble. This time he tried to digest meat with his acidified saliva, a digestive action which he had already claimed in his memoir of the previous July to have demonstrated.[19] But after fifteen hours there had "not been the least disaggregation; the piece of meat is as though one had placed it in acidified water. The saliva is nevertheless still acid." Attempting to resolve his difficulties with saliva on the following day, Bernard managed only to emphasize further the discrepancy between the phenomena and his views. With respect to starch he seemed at first able to vindicate his older theory, for an unacidified portion of saliva transformed the substance, whereas a lightly acidified portion of the same fluid did not; but he noticed when boiling the acidified salivary solution afterward that nothing precipitated from it (and therefore apparently that the explanation for its lack of action could have been that its active organic matter had been lost prior to the digestion in a deposit which had separated when the acid was added). To check this possibility he acidified another sample and rendered it alkaline again. Both it and a portion which had not been acidified digested starch, restoring perhaps his belief that the alkaline condition is essential to that process. Yet after boiling, neither portion would transform starch, so that he acknowledged "one could not invoke the alkali." It is impossible to tell whether he thought at this point that he had verified his theory of salivary action, disproved it, or merely reached a highly confusing situation. That he may have sensed the need for a broader basis on which to reason is suggested by his marginal note "to investigate the action of saliva, of urine, of bile, of sperm, etc. on starch solutions." In the case of salivary action on meat his dilemma remained simpler; once again placing a morsel of meat in acidified saliva, he observed it to be unaltered after twenty-four hours.[20]

With his digestive theories concerning the role of saliva in disarray, Bernard turned back to the gastric digestion of meat. In a new series of artificial digestions he compared the rates at which different kinds of nitrogenous aliments dissolve and the effects on the rate when air was excluded. He seemed for the moment to be probing without the guidance of his theoretical views, casting about, perhaps, for some new factor which might lead him in another direction. He did not escape his preconceptions for long, however, for he used the product of one of these experiments in an effort to demonstrate his hypothesis that there is in gastric juice an organic matter consumed in the digestion of nitrogenous aliments but not involved in the digestion of starch. Into a portion of the filtered juice remaining after one of the digestions he placed a new piece of meat. After three days, hardly any of this meat was digested. The other half of the gastric fluid, however, rendered alkaline and mixed with starch, caused the latter to disappear within six hours.[21] The experiment thus seemed to indicate that gastric juice can still act on starch after the principle which enables it to digest meat has been exhausted.

On October 24 Bernard tried to determine more definitely the chemical nature of the organic substance in the fluid filtered from gastric juice after digestion. He found that tannin precipitated a white material different in character from that formed by the same reagent with albumin or with undigested gastric juice. Although the distinction he was making seems from his own descriptions far from definitive,[22] and it would appear that he was also still far from resolving the various other problems he had encountered, Bernard was now ready to summarize "the principal results of the new experiments on digestion." The first and apparently primary conclusion for him was that "1° *Gastric juice possesses an organic material*, (precipitable by heat), *which disappears when one causes it to digest meat.*"

In the margin next to this statement Bernard added with emphatic strokes the word "Pepsin." [23] It is tempting to infer that this afterthought pinpoints the spot at which he recognized that his quest for the organic principle of gastric juice could be merged with the pepsin theory of Schwann and his followers. If so, however, the recognition was only nominal, for neither in concept nor means of identification did Bernard's organic material coincide with Schwann's pepsin. Bernard envisioned a substance which probably combined with the substances it digests, whereas Schwann regarded pepsin as acting by contact. Where Schwann had characterized pepsin by an extensive sequence of chemical reactions, Bernard's evidence for an organic material was simply a decrease in the amount of substance precipitated from the gastric fluid by heat after digestion. There was still little to indicate, therefore, that Bernard had become more than indirectly familiar with the pepsin theory as it was known among German physiologists.

Among the other general results of his experiments, Bernard put down in his notebook the "proposition" that "acidic natural gastric juice dissolves the nitrogenous principles—alkaline it destroys the amylaceous principles." [24] This was a direct generalization from several of the results themselves, but it represented also a reaffirmation of part of the theory of digestion expressed in his July memoir. Furthermore, it seems to contradict that part of his more recent hypothesis proposing that the acid of gastric juice is involved in digesting starch. The overall hypothesis which had formed the starting point for the investigation did not appear in Bernard's summary of its results. This circumstance leads one to wonder what had become of that hypothesis. Part of it survived, of course, in the first conclusion; but the hypothesis in its entirety seems simply to have dissipated during the two and a half weeks of the research. It is doubtful that Bernard ever systematically reasoned out the implications of the ideas which he had put down, especially since he did not even mention the strange anomalies inherent in it with respect both to his own previous theory and to the commonplace observation that acidic gastric juice does not digest starch. The hypothesis seems to have been a sudden inspiration, born of an immediate observation which he picked up without extensive critical analysis and as easily dropped once the investigation stimulated by it had taken form. Such a manner would be fully in accord with what he later described as the proper role of ideas in experimental science. "Feeling," he wrote in his *Introduction to the Study of Experimental Medicine*, "engenders the experimental idea, for it is that which calls forth the experiment . . . Without that one would not be able to pursue any investigation or learn anything; one could only accumulate sterile observations." [25] So crucial did he consider new ideas, yet so rare and difficult to come by through any methodical procedure, that Bernard believed it very important not to suppress those that did emerge, because of untoward concern for prevailing views. "We can follow our feeling and our ideas, can give free scope to our imagination, provided that all of our ideas be only pretexts for instituting new experiments which may furnish us conclusive or unexpected and fertile facts." [26] In the light of his early career, what Bernard advocated in his maturity seems less the result of a dispassionate analysis of scientific method than an expression of his own boldly imaginative temperament. In the present situation, as at other times, Bernard conceived new ideas easily, almost carelessly, without fearing to contradict what he himself as well as others had previously said. When the evidence did not support them, he often quietly abandoned them; but not invariably, as we shall see.

The proposition that acidic gastric juice digests nitrogenous aliments and alkaline gastric juice digests starch was already embraced by his previously published theory that the three principal digestive juices all act in this manner. That he now wrote down only the more limited statement undoubtedly reflects the perplexities he had just encountered with saliva, which at this point did not seem to fit into the broader generalization. Yet he had by no means given up the effort to make it fit. When he came to his conclusions about saliva he stated:

> Acidified (complex human) saliva eventually attacks starch. Its action is only retarded . . . at least if one does not receive an acidified liquid from the saliva. But in any case the acidified salivary principle does not bring about the digestion of meat. It will be necessary to go about it differently in order to demonstrate the identity of this principle with that of the gastric juice.[27]

Claude Bernard has been justly praised for his capacity to give up his theories when he met observations incompatible with them.[28] In his later discussions of scientific method he made much of the necessity to do so. One must, he taught, obliterate one's own opinion just as well as that of others when encountering the decisions of the experiments.[29] Discussing such a situation from his own work, he said, "In these researches I was guided by the principles of the experimental method which we have established; that is, in the presence of a well proven new fact in contradiction with a theory, instead of retaining the theory and neglecting the fact, I retained the fact which I had studied, and I hastened to abandon the theory." [30] The precept is a good one; but Bernard tended to remember best the cases in which it had worked for him, and it is easier afterward than at the time to perceive whether or not experience has passed its final judgment. The above paragraph recording Bernard's response to his experience with saliva portrays a different side of his scientific personality. In the face of facts which demonstrated, if anything, that gastric juice and saliva have characteristically different actions, he tenaciously sought to appeal the verdict against his own theory.

His determination seemed to be at least partially rewarded soon afterward, for on November 18, using acidic saliva which he had procured by placing a few drops of lactic acid in his mouth, he was able to digest half of a piece of chicken. The experiment proved, he concluded, "that saliva acidified by the means indicated possesses the digestive property." At the same time he made a few investigations with reagents such as mercuric chloride to precipitate the substances resulting from gastric digestion, and planned to try by similar methods to isolate the active principle of gastric juice.[31] Shortly afterward, however, he put aside the direct study of digestion for three months, probably because he had in the meantime come upon a more dramatic way to probe the deeper secrets of nutrition.

The key event behind Bernard's new approach to nutrition was a chance observation he later made famous as a paradigm in his *Introduction to the Study of Experimental Medicine:*

> One day, someone brought rabbits from the market into my laboratory. They were placed on the table, where they urinated, and I noticed by chance that their urine was clear and acidic. This fact struck me, because rabbits, by their herbivorous nature, ordinarily have turbid and alkaline urine; whereas carnivores, as we know, have on the contrary clear and acid urine. That observation of the acidity of the urine of the rabbits suggested to me the thought that these animals must be in the nutritional condition of carnivores. I supposed that they had probably not eaten for a long time, and that they were transformed by that abstinence into true carnivorous animals, living on their own blood. Nothing was easier than to verify this preconceived idea or hypothesis by experiment. I gave the rabbits grass to eat; and several hours later, their urine became turbid and alkaline.

After repeating the experiment many times with the same results and observing that a fasting horse also had acid urine, Bernard related, "I thus reached this general proposition[:] . . . that when fasting, all animals are nourished by meat, so that herbivores then have urine like that of carnivores." [32]

Bernard's laboratory notebook does not include any record of these particular events, but it is probable that his earliest observations of the phenomenon did occur in the manner he described; for the first recorded observations regarding a related situation show him to have been already aware of the result. However, in this concise account of the circumstances, which he gave as a model example of experimental research starting from a casual observation, Bernard naturally oversimplified what had happened. However accidental the fact that a fasting rabbit urinated on his laboratory table may have been, it was not purely accidental that Bernard noticed the unusual urine; for since the beginning of his research on nutrition he had, as we have seen, utilized changes in the character of urine as indicators of internal processes in animals. During just the period in which this event must have occurred, he was comparing repeatedly the urine of rabbits into which he had injected cane sugar with that of animals into which he had injected grape sugar.

Moreover, in his initial response to the discovery, Bernard did not appear to fix on the prospect of establishing a general proposition about the nutrition of fasting animals. Rather, the observation offered him a new opportunity to elucidate the physiological difference between grape and cane sugar which had just become the focus of his attention. On October 24, just about two weeks after being so impressed with that "enormous" physiological difference, he performed an experiment entitled "Injection of cane sugar into the jugular vein of a large rabbit having acid urine." He had prevented the rabbit from eating for twenty-four hours, until it rendered "an amber, lympid and very acid urine." After he injected one half gram of cane sugar the urine became slightly less acid, but never alkaline. Tests with Barreswil's reagent showed that a huge quantity of the sugar had passed into the urine. Bernard concluded that "1. Fasting rabbits have acid and clear urine. 2. After very little time this urine becomes again turbid and alkaline." These results probably served, however, only to confirm what he had already observed before. The "principal conclusion" of this experiment was that "the injection of cane sugar does not give urine an alkaline reaction, whereas grape sugar gives that reaction, proof that it [grape sugar] is digested???" [33]

What Bernard obviously had in mind was that alkaline urine taken as an indication that an animal is utilizing non-nitrogenous aliments for its nourishment provided a new criterion to judge whether a non-nitrogenous substance injected directly into the blood was assimilated and utilized. If so, the clear, acid urine of the animal hitherto feeding on its own nitrogenous substance should become turbid and alkaline. That it in this test did not was consistent with his previous indications, confirmed also in this case, that injected cane sugar is not utilized because it reappears in the urine. Bernard's statement leaves in doubt whether he had already run a similar experiment with grape sugar which is not recorded, or whether he was guessing, before he had tried it, that grape sugar would turn the urine alkaline. At any rate, he performed such an experiment on November 8, but it did not come out as unambiguously as he desired. After he had injected 5 decigrams of grape sugar the urine became much less acid, but not alkaline. He injected another gram of sugar. After ten minutes, he wrote down, the urine had become "very slightly alkaline." But he must have realized that his wishes were forcing his observations, for he corrected this to "still acid." Three quarters of an hour later the situation was still dubious. He put down that the urine was now "very turbid and alkaline." After two hours he wrote that it was "more turbid and more alkaline," but he had to line out the last two words and to add "nevertheless the acidity has not entirely disappeared." In a marginal note he modified this again to: "or rather it has returned." Even in his conclusions his expectation struggled with the outcome and lost. He wrote "The subcutaneous injection of grape sugar then renders the urine turbid and alkaline." Once more he crossed out alkaline and wrote "less acid." The experiment must obviously have been a disappointment. It was irregular in another way, too, for contrary to his recent experiments, the injected grape sugar itself appeared in large quantity in the urine. The next day the dog died, and Bernard convinced himself that the anomalies had arisen because the animal had been so weak and sick from prolonged fasting that it could not completely "digest" the injected sugar. He noted also in the margin that he should try a similar experiment injecting bouillon or albumin digested in gastric juice into a fasting rabbit. On the same day he extended the scope of his original observation of the acid urine of fasting herbivores by examining at the École Militaire the urine of a horse which had fasted for six days in connection with another investigation. He found its urine amber, lympid, and acid.[34]

Meanwhile, for several weeks Bernard had been carrying on a seemingly unrelated set of experiments, continuing his earlier efforts to determine the functions of the vagus nerves. Near the end of September he had formulated a theory that the diverse effects of sectioning this pair of nerves are indirect results of a primary disturbance of the heartbeat. The diminished force of its impulsion and consequent loss of pressures in the capillaries, he thought, would influence all of the secretions. "The withdrawal of blood from the gastric mucosa at the moment of the section of the vagus, and the cessation of the secretion of gastric juice is undoubtedly due to that influence of the eighth pair [of cranial nerves] on the circulation."[35] In order to verify his belief he set out to show that the blood pressure decreases when the vagus nerves are severed. The demonstration proved to be technically difficult, and Bernard performed a large number of experiments on different animals, using the "hemodynometer" invented by Poiseuille and Magendie[36] to measure the arterial pressure and cardiac impulse. The physiological changes after the operation and the state of various organs at autopsies showed that the modifications brought about were extraordinarily complex. Bernard found, for example, that although the rate and character of the respiratory movements were greatly altered, the respiratory process of oxygenating the blood went on unimpaired. In several cases he operated on dogs with gastric fistulas and followed the changes in the stomach lining after he cut the nerves.[37] These experiments were still continuing in December; on the 13th, he observed, for example, that "a portion of the mucosa was projecting from below; it is red and turgid. One cuts the right vagus nerve (it is sensitive) immediately paleness of the gastric mucosa." [38]

Six days later, in one of the most ingenious experimental conjunctures of his career, Bernard brought together this line of investigation with his newly discovered means of investigating nutritional conditions through the reaction of the urine. He was working at the quarters in which he ordinarily gave his private physiology course, 13 Rue Suger, which he used for his experiments nearly as often as he did the Collège de France or Pelouze's laboratory in this period.[39] The experiment was entitled "Influence of the vagus nerves on nutrition." Using a large rabbit, he sectioned the nerves in the usual manner, then immediately injected a solution of grape sugar under the skin. He compared samples of urine collected just before and at several intervals after the operation. His reasoning, though not stated, was evident. If the vagus nerves play an essential role in the nutritive assimilation of aliments, then the removal of this role might cause the normal process to cease, and this cessation should be detectable by a change in the properties of the urine. The outcome fit his expectation. Before the operation the urine was reddish, very turbid and alkaline. Forty-five minutes afterward it was transparent, colorless, and only slightly alkaline, and it contained a large amount of sugar. While the vagus nerves had been intact, Bernard could therefore infer, the grape sugar was assimilated into the blood, indicating by the shift in the reaction of urine to alkaline, that it was being used nutritively. After the section of the nerves, the injection of the sugar was no longer having these effects. In fact, the normal herbivorous nutrition previously taking place had also stopped. The result, however, inspired Bernard to leap far beyond these immediate interpretations of the experiment in the light of his conception of the meaning of the urine changes. He constructed from it a startlingly ambitious theory of nutrition. "The sugar," he concluded:

was no longer burned in the lung after the section of the vagi, because one has recovered it in the urine after the removal of these nerves—and it is because of this lack of combustion that it had not rendered the urine alkaline.
Reflection. The lung is thus the organ in which the chyle burns; in which in a sense it is digested. One might say that in the digestive system it is the stomach which destroys the substances–and in the assimilative system it is the lung which destroys the chylous substances and assimilates them. Now it is a

curious fact that it may be the same nerve, the vagus, which presides over these phenomena in the lung and in the stomach. And we have seen that this nerve abolishes in these 2 organs the phenomena which one could call more especially vital, whereas those which are purely chemical, such as the lactic transformation in the stomach, [or] the absorption of oxygen in the lung continue without the nervous influence, whereas the vital phenomena cannot go on. When one sees the relation which joins the stomach and the lung which concur to the same end (nutrition) in this sense, that the lung operates again on that which the stomach has already caused to undergo a first elaboration; one is no longer surprised, I would say, at the nervous union which exists between the stomach, the lung and the heart. [40]

To verify his views he planned a new experimental project consisting mostly of variations of the germinal investigation. He thought he would inject sugar into the stomach, or feed an animal starch, and see if cutting the vagus nerves would have similar effects. He would also try whether galvanising the severed vagus nerve might prevent these effects from occurring. [41]

Such was Bernard's enthusiasm for his new idea that he immediately sketched out the first part of a plan for a memoir based on it. He began:

> 1. I am doing research on the mechanical and chemical phenomena of respiration. Although that work is not yet finished, I have nevertheless selected from it a few experiments relating to the influence which the nerves exert on the chemical phenomena which occur in the lung, and I shall set them forth separately because they have appeared to me to present a quite special interest. etc. [42]

He then stated somewhat more elaborately the distinction between the chemical phenomena of the absorption of oxygen and exhalation of carbonic acid which persist after the section of the vagus nerves, and the burning of alimentary substances for nutrition in the lungs, which does not. Next he linked the action of the lungs with the preceding steps in nutrition, focusing particularly on the case of the sugars. "One demonstrates by experiments," he wrote, "that all of the sugars or the substances which can give rise to them are only capable of being destroyed by the lung after they have been transformed into grape sugar." [43] If the sugar which arrives at the lungs is not burned there, the result will be diabetes, so that diabetes can be considered a "nervous affection of the lung." [44]

With this statement Bernard had clearly discarded the conception expressed in his M.D. thesis, that gastric digestion produces a modification essential to the further assimilation of any nutrient substance. Instead, "only a very small number of substances," one of them glucose, were capable of the vital combustion in the lungs. Digestion converted other sugars and starch to glucose, but glucose itself did not require prior digestion, and could therefore be assimilated even when injected directly into the blood.[45] He did not indicate here, or in his later published statements, that his new formulation closely resembled that which Bouchardat and Sandras had already presented. The full version of their paper, with its detailed exposition of the idea, was not yet in print, and it is possible that Bernard had overlooked the importance of their brief statement in the extract which had appeared. It is hard to believe, however, that he had not studied carefully a paper in the official proceedings of the Academy which included prominent mention of his own experiments. As the preceding statement, "one demonstrates by experiments," suggests, he left it quite vague whether he considered the idea to have emerged from his own recent experiments or from the work of others.

Bernard's plan for his memoir ended on a statement in the form of a logical consequence of his theory: "Whenever one gives an animal amylaceous substances to digest, its blood should contain sugar, but only the venous blood after the entrance of the thoracic canal, for in passing through the lung that sugar is destroyed." [46] Two years later, when his work brought him back to related problems, Bernard returned to this idea and tried to demonstrate it experimentally. In view of the outcome of that later work it is interesting that here he still assumed that ingested sugar must pass through the lymphatic system, even though his mentor, Magendie, had long before challenged that exclusive view of the route of absorption, and Bouchardat and Sandras were arguing cogently that sugar is absorbed chiefly through the portal vein.

These outlines of a theory reveal a great deal about Claude Bernard's scientific approach at this stage of his career. They suggest that in spite of the experimental preoccupation with digestion, which seemed to have become over the preceding two and a half years his special field,[47] he was still searching ultimately for an overall understanding of nutrition; and that he still envisioned digestion as a first step in that process, inseparable from the rest. Perhaps his enthusiasm at this point was enhanced because he seemed to have encountered the best opportunity since his thesis to attach his immediate research directly to the broader significance of the nutritive process. The nature of his reflections also displays with particular force his proclivity for moving rapidly from one or a few striking special situations to the most general conclusions, and how elegantly but simply he attacked the underlying nature of physiological processes.

Bernard's nutritive scheme would have appeared less speculative to him than it seems in retrospect, because the role he was attributing to the lungs was not entirely original. It was a venerable idea, still widely held when he entered physiology, that the gradual process of converting aliments into blood was completed by some special action of the lungs.[48] Bernard must have felt that he was only giving more concrete meaning to this assumption. Nevertheless, his approach to the question was no less theoretical and deductive, nor much less simplistic, than the nutritional doctrines of those chemists whose reasoning had so bothered him. Not yet tracing the nutritional transformations into the interior of the animal, as he later imagined he had done from the beginning, Bernard, like Liebig and Dumas, was inferring these internal processes from the beginning and end products of nutrition. An already important difference, however, was that by means of his vivisection procedures he was able to manipulate the conditions under which those processes took place, and thus to gain some insights concerning the significance of the end products beyond what the methods of the chemists could achieve.

Bernard's reflections also display early forms of two general ideas which turned up repeatedly in his later thought. Just as he integrated his research on the nervous system here with that on the chemistry of nutrition to assert an "influence of the nerves on chemical phenomena," so afterward he brought other manifestations of these same two kinds of phenomena together over and over, seeking other ways to establish and elucidate that influence. Then, in distinguishing "vital" chemical transformations from purely chemical ones on the basis that the former require nervous involvement, he was postulating two fundamental classes of biological processes which he labored until the end of his life to delineate more distinctly.

"When any sort of phenomenon in nature strikes us," Bernard wrote in 1865, "we construct for ourselves an idea of the cause which determines it."[49] So swiftly had he responded to the phenomena that struck him on December 19, 1845, that he worked out all of the preceding idea of their causes before the experiment which inspired it was even ended. When he returned to inspect the animal the next day it appeared that the whole theory might have been built on an illusion. Suspecting from the character of the rabbit's cry and its respiratory movements that its vagus nerves might not really have been completely cut, he killed it and found by an autopsy that only one of the nerves was severed. On the opposite side he had merely separated the superior and inferior ganglions of the sympathetic nerve. Far from being discouraged by this development, however, Bernard saw in it an opportunity to extend the basis for his theory. The fact that in cutting only one vagus nerve he had managed anyway to render the urine clear and neutral encouraged him to think that he might find a way to isolate and sever the nerve branches which go only to the lungs. Then, in accordance with his theory, normal digestion should continue in the stomach, but the sugar produced by it should remain unburned and appear instead in the urine.[50]

Later that day Bernard repeated the original experiment. This time he obtained very distinct results equivalent to those he had obtained before. Now, however, following the first flush of excitement over his theory, he was already becoming more guarded. Recognizing, no doubt, that his demonstration was not exactly unambiguous if the same result occurred whether one or both nerves were cut, he decided that a complete experiment would require comparing in the same animal the effects of injecting sugar with both nerves intact, with one cut, and with both cut. The next day he began reflecting further on the experiments and his interpretation of them. As he surveyed various complexities and alternative possible explanations for them, he showed that his critical faculty could be quite acute in controlling his inspirations. The facts that after the severing of the vagus nerves the urine became clear and acid and that injected grape sugar then appeared in it were certainly remarkable, he declared: "But there are also [other] circumstances which must not be allowed to escape notice." Most notably, the amount of sugar which appeared in the urine seemed very small compared to what he had injected. There were, he thought, two possible explanations. One was that only a little sugar was absorbed at a time; but that possibility was ruled out because sugar had ceased to appear in the urine by the morning after the injection, so that the absorption must have been rapid. The other possibility was that some of the absorbed sugar had been destroyed in the lungs, whose action had not yet been completely lost so soon after the sectioning of the vagus nerves. But if this were the case, then by his own theory the sugar so consumed should have made the urine alkaline instead of acid. "Must one then suppose," he asked, "that the sugar is transformed into lactic acid in place of into CO_2?" If so one might search for lactic acid in the urine as the source of its acidity. But such a disruption of the normal outcome of respiratory combustion ran counter to an experiment by Provençal showing that after section-ing of the vagus nerves animals exhaled CO_2 just as before. Clearly aware now of the internal contradictions in his scheme, but not ready to abandon it, Bernard undertook new variations of the experiment on which it was based.[51]

One of the possibilities he raised was that when grape sugar is in-jected under the skin of rabbits a small quantity of it always passes into the urine. Such a situation, which would be contrary to the out-come of his experiments of two months before on grape sugar and cane sugar, would indicate, he was apparently considering, that the appearance of a little sugar in the urine after the vagus nerves were cut might not, after all, have the significance he was attributing to the phenomenon. On December 20 he injected grape sugar under the skin of the rabbit and did find it in the urine, a result which must have shaken further his belief in his theory, as well as in the earlier experi-ments.[52] Because he had injected 8 grams of sugar, however, he could still explain away this result as due to the unusually large quantity ab-sorbed.

After an interval Bernard returned to the problem on January 20 and immediately met another setback. This time he fed a fasting rab-bit a large meal of carrots. The urine became alkaline and contained considerable grape sugar. When he cut the vagus nerves the urine became acid as before, but the sugar ceased to appear in it. The ap-pearance of sugar before the operation he could explain as perhaps the result of extraordinarily rapid absorption in the intestine due to the prior condition of abstinence, so that the lungs could not burn the ab-sorbed sugar as rapidly as it passed through them. The lack of sugar in the urine afterward, however, just when according to his theory it should have appeared, was more baffling. He considered the unlikely possibility that sectioning the nerves had destroyed the absorptive ca-pacity of the intestine, but thought it more plausible that the digestive fluids stopped forming, so that sugar was no longer dissolved in the digestive tract. He contemplated performing another experiment in which he would inject water through an opening in the esophagus to compensate for such an effect. Thus, despite the growing troubles for his theory, Bernard still reasoned in terms of it, and still felt that he could resolve the difficulties by further experiments.[53]

Into the stomach of a second rabbit he injected a large amount of grape sugar. None appeared in the urine. Then he sectioned the vagus nerve and afterward still found no sugar in the urine. This case posed problems for him similar to the preceding experiment. Finally, on

January 28, he injected a gram of sugar into the stomach of another rabbit. After two hours the urine was clear and neutral. Next he cut both vagus nerves and injected another gram of grape sugar dissolved in distilled water. The urine samples he collected afterward were alkaline and free of sugar. Bernard stated his conclusions simply, but they imply at least disappointment.

2. There was no sugar in the urine in spite of the sectioning of the vagus nerves and the introduction of liquid into the stomach.
3. The urine has remained alkaline in spite of the section of the vagus, proof that the injected sugar has been digested.[54]

In the last statement he meant "digested" not in the usual sense of the process in the digestive tract, but in the sense that he had used the word elsewhere when discussing his theory—that the sugar had been destroyed in the general nutritive process.[55] Thus the foundations for his theory seemed at last to have crumbled, for this was just what the theory predicted would not happen. Another of his inspirations had proved inadequate to complex realities, and he could only perhaps console himself that this time he had been lucky enough not to have published his ideas. Furthermore, all was not lost, for Bernard soon salvaged from the wreckage most of the elements of his theory without the edifice itself.

The fact that he had conceived the hypothesis that sugar introduced into the blood is destroyed in the lungs Bernard later connected to the influence over him of the prevailing theory "that the sugar which exists in animals comes exclusively from foods, and that this sugar is destroyed in the animal organism by the phenomena of combustion; that is respiration." [56] Like so many of his recollections adduced long after the event to illustrate a general scientific precept, this one is only half true. He probably did derive his idea that sugar is destroyed somewhere in the blood by combustion from the view, common to the theories of Dumas and of Liebig, that that substance is a "respiratory nutriment." Among the projects for experiments to test his hypothesis which Bernard contemplated in December 1845, however, there is one which reveals clearly that by then he no longer believed the doctrine of the French chemists that an animal receives all of its nutritive substances preformed in its food. He was, in fact, already entertaining the thought that an animal may produce sugar from another, dissimilar aliment. "Give a dog a meal of meat with and without fat," he wrote, "cut its vagus nerves while it is digesting and see if one will find sugar in its urine—that experiment will be to judge whether a

material analogous to sugar can be produced from the digestion of fat
or from a certain principle in the meat." [57] The next day he returned
again to the same thought, and this time it became evident that he was
again seeking to challenge a whole method of approach to the chemistry of nutrition. Although not explicitly identified, the approach in
question was unmistakeably that represented in the theories of
Dumas: "May there be other substances than starch which are capable
of giving sugar. That is possible, for to believe that the stomach cannot go beyond that which we produce in our laboratories is one of the
whims of the human spirit, as Bacon says. Can fat perhaps give rise to
sugar?" [58]

The French chemists had already conceded under the pressure of
events the converse case, that animals can convert starch to fat, but
they had by then Pelouze's butyric acid fermentation to console them
that they could produce a similar transformation in the laboratory.
Bernard seemed to wish, on the other hand, to be free of the whole
presumption that one needed to provide such laboratory parallels as
evidence that a reaction takes place in the organism. He thought that
he possessed instead a way to detect certain nutritional reactions directly within the animals themselves by interfering with their normal
processes in such a way that an intermediate product normally destroyed within them would become observable in their excretions.
Unfortunately, the collapse of his theory prevented him for the
present from implementing his plan.

About this time, Bernard shifted the central thrust of his opposition
to chemically based deductions about physiological processes from the
theories of Dumas to the ideas of Louis Mialhe. The occasion was
most likely a book Mialhe had recently published containing some
strong criticisms of Bernard's own approach.

As noted earlier, when Bernard began to investigate absorption and
chemical reactions within the body in 1843, Mialhe had already developed a different approach to such phenomena, assuming that the
chemical reactions he could demonstrate outside the body take place
in the same fashion within it. [59] In 1845 Mialhe summarized his research on medicinal substances, which he had continued along the
same lines, in his *Treatise on the Art of Making Prescriptions, or Elements
of Pharmacy Applied to Medicine.* As an introduction he discussed his
general view that "the essence of life consists of an uninterrupted
series of chemical reactions." Using extensive quotations from Berzelius, Liebig, Dumas, and Chevreul to support his position, Mialhe as-

Louis Mialhe

serted that there are "two vastly different ways to study the phenomena of life." One way considers life to depend both ultimately and immediately on a peculiar vital principle, often represented as antagonistic to the forces of inorganic matter. In the other way, one refers "the phenomena of life to the forces which control inorganic matter." Mialhe avowed that he himself had chosen the second alternative. After quoting the analogy between the reactions of Prussian blue and blood which Chevreul had used to portray how vital phenomena might eventually be explained,[60] Mialhe added, "These remarks enable one to comprehend that all organic functions must be produced with the help of chemical reactions, and that a living being can be regarded as a chemical laboratory, in which operations take place whose totality constitutes life." [61]

Mialhe complained that many physicians refuse to admit that anything truly chemical, comparable to the reactions which "the chemist produces in his inert vessels," occurs in the human body. Others claim that "living chemistry" is entirely different from general chemistry. Since his own concerns centered largely on the processes by which medicinal substances are dissolved in and absorbed from the stomach or intestine, Mialhe related his general position especially to the actions occurring in those organs. "To those physicians who teach that in the study of the phenomena of digestion one cannot compare the stomach to a retort, I would answer that in that respect my opinion is entirely opposed to theirs." [62]

Such sentiments would in themselves probably have induced Claude Bernard to group Mialhe with antagonists to his own position on these issues. He could in addition identify Mialhe as a member of the school of chemists around Dumas, for Mialhe had been since 1842 in charge of the pharmacology portion of Dumas's course at the *École de médecine*. Dumas apparently played an important role in stimulating Mialhe's research. In dedicating the present volume to Dumas, Mialhe wrote gratefully: "You were the first person who deigned to encourage my efforts by declaring in your courses that my studies on mercurial drugs were suited to serve as the point of departure for a new therapeutics." His association with Dumas seems to have brought to life in Mialhe a latent experimental talent; for although Mialhe had graduated from the *École de pharmacie* in 1833, become chief pharmacist at the Saint-Antoine hospital in 1834, and obtained his medical degree in 1838, he had written no scientific papers up until 1842, with the exception of a note which had appeared in 1828. Then, during the same years that he taught under Dumas, he began to produce prolific investigations of drugs and of digestion.[63] Mialhe did not follow all of Dumas's physiological theories; his own theories of digestion were in fact incompatible with the views Dumas had expressed in his lecture on chemical statics. But at a more general level the two men brought such similar styles of reasoning to the consideration of the chemical phenomena of life that it is not surprising that Dumas lent his support to Mialhe or that Mialhe felt a special bond with Dumas.

As if to insure that he would appear to Bernard as an adversary, Mialhe was unkind enough to use as prime examples of ill-conceived ideas, which had caused some to doubt the value of chemistry in medicine, two of Bernard's own conclusions from his recent publications on digestion. These were examples, Mialhe asserted, of what happens when "experimenters, even highly skillful ones, sometimes hurry too much to draw general conclusions from scattered facts which they observe." [64] The first such hasty generalization was Bernard's definition of an alimentary substance as one which disappears in the blood when one injects it after having dissolved it in gastric juice.[65] This hypothesis could easily be refuted according to Mialhe. Some substances, such as albumin, fibrin, and gluten, require modification by the gastric juice, and cane sugar must be transformed to glucose by gastric action; but others, such as dextrin and grape sugar itself, are assimilated without the intervention of gastric juice. Salts of copper, on the other hand, are clearly not aliments, yet they dissolve in gastric juice and if "introduced into the economy" afterward, they remain there without being excreted. Furthermore, Alfred Donné had shown that milk injected directly into a vein gradually disappears within the blood.[66]

Mialhe's second complaint concerned the conclusion of Bernard's memoir of May 1844 about the influence of the vagus nerves in digestion. There, Bernard had used, as evidence that cutting the vagus nerves halts digestion, his own observation that emulsin injected with amygdalin into the stomach of an animal whose eighth pair of nerves were severed poisoned the animal, whereas the same injection did not poison an intact animal. He had interpreted these results to mean that in the normal animal gastric juice had so modified the emulsin that it had lost the property of acting on amygdalin to produce hydrocyanic acid. He had then added: "Thus in digestion in the stomach the aliments are, one could say, almost exclusively submitted to the powerful action of the gastric fluid; their natural affinities seem then in a sense destroyed, and no spontaneous decomposition can take place between the elements."[67] It was the phrase "their natural affinities seem then in a sense destoyed" which principally offended Mialhe. To accept the conception that gastric fluid can annihilate natural chemical affinities, he believed, would "set back the progress of physiology by more than half a century." Bernard's results were correct enough, but to explain them he had resorted to "a physiological cause, whereas it is nothing but the natural consequence of a chemical reaction." Mialhe pointed out that Liebig and Wöhler had shown long before that the reaction of emulsin on amygdalin is destroyed by acids. Therefore, it was a perfectly predictable result that in the acid condition of the normal stomach the reaction would not take place. Far from indicating some unique power of gastric juice, the results were just what "chemistry indicates that they should have been."[68]

That the reactions which take place within the organism are predictable from the chemical properties of the substances involved was the basis of Mialhe's whole approach to therapeutics. The internal actions of medicaments, he asserted, depend upon their being soluble, or capable of becoming so through chemical reactions occurring inside

our organs. These reactions he sought to establish by studying the reciprocal actions of inorganic salts on one another, operating "in inert
vessels, but expressly placing them in the same circumstances in
which they exist when they react in the midst of the human economy." That is, he carried out reactions in the presence of the same
organic materials, salts, acids, or alkalis that he thought were
present where the processes took place in the body. By such means,
he insisted, the reactions of medicaments in our visceral cavities
"could be explained and even anticipated." [69] Mialhe classified substances according to whether they were absorbable directly or only
after the action of acids or alkalies in the digestive canal; whether they
were assimilable in the blood or not, and whether they coagulated
with the alkalis or albumin of the blood. On the basis of these properties he predicted the order of rapidity with which the classes of substances so distinguished would, after being adminstered, be excreted
in the urine. For the case of the metallic chlorides he maintained that
they would enter the urine in the order of their solubilities. Clinical
observation has not yet sanctioned this theory, he admitted, "no physiologist having instituted comparative experiments on the passage of
metals into the urine; but everything leads me to believe that things
would actually take place as I foretell." [70]

It is easy to understand why a person with such faith in the predic-
tability of events within the body on the basis of chemical properties
viewed with alarm Bernard's statement about the action of gastric
juice; for it seemed to deny this whole premise of his own work. It is
more difficult to tell whether Bernard seriously intended to take the
position which his phrase literally suggested. The language was borrowed from familiar discussions of the preceding decades. Those who
believed that the composition and processes of the living organism
were maintained by forces not present in the inorganic world had
often expressed the belief that the chemical affinities which control ordinary reactions are counteracted by special forces which preserve the
more complex, unstable combinations of elements composing the constituent substances of the organism. After death, they supposed, the
ordinary affinities reassert themselves and cause these substances to
decompose into simple binary combinations of their elements.[71] Bernard's qualifying remarks, "one could say," and "in a sense" hint that
perhaps he was only adopting the language as a convenient shorthand.
The frequent shifts of position in his later discussions of this basic
issue show, however, that it was not easy for him to define just where
he stood between the vitalist and mechanist extremes. It may well be

that at this early period he had not carefully thought out his own philosophic attitude. For Mialhe, however, Bernard's statement must have identified him with those who believed that forces opposed to those of brute nature preside over vital phenomena. A man given to incisive yet starkly contrasted distinctions, Mialhe was not inclined to pay close attention to subtle qualifications. Bernard would probably have to fit into one or the other of the two camps he had portrayed, and this one sentence may in his eyes have revealed Bernard as a member of the opposition.

One can only guess at Bernard's reaction to Mialhe's comments, since he did not explicitly answer them. One would naturally expect him to resent them, however, and his later opinions about Mialhe do not diminish the likelihood that he did. It would not help much that in some respects Mialhe's criticisms were hard to deny. Already Bernard himself had had cause to modify his old definition of an alimentary substance, but it may only have been upsetting to see how his public statements could always be used against him, even after he had come himself to a different view. In describing Bernard as one who jumped hastily from individual results to broad generalizations Mialhe had put his finger on a distinct trait of Bernard in his early years, but it is not pleasant to be told such things. Public doubts about the soundness of his reasoning could not help him at a time when he was still struggling to establish some kind of professional scientific foothold. If Bernard had been a little careless in adopting the phrase concerning gastric action, he might have felt that Mialhe was blowing up one small point out of proportion to its importance in the overall context of his memoir.

Although Bernard did not explicitly reply to Mialhe's critique, he was, I think, primarily responding to him with a slightly veiled counterattack in two articles on digestion which he wrote late in 1845 or early in 1846. Only once did he refer directly to Mialhe's treatise, but it is hard to avoid the conclusion that he was addressing his arguments to the views of Mialhe when he began the second article by saying:

> If, following the example of certain authors, we had the idea that the role of the living stomach must be likened strictly to that of a laboratory retort, all of the facts which we are about to report relative to reactions which take place there would be completely insignificant, because their results could have been predicted by knowledge of chemistry alone.[72]

These two papers were unusual for Bernard at this time in that neither was constructed around a set of new observations or theory, and neither reflected his currently predominant research interests regarding digestion. Containing interesting observations of his own, but also much information which was generally known, the papers give the impression that they served primarily as occasions to express his view of the proper relation between chemistry and physiology.

The first paper appeared in January 1846 in a special supplement to the *Archives générales de médecine*,[73] a journal on which Bernard began to serve shortly afterward as an editorial consultant. He began his memoir by crediting both experimental physiology and organic chemistry for the recent development of knowledge about digestion. The chemists, he recognized, had brought undoubted progress to medical physiology; "their fruitful and brilliant application of [chemical] discoveries to the interpretation of the phenomena of life" seemed in fact about to sweep the medical sciences along with the rapid development of their own science. At the same time, he warned,

whatever may be the apparent simplicity and neatness with which chemical theories permit us to formulate a certain number of physiological phenomena and to account for them, it nevertheless becomes extremely important for the physician not to lose sight of the state of the living organism within which the different molecular reactions take place.[74]

In the case of digestion, the influence of life is manifest, for it determines the special nature of the fluids poured into the gastrointestinal tract. "It thus follows necessarily that the chemical mutations which operate there are no longer comparable to those which are produced in dead nature." Bernard's general view seems clearly to have been a rebuttal of the opinions Mialhe had professed. He did not, however, order his discussion of particular illustrations along any lines which Mialhe had staked out. Instead, he enumerated various conditions which affect the functional state of the stomach. The secretion of gastric juice, he reminded his readers, requires a stimulus, and he cited observations to that effect by Beaumont and by Blondlot. From his own experience Bernard added evidence that stimulation carried beyond certain limits disrupts instead of inducing normal gastric action. Moderate heat, for example, enhanced the digestive process, but boiling water introduced into the stomach severely injured the mucous lining. Similarly, illnesses often caused the stomach to react differently and arrested the formation of the digestive fluid. The conclusion from all these observations was that "one would have a completely false idea of the stomach if one regarded it as a sort of inert and passive pocket. The facts teach, on the contrary, that the stomach is perhaps the organ whose functions are the most susceptible of being modified." [75] Many of these facts were long known, and few could disagree with them, but Bernard was concerned that those with a predominantly chemical orientation simply overlooked them.

In his second article Bernard described specific chemical reactions which could be produced in the stomach, to show that their occurrence depended on the particular physiological conditions of that organ. Invoking a theme which he had tried unsuccessfully to apply a little while earlier in a different context, Bernard separated the actions of gastric juice into those depending "uniquely on its acid," and those which resulted from action by its "fermentable principle." The latter produced not ordinary chemical combination, but a special catalytic dissociation, or decomposition, of certain organic substances. This distinction may well have been a careful restatement of the idea whose previous manifestation had roused Mialhe's ire. It eliminated the vitalistic overtones in favor of a special category of reactions acknowledged in chemistry itself. By adopting it, Bernard was veering away from his previous notion that the organic material of gastric juice combines with the substances it decomposes, in favor of the more common view, which he attributed rather arbitrarily to Dumas. [76]

The action of the gastric acid he illustrated largely through its reactions with metals, and by his favorite reaction of lactate of iron with potassium prussiate. He may have been simply recounting old experiments, or may have recently performed minor variations of them for his purpose. Here his aim was to show that chemical reactions requiring the presence of acid conditions were more or less intense, depending upon the functional state of the stomach. In abstinence, when little gastric juice flowed, they took place much more slowly than when the stomach was digesting. The secretion of gastric acid could be stimulated also, he said, by small quantities of alkali. By now, Bernard had finally got around to an open and direct countercriticism of Mialhe. "One must therefore," he said, "not imagine that the stomach is an inert vessel in which alkalis will always saturate the acids which they find and destroy their action." Alkalis ingested into the stomach will, of course, tend to neutralize acid already present, but if not too concentrated, they will also provoke a further secretion of the gastric acid, because "the organism reacts." He continued: "It is through having considered only the chemical side of the phenomenon, and having neglected the physiological properties of the gastric mucosa, that M. Mialhe was led to say, in his *Art de formuler* . . ." that one should have a patient avoid drinking alkalies or other liquids when administering iron or one of its oxides. Assuming that Mialhe recommended this policy because he thought that the alkali or liquid would dilute the gastric acid, Bernard commented that "precisely the opposite" would occur.[77]

Bernard was apparently following a common tactic, but one which makes it difficult to pin down the critical issues in scientific as in ordinary disagreements. Perhaps because he sensed that some of Mialhe's criticisms had struck vulnerable positions, Bernard did not try to answer each of them. Instead, he chose terrain where he could catch Mialhe in an equally unguarded position easy to refute. One of Mialhe's citicisms, on the other hand, he clearly did answer, but without indicating that he was doing so. That was the explanation of the action of emulsin on amygdalin in the stomach. In the third section of his paper he considered the action of gastric juice on "substances of the nature of ferments." He had placed each of the three well-known ferments—yeast, diastase, and emulsin—either into the stomach of an animal or into gastric juice. In each case adding afterward the substance the ferment normally acted on—sugar, starch, and amygdalin, respectively—he found that none of the usual reactions took place. He noticed the appearance of the emulsin was changed after he removed it from the gastric juice. The general conclusion he reached was that "the fermentative principle was destroyed by the prolonged contact with the gastric juice," so that it was no longer capable of provoking the fermentation. To account for this action of the gastric juice, Bernard inferred that it had actually digested the ferment. Thus in his new explanation Bernard avoided references to the annihilation of chemical affinities; but he was not content merely to eliminate the grounds on which Mialhe had attacked his explanation, for he had found a way to dispose of Mialhe's own explanation. He reported that he had placed emulsin and amygdalin in water acidified to approximately the same proportion as the acid of gastric juice and that it "did not seem to me to prevent the reaction which emulsin exerts on amygdalin." [78] Had he cared to make it explicit that his target was Mialhe's discussion, he might have added that the prediction based on chemical properties had been too hasty.

After a section describing the abnormal fermentation reactions which can take place when the stomach is in a morbid state, Bernard concluded that not only the energy but the nature of the reactions which occur there are modified by physiological or pathological conditions of the gastric mucosa. "Consequently all chemical explanations of phenomena can only be rigorous on the condition that they be related to a definite functional state of the organ." [79]

The general views of Bernard and of Mialhe concerning the relation of chemistry to physiology were not totally irreconcilable. Mialhe acknowledged the necessity to duplicate the conditions in the organism under which reactions occur. Bernard's statements about the importance of physiological states did not deny that they controlled chemical reactions only indirectly by influencing what chemical substances would be present to react. Yet, whatever the logical relation between their opinions, Bernard came to identify Mialhe as a spokesman for that school of thought with which he had already taken it upon himself to contend. Whether because Mialhe saw Bernard as lending support to the conservative physicians who were his real adversaries, or because of more substantive differences in their results and conclusions, Mialhe continued to find reasons to criticize Bernard's work. Bernard continued to react with criticisms of Mialhe's views. There were important specific differences between them concerning the phenomena of digestion, and in practice, perhaps more significantly than in their statements, they represented different balances between the competing claims of chemistry and physiology. Yet it seems, particularly on Bernard's part, that the perception of the other person as representative of a rival approach became more compelling than the separation attributable to the inherent logic of their positions. This identification induced him to focus on his differences with Mialhe and to overlook the areas in which their respective investigations were neatly complementary.

XIII

Herbivorous and Carnivorous Nutrition—
a Success amid Further Setbacks

Through most of the year of 1846 Bernard contended with issues left unresolved by the intensive activity of the previous fall. His research moved in two directions, in one of which he retrieved with notable success that which remained after the debacle which overcame his grand nutritional theory in January. He spent at least as much of his effort, however, stubbornly striving to preserve the general theory of digestion which he and Barreswil had proposed.

On February 18 he began some experiments comparing the secretions of individual salivary glands, perhaps taking up again the questions which had engaged him during the summer before with the commission headed by Magendie. He placed samples of human parotid and submaxillary gland saliva in separate starch solutions and found, in contrast to Magendie's report, that both of these unmixed secretions transformed the starch. Instead of accepting this outcome, however, he suspected that he had not obtained the two salivas entirely pure. The next day he compared parotid saliva from a dog with mixed human saliva. This time he found what he expected; the parotid saliva did not change the starch, the mixed saliva did. He had, however, included as control tests boiled saliva and saliva acidified with lactic acid. The latter transformed starch, thus bringing up again those vexing experimental contradictions of his digestive theories which had caused him in the fall to leave the question with the remark that he would have to go about it differently. He renewed his attack on February 22 with a set of eight comparative tests of the action of filtered human saliva on starch. Two portions of the saliva were alkaline, two were boiled, one was acidified with hydrochloric acid, a second with lactic acid, and a third with an unspecified acid. Again, in spite of his theory, two of the acidified samples transformed starch along with the alkaline portions. Using human saliva obtained in a different way, by stimulating the secretion with tobacco smoke, Bernard obtained more hopeful results, for it transformed starch when alkaline and failed to do so when acidified. But another sample, which he acidified at the moment of its excretion by placing lactic acid in the mouth, dissolved starch even though highly acid. The situation seemed as confused as ever, and Bernard could only remark, "The fact is very curious and demands to be studied." [1]

The next day he prepared another series of ten comparative tests. Apparently suspecting that the type of acid and the manner in which the saliva was acidified influenced whether or not the digestion occurred, he added to one sample a trace of pure lactic acid, to a second dilute lactic acid, to a third dilute hydrochloric, to a fourth pure, concentrated hydrochloric acid, and to a fifth only a trace of concentrated lactic acid. One sample he acidified and then neutralized. All of these transformed the starch, although at different rates, except for the saliva containing concentrated hydrochloric acid. Although his method had not been quantitative enough to permit rigorous comparisons of the relative degrees of acidity in his samples, the outcome may still have suggested to him that saliva can digest starch if weakly acidified but not if it is strongly acid.[2] The next set of experiments, however, ran counter to such an inference. Of two tubes of saliva, one containing dilute lactic acid, the other dilute hydrochloric acid, the first did not transform the starch "even though the liquid is not very strongly acid to litmus paper," while the second left no trace of starch, even though "the liquid remained acid." He therefore repeated the same experiment. This time both tubes digested the starch. Then he compared the actions of two samples of saliva, both acidified with lactic acid, but of which he had then rendered one alkaline. Both digested equally well, but since the acidified saliva was only "faintly acid," he reacidified it with another trace of lactic acid and added more starch. This time there was "not the least transformation"; but neither was there when he made this saliva alkaline with sodium carbonate.[3] In spite of this last caprice the initial result of reacidifying the faintly acidified saliva seemed to him a crucial clue. "Then," he said, "I did the experiment again in another way." Taking two tubes of saliva acidified with lactic acid, he reacidified one with an additional trace of the same acid while he made the other alkaline with sodium carbonate. This time, when comparing their actions, he received perfectly distinct results. After forty-five minutes of digestion, iodine still produced an intense blue in the acid saliva. It gave in the other only a rose color, an indication that in the latter the transformation of the starch was under way; "so that," he ended with satisfaction, "the experiments are very conclusive—now it will be necessary to try it for meat; but for starch the matter is determined." [4] It was not the first time that, faced with results discordant with his views, Bernard reacted by manipulating the conditions of the experiments persistently until they came out the way he wished them to. That this was in this case his deliberate aim seems clear from a conclusion he put down after he had once more obtained the desired result and had observed that he was successful only when he made the saliva acid or alkaline before adding the starch solution: "Conclusions from all of the preceding experiments from which one must deduce the method of preparing the experiments in order to demonstrate plainly the analogy which exists between gastric juice and saliva." [5]

What the experiments seemed to have made clear was that the manner in which the saliva is acidified is the crucial point. If acidified two days after being procured it did not digest starch, but if acidified immediately it did. Filtered saliva, acidified lightly, retained its property of reacting with the starch but lost it when more strongly acidified. From such considerations Bernard devised a mode of preparation for the saliva which would enable the experiments to be carried out in a "regular and reliable manner." One should collect the secretion stimulated by tobacco smoke, allow it to settle for a day and filter out the mucus; then add dilute lactic acid, filter out the precipitate which forms, neutralize and add another trace of the acid. This preparation mixed with starch solution always leaves the starch unaltered, whereas the same preparation rendered alkaline always transforms the starch, provided only that one adds the starch after all the other steps. "Without this precaution the experiments fail to reach their goal." [6]

One then has a liquid which acts in reality like gastric juice in the sense that it is not precipitated by acids or by alkalis, and that being acid it does not transform starch, whereas being alkaline it transforms starch, and is made notably turbid by heat . . . One must cause that acid liquid to react with meat and examine comparatively gastric juice and the salivary fluid thus prepared. [7]

Tenaciously, therefore, Bernard held to his course. Before following out this plan, however, he pondered another possible direction.

Under the heading "desiderata," Bernard wrote that the first question he would have to examine in pursuing his experiments on saliva would be "to separate the *mucus* and examine its isolated action on starch (for Mialhe includes [mucus] in what he calls his diastase)." Bernard proposed a method for attempting to separate the mucus, by precipitating it with dilute acid, filtering and dissolving the precipitate in alkali. He thought he might also be able to precipitate in alcohol a second, distinct animal material from the filtered fluid. In general he wished "to search to determine the characteristics of these animal substances comparatively to those which one could find in the gastric juice and the pancreatic." [8] The motive for this interest came at least in part from observations he had made incidentally to his preceding experiments, for in some of them he had noticed that, if not filtered out of the saliva, mucus appeared to protect the active salivary principle from destruction by heat or strong acids.[9] The first passage suggests, however, that he was also feeling a need to come to grips with Mialhe's theory of salivary action, even while betraying a skepticism about it which later came out in the open. He may also have been casting about for an approach which would place him in closer touch generally with the efforts of his contemporaries who had dealt in greater depth than he had with the chemical properties of active organic substances. That he did not carry out these intentions may have been due to his impatience to settle the problems which had already plagued his own theory of digestion; or it may also reflect that his mastery of the highly refined art of isolating and characterizing the "animal substances" was not up to the level of the chemists who were more used to performing it.

At any rate, with his confidence undoubtedly bolstered by his apparent resolution of one of the two immediate obstacles to the vindication of his theory, Bernard headed straight toward a showdown with the more difficult one—the undemonstrated action of saliva on meat. With saliva prepared in his newly prescribed manner he tried to digest pieces of meat placed in tubes together with starch solutions. One sample was simply acidified, one was acidified and then re-acidified with a drop of lactic acid, one was rendered alkaline, and he added a control comprised of distilled water with a drop of lactic acid. At the end of an hour the meat had not yet been attacked in any one of them, but already in the first tube the starch was completely transformed. After five hours there was still nothing more to show than a little swelling of the meat in the twice acidified saliva. Even after twenty-four hours the most he could see was a little "defibrillation" of one of the pieces of meat, which was "not yet a real dissolution." He left two of the tubes for twenty-four hours more, but his patience brought him no closer to a noticeable dissolution of the meat.[10]

Undoubtedly feeling that, as with the starch, it was only a matter of finding the right conditions, he tried again. First he checked his procedures for preparing the acidified saliva, making certain that the samples with which he tried to digest meat were acidified in such a manner that they would not digest starch. Apparently the logic of his theory led him to believe that the conditions which preclude one process from taking place ought to be those which permit the other to occur. He began a new series of digestions on February 26, just as the first set finally ended. He compared the action on meat of saliva acidified with hydrochloric acid and then reacidified with lactic acid to the action of natural gastric juice and of gastric juice made alkaline with sodium carbonate. At the same time he tried to digest meat, gluten, coagulated albumin, and fresh albumin in ordinary filtered saliva. After twenty-four hours the reacidified saliva had again failed to alter the meat, in sharp contrast to the gastric juice, which had almost completely dissolved its meat. Neither did the gluten or albumin dissolve. As discouraging as this repeated failure must have been for the central problem, Bernard did find some encouragement in another quarter for his theory; for the alkaline gastric juice nicely transformed the starch in its tube, though it also partially dissolved the meat.[11] On February 28 he ran another similar group of comparative digestions. This time the gastric juice gave a more distinctly positive result, for when alkaline it transformed starch and only softened beef in a manner "different from digestive dissolution." However hopeful this may have been for one segment of his theory, nothing could help the situation for saliva. Once more the acidified secretion merely discolored meat, while ordinary acid gastric juice under corresponding conditions was dissolving the same substance.[12] Bernard ran no further tests of saliva with meat. By now it must certainly have seemed that the long and tedious effort to substantiate his theory that saliva and gastric juice are equivalent when they act under corresponding conditions of acidity or alkalinity was ending in an impasse. The persistence which rewarded him when he dealt with the first half of the problem proved for the second half to be futile.

While his repeated efforts to digest meat with saliva were only reinforcing the unfavorable outcome, Bernard shifted back to the concern with which he had begun this series of experiments ten days before, the comparison of different types of saliva. Simultaneously with his last tests with meat he investigated the action on starch of saliva from various sources, including secretions obtained four days before from the submaxillary and sublingual glands of horses by sectioning their ducts. He compared also some twelve-day-old saliva from the parotid gland of a horse, various serous fluids from human patients, and diastase. All of these transformed the starch, a result of no help to him in his attempts to make distinctions.[13] On March 12 he collected submaxillary and parotid gland saliva separately from a dog by creating salivary fistulas, and this time he had better luck differentiating their properties from those of ordinary mixed saliva. The latter rapidly digested starch, whereas the individual secretions, which were fresh this time, acted only very slowly on a filtered starch solution. On March 29 he collected some very pure submaxillary saliva from a dog and found that after sixteen hours of digestion it had not noticeably transformed the starch solution.[14] During the same period he was improving his procedure for detecting the transformation of starch to sugar. Instead of relying exclusively on the disappearance of the iodine test for starch, he now began to check by means of Barreswil's reagent whether grape sugar had actually formed.[15] In spite of these progressive steps, Bernard's interest in the digestion experiments seemed to decline after his failure to achieve the salivary digestion of meat; the laboratory record suggests that the few such experiments he did during March had a rather fragmentary quality. At the end of the month they stopped. This may have been in part due to discouragement at the fate of the inquiry most important to him, but it may also be because he was concentrating his attention on another line of investigation which had turned out to be far more rewarding.

At the end of January Bernard's investigation of effects that diet, injections of sugar, and severing the vagus nerve have on the properties of urine seemed to come to a halt just as the nutritional theory based on it disintegrated. It soon became apparent, however, that some of the experiments themselves were beginning to attract unusual attention within the scientific and medical community of Paris. On February 14, at his own laboratory on Rue Suger, Bernard demonstrated some of the effects he had discovered to "MMrs. Rayer, Mandt, Galtier, Caheu, Villemain, and Hervé." He fed a carrot to a rabbit which had fasted for thirty-six hours, and showed that its previously clear, acid urine became turbid and less acid. He demonstrated also the divergent effects on the urine of injecting grape sugar and cane sugar respectively into the jugular veins of two rabbits.[16] The first person

mentioned, Pierre-François Rayer, must have been particularly interested in the phenomena he witnessed, for this eminent physician had
for a long time studied the alterations of the urinary secretions which
accompany diseases. In 1839 he had published a massive pioneering
treatise on that subject.[17] Rayer had taken a close interest in Bernard
and his work ever since Bernard had assisted him at the Hôpital de la
Charité in 1840.[18] Rayer often supplied Bernard with urine from
diabetic patients, and with other specimens; perhaps he also offered
Bernard some guidance in these investigations. Interest in Bernard's
demonstration continued to spread, so that a few days later he was
repeating it for another group, including the distinguished medical
scientist and clinician, Gabriel Andral, who had succeeded to the
professorship of general pathology and therapy of the famous Brous-
sais; and the medical historian Charles Daremberg. The experiments
"succeeded admirably." Soon afterward he had equally good fortune
demonstrating them for three other people. Finally, facing the pin-
nacle of the Parisian establishment, he performed them successfully
for Dumas and the very influential toxicologist, Matheo-José-
Bonaventure Orfila.[19]

Although Bernard's earlier work had already received favorable notice, nothing he had done before had attained such sudden prominence in the eyes of his colleagues. This development must have been
a welcome consolation for the failure of the theory which he had tried
to construct from the same investigations. Perhaps because of the
special attention which his results received, he was more cautious than
he sometimes had been about publishing his conclusions. First he
sought to strengthen them by further experiments, interspersed with
the previously described researches on salivary digestion. One experiment, which he recorded very concisely, provided a further differen-
tiation of the effects of varied diets:

> 3 rabbits nourished, the one
> No. 1 with carrots
> No. 2 with bread
> No. 3 having fasted for 24 h[ours].
>   Result
> No. 1 urine turbid, lactescent and alkaline
> No. 2 very opalescent, resembling human urine, (very acid).
> No. 3 urine acid and clear.[20]

Bread, made from plant matter but containing more nitrogenous substance than carrots do, thus produced a result intermediate between

that produced by carrots and by abstinence. This must have indicated to Bernard that the character of the urine depended not on a simple distinction between food derived from plants or animals, but on the proportion of nitrogenous to non-nitrogenous constituents in the food.

On February 26 he investigated again a phenomenon which had given him some trouble in the past, the effects of injecting grape and cane sugar on the urine of a rabbit. Injecting the two sugars respectively under the skin of two rabbits, he now obtained for grape sugar an unequivocal change from slightly acid urine to a whitish, turbid, and "very clearly alkaline" excretion. The sugar did not appear in the urine. Cane sugar did appear in the urine of the other rabbit; but for some unexplained reason he had used an animal whose urine was already alkaline, so that the two cases were not strictly comparable.[21]

On February 28 Bernard confronted a crucial test of his explanation of the changes in the urine of fasting rabbits. If the clearness and acidity indicated that they were in a state like carnivores, nourished by their own flesh, then these animals should excrete such urine also if they were given a diet of pure meat. He therefore fed raw beef to two rabbits which had fasted for twenty-four hours. They ate the unaccustomed food very well. For comparison he fed a third rabbit carrots. After five hours, however, he appeared to be in for another disappointment. One of the rabbits on meat would not secrete any urine at all. The other, he noted emphatically, gave "turbid, whitish urine, little acid, almost neutral!" Two hours later the situation was still worse, and his heavily penned exclamation points betray his growing anxiety. The urine was "turbid, whitish, very alkaline!!" This occurred the same day that he began his last futile effort to digest meat with saliva, so it would not be surprising if he were all too easily disposed to fear another impending defeat. The next day brought relief. By now the rabbit was acting as it should, excreting "very amber, very acid [urine], exactly like that of a dog in appearance." The second rabbit had finally produced one drop of "extremely acid" urine, while the rabbit on carrots continued to give turbid, whitish, very alkaline urine. The moment of alarm had given way to a very satisfactory outcome.[22]

With the basic phenomenon now apparently on firm ground, Bernard returned a week later to a more troublesome facet of his earlier investigation, the attempt to demonstrate by the change of urine that sectioning of the vagus nerves stops digestion. Here he was again frustrated on his first try, however, for when he cut the nerves of a rabbit nourished with cabbage the urine remained over the next five hours constantly turbid and alkaline. He had to conclude that the digestive process had not been arrested, but he refused to accept the result as decisive. Instead, he decided that digestion had continued only because gastric juice had already been secreted prior to the operation. He claimed that the result would be different if he cut the nerves at the beginning of the period of digestion.[23] Bernard had better luck that day refining his studies of the actions of different sugars injected into the circulation. Comparing cane sugar "inverted" by reacting it with sulfuric acid to unmodified cane sugar, he found that the former did not pass into the urine, and concluded that "invert" sugar "behaves exactly like commercial hydrated grape sugar." By means of "a multitude of small tests" he also perfected his procedures for detecting sugar in the urine.[24]

During the next few days Bernard continued to alternate between further experiments on each of the related aspects of his investigation. The next step he took was to vary the basic nutritional effect by nourishing a rabbit for two days on a diet of bread and milk. Its urine became turbid but very acid. Then he switched it to carrots, which caused turbid, very alkaline urine. He concluded that acid but turbid urine was an indication of an animal nourished by a largely, but not exclusively, herbaceous alimentation. As this experiment ended he tried once more to demonstrate the action of the vagus nerves on digestion. This time everything worked. Three hours after he fed carrots to a fasting rabbit its previously clear, acidic urine had become turbid and alkaline. Then he cut the vagus nerves. Within an hour and a half the urine was almost neutral. In another hour it was distinctly acid, and thirty minutes later it was very acid and clear. An autopsy showed that the nerves had been cleanly severed.[25]

On March 17 Bernard ingeniously carried the last experiment a step further. After repeating the previous procedures with equal success, he injected through the esophagus of the rabbit 100 grams of gastric juice. The urine remained acidic and became even clearer.[26] Apparently he was reasoning that if the sole cause of the cessation of digestion was that severing of the vagus nerves halted the secretion of gastric juice, then the injection ought to have restored the digestive action, so that the urine ought to turn alkaline again. The contrary result would seem to imply, therefore, that the vagus nerves were essential to some deeper aspect of the digestive or nutritive process. There is no evidence, however, that this outcome emboldened Bernard to revive his speculations concerning the internal processes of nutrition. Instead, he cautiously returned to refine the basic demonstration of the effects of alimentation on urine. On February 20 he fed a fasting rabbit a small meal of carrots, but found the urine unchanged the next morning. When he fed it more carrots the urine turned turbid and alkaline. Apparently he was varying the procedures to establish those best suited to display the phenomena. Reviewing the conditions of his past experiments, he noted that the times required for the "urine of abstinence" to change to that of digestion and the reverse were highly variable. To produce the shifts most rapidly he judged that the rabbits should be kept in abstinence for thirty-six hours. Then a small meal of carrots would make the urine alkaline for a short time, after which the secretions would again become acidic. Another small portion of the vegetable would bring about the same cycle of changes again. "In short," he said, "one must regulate the meals of the animal and not allow it to eat continually; one must always give it small meals at a time." [27]

Evidently assured now that he could control the urinary changes at will, Bernard was ready to make his conclusions public. Two days later he submitted to the Academy of Sciences a memoir on "The differences which the phenomena of digestion and nutrition present within herbivorous and carnivorous animals." [28]

His memoir, at least in the condensed form in which it was published, was a model of concise reasoning and forceful conclusions. It embodied the kind of elegant generalization for which he had often striven in the past, but without the forced quality that marked some of his earlier theories. This time the conclusion seemed to be the inevitable result of striking experimental observations. The central question he raised was whether the anatomical differences between the digestive systems of carnivorous and herbivorous animals affected only the mechanical aspects of digestion, or whether they were related to more profound differences in the phenomena of digestion and nutrition inherent in these two classes of animals. An indication that the chemical processes also differed Bernard saw in contrasting properties of their chyme, chyle, and urine. The chyme in the small intestine of carnivores was acid, that of herbivores alkaline; the chyle of the carnivores was a homogeneous milky white, that of the herbivores clear or slightly opalescent. These distinctions he had observed in animals which he had sacrificed while they were in digestion. Finally, there was the fact that carnivores secrete clear, acid urine and herbivores produce a turbid, alkaline fluid.[29]

It was, of course, primarily through his recent experiments concerning the urine that he was able to judge the general question. The differences were not due to basic differences in the nutritive functions of the animals. Summarizing the way in which he had been able to alter the urine of rabbits by placing them in a fasting condition, he concluded that "without feeding, *the urines of herbivores and carnivores present primitively the same appearance and reaction.*" The ordinary modi-·fication from this condition of the urine of rabbits derives from the nature of their aliments, he contended, and adduced as evidence the experiments in which he had "inverted" their alimentation by feeding them meat. He invoked also a converse experiment, not mentioned in his notebooks, in which he had caused dogs to secrete whitish, alkaline urine by feeding them carrots and potatoes. By sacrificing some of these animals during digestion, he reported, he had seen corresponding inversions of their chyme and chyle.[30] (Unfortunately there is no indication of when he performed the experiments on dogs and made the last-mentioned observations. Obviously the interpretation I have given of the notebook record does not take them into account; but without knowledge of where they fit in the sequence of investigations, I cannot tell in what way the significance I have attributed to the individual recorded experiments ought to be modified.)

From these facts Bernard concluded that the differences in the alimentary apparatuses of the two classes of animals do not extend beyond the mechanical actions in the mouth and stomach, for, he explained,

the experiments inform us that in herbivores and carnivores the chemical part of the digestive function does not vary, in the sense that the intestinal juices always act in the same manner with the same alimentary principles, whether the digestive phenomenon be performed in the intestine of a dog or in that of a rabbit. The assimilation into the blood is equally brought about in an identical manner, and the *alkaline* reaction of the urine has always provided us with an indication, in all animals, of the assimilation of non-nitrogenous substances. Instead, therefore, of saying that *turbid* and *alkaline* urine is that of herbivores, it is more accurate to say that it pertains to the assimilation of non-nitrogenous aliments.[31]

The character of the urine, Bernard continued, provided a diagnostic indication which could help to resolve other important physiological questions involving digestion and nutrition. From his recent research he provided two examples. The first was the injection experiments in which grape sugar turned the acid urine of a fasting animal alkaline, whereas cane sugar did not. The difference resulted, he said from the fact that grape sugar is directly assimilated and destroyed in the blood, whereas cane sugar . . . can only be assimilated after having previously undergone the influence of the stomach, as I have proved elsewhere. This very remarkable physiological difference between the two sugars, suspected or indicated by several chemists, is proved beyond any objection by the difference in their influence on the urine.[32]

Here Bernard was publicly stating for the first time the position he had adopted during the previous fall. His statement, "as I have proved elsewhere," however, implies that this is what he had maintained all along, in spite of the fact that in his earlier published discussions he had said that all nutrients, including grape sugar, must undergo the influence of the stomach. By this time, apparently, Bernard had banished from his view the fact that he had changed his mind, or that he was not the first to demonstrate what he now advocated. Bernard is not alone among eminent scientists in having resorted to unacknowledged "editing" of a former conclusion to make it conform to his later opinion.

The second example of the diagnostic value of the urinary changes which Bernard gave was the experiments in which sectioning of the vagus nerves changed alkaline urine to acid. This result proved also beyond any further doubt, he claimed, that the severing of these nerves "arrests completely the phenomena of digestion." [33]

Though the results Bernard presented were original and significant, his memoir fosters an impression that the general conception he drew from them was more novel than it actually was. His presentation implies that until then the distinction between herbivorous and carnivorous urine was generally attributed to the organization of the animals themselves rather than to their diets. It is true that textbooks of the time commonly made the general distinction that the urine of carnivores is clear and acid, whereas that of herbivorous mammals is usually turbid and alkaline.[34] Nevertheless, there was ample evidence from earlier investigations that the properties of urine vary according to the type of food an animal consumes. One of the most striking demonstrations had come out of the research of Bernard's own teacher. While Magendie was carrying out the famous experiments in which he tried to maintain dogs on non-nitrogenous foods, in 1816, he asked Chevreul to analyze the urine and bile of the animals. In the urine of a dog which had died after twenty-three days on a diet of pure sugar, Chevreul "found almost all of the characteristics which belong to the urine . . . of herbivorous animals; that is, instead of being acid like that of carnivores, the urine was noticeably alkaline, and showed no trace of uric acid or of phosphates." He obtained similar results in the other cases.[35] Magendie repeated this description from his original memoir in his later textbooks, Friedrich Ludwig Hünefeld referred to it in 1826 in his *Physiologische Chemie*, and Johannes Müller thought it important enough to mention more than once in his *Handbuch*. Rayer also inserted it in his medical treatise on the alteration of the urinary secretions.[36] The observation, therefore, was widely known.

There was considerable other evidence that urine varied with dietary changes. In 1810 William Hyde Wollaston observed that birds eating animal food produce much greater proportions of uric acid in their excrements than do those feeding on vegetable substances.[37] In 1826 Charles Chossat, an industrious Tuscan physician, made an extraordinarily painstaking study of the variations in the quantity of solid matter secreted in human urine over a given time period. He showed that increases occurred consistently at a certain interval after he had taken his meals, that the amount of increase varied according to the quantity of food, and that it was larger when he ate "animalized," or highly nitrogenous aliments. The changes in the amounts of the solid portions of urine secreted displayed such an "intimate, direct" relation to the digestion of aliments, that Chossat felt he had proved that the character of the food, and consequently of the chyle, determined the quantity and nature of these constituents of the secretion. In an appendix to his study he tried to account for the clarity or cloudiness of urine in terms of the diet, suggesting that the latter condition always occurred when there were fibrinous constituents in the food.[38] These early indications of the relation between the properties of the aliments and the qualitative character of the urine may have been too fragmentary to establish conclusively that there is a close interdependence. In 1842, however, a young physician at Leipzig who had devoted himself for several years to physiological chemistry,[39] undertook a very careful and complete study of just that question. Carl Gotthelf Lehmann [40] began with a critical evaluation of the methods used for determining qualitatively and quantitatively each of the major constituents recognized in urine—urea, uric acid, free and combined lactic acid, mucus, sodium and ammonium chloride, alkali sulfates, sodium, calcium, and magnesium phosphate, and an "extractive material." Then he compared the quantities of each of these in his own urine when he was on a normal mixed diet with the corresponding quantities when he was on a purely "animal diet" of eggs for three weeks; on a pure vegetable diet for two weeks; and on an exclusively non-nitrogenous diet of starch, sugar, and oil for three days. He

Carl Gotthelf Lehmann

was able to show that certain constituents, such as the total of all solid matter, the urea, and the extractive matter varied substantially with these dietary changes; whereas others, including uric acid, were relatively little affected. Although he was most interested in these quantitative analytical differences, Lehmann did note that certain qualitative distinctions were observable in the urines. That produced during the time of the "animal" diet was "straw yellow, limpid," and "distinctly acid." That pertaining to the vegetable diet was also distinctly acid, but more brownish and deposited more sediment. From the non-nitrogenous regimen he obtained an almost reddish brown urine. It had "a very slight acid reaction; however, it was never entirely without an acid reaction." [41]

In 1844 Liebig tried to determine what constituents of human urine were responsible for its normal acid reaction. His arguments were subtle and based on complex analytical factors. He remarked, however, that the acid reaction was really accidental, for the character of urine is easily altered by the nature of the food eaten. Thus animals which live on vegetables, grass, herbs, or roots have alkaline urine, he claimed, because all of these foods contain alkali salts of vegetable acids, which produce alkaline carbonates in the urine. "The acid, neutral, or alkaline reaction of the urine of healthy individuals," he added, "does not depend on a difference between the digestive, respiratory, or secretory processes in the different classes of animals, but from the aliments and the alkaline bases introduced with them." Analyses of urine which ignore the nature of what has been eaten, he warned, teach nothing about the nature of physiological or pathological processes.[42]

In the light of these developments previous to his own investigation, Bernard's memoir would appear to fit logically as one more contribution to a fuller understanding of a general problem which others had already probed with success. By omitting to connect his work with the work of his predecessors, however, Bernard's memoir seemed to imply that it comprised a venture into a new area of inquiry. Perhaps, as in other cases, he was unfamiliar with the recent papers of the German chemists, although he must have known of Magendie and Chevreul's older discovery. Undoubtedly he himself came to this problem through the logic and accidents of his own research rather than from the leads of others. Clearly he did not survey contemporary efforts to deal with the same problem, but followed what he conceived to be his own path. It may have been true, as he later asserted, that it was better to investigate things for oneself without too much regard for what had previously been said on the subject, even if one sometimes ended up discovering what was already known.[43] Nevertheless, his casual attitude toward the literature in his field here led him to ascribe a broader significance to his own discoveries than the situation warranted. The connection he sought to establish between the character of urine and of aliments was only a particular manifestation of a general relation which other scientists were already finding.

Furthermore, by comparison with a study such as that of Lehmann, the criteria by which Bernard judged various samples of urine to be the same or different in character were almost primitive. Lehmann and others were dealing quantitatively with specific chemical constituents, whereas Bernard was utilizing only the appearance and a simple test of the reaction of the urine (excluding those aspects of his memoir which involved tests for sugar in the urine). Bernard himself acknowledged that his present conclusions were based only on "inspection" of the urine and its reaction, and indicated that he hoped with Barreswil's help to investigate the actual composition of that secretion produced by different dietary conditions.[44] For all that, however, Bernard had added considerably to the elucidation of the general question. Superficial though the changes he reported may have been, they were more striking than those which others had reported, and in physiological terms they dealt most directly with the purported distinctions between the nutritive processes of herbivores and carnivores. Lehmann had found that non-nitrogenous aliments decreased the acidity and modified the appearance of his urine, but he did not detect anything as persuasive as the "inversions" Bernard found. Lehmann reviewed his own investigation later in his *Lehrbuch der physiologischen Chemie* and listed among the conclusions to which it had led that "with a nitrogen-free diet [the urine] completely loses" its free acid.[45] Since he was summarizing the same data that in 1842 had revealed only a lessened acidity, it may well be that Bernard's more dramatic results in the meantime had influenced Lehmann to see more in his own results than had originally been there.

The strong impact of Bernard's discovery on his immediate scientific surroundings may be measured by the influence it exerted on Magendie. During the spring of 1846 Magendie chose digestion as the topic for his course at the Collège de France and repeated publicly, as he customarily did, many of the important experiments recently published on the question. In the course of these demonstrations he made several interesting observations, which he reported to the Academy in July in his "Note on the normal presence of sugar in the blood." The central feature of this paper, the detection of sugar in the blood for a time after an animal has digested starch, has already been discussed in connection with Boussingault's reaction to it.[46] This observation grew out of experiments on the artificial digestion of starch, in which Magendie found that, besides saliva and pancreatic juice, all of the fluids he drew from the animal, including blood, could transform the substance into sugar. The outcome raised some doubt, Magendie remarked, about the specific catalytic properties which were attributed to saliva and pancreatic juice as a result of the research of Mialhe, Bouchardat and Sandras, and others. The fact that Bernard also tested other animal fluids along with his digestion experiments with saliva and gastric juice during this spring indicates that he was probably keeping in close touch with Magendie's research, even though he no longer assisted in the course. After finding that extracted blood changes starch to sugar, Magendie tried injecting starch directly into the circulating fluid of a rabbit, charting its conversion by withdrawing samples for analysis at hourly intervals. But he also resorted to a more indirect method. It was based on "a recent work of MM. Bernard and Barreswil" [47] showing that the urine of fasting herbivores is comparable to that of carnivores. Having injected starch into the blood of a rabbit whose urine was clear and acid, Magendie and his *préparateur*, M. Ferrand, found that its urine acquired in a short time the turbid, alkaline state normal for a digesting rabbit. "That is a new proof," he asserted, of the "close connection which exists between the composition of the blood and that of the urine." [48] The conclusion was typical of the cryptic, abbreviated interpretations which Magendie all too frequently gave his observations. He certainly implied that the urine change was evidence that the starch was converted into sugar in the blood. One cannot tell, however, whether he accepted an explanation according to Bernard's theory, that the alkaline urine indicated that the non-nitrogenous aliment was assimilated after conversion to sugar in the blood, or whether, in his less theoretical fashion, he reasoned no further than the literal meaning of his statement.

Magendie also performed an inverse experiment which Bernard had contemplated too but apparently had never carried out. Injecting meat bouillon into the vein of a rabbit whose urine was turbid and alkaline, Magendie found that in a few instants the urine became clear and acid and contained an abundance of urea. "Can one not conclude from these experiments," he asked, "that the presence of urea in the urine is connected with the composition of the blood, and that the origin of that material is not always that which is generally attributed to it?" [49] Unfortunately Magendie did not specify to what origin urea was generally attributed, so that it is hard to tell what view he was questioning. Perhaps he was aiming at Liebig's belief that all nitrogenous nutrients must become organized constituents of the animal and contribute to the "metamorphosis" of its tissues before they can be decomposed into waste products. [50] On the other hand, the result also contained an implied criticism of Bernard's own view of the phenomena, for the nearly instantaneous change of the urine suggests that the connection between the composition of the blood and of the urine was too immediate to be a reflection of intervening alterations in the more profound processes of assimilative nutrition. There is no record, however, of any confrontation over this issue between the teacher and his former student.

Bernard must have been heartened by the recognition his discovery had won. His success could not have come at a time when it was more needed, for there was much to discourage him. The experiments on digestion which had been his steady concern for so long had gone badly again. A year and a half after leaving his position as Magendie's assistant, he was still struggling along without material support for his research. His unfulfilled need for some professional status is, I think, poignantly reflected in the titles which he listed at this time under his name in some of his published articles. "By Dr. Cl. Bernard, ex-preparateur of the course of physiology at the Collège de France, former intern at the hospitals, private professor of anatomy and physiology." [51] That the scientific establishment of Paris could not make better provision for the best student of its most eminent physiologist, a young man already clearly marked as an experimentalist of great promise, illustrates dramatically why France was rapidly losing its scientific preeminence to Germany.

During April and May Bernard does not seem to have pursued any of his investigations of nutrition or digestion. In the summer, however, he began to extend his observations concerning the effects of nutritional conditions on the urine. On June 6 he and Barreswil placed themselves on non-nitrogenous diets. The previous evening Bernard had dined on an ordinary mixed meal and found his urine to be colored and very acid. It deposited uric acid when cooled. The next morning he began his regimen with a porridge composed of potatoes and butter. At ten o'clock his urine was unchanged. At noon he ate carrots and cabbage sautéed in butter, lettuce salad, and sugar. At two o'clock and four o'clock in the afternoon his urine was still acidic. For dinner he had vegetable soup, fried potatoes, buttered peas, and fresh potatoes in place of bread. At ten o'clock in the evening his urine was still acid, but by the time he went to bed at midnight it seemed a little less so. Waking early, at six o'clock, he was rewarded by finding that his urine had become clearly alkaline and no longer formed deposits of uric acid. The excretions remained alkaline for the rest of the morning. At noon he switched to a meat diet, and the excretions gradually returned to their ordinary state. Aside from the general success of the experiment, what interested him most was that when he perspired his sweat was acidic, even while his urine was alkaline. [52]

Barreswil's constitution was as uncooperative as ever. Bernard commented: "Barreswil subjected to the same regimen as I was did not observe his urine alkaline because he did not follow the regimen long enough; he claims that it is because he walked and perspired much more than I—nothing up until now substantiates such an opinion." [53]

On July 26 Bernard tested the urine of a horse which had been given no solid food for eleven days and found it acid. When ridden until it perspired, its sweat turned out to be very alkaline, a result which was puzzling to Bernard. The sweat of the horse was opposite in reaction to that of humans, yet in neither case did this seem to be related to their dietary differences; for when Bernard switched the diet of each, the sweat, unlike the urine, remained what it was normally. He considered doing some further experiments on the perspiration of dogs and rabbits, but apparently did not carry them out at this time.[54] On August 27 he examined three calf fetuses at the slaughterhouse of Popincourt, one of which was two or three months old, the other two near birth. Their urines were neutral. Five days later, however, he found the urines of four other fetuses to be alkaline, as were their other body fluids. This "remarkable" fact made him wonder whether the urine of a fetus is simply like that of its mother, and in what form nourishment passes from the mother to the fetus. The paradox, in view of his earlier experiments indicating that a nitrogenous diet produces acid urine, was that the aliment of the fetus ought to be the blood of its mother. He thought that in order to elucidate the matter further he ought to compare the urine of the fetuses of carnivores, as well as of herbivorous mothers either fasting or placed on meat diets.[55]

Meanwhile, he was following the effects of a long fast on another horse. On August 31, when it had been without food for seventeen days, its perspiration was alkaline. The soldiers attending the horse observed with litmus paper that its urine was very acid. On the twenty-first day of its fast Bernard was able to collect its urine, even though the horse was still strong and vicious enough to make approaching it difficult. Bernard boiled a portion of the urine, producing a white cloudiness which became clear and dark when he added nitric acid. The latter reaction was a test which Rayer had suggested to him as a way of distinguishing the coagulable material from albumin. When Bernard added nitric acid to another unheated portion, alterations took place which made him think there might be bile present in the urine. The next day he evaporated a semiliter of the urine to dryness, macerated the residue in alcohol for thirty-six hours, filtered it and washed the residue again. Upon further evaporation he obtained a large quantity of crystals of urea. Apparently this was as far as his own analytical experience could carry him; for he sent the urine for further analysis to a student of Barreswil, who reported that it contained "prodigious quantities" of urea, but no uric or hippuric acid and no carbonate or phosphates.[56]

Bernard's research over the summer had gone at a rather slow pace compared to former times. His experiments on nutrition were in addition carried out mostly outside of the laboratory—on himself at home, on horses at the stable of the École Militaire, on calf fetuses at the slaughterhouse. This pattern raises a possibility that in these months he had less access than usual to laboratory facilities. Possibly also he could have been distracted by the birth and early death of his first son during this period.[57] Nevertheless, he seemed to be finding profitable ways to follow up his earlier discovery. He was extending the range of its applicability and discovering related questions which promised to open up interesting new investigations. In the last experiment he appeared finally to be starting to implement his announced intention of making detailed studies of the effects of dietary changes on the chemical constitution of urine. Just at this juncture, however, he turned away from this path to return once again to his unsolved problems concerning gastric and salivary digestion. That he should revert from his most successful venture back to the source of some of his most frustrating experiences is explained, at least in part, I think, by the fact that in August Louis Mialhe had delivered a strong criticism of his troubled digestive theory.

XIV

Claude Bernard and Louis Mialhe

While Claude Bernard was still mired in his struggle to save his ideas about digestion, Louis Mialhe was forging ahead with his own approach to the same problems, buoyed by the warm approval which the Academy of Sciences had recently given to his discovery of animal diastase. In spite of the debate which his theory of salivary action had engendered in 1845, a commission comprised of Magendie, Flourens, Milne Edwards, and Payen verified his results and judged them so important that they reported in March 1846 that "his numerous experiments have changed the face of the question." [1] Now Mialhe turned to the digestion of nitrogenous, or albuminoid, aliments. On August 3, 1846, he read a memoir on that subject at the Academy. In it he made a significant contribution and he also presented an unusually cogent discussion of the whole problem of digestion as it had developed from Spallanzani to his own day. He debated with recent positions taken by Blondlot, Bouchardat and Sandras, as well as by Bernard and Barreswil. Mialhe dealt with three major questions. First, he discussed the composition of gastric juice, comparing the properties of Schwann's pepsin to the chymosine of Deschamps and the gasterase of Payen. Then he refuted Bernard and Barreswil's contention that the active organic principles in the digestive juices are the same. Finally, he demonstrated conclusively that the action of gastric juice on albuminoid materials is different from that of its acid alone, and in so doing developed a new theory of chymification. [2]

Mialhe fully accepted the view that the pepsin discovered by Schwann was the active principle of gastric juice. Of the means for extracting it worked out successively by Pappenheim, Wasmann, and

298

August Vogel, Mialhe preferred the method of Vogel, basically an extension of Schwann's own efforts to separate the substance by precipitating it with lead acetate.[3] Mialhe regarded the pepsin obtained this way as still impure, but sufficiently isolated so that its physical and chemical properties could be meaningfully described. The material which Michel Deschamps had obtained from calf rennet and named chymosine[4] Mialhe considered to be only pepsin combined with other casein-like materials which made it insoluble in water. With another method of extraction he got from the same source a material whose properties were indistinguishable from ordinary pepsin. Gasterase, a preparation which Payen had given this name because he claimed that it differed from pepsin,[5] was, according to Mialhe, only pepsin in a much purer state because Payen had separated it from natural gastric juice instead of the mucus of the stomach. Mialhe himself used Payen's procedure to procure large quantities of pepsin from the gastric juice of cows, which he could bring home by the liter from the slaughterhouse. There was, Mialhe concluded, only one gastric ferment, and it was therefore appropriate to retain the name which Schwann had first given it.[6]

It would be going too far, however, Mialhe asserted, to conclude with Bernard and Barreswil that there was only one digestive ferment altogether. He believed that his own experiments had proved just the opposite: that "pepsin and diastase are two entirely distinct active principles, having no other characteristic in common but that of belonging both to the class of chemical agents operating in infinitesimally small amounts." Mialhe found that diastase uniquely transforms starch to dextrin and glucose, whereas pepsin uniquely brings about the physiological transformation of meat and related albuminoids. He checked for himself the "proposition" of Bernard and Barreswil that gastric juice made alkaline ceases to digest meat and transforms starch instead. Mialhe, too, succeeded with this experiment when he used gastric juice from humans or from dogs, but not with the juice from calves. The reason, he asserted, was that the gastric juice of those mammals with single stomachs always contains some pure saliva, whereas the saliva of herbivorous animals is altered in the gastric cavities anterior to the source of their gastric fluid. Therefore, when Bernard and Barreswil neutralized the acid of their gastric juice, they had only restored the digestive properties of the saliva mixed with it. To confirm his explanation, Mialhe mixed equal parts of diastase and pepsin in faintly acidifed water. The solution dissolved meat very well. Then he saturated it with sodium carbonate;

the fluid thereupon lost the capacity to digest meat, but acquired the power to transform starch. Mialhe thus accepted Bernard and Barreswil's results, but disagreed with their interpretation. In the case of their claim that acidified saliva digests meat, however, Mialhe found his own "researches in complete disaccord" with theirs. Acidified saliva for him only caused fibrin to swell and become hydrated, just as fibrin did with very dilute acid alone; the secretion never caused that aliment to undergo the transformation of digestion. Acidified pancreatic juice did seem capable of dissolving fibrin as Bernard and Barreswil had observed, Mialhe acknowledged, but he attributed this action to a putrefaction rather than a true digestion.[7]

Mialhe's refutation of Bernard and Barreswil's generalization was based on experimental results which others readily sustained. As we have seen, Bernard himself was finding it impossible to confirm his assertions about saliva. In 1847 Joh. Carl. Strahl wrote that "one must be amazed at the boldly erected hypothesis" of Bernard and Barreswil. "Here in Germany we have not yet been able to digest albumin with acidified saliva."[8] In the next two years investigations by Jacubowitsch and Frerichs further refuted the theory of the two French collaborators, and in 1853 Lehmann, an admirer of Bernard, wrote that "anyone can easily convince himself that it is untenable, simply by repeating the investigations employed by Bernard and Barreswil." In Paris, too, the verdict of other scientists was against their theory of digestion. In 1848 Pierre-Honoré Bérard said in his course that it seemed to him that Mialhe had completely disproved it. Bernard did not publicly recant in the face of these adverse judgments, but Bérard reported: "I have some reason to believe that the authors of that doctrine no longer adhere very much to it today."[9]

Nevertheless, Mialhe's opposition was as much conceptual as empirical, for he, as much as Bernard and Barreswil, sought to reduce the complexities of nutrition to a simple explanation. Where they saw this simplicity in the idea of a single organic principle modified by its milieu, Mialhe sought it in the doctrine that there is one specific ferment for the digestion of each of the three major classes of food. He was sufficiently confident of this scheme that he believed that after proving it for starch and albuminoids he would have little trouble completing the demonstration for the remaining class. "One may conclude," he said,

that nature, so admirable in the simplicity and uniformity of its means, manages the assimilation of fatty materials comprising the third alimentary group by a similar reaction, by a special ferment, in a such a way that the same law presides over the act, in appearance so complicated, of nutrition. It is that which I propose to demonstrate in a subsequent memoir.[10]

That was a demonstration fated to fall not to Mialhe, but to Bernard. Meanwhile, however, Mialhe had achieved a result nearly as significant in his study of the way in which albuminoids are digested. Even though several authors, he pointed out, had already refuted the idea that the gastric acid by itself is capable of digesting these aliments, Bouchardat and Sandras had recently reasserted that fibrin, albumin, gluten, and casein are digested in that way.[11] To refute their claim, Mialhe showed that although the substances do dissolve in dilute hydrochloric acid, the products are quite different from those obtained when the same materials are placed in this solution together with pepsin. Fibrin dissolved in acid had properties analogous to casein. It became clouded by heat but did not coagulate. It was precipitated by acids and alkalis, and like casein it was precipitated immediately by an addition of pepsin. Fibrin dissolved with pepsin in the same acid had "totally different chemical characteristics." It was not coagulable by heat, nor precipitated by alkalis or by hydrochloric or nitric acid, and was not affected by a further addition of pepsin. The result proved, he said, that pepsin not only dissolved the fibrin, but caused it to undergo a "complete constitutive metamorphosis." Gastric acid clearly facilitated this process, but only by dividing and hydrating the aliment so as to prepare it to react more rapidly.[12]

By similar experiments Mialhe showed that the properties of gluten, albumin, and casein digested with pepsin also differed from the products of these substances dissolved in acid alone. Such distinctions had been discussed long before, by Müller and by Eberle among others; but Mialhe added a very significant new generalization. All of these products of digestion with pepsin, he claimed, had exactly the same properties. He admitted that perhaps their elementary compositions would differ slightly depending on the source, but their chemical reactions were identical. On the basis of these results Mialhe proposed that pepsin transforms all albuminoids into one substance, which he named "albuminose."[13] "This product of metamorphosis plays an immense role in the grand act of animal nutrition," he asserted, "for it is to the nitrogenous aliments what glucose is to the carbohydrate aliments of the amyloid family of substances."[14] Just as glucose is the only member of the latter group which can be assimilated, so albuminose is the only member of the former group which can be.

To demonstrate the validity of this view Mialhe recalled how Claude Bernard had shown that albumin merely dissolved in water and subsequently injected into the veins of an animal is rejected in the urine, but the same substance injected after digestion with gastric juice is assimilated. Mialhe himself repeated Bernard's experiment successfully, and extended its scope by replacing albumin with casein and getting a similar result. With fibrin he also confirmed the generalization, except that in this case the undigested fibrin immediately killed the animal by blocking the capillaries of its lungs.[15] By borrowing Bernard's physiological methods to verify a conclusion derived from his study of the chemical reactions and properties of the substances involved, Mialhe seemed to be growing beyond his old presumption that the latter results form by themselves a sufficient basis for deducing physiological phenomena. His movement in this direction, however, was limited by the range of his own experience. Just as Bernard the physiologist required the aid of a chemist when his research led him into complex analytical problems, so Mialhe the chemist now needed help for the physiological aspects of his experiments. "All of the experiments which required any vivisections have been performed," he acknowledged, "in common with my friend Doctor Martin Magron, to whom I repeat here the assurance of my gratitude."[16]

Mialhe's memoir showed the sometimes controversial scientist at his best. His discussion was elegant and incisive, displaying a sure instinct for the central problems concerning digestion. As he noted, his predecessors had already observed various chemical transformations of albuminous aliments in the stomach, and some of the digestive changes were similar to those he was describing. But the past reports were fragmentary and had not revealed a common meaningful pattern. Mialhe quoted a comment of Burdach in response to a claim that the different nitrogenous aliments are converted to albumin during digestion. If there is any common product of digestion, Burdach had predicted, it will not be a constituent of the blood, but some neutral rudiment of the diverse alimentary substances from which each of them can be formed. This characteristic, Mialhe added, applied perfectly to albuminose.[17] Undoubtedly Mialhe set out with a predisposition to find a substance which would solve the riddle inherent in Burdach's proposition, so that his albuminose was probably as much a product of his will as of his analyses. Other commentators were less certain that it existed in as sharply defined a manner as he proposed. Friedrich Theodor Frerichs found in his own experiments that the product of the digestion of albumin had properties similar to those Mialhe had described. He was willing "for the sake of brevity to call it albuminose with Mialhe," but he doubted that the elementary composition of the albumin itself had really been changed during the digestion.[18] Lehmann criticized a subsequent effort by Mialhe to define albumin, the casein-like products of its solution in acid, and albuminose, as the three stages in the physiological conversion of albuminous materials to an assimilable nutrient, and rejected Mialhe's later claim that blood albumin is albuminose.[19] Obviously Mialhe overreached in his determination to support a rational theory of digestion. Yet he brought sufficient experimental skill to his task so that, even though some of his conclusions had to be modified, the nucleus of his discovery held up. Lehmann found, for example, that Mialhe had gone too far in claiming that the soluble products of the digestion of all protein substances and gelatin were completely identical. He himself found slight differences in the properties of the products of some aliments of this class, and he renamed the products peptones. Nevertheless, he recognized Mialhe as the first person to have investigated these products closely, and acknowledged that the properties by which Mialhe had identified albuminose actually were common to most of the peptones.[20] Milne Edwards described Mialhe as the first to "call the attention of physiologists to these metamorphoses of the alimentary material." [21] Clearly Mialhe's solution to the problem of the digestion of albuminous materials was not definitive in the sense he believed it to be, but clearly also it marked a new phase in the investigation of the problem.

Mialhe's success was not a result of his analytical and logical talent alone, for he had also a remarkably comprehensive awareness of the way in which knowledge of digestion had developed. He summarized the historical significance of the contributions of each of the recent and earlier participants with such cogency as to make it quite likely that, unlike many of his colleagues, he had carefully read most of the original memoirs. Consequently, he had a good feel for the direction in which the problem was going, and this sensitivity helped him to place his own effort at the heart of the currently unresolved questions. Most important of all, perhaps, he alone of the French physiologists appreciated German and French contributions equally and understood that all investigations of gastric digestion must begin with the foundation of the pepsin theory formulated by Eberle, Schwann, and their German successors.

Though Mialhe had a certain taste for disputation, to all appearance he singled out Bernard and Barreswil's theory for criticism because of the discordance of their results with his, and because of the disparity of their views with his own conception of digestion, rather than because of any animosity. As we have seen, he supported and utilized Bernard's injection experiments, and he also took the opportunity to mention that his research agreed with that of Bernard and Barreswil concerning the nature of the gastric acid.[22] He reserved his enthusiasm, however, for Dumas, to whom he again dedicated his publication. This time he wrote, "In this memoir experiments are reported which achieve the confirmation of several of your theories; it was therefore an obligation for me to offer the dedication to you." [23] This was plainly a forced interpretation of the situation. Mialhe did find some statements by Dumas, to the effect that digestion was a kind of ferment action and that chymosine was probably identical with pepsin, which he could cite as anticipations of his own conclusions. Somewhat more convincing was the fact that Dumas and Cahours had found differences in the physical properties of fibrin digested with pepsin and that dissolved in hydrochloric acid alone, from which they inferred that there are two agents in gastric juice. This "capital experiment," which Mialhe repeated "a great number of times," might have served as the prototype for his own more extensive investigations.[24] But on the most important point of his paper—that digestion produces a true chemical metamorphosis—Mialhe flatly contradicted Dumas's assertion that digestion is a mere dissolution. He even quoted Dumas's view as that of "a great scientific authority" [25] in order to emphasize how divided opinions were over the question which he believed he had resolved. If Mialhe nevertheless represented himself as in general confirming Dumas's theory, his desire to identify himself personally as a follower of Dumas in animal chemistry must have transcended any logical coincidence of their scientific positions. Had he chosen to identify himself with Bernard instead, he could with better reason have portrayed his results as a confirmation and chemical specification of the general view of digestion which Bernard had advocated in his M.D. thesis.[26]

The entire memoir which Mialhe read did not appear in print until 1847, but an abstract was published in the September 1846 issue of the *Journal de pharmacie et de chimie*, as well as in the *Compte rendu* of the Academy. This shorter version contained, in somewhat blunter terms, most of the essential arguments which he had made to "reverse the opinion of Bernard and Barreswil." [27] For a subject which so directly concerned him Bernard surely must have heard most of the details from friends soon after the meeting itself in August.

It cannot be proved beyond all doubt that the experiments on digestion which Bernard undertook in September were a direct reaction to Mialhe's memoir. They did not exactly parallel those which Mialhe had used to reinterpret Bernard and Barreswil's conclusions about the actions of gastric juice and of saliva, and they had sufficient connection with his own research of the previous spring to be explainable simply as a continuation of these. Yet their timing, and the fact that they consisted chiefly of tests involving gastric juice mixed with saliva, give a strong impression that he was influenced to do them, at least in part, because of Mialhe's comments. On September 17 Bernard began a series of "experiments on the properties of saliva." In the first four of six test tubes he compared the action of normal alkaline human saliva with acidic saliva taken from a diabetic patient. Both kinds transformed starch within half an hour. The last two runs, however, came to occupy most of his attention. In them he compared the action upon starch of normal acidic gastric juice from a dog with that of the same juice to which he had added an equal part of fresh human saliva. The reaction of the latter mixture remained acid. After thirty minutes the iodine indicator was still "excessively intense blue" in the former, whereas the color had disappeared in the other, indicating that the starch had been completely transformed there. The conclusions, he wrote, were "easy to draw," though he did not state them. Next, he mixed the two tubes and observed that the starch from the first tube was then also transformed, evidently a further indication that the presence of saliva was the essential factor in the reaction. As he tested the effects of mixed secretions further, however, he encountered contradictory results. He took gastric juice impregnated with bread and added an equal quantity of his own saliva, but this time the blue coloration with iodine remained very intense.[28] When there was still no evidence of any transformation after an hour, the unexpected turn of events drew from him an interesting train of thought:

> This experiment is curious in this sense, that one sees that bread soaked and macerated in the gastric juice is not transformed into sugar by an equal quantity of saliva. It is true that the reaction has remained acid—but it has appeared to me that in the case where animals ate bread, even though the reaction remained acid in the small intestine, nevertheless, one would no longer find starch by the tincture of iodine. That will be a fact to look at again.[29]

That is, if the acidity were sufficient to prevent saliva from transforming starch, then it was hard to understand how saliva could be responsible for the conversion in situations in which the reaction was continuously acid where it occurred. That being the case, he wondered if it was rather a combination of the bile and pancreatic juice which caused starch to disappear in the intestine. This thought led him to recall that in dogs there is a small pancreatic duct joined to the hepatic duct. Whether he considered that this arrangement supported the idea that the two juices act together, or whether the observation merely occurred to him by the coincidence that it also involved a connection between the two fluids, is not discernible. At any rate, the anatomical remark led him in turn to another idea, which he interjected with a parenthesis, that such a joining of the ducts might cause the bile by the time it reaches the mucous lining of the intestine to be in a condition different from that in the bile duct. Still wandering by free association from one idea to another, he wondered if there might not be an analogous explanation for some puzzling observations he had made concerning the different properties of saliva obtained in different ways:

for when I collect saliva with my little tubes [from around the openings of the ducts] it has properties nearly like that of the mouth, even though it has not stayed there and it has been collected as it leaves the duct.—Moreover, I believe that this chemical action of saliva is only an accident more pronounced in man than in the animals whose saliva even when mixed is always less active chemically than in man.[30]

The source of the perplexity embodied in the first part of this passage is that his own earlier experiments, as well as those of Lassaigne and the commission on equine nutrition, had shown that mixed saliva from the mouth digested starch, whereas the individual secretions obtained by sectioning the duct of a gland did not.[31] If this difference were due to a change in the conditions of the secretions after they entered the mouth cavity, however, then that change should not yet have occurred to saliva collected just as it enters the mouth. He was contemplating the possibility, therefore, that something happens to saliva near the end of its duct, just as something might happen to bile near the end of *its* duct because of a conjunction of its duct with a pancreatic duct. These were merely hints of explanations, passing thoughts typical of the way Bernard's mind searched around for clues to make sense of anomalous observations. The last statement in the above passage does not follow obviously from the preceding one, but has a certain connection with it, in that it was apparently the variations in the properties of saliva obtained from different sources which started him contemplating that the ability to transform starch of those samples of saliva which do possess it is only accidental. Magendie's conclusion that the property is common to other body fluids [32] would also support such an inference; yet it was a surprising conclusion to entertain, especially in view of Bernard's past attempts to demonstrate a chemical role for saliva in digestion.

This record of some of the thoughts that went through Bernard's mind in the midst of his experiment provides a fascinating glimpse of a mental process which he described vividly several years later in another notebook:

> Ideas develop spontaneously in the mind, and when one abandons himself to his ideas, one is like a man at the window who watches the travelers go by. In a sense, therefore, one watches his ideas go by. That does not require any effort; it has even a great charm.[33]

Not all of these ideas simply passed by, however, for some of them were the germs of well-defined positions which emerged during the following weeks. That part of the process, too, Bernard later portrayed in the continuation of his simile. "Where the labor, the wearisome toil is, is to hold the idea by the collar, as one would stop the traveler in spite of his desire to escape, to remember it, to fasten it, to give it its character, etc." [34] That is what he did with some of the ideas which came to him on the present occasion; as he gave his idea concerning the chemical properties of saliva more character and definition, it became the base for a drastic shift in his conception of the function of that secretion.

Following up the thought that in digestion starch may be transformed by something other than saliva, Bernard contemplated adding bile to gastric juice and bread. Instead he went on with the experiments he had begun. The test of mixed gastric juice and saliva which had stimulated these meditations was still going on. After fifteen hours the solution still had not transformed the starch; but after twenty-four hours the tube displayed in its blue coloration a reddish reflection which indicated to him that a little dextrin had formed. This nuance might not have constituted very impressive evidence of a specific effect due to the saliva, except that a second control sample without the saliva was still completely blue. The situation was therefore now even more ambiguous than it had seemed to be when he put down his reflections. He then added more saliva to the first tube until the reaction became clearly alkaline to litmus paper. When the resulting solution was exposed to a warm bath, "the starch disappeared almost instantly." Perhaps at this point Bernard was hopeful that he was on the way to reaffirm his old theory that it is the gastric juice itself which digests starch when it is alkaline; for the addition of saliva had caused only a slight transformation so long as the mixture remained acid, in contrast to the nearly instantaneous reaction as soon as it became alkaline. He remarked, "It is therefore because the reaction had become alkaline; to convince myself of that I am doing the experiment again in the following manner." Varying his procedures slightly, he repeated the experiment three more times with the same result. He was cautious, however, about jumping to a conclusion: "It is curious that it is necessary to render the liquid entirely alkaline. But would that depend rather on the fact that it is necessary to increase the quantity of saliva, which is then in excess, or else is it uniquely a matter of the alkaline reaction[?]" [35]

To decide between these alternatives, Bernard prepared three tubes containing bread macerated in gastric juice. To one he added enough saliva to make the mixture alkaline; to the second he added only a little saliva and then enough potash to render the solution alkaline. The third he made alkaline with potash alone. The outcome was quite clear. After fifteen minutes the starch in the first tube was gone; in the second tube it was still present, but a rose tint indicated that dextrin was forming. In the third tube a voluminous blue precipitate showed that "the starch did not appear to have undergone the least transformation." The conclusion to draw seemed unmistakable: "the alkaline reaction is not sufficient, there must be saliva." [36]

On September 19 Bernard macerated a little bit of starch for half an hour in gastric juice, then added saliva until the mixture was alkaline. The iodine reaction disappeared within fifteen minutes. A second bit of starch he treated in the same way except that he substituted ordinary water for the gastric juice. The result was the same. He concluded that the nonacidity of the liquid in which the starch was soaked in the latter case "had not noticeably retarded the transformation." What he did not say, even though it would seem to be the principal result of the experiment, was that gastric juice appeared not to be a significant factor in the transformation of the starch. [37]

On September 25 Bernard compared the action of acidic human diabetic saliva and of mixed saliva from a dog. The experiment led to a rather equivocal conclusion: "The mixed saliva of the dog, obtained from its mouth, thus transforms the starch, more slowly it is true than that of man." Two days later he compared the actions of canine saliva, normal and diabetic human saliva, and nasal mucus from a person suffering from an acute cold. The inclusion of the latter probably reflected the influence of Magendie's views concerning the actions of other body fluids on starch. Each of the fluids transformed equal quantities of starch solution within two hours. When he added more starch, however, only the two kinds of human saliva were able to act on it. "[Human] saliva," he inferred, "although not alone in having the power to transform starch, possesses it therefore in a higher degree than the [other] fluids indicated above." [38] In these experiments Bernard seemed to be exploring the variability in the transforming power which had induced him in his reflections a few days before to believe that that power was accidental to saliva.

Bernard must have continued his research on variations in salivary secretions sometime during the next four months, but the laboratory records of the experiments are gone. By the end of the above series the evidence would seem to have been overwhelming that his theory of gastric action was untenable and that Mialhe's explanation of his results as due to a mixture of gastric juice and saliva was correct. It would seem also that it ought to have become less important to Bernard to maintain that theory, since his failure the previous spring to confirm the corresponding theory of salivary action had apparently already destroyed the identity he had sought to establish in the nature of the digestive fluids. Yet Bernard was still not ready to give up. It seems evident that he had come to cherish his idea that an acid or alkaline reaction specifies the action of a more general transforming power of a digestive fluid. Attacks on this view from others, and even mounting evidence against it from his own research, still had the effect only of stimulating him to try harder to prove its validity. His response was in that sense similar to the response of Boussingault in 1844 to the multiplying arguments against the exclusively nutritive origin of animal fat. Like Boussingault also, Bernard's desire to prevail may have been sharpened by the fact that the criticism of his view came from someone whom he had come to identify as a rival.

In January he returned again to this basic question and, to judge from the character of the entry in his notebook, he approached it with an air of assurance which in the light of the previous developments seems astounding. He began:

Experiments on digestion–taken up again on the 9th of January, 1847 and repeated definitively with great care.
(1st new proposition resulting from my earlier researches)
Natural and acid gastric juice dissolves the nitrogenous principles–Alkaline, it destroys the amylaceous principles. [39]

This heading he wrote in what was for him an extraordinarily precise, formal hand, giving the distinct impression that he expected it to

Page from Claude Bernard's laboratory notebook describing the beginning of a series of experiments on gastric digestion. MS C. VIIIe, 7c, p. 151. See text, p. 309.

be the definitive statement on the problem. Beneath it, on January 10, he began "Experiments to support it." Working late in the evening, he prepared four tubes for gastric digestion. Two were naturally acidic and contained meat. The third was also acidic but contained starch, while the last one containing starch was saturated with potash until it was slightly alkaline. By midnight the pieces of meat were already beginning to digest, but the iodine indicator in the two tubes with starch was still intensely blue.[40]

Checking again at ten o'clock the next morning, Bernard found that the blue was still intense in the alkaline tube with starch. By Barreswil's reagent he found that no sugar had yet formed. His reaction to this news is recorded only as an exclamation mark in the margin of his notebook. There was no change either in the tube containing normal acidic gastric juice with starch, but this was to be expected. Separating the latter into two portions, he added an excess of beef bile to one of them. Presumably he was here investigating a hypothesis similar to the one he had put down in September, that a secretion other than saliva transforms starch in the digestive canal where the contents remain acid. After two days, however, there was no sign of a transformation in this portion. More critical, because it affected his more deeply entrenched views, was the situation in the alkaline tube, which he had kept at body temperature for the same time:

> end.
> Tube B after 2 days of digestion, there is ever an intense blue with the tincture of iodine and no reduction by boiling with the blue liquid [Barreswil's reagent]—There has therefore not been a verification of the denoted property. That is to say that gastric juice made alkaline as described has not transformed the starch into glucose.[41]

With that simple statement the long, arduous quest was over. Although Bernard qualified the negative result by relating it to the particular manner in which he had made the gastric juice alkaline, he did not, as far as is recorded, make any further efforts to reverse the outcome. For eighteen months he had done everything in his power to justify a digestive theory which he and Barreswil had apparently conceived in a burst of enthusiasm and published in haste. The theory had been very enticing in its simplicity, even though it ran against the general explanatory trend of the times as well as against available evidence. In persisting so stubbornly to retain it, Bernard displayed a willful streak in his scientific character which sometimes led him astray. The same quality, however, was partly responsible for the extraordinary successes he later achieved.

In the meantime Bernard had also been developing another line of investigation, elaborating and seeking to establish the belief he had put down in September that the chemical properties of saliva are accidental. He began with the experiments which he had already performed or participated in at various times since Magendie's commission had taken up the question. Probably Bernard added some new refinements and extensions of this research. Unfortunately the lack of a laboratory record makes it impossible to reconstruct the steps by which his thought and work on the problem unfolded, a process which must have been particularly interesting because it involved a reversal of the whole tendency of his earlier efforts to define a chemical role for saliva. At any rate, he had reached a full formulation of his new view in a memoir which was published in the January 1847 issue of the *Archives générales de médecine*, but which may actually have appeared in February.[42] By this time he had not only come to deny any physiological significance to the property of saliva of transforming starch, but he was aiming his whole argument against Louis Mialhe's theory of a specific salivary digestive ferment.

Bernard's primary argument against the existence of a *salivary diastase* derived from the experiments showing that only mixed saliva can cause starch to disappear. To experiments of the type described earlier[43] he added another in which he had found, contrary to his own expectations, he said, that when he placed parotid and submaxillary gland saliva together so as to reconstitute mixed saliva, there was still no transforming action. Thus the salivas apparently had to be mixed within the mouth in order to acquire that power. It seemed to him evident, therefore, that "salivary diastase does not exist in the saliva at the moment in which it issues from the glands."[44]

In the second part of his paper Bernard developed his own theory that the source of the chemical properties of mixed saliva was not the saliva at all, but the mucous membrane lining the mouth. He drew the inspiration for his explanation from the influential paper on lactic acid fermentation which Boutron and Edmond Frémy had published in 1841.[45] Following the general viewpoint popularized by Liebig, that animal matter undergoing decomposition induces the fermentative decomposition of other substances, Boutron and Frémy had tried to demonstrate that lactic acid is produced "under the influence of substances of an animal nature which are submitted to a special force of decomposition, and which have the property of transmitting an action to certain bodies with which one places them in contact." Although almost all animal materials can exert such effects, they found it most convenient to utilize membranes, particularly those of the stomach and the bladder. They showed that these acted upon sugar, gum, milk sugar, starch, and dextrin in different ways, depending upon the degree of alteration which the membranes had attained. If the latter were decomposing rapidly, the nature of their actions also changed rapidly, producing a mixture of substances; but when Boutron and Frémy used more stable dried membranes, they could selectively obtain pure products, including lactic acid. In order to place the membranes in the proper state of decomposition to act as ferments, they exposed them to the air, but the fermentations themselves could take place without air.[46]

Bernard followed Boutron and Frémy's procedures closely as he applied the same reasoning to explain the actions of saliva. Exposing the lining material taken from the mouth of a horse to air for twenty-four to thirty-six hours, he then covered it with a starch solution, which was transformed within twelve hours to glucose. He could produce the same reaction without the membrane itself, by soaking it in water and mixing the filtrate with a starch solution. If he used parotid saliva in place of the water he could impart to that secretion the properties of mixed saliva. The power to transform starch, he therefore asserted, resided in "organic animal particles" on the surface of the mucous membrane, which are "habitually exposed to air," and are dissolved in the saliva which comes into contact with them. Even these particles were "far" from constituting a special salivary ferment, for he could obtain the same result with an infusion of saliva and any other mucous membrane. Explicitly imitating Boutron and Frémy's experiments, Bernard then showed that saliva itself can produce other materials besides glucose, depending on its state of decomposition. "In substituting the action of human or animal saliva for that of the membranes and the casein employed by these chemists, one can see that I have obtained entirely analogous results." In twelve hours a solution of starch and saliva produced glucose, but after three or four times that period lactic acid also appeared. In another case he obtained butyric acid, which Pelouze had shown in 1843 to be another product of the fermentative action of animal membranes.[47] Thus Bernard undermined the idea of a specific action of saliva both by duplicating its action with other animal materials and by imitating with it other actions of animal membranes. As further support for the former point he adduced Magendie's observation that other animal fluids transform starch and added similar observations of his own. Altogether Bernard felt that he had proved by many facts that the ferment in mixed saliva "contains nothing special, and that it acts in the manner of a great number of animal materials which . . . are entering the process of decomposition." [48]

Although Bernard's opposition to Mialhe's salivary theory was based on the different kinds of experimental evidence which the two men respectively brought to bear on the problem, their divergence was also due partly to a conceptual problem growing out of contradictory elements within current theories of fermentation. The views of Boutron and Frémy, on which Bernard depended, illustrate the difficulty well. Citing the examples of diastase and emulsin, whose discovery "had truly opened a new way in organic chemistry," they generalized that there is "a great number of organic materials which can be modified under the influence of ferments; that the same ferment does not appear suitable to determine different fermentations; finally that each material requires a special ferment to ferment it." [49] Yet the decomposition theory of ferment action which they accepted ascribed the specificity of these ferments not to permanent properties of specific substances but to particular modes of alteration which any of a great number of animal materials undergo. In support of this view Boutron and Frémy found that even diastase would transform starch into lactic acid rather than into sugar if the ferment were first modified by exposing it to air for three days. [50] How such a general process of decomposition could produce from any animal matter substances with such well-defined properties as diastase, emulsin, and, as chemists were coming to believe, many other yet unidentified ferments, they left unmentioned. Conceived at a time when fermentation was considered to mean only one or two reactions, the decomposition theory could not adequately account for the growing number of distinct processes which chemists were investigating. Under the circumstances it was easier to grasp one or the other half of the theoretical dichotomy, according to the phenomena one wished to explain, than to reconcile them. Mialhe chose to focus on the specificity of ferments, and he justified his approach by separating from saliva a material with distinct chemical properties, and which in very small quantities exerted a powerful action, just as his predecessors had done with vegetable diastase, emulsin, and pepsin. Bernard focused on those experiments which seemed to indicate the differing effects of specific *conditions* on unspecified animal matter. Neither reconciled his views with the observations explained by the views of the other. Perhaps it was a similar choice of priorities which had led Barreswil and Bernard to ground their theory of digestion in the conception of a common organic principle in the various digestive fluids, acting differently according to the conditions specified by its milieu. In his effort to expose the inappropriateness of Mialhe's theory of animal diastase through Boutron and Frémy's conception of fermentation, Bernard went further than Boutron and Frémy, who had tried to balance the two theoretical viewpoints, would probably have gone. For even though they had shown that decomposing vegetable diastase could produce lactic acid, just as Bernard showed saliva could, they did not doubt that vegetable diastase is a specific ferment whose special action is to convert starch to glucose.

After completing his case against the significance of the fermenting principle of mixed saliva, Bernard went on to his second major argument, that no matter what may be the cause of the chemical action of saliva on starch, that action played no important physiological role. From observations on dogs with gastric fistulas and horses with sectioned esophaguses he had found that their food reaches their stomachs not much more than a minute after it enters their mouths. Saliva requires several hours to transform starch in the solid forms in which it is ordinarily eaten, so that the reaction could not take place in the mouth. The explanation usually given, that the saliva continues to act in the stomach, he asserted to be untenable, because his experiments, as well as those of Boutron and Frémy, had shown that the transformation of starch by animal ferments ceases when the reaction becomes acidic. Furthermore, he added, he had found many times that animals sacrificed at any period of digestion after being fed large amounts of potatoes contained starch in their stomachs and little or no detectable sugar. It was only in the intestines that the starch disappeared. From all of this evidence he concluded that "in reality the chemical role of saliva in digestion is almost null." [51]

The rest of Bernard's memoir was a persuasive demonstration that saliva does play an important mechanical role in digestion. Using data compiled by Lassaigne and by the equine commission, together with an experiment of his own, he showed that the amount of saliva a horse secretes is proportional not to the starch in its food but to the dryness of the food. Clearly a principal function of the secretions was to moisten and soften food, as many physiologists had assumed all along. A horse with its parotid gland ducts sectioned, so that the secretion issued outside its mouth, could only swallow with difficulty. Bernard distinguished also between this moistening process, which he attributed to the more aequous parotid secretion, and the function of the more viscous submaxillary gland saliva. The latter covered the alimentary bols with a slippery surface to make them easier to swallow.[52]

Bernard's article contained important observations, and the opinions he introduced exerted a significant cautionary influence upon theories of salivary action during the following decades. Yet he showed himself to be at least as adroit a debater as he was able an experimenter. As on some previous occasions, he was in part imposing upon the evidence a theory which he found attractive, by carefully selecting the arguments and data that would best support it. He knew, for example, that the mucus lining of the mouth contained dispersed secretory glands,[53] but he did not discuss the possibility that these might be the source of the salivary ferment he attributed to the lining. To derive that substance from the decomposition of the membrane itself better conformed to his viewpoint. He depended on the general argument that saliva cannot digest starch when it is acid, although he was well aware that the manner or degree in which the solution is acidified was a crucial factor. Repeatedly in his own experiments he had encountered instances in which lightly acidified saliva did act on starch.[54] He did not attempt to establish that the degree of acidity in the stomach is equivalent to that which he and others had found to be sufficient to halt the process.

Although Bernard's theory of the source of the salivary ferment was a novel and distinctive adaptation of Boutron and Frémy's view of fermentation, some aspects of his discussion were less novel than he implied. The primacy of salivary action in the digestion of starch had already come under question in the debates in the Academy of Sciences in 1845. There Bouchardat and Sandras had already reported that they found starch to be transformed principally in the intestine, and they had attributed this action to the properties of pancreatic juice.[55] Bernard could well have presented his views as a further development of theirs, or at least have used their observations in support of his own. Instead, he restricted the discussion of this point to his own investigations.[56]

Bernard used his adeptness at argument also to achieve another purpose which may have been even more important to him than his own theory. That is, he wished to turn the situation into another object lesson concerning the proper relation of chemistry to physiology, and to portray Mialhe as the principal violator of that relationship. He sought not merely to correct Mialhe's theory of salivary action, but to discredit it as an example of exclusively chemical reasoning. In his opening paragraph he set the theme which he carried through his discussion: "For several years one has been led to essentially chemical views concerning the uses of saliva, and one has tried to assign to that fluid an entirely special action which would be indispensable to the digestion of amylaceous alimentary substances." [57] Near the end he referred again to "the chemical theory emitted concerning the role of the salivary fluid," [58] which he believed he had now refuted. He gave the clearest expression to the basic issue when he said: "All of the observations made by MM. Leuchs, Mialhe, the hygiene commission, and myself, which are true when they occur in glass tubes, outside of the individual, only represent an impossible theory when one tries to apply them to digestion in the living gastrointestinal tube." [59]

This was the same general point Bernard had been making since 1843, and the statement was very like those in his articles on gastric digestion the year before. But generalizations become meaningful only in the context of their manifestations, and he was able to make his meaning clearer than before because he had found a situation in which he could more effectively apply the principle to judge a particular theory. Moreover, it was a theory which stood at the forefront of current discussions of digestion. In his M.D. thesis he had confronted the central question of whether digestion is a dissolution or a chemical change, but it was mostly the fact that the sponsors of the alternative Bernard opposed were chemists that made that theory a "chemical" one. In his papers of 1846 he had brought together sundry examples of physiological circumstances which affect the chemical processes of digestion, but, with the exception of the peripheral opinion of Mialhe regarding the therapeutic administration of alkalis, he could not bring these arguments to bear on any current theories. Now he was finally in a position to use physiological considerations such as the dependence of the properties of saliva on its source, the timing of the movement of food through the alimentary canal, and conditions within the stomach, to assert that the chemical processes involved could not take place in the manner that the behavior of the same substances outside of the body indicated they should. Lehmann caught the paradox in the situation very well when he said a few years later: "We have therefore as much through Bernard's earlier observations as through Bidder and Schmidt's more recent investigations reached the result that in spite of the energetic action of saliva on starch and in spite of its ample secretion, nevertheless no significant influence on the digestion of that substance can be ascribed to it." [60]

Bernard did not use only logical arguments against Mialhe's theory.

He resorted also to ironic phrases which tended to make it appear as an arbitrary interpretation. Bernard introduced the term "salivary diastase" as a name "imposed by M. Mialhe on the active principle of saliva." In another place he referred to the principle "which one had decorated with the name of *salivary diastase*," and he spoke of the phenomena "for the explanation of which one has invoked the existence of a *salivary diastase*."The term itself he characterized as "doubly faulty [*vicieuse*]," because, he claimed, the ferment was neither specific nor derived from saliva.[61] Moreover, in his review of the history of the problem he nearly reduced the contribution of Mialhe to "the chemical explication of the fact" which Leuchs, Schwann, and Sebastian had discovered, that human saliva transforms starch into glucose or dextrin.[62] His version contrasts sharply with the opinion of the commissioners of the Academy. They praised Mialhe for *discovering* the active principle in saliva; for demonstrating, not simply deducing, the similarity of its properties to ordinary diastase; and for investigating the transformation itself so much more thoroughly than his predecessors that he brought clarity to conclusions which had previously been vague and inexact.[63] All of this suggests that Bernard's attitude toward Mialhe's work reflected some feeling deeper than the simple disapproval of his overly chemical orientation. One startling passage in Bernard's memoir greatly strengthens such an impression. Referring to the fact that natural gastric juice taken from the fistula of a dog has no action on starch, he said:

Nevertheless this gastric juice is itself nothing but a mixture of pure gastric juice with saliva which the animal swallows as it forms. Why, therefore, has that saliva lost its action on starch by mixing with gastric juice? It is evidently because the latter has an acid reaction. In fact it is sufficient, *as I have shown elsewhere*, to saturate the acid of gastric juice, with a little sodium carbonate, for example, in order to make the property of the saliva which was mixed there reappear.[64]

The only published statement which Bernard could have meant by "as I have shown elsewhere" was in his paper with Barreswil of July 1845. But there they had said that gastric juice itself can digest starch when it is saturated with alkali. It was Mialhe who had corrected their interpretation by asserting that there had been saliva mixed with the gastric juice. Now, without referring to Mialhe's statement, or acknowledging that up until almost the present time he had still hoped to prove the other explanation, Bernard pretended that this was what he himself had said from the first! One can only wonder whether his lack of generosity toward one who had bested him on this particular question derived from simple annoyance at having been proved wrong, or from professional insecurity which gave him little room for acknowledging error.

Though Bernard intended to refute Mialhe's theory, the views of the two men turned out to be complementary in that each contributed to the problem of salivary action something which the other could not adequately treat. Mialhe, who thoroughly understood the significance and contemporary methods of the search to isolate active organic principles from complex body fluids, was unfamiliar with the physiological complexities which Bernard could bring into play from his experience in vivisection. Bernard, on the other hand, used less sophisticated analytical methods than Mialhe did when investigating the digestive process outside of the body, and he did not fully appreciate the chemists' standard for the identification and characterization of organic principles. It was typical of the difference in their approaches that Mialhe mixed pepsin, diastase, and dilute acid to simulate the properties he claimed to be those of the fluid in the stomach, whereas Bernard simply mixed gastric juice and saliva. Thus the experience of neither man was comprehensive enough to embrace all of the factors essential to a fully satisfactory explanation of salivary action. The situation was so complicated and uncertain, however, that probably no one during this period could have produced an unobjectionable theory. On each of the crucial questions, such as whether saliva transforms starch when it is acidified, and whether starch disappears in the stomach and sugar appears there, the best investigators of the time obtained widely discordant results.[65]

Contemporaries judged that the truth lay somewhere between the opinions of Bernard and Mialhe. Lehmann, whose assessments were usually careful and balanced, agreed with Bernard that saliva did not play an essential role in the digestion of starch. He doubted that Mialhe had separated the active principle of saliva, for after believing for a time that he had confirmed the effects Mialhe described, he could not afterward repeat them. He felt, on the other hand, that it was unscientific and only closed the doors to further understanding of the problem to "lull to sleep" the search for the specific ferment with the fiction that the cause of all fermentations is merely organic matter undergoing alteration. Tactfully, Lehmann omitted to mention that this was Bernard's view.[66]

For the longer run, as Lehmann's remark suggests, it was Mialhe rather than Bernard who had grasped the central ground. Whatever may have been the inadequacies of his own diastase preparations, he saw before Bernard did that it was only the isolation of specific ferments which could lead to the heart of the question of digestive processes. Bernard's physiological observations led to important qualifications of the theory of salivary digestion, such as the necessity to take into account variations in the individual secretions, and not to overestimate the physiological significance of the chemical action; but later physiologists did not agree with him that the action has no significance. The qualifications, moreover, were added to a theory which descended directly from that of Mialhe. Later investigators were able to isolate the salivary ferment; to show that it did derive from some, although not all, of the individual secretions; and to conclude that Mialhe's diastase did contain that ferment in impure form.[67] In short, it was Mialhe who had best sensed the direction in which the problem was moving, even if he may have underestimated the distance it still had to travel.

XV

A New Look at Old Projects

Two obvious choices lay open to Bernard in 1847 for his researches in animal chemistry. Although his central endeavor to elucidate gastric digestion had come to an apparent dead end, his new views of salivary action posed problems for further investigation. He also had unfinished work to do in relation to the differences he had discovered between carnivorous and herbivorous urine. Eventually he took up both of these, but not until late in the year. We have seen that Bernard tended to work intently on one problem for several weeks, then switch to another of the several lines of investigation which he had previously developed. In the winter of 1847, perhaps needing some relief from those problems which his recent efforts had left unsolved, Bernard turned to two projects from the past. One of these concerned the secretion of urea after the extirpation of the kidneys, a phenomenon which he had studied for a time two years before. The other project took him still further back, to the very beginning of his experimental career. For he resumed the investigation he had pursued in early 1843 of the places within the animal organism in which various easily identifiable chemical reactions can take place.

On January 27, 1847, Bernard injected successively into the jugular vein of a large rabbit 12 grams each of a saturated solution of ferric lactate and a 1 percent solution of potassium prussiate. Afterward, he found prussiate in the urine, but no iron there. By an autopsy he found that there was no blue coloration anywhere within the animal to indicate that any reaction had taken place.[1] The experiment was very much like some of those he had been performing just four years before.[2] There is no indication whether some recent observation had

321

caused him to see a new link with his old research, or whether he simply went back to see if he could do something more with a question from which he had gradually drifted away as he came to focus on the stomach. He next tested the effects of ether on rabbits and a cat, but this experiment was probably unrelated to the previous one. The general excitement which the anesthetic effects of ether was beginning to arouse among physicians and physiologists in Paris at that time would sufficiently explain why Bernard began to work with that gas.[3]

Five days later, on February 1, he performed an experiment similar to that with the iron salt and prussiate, but using injections of amygdalin and an emulsion of oil of almonds. As was well known, the ferment emulsin in oil of almonds acted on the amygdalin within the animal to produce the toxic "essence of bitter almonds" and the highly poisonous hydrocyanic acid. It must have been no surprise, therefore, that the rabbit began to respire rapidly, fell to the ground, entered into convulsions, and quickly died. Bernard could smell the hydrocyanic acid on its breath and the essence of bitter almonds when he opened its thorax.[4] Following the record of the experiment he made three remarks whose juxtaposition there suggests that he was particularly interested in comparing different types of chemical reactions to see which can occur within the organism and in what parts of it. The first was "Try gastrate of lead [his term for a salt made with the gastric acids] and dilute sulfuric acid, and try also other chemical indications." Below that he wrote "There are substances which decompose in the blood—ex: *cyanides*. exp[eriments] with the lungs. It is curious. (a kind of platinum sponge)."[5]

In the second note Bernard was undoubtedly referring to some experiments which he had made in 1843 with cyanide of mercury. Injected into an animal, that salt poisoned it by decomposing to give cyanic (prussic) acid. His experiments had been designed to locate where the reaction might take place. Placing solutions of the salt in contact with the mucous lining of various portions of the stomach, he had obtained the odor of the acid from one portion. He had also obtained it by placing the solution on pieces of lung and kidney. One sample of urine mixed with the solution gave the reaction, another did not, whereas no odor developed when he mixed the solution with warm blood. To establish whether one of the tissues which had produced the reaction outside the body was a site for it within the animal, he had removed the stomach of a small dog, injected cyanide of mercury into its circulation, and observed that it was poisoned in the usual way. The acidity of the stomach could not be the cause of the reaction. "Where, therefore, did the decomposition take place," he had asked; "is it in the general capillaries?" To test this possibility he had separated the hip of a dog from its body except for an artery and a vein, then injected the salt into the artery. Opening the vein immediately, he had collected two samples of blood from it, and detected only "a barely appreciable odor of prussic acid." That odor, he thought, might have derived accidentally from a little of the salt which had fallen on some urine present. When he added hydrochloric acid to the venous blood, it disengaged prussic acid, proving that the mercuric cyanide was present in the samples. Because of the faint odor already there, he could not "conclude absolutely that the combination did not take place in the general capillaries," but he was obviously convinced that it did not. From the preceding experiments he had already come to believe that the lungs were the probable place, for "these conditions exist in the lungs, and in the lungs the gaseous substances form which must have that organ as their emunctory." The condition which he had then had in mind was the necessity of an acid to displace the hydrocyanic acid from its salt, supplied in the lungs by the carbonic acid which is exhaled there.[6] Now, as he recalled these experiments in 1847, however, he seemed to prefer an explanation in terms of some special catalytic action of the lungs, analogous to the effects of finely divided platinum.

The third note appended to his experiment with amygdalin and oil of almonds stated, "One could not say that the Prussian blue is soluble in the blood, because I have injected it already formed into the blood of a cat." [7] Here he was countering a possible objection to his conclusion that lactate of iron and prussiate do not react in the blood. If there were some special solubility of the product in that fluid, so that the usual blue color was undetectable, then Prussian blue itself should disappear when injected, but he had already tried that in 1843 and found the blue deposited in the lungs.[8]

While Bernard pondered over connections between old and new investigations, however, he still had an unsettled doubt about the result of his current experiment. Having injected both the amygdalin and the emulsion of almonds with the same syringe, he was afraid that even though he had washed the instrument in between, enough of the first substance might have remained in it to produce some reaction before the second injection. To guard against that, he repeated the experiment very carefully, using separate syringes. The outcome was the same, but now a second complication arose, for when he injected the almond emulsion alone into a second rabbit that animal died also.

There was no odor on its breath, however, and Bernard thought that its death was due to a mechanical effect, that the emulsified oil had blocked its lungs. Nevertheless, he felt that in order to be sure to eliminate "this cause of error," he ought to use emulsin isolated from the oil. To prepare the ferment in this way required the specialized skill of a chemist experienced in the separation of organic materials by means of solvents and precipitation reactions. Probably for this reason Bernard wisely asked Pelouze to have it done for him in his laboratory. Meanwhile, he seemed to be formulating somewhat more specifically the point he hoped to make with these investigations. "One could, as a demonstration," he remarked, "place that combination of the emulsin and the amygdalin in the blood opposite to the non-combination of prussiate, iron and lactate." He contemplated injecting the emulsin under the skin and the amygdalin in the blood, and treating similarly yeast and sugar. The latter experiment would evidently compare the action of another ferment to that of emulsin.[9]

While waiting for his emulsin, Bernard performed on February 10 another experiment with lactate of iron and potassium prussiate. Its unusual outcome led him to propose an explanation for the fact that these two salts do not react in the blood. Injecting the iron salt under the skin of the neck of a rabbit, and the prussiate in its hip, he found that the tissue in the former region became intensely blue, whereas that of the latter area did not. Prussiate appeared in the urine, but not iron. Two days later the rabbit died. At its autopsy Bernard saw that the blue color had spread down into the abdominal connective tissue, and that the muscle tissue in the affected portions was altered. The blue had become paler than it was at first, but he was able to restore its original intensity by moistening it with sulfuric acid. All of this Bernard explained by the hypothesis that the iron salt formed some kind of combination with the tissue, preventing it from entering the circulation. The prussiate formed no such combinations, so that it was carried freely throughout the body in the blood. The two substances reacted, therefore, where the prussiate reached tissues into which the iron salt solution had directly infiltrated. The later fading of the color was due to other alkaline fluids which had exuded into the tissues and partially decomposed the Prussian blue. That was why the sulfuric acid again produced the blue color.[10]

This elaborate theory illustrates very well how freely Bernard sought to satisfy his great curiosity about the reasons for unexpected phenomena. It is not convincing, even in its own terms. To account for the fact that prussiate combined with the iron, he had to postulate that there was present an excess of the iron above the amount which combined with the tissues.[11] Yet it was only the latter combination which he supposed prevented the iron from entering the blood; logic would suggest that the excess ought to have circulated and become available to react with prussiate elsewhere. His reasoning was therefore more ingenious than rigorous. In spite of that, he was confident enough to apply his explanation to other "analogous cases" in order to understand why certain reactions do not take place in particular parts of the organism:

1. In all of the animal liquids except the gastric juice, the reactions are masked.
2. This masking of the reactions occurs only for metallic substances and double decompositions—for the fermentations, that does not take place ex: *amygdalin and emulsin—sugar, yeast etc.*
3. This masking of reactions depends on the fact that the metallic salt enters into some combination with the organic material.[12]

There is an obvious resemblance between these reflections and Bernard's youthful idea of four years before that chemical combinations are produced nowhere but in the stomach (and glands). Yet his thought had clearly matured in the sense that he was no longer content with the explanation that there are certain "selected places" in the body for chemical changes to occur;[13] now he sought an explanation in terms of the chemical conditions existing in different parts of the body, and he differentiated their effects according to the class of reactions involved.

By February 27 Bernard had received from Pelouze "very pure" emulsin and amygdalin. With these he repeated his earlier experiments. The results fully supported the interpretation he had made then, for neither substance affected the rabbit when injected alone, whereas the two injected into the same animal poisoned it as before.[14]

Satisfied with that outcome, Bernard went on two days later to investigate the action within animals of yeast on sugar. He hoped that if alcoholic fermentation could take place in the blood the product would make the animal intoxicated, so that by its behavior he would be able to detect the reaction. When he injected both substances into the jugular vein of a dog, however, the animal appeared unaffected. It did not seem either sleepy or drunk. After two days it became quite sick, and on the third it died. Bernard found widespread inflammation and other alterations in its stomach, intestines, and pancreas. He thought that the changes indicated that the yeast had caused a "profound alteration of the blood," but he could not tell whether this was an effect of the action of the yeast on sugar or some direct toxic effect of the ferment alone. Therefore he had to think of another way to trace whether the yeast transformed the sugar. His many earlier experiments had shown that cane sugar injected under the skin passed into the urine. Now it occurred to him that if he first injected yeast into the blood, then cane sugar into the connective tissue, he ought to be able to tell by the appearance or non-appearance of sugar in the urine whether or not the yeast acted on it. "It will be curious," he anticipated, "if one does not recover sugar in the urine it is because it will have been destroyed in the blood by the yeast." Again he was disappointed, for two hours after he had performed the injections on a rabbit, its urine contained "huge quantities" of cane sugar. Ironically, in this case the animal became very quiet, and sat in a corner with its eyes half closed. Like the dog, the rabbit later died, with inflammations in its intestinal tract.[15]

On this rather unsuccessful note the series of experiments apparently ended. Bernard did not publish the results until 1848, when they appeared in two installments in the January and February issues of the *Archives générales de médecine*. In the intervening months he must have carried out additional investigations similar to those already described.[16] His memoir, "Experiments on the diverse chemical manifestations of substances introduced into the organism," was derived primarily, however, from the research he had performed between January 27 and March 4, 1847, together with a number of the older experiments dating from the spring of 1843.

In his paper Bernard was able to establish only loose connections between the categories of reactions in the organism which he brought together. His original goal, he said, had been "to search for places in the body where combinations and decompositions take place." He had directed his study according to "the ordinary ideas of chemistry," but soon observed various phenomena which were unforeseen. When he pursued these, it seemed to him that in the fluids and tissues of the living body there were "particular circumstances, still little known to chemists and physiologists, capable of modifying the reactions of certain substances whose properties in other respects have been completely examined."[17] In other words, Bernard was again using his results as an occasion to draw the moral that it is not safe to predict what will occur within the body from the chemical properties of substances outside it. He was not entirely frank when he implied that he himself had set out believing that the "ordinary ideas of chemistry" would suffice, because he had been skeptical of that view almost from the first. What he now asserted was, in fact, an elaboration of what he had put down long before in his notebook, that "between the chemistry of the living animal and that which occurs in the crucibles there is analogy but not identity." [18]

Bernard illustrated chemical "combinations in the blood and different liquids or tissues of the body," by the reactions of ferric lactate and potassium prussiate which he had so frequently studied. He described some of the early experiments in 1843 which had led him to choose the lactate as the only iron salt which did not harm the animals. In all these cases in which he had injected both substances into the blood, he reported, no blue color had formed anywhere. Next he turned to four later experiments, including the one performed on January 27, 1847, described at the beginning of this chapter; these showed that higher doses of the reagents still caused no reaction in the blood, although in some cases they produced a blue color in the stomach or urine.[19] Then he undertook to explain why these two salts "could have circulated simultaneously in large quantities in the sanguinary fluid without giving rise to Prussian blue," and why that combination formed only in the gastric juice and sometimes in the urine. He rejected the possibility that the acidity of the latter two fluids was the reason, because he had repeated the injection experiments on fasting animals without finding blue in their acidic urine. The real cause, he said, was that everywhere in the body except in the gastric fluid, "an organic material . . . conceals the properties of the iron and impedes it from reacting with the prussiate." This was the same explanation which had occurred to him on the occasion of the curious outcome of injecting the iron salt in the tissue of the neck of a rabbit and prussiate in its hip. Since then, however, he had modified the explanation of that result and had broadened the experimental support for the general conclusion. The primary evidence he now brought to bear was based on the properties of gastric juice, blood serum, and acidic urine. To equal quantities of each of these fluids he added several drops of ferric lactate, agitated the solutions, and then put in a few drops of potassium prussiate. A reaction took place only in the gastric juice. To substantiate his inference that an organic matter had prevented the iron from combining in the other fluids, he showed that one could also impede the reaction in water by adding egg albumin to it. Sometimes he could get a reaction in urine if he added prussiate immediately after the iron salt, but not if he added it some time later. This effect he took to be evidence that the organic material took some time to combine with the iron. Concentrated acids made the reaction appear in all of the fluids, because, he asserted, the acid destroyed the organic material. Gastric juice permitted it to occur because that fluid has a lower concentration of organic constituents than other body fluids.[20]

By now the experiment involving injections in the neck and hip, which had stimulated Bernard's idea for "masking" in the first place, had become merely confirming evidence. To that experiment he had added two others. In one he injected the iron salt into the hip tissue and the prussiate into the blood, and showed that the blue color appeared around the first injection. In the other he inverted the injections and found no blue color anywhere in the animal. He explained all of these as he had previously explained the first case, but with the more general basis he now had for his theory he was able to dispense with the inconsistency in that earlier explanation. He no longer maintained that a combination between iron and the tissues prevented the iron from entering the circulation, but only that whatever iron was absorbed into the blood "would circulate in combination with the organic matter of the blood," so that it would not be free to react there.[21] Again Bernard had "held by the collar" an idea which had passed through his mind in response to a particular observation. Allowing free scope to his imagination, he had used it as a pretext for instituting further experiments, developed it, and supported it by enough circumstantial evidence to make it plausible.

While describing his efforts to make the two salts react in gastric juice, urine, and blood serum, Bernard emphasized that "outside of the organism, I observed that matters were singularly like that which happens in the living animal." This remark is important for understanding his general position. It makes clear that in insisting that the phenomena in animals are unpredictable from the general ideas of chemistry alone, he was not maintaining that some vital principle in organisms causes phenomena to deviate from the general laws of nature. What was not predictable was only the special material conditions which are present in the organism. Though he might be vague on the identity of the organic material which he supposed in this case to interfere with the expected reaction, it was nevertheless in principle a chemically definable substance which could exist "inside the organism the same as outside of the individual."[22]

Bernard claimed that he was reluctant to generalize from one particular reaction, but since he had tried many other experiments of a similar nature, he thought he could at least say that it seemed to him that "the composition of the blood prevented a very large number of double decompositions which usually occur in the laboratory between substances of an inorganic nature." [23] Next, he turned to a class of reactions involving organic instead of inorganic substances, and decomposition instead of combination. These were the fermentations. Summarizing those experiments with emulsin and amygdalin and with sugar and yeast which he had performed in the winter of 1847, he concluded that both of these reactions can take place in the blood. "In brief," he ended, "it therefore appears that the *fermentations constitute phenomena to which the chemical composition of the blood presents no obstacle.*" [24]

Unfortunately Bernard was so anxious to make this generalization that he apparently falsified his own result. In the experiment he had performed to see whether sugar injected into the tissue of an animal after yeast has been injected into the circulation is destroyed in the blood instead of entering the urine, his laboratory record states, as has been mentioned already,[25] that huge quantities of cane sugar appeared in the urine. In his memoir Bernard reported what is undoubtedly the same experiment, but he wrote, "The sugar had not arrived in the urine, from which I conclude that the yeast had destroyed it, and had produced alcohol from it." [26] We have already noticed that Bernard's ideas had more than once colored his view of his observations; in this more egregious lapse they seem to have caused him to see black as white. Many years later he mused: "In youth I could believe that science was all in the mind. Then that leads [one] to deny, to twist results, in order to remain logical, believing that that is necessary." [27]

In the second half of his memoir Bernard treated other decompositions which can "take place in more limited points of the organism." [28] He focused principally on the decomposition of mercury cyanide. One cannot be certain whether he was relying entirely on his experiments of 1843, which have been summarized above,[29] or whether he had more recently performed others very similar to them. The fact that the experiments he now described correspond closely to those in procedure and language, and that his present discussion was based on essentially the same set of investigations he had done at that time, suggests the former alternative. Yet one crucial experiment is described just differently enough so that, if it is the one recorded in his notebook, he was once more altering his account of it to give the appearance of firmer support for his conclusion. This was the experiment in which, according to his notebook, he had removed the stomach of a dog and found that an injection of mercury cyanide poisoned it anyway. The experiment he reported in his memoir was almost identical except that he stated that he had "removed, through a large wound made in the abdomen, 1. the stomach, 2. the kidneys, 3. the bladder." [30] Done in this way, the experiment would provide more persuasive evidence for his contention that it was not an acid liquid in the body which decomposes the salt; for it would eliminate all of the organs in which he believed such a liquid may be found. After eliminating the possibility of the general capillaries, by the experiment described previously, he now asserted positively that the decomposition occurs only in the lungs. Like certain bicarbonates which he had also shown to decompose in the lung, forming carbonic acid, "the cyanides decompose while crossing the pulmonary tissue as if they were submitted to the action of an acid." The lungs appear, he concluded, "to be the special theater for these types of chemical changes." [31]

Unlike the case of the Prussian blue reaction, Bernard did not attempt to specify what chemical conditions in the lungs gave the organ this special quality, for he did not contend that the salt actually encountered an acid there. On the contrary, he stressed the paradox that a reaction ordinarily requiring an acid can occur here in the alkaline blood. [32] Thus in this instance he seemed to espouse the more radical position that within the animal a reaction can take place under conditions different from those needed outside of it. It is not clear, however, whether he meant deliberately to suggest such a view. Perhaps the best clue to his intentions is the remark in his notebook that the lungs act in some way like a catalyst.

Bernard presented in the last section of his memoir some evidence that iron is oxidized partially or wholly to the peroxide (ferric) state in the stomach, whereas a peroxide of iron in the blood or urine is reduced to the protoxide (ferrous) state. He raised the possibility that such changes might provide an alternative explanation for the inability of iron salts to react with prussiate in the blood. [33] In his conclusion he said that each group of the experiments he had brought together led to "partial deductions." These were mostly restatements of the conclusions of each section, with the suggestion that some of the results might form a guide for therapeutic measures against poisons. "If now we wished to proceed from these partial deductions to lift ourselves to more general conclusions," he added, "I believe that we would be in great danger of falling into error." [34] This negative warning seemed, in fact, to be the main point of Bernard's paper. The diverse and little known ways in which the organism affected the outcome of chemical reactions made it impossible to foresee a given result in advance or to generalize from an examination of one type of reaction what the result would be for others. Out of this situation Bernard derived one of the clearest expressions of his career of what he meant by the proper relation between chemistry and physiology. The lesson which his observations had taught him, he said,

is that it appeared to me impossible to foresee rigorously, from the ordinary ideas of chemistry, all of the results of the experiments contained in this study. Now, when sometimes one explains and predicts in advance in experiments of this nature, basing oneself in other respects on very positive given scientific facts, it seems to me that one begins where one ought to finish; that is to say, that first of all it is necessary to make the experiment on the living animal, because it often occurs, as the examples furnished in this memoir demonstrate, that one encounters unexpected circumstances, which nevertheless can be explained afterward, but which make one see the matter entirely differently than one had judged them beforehand. If this were the proper place, I would be able to prove that for different parts of physiology, and in particular for digestion, it is the source of much disagreement. In fact, there are physiologists, and I am among them, who begin directly from the observation on the living animal, in order to go afterward into the laboratory to search for the explanation of what they have seen; whereas others descend more particularly from the laboratory in order to explain the living animal according to their studies. The latter can undoubtedly sometimes happen to be right [tomber juste]; but very often also, proceeding in that way, they are in danger of understanding the phenomena not as they take place, but as they might exist theoretically.[35]

The special importance of this statement in its context is, I believe, that it leaves little doubt that Bernard's primary concern with the growing influence of chemistry over physiology related to the way one acquired explanations of physiological phenomena, rather than with the ultimate nature of the explanations. Some of his other general statements, including the one with which the present story opens, were ambiguous on just that point. Here he did not deny that processes occurring within the organism could be reduced to chemical explanations, but only insisted that the explanations should come last instead of first. The approach to which he objected could apply to Mialhe, to Liebig, or to Dumas, regardless of whether they regarded life as a collection of chemical reactions or believed in distinct vital principles. The crucial question was whether one went from the physiological operating table to the chemical laboratory, or started and finished in the latter. The procedure Bernard advocated, however, was not easy to execute perfectly. As we have repeatedly seen, the fact that he began with experiments on living animals did not invariably protect him from understanding phenomena as they might have existed theoretically rather than as they actually took place.

The other investigation to which Bernard returned early in 1847 was the study of the ways in which an animal excretes urea after its kidneys have been removed. The experiments, which he performed in cooperation with Barreswil, were a continuation of those that they had carried out between January and March 1845.[36] By that time they had already observed urea in the blood in several cases, confirming the observations of Prévost and Dumas and others, and they had made the new observation that ammonia appears in the fluids of the stomach. But they had got into difficulty over the fact that in some other cases they could not detect urea in the blood a day or two after the extirpation of the kidneys. Their procedure for identifying the substance followed the method Prévost and Dumas had applied to the same situation twenty-four years before. They dried the sample of blood, treated it in boiling water, and extracted in alcohol the residue left by evaporation of the water. The residue left in turn by the alcohol they reacted with nitric acid; when urea was present, a mass of white crystals of nitrate of urea formed.[37] When in several of their experiments they could produce no crystals with nitric acid, but obtained instead only a mysterious effervescence or a precipitate lacking the distinct properties of nitrate of urea, they suspected that the method was not adequate, and they made some efforts to modify it; [38] but they recognized also that the inconsistencies might derive from variations in the physiological conditions. At one point Bernard remarked that it was essential to keep the dogs alive for a few days after the operation in order to succeed. This was not the only possibility he considered, however, for he noted also that in "two or 3 animals where we have found the urea in a very evident manner, it was with dogs which had eaten—perhaps that is a favorable condition for the production of urea?" [39]

It is uncertain when Bernard and Barreswil again took up these questions after March 1845, for their later experiments are not preserved in Bernard's notebooks. They had, at any rate, resolved their difficulties sometime in the spring of 1847, and published their results in April. The key turned out to be the factor at which Bernard had already hinted, that the presence or absence of urea in the blood depended on the length of time after the operation. In the original experiments demonstrating urea in the blood after the removal of its normal pathway of elimination, Prévost and Dumas had found that if they removed one kidney first, and waited until the wound healed before removing the other, the animals would survive between five and nine days after the second operation. They usually took their blood samples for analysis when the animal was nearing death, although they did claim that enough urea collects in the blood by the end of two days to be detected easily.[40] Bernard excised both kidneys at the same time,[41] a procedure which Prévost and Dumas had pointed out reduced the length of time that the animal survived.[42] Some of the animals Bernard operated on died rather suddenly of complications, while they appeared still generally vigorous; others lived three or four days but became very weak near the end. This difference turned out to be not only the resolution of their difficulties, but the foundation for their principal contribution. For at some point they realized that the animals which died soonest were always the ones which yielded no urea in their blood, whereas those which lived longer did. With this recognition, the information already gathered became as enlightening as it had earlier been confusing, and they could again use Prévost and Dumas's method of analysis with confidence. In their memoir of April 1847, therefore, Bernard and Barreswil were able to use some of the experiments they had already done in 1845, together with some which they probably had carried out more recently.[43]

If all of the urea which is ordinarily secreted by the kidneys were retained in the blood after the removal of those organs, Bernard and Barreswil argued, then it should not take several days for enough of it to accumulate to be detectable. From Prévost and Dumas's figures for the amount of urea which a dog ordinarily excretes, Bernard and Barreswil calculated that there ought to be within a day four to five times as much in the blood as would be necessary in order to observe it by analysis. Clearly the substance was being lost somewhere else in the meantime. The answer lay in their discovery of ammonia in the digestive fluids. They contended that these intestinal secretions substituted for the urinary excretion so long as the vitality of the animal permitted it. Only after its general loss of strength caused the intestinal secretions to diminish did urea remain trapped in the blood. They supported this conclusion very nicely by repeating the operation on a dog with a gastric fistula. By collecting gastric juice at intervals, they showed that during the first two days an unusually large amount of gastric juice, containing "very great quantities" of ammonia, was secreted, even though the animal had had nothing to eat. During the last two days the flow progressively decreased until it nearly vanished.[44]

The idea that other organs might substitute for the excretory function of the kidneys was in itself not new. Prévost and Dumas themselves had mentioned [45] that Anthelme Richerand, the one person before them to try the operation of removing the kidneys, had noticed that after the animals died their gall bladders were always gorged, "as if the urea had sought to leave by that way, joined to the biliary fluid." Richerand thought that this result showed that "nature could substitute by other excretions for the evacuation of the urine." [46] In 1824, in his classic "Investigations of the passage of materials into the urine," Friedrich Wöhler discussed this problem of replacement in relation to Prévost and Dumas's discovery. While it would be improbable, Wöhler thought, that one organ could take over for another the production of urea, he thought it perfectly reasonable that another organ would be capable of exchanging the function of simply removing the substance from the blood. Therefore, observations such as a urinous smell in the perspiration and vomited material of patients with disrupted urinary functions, he considered to be evidence in favor of their conclusion that the kidneys merely removed urea and did not form it themselves. [47] Eilhard Mitscherlich, Tiedemann and Gmelin apparently made similar assumptions when they confirmed Prévost and Dumas's discovery in 1833. They searched for urea not only in the blood of a dog whose kidneys they had removed, but in its bile, intestinal contents, faeces, and the material it had vomited. They found the substance definitely, however, only in the blood, and possibly in the vomited matter. [48] Bernard and Barreswil therefore had found an answer to a question which others had raised but had not been able to resolve. [49] Their success lay largely in their recognition that the substitute secretion was not urea itself, but a product of its decomposition. [50]

While formulating the explanation which he and Barreswil presented, Bernard apparently abandoned the hope he had entertained in 1845 that the conversion of urea to ammonia would lead him to a general theory of secretion. [51] Then he had imagined that the process would illuminate the way in which each secretion results from an alteration of a constituent of the blood to form a special product. Now, however, he and Barreswil regarded the transformation as accidental. They believed that the urea itself is secreted into the stomach, where it is swept into the decomposing influences that nutrients and many other substances introduced there undergo. They supported this interpretation by showing that urea placed in the stomach of a living animal, or in contact with an intestinal membrane, was also converted to ammonia.[52]

Bernard and Barreswil's memoir on urea does not rank with those for which the former is remembered, but it was nevertheless one of the most attractive of his early years. It contained novel insights and made a real advance in an area in which other eminent scientists had looked without seeing quite as far. It required a perceptive chain of reasoning to form a pattern out of results which had at first seemed only inconsistent, yet it did not involve deductions remote from the data themselves. The authors emulated the plan and procedures of Prévost and Dumas and presented their experiments realistically as an addition to the fundamental discovery by their predecessors. Their study was, in fact, a good example of the fruitful secondary contribution which a germinal discovery stimulates. Prévost and Dumas's investigation had been a major stimulus to physiological thought and research during the intervening decades. It was generally taken to be "of the highest importance." [53] Tiedemann and Gmelin had set out to repeat it even after Vauquelin and Ségalas had confirmed it, because the result was "of such great influence on the theory of secretion." [54] Magendie commented that Prévost and Dumas had proved that the kidneys do not create urea, "as one generally used to believe, but that they simply separate it from the blood, where it forms." [55] Their experiments did not merely resolve that question decisively, but raised equally important new questions for further research. Physiologists wondered if their findings for urea would apply to other constituents of urine; in addition, since urea was considered the special defining constituent of urine, the result brought into doubt the assumption that other glands create the special substances characterizing their particular secretions.[56] Further, it forced physiologists to consider where the urea may be produced, for Magendie's answer that it formed in the blood was no solution. Müller asked whether there is another specific organ, or whether it forms in various tissues; whether it results only from the decomposition of the substance of the animal or also directly from unused nutrients.[57]

Prévost and Dumas's memoir was important in a more fundamental sense for the emergence of experimental physiology. It was one of the earliest and most persuasive demonstrations that a combination of vivisection and sophisticated chemical analysis is essential for the resolution of many physiological problems. Bernard, who reacted against the method of the later Dumas, could have found no better model for the approach he espoused than this investigation in which the young Dumas had taken part.

About the time that he was finishing his memoir on urea, Bernard received the welcome news that he had at last a professional scientific position. On March 14, 1847, the assembly of professors of the Collège de France voted to authorize Magendie to have Bernard serve at his request as his substitute in his course during the first semester of the academic year. That duty would have begun the following December; but the assembly two weeks later authorized the same arrangement for the second semester of the academic year 1846–47, so that Bernard actually began to teach early in May.[58] According to Olmsted, Bernard took over all of the first semester course, while Magendie continued the second semester, or winter course.[59] Records from 1850 and 1851 indicate that generally each man gave slightly more than twenty lectures per year.[60] Bernard was probably not required to divert his attention very far from his current concerns, for the title of the course was "The Most Recent Discoveries in Physiology and Medicine," and he later noted that his lectures had revolved around his own investigations. The course met on Tuesday and Thursday at noon.[61]

Bernard's new title of *Suppléant* to Magendie can be translated either "substitute" or "assistant." Both meanings are appropriate, for he was expected to teach in Magendie's "absence," [62] but he also worked closely with Magendie on research projects immediately afterward.[63] It was an irregular but common position; at the time of Bernard's appointment, five other *suppléants* to professors of the Collège de France were similarly authorized.[64] Because professorial chairs seldom became available in Paris until a senior scientist retired or died, this device was used to help support those who were expected to succeed them during the long wait which often intervened. Scientists sometimes held the position even when they were already established. Pelouze, for example, served as *suppléant* to the distinguished Baron Louis Jacques Thenard from 1838 until 1846, even though he was already a professor at the École Polytechnique and had made his private laboratory one of the foremost centers in France for chemical training. When Thenard finally retired, Pelouze became professor of chemistry at the Collège de France.[65] Bernard's new post, therefore, was quite different from the apprenticeship he had served earlier as Magendie's *préparateur*. His situation now permitted him to use the laboratory of the Collège regularly, so that he was able to discontinue the burden of maintaining his own. Magendie, who was by then sixty-four years old, had already begun to reduce his medical practice. Before long he ceased active research as well,[66] so that the resources of the laboratory must have been largely at Bernard's disposal. Clearly the prospect of succession came with the appointment.[67] Nevertheless, the arrangement was makeshift. The budgets for the Collège de France during this period contained no provision for regular salaries for the *suppléants*, only for professors and for *préparateurs*.[68] Not until 1852, apparently, did Bernard receive, through Magendie's request, the first of three special yearly indemnities of 1000 francs out of unexpended funds, for "his honorable investigations which have been so justly esteemed." [69] Even the experimental resources to which he had access, beginning in 1847, were modest. Although by then the laboratory of the Collège was of more comfortable size than it had once been, Magendie had continual difficulty obtaining funds for his research expenses.[70] The reluctance to provide adequate support came partly from hostility to his vivisection experiments, partly from a general financial stringency. The buildings of the institution had recently been rebuilt and expanded, and new courses added, but the operating budget had not been raised to cover the increased expenses of running the enlarged establishment. Consequently, there was seldom enough money to cover the needs of any of the laboratories when they exceeded their meager allotments.[71] Thus while Bernard's situation after May 1847 represented a major improvement over what it had been, it still continued to illustrate the paucity of opportunities for young scientists in what had recently been the scientific capital of the world.

The hardships Bernard had faced before this time made a lasting impression on him. Long afterward, while pleading for more public support for physiological laboratories, he used his own experiences from that period to illustrate the material obstacles which discouraged young physiologists in France from pursuing that career. "Twenty-five years ago, when I entered the career of experimental physiology, I found myself in circumstances where I myself, like others, had to undergo all of the hindrances reserved for experimenters. One had then to be sustained by a true passion for physiology and to have patience and often great courage to avoid being disheartened." [72] Having to be on his own had exposed him particularly to the harassment of other residents in his neighborhood who objected to his experimentation on living animals. It was only through an accident by which he won the protection of a local police official that he was able to maintain his

private laboratory through these years.[73] Fierce opposition, he recalled, "was then the sad destiny of beginners in experimental physiology, when they had not been able, through special circumstances,
to become secluded or tolerated in some public establishment." [74]
Lack of protection from such hostility was the most emotional trial
Bernard had to endure, but his activities were probably more effectively limited by the absence of regular financial support. "I have
known," he wrote, "the anguish of the scientist who, because of the
lack of material means, cannot undertake the experiments which he
conceives, and is obliged to renounce certain research or to present his
discovery in a preliminary state." [75] This remark did not apply exclusively to Bernard's early years, for even after he acquired a secure professional position his activities were still constrained by inadequate facilities; but such frustration must have been most acute at that time in
which he had the least help. The laboratory notebooks describing his
experiments during those years say nothing about the exertions it
must have cost to procure the many animals, the operating instruments, and the chemical supplies he needed; or about the time lost
searching for ways to augment the income on which he had to support
both his research and his family. Undoubtedly, Magendie and Pelouze gave him as much informal assistance as their own resources
would allow and made it possible for him to continue at all.
Frequently he was able to perform experiments in their laboratories.
Nevertheless, the two years and four months in which he remained in
this sort of professional limbo must have seemed to him much longer.
The language in which he later recalled the period at least suggests as
much. He had maintained his own laboratory and continued his private course in physiology for "several years," he wrote, "up until the
time when I was at last named *suppléant* to Magendie at the Collège de
France." [76]

Under the circumstances he had done remarkably well. Whatever
faults one can perceive in the research and ideas which Bernard produced between 1844 and 1847—if he sometimes reached conclusions
before he had sufficient data to support them, if he occasionally presented his theories too hastily, if he clung to a few generalizations too
adamantly in the face of unfavorable evidence, and if there were some
deficiencies in his practice of chemical analysis; if he did not find time
to become familiar with all of the significant contributions in his field,
and if it was not always easy for him to recognize or acknowledge
where his colleagues were ahead of him—all of these shortcomings
pale by comparison with the achievement of having performed, in the

midst of great stringency, highly competent, independent and imaginative research month after month; of having made several discoveries which attracted favorable attention; of having proposed theories which were taken seriously even when not wholly accepted; and of having impressed the leaders of the Parisian scientific community with his talent. Claude Bernard had been severely tested and had survived.

XVI

The Persistence of Claude Bernard

If Claude Bernard appeared to do little with his investigation of digestion and nutrition during the first half of 1847, that was not entirely due to his occupation with other activities; for in the one direction in which he tried to move his study of digestion he was frustrated by technical obstacles. It may have already seemed unusual that even though pancreatic juice was a crucial factor in the digestive theory which he and Barreswil had proposed in 1845, Bernard had afterward dealt mostly with the properties of saliva and gastric juice. The reason was probably not that pancreatic juice was less interesting to him, but that he had evidently been trying unsuccessfully to contrive a better way to procure it. We have seen previously that in September 1845 he had envisioned the possibility of collecting it by means of an intestinal fistula.[1] By early 1847 the outcome of his study of saliva would seem to have made it more imperative than ever for him to explore the actions of those secretions which mix with aliments in the small intestine. Although his notebook makes only one mention of efforts at this time to obtain natural pancreatic juice, that entry shows that he had been quite concerned about it. On February 12 he tried to form a pancreatic fistula in a dog, but the animal apparently died. Bernard commented:

I have sacrificed a great number of dogs (at least 15 to 20) for the sake of making pancreatic fistulas in them, and all have died (with one exception, on which it did not succeed [because] the duct reformed). Ordinarily dogs do not die so easily when one handles another part of the gastrointestinal tube. I believe therefore that lesions of the duodenum and of the pancreas are more grave than those of other parts of the gastrointestinal tube.[2]

In March, during his experiments on the injection of yeast into a rabbit, he glimpsed another possible way to investigate the action of pancreatic juice. At the autopsy he noticed the unusual separation of the biliary and pancreatic ducts in the rabbit. The latter opened into the duodenum at a considerable distance lower than the former. "One could," he remarked, "easily collect aliments before and after the pancreas in order to understand the alteration which they will have undergone by the action of these two fluids." [3] This observation was a crucial one for Bernard later, but like his attempts to establish a fistula, it apparently did not bear fruit for nearly another year.

The immediate effect of Bernard's new academic appointment was probably to divert him from his studies of chemical physiology, as he concentrated on studies of the nervous system which particularly interested Magendie. On March 4, shortly before the appointment was authorized, he and Magendie experimented on the facial nerves of a horse at the École militaire. Over the next two weeks Bernard carried out similar experiments with rabbits for his private course in his own laboratory, perhaps the last research he did there. On March 25, nine days after the first vote on his position had gone through, he transferred his operations to the Collège de France and began a series of experiments with Magendie on the spinal nerve roots. [4] The move to the Collège caused him to collaborate more closely than before with his former teacher, whose advancing age forced him to rely heavily on Bernard's operative skill and energy. Through the summer and most of the fall the two worked intensively together to resolve inconsistencies in Magendie's earlier observations that had led some other physiologists to question his famous discovery of the distinction between the dorsal and ventral roots. They demonstrated their new results repeatedly to a distinguished succession of local and foreign scientists. Bernard presented two papers on the topic during the summer, and Magendie published one in December based largely on his former student's work. It was, according to Olmsted, the older man's last experimental investigation. [5]

In spite of the excitement attending this project, Bernard also took up again near the end of the summer his own unfinished business concerning digestion and the dietary alterations of urine. On August 10 he began an experiment on "the time necessary for the urine to become acid in rabbits." Depriving two animals of food, he examined the changes in their urine in the accustomed way. Except for observing at the beginning that he could disengage a "great abundance" of carbonic acid from the alkaline urine of one animal with hydrochloric

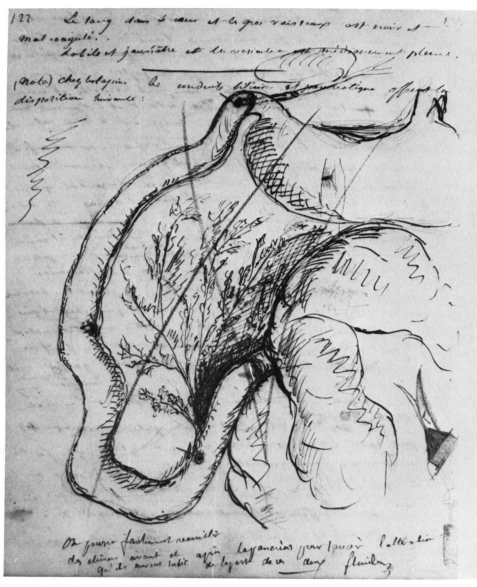

Claude Bernard's sketch of the locations of the biliary and pancreatic ducts along the intestinal tract of a rabbit. MS C. VIIIe, 7c, p. 122. See text, p. 341.

acid, and that the rabbits' ears became cold during long fasts, he
carried out the experiment in much the same way he had done similar
ones a year earlier. But the unexpected was never far off in Bernard's
investigations, even in the seemingly routine ones. Having begun the
experiment either at home or in another laboratory, he carried one of
the animals to the Collège de France on the second day and continued
there. For nine days he allowed the rabbit to feed on ordinary grass,
then put it in a zinc box shut off from all sources of nourishment.[6]
The next day he caused it to urinate by pressing its bladder. The fluid
was acidic and contained much urea. Ten minutes later he pressed the
bladder further until it was empty; "but how surprised I was [*quel n'est
pas mon étonnement*]," he declared in his notebook, "to see that the
urine was turbid and very plainly alkaline." Testing it with nitric
acid, he found no trace of urea. The contrasts between these two
urinary excretions obtained almost at the same time struck him as "apparently inexplicable incongruities." [7] Bernard nevertheless could not
forebear to try to explain them.

His explanation was ingeniously contrived. If urine descends into
the bladder drop by drop, he thought, so that the urine of abstinence
comes into contact with urine of digestion already there, the lactic
acid which he supposed responsible for the acidity of the former
would decompose the carbonates which make the latter turbid and
alkaline. Both carbonic acid and bicarbonates would form. If the latter
were in greater proportion, the resulting urine might be clear and
alkaline, but it would become cloudy again when warmed, because
carbonic acid would be disengaged and carbonates would reform.
This was the situation, he believed, in horses. If the carbonic acid
were in greater proportion, the urine might be acid at the time it was
emitted, because, so long as the fluid was under pressure in the bladder, the carbonic acid would remain in solution. When the urine came
into contact with the air, however, the carbonic acid would evaporate,
leaving the fluid again alkaline. He was still left, however, with the
problem of how there could be urines of "two qualities" at the same
time in the bladder of this rabbit. This he thought might be accounted
for by there being only incomplete mixing of the fluids successfully
secreted into it, so that the organ could contain distinct layers forming
a gradient between the properties of fasting and of digestive urine.[8]
This was another one of those ideas which passed frequently by the
window of Bernard's mind, and probably little more came of it. It is
interesting, I think, primarily because it again illustrates the intensity
of his desire to construct *some* explanation for every anomalous phe-

nomenon he encountered. To his own innate curiosity may have been added a compulsion to explain because he felt that his mentor Magendie had too often left things in a state of confusion by not finding reasons for apparently discordant results. Later on Bernard wrote among his notes for his course:

> Magendie was in his manner an empiric, because he used to say: disturb the phenomena, that is, experiment and *simply verify without explaining anything*. That was still not a complete experimental method at all, because in the experimental method it is necessary to explain. Only it is necessary first *simply to confirm* the results of the experiment. But afterward it is necessary to explain and to reach a determinism.[9]

Temkin and Schiller have both pointed out that this is an incomplete picture of Magendie,[10] but it was nevertheless Bernard's impression. The present instance suggests that the younger man may sometimes have overcompensated for what he considered to be the deficiency in Magendie's approach. Spontaneous private remarks should not be used as indications of a man's considered judgments, but in this case they illustrate in a freer, more striking manner a propensity which in a more controlled form manifested itself also in some of the ideas Bernard made public.

In the midst of writing down his explanation, Bernard interjected the following thought, stimulated by his consideration of carbonic acid in the urine: "By the way, the chemists who try to measure the carbonic acid of the aliments by the respiration seem to me to be furiously in error, for the urine eliminates carbonic acid considerably." [11] Liebig and Dumas were the most prominent proponents of treating the carbon of the carbonic acid exhaled in respiration as a measure of the carbon ingested in food, as well as the converse.[12] Bernard's remark therefore reinforces the impression of the depth and persistence of his desire to counteract the influence of their approach. That motive came quickly to the surface when an opportunity seemed to present itself to channel his general opposition into a specific proof of their errors. This time, as on several previous occasions, nothing more came of the idea.

Meanwhile, the experiment itself continued. Bernard kept the rabbit from eating for three more days, but nothing else unusual turned up and the later urinary excretions were always acidic.[13] Early in September Bernard made an autopsy on a dog sacrificed for another experiment after it had refused food for three days. The urine was not only acid, he noticed, but when treated with nitric and nitrous acid it gave reactions which suggested to him that some bile may have been present in it. He recollected a similar observation on the urine of horses a year earlier. He also noticed that there was some acidic material along the entire length of the small intestine, even though the pancreatic juice and bile were alkaline. In another dog he found the intestine acidic although the reaction was alkaline in the pancreatic duct. "The bile did not appear to be distinctly acid (nevertheless that should be looked at again)." [14] These observations apparently induced him to consider that dietary changes might modify in some way the reaction of intestinal secretions as well as the urine, and to watch particularly for variations of the bile.

Between September 15 and 20 Bernard kept a rabbit without food in order to follow the changes in its urine until it died of hunger. He paid special attention to changes in the quantity of urea secreted over this period, to see if it would diminish near the end, and he also tested for lime and magnesia by treating the urines with ammonium oxalate. His intention was frustrated because the animal died prematurely, apparently from having injured itself while in a weakened condition. [15] At its autopsy the most remarkable observation he made concerned the bile:

It presents a very distinctly acid reaction. The fact was curious enough so that I took care to assure myself of it completely and repeatedly with litmus paper . . . That acidity of the bile is a new fact which would indicate that bile is an excretion. What is the acid which renders it acidic? [16]

In the next few days Bernard followed up this observation, but meanwhile he had been attempting simultaneously with this investigation a bold operation to examine an even bolder idea. In the preceding experiment his reason for wanting to know whether urea persists during "the last days which precede death by abstinence," was that "one says that the lymph then diminishes." [17] What he had in mind, apparently, was a hypothesis that the general lymphatic circulation is the pathway by which urea is carried from the sites of its formation to the blood. If the flow of lymph and the excretion of urea both decreased together, such a theory would become more plausible. An operation he carried out on a dog the same day that he began the experiment on the rabbit seems to have been intended as a means to test this idea more directly by suppressing the entry of lymph into the blood. After studying the operative procedures on dead animals, Bernard exposed on a living one its left external and internal jugular and brachiocephalic veins. He tied all of these veins and their branches, so that the lymph which enters the brachiocephalic vein could not pass into the general circulation. Then he destroyed the valves in the external jugular vein with a sharp instrument, and inserted a tube into it to form a "chylous fistula" from which he could collect the lymph. The lymph clotted, however, and the animal grew weaker until it died six days later. At its autopsy Bernard found its urine acidic. With the nitric acid reaction he could not at first obtain any crystals of nitrate of urea. After concentrating the urine he still detected only a small quantity. The animal had nevertheless been in abstinence, a condition which ordinarily resulted in large amounts of urea. Bernard could not be certain, however, whether the cause of the difference was "that I have prevented a part of the lymph from pouring into the blood," or whether the illness of the animal had prevented the formation of urea near the end.[18]

The possible relation between lymph and urea came up again during the next group of experiments, although Bernard carried these out chiefly to determine more fully what conditions caused the bile to become acidic. Clearly his earlier observations predisposed him to regard the phenomenon as a result of fasting, corresponding to the situation for urine; but his next findings were somewhat equivocal. On September 24 he examined two dogs which had been sacrificed after serving for other experiments deriving from his collaboration with Magendie. One of the animals, which had eaten very little for four days, had "manifestly" acid bile, as well as acid urine containing a substantial amount of urea. The bile of the other animal was neutral or alkaline when he first examined it, but he took a sample of it home with him in the evening and found it then "very distinctly acid." He wondered whether he had been mistaken in the morning or whether in the intervening period the bile might have been made acid by inadvertently coming into contact with the gall bladder of the first dog. Later he "examined the phenomenon more closely," and had to acknowledge that the bile was "really very little acid." Moreover the bile might become acidic after death by the admixture of gastric juice which reached it by endosmosis from the stomach. On the 26th he observed that a rabbit which he considered to be fasting, since it had eaten very little for twenty-four hours, contained bile that was "noticeably alkaline, although not very strongly so." He compared this to the acid bile of the rabbit which had died of starvation, but did not say what he thought the difference indicated.[19] The next experiment only added confusion, for a rabbit which he examined in Rayer's laboratory had acid bile and acid urine, though it had been nourished with

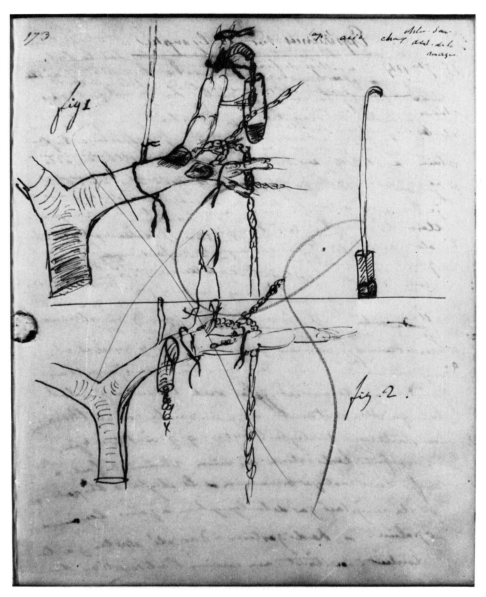

Claude Bernard's sketch of an operation to form a "chylous fistula" for collecting lymph, MS C. VIIIe, 7c, p. 173. See text, pp. 345–346.

bran and oats. The only observation on this animal which fit Bernard's conceptions was that the urine did not produce a mass of nitrate of urea.[20]

Bernard had also begun on the 25th another experiment comparing the urine of a fasting rabbit with that of a rabbit on a diet of carrots. After twenty-four hours, the urine of the latter was alkaline, that of the former still slightly alkaline. By now, however, Bernard had shifted his emphasis almost entirely to the question of the relative quantities of urea produced in the two situations. With the usual nitric acid reaction he obtained a "prodigious" precipitate of urea from the urine of the fasting rabbit, and none from the other, for which he did not bother to try more sensitive procedures. "This experiment, although roughly done," he wrote, "is therefore entirely conclusive, for it is clear that the fasting rabbit, although its urine was not acid . . . has produced in 24 hours a quantity of urea enormously greater than the rabbit on carrots." He thought, however, that he should still measure the quantities of urea more exactly. At this point he sacrificed the fasting rabbit in order to make one of the examinations of bile mentioned above. Then he gave the other rabbit no food for four days before returning it to a diet of lettuce on October 1. Comparing the urines from the period of abstinence with that excreted while the animal was on a herbivorous diet, he confirmed that the former contained a "huge" amount of urea, the latter so little "that it is difficult to perceive it by its nitrate." [21]

After the first of these comparisons Bernard wrote that when he had measured the quantities of urea more exactly he should "next seek to suppress the lymph to see if the urea will disappear." [22] The result encouraged him, therefore, to pursue his idea that the lymph carries urea into the blood. Presumably he intended to repeat his attempt to form a thoracic fistula. Apparently, however, he did not implement his plan. One reason may have been that before he completed the preceding experiment itself he made another observation which called his interpretation into question. From the bladder of a dog which had died from the effects of a spinal nerve root operation Bernard obtained urine which was acid but contained no urea, despite the fact that the animal had fasted for several days. It was therefore, he decided, the general sick state of the animal which may have prevented urea from forming. He thought he should examine the urine of humans after death to see if the same phenomenon occurred. "Would that be due to the arrest of the lymphatic circulation," he wondered, "or to the arrest of the secretion of bile or to some other cause?" At any rate, he added,

"This fact invalidates a little my observation made on the dog with the chylous fistula." [23] That is, in the animal whose flow of lymph he had blocked, the decrease in urea may not have resulted from that specific effect, but from the general debilitation of the animal, just as it probably had in the present case. He had already considered that possibility at the time, but had probably not believed it so likely as he now had to acknowledge that it was. The passage suggests that Bernard still did not give up entirely his theory of the relation of lymph to urea, but perhaps his confidence in it was weakened sufficiently to deter him from undertaking again the difficult operation required to pursue it further. [24]

The boldness of the plan which Bernard had contemplated is perhaps not apparent without some discussion of its implications. What Bernard seemed to envision would have amounted to an effort to answer the central question which Prévost and Dumas's experiments had raised; that is, what is the source of the urea which ordinarily passes from the blood into the urine? If it enters the blood from the lymphatic system, as Bernard thought it might, then urea must arise not in some special organ, or in the blood itself, but in the general body tissues; for the lymphatic system was considered to absorb the materials produced there. (It is possible, but I think improbable, that he was considering the source to be digested materials in the intestine, absorbed through the lacteal portion of the lymphatic system). Bernard's approach would have fitted the broad strategy he had also followed in his unsuccessful attempt to establish the role of the vagus nerves in nutrition. That is, he would have tried to locate a chemical phenomenon within the body by means of vivisection operations designed to interrupt a process, and of chemical analyses of the ultimate product of the process, to detect indirectly whether the operation had caused it to cease. If he had pursued his investigation, Bernard would not have succeeded, for he was not looking in the right place, but his manner of attack on the problem would have been in more general terms a step in the direction of the solution. [25]

Taken by itself, Bernard's abortive investigation would seem to have embodied the goal of substantiating physiologically the theory that urea is the decomposition product of the organized nitrogenous constitutents of the body tissues. Most elaborately formulated in Liebig's *Animal Chemistry*, this idea had deep roots. It derived originally from the chemical consideration that the high nitrogen content of urea made it the most obvious vehicle for the elimination of excess nitrogen from the body. [26] That basic relation seemed to apply, whether the source of the nitrogen was the organized material of the body itself or unusable portions of the aliments. In 1838 Richard Felix Marchand carried out an investigation which appeared to demonstrate that at least part of the urea excreted must come from the former source. Marchand fed a dog exclusively on sugar for twenty days. The percentage of urea in its urine decreased only from 3 to 2.8 after six days, and by the end, when the animal had grown very weak, it had reached a steady minimum of 1.8 per cent. The fact that the secretion continued even with no nitrogen in the diet was for Marchand convincing evidence, although not direct proof, he admitted, that the urea "is created from the living, already-formed animal substance."[27] Supported by this conclusion and his own conviction that it "would be irrational" to think that nitrogenous aliments were converted immediately to waste products without first serving as parts of the organism, Liebig asserted that the formation of urea is a direct measure of the decomposition of the nitrogenous constituents of organized tissue. The compound is produced in the tissues, he believed, and then passes "through the absorbent and lymphatic vessels into the veins."[28] Bernard's hypothesis concerning the relation of lymph flow to urea formation would seem to fit in very well with these general conceptions. At the end of the experiment in which he found that the urine of a fasting rabbit contained much more urea than that of one on a herbivorous diet, however, Bernard wrote down a query which reveals that his ideas on the question were quite out of step with these trends of his time. For it appears that he was willing to disregard either the idea that the product of the decomposition of the nitrogenous substances in the body is urea, or else the idea that this process goes on continuously within the organism. He wrote:

There will even be a possibility of preventing all formation of urea by making [the animal] digest in a continuous manner.—Is that different in the dog and the rabbit??

The carnivores do not produce a greater quantity of urea because they are carnivores, but because their digestion is more rapid.

Could one give substances which, being more or less rapidly digested, would thus give more or less urea independent of their composition?[29]

The second and third of these statements are somewhat cryptic. To be consistent with the first and with the experiment which inspired them, however, Bernard could not have meant that rapid digestion produces more urea by more rapidly supplying matter to be converted to it; rather that by being over more quickly it leaves longer periods of fasting between the times when aliments are being absorbed. The second statement, in particular, seems to be a denial that nitrogenous aliments are the source of increased urea.

These suggestions were consistent with Bernard's earlier efforts to find sharp contrasts between the urine of fasting and of digestion, but they made no sense within the general framework of current nutritional theories. If urea formation could be suppressed simply by keeping an animal in continuous digestion, then the processes which produce urea would not be essential to the life of the organism. In terms of current ideas it would be possible, according to this scheme, for an animal to subsist by consuming non-nitrogenous aliments alone, and urea must be formed only when it is necessary in the absence of this alimentation for the animal to consume its own substance. Such an adjustment of nutritional theory, however, would be hard to reconcile with the basic investigation by Magendie showing the insufficiency of non-nitrogenous nourishment. That Bernard should entertain ideas containing such implications poses an interesting question. Had he thought through the basis of current theories and concluded deliberately that they were not indispensable? Or did he more simply respond to what he observed before him with little attention to contemporary thought? The impossibility of answering with certainty illustrates how fragmentary a picture of a man's thoughts even a very extensive written record of his daily investigations must be. I believe it is more probable, however, that he did not make an analysis of other theories, but again gave "free scope" to his imagination. Not only would the latter course be in keeping with his manner on other occasions, but the alternative would presume that he had been able to reason away formidable obstacles. Given his attitude toward the theories of the chemists, it would not be surprising for him to reject Liebig's contention that urea is a direct measure of the quantity of muscle tissue decomposed; but to deny that such decomposition of organized nitrogenous substance did occur during all vital activity and was responsible for at least some continuous formation of urea, whether or not the animal is in digestion, was to break more radically with a broader spectrum of physiological opinion. Simply to consider how deep the reformulation of current thought implied in Bernard's ideas would be is to make it implausible that he himself had attempted it.

"In biology," Bernard later wrote, ". . . theories are so precarious that the experimenter keeps almost all of his freedom. In chemistry and physics the facts are becoming simpler, the sciences are more advanced, the theories are firmer, and the experimenter must take greater account of them and grant a greater importance to the conclusions of experimental reasoning based on them." [30] The above incident helps, I think, to clarify how seriously he meant that statement, how little account he felt it was necessary to take of the biological theories of his time. It suggests also that he might sometimes dispense with them too easily; for, if not established beyond doubt and in detail, the general direction of thought represented in the doctrine that urea is the ordinary end-product of an essential metamorphosis of nitrogenous substances in the body was sound and productive. Perhaps I am again making too much of mere surmises which Bernard may have put down casually, with little commitment, and which he probably did not pursue. It is perfectly possible that he did begin to assess the relation of these ideas to other nutritional theories and that their discordance led him to drop his own suggestions. Yet the freedom from the restrictions of contemporary theories which he allowed himself here, even if only momentarily, was a heightened degree of the freedom which he maintained for himself in his public opinions, and which, according to the preceding general statement, he considered fully justifiable.

Bernard apparently interrupted his investigation of the dietary alterations of urine and bile, just as he had dropped a similar investigation in 1846, at a time when he seemed to be in the midst of unresolved but absorbing questions. He must have performed at least a few more experiments after the beginning of October, when the laboratory record ends, for when he presented a note on the "Physiological constitution of urine and bile" to the Philomatic Society of Paris in February 1848, he described certain results as more definitive than they had appeared in the notebook. He was now able to state that in either herbivorous or carnivorous animals, "bile acquires, in complete abstinence from aliments, a very manifest acid reaction." In herbivorous animals this change occurs in 36 to 48 hours, and as soon as one again nourishes them with herbaceous foods the reaction becomes again distinctly alkaline. Carnivores, on the other hand, have normally acidic bile. His very brief description provided no experimental details, but it is clear from the fact that he said he had investigated cattle as well as dogs and rabbits, that he had extended his research further and must have achieved more consistent results than he was getting at the end of September. On February 10 he had found "very manifestly alkaline bile" in a rabbit digesting potatoes, whereas a dog on its ordinary meat diet had "strongly acidic" bile. Perhaps this clear contrast encouraged him to draw his conclusions out of the earlier investigations, for it was two days later that he presented his note.[31]

The data he already had in September may have sufficed for his discussion of urine. He asserted that urea is present in abundance in the urine of all fasting animals. Other constituents of urine produced during digestion, such as the hippuric acid and carbonates of herbivorous animals and the uric acid of carnivores, disappear in abstinence. The information concerning urea came primarily from the experiments of September; that on the other constituents might have derived from investigations during the summer of 1846.[32] Now he concluded that "urea is then the sole principle of urine which corresponds to that nourishment which I would call normal." By "normal" he meant that since only the urine of abstinence has always the same characteristics, it should be considered typical and serve as the point of departure for all research on the variations caused by digestion. With these remarks Bernard felt that he had fulfilled the promise in his earlier memoir on the subject to show that the distinctions between the urine produced during fasting and that produced during digestion applied to their chemical composition as well as to their appearance and reaction. He again characterized the urine of all animals "subsisting on their own substance" as carnivorous, without appearing to notice the contradiction with his own statement that digesting carnivores secrete uric acid and urea, whereas fasting animals secrete only urea.[33]

Once again Bernard represented the main objective of his investigation as a demonstration of the importance of physiological considerations in the chemical analysis of organic materials. "All of the disagreements" among the ablest chemists who had analyzed urine and bile he believed to have resulted from their neglect of the physiological condition of the animals involved. His argument would have been stronger if he had invoked specific examples, for there were at least some outstanding chemists, including Liebig and Lehmann, who were quite aware of the dietary influences by which Bernard substantiated his contention. Moreover, many of the disagreements which prevailed resulted from the chemical complexity of the fluids, particularly of the bile.[34] Bernard, however, was less concerned with particular individuals or investigations than with the principle. "It is evident, in fact," he ended, "that in the analysis of animal fluids, the physiological question must dominate the chemical question. And if one does not take into account the physiological state of the animals on which one experiments, it becomes impossible to apply the divergent analyses of chemists fruitfully to the study of vital phenomena."[35] By now this theme had almost become the banner by which Bernard sought to mark the ground on which he stood. Most of the discoveries he had made during his studies of physiological chemistry he had engaged in the service of this cause.

Bernard's communication to the Philomatic Society summarized the studies of dietary influences on excretions which he had carried on intermittently for more than two years. It embodied some significant distinctions which he had worked hard to establish. Yet the nature and brevity of the note give it more the appearance of a convenient halting-place than of the achievement of his aims. As we have seen, both in the early stage of the research and in his more recent efforts he had sought to use the distinctions he found as means to penetrate to a deeper understanding of nutritional processes. None of these hopes were satisfied. The use of his results to support his stand on the relation between physiology and chemistry may only have been a consolation for him when he saw that the particular path he was following had taken him only to the edge of the territory he wished to enter.

One can only wonder why he ceased to pursue the deeper questions he had raised. Perhaps he came to feel that the phenomena were too complex for the technical means by which he had planned to approach them. There is no direct evidence, however, that he explicitly reached such a decision. The investigation simply came to an end. Perhaps that was in part because his main effort in the fall of 1847 was once again attracted by the magnetic lure of his unsolved problems concerning digestion.

As he pursued a new series of researches on digestion from September until early December, Bernard became involved in an intricate tangle of observations and explanations. He seemed to begin in an effort to follow through certain conclusions from the memoir on saliva he had presented six months before. Having stressed then that starch is not transformed by saliva in the mouth or stomach, but starts to form sugar only in the intestine, he now began to look in the latter organ for further evidence of the existence and cause of that reaction. As he continued, however, he kept coming back to his old idea that a common material principle underlies the actions of all digestive juices, and this theme appeared to distract him in part from his intent to locate the transformation of starch at a particular level in the digestive tract. That old idea also took on a new form, for he now came to feel that the theory of ferment action which he had applied to saliva in his memoir could be extended to the other digestive juices. According to this view, the degree of decomposition of the fluids would determine the nature of their digestive actions. To complicate the matter further, however, he reverted intermittently to his former view that it is the acid or alkaline reaction which specifies the actions of the various juices, and by focusing on the intestinal fluids he sometimes seemed on the verge of succeeding with the demonstration which had so often frustrated him.

On September 3 Bernard sacrificed a rabbit which had been fed bran flour and potatoes for three days. With a microscope he observed that the fluid drained from its stomach contained many intact starch granules. Iodine colored the fluid blue, whereas potash did not "very noticeably" turn it brown—"proof," he wrote, "that there is only infinitely little sugar, if in fact there is any." With the intestinal contents iodine did not give a blue color, yet he could still see starch granules there under the microscope. Thinking, therefore, that the bile that mixes with the alimentary mass in the intestine had altered the starch in some unknown way which masked the usual test for it, he added some bile to a portion of the stomach contents to see if it would cause a similar change. It did produce a precipitate, and afterward the iodine reaction would no longer take place. "What action, therefore, could the bile have on the starch?" he asked. "It will be necessary to search for it with great care." It seemed to him also that the pancreatic juice dissolved, or at least modified, the precipitate formed by the bile; but, he added, "These observations must all be made again very carefully." [36] Bernard's experiment thus supported his earlier conclusion that the transformation of starch into sugar did not take place before the intestine; but, more important to him, it seemed to call for further investigation of the involvement of bile and of pancreatic juice in whatever processes comprised this conversion.

It may well have been these observations which induced him to renew his attempts three weeks later to create a fistula in order to collect these two juices in pure form. Using two dogs which he had killed in order to see whether their bile was acidic,[37] he "studied the best procedure to follow in order to make a biliary or pancreatic fistula. Here is the one on which I have settled." [38] He drew a careful sketch of the operative arrangement, but the procedure must still not have been satisfactory, because he did not record any such operations on living animals and did not use juices procured in this way for the ensuing experiments.

Bernard continued instead to examine the alimentary canals of rabbits in order to ascertain what happens to starch in natural digestions.

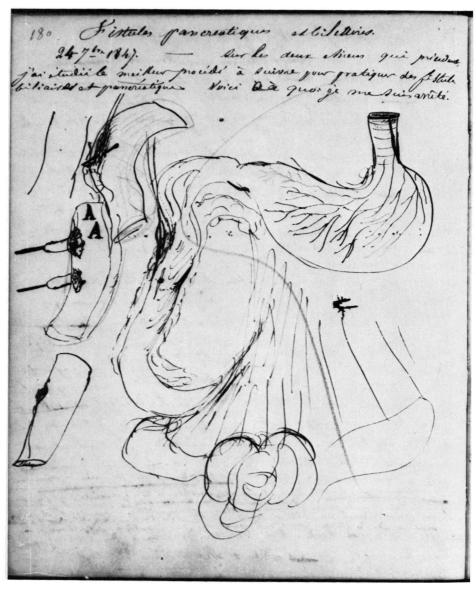

Claude Bernard's sketch for an attempt to create a pancreatic and biliary fistula. MS C. VIIIe, 7c, p. 180. See text, p. 355.

He was perhaps influenced to follow this approach, closely resembling that Bouchardat and Sandras had used,[39] by the fact that the research on the nervous system was leaving a supply of injured animals which would have to be sacrificed anyway. In one case he found starch granules in various stages of alteration throughout the stomach and intestine, and no sugar until the level of the cecum. This result made him suspect that in rabbits the cecum serves as a "second stomach," transforming starch to sugar or lactic acid. On October 17 he withdrew from the intestines of two rabbits, juices which rapidly transformed starch solution to glucose. Three days later, however, he encountered "a great quantity of glucose" in the stomach fluid of a rabbit nourished with carrots, whereas he could detect none in the intestinal fluid. This result was clearly contrary to his expectations and his conceptions. "Whatever is the cause of that?" he wondered. "Look again to see if that might be the mixture of the glucose with bile which would have changed it in some way? Mix this gastric juice with bile." [40] The investigations on these animals thus turned out to be rather puzzling and to constitute less than ideal support for his earlier assertions: perhaps for those reasons he switched his approach to artificial digestion.

Digesting pieces of boiled beef in gastric juice obtained by filtering the stomach contents of a rabbit, Bernard found that the addition of a small quantity of bile to the juice "perhaps impeded the action of the gastric juice a little rather than favoring it." An infusion of pancreatic tissue mixed with the gastric juice also seemed to retard the digestion, an effect which he attributed to the fact that the pancreatic material neutralized the acid of the gastric liquid. Bernard also added bile to saliva and to intestinal juice, but it did not alter the action of either fluid on starch. These observations seemed mostly negative or inconclusive, but in the midst of them Bernard had a sudden idea. Noting that fresh bile by itself does not act on starch, he wondered whether aged bile might. "This is in agreement with my other observations that the destruction of starch is due to materials in decomposition," he reflected. "The acidic reaction of gastric juice, resisting that decomposition, resists that transformation of starch; when one renders it [the bile] alkaline, its decomposition being able to take place, it acts on the starch." [41] Thus Bernard glimpsed an opportunity both to explain the transformation of starch in the intestine, where he believed it chiefly occurs, and to expand his doctrine of salivary fermentation to include other digestive fluids.

On October 23 Bernard carried out thirteen artificial digestions, using gastric, intestinal, and pancreatic juice from a turkey and from a rabbit. The purpose of these tests is not entirely clear, since he did not make those with the different digestive fluids strictly comparable. He was, however, generally interested in the effects of altering the reaction of the fluids. He observed that the general intestinal fluid of the turkey and of the rabbit digested meat when acidified, but the latter did not act on starch. With a pancreatic infusion Bernard seemed to achieve the result which had eluded him in his prior investigations of saliva and gastric juice. When he acidified the fluid it digested meat but did not act on starch, whereas it converted the starch to sugar after he had rendered it alkaline with sodium carbonate.[42] The persistence of his conception that the various digestive juices are interchangeable is suggested in the fact that he changed the title of one section of his record from "pancreatic juice" to "gastric juice with pancreas." His retention of this notion was revealed more clearly a little later when he remarked that "the pancreas of the rabbit did not appear to me to be good for making artificial gastric juice. It will be necessary to investigate on other animals." [43]

During the course of another experiment on artificial digestion with gastric juice filtered from the stomach contents of a rabbit, Bernard made with the same animal a very interesting attempt to ascertain the region in which a crucial digestive process takes place. "I intended," he said, "to see where the lacteal vessels began." That is, he wished to see at what point along the intestine were located the first of the lymphatic vessels which carried the whitish material known as chyle from the alimentary canal. But "the experiment did not succeed from that point of view." The lacteals contained only lymph, although he had killed the animal rapidly and opened it immediately. "To what must one attribute the absence of white lacteals? To the fact that there was not enough fat, or rather to the fact that the animal had ceased to digest?" [44] It is not entirely clear what purpose Bernard had beyond his stated plan. Since he had previously noticed that in rabbits the pancreatic duct is unusually placed at a distance from the bile duct,[45] it is tempting to infer that he wished to find out if the chyle formed at that point in the alimentary canal at which nutrients mix with one of these secretions. From the context of the investigation of the digestion of starch and of meat which he was carrying on, and from the fact that this particular rabbit was nourished on bread and meat, one would suspect that if that was his aim, he had in mind chiefly the influence of the digestive juices on those two nutrients. On the other hand, his reference to fat, taken in conjunction with the view of Bouchardat [46] and others that it is only this class of aliments which forms the whitish chyle, would suggest that he was interested in the digestion of that substance. He himself had performed only a few scattered experiments on the digestion of fat,[47] however, and there is no indication that he yet associated it particularly with the pancreatic juice. Whatever his intentions, he did not immediately pursue the question after this negative outcome, but his interest in it eventually helped lead him to some of his most significant discoveries.

After a lapse of two weeks, during which he was probably busy doing experiments for Magendie,[48] Bernard resumed his study of digestion on November 3. He now went back again to his favorite question: "Does the reaction modify the digestive action of fluids?" This time he compared the action of infusions of stomach and duodenal membranes. After macerating each tissue for six hours in weakly acidified water, he put pieces of meat in each tube. The liquids, which seemed on the edge of putrefaction, digested only feebly. When he put both membranes together for another 12–18 hours in hydrochloric acid, they yielded a liquid with "very active digestive power." Made alkaline, however, this liquid did not transform starch. Not satisfied with these experiments, Bernard remarked that "they must be pursued differently." [49]

Shortly afterward Bernard had another opportunity to examine the intestinal contents of a dog sacrificed for one of the spinal nerve experiments. The animal had been fed potatoes one day before. Bernard found that the stomach still contained some recognizable potatoes, as well as "very large quantities of starch." There was "no trace" of sugar. He analyzed separately a portion of the contents of the duodenum removed from just beyond the pylorus, and another taken from somewhat further along that canal. The former gave very little reduction with Barreswil's solution, whereas the latter produced a great amount.[50] "From this experiment," he concluded,

it follows clearly that the sugar did not begin to be evident until the beginning of the small intestine—there were no traces in the stomach and there was much starch—there was little [starch] at the beginning of the duodenum, the presence of the bile prevents the confirmation of starch by iodine. In the small intestine, below the pancreas, there is much sugar.[51]

With the microscope he could observe that in both portions of the intestine there were still some particles of starch undergoing alteration.

Bernard's initial reaction to these results was to "ask whether it is the bile which acts on the starch to transform it into sugar," a natural response in view of the fact that he had already been contemplating that possibility. In the animal, however, some bile had mixed with the stomach contents near the pyloric end, and he could not find any sugar there. Perhaps following up his idea that the bile may react with starch only when alkaline, he then mixed gastric fluid, bile, and potatoes with a little sodium carbonate; but even then "the bile appeared to have no action on the starch." In contrast, when he placed portions of gastric and duodenal mucosa together in a solution of sodium carbonate, the starch disappeared. From this result, together with his observation that in the intestine the sugar appeared "below the pancreas," one might expect that Bernard would have been anxious to pursue the question of where and by the action of what secretion this conversion took place. Instead, however, he was attracted to another feature of the last test: the tube containing the gastric and duodenal material and the starch had been in a warm water bath for several hours, when the liquid began to putrefy, and it was at this point that the starch disappeared rapidly. But as that occurred, it also became "very difficult to seize the glucose in transition, if it nevertheless necessarily exists." Rather than try to locate the natural process, therefore, he examined further which of the conditions involved in the artificial reaction might have been responsible for these peculiar phenomena.[52]

Returning to this question on November 12, he used an ingenious new technique for producing alkaline digestive fluids. Sacrificing a dog, he injected a sodium carbonate solution into its abdominal aorta and portal vein. The solution impregnated the tissues of the stomach and intestines. Then he stripped off pieces of membrane from each organ and, placing them in water, made with each a "perfectly alkaline" infusion. After the preparation from the stomach had been exposed to air for 8–10 hours, it transformed starch to sugar, "at the moment in which putrefaction seized the mucous [lining membrane]." After a somewhat longer time the same thing occurred with the preparation from the intestine. Although he had started with a method to produce alkaline digestive juices, he could not in the end ascribe these reactions to their alkalinity:

Without doubt there is a transformation of the starch there, but as a consequence of the putrefaction of the membranes, and that transformation is more complete when there are fragments of membrane than when their infusion is filtered or decanted. Nevertheless, it is a long way from this transformation to that which is obtained so rapidly with the pancreas, or mixed human saliva, serum, etc.[53]

Equivocal as this outcome therefore was, it nevertheless encouraged Bernard to pursue the possibility that in these digestive processes, too, the decomposition of animal membranes was the crucial factor. He left the same gastric and duodenal membranes exposed to cool, humid air for twenty-four hours longer, and then placed them together in water to make a new infusion. The resulting liquid dissolved starch rapidly, but he recognized that the mixing of the two membranes and the possibility that fragments of pancreatic material were present in addition, had produced a "complex" situation. Searching in the solution, he found such fragments, so that the experiment "perhaps does not mean anything." Therefore he isolated some of the pieces from the stomach, put them in fresh water, and added more starch. Once more the starch disappeared in a short time. "The stomach membrane therefore actually appeared to have acquired the property of transforming starch rapidly into sugar," he concluded. "It is a peculiar fact that that membrane did not have that property to the same degree on the first day." [54]

By now Bernard must have begun to feel that he had at last discovered the key to a general digestive theory which had for so long escaped him. If it was not the acid or alkaline reaction which accounted for the particular actions of the digestive juices, then perhaps it was the different states of decomposition of animal membranes. Thus Boutron and Frémy's fermentation theory might serve as the means by which a unified explanation for the properties of all of the digestive fluids would be found. Over the next two weeks Bernard proceeded at the intense pace that marked periods in which he sensed he was on the track of something especially important. The following day he took another portion of the same gastric membrane, which had remained exposed to air on a tray in the lecture hall. After preparing another infusion, he found that this liquid also "rapidly transforms a starch solution into sugar." His excitement must have been growing. He wrote, "This fact is becoming more and more interesting." To make certain that the phenomenon was not again due to some unnoticed bit of pancreas, he examined the preparation closely and found none. Then he carefully separated the mucous membrane from fragments of muscular and vascular tissue which had remained attached to it and made another infusion. When he reacted it with starch the result was less favorable. "It no longer transforms starch into sugar as plainly." Some dextrin appeared, but Barreswil's solution produced no reduction. The next day he divided the infusion into two parts. One he acidified, and placed a piece of beef into it. The meat began to dissolve in four hours and was completely digested in twenty-four. The unacidified portion he mixed with starch, but at the end of four hours the latter had not changed. "In the end," he commented, "the transforming power was lost. Do that over." It also seemed to him now that when he left the membranes in the infusions, the starch disappeared, but instead of sugar lactic acid appeared. "That fact is important," he thought, for when the filtered liquid was itself on the verge of putrefaction, it still produced sugar. He wondered, however, what would happen if the putrefaction of the liquid were more advanced.[55] Perhaps he saw here more parallels to Frémy's lactic acid fermentation and to his own demonstration that saliva could produce that substance. Thus, after the initial observations which had aroused his interest, the phenomena were again beginning to appear more complex, but Bernard probably still thought that the varying results could be fitted nicely into the conception that they depended upon the state of decomposition of the organic matter.

The next day Bernard began to broaden the scope of his inquiry by including pancreatic infusions and by attempting to digest meat with the intestinal infusions. Using material from the same dog he had injected with sodium carbonate three days before, he found that the fluid prepared with three-day-old pieces of pancreas did not digest starch, whereas the corresponding preparation from the small intestine did. Then he divided the latter fluid, still containing the sugar it had produced, into two portions, one of which he acidified. Neither portion was able to dissolve meat. Twenty-four hours later, however, he noticed the "extraordinary" fact that the sugar had disappeared from the unacidified portion, but not from the acidified one. "That is in accord," he commented, "with the experiment of Frémy concerning the influence of very strong acidity—the lactic fermentation is stopped."[56] But if that unexpected aspect of the experiment seemed to support his general hypothesis, Bernard had yet to show that his conceptions could apply to meat.

In the preceding experiment Bernard seemed to be attempting to blend his new approach with his older view that the acidity or alkalinity determines whether a digestive juice attacks meat or starch. In his next effort, on November 16, he followed this pattern more distinctly. He placed one part of an alkaline infusion of the small intestine of a rabbit in a starch solution and immersed another portion for fifteen hours in warm water acidified with hydrochloric acid. The former transformed the starch, but the latter was unable to digest meat. He took another piece of duodenum which was already beginning to putrify, and treated it similarly. It, too, transformed starch, but when he acidified it he still did not succeed in digesting meat.[57]

Bernard continued to test his infusions under varying conditions. He was able to digest starch with an infusion of fresh membrane from the small intestine of a rabbit.[58] He compared the action on starch of an infusion of fresh pancreas from a dog with that of the same material made alkaline with sodium carbonate. The alkaline liquid, he found, "did not lose its property with respect to starch, it was only retarded." On the other hand, "gastric juice" made by macerating a piece of small intestine for two days in alkaline solution and then acidifying the membrane until it dissolved, failed to digest boiled beef.[59] He also made a more unusual "gastric juice" from infusions of calf brain. Placing some of the tissue in acidified water, the rest in alkaline solution, he left each to stand for 8–10 days, until they began to putrefy. Then he acidified the latter. With each resulting fluid he tried without success to digest a piece of boiled beef.[60] That he should try this last experiment indicates how far he had been carried along by his new expansion of the idea that digestive actions result from particular stages of decomposition. Not content with attempting to show that the tissues that produce the digestive fluids have this property in common, he apparently envisioned demonstrating that animal tissues in general possess it.

At this point Bernard reviewed some of the properties of the digestive juices he had so far observed. An infusion of gastric fluid made alkaline does not transform starch on the first or second day, he noted, but it does on the third day after exposure to air. "But that transformation seems temporary in that the first infusions do not produce that transformation. It is at the moment in which the tendency to putrefy manifests itself that the transformation of starch takes place. But as soon as the putrefaction has got underway, there is no more transformation." Both pancreatic juice and human saliva produce sugar rapidly when they are fresh; later they produce lactic acid.[61] These comparisons might seem to imply either the similarity or the distinctness of the digestive juices. In the context, however, Bernard probably meant to show that they have common basic properties, but that they require different conditions to manifest the same action. In his next experiments he seemed to be making another attempt to show that under the proper conditions of both decomposition and reaction, these common properties extended to meat as well as starch. If so, the outcome again defied his intention. First he prepared an "artificial gastric juice" from a stomach membrane rendered alkaline by an injection (presumably of sodium carbonate through the aorta and portal vein, as before); just at the moment putrefaction began to show, he dissolved the membrane in hydrochloric acid. The result was "a very good gastric juice," which digested a piece of roast beef very rapidly. After saturating some of this gastric juice with sodium carbonate, however, he failed to transform starch with it. A piece of small intestine macerated for 8–10 days gave an infusion with opposite properties. Alkaline, it transformed starch to sugar, but when he acidified it, it had only a slight digestive action on meat. Somewhat more hopeful for Bernard's general viewpoint was an artificial gastric juice made with tissue from a spleen, for it digested a piece of beef in twenty-four hours.[62]

During the last days of November Bernard continued to contend with the diverse complicating factors which his research was turning up. On the 28th he noted a few of the conditions which seemed to influence his results. Infusions acidified with hydrochloric acid produced active digestive juices, whereas those treated instead with nitric acid did not. Gastric juice made from an infusion of the stomach membrane digested more actively if the membrane had first been made alkaline by injection. On the other hand, if after he acidified the infusion he again made it alkaline, it did not seem to dissolve starch at all. He wondered if perhaps the hydrochloric acid united so intimately with the organic material that it could no longer be separated. Cooked beef, he thought, digested more easily than boiled or uncooked meat. "Gastric juice made with gastric mucosa at the moment in which it turns to putrefaction seems to me to be more active than that made with fresher mucosa."[63] This rather weak statement reveals the frailty of Bernard's basis for his idea that digestive actions depend on the decomposition of organic matter. So far, he had only one apparently persuasive case, and that was the ability which some gastric juice had acquired after a period of aging to digest starch. Here he was trying almost wishfully to make out something of a parallel in the action of that juice on meat.

On November 30 Bernard observed that, contrary to what he had thought, uncooked beef was digested a little more quickly than roast beef, and two to three times faster than boiled beef.[64] The same day he had a special opportunity to examine the properties of pancreatic juice, because Rayer gave him a sample taken from a female patient who was supposed to be afflicted with a pancreatic fistula. The fluid was already a little altered. It transformed starch slowly, and when slightly acidified it had only a "very equivocal digestive faculty" for meat. "One must have that liquid fresh," he decided, "in order to know precisely what to believe concerning its properties." [65] So long as his attempts to create a fistula remained fruitless, however, he could not readily procure fresh pancreatic juice. He went on with his studies of digestive juices prepared from membranes. The following day [66] he compared the digestive actions of fluids prepared from the mucous membranes of two regions of the stomach. He macerated both membranes in dilute hydrochloric acid, but in a period of thirty-six hours neither was able to digest pieces of grilled pork. Then he prepared new fluids in a similar manner from the same membranes. This time the infusion made with a piece from the pyloric region of the stomach digested most of the meat in twenty-four hours; that from the area of the fundus scarcely digested any. He did not comment on what he thought these differences might indicate. Then he made the gastric juice alkaline and added a starch solution. The starch disappeared, but no sugar appeared. This result, similar to what he had observed in some analogous situations, now struck him again as "of the greatest importance, and deserves to be repeated." "What has become of the starch, therefore," he asked, "since there was no sugar—has it become dextrin or lactic acid?" [67] The observation was undoubtedly of special interest to Bernard because of its relation to his conception of the variable products of fermentation; he recorded no clue, however, about whether this experiment provided some new insight into the question or merely reinforced the earlier cases.

Bernard tried another variation of the same kind of experiment on December 3. This time he macerated for an hour in water a piece of the stomach of a dog containing all of its tissue layers. Then he added a few drops of pure hydrochloric acid, which dissolved the mucous layer. Filtering a portion of the fluid, he placed a piece of beef in it, and another piece in an unfiltered portion. The former portion caused the meat to soften a little, but did not hydrate it. The latter digested it "rapidly and in an admirable manner." Another unfiltered portion he made alkaline and found that it would digest starch. In contrast to the previous experiment, sugar was produced. [68] The very success of the digestions must have posed a certain dilemma. Although Bernard used stomach tissue from a dog which had died the day before, he did not expose it for any extended period, and he made no mention of its having been altered in any way through aging. The result would seem, therefore, to be more favorable to his old view, that gastric juice operates on meat or starch according to its acid or alkaline reaction, than to his new idea that certain combinations of reaction and stages of decomposition determine the digestive transformations. Perhaps he had such questions in mind the next day when he reflected, "The gastric juice produced with a fresh membrane is very active: it will be necessary to see if there is really any difference from the old membranes when they are entirely putrefied." [69] If there was a hint of doubt here, however, that did not deter Bernard from continuing to reason in terms of a decomposition theory when he launched into a new explanation of some aspects of gastric digestion.

There existed, he thought, "two species of gastric juice." One was "neutral," in the sense that it contained only enough acid to combine with the organic matter; the other had an excess of acid. Both digested meat, but only the latter hydrated it first, and then digested the substance more rapidly than did the former. When one placed some uncooked meat in acidified water the meat also became hydrated and dissolved after twenty-four to thirty-six hours, whereas cooked meat did not. The reason for this difference, he asserted, was that "a part of the [uncooked] meat, tending to decompose, combined with the acid and produced gastric juice which digested the rest of the piece of meat." For the same reason, when he had macerated stomach membranes for long periods in acid they themselves had sometimes disappeared. Boiled meat, in contrast, would not dissolve in acid because "having been submitted to a prolonged ebullition, it had lost the properties of a ferment capable of uniting with the acid to make an artificial gastric juice." Thus he conveniently incorporated into his scheme an observation which a few days before had been a surprise to him concerning the rates of digestion of cooked and uncooked meat. His hypothesis also led to a simple explanation for Bouchardat's minority opinion that hydrochloric acid can digest meat by itself.[70] Bouchardat had probably used meat which had been cooked very little or not at all, Bernard surmised, so that the aliment itself had produced an artificial gastric juice in the acid. From these ideas, "it also results," Bernard added sweepingly, "that the more meat is cooked the more difficult it is to digest." [71]

All of this was a quite logical development from the premises with which Bernard began. If he accepted the common opinion that many transformations of organic substances are caused by ferments formed during the decomposition of other organic matter, then he could easily include the digestive transformations in this category. If the membranes surrounding the cavities in which the digestive changes occur can serve as sources of active digestive juices, especially when they are beginning to putrefy, then it is reasonable to consider that it is the decomposition of these membranes which produces the ferment. If, however, the production of such ferments is a general property of decomposing animal matter, then other tissues ought likewise to be capable of forming digestive juices. Then it is only a small step to reason that animal tissue which happens to enter the alimentary canal of another animal can also be a source of digestive ferments. But it illustrates the strange conclusions to which logic can lead, that Bernard had reached the point where he could believe that aliments might supply the ferments for their own digestion.

Later on, when he became more self-conscious about the methods he employed in scientific investigation, Bernard wrote: "It is always necessary that we begin from something which we admit without proving it." Mathematics begins with postulates or axioms. It is pure logic. "In the natural sciences, we wish to apply the logic which is in our mind and we think that that logic is found there; but the difficult part is to have a point of departure for the deduction, for deduction is the only method which the mind entirely understands." [72]

The preceding experiments show that for Bernard it was still also a point of departure that the digestive juices were in some way interchangeable. Yet he had to admit, as he meditated on the results, that he had again not been fortunate in his efforts to form one from another. "I have tried," he commented, "to make artificial saliva with different parts of the mucous membrane without great success." With these membranes (presumably he meant from the stomach), he had obtained liquids which transformed starch into sugar, but "always slowly and in a manner incomparably more feeble than what takes place for saliva." Conversely, he had endeavored to make artificial gastric juices "with different fresh or old mucous membranes macerated in hydrochloric acid. The gastric membrane is the only one which has succeeded well." Had his predisposition been less persistent such an acknowledgement might have led him finally to consider that each digestive juice may have a particular action. Instead, he imagined various ingenious ways by which he might create conditions under which mucous and other animal tissues would decompose so as to dispose them more favorably to act as artificial salivas and gastric juices. [73]

Bernard did not carry out such plans; in fact, his systematic research on these questions had nearly come to an end. On January 16, 1848, however, he received another sample of pancreatic juice from the patient of Rayer. This time it was very fresh, for Bernard had observed it flow from the fistula himself. He placed it immediately in a starch solution, but after two days of digestion, which he maintained by carrying the test tube around in his pocket, the starch had not disappeared. He concluded that pancreatic juice does not act when it is completely fresh; only later, just as it begins to decompose:

> Thus this *recent* fluid does not act; too old, it no longer acts. There is an intermediate moment to seize. It is the same with the parotid or other saliva or mixed saliva of animals. (—Does putrefied saliva still act?) I have tried with the [pancreatic] fluid of the young lady and a little hydrochloric acid to make an artificial gastric juice. I did not succeed.[74]

The final sentence could equally well sum up the whole of Bernard's latest bout with the question of digestion. Endeavoring still to make the phenomena conform to his old premises and to the theory of fermentation he had adopted, he seemed to be getting further and further into a morass. Whether he recognized this when he broke off the investigation in January is hard to tell, but it seems in retrospect another in the long list of wrong turns which he had made ever since he took up the problem of gastric digestion. We ought to be cautious about judging that warning signs should have been visible to Bernard that he was following a false trail; for it is by later events that we can see most easily that the other direction, in which Mialhe followed Schwann, led to the destination. Yet there were certain flaws in Bernard's approach which do not require the evidence of later outcomes in order to be recognized.

Part of his trouble was evidently chemical. He relied on simple chemical methods, considerably less precise than some of his colleagues used, to deal with very complex situations. At a time when others paid careful attention to the quantities of acid or alkali in digestive preparations, Bernard was ordinarily satisfied with litmus paper tests and gave impressionistic descriptions such as that a solution was "barely," "noticeably," or "distinctly" acid or alkaline. He only occasionally recorded accurately measured proportions of reagents. At one point he recognized that he needed to be more careful, noting, "It will be necessary to measure the weight of the mucus, the water, and the starch in order to make gastric juice with identical activity." [75] It is far more revealing that he had not regularly done this before than that it occurred to him to do it. Furthermore, there is little evidence that his methods afterward became significantly more quantitative. One has only to compare the records of Bernard's experiments with the elaborate study Lehmann published not long afterward concerning the effects of digestive activity of variations in the quantities of each constituent of artificial gastric juice preparations,[76] in order to appreciate how far the French physiologist fell short of the most rigorous analytical standards then being applied to such questions. As much probably as any other factor, Bernard's cursory treatment of such analytical details prevented him from attaining sufficient experimental control to produce consistent distinctions with respect to the conditions he wished to compare. Whether he used gastric, intestinal, or pancreatic infusions, fresh or decomposing membranes; whether he reacted them with starch or with meat, he sometimes achieved digestion and sometimes not; sometimes energetic action and sometimes feeble action.

The most prominent and surprising shortcomings in Bernard's latest ideas, however, were physiological. On other occasions he had criticized theories of his colleagues which might be feasible for test tube reactions but were impossible in the conditions of the living organism. Now he seemed to be forgetting his own precept. It is hard to see how he could have envisioned that a digestive juice whose activity depended upon its having reached a certain ephemeral stage of incipient putrefaction would function in the animal. That would require that the animal anticipate what it was going to eat in such a way as to have prepared its digestive juices just far enough ahead of time so that they would reach the proper state of decomposition at the same time as the food reached them. One wonders if he noticed the incongruity of the fact that in the case of saliva he had earlier used the same conception of the nature of its action to argue that its digestive effects were accidental.[77] It is not certain from his remarks that he regarded natural digestive juices as operating in the same manner as the artificial juices he was preparing. Unless he did, however, it would not be easy to see what he hoped to learn about physiological processes from his experiments. It would be unfair to judge that Bernard was in error to follow the approach he did, for all of these objections could have appeared at the time to be the kind of temporary difficulties which accompany any investigation before it is completed. Nevertheless, it is evident that he was following a path which was in fact placing him in danger of becoming stalemated in ever deepening perplexities.

I suspect that Bernard himself later came to regard these and some of his previous investigations of digestion in that way. In one of the rare criticisms of his own performance which he recorded, he wrote:

If a man is abandoned to himself he never arrives at that 3rd period at the first try. He will pass necessarily through the first two. I lost 4 or 5 years of my youth floundering painfully in the first two; I had . . . [illeg.] made on a few facts . . .[illeg.] lightly published . . . [illeg.], when having arrived at the second period I added for the . . . [support?] of my hypotheses facts obtained without *counter proof.* I was fortunate enough not to publish the . . . [results?] of my first period. They remain in my notebooks . . . [illeg.] as witness of the [wanderings?] which an intellect underwent in that way.[78]

It cannot be proved exactly what investigations or years Bernard had in mind in this hastily written note. His intent was to compare his personal progress with the stages of development which he believed a science itself goes through while it is imperfect. He was therefore more concerned to identify the periods of his career philosophically than to relate literal biographical information. Yet the fact that the "4 or 5 years" he mentioned could neatly encompass a period in the youth of his career in which he had conceived of a procession of ill-fated theories of digestion makes it at least plausible that these events were the principal source of Bernard's recollection. At a time in which he became very concerned to define proper scientific methods it was natural for him to ascribe his early mistakes to his not yet having acquired a full understanding of those methods. I think, however, that his later successes did not arise from his entering at some point a "third period" in which he came to comprehend the use of counterproofs in a way that he had not before. For the same willful pursuit of his favorite ideas and the bold leaps from specific observations to generalizations which got him into his difficulties were involved in his most impressive successes, and remained characteristic of much of his later thought.

Sometime during this phase in his long struggle with the tangled problems of digestion, Bernard decided to write a general treatise on the subject. In a large notebook he began by outlining the procedures others had used to prepare artificial gastric juice. Then, apparently starting over, he wrote out a more extensive "history of experiments on digestion," beginning with Réaumur and including Spallanzani, Montegre, Tiedemann and Gmelin, Beaumont and Blondlot. Next he described the properties of gastric juice and its action on the major types of alimentary substance. After shorter sections on saliva and pancreatic juice, he tried out several versions of possible introductions or prefaces for the treatise.[79] At that point he apparently dropped the project for the time being.[80]

Bernard's first sketch of his plan for a book marks an important transition; although he undoubtedly did not conceive it as such, it represents the end of the period of his preoccupation with gastric digestion, and contains as well the earliest surviving formulations of some more general questions that concerned him increasingly in future years. One can only guess at his original motives for trying to write a comprehensive account of digestion. Possibly his new teaching responsibilities stimulated him to examine in broader scope the topic to which he had devoted so much of his research effort; or he may have been prompted by the feeling that he had reached a stage in his career in which it would be useful to publish a textbook. A more intriguing surmise is that his own frustrations with the subject might have induced him to evaluate, more systematically than he had done before, the achievements of other men in the field. His notes comprised a generally conventional review of the topic, but included some interesting features. In his discussion of artificial gastric juice he seemed finally to recognize the priority of the recent German line of investigations, for he began with summaries of the experiments of Eberle, Müller, Schwann, and their followers. He seems, however, to have relied more heavily on Burdach's textbook for his information concerning them than he did on their original writings.[81] Bernard ended his historical discussion of digestion with the appearance of Blondlot's work "in 1842" (actually 1843), adding that "Between 1842 and the present the physiological and chemical history of gastric juice was completed (my thesis 1843). But that history having been actually completed with respect to the important points, attention has been turned to the other intestinal fluids, the *saliva, pancreatic juice,* and *bile.*" [82] In the light of the efforts Bernard himself had expended over questions concerning gastric digestion that he had not resolved, that judgment appears more as a statement of resignation than of accomplishment. In his discussion of gastric juice itself, he utilized almost entirely Blondlot's description of its properties and actions on different aliments, even though he had characterized Blondlot's book as "filled with errors in many respects." [83] Bernard's summary of the digestive action of gastric juice followed the generally accepted conceptions of the time, making little mention of the special theories he had sought to establish. His discussion of saliva, on the other hand, centered on the ideas of his own recent memoir.[84] The contrast suggests that implicitly he recognized that his efforts had failed to win him a central place in the development of knowledge about gastric digestion.

It is quite likely that Bernard did not carry out his plan for a treatise on digestion because in the process of surveying the subject he conceived the idea of doing something more ambitious. His search for a definition of his goal is evident in the several successive attempts he made to outline a preface for his work. In his first try he began: "What is experimentation? What is observation?" Observation, he decided, is the examination of natural phenomena in their normal disposition and order. "Thus the study of the phenomena of digestion as nature gives them is observation." If one opens the stomach to view its action, that is vivisection for the purpose of observing better. Experimentation he defined as "the counterproof of observation," which one produces by disrupting processes. A good experiment, he concluded, is one which "responds clearly to the solution of the problem in question." [85] Bernard then tried another way to begin his preface. He had thought, he wrote, that his book would portray "faithfully the present state of physiology." The accumulation of new observations, however, was so rich that he "would almost say they encumbered the science;" from an appreciation of these facts would come a doctrine which must within a few years "destroy or deeply modify certain dominant but imprecise ideas." On the following page he distinguished physiological, physical, and chemical phenomena. That discussion, too, he thought, should "find a place in the introduction." [86] In his next "Preface" he rephrased his previous statement about trying to represent the present state of physiology. Underneath that he added:

> I have not wished to be a historian leaving the responsibility for opinions or experiments to their author with a condemnable complaisance and very great facility. I have criticized everything, I respond to everything except when I say it. I take responsibility for all of the experiments—and I defend that which I approve with the same conviction [with] which I support what I defend.

Again he was led to distinguish experimentation from observation. "What does one mean by experiment? In observation, Tiedemann has said, 'we spy on nature; in experimentation we interrogate it'." He developed again the idea that in observation we study normal phenomena, in experimenting we study phenomena disturbed "by our will," and concluded that he should "reflect on these definitions." [87]

Thus began several quests that Bernard carried on for the rest of his life—to provide a critique of the experimental efforts of his colleagues, to forecast and participate in a general renovation of physiology, and to define the basic nature of scientific activity. These were grand aims for a man who was still securing his own credentials in his calling. Perhaps he had had such ideas in mind even before this, and only used the projected book as an occasion to try to write them out; but it is plausible that these questions came into focus for him through the examination of the literature in his field that he had to undertake in order to outline his treatise. In fact, before he posed the question of experimentation in general terms, he had already been led to discuss its nature during his summary of the memoirs on digestion of Réaumur. "These experiments," he remarked,

are so well-known and so justly celebrated that it will suffice for me to recall them. I would only add that the two memoirs which de Réaumur has left us ought to be read and pondered by every young physiologist. They are worthy of being taken as models, because of the elegant and precise form in which the experiments are laid out, and especially by the acute and severe logic which shows at each instant. It does not suffice, in fact, to qualify as an experimenter, as some people believe, to be equipped with a certain propensity or a certain manual dexterity for practicing vivisection. That is only an accessory quality. What distinguishes the experimenter of genius is not the hand which performs the experiments, it is the mind which imagines them and institutes them in such a way that they may be decisive; which judges them and discerns the truth, often in the midst of very complex elements. Now there are few men who possessed these qualities in so high a degree as de Réaumur.[88]

The ideas touched on here echo through many of Bernard's later discussions of experimentation, and the similarity is too plain to be missed between this passage and the following statement near the beginning of his *Introduction to the Study of Experimental Medicine:* "We cannot separate these two things: head and hand. An able hand, without a head to direct it, is a blind tool; the head is powerless without its executive hand." [89] At the end of his discussion of Réaumur's investigation, Bernard wrote, "He thus established the *artificial digestions* which we are still repeating today. De Réaumur foresaw all of the future and the path which he had just opened up for the investigation of digestion." [90] Thus, by pausing to take a longer view of the subject in which he had been immersed, Bernard was able to see his own activity as the continuation of an old tradition, and to discover a kindred spirit in the work of a man separated in time from him by more than a century. Obviously he had derived inspiration from Réaumur, and perhaps also a clearer perception than he had had before of the purpose and nature of experimental physiology itself.

The last theme which Bernard put down "for the preface" began with an argument he had made before. "It seems to me," he wrote, "that one ought always to have a physiological goal in the study of sciences." Anatomy does not exist for itself. "I have therefore always had a physiological question as an objective; I have studied anatomy, physics [and] chemistry in order to explain it, and I have never chased after discoveries as some people do." There are people, he remarked, who do anatomy merely in order to find something which others have not seen, a goal which he had heard Rayer call ridiculous. Others study science only to know and relate everything that has ever been said on the subject, displaying a sterile erudition. "As for me, I have tried to clarify and resolve [, to] prove. I have used all possible means to reach [that goal]." [91] With that reflection on himself he stopped.

All of these passages are important for more than the evidence they provide that Bernard had begun meditating on the questions he treated in his *Introduction* sixteen years before he wrote that book. The circumstances under which he expressed these thoughts suggest that even his interest in the most general principles of scientific investigation emerged from his examination of specific problems in his special field. Undoubtedly his views were conditioned as well by more general philosophical influences. Georges Canguilhem has pointed out that during the first four decades of the century a large number of dissertations had been written in Paris on such questions as observation and experimentation in biology, and the relation of physiology to physics and chemistry and to philosophy. Some of these developed quite closely the order of topics that Bernard followed in his later general writings. [92] Yet by the evidence of Bernard's first effort to formulate his thoughts, such influences were not initially at the forefront of his concern; for he connected his ideas concerning the nature of experimentation not with any of those authors, but with Tiedemann and Réaumur, two of his most eminent predecessors in the study of digestion.

These pages have a special significance also because they are not the pronouncements of a distinguished scientist describing the principles responsible for his success. Rather they are the views of a man still seeking his place in a scientific world he had yet to conquer. By 1865, when he had turned these musings into closely reasoned expositions, he found all of his models in his own work, for by then he regarded his investigations as the best expression of his scientific ideals. Here, in contrast, he drew inspiration from the example of a great predecessor. In 1865 he was able to elucidate his objectives with greater precision, because he felt he had already achieved many of them. Here he was defining his hopes for himself as much as his accomplishments; and perhaps his phrase, "I have not chased after discoveries," reflects a certain need to explain to himself why after five years of intense effort he had still not produced a discovery of a scope commensurate with the breadth of his aims.

Bernard made another highly interesting comment on Réaumur's famous experiment. After describing the manner in which Réaumur had prepared a perforated tube containing a piece of meat protected from the mechanical action of the stomach, Bernard added:

The result must therefore be the judge of the question and the demonstration of a digestive action other than triturition. The emotion with which de Réaumur describes his anxiety while awaiting the end of his experiment rings true for all persons who have devoted themselves to experimental research and who have experienced similar feelings. In fact, at the time when one is in pursuit of a physiological phenomenon and one feels that he is at the point of wresting a secret from nature, the final experiments become decisive. At that moment the mind, made tense by the expectation of the result, awaits it with a mixture of resignation and a secret joy which one does not yet dare to confess to oneself. De Réaumur, seeing the tube returned by the bird of prey which he had forced to swallow it, felt his emotion increase in proportion as he unwound the thread, and finally he looked at the bottom of the thread with timidity, but his eyes did not deceive him, he saw well; the meat had disappeared: it had been dissolved by the gastric liquid, of which the remainder was still coating the walls of the tube. There was, therefore, the gastric juice demonstrated. From then on de Réaumur's genius redoubled to imagine new ways to obtain that juice.[93]

This glimpse of Bernard's inner feelings, which he seldom unmasked, reminds one more of the romantic youth who had hoped to be a playwright than of the calmly rational scientist he later appeared to be. When he recalled his own investigations in later years he analyzed lucidly the intellectual processes he believed he had gone through, stressing the role of reasoning, intuition, and doubt. Rarely, however, did he admit to a deep emotional involvement with the outcome of his experiments. On the contrary, he cultivated the image of the scientist so detached from his own ideas that he could drop them without effort when an experiment turned out unfavorable to them. That ideal he expressed well in this passage from his *Introduction*:

The experimenter must now disappear or rather change himself instantly into an observer; and it is only after he has noted the results of an experiment exactly, like those of an ordinary observation, that his mind will come back, to reason, compare and decide whether his experimental hypothesis is verified or disproved by these very results.[94]

We have already seen that, in his early years at least, Bernard did not always respond to such situations in that ideal way, but we have had to infer from his actions what feelings may have accompanied them. His portrayal of Réaumur's experiment suggests, I think, that Bernard reacted to his scientific work with more intense feeling than he would afterward have others believe. The passage says more, in fact, about Bernard's reactions than about Réaumur's, for much of the description Bernard read into Réaumur's account. Réaumur had implied that he was impatient to see the outcome of the experiment, especially with his remark that he "did not let the day pass without going many times to see if the buzzard had emitted anything from its beak"; [95] but the narrative details Bernard supplied came from his own imagination, expressing, I believe, how he himself would have felt in Réaumur's place. If, as seems evident, Bernard was ordinarily reticent about revealing his inner emotions, perhaps it was easier for him to express them under the cloak of depicting the reactions of another man. In later years his reactions in the laboratory may have become more subdued, as normally happens when one has been involved repeatedly in the same type of situation. At any rate, if the passage does express a trait of Bernard's personality more prominent in his earlier years, one might add that the anxiety and suspense he experienced when approaching the results of decisive experiments must have been conditioned by the number of times those outcomes had disappointed him.

XVII

The Pancreatic Juice: "A Different Field of Activity"

If my contention that Claude Bernard had become bogged down in his studies of animal chemistry at the beginning of 1848 is valid, then he emerged from this state with remarkable speed. The immediate cause of his sudden change of fortune was that he finally succeeded in creating a pancreatic fistula which could supply enough fresh pancreatic juice for digestion experiments. He had failed in numerous attempts more than a year earlier, because the animals succumbed so easily to injuries of the duodenum and pancreas.[1] According to Bernard's later accounts, he had been working on the problem since early 1846.[2] Whether success came in the spring of 1848 by chance or because he intensified his efforts at that time he did not say, but there is reason to favor the latter possibility. His most recent studies of digestion had brought the properties of pancreatic juice to the center of his attention, and his tests with altered pancreatic juice from a hospital patient caused him to feel more acutely the need to procure a supply of the fresh fluid. Moreover, the uninviting prospects for his other digestive investigations by early 1848 may have induced him to press harder in this direction.

Bernard was not the first person to collect natural pancreatic juice from the duct of its secretory organ. Magendie, Tiedemann and Gmelin, Leuret and Lassaigne, and Bouchardat and Sandras had all done so previously. They had obtained small amounts, ranging from a few drops to three ounces.[3] The chief improvement Bernard made was to perfect the operative technique to such a degree that he could collect the secretion with a minimal disturbance of the animal. Through an

377

incision only five centimeters long he could withdraw a small loop of
the duodenum, locate the pancreatic duct, cut it open, insert a small
tube into it, replace the intestine, and sew up the wound with the end
of the tube protruding. When everything went smoothly the entire
operation took only five minutes. Consequently the intestine and pancreas suffered very little from bruising or exposure to air, the animal
recovered quickly, and Bernard could collect within the first day as
much as twenty-five grams of the fluid. During the next two days
even larger quantities flowed, but the properties of these later secretions were altered, due, as Bernard thought, to the inflammation of
the pancreatic tissue.[4]

The first such operation which Bernard recorded in his notebook
was on March 24, 1848. Inserting a small silver tube into the larger of
the two main pancreatic ducts of a very large dog, he afterward attached a hollow rubber bulb which he had first squeezed. As the bulb
slowly expanded again, it exerted a suction which helped to draw the
fluid into it. On the first day he received only 1 gram of fluid, because, he thought, the silver tube was too narrow.[5] Nevertheless,
on the following day he ran a large number of experiments, using for
each one a few drops of pancreatic juice freshly dripped from the
duct. The way in which he utilized these first samples of the natural
digestive fluid readily available to him displays the continuity of his
research on digestion; for with the material he repeated experiments of
the type he had earlier been doing with infusions of pancreatic tissue.
In two trials he confirmed that the natural juice rapidly converts
starch solutions to sugar. Then, adding four drops of the fluid to a
tube containing lightly acidified water, he placed a piece of mutton in
the solution and observed after twelve hours that the meat was partially dissolved. Bernard was more careful in these experiments than
he had sometimes been, however, to use controls with his tests. Comparing a tube similar in every respect except that he had not added the
pancreatic juice, he found that "the digestion proceeded almost the
same amount in one tube as in the other. It is not a true digestion."
The pancreatic juice therefore did not appear to impart any action
beyond that of the acid alone on meat. He then added starch to both
tubes and found that neither solution transformed it. "The acid therefore prevented the pancreatic fluid from acting on the starch." Next he
placed equal quantities of both meat and starch into each of two tubes
containing natural gastric juice, adding to one of them two drops of
pancreatic juice. The meat was digested at about the same rate in both
tubes, whereas the starch disappeared only from the tube containing

pancreatic juice. "Hence," he inferred, "pancreatic fluid in the gastric juice does not seem to have accelerated the digestion of meat, and the gastric juice did not prevent the pancreatic juice from acting on starch." These results, exhibiting the independence and distinctness of the two juices placed even in identical conditions, ought to have diminished further the plausibility of Bernard's idea that the digestive juices embody a common organic principle modified by the circumstances under which it acts; yet he still returned afterward from time to time to his old view. He finished this group of experiments by finding that pancreatic juice can convert dextrin to glucose within three minutes and that the juice coagulates like albumin when treated with a drop of nitric acid.[6]

During the same day Bernard carried out a second series of digestions, using the pancreatic juice he had collected the day before in the rubber bulb. This time he tested whether pancreatic juice mixed with boiled gastric juice would digest meat. Perhaps he thought that if it did so, he could yet find a way to prove that it was not the specific nature of the gastric ferment, but some accompanying conditions which enabled it to digest meat, and that the organic matter of pancreatic juice placed in exactly the same conditions could replace it. He controlled the experiment carefully with tests using unboiled gastric juice and pancreatic juice, boiled gastric juice alone, and unboiled gastric juice alone. The outcome merely strengthened the appearance of specificity, for only the two preparations which included fresh gastric juice were able to digest meat.[7] After four more tests involving the digestion of starch, cane sugar or meat, he performed a last experiment which was quite different from all the rest:

9th *exp*. About ½ gram of pure pancreatic juice to which one has added about 5 centigr[ams] of candle tallow—after 8 h[ours] of continued digestion (the liquid is very plainly alkaline), a white, perfectly homogeneous emulsion has formed. The liquid does not rise to the top at all while cold, nor while warm. But the emulsion is fine, like milk, and does not show . . . [illeg.] at all. There has been, therefore, a peculiar [*singulière*] action of the pancreatic juice on the fat. (the emulsion liquid had remained very alkaline). It will be necessary to make other comparative experiments on this subject.[8]

The next day he added a starch solution to the emulsion and found that the starch was not transformed. He wondered if that result indicated that the organic material in the digestive fluid had combined with the fat and become inoperative. Although Bernard clearly considered his new observation to be remarkable, he did not at once drop the other aspects of his investigation for it. When he continued the next day his first concern was to see whether the pancreatic juice two days after its collection would still act on starch. It did so, but slowly, a result which persuaded him that "the juice seems to have lost some of its energy." Then he turned again to the newly discovered action on fat. First he tested whether fluids other than pancreatic juice might have a similar effect. When he placed candle tallow in human saliva he observed that "the fat was not emulsified at all." Distilled water containing a little potash did act on the tallow, but he persuaded himself that the resulting emulsion was "less thick and heavy than in the case of pancreatic juice." [9]

Needing another supply of pancreatic juice in order to continue, Bernard performed a second fistula operation on March 28. The dog was smaller, however, and he could insert only a very thin tube into its pancreatic duct. Not able to obtain enough juice to use for experiments, he removed a small piece of the pancreas of the animal and made artificial pancreatic juice with it in the way he had often done before.[10] He then carried out eight experiments to examine the conditions under which fat is emulsified. He compared the actions of bile, of bile plus the fresh artificial pancreatic juice, of the original natural pancreatic juice, now four days old; of the preceding plus bile, of the artificial pancreatic juice alone, and of fresh alkaline blood serum from three different sources. The results were very clearcut. In each of the digestions involving either type of pancreatic juice, there was after twelve hours a perfect emulsion, whereas none of the solutions excluding pancreatic material produced such a change. The fact that the aged natural juice was still able to act must have been particularly interesting to him, for two days earlier it was already losing its power to transform starch. Another observation which acquired special significance for him was that the two preparations of pancreatic juice and bile, alkaline at first, became during the course of the action on fat distinctly acidic.[11]

At this point Bernard wrote down six "corollaries of the first experiments on the pancreatic juice," a heading which perhaps suggests that he now felt himself to be at the beginning of a new stage in his research. His corollaries were straightforward summaries of his results. The emulsifying action of the pancreatic fluid on fat came last on this list. To the basic observation, he added: "The artificial pancreatic juice produces the same effect [as the natural juice], only with less energy." [12] This placing of his statements about fat after several conclusions concerning starch and meat seems to imply that in his mind the new discovery did not yet entirely overshadow those aspects of the investigation more closely related to his earlier interests.

Bernard's long preoccupation with the acidity and alkalinity of animal fluids now began to prove very rewarding. Fixing upon the changes of reaction which he had observed during the preceding investigation, he found when he resumed his experiments on March 31 that a mixture of tallow, neutral bile, and neutral artificial pancreatic juice became very plainly acidic. The bile also lost its fatty characteristics. When he mixed the bile and pancreatic juice alone, however, this solution also turned acidic, so that he was somewhat misled to infer that "the acidity is therefore independent of the tallow." In the next test he observed that, even though his natural pancreatic juice was now seven days old, when mixed with tallow and bile it could still produce an emulsion and an acidic reaction. By contrast, bile and tallow without the pancreatic liquid remained neutral.[13]

The new factor of a change of reaction enabled Bernard to ascertain a clearer distinction between the action of pancreatic juice on fat and that of a dilute alkali. A solution containing sodium carbonate produced a complete emulsion, but the liquid remained very alkaline. Continuing to compare the actions of other liquids, he found that neither distilled water nor alkaline serum from the portal vein produced an emulsion; but an anomaly appeared when he tried serum taken from the right ventricle of the heart, which was "chylous." The same material had caused no reaction three days before, but now it produced both an emulsion and a "manifestly acidic" reaction. He discovered, on the other hand, limits on the duration of activity of artificial pancreatic juice, for three days after its preparation it produced only a "very imperfect" emulsion and remained alkaline.[14]

Although Bernard was now fastening his attention increasingly on the new phenomenon of pancreatic action on fats, he was not too absorbed in that problem to preclude a brief diversion back to problems of gastric digestion. On April 4 he obtained juice filtered from the stomach of a horse which had eaten hay and oats. To his surprise the fluid would not digest meat, a result which made him think that horse gastric juice might not contain pepsin. He then considered other tests by which he could explore this new anomaly further. Meanwhile, he digested several combinations of animal fluids, including blood serum and chyle, serum and bile, chyle and gastric juice, chyle and starch, chyle and bile, chyle alone, and chyle and tallow. His intention is not entirely certain, but perhaps the unexpected effect on fat of "chylous" serum from the heart had induced him to try to establish what had caused the emulsion and acidity in that experiment. None of these combinations duplicated that result, so that he probably was able to allay any doubts the earlier test had raised over whether or not the action of pancreatic juice is a property special to it.[15]

In need of a new supply of pancreatic juice by now, Bernard performed another fistula operation on a large hunting dog. The animal was hard to manage, and he had no assistance except for Julian, the laboratory boy. Consequently a large portion of the intestine was accidentally forced out through the incision, and Bernard had to reinsert it. In spite of this inconvenience and the fact that the dog was sick afterward, he collected a substantial amount of pancreatic juice. Deciding that he should investigate more extensively the chemical properties of the juice, he observed that boiling, and concentrated acetic or hydrochloric acid, coagulated it. The same acids diluted did not. "This organic matter gives almost the characters of albumin," he thought; "nevertheless physiologically it differs from it considerably." It was typical of Bernard to regard physiological properties as more discriminating tests of chemical distinctions than conventional chemical tests were, so he assumed that there must be a chemical difference as well. "Search for the chemical characters of that material distinct from albumin," he concluded. "Separate it and perform an elementary analysis." [16] Comprehensive chemical analyses of that sort were, however, beyond the range of Bernard's normal experience. He used the fresh supply of juice instead for more digestion experiments.

Broadening the observations first made on tallow, he now digested two cubic centimeters of ordinary salad oil with the same quantity of pancreatic juice. They formed a "perfect emulsion" and became very acidic. He then compared the action of bile on the same oil. When agitated, they too produced an emulsion, but unlike the previous one, it separated within twelve hours and remained neutral. These two experiments he did along with ten more devoted to other aspects of pancreatic and gastric digestion. He again found that the pancreatic juice transformed starch to glucose, but it did not alter either glucose itself or cane sugar. In the cases where no change occurred, however, he recognized that the cause might have been that the temperature in the water bath had gone too high. He continued also to try to ascertain whether horse gastric juice was really incapable of digesting meat, and he was able to transform starch with it.[17] Thus Bernard was still dividing his attention between several questions concerning digestion, but it was only his study of the pancreatic action on fats that seemed to be progressively uncovering clearer outlines of the nature of the process. Perhaps it was for this reason that in his next experiments he concentrated all of his effort on that problem.

When he mixed pancreatic juice with butter, Bernard made the important observation that the emulsion which formed not only became "very strongly acidic," but also "emitted a very pronounced odor of butyric acid." Although he did not record his reaction to this clue, it must undoubtedly have led him to think, if he had not before, that pancreatic juice may decompose fats into their fatty acids. He then tried lard. This emulsion also became very acidic, and gave off "an odor analogous to that of sharp cheese." Repeating the reaction with tallow, he now noticed that here too an odor arose, that of rancid tallow. A similar odor appeared when he used salad oil, and also when he used salad oil together with bile. Clearly Bernard had detected a highly significant scent. To test whether the material resembling albumin was essential to these actions, he precipitated that substance from the pancreatic juice with concentrated acetic acid. The remaining fluid no longer produced an emulsion with butter. When he used more dilute acetic acid, which formed no precipitate, the acidified pancreatic juice was still capable of its normal action.[18]

On April 11 and 12 Bernard injected 50 grams of butter and tallow into the stomach of a rabbit. During the night it died, and he performed an autopsy the next morning. The most important observation he made was "I do not find chyliferous vessels until the jejunum, farther along consequently, than the pancreatic duct. There is milky white chyle in the mesenteric ganglions and in the thoracic canal."[19] The experiment as described seemed to have an element of chance in that he had not expected the animal to succumb, yet it is quite likely that he anticipated the observation itself. As previously described,[20] he had over a year before noticed the exceptional position of the pancreatic outlet in the intestine of rabbits, far below the bile duct, and had remarked that the arrangement might facilitate the study of the changes pancreatic juice produces on aliments. Now that his artificial digestion experiments had taught him about the special effects of the pancreatic secretion on fats, it would be natural for him to suspect that its action is responsible for the emulsified fats which give chyle its milky appearance. If so, then the chyle should appear only below the point in the digestive tract where these substances mix together. That Bernard was by now clearly considering that pancreatic juice may also decompose fats to fatty acids is evident from the fact that he wondered if their production from the large quantities of ingested fats might have caused the death of the animal.[21]

Probably eager to verify an outcome which so neatly complemented his earlier results, Bernard fed another animal 60 grams of melted lard at ten o'clock on the same morning. At five o'clock in the afternoon the rabbit was healthy and lively. He killed it by sectioning its brain stem, and exposed its intestines. The view could not have been better: "There are no white milky chyliferous vessels in the duodenum. At the level of the pancreatic canal there are two or 3 slightly opalescent vessels, but at 2 or 3 inches below that duct superb milky white vessels are visible, which exist along all of the small intestine and end 3 or 4 inches before the cecum." [22]

Early on the morning of April 15 Bernard performed a pancreatic fistula operation in Pelouze's laboratory. He undoubtedly had a special reason to transfer his activity there, for he wished to obtain aid in the chemical identification of the products of pancreatic action on fats. The operation itself was particularly successful. Using a big dog which had just begun to digest its meal, he found its pancreatic duct very large and swollen with fluid. Large, pearly, viscous drops of pancreatic juice began to flow as soon as he introduced the curved silver tube into the duct. Between nine in the morning and five in the afternoon he collected over 16 grams. Mixing half of this juice with 6 grams of olive oil, he obtained a large enough quantity of the emulsion for Barreswil and another chemist, Frédéric Margueritte, to analyze. They extracted the material in ether, evaporated, and treated the residue with alcohol. The matter which dissolved in the latter solvent saponified in a cold sodium carbonate solution. When they added hydrochloric acid it yielded a material recognizable by its properties as a fatty acid. Bernard was now confident that it was a special property of pancreatic juice to separate fatty acids from fats, as well as to emulsify the latter. He found also that if he boiled the pancreatic juice, it lost those properties. A more puzzling observation was that the natural juice did not coagulate milk, whereas his artificial pancreatic infusions had. By April 18 the pancreatic juice procured in the operation had changed in appearance and become more alkaline. It would no longer form a perfect emulsion with olive oil or castor oil, but did still transform starch energetically into glucose. This result must have seemed strange to Bernard, for in a previous case he had found the juice able to emulsify fat after it had begun to lose its action on starch. In spite of these minor anomalies, his new experiments were continuing to sharpen the definition of the new "special" property of pancreatic juice. Paradoxically, Bernard nevertheless referred still to a preparation of calf pancreas and hydrochloric acid as an artificial gastric juice. He attempted unsuccessfully to digest meat with it. [23]

During the same day Bernard tried his pancreatic fistula operation on a rabbit. He failed, because he could not insert a tube into its small pancreatic duct; but he demonstrated his experimental resourcefulness anyway, by using the situation to attempt a counterproof for his earlier discovery that the whitish chyle vessels appear only beyond the point where pancreatic fluid mixes with aliments. He tied the duct off, then introduced 50 grams of melted lard into the stomach of the animal. Two and a half hours later he killed it and examined its intestines. Unexpectedly he saw whitish chyliferous vessels beginning 10 centimeters beyond the pylorus, though they were much finer than ordinary. He checked the pancreatic duct and found that it had been fully blocked, so that there must be some other explanation for the fact that the formation of chyle had not been absolutely prevented. He considered that perhaps the glands of the intestinal lining (glands of Brunner) serve as a "secondary pancreas," or else that some pancreatic juice secreted before the operation might have produced the chyle. To obviate the latter possibility he planned to do another experiment in which he would tie the duct the night before he injected the fat. He also thought he might test whether the intestinal mucosa containing the glands of Brunner possesses the same properties as pancreatic tissue.[24]

At this juncture Bernard veered once more back to his old preoccupation with artificial gastric juices. Perhaps because another possible explanation for the preceding observations was that bile may be able by itself to emulsify fat in the intestines, he mixed lard with some of that fluid, but obtained no emulsion. As soon as he added pancreatic juice, the emulsion formed and turned acidic. That confirmation of his original discovery seemed to interest him less for the moment, however, than the fact that he filtered the acidic fluid, diluted it with water, and found that it "digested meat perfectly well." When he repeated the experiment on April 21 and saw that the fluid digested meat "absolutely like ordinary gastric juice," he considered that he had a "new formula for artificial gastric juice." In a third trial he mixed pancreatic juice and bile first and found that it remained alkaline. When he then added a little lard and shook the solution, it became very acid, so suddenly that he exclaimed "What the devil happened at that moment?"[25]

By now, however, even such fascinating observations could not for long divert Bernard from his new path. He returned to the digestion of fat. Feeding that substance to a dog which he had partially anesthetized with ether, he opened its intestine an hour and a half later. He found the contents neutral, when he thought they ought to have been acidic because of the action of the pancreatic juice on the fat. He attributed the anomaly to an unusually large flow of bile stimulated by the ether and decided to avoid such complicating factors in the future. At this point an explanation of a scientific dispute involving his mentor occurred to Bernard. Benjamin Brodie had claimed that bile is essential to the formation of chyle, because when he tied off the bile duct in a cat that process ceased, the lacteal vessels becoming clear and transparent. Magendie, on the other hand, had observed the opposite in dogs and other animals.[26] The difference, Bernard thought, might have arisen from the fact that in cats the bile duct merges with the pancreatic duct, so that Brodie had probably inadvertently blocked both secretions. In dogs, however, the two ducts are separate.[27] Later, Bernard elaborated on this explanation in a paper on the pancreatic juice,[28] and he referred to it again in his *Introduction to the Study of Experimental Medicine* to support his general belief that in physiology "experiments can be rigorous and provide identical results every time that one operates under exactly similar conditions." [29] Apparently by then, however, he had forgotten that in his comprehensive memoir on the pancreas in 1856 he retracted his explanation, having found out in the meantime that cats always possess a second smaller pancreatic duct separate from the bile duct.[30]

To return to April 1848: on the 25th Bernard tried again to halt the formation of chyle by blocking the pancreatic secretion. This time he tied both pancreatic ducts of a medium-sized dog. The animal struggled so violently that its intestines were forced out of its abdomen, and they became somewhat bruised as Bernard replaced them. After completing the operation he immediately injected melted lard into the stomach of the animal. Five hours later he sacrificed it. He found only a few "excessively slender" chyliferous vessels near the lower end of the duodenum. Most of the lymphatic vessels and the thoracic duct itself contained only transparent lymph. The amount of chyle produced was so slight, he thought, that if any cause of its formation other than pancreatic juice did exist, its role was "very minimal." Nevertheless, he realized that the disturbances to the intestines might have complicated the outcome, so that it would be best to repeat the experiment.[31] It is questionable, however, that he waited to do that, for there is no record of another one soon afterward, and just four days later he presented to the Philomatic Society his note "On the functions of the pancreatic juice." The simplicity and brevity of his report contrast with the extent of its importance.

"The pancreatic juice," he began, "is a clear, viscous, alkaline fluid, having physical properties analogous to those of saliva, but differing completely with respect to its physiological properties. I have found that the pancreatic juice is the indispensable agent for the digestion of fatty matters." He then enumerated briefly the emulsions which he had formed with pancreatic juice and various kinds of fats. "No other fluid of the economy possesses that remarkable property," he claimed. He did not consider the essential action on fats to be "a saponification or chemical combination," but simply a very fine division of the matter, produced "under the influence of a particular organic substance which the pancreatic juice contains." Nevertheless, that substance also causes a more profound modification of the fats. The odors which he had noticed during the process, together with the chemical examination he had made with Barreswil and Margueritte, provided the clearest recognition that "the neutral fat had been decomposed into fatty acid and glycerine." Bile does not produce such effects. Its well-known property of removing spots made by fats is due to its ability to dissolve fatty acids. Bernard did not believe that this result proved that fats can only be absorbed after they are decomposed; on the contrary, he thought that they ordinarily entered the lacteal vessels in the state of simple emulsion, which gave rise to the milky appearance of the contents of these vessels. Without pancreatic juice, he asserted, "there is no emulsion, and consequently no absorption of fatty bodies." This he had proved, he said, by tying the two pancreatic ducts on dogs and the single pancreatic duct in a rabbit; the result was that the chyliferous vessels afterward contained no fat, whereas the intestines were filled with unemulsified fat.[32] Unless he had repeated these experiments at the last minute, Bernard on this point, as on some occasions in the past, was making his results sound more certain than they were. "In ending," Bernard added,

I would say that this action of the pancreas on fatty matters, which, I believe, has not yet been pointed out by anyone, gives that organ a great importance in the phenomena of digestion. I would remark besides that this role of the pancreas is entirely different from that of the salivary glands, and that the denomination of *abdominal salivary gland,* given to the pancreas, is utterly incorrect.[33]

In later years Bernard developed the final remark as part of a general argument against the validity of physiological deductions made from a knowledge of the anatomy of organs alone. Paralleling his case against deductions from chemistry alone, he asserted that the anatomical localization of a function must be the end result of physiological experimentation, not a starting point. Anatomical deduction had led to the false conclusion that the salivary glands and the pancreas have the same function, because of the misleading similarity in their appearance.[34] Nevertheless, I suspect that initially, as he made the point above, Bernard was primarily enjoying a little triumph over his rival, Louis Mialhe. For it was Mialhe who had reacted to Bouchardat and Sandras's discovery of the action of the pancreas on starch by referring to the organ as an abdominal salivary gland.[35]

More significant was the fact that Bernard's new discovery had caused him to reverse his whole previous approach to digestion. After trying for three years to demonstrate that all digestive juices operate by means of a common organic principle, he ended up asserting in language as unequivocal as Mialhe applied to diastase and pepsin, that there exists in pancreatic juice a special organic principle having a unique digestive action. He had, in fact beaten Mialhe to Mialhe's own goal of finding the substance responsible for digesting the last of the three major types of aliment.[36] For a long time Bernard still resisted the application of the concept of specific digestive principles to the question on which he had most stubbornly opposed it; that is, he continued to attribute the transformation of starch by saliva and pancreatic juice to a simple property common to many organic materials rather than to anything particular to these juices.[37] Nevertheless, in the area in which he made his own major contribution, he adopted fully the view of his adversaries, that the digestive action is produced by a specific ferment.[38]

The presentation of his first paper on pancreatic juice marks the most important turning point in Claude Bernard's career, for that short communication embodied the first of what are regarded as his "major discoveries." [39] In that light the remarkable ease with which he achieved such a result in just one month contrasts dramatically with the tortuous, far less successful researches on digestion he had carried on for nearly five years. From his first observation of the peculiar action of pancreatic juice until he was able to state his conclusions in public, he made unusually steady progress. Only a few secondary discrepancies turned up, and most of his results firmly supported his interpretation. That was not at all like his earlier experiences, in which he frequently encountered results that seemed contrary to what he expected and needed to confirm his theories. This change of pace induces one to reflect on whether Bernard had in some way suddenly matured as a scientific investigator; whether he had adopted some methodological principle that formerly had escaped him, and which now began to smooth his path. The new experiments did in fact have an aspect of greater rigor than much of his earlier work. The results were more definite, more systematically controlled, more immediately persuasive. He seemed to exert more care in his comparative experiments to maintain corresponding conditions in every respect except the factor being tested. It might almost appear that he had in fact reached that "third stage" of scientific development he later described, in which all theories are subjected to strict counterproofs. Yet it would be hard to identify any new influence just at that time which could have impressed on him some general scientific precepts that he had overlooked up until then. His experiments looked better, but his approach was not fundamentally different from what it had been all along.

A more important factor may have been a certain quality of Bernard's personality. At his death in 1878 his best-known student, Paul Bert, recalled his manner of writing in a way which perhaps gives a clue to a more general insight about him:

His style, whether spoken or written, is the equivalent of his ideas. In episodical narrative, he is often dragging and confused; but when a hard problem presents itself, when his thought is forced to fall back as if to conquer an obstacle or make a bound, then he concentrates, purifies and accentuates himself in definite formulae and often in verbal imagery.

As he was in his books, so was Claude Bernard in his courses and his conversation. His was not a docile thought, speaking every language and playing every role; and he never disciplined it to any conventions of profession or social custom.[40]

Not all of the traits mentioned are transferable directly to Bernard's way of carrying on research at a much earlier period of his life, but I think that Bert's portrayal reveals something about Bernard deep enough to help explain that too. It suggests a man who at his best was very much better than his average performance; one who might sometimes drift indecisively, sometimes be confused, careless, or impetuous; who might as easily ignore factors essential to success as he ignored professional conventions. But it also portrays someone who at other times could seize an opportunity, pursue it with inspiration, and rise to a level of experimental genius which was unsurpassed.

On the other hand, a good case could be made that nothing had changed about Claude Bernard except that fortune had suddenly favored him; that he had lavished as much skill and ingenuity in his efforts to perceive general theories where they happened not to be as he did to exploit the important discovery which he chanced upon. He himself commented that it "is so simple and so easy to demonstrate that it is the pancreatic juice and not the bile which emulsifies fat," that he wondered why that fact had not been known long before.[41] After he had made his first indisputably major discovery, it was perhaps easier for him to go on to further successes, in part by the very fact that he probably felt less pressure to produce distinctive theories before nature was ready to yield them to him.

The preceding narrative of Bernard's experiments leading to his discovery of the function of pancreatic juice ignores one very crucial factor: his own account of its origin. In 1856, in his long memoir on the pancreas, he recalled:

During the winter of the year 1846, I was studying, comparatively on herbivorous and carnivorous animals, the digestion of diverse alimentary materials. Having injected fatty materials into dogs and rabbits, I was following the physical or chemical changes which these substances undergo in order to be digested and absorbed by the chyliferous vessels. Now I noticed, in opening the intestines of the animals, that in the dogs the fatty material had been emulsified and absorbed by the lacteal vessels from the beginning of the small intestine . . . whereas in rabbits the phenomenon did not become very evident until much farther down.

"Struck by this difference," he continued, he searched for a particular anatomical disposition to explain it, and found a corresponding difference in the locations at which the pancreatic secretions entered the intestine in the two kinds of animal. From this relation he was "naturally led to think that it was to this liquid that the property of modifying fatty material to render it absorbable must be attributed." To confirm his hypothesis, he set out to devise means to collect pancreatic juice, a task in which he only succeeded in early 1848.[42] In May 1855 he had already given a similar but more leisurely account of the discovery during his lectures, in order to instill in his listeners "the conviction that it is not in starting from the anatomy of an organ that one can expect to deduce the functions, but it is on the contrary in orienting oneself from a physiological point of view and pursuing a phenomenon in the different phases which it undergoes in contact with the organism." [43] He repeated the same story briefly in his *Introduction to the Study of Experimental Medicine* as an example of experimental research whose starting point is a chance observation.[44] If Bernard's own description were entirely accurate historically, then the sequence of events would not only have been nearly the reverse of what the laboratory record suggests, but would represent a quest lasting for two years rather than a problem which he resolved in barely a month.[45] The fact that he used this story in the first place to teach a general scientific lesson might cause one to suspect that he shaped it somewhat to fit that purpose; yet the observations he ascribed to the winter of 1846 are too definite to be discounted as tricks of memory. I think it most likely that he observed just what he said he had, but that the consequences of what he saw were not as clear to him then as they appeared to have been when he recalled the occurrences long after his discoveries of 1848.

If Bernard were already strongly impressed in early 1846 that pancreatic juice digests fat, it would be hard to imagine why he should have waited for two years to test his view directly. He need not have postponed such a test until he could procure fresh natural juice, for, as he found as soon as he did discover the action upon fat of the fluid collected from the fistula, he could easily reproduce the phenomenon with artificial pancreatic juice. Now Bernard had been using artificial pancreatic juice frequently for digestion experiments on starch and meat during that period, but apparently never on fat. Moreover, even after he had natural juice available, he was at first more interested in applying it to the previous type of investigation than in reacting it with fat. On the other hand, the very fact that he did try an experiment with tallow in the midst of the others implies that he already had some expectation that the fatty material would be modified. If there is a way of reconciling the two seemingly contradictory versions of Bernard's discovery, I think it must be as an illustration that an idea which has once occurred to a person does not necessarily remain to guide his thoughts ever afterward. An idea is often lost when one turns his attention in other directions and may again be recovered when another experience comes along to reinforce its initial source. Thus Bernard may well have made the inference in 1846 that pancreatic juice digests fats, have nearly forgotten about it afterward while he dealt with other problems, and have recalled it again when the success of his operation provided a particularly favorable opportunity to examine the various properties of his newly available natural secretion. Similarly, the fact that he did strive for over two years to achieve the fistula operation does not necessarily mean that he was steadily occupied with that effort over long stretches of the time. Rather he may have returned to the problem intermittently, when he found some new reason to enhance his interest in the role of pancreatic juice.

One consequence of Bernard's spotty acquaintance with the research of his contemporaries on problems of digestion was that when he discovered the action of pancreatic juice on fats he did not know that an important predecessor had already described the phenomenon. J. N. Eberle's treatise on digestion had included an experiment in which he added a little oil to artificial pancreatic juice, shook the mixture, and obtained a white, creamy emulsion. Eberle had concluded that the digestive action of fats attributed to bile belonged instead to the pancreatic secretion.[46] After Bernard published his investigation, some commentators noted Eberle's earlier result. Françis A. Longet, who had repeatedly clashed with Magendie, went so far as to describe Eberle's observations in greater detail than those of Bernard, treating the latter only as results "confirming the doctrine of Eberle."[47] Bernard indignantly objected that these incomplete and forgotten observations were being "exhumed" only in order to oppose him. It is indicative of his attitude toward the scientific literature that after five years of research on digestion Bernard did not know about an experiment reported in one of the most influential treatises in that field, on a subject which directly concerned him. Nevertheless, he was justified in discounting Eberle's observation on this particular question. It had been isolated, and unlike the rest of his treatise, it went nearly unnoticed. Bernard was, as he claimed, the first person to investigate the phenomenon thoroughly, with natural pancreatic juice, and to obtain an instantaneous, permanent emulsion.[48] For an initial attack on the problem he had achieved a great deal in four weeks. Not only had he reproduced the basic emulsifying action under a variety of conditions, but he had adduced supporting evidence of various kinds for its physiological significance. His discovery comprised, in fact, an ideal realization of what he had long advocated as the proper relation between chemical theory and physiological experimentation. He showed that pancreatic juice as a chemical reagent has the property of emulsifying fats and producing fatty acids; but that was not enough from his point of view. He gave evidence as well that the process actually occurs in the intestine only where fats and the pancreatic secretion come together. As he emphasized later, he had examined the action both outside and within the living animal.[49] There is no doubt that he considered the underlying nature of the phenomenon to be chemical. He did not have to investigate the chemical transformations themselves in close detail, because the careful research of Chevreul twenty-five years before had already established their character. From rather simple evidence for the presence of a fatty acid, he could therefore assume that a reaction had taken place by which a fat or oil is decomposed into its components, glycerine and fatty acids. Just as Tiedemann and Gmelin had drawn on prior chemical knowledge of the transformation of starch, so Bernard gave physiological significance to another reaction whose detailed analysis the chemists had already provided.

When he discovered the action of the pancreas on fats, Bernard had happened upon a problem for which his particular talents were remarkably well suited. Its solution required the surgical ingenuity and dexterity in which he excelled, but involved less demanding chemical tests which he could handle with some help from his chemist friends. His relative detachment from the dominant directions of research in the field of digestion probably made it easier for him to follow clues revealed in his own investigations, toward a phenomenon which was neglected even though previously noted. Other scientists more closely in step with current trends were more likely to stick to the developments which were agreed to be most promising, such as the pepsin and diastase theories. The very fact that no one had chanced to pursue Eberle's conclusion about the role of pancreatic juice obviated any disadvantage Bernard might otherwise have incurred for his inattention to contemporary German research. The paucity of literature on the subject enabled him to make a crucial contribution without having to acquire a systematic knowledge of what others had been doing. So long as he had worked primarily on the digestion of starch and the nitrogenous aliments, on saliva and gastric juice, areas which were already crowded with other investigations, his neglect of some of the best work of other men prevented him from becoming a master of the situation. Endeavoring to go his own way, he had merely traveled byways, while the main movement continued along the same road it had previously taken. Now he had, by alertness and good luck, turned up an opening where others were not looking. As Frerichs commented, Bernard was seeking to establish "a completely different field of activity" for the pancreatic glands.[50] More crucial still, the new field he found was at the same time a solution to a question whose importance was already recognized; for the development of knowledge about the digestion of the other classes of aliments was pointing up with increasing sharpness the lack of information concerning the digestion of fats. Thus Bernard had for once been able both to preserve the individuality which he valued and to move into the center of an area of contemporary concern.

These attributes of Bernard's discovery assured that it would have an immediate impact. As soon as his results were known, physiologists in Germany began to do similar experiments.[51] In the French Academy his work met an enthusiastic response. A few months after his preliminary note had appeared he submitted to that body a more extended memoir on the topic. To a commission composed of Magendie, Milne Edwards, and Dumas he demonstrated the principal experiments. The commission reported to the Academy in February 1849 that it found Bernard's results novel, precise, logical, and important. The emulsifying action of natural pancreatic juice was "incontestable." Bernard's demonstration that chyliferous vessels begin at the region of the intestine where the pancreatic juice enters "offered all of the distinctness of a chemical operation carried out in the laboratory and all of the beauty of the most perfect injections." It was not merely the quality of the investigation itself, however, which impressed the commissioners. The recent experiments of Bouchardat and Sandras, Mialhe, and Barreswil and Bernard himself, they noted, had proved the existence of a ferment to transform starch in digestion, and shown that gastric juice digests nitrogenous matters. "There remained still to discover the true agent of the digestion of fatty bodies, that is, the agent of the formation of the fatty substance of the chyle." By establishing the role of the pancreas in this process, they concluded, Bernard "has made complete the general character of the theory of digestion." [52] Thus, unlike Bernard himself, who saw his previous digestive theories as refutations of the ideas of Mialhe, the commissioners assimilated his work with Mialhe's into a progression of developments which together comprised a unified framework. If their view was more comprehensive than Bernard's, they remained narrowly provincial in crediting the three facets of the theory of digestion exclusively to their French colleagues. It was also ironic that the man selected to report the evaluation of the commission was Dumas, for in completing the "theory of digestion," Bernard had also completed the ruin of the conception of digestion Dumas had himself proclaimed eight years before in his *Chemical Statics.* Now for each of the major classes of nutrient there was persuasive evidence that some chemical metamorphoses, not simple dissolution alone, take place.

The combination of originality and direct relevance in Bernard's new discovery greatly altered his position in the field of digestive physiology. Previously he had been seeking to make a distinctive mark on a large problem already defined by the work of others. Now his own endeavor had defined a new special area of that problem into which others had to follow him. After six years of running somewhat behind the leaders in the field, he had now reached a zone where no one was ahead of him.

Bernard's new leadership did not go uncontested. The German investigators who took up his results found considerable fault with them. Friedrich Theodor Frerichs, a young pathologist who was also serving as an assistant in the physiological institute at the University of Göttingen, had been doing extensive research on digestion in order to prepare an article on that subject for the *Handbook of Physiology* edited by his professor, Rudolph Wagner. In the summer of 1848, following news of "the recent work in France," Frerichs began to experiment with pancreatic juice collected from a donkey. He found that the juice did emulsify fats, but that the emulsion eventually separated. Moreover, a comparison with the action of serum, bile, and saliva on fat revealed "only a slight difference in favor of the pancreatic juice." In various ways Frerichs blocked the access of pancreatic juice to all or portions of the intestines of cats and of dogs and observed that although less milky chyle formed there afterward than otherwise did, some nevertheless appeared. This result was not entirely different from those recorded in Bernard's own notebook, but in sharp disagreement with Bernard's published statements. Frerichs concluded that "the results of my own observations are not in accord with the view that the digestion of fat is the only or even the principal function of the pancreas." He thought that the chief role of its secretion was still the transformation of starch, and that the fluid also decomposed the bile into insoluble excretory products.[53] Bidder and Schmidt and Lehmann also repeated some of Bernard's experiments with results that seemed to contradict his in almost every respect except for the basic property of pancreatic juice outside the animal to emulsify fat.[54] Several other physiologists, both in Germany and France, raised similar objections, while still others came to Bernard's support.[55]

Much of Bernard's research on the pancreas over the next seven years was an effort to overcome such criticisms and to develop confirming evidence for the conclusions he had reached. Over the substantive issues he prevailed. He was able to show that in the cases in which his opponents found whitish chyle after they thought that they had blocked the pancreatic flow, they had not totally prevented pancreatic juice from reaching the intestines. He asserted that, when Frerichs and others found that pancreatic juice did not act in a unique way on fats, it was because the secretions they utilized had become altered, like those which his own fistulas delivered after the first day. He drew important new chemical support from a brilliant young as-

Friedrich Theodor v. Frerichs

sistant to the professor of chemistry at the Collège de France. Marcellin Berthelot demonstrated conclusively for Bernard that the pancreatic juice decomposes fats; he was able to isolate both the fatty
acids and the glycerine produced in the reaction.[56] The function
which Bernard defined for pancreatic juice has been regarded ever
since as a basic aspect of digestive theory. Even the question which he
left uncertain, whether the fats can be absorbed in the form of a
simple emulsion, or must first undergo decomposition, has continued
until recent times to serve as a source of new investigations and
thought. The same dilemmas which that problem posed for him have
caused opinions to fluctuate even down to the present.[57] The very fact
that Bernard's conclusions were controversial from the first added to
his stature in digestive physiology; for it is not necessarily the indisputable final result so much as the conclusion which others try to challenge that often makes the work of a scientist a focal point in his field.

As in some of his previous investigations, Bernard reached beyond
the immediate results of his research on the pancreas to a bolder interpretation. He thought not merely that he had found a new property
of pancreatic juice, but that its action on fats constituted "the essential

and special role of pancreatic juice in digestion." He did not believe that his results made invalid Bouchardat and Sandras's observation of the transformation of starch by that fluid, but he did maintain that what they had discovered was not a special function; it was merely a general property common to many other animal fluids.[58] Bernard's opinion was an outgrowth of his own peculiar theory that the transformation of starch arises from the general decomposition of animal matter rather than the action of a specific ferment. By persisting along that idiosyncratic line of reasoning, he was led sometimes to disregard the contributions of his colleagues. Thus in 1855 he pronounced during a lecture, "You see, gentleman, that the properties of pancreatic juice were not at all determined and that its functions were not known when we were led to study the role of the pancreatic juice in 1846." [59]

This incident suggests that, just as Bernard preferred to follow his own path when he undertook research on a problem, so after he had achieved success he tended to view the whole development of the problem from the perspective of his own role in it. Numerous other examples can be found in his later writings, but one is especially relevant to the developments we have been following. In his course at the Collège de France for the spring of 1855 he dealt with the functions of the digestive secretions. He devoted five lectures to the salivary glands, nine to the pancreas and other intestinal secretions, and only two lectures to gastric digestion. In the latter he described in detail some of his earlier experiments, such as those on the nature of the acid, but spent less than two pages on pepsin.[60] This distribution is understandable in view of the fact that he habitually organized his course around his own research. Beyond that, however, when he did discuss the function of gastric juice, he treated it in a curiously negative manner. He stressed that "the gastric juice has only a very limited action in the phenomena of digestion." Digestion in the stomach, he said in another lecture, "is only a preparatory act" for the transformations which occur in the intestine. He taught that gastric juice dissociates the anatomical elements of nitrogenous food by dissolving the substances capable of forming gelatin. Its most general action, therefore, he concluded was similar to the effects of prolonged boiling. Mialhe's theory of gastric digestion he implicitly dismissed with a reference to "that vague product which one has designated by the name albuminose." [61] All of this contrasts sharply with the exalted view of gastric action which Bernard had set out to establish in the first years of his career, as well as with the importance which most of his colleagues attributed to the action of its specific ferment. Perhaps his physiological orientation made it difficult for him to appreciate the subtle criteria the chemists used to decide when the properties of an organic material seemed distinct enough to justify calling it a particular substance such as albuminose.[62] Perhaps also he could still not view a contribution by Mialhe objectively. I believe, however, that there may have been a broader underlying trait of his character involved. In spite of the breadth of his vision in some directions, Bernard took a highly personal view of physiology and felt great pride in his own position within it. It seems to me almost as though he could not depict gastric juice as a process as significant as intestinal digestion because he himself had failed to discover anything as significant about the former as he had about the latter. After seven years of scantily requited labor, he seemed to have turned his view away from the topic in favor of those which had proved more rewarding to him.[63] Later in life his perspective deepened in many respects, but he still scanned the development of physiology largely in terms of those questions which he personally had been able to elucidate.[64] When he submitted a report in 1867 to the Minister of Public Instruction concerning the progress of physiology in France, he oriented his review so heavily toward his own view of the science that some members of the Academy of Sciences were said to have complained that he had "circumscribed his subject to the point of saying '*La physiologie, c'est moi.*'"[65] The charge was exaggerated, of course, but not baseless.

Frerichs in 1849 criticized not only Bernard's conclusions concerning pancreatic juice, but most of the general ideas that he had published up until then on the subject of digestion. Bernard and Barreswil's claim that gastric juice, pancreatic juice, and saliva contain the same organic principle was an error "which is suitable only to bring back into the theory of digestion the confusion of earlier times." According to Frerichs's own research, saliva did not digest coagulated albumin, even when acidified, and he implied that Bernard and Barreswil's assertion that it did was a product solely of their theory that the digestive ferments are identical. Frerichs had tried to transform starch with material from the mucous membrane of the mouth and found that it did not have the strong action which Bernard's theory of salivary fermentation attributed to it. Although he agreed with Bernard and Barreswil's conclusion that gastric juice contains lactic acid, he judged that their own investigation of the question "unfortunately proved little." He thought Bernard's belief that when animals fast or drink, no saliva is secreted, was an unlikely idea, because the continuous need to swallow the fluid indicates that small amounts are steadily produced. He repeated the experiments in which Bernard had injected albumin and sugar into the blood, had found them again in the urine, and had asserted that the result proved that gastric action was essential to render aliments assimilable. Frerichs commented, "I cannot confirm Bernard's investigation in all respects, and I believe also that this complicated question is not resolved by it." In several other places in his review of digestion Frerichs added similarly unfavorable judgments of Bernard's work and acknowledged only faintly that he had made any positive contributions.[66]

Taken together with his opposition to the discoveries concerning pancreatic juice which the French Academy had highly praised, Frerichs's remarks might seem to indicate that he was biased against Bernard. Perhaps, like Blondlot, he wished to revise the whole subject of digestion in his review, and simply regarded all prior work as less reliable than his own experiments. Frerichs did reveal traces of such an attitude, yet his judgments were in general both more cautious and more comprehensive than those of Blondlot. He was thoroughly familiar with the entire development of the field, and his review came to be regarded as an authoritative, even a "classic" treatment.[67] It was, in some respects, a German view of the subject. All of the great landmarks he saw were by German authors, Tiedemann and Gmelin, Eberle, Schwann, and their successors.[68] He generally trusted the results of contemporary German physiologists more easily than those of their French counterparts. Yet he acknowledged, even if with less enthusiasm, some of the contributions of French contemporaries, including Mialhe and Bouchardat and Sandras.[69] I think a more cogent reason for Frerichs's attitude was that Bernard's early published work was highly vulnerable to criticism. He had made a sufficient number of errors and unverifiable generalizations so that a reviewer of his articles on digestion, comparing them to other contributions, might well make up his mind that Bernard's thought was erratic and his work unsound. Instead of sifting the valuable aspects of the papers from the refutable, Frerichs probably formed a generally negative impression. It was the nature of Bernard's approach itself which invited the risk of such a response. His boldness, his readiness to publish general conclusions before subjecting them to rigorous criticism, his failure fully to grasp what others in the field had accomplished, all left him open to severe judgment. It is not surprising that in 1849 Frerichs failed to recognize that the same traits could also comprise the ingredients of a work of genius; that he greeted Bernard's latest discovery with mistrust rather than with the adulation which Bernard's more sympathetic colleagues in Paris accorded it. The rising young leader of German physiology, Carl Ludwig, sensed both sides of Bernard's early scientific character when he wrote in July 1849 to his friend Emil Du Bois-Reymond: "Bernard is a great talent, but very hasty." [70]

Claude Bernard's contribution to the field of digestion was of a magnitude comparable to that of his rival, Louis Mialhe. Yet Bernard's discovery of the action of pancreatic juice on fats is much better remembered than Mialhe's discovery of salivary diastase or of the formation of albuminose. One may wonder what accounts for this discrepancy. One reason, of course, is that as Bernard made equally important discoveries in other areas of physiology, his stature grew until the aggregate of his achievements lent added luster to each individual discovery. Another factor derives, I think, from their contrasting positions with respect to the development of digestive physiology. As we have seen, Mialhe perceived more clearly than Bernard the movement of the mainstream in the problem, and made his contributions at the center of that current. He advanced the subject in the direction it was already headed. He was no less bold than Bernard, nor any less imaginative in grasping theoretical consequences beyond immediately demonstrable evidence; but his ventures only placed him in a procession of distinguished contributions reaching from Tiedemann and Gmelin, Eberle, and Schwann to himself, and linking smoothly with those who came after him. Bernard was less successful when he tried to swim in the mainstream, because he did not know its currents as well—in fact, he nearly went aground. But the same detachment and will to proceed in his own way made his investigations the kind which, when they did work out, could result in contributions which were not only important but surprising. It was Bernard who was best equipped to detect the unexpected clue which could give rise to a new stream of development. Though not necessarily more significant than Mialhe's discoveries in digestion, therefore, Bernard's were more exciting. His discovery concerning the pancreas was the first of several during the ensuing decade which had that dramatic quality that enabled the "unprecedentedly fortunate discoverer," as Du Bois-Reymond described him in 1858, to "keep all eyes fastened on the vivisection table of the Collège de France." [71] Such discoveries not only stir special interest among contemporaries, but engage most readily the attention of historians.

XVIII

The Search for Sugar

Shortly after Bernard communicated to the Philomatic Society his first note on the uses of the pancreatic juice he helped found a new society devoted especially to biology. In May 1848 he and a number of physicians and naturalists began meeting together every Saturday in the lecture hall of the histologist Charles Robin, at the École pratique. They constituted themselves officially as the Société de Biologie.[1] Bernard's friend Rayer became the first president, while he himself and Robin served as vice-presidents. In 1849 the society began publishing the memoirs and reports read at its meetings. The organization was more than a forum for scientists with related interests to exchange views, for it represented an effort to attain recognition of biology as an independent, unified science. The term biology itself was relatively new. At the beginning of the century J.-B.-P.-A. Lamarck and Gottfried Treviranus independently applied the word to the sciences which collectively treat the phenomena of life.[2] German naturalists adopted the term more quickly than did their French counterparts. In Paris, however, Ducrotay de Blainville introduced it into the lectures in comparative anatomy and physiology which he taught for many years at the Faculté des Sciences, the Collège de France, the Jardin du Roi, and the Atheneum. De Blainville asserted that "biology" was a more suitable term than physiology for the science of life, because the idea of physiology was closely related to the conception of nature itself. Since the word biology applied to all organisms, however, and he dealt primarily with animal life, he coined the term "zoobiology" to refer to his own subject. He defined it as "the science which analyzes, in animals, the phenomena of life in regard to their production, and their relation either to the organization or to the external circumstances; and which seeks to explain them by connecting them to the general laws of nature whenever they are susceptible to that." [3]

Auguste Comte, who followed de Blainville's lectures and incorporated much of his thought into his own discussions, adopted the term biology and defined it as a science having divisions similar to those de Blainville had described. Biology, according to Comte, encompassed both anatomy and physiology. It dealt, in addition, with the relations between organisms and their environments. Because it was not limited to the study of one organism, but investigated the characteristics common to "the entire hierarchy of living beings," its domain extended to all kinds of animals and to plants as well. Comte made the science of biology one of the basic branches of his "positive philosophy." It was, however, much more imperfect than physics or chemistry. He argued that the time had come for biology to develop free from any adherence to its useful applications. Admitting that the needs of medical practice had first stimulated progress toward positive knowledge of vital phenomena, and that the development of physiology had continued in extraordinarily close association with the art of medicine, Comte nevertheless believed that biology had reached a stage of maturity at which continued dependence, with the attendant expectation that its research be immediately applicable, could only narrow and impede its growth. The science needed a period of abstract, speculative development, consecrated solely to the discovery of laws of nature. Afterward it could return to medical practice benefits which would never be reached if its research had to be directed immediately to that end. [4] Comte's program seems to have provided a principal motive for the establishment of the Société de Biologie. Charles Robin followed his arguments closely in describing the "aims which the founding members of the Société de Biologie proposed in joining together." Robin divided biology into the same areas as Comte had, and he asserted that the collective effort of the members was to promote the study of the whole vast subject of life in all its forms, "independently at first of all idea of application." [5]

The establishment of a society with such aims must have been especially welcome to Bernard. Trained to be a physician, he had after wavering for several years foregone the thought of practicing medicine in order to devote himself to scientific research. Yet he remained heavily dependent on medical institutions. He was assistant at the Collège de France to the professor of experimental medicine, who was also an active physician. Later on, when Bernard filled the chair himself he was sometimes criticized for making his courses entirely physiological. Such circumstances probably helped induce Bernard to justify physiology repeatedly as the principal basis for medicine, at a time when the tangible services which the science could render to practice were still rather slight.[6] He must therefore have been glad to belong to a group which believed that the study of the phenomena of life was an end in itself. Perhaps the broadening from mammalian physiology toward the fundamental phenomena common to all of life which his investigations began to undergo during the next decade was stimulated in part by his involvement with the society.

The influence of Auguste Comte on the objectives of a society which Claude Bernard helped to found naturally raises the question of how much Comte affected Bernard's own thought during the early years of his career. That question takes on a special interest by the fact that in his *Cours de philosophie positive* Comte had argued strenuously for a relation between chemistry and physiology resembling the position Bernard took. According to Comte, chemists had appropriated the investigation of many phenomena which belonged to the domain of physiology, but which physiologists had been unable to carry out successfully because they were unfamiliar with the chemical methods required. Chemists were analyzing materials that were undoubtedly biological in character, such as plant sap, blood, and the products of respiration. If these usurpations continued, Comte warned, chemists would soon have taken over the research concerning nutrition and secretions, leaving physiology only the study of what Bichat had called *la vie animale* and of the laws of development. Such a dismemberment of the science of biology was inevitably deleterious to its progress. Although chemistry was of the highest importance to biological studies, exclusive consideration of the chemical phenomena would lead to incomplete, erroneous views. Chemists were essentially unqualified to deal with these subjects, for they were unable to recognize the distinctions de Blainville had established between the *elements* of an organism and its simple *products*. Since they could not appreciate the differences between tissues, parenchymas, and organs, they could not properly choose the subjects for their analytical operations, nor establish the conditions essential for their analyses. A rational solution to biological questions could only be achieved by the "general . . . subordination of the chemical point of view to the physiological point of view, and consequently by the use of chemistry by physiologists themselves, for whom chemical analysis, although indispensable, could be only a simple means of exploration."[7]

Comte gave several examples of studies he considered to be inadequate because of the limited point of view of the chemists who had carried them out. Thus when a chemist analyzed blood or other body fluids and solids, he usually contented himself with a single sample of material, taken without regard for the condition of the organism from which he obtained it. When chemists attained divergent results because of this neglect of physiological sources of variation, they mistakenly attributed their differences to discordant analytical methods. Although the experiments of Priestley, Senebier, and de Saussure on the chemical exchanges between plants and the atmosphere had provided the first positive knowledge of the "plant economy," subsequent studies had shown that the investigation could not be reduced to the simple state imagined by the chemists. They had viewed the whole process as the absorption of carbonic acid and the exhalation of oxygen, because they failed to appreciate the double movement of composition and decomposition inherent in all vital activity. In their examination of animal respiration, chemists had ascribed the conversion of arterial blood to venous blood solely to the transformation of oxygen to carbonic acid, even though the process was obviously far more complex. With similar naiveté they had tried to explain animal heat as the result of a simple combustion in the lungs. The fact that nitrogen is as abundant in herbivorous animals as in carnivorous animals, even though the food of the former contains very little of that element, had caused great difficulties for chemists. According to Comte, that situation proved that the chemical composition of "anatomical elements" cannot be directly explained, as chemists attempted to do, by the composition of the external materials from which they derive. Comte counseled physiologists to reclaim all such studies which they had abandoned to the chemists. Biological considerations, he asserted, must clearly be preponderant "in order to direct at every instant the judicious use of chemical methods, and for the sound interpretation of the results they provide."[8]

Comte's ideas attained such prestige that, according to Georges Canguilhem, "there was not a biologist or physician in France between 1848 and 1880" who did not have to deal directly or indirectly with Comte's biological philosophy in order to define the sense and extent of his own work.[9] Numerous commentators have pointed out the similarities between Bernard's later general philosophical propositions and those of Comte. Moreover, Comte expressed the above ideas in one of his most important works just as Bernard was beginning his scientific career. It might therefore appear nearly self-evident that

Bernard's early attitudes concerning chemistry and physiology must have derived in part, or at least have been strongly affected by, the views of Comte. Of the various statements Bernard made on the subject between 1843 and 1848, one of them—his brief description of the discordant results chemists had obtained by analyzing body fluids without regard for physiological conditions—was enough like Comte's description of the same situation to make it plausible that Bernard could have been directly inspired by that passage from Comte's book.[10] There are, however, reasons to doubt that Comte served as a decisive source for Bernard's opinion. D. G. Charlton has suggested that the strength and generality of Comte's influence has been accepted without proof, and that his *Cours de philosophie positive* may have been largely ignored in France during the first years after its publication.[11] Furthermore, the resemblances between Comte's views and those Bernard espoused were rather superficial. The physiology that Comte believed should dominate chemistry was quite different from the physiology with which Bernard identified himself. Comte regarded the observation of natural variations in biological phenomena, the comparison of the same function in different members of the animal series, and of normal states with pathological states, all to be more important than direct experimentation. Meaningful experiments were very difficult to attain in physiology, Comte thought, because there were so many variable conditions. Vivisection he considered to be the least useful of all possible types of physiological experimentation, because it disrupted the entire life of the animal so drastically and suddenly that specific effects could not be observed. Comte's reasons for denying chemists the competence to treat physiological questions adequately were also mostly different from Bernard's reasons. Comte wished to establish a rational division of the sciences in which each science would deal with a homogeneous subject matter. Organic chemistry, which treated partly chemical and partly biological phenomena, did not meet such a criterion, and Comte wanted to divide the science up. That which was properly chemical would become part of a new unified chemistry, that which was biological would become part of physiology. Furthermore, although the examples Comte used to illustrate the limitations of chemists investigating biological questions were in some respects like the cases Bernard used, the more basic reason for Comte's view was that he placed biology after chemistry in his general hierarchy of the sciences. By his philosophical principles this ordering automatically made chemistry capable of furnishing physiology only analytical tools to be used by physiologists.[12] If Bernard was concerned with these general, abstract issues during the first five years of his research, he left no record of that interest; in contrast we have seen clear traces of more immediate sources for his position with respect to the relation of chemistry and physiology.

These considerations do not necessarily exclude the possibility that Comte's writings were relevant to the early development of Bernard's views. It is very often difficult to establish the immediate point of impact of general ideas on the thoughts and actions of men engaged in concrete investigations. Even though Bernard was reacting most directly and consciously to certain specific activities of contemporary chemists, the presence of Comte's arguments might at least have reinforced his attitude. Since Comte was not within the scientific arena in which Bernard had to contend, however, Bernard may have been less aware of the effects of Comte's writings on him or else did not think of mentioning them in publications and notebooks oriented toward research questions.

About the time that Bernard was finishing the research for his first publication on pancreatic juice he filled ten pages of his laboratory notebook with random reflections concerning past work, possible future investigations, and general physiological issues. His thoughts ranged from new ways to study salivary, gastric, and pancreatic digestion to questions regarding the effects of poisons and methods for measuring the quantity of blood in animals. Among other things, he speculated that if he injected potassium chlorate into the circulation of an asphyxiated animal that substance might be able to supply the oxygen needed by its blood.[13] One of the most interesting trains of thought he sketched out was the following:

A fertilized egg ferments and produces a creature.

An unfertilized egg ferments and produces gas.

Its elements decompose into others less organized; whereas in the first case they decompose into others more organized.

In spontaneous or chemical decompositions the bodies are divided [*se dédoublent*]. All that belongs to dead nature.

In living nature these same principles redouble or are joined together.

It is that which distinguishes the living force from the dead force—in the one there is destruction [*deconstitution*], in the other there is reconstitution of bodies.[14]

In 1845, while attempting to construct a nutritional theory, Bernard had already differentiated vital transformations, which required "nervous influence," from purely chemical reactions which could continue within the body in the absence of that nervous factor.[15] At that time, however, he had not based the distinction on the intrinsic nature of the transformations themselves. Now he seemed to have formulated such a basis in his assertion that synthetic reactions are vital, whereas decompositions are purely chemical. This was his first clear written expression of a view which in later years became a very prominent feature of his thought. It is also one of the few of his early statements implying that he objected to purely chemical explanations of physiological phenomena on philosophical as well as operational grounds. Although this brief passage leaves unclear the sources or full meaning of his ideas, they at least suggest that he accepted that there were forces and processes in "living nature" unlike those in nonliving nature. A little further on he speculated that different species of electricity might direct the phenomena of inorganic, vegetable, and animal nature respectively, causing the same material elements to undergo different kinds of combination in the three realms.[16]

Of the numerous possible sources of the ideas which Bernard incorporated into this statement a major element must have been the deep influence the writings of Xavier Bichat still exerted on French biological thought. It was Bichat who had sought to contrast in every respect the properties of "vital forces" with those of physical laws. "An immense interval" separated physics and chemistry from the science of organized bodies, Bichat had written in 1800, "because an enormous difference exists between their laws and those of life." [17] In the following decades physiologists came to reject the extreme form in which Bichat had separated vital from physical laws. As Comte wrote, "that great physiologist . . . continued to be preoccupied with the false idea of an absolute antagonism between dead nature and living nature." [18] Nevertheless, even in the 1840's the lingering attraction of Bichat's teachings were still strong for French physiologists; [19] they may well have induced Bernard to contemplate what features differentiate the phenomena in these two natures. Bichat emphasized another conception which might have aided Bernard in his choice of the particular distinction he made. "A double movement also takes place in the organic life," Bichat wrote; "one unceasingly composes, the other unceasingly decomposes." [20] De Blainville quoted Bichat in his lectures, and even defined life itself as such a double movement. Bernard wrote down in his notes of De Blainville's course in 1840 a very similar statement: "Organic life is composed of a successive and alternative movement of composition and decomposition." [21]

Bichat had not defined the physical nature of composition and de-composition as Bernard was attempting to do. Bernard could easily have drawn his characterization, however, from the view common in early nineteenth-century organic chemistry that the synthesis of organic compounds requires living organisms, whereas ordinary chemical forces can produce only decomposition reactions. By comparison with Bichat, Bernard was diminishing the opposition between vital phenomena and inert processes, narrowing the specially vital transformations to one class among the reactions which occur in organisms. In making this distinction, however, Bernard fell into a limitation of vision which was the converse of that to which he objected in the school of Dumas. They restricted the chemical reactions which they imagined animals can produce to the types they had been able to carry out in their laboratories, not comprehending, as Bernard complained, that nature has more ample means of operating.[22] He, on the other hand, would only designate as purely chemical the kind of reactions in the body which chemists had duplicated outside it, even though nature's more ample means might suffice to explain the others without recourse to a vital directing agent. Both views identified the boundaries of chemical phenomena in the living organisms with the present achievements of chemists rather than with future possibilities.

The above statements about chemical destruction and vital reconstitution Bernard applied to a more specific situation:

> In the intestinal tube there is a destruction of bodies, that is, actual decompositions in the stomach for nitrogenous materials and in the intestines for the others. Then it is in the blood that the reconstitution takes place . . . Everything is transformed into albumin—for the nitrogenous materials, then in the blood that albumin gradually becomes fibrin, then muscle, etc. These are the nervous attractions.[23]

The concrete example of a nutritive transformation was not novel. Before Mialhe defined albuminose such sequences were commonly proposed. Among others, Johannes Müller believed that the purpose of digestion was to convert all nutrient materials to albumin. Müller thought also that some of this albumin was changed into the fibrin of the blood, although he and others were uncertain about whether that process took place in the blood itself or during the passage of chyle through the lymphatic vessels.[24] Finally, it had been a common theory for over sixty years that blood fibrin is transformed into muscle fiber. But if Bernard was merely reiterating such ideas, his interpretation that the changes amounted to a decomposition of the aliments and then a reconstitution of constituents of the animal was more novel. Because of the similarity in the composition and properties of the above substances physiologists and chemists tended to think that the conversion of one to another involved only minor modifications of their composition. Liebig and Dumas had carried this idea to its logical extreme when they deduced from the apparently identical elementary composition of these substances that only superficial changes of form were required and that animals therefore essentially received the constituents of their blood in their aliments. Bernard was attributing a more complex nutritional role to animals. It is improbable that he inferred this from any knowledge of specific chemical changes, especially in light of the illustration he chose. Probably he was drawing on a more traditional physiological belief that animals must impose basic changes upon their nutrient materials in order to impart to them the specific properties of their own substance. It was such a view that Alfred Donné had expressed in his criticism of Dumas in 1843.[25] Here, too, Bichat may have provided a general image of animal nutrition which could serve as a counterforce to Dumas's scheme. In contrast to Dumas's characterization that the processes in animals and in plants are opposite, Bichat had depicted animals themselves as embodying both an "animal life" and an "organic life." The latter "all organized beings, animal or vegetable, enjoy in a greater or less degree." [26] The most fundamental feature of this organic life which all organisms share is the double process of composition and decomposition. Bernard was not merely restating Bichat's general conception, however, for Bichat included digestion as a phase of the phenomenon of composition.[27] Neither did Bernard necessarily connect his idea with that of Bichat; but it is nevertheless important to recognize that there were in Bernard's intellectual milieu alternative conceptions of animal nutrition to those imposed by the doctrines of Dumas or of Liebig. For present purposes the most significant point is that in the spring of 1848 Bernard was able to view the problem of nutrition in a framework quite independent of the popular theories of those chemists. That factor suggests a somewhat different interpretation from the one he afterward gave of the path he followed during the next few months to his best-known discovery.

After presenting the first results of his pancreatic research Bernard continued to investigate the same problems and some related digestive phenomena. On May 1, for example, he examined the effects of bile on the properties of gastric juice. He also performed a new pancreatic

fistula operation and noticed, probably because the weather was becoming warmer, that pancreatic juice is altered extremely rapidly.[28]
On May 24, however, he again changed directions, going back to his
long-standing preoccupation with the behavior of different kinds of
sugar injected into the circulation. He also returned for much of the
ensuing research to Pelouze's laboratory, probably because he wished
to work more closely with Barreswil. In the first experiment, carried
out in his usual manner, he injected into the jugular vein of a dog 2
grams of molasses which he had found beforehand to contain both
cane sugar and grape sugar. Only the cane sugar appeared in the
urine, and he concluded that the grape sugar "has been destroyed."
His conclusion, that he had resolved the question of the composition
of molasses, seems rather trivial, since he already knew that from the
prior analysis.[29]

The next day he returned to the Collège de France and injected into
a large rabbit 3 decigrams of "diabetic sugar." Théodore-Auguste
Quévenne, a physician interested in that disease, had isolated the
substance from the urine of a patient. No sugar appeared in the urine,
and Bernard concluded that "the diabetic sugar was destroyed like ordinary grape sugar." Later that day he demonstrated, in a private
course he was teaching, his standard experiment of injecting cane
sugar into one rabbit and grape sugar into another.[30] On the same
busy day he began another series of experiments on gastric juice. He
compared preparations made with stomach membranes and intestinal
membranes, and the effects of making the membranes alkaline prior to
composing the digestive fluid. He also compared the effects upon
otherwise identical preparations of varying the concentration of hydrochloric acid, using respectively 2, 1, ½, and ¼ percent solutions.[31]
This was a refinement to which he had rarely resorted, although it
was common practice for some of his contemporaries working on similar problems. He broke off these experiments without recording any
definite results, however, perhaps because a certain aspect of the preceding experiments with sugars had occupied his attention in a new
way. That he assumed those sugars which did not appear in the urine
had been destroyed was not a new idea; for as we have noted, from his
first discussion of the phenomenon in his medical thesis of 1843 he had
described that sugar as "assimilated" or "decomposed" in the blood. In
the theory of nutrition which he entertained in 1845 he had imagined
that process occurring in the lungs.[32] Now for the first time, however,
he set out to ascertain by direct means where that destruction might
take place within the animal. He began with the following experiment:

Destruction of sugar.

May 26, 1848. A rabbit having been killed by asphyxia by means of carbonic acid, I took its lungs, ground them in a mortar with the blood which they contained and added a little grape sugar and a little ordinary water and I submitted them to the water bath at 40 to 45°. The next morning after 10 to 12 hours of digestion the sugar had disappeared and the whole emitted a very characteristic odor of butyric acid.[33]

That Bernard should attack the problem in this manner is interesting and somewhat unexpected. It was logical for him to look first at the lungs as a possible source of destruction, in view of his earlier nutritional theory. In that theory, however, he had assumed that the "assimilative combustion" of sugar in the lungs was a vital action which could not continue without a presiding nervous influence. Now he had so far reversed that conception that he was attempting to duplicate the physiological action of the lungs with ground-up pulmonary tissue. Perhaps his recent classification of decomposition phenomena as purely chemical had prepared him to take this new approach. If so, it would be, I think, an instance rare in his early career, when a basic, consciously formulated philosophical attitude toward the relation between organic and inorganic nature immediately influenced his choice of experimental procedures.[34] It is likely that he had in mind also that some ferment contained in the lungs produces the reaction he was seeking. This first effort must have pleased Bernard, for it seemed to indicate that he had indeed found the place in which the destruction of sugar occurs. He repeated the effect equally successfully with the lung tissue from another dog killed with hydrogen sulfide. The situation grew more complicated, however, as soon as he compared the actions of other tissues. Grape sugar disappeared also in liver, although he thought more slowly than in lung substance. Pancreatic tissue mixed with the sugar acquired an acid reaction similar to the previous cases. He interpreted this as due probably to lactic acid. Presumably he guessed that it derived from the destruction of the sugar, but he did not mention whether the sugar itself disappeared.[35]

Bernard continued the investigation on May 27, using beef liver and lung tissue he had bought from a butcher. The new results, however, were still more equivocal. Placing chopped liver in one tube and chopped lung in another, he added grape sugar and water to each. After three hours the amount of sugar did not appear to have decreased in either tube. At the end of twelve hours the sugar had still not completely disappeared. There was evidence that some reaction had taken place, however, for in both cases the acid reaction and odor of butyric acid appeared and gas was disengaged.[36] Although this outcome did not necessarily refute his first result, it could hardly have enhanced Bernard's confidence that he was dealing with a special action of the lungs.

Two days later Bernard made a more extensive series of comparisons, using chopped liver, heart, spleen, and thymus tissue from a rabbit. Liver did not alter *cane* sugar, a result which was compatible with his expectations; for he believed that this substance could not be utilized in nutrition without a prior digestive conversion to grape sugar. Less favorable was the fact that chopped liver without sugar became acidic and acquired the odor of butyric acid, for this showed that he had been hasty in using such signs as indications that a given tissue had acted on sugar. Worse still, when he mixed grape sugar with chopped lung, "much sugar" remained twelve hours later. Similarly, the liver tissue left after twelve hours an "enormous" amount of sugar. The last result was eventually enormously significant to Bernard, but at this point he probably considered it to show simply that the liver did *not* destroy sugar. In contrast, the heart, spleen, and thymus tissue caused the sugar to disappear almost entirely. From these reversals of his first results Bernard could only conclude: "Thus the sugar seems to have been destroyed by all of the tissues except for the liver and the lungs. It will be necessary to do the experiments again with still other tissues, while weighing the quantities of sugar." [37]

Instead of doing that, Bernard approached the same question in a different manner, by trying to trace the actual course of the sugar within the circulation of a living animal. On May 31 he injected one gram of grape sugar into the right jugular vein of a dog. He then removed from the right carotid artery three samples of blood at 30-second intervals. The blood into which he had injected the sugar would thus have had to pass through the lungs before he collected what he hoped would be portions of the same circulatory fluid, and by testing the latter for sugar he hoped to detect the effects of that passage. "I found," he reported,

sugar (and much of it) in each of the bloods except for the first withdrawn. (The urine was not examined.) That would indicate therefore that it is not the lungs which destroy the sugar. Would it therefore be in the general tissues? It will be necessary to do that experiment again with great care and it will be necessary that the animal not lose so much blood, which might have modified the circulation in the lungs. [38]

Despite its indecisive and negative outcome, this experiment was one of the most crucial that Claude Bernard ever performed, for with it he attempted for the first time to intercept the path of the reactions a nutrient substance undergoes after it has been absorbed into the blood. That is what he described afterward as his general contribution to the chemistry of nutrition. "I am the first," he believed, "who has investigated the intermediary [steps]. One knew the two extremes and one created the physiology of probabilities with the rest." [39] To follow "experimentally step by step" the transformations the chemists were trying to deduce, he stated in 1865, had been his approach from the start. [40] In one sense it had been. As we have seen, he first imagined that he might discover the laws of animal chemistry by injecting reagents whose reactions he could follow within animals by means of their conspicuous products. [41] Yet in these early experiments he had not traced the course of nutritional transformations themselves. Like the chemists, he had dealt with those processes only indirectly. He would alter the digestive or physiological state of an animal, or inject a nutrient material into its circulation, then from the resulting changes in the urine he reasoned about what might have occurred within. Already in the injection experiments, however, he had diminished the range of the unknown intermediate steps by bypassing those of digestion. In a sense the new experiment only narrowed that range further by comparing the condition of a nutrient before and after it passed through an organ (or rather in this case two organs, since the blood traversed the heart as well as the lungs before he could recover it). He was trying to strike a balance between what the organ takes in and gives out, analogous to what the chemists were doing for the whole organism. He still had not reached the site of a reaction itself, certainly not the individual steps of a process, and we can see by hindsight that he was much further from that goal than the concepts of his day would lead him to suspect. Nevertheless, he had sufficiently narrowed the target area so that he clearly had made a major move toward, even if he had not fully achieved, a direct examination of what chemists had "explained theoretically." Bernard's approach can also be viewed as an extension into the circulatory system of the same basic methods that his predecessors and he himself had utilized to study digestion. His mixtures of sugar with ground tissues corresponded to artificial digestions, whereas the injection of sugar into a vein and its recovery after it had passed through a portion of the vascular system corresponded to the tracing of the course of aliments within the digestive tract itself. The collection of the arterial blood was thus a procedure analogous to the collection of the contents of the stomach through a fistula of the type devised by Blondlot. Some would object that these situations are different in principle, since the intestinal cavity, unlike the interior of the blood vessels, is morphologically external to the organism. Practically, however, that distinction is less significant, since both cases involved operations to remove substances through structural layers of living animals from cavities internal to those layers.

As soon as Bernard had seized on the general strategy of injecting sugar and removing blood from a point in the path the injected material followed, he could begin to imagine variations on the original experiment. Its outcome, indicating to him that sugar may be destroyed in the general tissues rather than the lungs, immediately suggested other experiments to test that alternative. He planned to collect blood next time not only from the carotid artery, but from the jugular vein on the other side, in order to see whether the sugar still remained in the blood as it returned from the tissues in the head. Similarly, he considered injecting sugar in the crural artery of the leg of an animal and collecting the blood from the corresponding vein. If it were in the tissues that sugar disappeared, he surmised, then an animal digesting starch ought to contain sugar in the blood of its "arterial portal vein," but not in the returning venous blood.[42]

On June 1 Bernard performed at Pelouze's laboratory an experiment on the digestion of fat, during which he searched unsuccessfully for fatty acids in the intestine of a dog nourished for eight days on mutton fat. With the same animal he carried out his plan to test whether sugar is destroyed in the general tissues. Injecting the substance into a crural artery and collecting the blood on its return through the crural vein, he "found sugar in that blood, but not in huge amounts, so that I think that it was in very large part transformed. Only the quantity of sugar was too great." That is, he apparently thought that it was only because he had injected too much that it had not totally disappeared.[43] The following day, however, after he performed the other of the two experiments he had planned, he was forced to doubt this opinion. Injecting sugar into the right jugular vein of a dog, he immediately afterward collected blood from the right carotid artery and the vein into which he had made the injection. There seemed to be as much sugar in the vein as in the artery, "which would seem to indicate," he acknowledged, "that the transformation of sugar which had not taken place in passing through the lungs would not have taken place either in passing through the capillaries." Nevertheless, the divergent result of the previous experiment encouraged him to try again. He felt that perhaps in removing the blood from the same vein into which he had injected the sugar he might have incurred some error from reflux of the blood through anastomozing veins. He thought also of testing whether the liver might destroy the sugar (thus implying that he did not regard the results of the experiments with crushed tissue as decisive). To do this he planned to inject the sugar into the mesenteric veins and collect the blood from a tube inserted into the right auricle of the heart.[44] The latter would be the first point beyond the liver from which he could conveniently collect blood of which part had passed through that organ.

Two days later Bernard injected one-half gram of grape sugar into the jugular vein of the same animal. He collected blood this time from the left crural artery and the right crural vein. In the first, which would have passed through the lungs, he found "very evident sugar"; in the second, which would in addition have returned from the tissues of the leg, there were "traces" of sugar. Sensing, perhaps, that the situation was too complicated to handle with such simple qualitative distinctions, he repeated the experiment the next day and attempted to compare quantitatively the relative amounts of sugar in the blood samples. He probably used as his measure the amount of copper oxide which a given volume of serum precipitated with Barreswil's reagent. In the blood from the crural artery collected one minute, and one minute fifteen seconds after the injection, the sugar was "as 200." That collected from the crural vein during the injection gave sugar as "100"; the next two samples extracted from there contained no sugar, the last one sugar "as 10." After releasing the ligature he had used during the injection, he collected from the jugular vein blood which included sugar "as 10." [45] Bernard did not state whether or not he could discern in the results of this refinement of the experiment any clarification of his original question.

Recognizing perhaps that the direct injection of sugar produced an artificial situation, or that the effects were too transient to follow effectively, Bernard decided to follow the path of sugar which entered the circulation from natural digestion. He fed a large amount of cane sugar, together with a little grape sugar and starch, to a dog. Three hours later, when these aliments were presumably absorbed as grape sugar, he collected samples of blood. He found much sugar in the right crural vein, the right crural artery, and the heart. In the portal vein there was "a huge amount of sugar," a result which he noted without evident surprise. Since that vein forms the route of absorption of sugar from the intestine, the finding would not appear anomalous.[46] Then he injected one-half gram of grape sugar into the portal vein and collected 10 seconds afterward "enormous" amounts from the heart and crural arteries.[47] Far from providing any additional clue concerning the place in which sugar is destroyed, this experiment seemed only to contradict whatever pattern he might have been able to perceive in the preceding injection experiments.

Thus Bernard's first endeavor to trace the fate of sugar within the animal failed to bring the distinct result for which he had hoped. Part of his trouble lay in formidable technical obstacles. The more basic difficulty, however, was his conception of the problem itself. His experimental procedure embodied the assumption that sugar contained in any portion of blood would disappear almost instantly when it encountered that region of the body responsible for its destruction. That was an extraordinarily simple conception of the physiological process, even for his time. It may have been in accord with the fact that none of his predecessors had found sugar in the blood of animals except when the animals had recently been fed alimentary sources of the substance. Yet it is hard to see how he could reconcile such an expectation with the continuous nature of respiratory combustion. If sugar were destroyed almost as soon as it entered the blood, as he supposed, then both the respiratory gaseous exchanges and the heat production of the animal ought to fluctuate far more drastically than either common experience or the numerous experiments undertaken to measure these processes indicated. Bernard's position could only have been plausible if he did not take very seriously the contention of Liebig and of Dumas, as well as of their predecessor Lavoisier, that the principal source of animal heat is the combustion of the "respiratory aliments," and that the amount of heat produced is proportional to the quantities of nutrient matter burned. Given his general skepticism toward the theories of the chemists, that was quite likely his attitude, but it would suggest that Bernard was less adept than some of his contemporaries at discriminating between their fundamental insights and their speculative excesses.[48]

Meanwhile Bernard had been making a little more progress on a related question. Ever since he had observed, two and a half years earlier, that cane sugar injected into the circulation appears in the urine, but that grape sugar does not, he had been troubled by his inability to demonstrate decisively that cane sugar is converted into grape sugar during digestion.[49] As he took up his injection experiments again at the end of May, that subject arose once more. "Gastric juice does act on cane sugar to transform it into grape sugar," he wrote, "that is indisputable, because cane sugar injected into the stomach does not appear in the urine." After speculating that the organic material of the gastric juice rather than the acid must cause the transformation, he remarked that he would have to do new research on the problem.[50] This he undertook on June 2. From two preparations of artificial gastric juice he was able to produce a rapid transformation of cane sugar to glucose. In one case natural juice also caused a transformation, but in two others it failed to act. From a dried stomach membrane and a solution of cane sugar he obtained after two days both glucose and an acid, the latter of which he assumed to be the result of lactic fermentation. Somewhat cryptically he commented "It is probably in this manner that cane sugar is altered in the stomach." [51] Following up this conclusion, he next tried to follow the process within animals. On June 8 and 9 he injected respectively into the stomachs of a dog and a rabbit two ounces of cane sugar. In the first case he found five hours afterward no sugar in the stomach, grape sugar and a little cane sugar in the urine. In the second case he found a little of each sugar in the urine and a trace of glucose in the blood of the crural artery, but none in the vein. The next day the rabbit was dead from the bleeding, and Bernard found sugar in the blood of several of its arteries and veins.[52] Although these results were hardly definitive, Bernard may have gained from them some needed support for his conviction that during digestion cane sugar must be converted into glucose.

At the same time he was continuing to try to ascertain by reactions outside the body what might cause the destruction of glucose within it. On June 2 he mixed five drops of a glucose solution with each of several tubes containing respectively blood serum, blood serum made alkaline, a concentrated solution of sodium carbonate, and caustic potash. After twenty-four hours the sugar had disappeared only in the last of these. The same solution mixed with various tissues from a rabbit disappeared in ten hours from kidney tissue and in twenty-four hours from heart and brain tissue. But at the end of that time traces still remained in the liver tissue, a "sensible amount" in the lung tissue, and an extraordinary quantity in the muscle tissue. He did a similar set of tests on the 11th, but some of the results diverged from those of the last group. Now glucose disappeared in serum, although not in acidified serum. Most of it disappeared also from kidney tissue within two hours. In several cases he showed that boiling the mixture with two drops of sodium carbonate halted the disappearance of the sugar. Probably he was looking again for a ferment action.[53]

On June 9 Bernard also repeated the experiment of injecting glucose into the jugular vein of a rabbit and collecting blood immediately afterward from several points. He found that portions extracted from the opposite carotid artery, a crural artery, and a crural vein each contained "manifest" sugar: a result which could only tend to erase further the impression some of the earlier experiments of this type had given him that they were leading him toward a specification of the places along the circulation in which the sugar disappeared. For some reason he apparently had given up his attempt to compare the amounts of sugar quantitatively. On the 11th he injected starch into the stomach of a rabbit, and after killing it five hours later found sugar in each of the samples of blood he examined. There was, however, only a "feeble quantity" in the jugular vein, much in the vena cava after the liver, and still more in the portal vein before the liver.[54] Such a result may have suggested that the sugar diminished in the blood from the time it was absorbed from the intestine, which still contained large quantities of the nutrient. On the whole, however, the research which he had pursued on the problem for the past two weeks had yielded no consistent answer to his quest for the manner in which glucose is destroyed. None of the individual experiments was decisive, and the possibilities they suggested were divergent. Perhaps for this reason he dropped the investigation for some time, returning to a project whose fruitfulness was already proven. On June 21 he performed another pancreatic fistula operation.[55]

Bernard's progress was interrupted again, however, this time by a more extraordinary occurrence. Since the riots and abdication of King Louis Phillippe on February 23 and 24, Paris had been the scene of tumultuous events. These upheavals had little visible impact on Bernard, although his notebook shows no experiments dated during the two weeks following the end of the monarchy. His next entry began "March 10, 1848, at the course of the Collège National de France. République Française."[56] Laboratory notebooks are not the usual places for setting down reactions to political events. This brief indication of the changed situation of the Collège de France and the French nation suggests that the changes may have occupied his thoughts more than he revealed publicly. Nevertheless, he carried on his research as usual. By late June, however, the situation in the city was very tense. On the same day that Bernard undertook the new pancreatic investigation, laborers were being driven to take up arms by a decree closing down workshops which had earlier been provided for the unemployed. By June 23 they were building barricades all over Paris. On that day Bernard went to the laboratory to examine the state of the animal on which he had operated. He saw that it was still producing pancreatic juice, but he did not have time to examine the fluid. "I departed from the Collège de France at that moment," he recorded; "one was forming ranks and building barricades in the Rue St. Jacques." It would be very interesting to know what he thought and did during the next few days, while the National Guard was subduing the insurgents. Unfortunately he noted only that "the dog was not seen again until after the events of June." [57]

Compared to those around him, Bernard was remarkably undistracted by the troubled political situation. In the laboratory in which he was performing many of his experiments during this period he must have heard the upheavals discussed with fervor; for Pelouze was a man of outspoken republican views, and he was deeply caught up in the changes. After they were over Pelouze wrote Liebig that "the great and important events which have taken place in France and in Europe, and the conflicts of February and June, have slackened the zeal for research among all of the chemists, and all of their time, like that of every citizen, is absorbed by politics." [58] Bernard, on the other hand, was so absorbed in his science that he achieved during that same time one of the most productive research spurts of his career. Whether he was impervious to the social issues, or whether the sudden favorable turn in his investigations made him determined to press on despite all, he did not allow himself to be diverted.

When Bernard was able to return to his research he resumed simultaneously his studies of the digestion of fat and his "search for sugar in the economy." He tried to accomplish both with the sacrifice of a single animal, by nourishing a dog for several days on fat, then feeding it 200 grams of starch five hours before he killed it on July 1. Again he was unable to find fatty acids in the digestive tract. Tracing sugar absorbed from the starch, he found, as in the most recent similar experiment, that the portal vein contained much sugar, the jugular vein less but "evident" amounts of it. He extended his search also to other fluids. Barreswil's reagent was reduced by both the cerebro-spinal fluid and the vitreous humor of the eye, but he was not certain that sugar was the cause of the reaction. [59]

During one of his earlier experiments Bernard had been astonished to observe that a sample of clotted blood, whose separated serum had by the cupric tartrate reaction revealed a considerable quantity of sugar, did not itself seem to contain any. He had thought then that perhaps the fibrin somehow interfered with the reaction, and consulted Barreswil about the problem. Now he considered that question again. On July 2 he killed another rabbit several hours after injecting starch solution into its stomach. After allowing the blood to coagulate and the serum to separate, he confirmed that the latter, when reacted with Barreswil's reagent, appeared to contain a large quantity of sugar. Recalling that the blood cells and fibrin (that is, the clot), do not give the same result as the serum, he constructed a theory to explain the divergence. In whole blood, he surmised, sugar does not reduce the cupric tartrate because fibrin yields its oxygen to the sugar more easily than the copper does. If that is so, he went on, then in the circulation fibrin may serve an important role as "a sort of oxidizing agent which attacks the sugar in the blood." To test that hypothesis he thought it would be necessary to find out whether sugar disappears more quickly in blood containing fibrin than in blood from which that substance has been removed.[60] Although he did not say so, Bernard's explanation would be in accord with the experiments which suggested that sugar diminishes over the general course of the circulation, instead of disappearing all at once at a certain point in it as he had originally imagined. Thus he attempted to turn a technical difficulty into an opportunity to resolve the physiological question itself; how is sugar destroyed in the organism?

At Pelouze's laboratory the next day, however, Bernard obtained a result surprising enough to divert him away from that question. A female dog previously nursing puppies and still containing milk in its mammary glands had been kept in the laboratory for eight days on a mixed diet. Then for one day it had been placed in total abstinence, although it managed to eat a few bones. On July 3 Bernard injected potassium prussiate into its jugular vein to see if that substance would pass into various body fluids, and then he sacrificed the animal. Next he searched for both prussiate and sugar in the blood serum, chyle, cerebro-spinal fluid, and the vitreous humor of the eye. He looked for sugar also in the stomach and intestine. He found prussiate only in the urine. Sugar appeared in the serum, chyle, and vitreous humor, but not in the cerebro-spinal fluid, the stomach, or the intestine. "From where, therefore, does this sugar, or that cause of reduction in this blood, the chyle, the vitreous humor, come," he wondered, "whereas in the stomach there was none. Could it be that that could have come from the fact that the dog was nursing a few days before, and that its organization produced milk sugar? All of that is very curious and needs to be elucidated by new experiments." [61]

Clearly this was a very crucial experiment in Bernard's investigation. Its result switched his attention from the problem of the destruction of sugar in the animal to that of its source. It is not easy, however, to ascertain the purpose for which he undertook the experiment. Seventeen years later, in his *Introduction to the Study of Experimental Medicine,* he asserted that he had not previously doubted that the sugar in the blood came from the food, but that he nevertheless performed a comparative experiment excluding the alimentary source of sugar, because he believed that one must always do so as a matter of principle even when one does not foresee that it will be important.[62] The actual course of events does not readily fit this explanation. In the first place, the comparative experiment he outlined in the *Introduction* is different from the preceding experiment, and must have been a subsequent one, as will be seen below. Second, although a comparative test of the sort he afterward depicted might have been one of his aims, it could not have been his sole intent. If it had been, there would have been no reason to complicate the situation by searching for sugar in several places, nor by combining the test with a search for prussiate. Bernard seems to have been at least in part continuing the investigation he had taken up two days before of the passage of substances from the blood into other humors. The fact that he looked for sugar in various places even appears to imply that he probably thought in advance that he might find some somewhere. Otherwise he would have needed only to check where he had found it to be most evident in the case of an animal digesting starch—that is, in the blood of the portal vein, the vena cava, or the right ventricle. On the other hand, it would be going beyond any available evidence to suppose that he already suspected beforehand that there would be sugar in the blood when none was reaching the animal from its food. A possible solution to this dilemma would be that he was not expecting the animal to be totally deprived of alimentary sugar from its relatively short fast, until he observed that there was no sugar left in the intestinal canal. That recourse leaves unexplained, however, why the animal was deliberately kept in abstinence. Thus no unobjectionable interpretation of the experiment itself seems possible from the remaining record. Whatever may have been Bernard's intentions, it is with respect to his later account most striking that he expressed only moderate surprise over the outcome, and that he conjectured with little hesitation that the animal may have produced sugar from something else because it was nursing. His reaction suggests that if he had previously assumed that the sugar present in the blood derived from alimentary sources, that was probably because both Magendie and he had found it there in animals conspicuously fed such nutrients, rather than because he believed as a general rule that animals cannot form sugar from other substances. We have seen, besides, that he had already contemplated several years earlier that animals might produce sugar from fat or meat.[63]

Although his investigation of the physiological role of sugar now invited further efforts in several directions, Bernard let the topic lie mostly fallow for about a month. Meanwhile he pursued another objective which repeatedly eluded him, the creation of a permanent pancreatic fistula. He constructed an ingenious canula with an inner rotating tube intended to permit pancreatic juice to secrete normally into the intestine except when he wished to collect it. In two different operations, however, he was unable to insert it so that it would function properly. During this time he carried a dog with an ordinary fistula to a meeting of the Société de Biologie to demonstrate the collection and properties of pancreatic juice.[64]

When Bernard returned in early August to the investigation of sugar in the blood, he had evidently made up his mind to fasten onto the question of whether that substance may be present when an animal has not been receiving sugar or starch in its food. To ensure that the latter condition existed in his experiment he took thorough precautions. He deprived a dog of all solid aliment for six days, giving it only water. Then he examined blood from its jugular vein. There were "traces of reduction" with Barreswil's solution, and a "barely sensible" fermentation when he added yeast to a part of the serum. Although he recognized that the small amount of serum he had used made the tests less certain, he concluded that "the quantity of sugar would have to be very slight, if there was any of it." [65]

In the sequel, however, the result was quite different. He fed the same animal exclusively raw meat for eight days, after which he killed it by sectioning its brain stem so that he could obtain its "different bloods." He extracted and tested with Barreswil's reagent serum of the blood from the portal vein, the heart, and the wound in the neck of the animal, and chyle from the thoracic duct. The latter two gave little or no reduction. The blood of the portal vein produced an "enormous reduction," whereas that from the heart yielded a "very clear reduction, but less abundant than the blood of the portal vein." [66]

"How did it happen, therefore," Bernard asked, "that there was sugar (or a material which reduces) in the blood of the portal vein?" Since that vein was considered to absorb materials from the alimentary canal, he naturally thought first of searching in the stomach and the intestines for the source of the sugar; but fluids collected from each of these places caused no reduction with copper tartrate. Now baffled, Bernard exclaimed:

This experiment is exceedingly strange. From it one can comprehend nothing. [*C'est à n'y rien comprendre*]. Would sugar form in the portal vein, by what organ, by what mechanism?

It will be necessary to take this blood from the portal vein of a dog in abstinence and see if one will find there that material which reduces.

If sugar is formed from an alimentation other than that of starch, the question of diabetics is singularly complicated.

It will be necessary to see if this material which reduces may not be uric acid?

That reducing material (sugar or other) disappears quite rapidly, for the blood of the heart contained less of it and the blood from the neck only in a very equivocal fashion.

What therefore is the organ which would form that sugar or that reducing material? [67]

If we accept literally the well-known account which Bernard related in his *Introduction to the Study of Experimental Medicine*, the amazement with which he responded to this outcome derived from its incompatibility with the "prevailing theory" of Dumas that "the sugar present in animals came exclusively from foods, and that it was destroyed in animal organisms by the phenomena of combustion." As Bernard depicted the situation, this theory had served as his starting point in his search for the place in which the sugar disappeared.[68] In the prior experiments, in which the animals obtained sugar from their aliments, he said, it was "entirely natural and, as one says, logical," to think that sugar found in the portal vein was the same as that he had given them in their food. "I am certain," he continued,

that more than one experimenter would have stopped there and would have considered it superfluous, if not ridiculous, to perform a comparative experiment. Nevertheless, I made the comparative experiment, because I was convinced on principle of its absolute necessity . . .

I therefore took, for comparison with the dog fed on sugary soup, another dog to which I gave meat to eat, taking care, furthermore, that no sugary or starchy material entered its diet; then I sacrificed the animal during digestion and examined comparatively the blood in its superhepatic veins. But my astonishment was great when I ascertained that this blood from the animal which had not eaten sugar equally contained it.[69]

The surprise and disbelief which Bernard recorded in his notebook in August 1848 seem to support his later interpretation. For that reason M. D. Grmek, who first drew attention to this "crucial experiment" in Bernard's notebook, quite reasonably identified it as the point at which Bernard was, as he himself said, "led to see that the theory about the origin of sugar in animals, which served me as a starting point, was false." [70] To Bernard's own testimony Grmek adds, "Bernard's notes express his astonishment. Actually, the discovered facts completely contradicted his working hypothesis and the generally accepted ideas on animal physiology. The presence of sugar in the blood of an animal without an alimentary supply of carbohydrates was such an incredible finding that Bernard, as we see from his journal, doubted the specificity of the copper reagent." [71]

Professor Grmek's finding therefore seems to provide a strong case for Bernard's own account; yet I believe that, in the context of the whole sequence of earlier events, Bernard's recollections of his reasoning present difficulties which can best be resolved by a different explanation of the cause of his surprise. If it were really true, as Bernard maintained, that his insistence on doing comparative experiments brought him to the entirely unexpected discovery of sugar in the blood independent of alimentation, then this particular experiment could not have been the one in question. For the earlier experiment of July 2 had already made him suspect that an animal may sometimes produce its own sugar. He must, therefore, have approached the second experiment anticipating that he might find sugar in the blood. Neither could the earlier experiment have been that to which Bernard later referred, since the descriptions are quite different. The only way to save Bernard's interpretation, then, would be to assume that he was remembering some other experiment prior to these two, and unrecorded in his notebooks. Even then it would be hard to see how he could have been caught by surprise twice by the same phenomenon.

If it was not a routine counter experiment which led Bernard to his result, was he nevertheless in some sense following or testing the prevailing theory of nutrition when he searched for the place in which sugar is destroyed? This is also unlikely, for in his record of the investigation he nowhere alluded to that theory. The objection would not be cogent if only the two experiments his later account mentions were involved; but since he actually conducted a series of experiments, we might expect somewhere among them a hint that this was his purpose. In other situations he had been quick to note down observations or ideas which had some bearing on the theories of the chemists. When he did find sugar in the blood independent of an alimentary source, he immediately thought of such a broad implication as the problem of diabetes, but he was not moved to comment on the meaning for the general theory of nutrition.

There is no obvious reason why Bernard should have been especially concerned with Dumas's general nutritional theory in the summer of 1848. There were no notable new developments concerning that theory to cause him to take it more seriously than he had in previous years when it had been a focus of scientific attention. Furthermore, Bernard had for so long been skeptical about the whole approach represented in that theory that it is difficult to believe that at this time he could have had such confidence in it as to use it as his starting point, and to be unprepared for a finding contrary to it. Already he had publicly maintained that the methods of those who formulated it showed only how things theoretically might be rather than how they actually were. The influence of that theory, "established and supported by the most illustrious contemporary chemists," [72] is not essential to explain why Bernard had been carrying out his research; for we have seen that it was a logical development out of his own previous concerns. He assumed that glucose was destroyed in the circulation because when he injected it there it did not reappear in the urine. His first experiments on the place of destruction in living animals involved such injections of sugar, rather than a natural alimentary source of sugar as one might expect if his starting point had been the general theory of nutrition. These considerations taken together make it evident, I think, that the view Bernard afterward took of his reasoning in the period prior to the discovery was an artificial reconstruction he imposed on the events, for reasons which will be discussed further on.

If this is the case, why then was Bernard so surprised at his result? I think that a careful reading of his remarks suggests that it was not merely that he found sugar in the blood, but specifically that he found it in the blood of the *portal vein*, which he could not understand. It was not difficult, I would argue, for him to comprehend that the animal can produce sugar, since he had already entertained such ideas; rather he could not see how the substance could be produced where there was no evident organ available for that purpose. He apparently assumed that the sugar would have to be formed somewhere along the short path between the capillaries which absorb materials into the portal vein and the entrance of that vein itself into the liver. That is why he immediately queried *what organ* could form the sugar. One might object that the sugar might be produced anywhere in the body and pass around in the circulation until it reached the portal vein; but, as his comments and his previous investigations show, Bernard believed that sugar disappeared too rapidly in the circulation for it to have arrived at the portal vein after a lengthy circuit.

XIX

The Source of Sugar in Animals

Whatever Bernard may have expected before he undertook the experiment in which he detected sugar in the portal vein of a dog that had not eaten starch or sugar for eight days, its startling outcome determined the direction of his subsequent investigations. On August 17 he anesthetized with ether a dog which had eaten some meat and a little milk eight hours earlier. He drew blood from its portal vein and its heart. The serum from each sample reduced copper tartrate "enormously," and when he added yeast, each "fermented with an unbelievable activity, so that there is evidently sugar, and much sugar there. From where does it come? The dog had eaten a little milk in the morning but it must have digested that already." Examining the intestinal liquids, he found no evidence of sugar in them. He thought that perhaps the ether had something to do with the "enormous production of sugar in the blood." Another possibility was that the milk sugar contained in the milk might have been the source, but there were two difficulties with this explanation. First, his conception of the rapid destruction of sugar in the blood made it difficult to accept that sugar digested long enough before to have disappeared from the intestine could have supplied the substance still present in the blood. The second problem was that milk sugar was a different type from the sugar of the blood. The former did not ferment, so that it would have had to be transformed to glucose during digestion.[1] This factor, however, actually attracted Bernard to the explanation, for he had already been contemplating a theory that milk sugar is converted to glucose in the intestine. During June he had extended the injection experiments on different types of sugars, the starting point for the whole investiga-

426

tion, to milk sugar. Finding no milk sugar in the urine of a dog after injecting it into the circulation, he had assumed that it disappears into the blood as glucose does. He had then fed the animal a large quantity of milk sugar and looked unsuccessfully for sugar in its blood. Nevertheless, he continued to believe that somehow milk sugar must be converted into glucose in the intestine.[2] On August 5 he had tried the injection experiment again, but this time the milk sugar was excreted in the urine.[3] Undoubtedly these efforts came to mind as he reflected on his latest experiment on the source of blood sugar. On the next day, August 18, he repeated the injection of milk sugar and again found that it was not assimilated into the blood.[4] Perhaps he construed the result as support for his view that milk sugar, like cane sugar, must first be converted to glucose during digestion, but he did not at the time pursue the question. The question itself was now a side issue, for the central problem was to account for the presence of glucose in the blood of animals which had no immediate alimentary source of any kind of sugar. On August 21 Bernard brought himself back to that main task.

Since Bernard entitled his next experiment "Digestion of fat—formation of sugar at its expense," it appears that he may have revived and intended to test his old conjecture that fat might be a source of the sugar in an animal. If so, however, his procedure was confusing. He used an animal which had eaten only meat scraps for some time, but which had a copious meal of meat and lard on the morning of the 22nd. Early in the afternoon Bernard killed the animal, collected samples of blood, and examined the intestines. Only the fat had reached there, and the chyliferous vessels were full. He inferred, therefore, that whatever phenomena he observed belonged "especially to the digestion of fat." Yet he had earlier tied off the pancreatic duct, so that it would seem that he must have planned to inhibit the digestion and absorption of fat.[5] Whatever he had in mind, this aspect of the experiment became unimportant, for he found during the course of it a more effective means of pursuing the general problem. There were two ways to seek the source of sugar; the first, illustrated by this attempt, was to identify some other aliment with its presence. The second was to locate more precisely, if possible, the point at which the sugar originated. In his initial surprise, as we have seen, he assumed that the sugar must form in the portal vein, even though there were no organs along the main nutritional pathway to account for it. As he recalled a few weeks later, however, it was unlikely that the walls of the portal vein had the property of secreting the substance. The only alternatives were the neighboring organs.[6] If one of them were responsible, the sugar might be most concentrated in the portion of the vein or its branches where that organ secreted it. It was probably such reasoning which led him to compare blood from the "furthest branches" of the vein with that from the other end of it, at its entrance into the liver. To force out the latter blood he pressed both on the liver and the intestinal mass. Serum from the former blood gave only "traces of reduction," while the latter produced an "enormous reduction." Then he searched for sugar in the tissues of organs connected with the portal system. "The tissues of the [mesenteric] ganglions [of the lymphatic vessels] and of the spleen did not show sugar distinctly," he observed, "but the tissue of the liver contained it enormously." These striking contrasts convinced Bernard that, despite the awkward fact that blood flows from the portal vein into the liver, not from the liver into the vein, that organ must somehow be implicated in the production of the sugar appearing in the vein. Remarking that next time he should compare arterial blood as well, he added cryptically "equilibrium of the liver and the lungs." The phrase hints that he was beginning to think that the liver forms sugar which the lungs destroy.[7] Immediately he began an intense investigation of the tissues of livers from other animals.

Even before he had completed this experiment, Bernard purchased a beef liver and a calf liver from a butcher. He found in each great amounts of sugar, by Barreswil's test as well as by fermentation. The next day, the 23rd, he went to the Hopital de la Charité to get pieces of liver tissue from three deceased patients. One of them, from an elderly person who had died in a very emaciated condition, contained no sugar. A second piece from an obese woman who had died of unknown causes also gave no reaction; but in the liver of a healthy young man who had been poisoned he found by both tests a great amount of sugar. On the 24th he observed that the liver of the dog in which he had first discovered sugar still contained it, three days after the death of the animal.[8]

Bernard soon began to encounter technical problems in his analyses of the tissues for sugar. He tried, for example, to extract the substance from a beef liver in alcohol. The solution he obtained reacted with Barreswil's reagent, but did not ferment. He attributed the discrepancy to the inhibiting effect of the alcohol, which he had not entirely removed, on the fermentation.[9] Another complication also attracted his attention: "Often I believed that there was not any sugar in the livers when I examined them fresh—upon what does that depend? It is undoubtedly that the liver tissue is too hard and does not easily yield the sugar.–It will therefore be necessary to grind them well and pound them in a mortar and boil them with water." Not until seven years later could Bernard appreciate the full implications of that observation; when he did, it was by means of a famous experiment the germinal idea for which may have been his next thought at this point: "It will be necessary to inject different liquids into the liver, wash them with warm water or other serum . . . to learn if one would carry out sugar and with which liquid one will carry it out most easily." [10]

Such distractions, however, did not divert him from his immediate objective. He found on the same day much sugar in livers taken from a rabbit and from a capon. A day later, on the other hand, he detected only traces in the livers of two persons who had died of heart disease, one after a long illness. He also examined that day livers from four cold-blooded animals. That of a lizard gave "insignificant traces" of sugar, a frog liver contained "very evident traces of sugar in small quantity," and two fish livers gave no sign of the substance. Still on the same day he went to the slaughterhouse and obtained livers from three fetal calves of eight, six, and two months gestation respectively. Examining them he found that the oldest contained a great amount of sugar, the next a noticeably smaller quantity, and the youngest none at all. [11]

With a burst of activity typical of his response to an observation of unusual interest, Bernard had produced in four days an impressive range of confirmatory evidence that the presence of sugar in the liver was a phenomenon of widespread significance. We have seen that after such rapid advances he often made his results quickly public. At this time, however, Bernard was probably not ready to report his discovery, despite its exciting nature, because he still had too many unsolved problems. He had uncovered something very important, but it is doubtful that he could yet give a coherent interpretation of all of his findings. To assure his priority for them while he worked out the remaining difficulties, he followed a time-honored custom and deposited a sealed note at the Academy of Sciences on August 28. [12]

During the same busy days in which he analyzed so many livers, Bernard also found time to carry on his injection experiments with different sugars. When he next tried milk sugar, only a little of it appeared in the urine, so that he considered that it can be assimilated, "but considerably less so than grape sugar." Comparing ordinary grape sugar with sugar from a diabetic, he observed that he could inject more of the latter without causing it to be excreted. "Diabetic sugar is at least twice as destructible as grape sugar," he inferred with dubious logic.[13] For many years Bernard regarded diabetic sugar as physiologically distinct from glucose. For now, however, his main preoccupation remained the source of sugar in the blood.

On August 25 Bernard performed on a dog the first of several investigations of the "natural sugar in the blood." This simply meant that he used animals just as they arrived in the laboratory, without submitting them to any special diet or injections. Drawing blood from the carotid artery, the right jugular vein, and the inferior vena cava, he found "notable sugar" in the serum of each. To reach the vena cava he had to insert a tube from the jugular vein through the heart, a procedure which reveals the growing refinement of his methods. As he learned thus to procure blood from strategic sites deep within the circulation of living animals, he was laying the foundation for the goal he later described as following step by step the reactions supposed to take place in the organism.[14] In this case he was apparently trying to collect the blood just after it had passed through the liver. He noted afterward, "It will be necessary to try with the tube to penetrate into the subhepatic veins, for that time perhaps I did not go far enough. Do it over." [15]

In the next experiment on "natural sugar," again with an animal brought into the laboratory the same day, Bernard compared the blood of a crural artery with that from a crural vein. There was sugar in each, but "sensibly more in the arterial blood than in the venous blood." This experiment shows that despite the absorbing problem of the source of sugar Bernard was maintaining his concern with what afterward happens to it; here he was again trying to trace it through the general circulation. Two hours later he examined both serums again and saw that the sugar had almost entirely disappeared from them. The rapid depletion, he remarked, "explains how having brought blood from the slaughter-house I did not find sugar in it. It had disappeared on the way. It will be necessary therefore to coagulate the blood with alcohol as soon as it leaves the vein." [16] This phenomenon proved the key to many puzzling results then and later; perhaps Bernard recognized it as one reason why sugar had not before been noticed as a normal constituent of the blood. The disclosure of this cause of irregularity in the analyses did not, however, bring an end to discordant results in his subsequent research.

There were two ways in which Bernard could explain the existence of sugar in animals not digesting a known source of that substance. Either some other kinds of aliment were capable of giving rise to sugar, or else animals could produce sugar independently of the nature of their alimentation. From his remarks and investigations after he discovered this phenomenon Bernard apparently entertained both interpretations, although it is not clear how consciously he posed them as alternatives. At any rate, the critical test between these possibilities would be whether fasting animals maintained sugar in their blood and livers. On August 24 he had already started a dog on an extended fast in order to examine this situation. By the time he was ready to carry out the investigation seven days later, however, the animal had grown very thin and contracted pneumonia. Sacrificing it, he collected blood from the neck, the two ventricles of the heart, the portal and subhepatic veins, but none of them gave any evidence of sugar. Not even the tissue of the liver contained it. The lungs were altered by the effects of the pneumonia. "Therefore," he concluded, "the pneumonia has made the sugar disappear." Although significant in itself, the complication obscured the main issue. On the next day, Bernard examined a rabbit which had appeared very ill and eaten nothing for three days. In contrast to the previous case he found much sugar in the blood of its portal vein and heart.[17]

On August 30 Bernard had placed another dog in abstinence. On September 3 he found sugar in its crural artery and vein. Three days later, however, when he sacrificed the animal and collected blood from the chambers of the heart, the neck, and the inferior vena cava, he found none. There was not even any detectable in the tissue of the liver, which he examined with special care. With each experiment the pattern was now getting less clear, as Bernard's puzzled reflections on this one indicate:

> In this dog there was not any sugar in the liver or in the bloods. Nevertheless there were no diseases apparent in the lungs or in the other organs. Still the dog had had two wounds in its groins—its leg was swollen and the animal was dragging it. The wound was suppurating extensively. Is that of some importance in the result? Or rather might sugar disappear after that length of abstinence?[18]

There was no recourse except to try again to ascertain the effects of abstinence free of other concomitant conditions. On September 8 Bernard started another dog on a ten-day fast. Meanwhile, he favored the view that the absence of aliments was the decisive factor, and speculated on further consequences of that interpretation:

> When an animal has fasted a certain time, there is no longer sugar in its liver–and then its urine is alkaline? Is it that the liver is exhausted, then if one would give acid to this dog would it be diabetic [?]. Would the liver recover

its role [?] Magendie has observed that dogs did not recover after a certain period of fasting. That is undoubtedly on account of that. Because once the functions of the liver have been suspended one cannot live much longer.[19]

On September 15 Bernard found another way to "exhaust" the liver. He cut the two vagus nerves of a healthy, vigorous rabbit. The next day it had died, and he could find no trace of sugar. *"Therefore there is no sugar in the liver after death by section of the pneumogastrics."* That result he thought fitted in well with the observation that the respiration and temperature of the animal had diminished before its death.[20]

Two days later Bernard was ready to examine the fasting dog. It had become thin and had developed a tremble, but did not appear sick. He killed it and analyzed a lobe of its liver. There was no trace of reduction with Barreswil's reagent, and no fermentation. After performing a control test to make sure that fermentation could take place in the liver tissue if sugar were added, Bernard felt that the issue was settled: "Therefore after having fasted a certain time dogs no longer have sugar in the liver, even though they do not appear ill–do they then have any in the blood? And do they then give off carbonic acid in as large quantity by respiration–No, they render less of it." [21] Evidently Bernard was beginning to see in these results the possibility of a general theory something like the following: the liver produces sugar which it supplies to the blood to be consumed in respiration, in accordance with currently accepted views that combustion is the source of carbonic acid and animal heat. The liver cannot form sugar, however, without using some alimentary substances, so that in abstinence its provision of sugar is gradually used up. As the amount the organ is able to supply dwindles, so must the consumption of sugar, and consequently respiration itself, decrease. It is hard to see why, in the experiment, Bernard did not examine the blood as well as the liver, for it was crucial to his reasoning that the circulating fluid not contain sugar after the liver has ceased to furnish it.

If Bernard's theory were correct, then in a fasting animal the product of respiratory combustion, carbonic acid, should decrease in the blood as the supply of sugar failed. To check this, on September 24 he compared beef blood obtained at the slaughterhouse with blood from the fasting dog which he had used for the last experiment. Utilizing barium chloride to precipitate carbonates from the blood samples, he persuaded himself that there were carbonates in the beef blood but none in that from the dog.[22] The comparison fitted nicely into his scheme. His reasoning and results, however, were drawing him into a very strange position. Since he found no sugar at all in the liver and no carbonate in the blood of the fasting animal, the implication of his view is that respiration can essentially cease while an animal is still alive. Because Bernard did not fully state the hypothesis which he evidently had in mind, it is impossible to tell whether he actually made that inference, assumed that there was still present an unmeasurable quantity of sugar and carbonate accompanying a diminished respiration, or did not think the question through. Nevertheless, he contemplated extending his approach by comparing for carbonates the blood of a fasting dog with that of one digesting meat.[23] At this point he encountered a result which seemed incompatible with the whole theory.

Having by bleeding killed a dog which had been deprived of solid food for eight days, Bernard searched this time both in its blood and liver for sugar. He found "evident" sugar in the blood, but only "insignificant traces" in the liver. Puzzled again, he asked:

How therefore can one explain the presence of sugar in the blood and its absence in the liver? Without the hemorrhage would the blood have washed out the liver in passing through it [?] Or rather would the kind of agony which preceded the death by hemorrhage have made the blood [*sic*–probably intended "sugar"] disappear in the liver?

Bernard concluded that henceforth he should kill the animals by a blow on the head rather than by bleeding.[24]

Thus in the weeks since Bernard had discovered that animals can contain sugar without a direct alimentary source of the substance, each of the possible explanations of its source which he could pose had met serious experimental obstacles. The few efforts he had made to identify another alimentary source had not led to anything. The view that the formation of sugar was independent of alimentary conditions appeared contradicted by the disappearance of the sugar in fasting animals. Now even the demonstration that, whatever the material source of the sugar, the liver was the site of its formation, seemed endangered by this observation that the blood could contain sugar when the liver did not. As his reaction suggests, however, Bernard was not prepared to give up his idea that the liver supplies the sugar in the blood because of such a finding. Rather, he decided to change the experimental conditions in the hope of eliminating the inconvenient result.

Some of his trouble, Bernard recognized, arose from difficulties in the methods for identifying sugar in tissues. On the same day that he encountered the preceding experimental setback he tested the livers of some rats with two different preparations of Barreswil's reagent. One indicated the presence of sugar, the other did not, so that he decided he would have to rely more on the check of the fermentation reaction.[25] Perhaps such uncertainties helped sustain his belief that other inconsistencies arose from technical difficulties rather than from his conceptual approach. He had already thought that it would be an advantage if he could extract the sugar instead of merely inferring its presence from the two characteristic reactions. At one point he thought he had discovered a way to do it. "After much groping," he remarked, "I have settled on the following procedure." He described a sequence of operations by which he extracted substances from the ground pulp of liver in alcohol and water, then removed the albuminous and fatty matters. He was not satisfied, however, for he could not sufficiently separate chlorides from the sugar to enable the latter to crystallize. He envisioned various "physiological analyses" which he thought might be superior to ordinary chemical techniques, but he did not carry them out.[26] Instead, he contented himself with the usual means of identifying sugar and concentrated on the physiological aspects of the investigation.

In early October most of Bernard's difficulties disappeared, along with the general theory he had been constructing about the effects of the exhaustion of the liver. He began to find sugar in the liver and blood consistently. His accumulating experience with the procedures may have helped, but more important was a change he made in the conditions of the experiments. He continued to use animals which had fasted, but not for the prolonged periods which had produced such uncertainties in his previous tests. Instead, he examined some animals immediately after fasts of a few days. Others he subjected to a fasting period followed by nourishment with foods which excluded sugar or starch. On October 8 he found sugar, though less than the ordinary amount, in the liver of a dog which had fasted for six days. Another dog, deprived of food for eight days, then nourished only with fat for seven more, contained an "enormous" amount of sugar both in its liver and in its blood. Bernard repeated the experiment on a third dog with a nearly identical result. In each of these cases he killed the animals by blows on the head, so that he probably decided he had been right when he conjectured that in the puzzling earlier case bleeding had drained the sugar out of the liver. A duck which died after eleven days on a pure fat diet had no sugar left in its liver, but another which survived for fifteen days on washed egg whites contained much sugar in that organ.[27] From such experiments Bernard was able to conclude that "the formation of sugar in the liver is independent of aliments." [28] That phrase, which he used in his first memoir on the subject, was adroitly chosen. It encompassed the result which he had clearly established, that the direct alimentary sources of sugar, starch and sugars themselves, were not essential to the process. It implied as well that no particular alimentary source was necessary, but did not state that so explicitly as to confront those earlier results which had indicated that the sugar disappeared during a long abstinence. It left wisely unanswered the question of what was the initial source of the sugar.[29]

Just at the last, climactic stage of his investigation, Bernard kept an unusually cursory record of his experiments.[30] The sketchiness of his notebook leaves uncertain just when or how he discovered the key which unlocked the final, critical puzzle for him. As we have seen, the most incomprehensible aspect of his observations was that sugar should exist in the portal vein, when there was no obvious organ in a position to produce it. Since that initial discovery he had uncovered persuasive evidence that the liver was the source of this sugar; yet the paradox remained that the flow of blood was the wrong way to account for the appearance of the substance in the portal vein. There is an entry in the notebook which may indicate the point at which Bernard came upon the means to resolve the problem, although there is no guarantee that it represents the first such observation. Unfortunately it is undated, but the sequence in the notebook suggests that he probably wrote the note between September 24 and October 8. At the time he was pursuing a new hypothesis—that "the substance of the liver can play the role of yeast." From liver tissue he had extracted in alcohol a substance which partially redissolved in water. The soluble portion precipitated with heat and with acids. He called the substance "hepatine" and found that it could convert cane sugar to grape sugar. That result was very significant, he thought, "because the liver might be able to reduce all sugars to the same type." Apparently he was embarked on another of the bold conjectures which served so frequently to inspire his new paths of research. This one did not endure, however, possibly because of a more immediately significant observation which he made during the same investigation. At the bottom of the page he appended to the previous description:

Serum of the portal vein

The portal vein, tied on the preceding animal before opening the abdomen, did not contain sugar, whereas the liver contained a huge quantity of it.[31]

This observation, or another like it,[32] provided the answer to the riddle. As is well known, Bernard deduced from it that the sugar he had found in the portal veins of animals without an immediate alimentary source of the substance derived from a reflux of the blood out of the liver after he had opened their abdomens and the normal circulatory movements had ceased. What the record does not reveal is whether the explanation occurred to Bernard first and he deliberately tied the vein to test it; or whether he tied the vein for some other reason connected with this or another experiment and so solved his problem by chance.

On October 21 Bernard presented the results of the investigation he had been carrying on since late May to the Société de Biologie. His memoir, entitled "On the origin of sugar in the animal economy," was the first formal paper he read to that group, and one of the masterpieces of his career. Besides containing his most significant discovery, it was a beautiful example of closely interlocked reason and experiments. He constructed his demonstration so carefully, in fact, that it bore little trace of the obstacles he had met or of the shifts in the nature of the question during the course of the research. He also attained with apparent ease the goal toward which he had often strained in the past; that is, he was able to draw from the experimental proof of a specific phenomenon very broad consequences concerning the roles of physiology and of chemistry. Bernard posed the central issue clearly in his opening paragraph:

Sugar is spread profusely within the vegetable kingdom, but it exists also in animals. Plants cannot find it already prepared in the earth, and it is evident that they form it in their organs. Within animals does the same thing occur? Or rather is the sugar which one encounters in their bodies furnished exclusively by the sugars and starches of the plants which serve them as aliments? [33]

He enumerated the three types of sugar and starch which, according to "the ideas now reigning concerning nutrition," were the only sources of the sugar found in the blood. It was, he added, because only starch among the aliments could be transformed into sugar by means of known chemical operations, and because of "the ingenious idea that animals create no immediate principles and only destroy those which are furnished by the vegetable kingdom," that people believed themselves "authorized to refuse" to animals the faculty of forming sugar. His own work would show, however, "that physiology opposes . . . that point of view." [34]

By this time Bernard obviously did see his discovery as a new challenge to the chemical theories of Dumas. That does not mean, however, that he had necessarily set out either with Dumas's theory as his guide or with the objective of refuting the reigning nutritional views. Undoubtedly he was aware throughout the investigation of the connection between his findings and the prevailing belief that sugar in the animal is exclusively of alimentary origin; yet, as I have maintained in the preceding chapter, such considerations were probably not the driving force in his investigation. We have seen that Bernard had always been alert for any outcome which he could turn into an occasion to demonstrate the weaknesses of the theories of the chemists. I think it most probable that, once he had accumulated evidence that sugar is present in the blood under conditions in which it could not have derived from the accepted alimentary sources of that substance, he began to realize that he had at hand the most powerful rebuttal yet to the whole approach of the chemists. Then he recast the emphasis of the research itself to make that refutation his central point.

The recasting was substantial. In his memoir Bernard presented four "series of experiments" which led by logical steps to the conclusion that the liver forms sugar independently of the nature of alimentation. The sequence did not represent literally the order in which he had performed the research. He did not claim that it did, although he left a distinct impression that he had followed the same progression he presented. He omitted results which did not contribute to his conclusion, and relegated to an inconspicuous sentence in the last paragraph the fact that sugar diminished or even completely disappeared in "animals enfeebled by a very long abstinence, or having become sick or dead of disease." [35] Among the carefully selected experiments he described he sometimes left out elements which were not essential to his case.[36] He gave only one hint that he had not sailed on a straight course toward the objective which his memoir embodied. When he had begun to consider where the sugar in the blood of animals nourished with meat came from, he said, "After some groping which I believe is useless to report here, I was led to search for the source of the sugar" in the abdominal organs.[37] He was, of course, perfectly justified not to clutter up his memoir with digressions which would detract from the force of his argument. The argument, however, can easily be mistaken for a historical account of his discovery.[38]

The first series of experiments, one on a rabbit and three on dogs, showed that whether an animal is fed carrots, starch, or meat, or is left for two days without food, its blood contains sugar. Bernard reported that he had reproduced these experiments "a great number of times with similar results." The next question, he continued, "for the solution of which we must now institute new experiments," is where the sugar in the blood of animals on a meat diet or in abstinence comes from. That search constituted the second series of experiments. The first two of these, one on a dog fed meat, the other on a fasting dog, showed that the portal vein contained much sugar, the blood in the heart somewhat less, the stomach and the thoracic lymph none. These investigations, which he also "repeated many times," led him to conclude that the source must be some abdominal organ neighboring the portal vein.[39] Here we can see that Bernard had separated into two logical stages experiments which were originally mingled together. He had discovered the sugar in the portal vein in the second experiment showing sugar to be generally present in the blood in the absence of a known alimentary source. Then he immediately tried to ascertain the source of the sugar. Later he went back to the problem of the dietary conditions under which sugar was present. Thereafter the two efforts sometimes alternated, sometimes merged.

The last experiment Bernard placed in the second series in his memoir was one in which he ligatured the branches of the portal vein connected to the small intestine, the spleen, and the pancreas, and the central trunk of the vein near the liver. Drawing blood from the portions of the vein adjacent to each of these organs, he found sugar only in the blood next to the liver. He then analyzed pieces of each organ and found that only the liver tissue contained sugar. "From that time," he said, "it was evident that it was from the liver that the sugar was issuing." [40] Here his account followed rather closely the manner in which he did reach that conclusion, except that he substituted for his original experiment a more elaborate and decisive refinement.

Dealing next with the question of how the liver could be the source of the sugar in blood which was not leaving but entering the organ, Bernard described how he had ligatured the portal vein at the liver immediately after killing an animal. Then no sugar appeared in the vein. He explained that in the cases in which he had not followed this procedure the expansion of the vein when he opened the abdomen, the loss of pressure in it, and the lack of valves in its lumen could easily account for a reflux of blood from the liver into the vein. "From which it follows," he asserted, "that in the physiological state sugar does not exist in the blood which enters the liver." [41] This was a reasonable deduction from his data. It was also important for his understanding of the situation, largely because of his belief that the sugar is rapidly destroyed in the blood. It was not accurate, of course, and the validity of his theory that the liver produces sugar which it secretes into the blood did not require it to be true. A few years later his insistence on it caused him difficulties. In 1855 Louis Figuier attacked his theory. Some of Figuier's arguments were gratuitous, but he made the very serious claim that he had found sugar in the portal vein. As Bernard defended himself he utilized at first his whole range of evidence, of which by then he had accumulated a great deal. Meanwhile, however, Lehmann published a confirmation of Bernard's opinion that there is no sugar in the portal vein. Thus encouraged, Bernard made that particular issue the fulcrum on which his whole theory rested. "All of the arguments relative to the question of knowing whether the liver fabricates sugar or not," he stated at a meeting of the Academy, "must be led back to that fundamental experiment . . . as long as it remains established that the blood which enters the liver does not contain sugar and that the blood which leaves it contains considerable proportions of it, it will be necessary to admit that sugar is produced in the liver." [42] By thus oversimplifying the problem Bernard made his own position unnecessarily vulnerable. He won the debate officially, largely because the commissioners of the Academy chosen to judge the dispute did not give Figuier's method a fair hearing.[43]

The "third series of experiments" which Bernard presented in his memoir of October 1848 was actually a description of his methods for detecting sugar in liver tissue, and some related considerations. In the final series he met the possible objection that the liver merely accumulated sugar previously derived from aliments and returned it to the blood when the animal was not receiving any in its diet. Although he acknowledged that the liver might do that in some circumstances, he argued that such an interpretation could not account for the result of an experiment in which he had deprived a dog of all food for eight days, then fed it meat alone for eleven days. At the end of the time, both blood and liver contained normal amounts of sugar. Sugar stored from prior food would have been eliminated long before then, he thought. To demonstrate that it disappears rapidly when something interrupts its formation, he summarized the experiments in which he had severed the vagus nerves of a dog and of a rabbit. When the animals died, within two days, sugar was gone from both blood and liver. The liver is, Bernard now concluded, "at the same time both the *source* and the *origin* of the saccharine material in animals." [44]

Bernard had not lost his original interest in the destruction of sugar in the body. That question was merely overshadowed by his discoveries concerning its origin, and he promised to discuss the destruction in a later paper.[45] The brief remark in his memoir was probably related to an entry in his notebook which reveals that he may have been considering another boldly speculative hypothesis. Noting the progressive disappearance of the normal sugar in blood samples, he wondered if that type of sugar might be "more easily destructible than the true sugar of diabetes." If such were the case, then the cause of diabetes could be a failure of the body to manufacture the more destructible sugar. "Perhaps," he went on, "the lungs [normally] modify that sugar in such a way that it would be more destructible? To resolve that question it will be necessary to find out if diabetics exhale carbonic acid." He conjectured further that perhaps diabetic sugar is destroyed as lactic acid and ordinary blood sugar as carbonic acid. "Would it be in the lungs that by taking up oxygen the sugar acquires the power to change into CO_2?" [46] These thoughts would only have got Bernard into further difficulties if he had pursued them then. Diabetic sugar was not really different chemically from ordinary glucose. Bernard's effort to determine where sugar is destroyed was based on his oversimplified view of the nature of the destructive process, abetted by analytical techniques inadequate to detect the sugar in the blood in the concentrations that are normal to all parts of the circulation. Furthermore, the simple qualitative tests for sugar he was using in 1848 could not have revealed the small decreases in the concentration along the course of the circulation which would accompany a gradual consumption of the substance.[47] Thus his conception and his methods had constrained him to look for a more drastic, localized process of a sort which does not exist in animals. He could not have succeeded with the plan on which he was embarked in the summer of that year. The unexpected observations which shifted his effort from that problem to the source of the sugar rescued him from the danger of floundering in another doomed venture.

Bernard's discovery of the source of sugar, like that of the action of pancreatic juice on fats, arose out of circumstances remarkably well suited to his special experience and talents. It required extraordinary surgical skill as well as alertness to operative opportunities. The means he used to collect blood from deep within the circulating system of living animals, and the ligaturing of the portal vein so quickly as to prevent a reflux of blood from the liver, illustrate crucial aspects of the experiments demanding skills in which few could equal Bernard. The chemistry required was again relatively uncomplicated. He utilized chiefly two tests for sugar—fermentation and Barreswil's reagent—which he had long used routinely.[48] Finding the conditions under which blood and liver tissue yield consistent results with these tests was an important achievement; but he himself maintained that "nothing is so simple or so easy as to confirm the presence" of sugar in the liver. The investigation of sugar in the blood was also "very simple." With the more complicated chemical problem of extracting the sugar from the liver he did not succeed; but "from my point of view," he said, that did not seem essential, and he gladly left it for the chemists.[49]

Bernard's discovery of the origin of sugar in animals set the course for much of his activity for the rest of his career. During the next decade, his most productive, he added to the basic achievement equally imposing further developments. By 1857 he had isolated the substance within the liver from which the sugar was formed, and duplicated the reaction outside the organism.[50] The investigation moved him to the forefront of the rapidly expanding field of nutritional physiology. The impact of the initial discovery, like that of the pancreatic function, was especially strong because it was not along a line others had been following, yet immediately relevant to current concerns. As Henri Milne Edwards afterward put it:

> For a long time we knew also that the digestion of starchy materials furnishes to the organism a considerable quantity of glucose, and consequently that one could, at first, suppose that all of the substances of that class which appear in the animal economy derive from that source . . . but an unanticipated discovery and one of great importance came, in 1848, to change the ideas of physiologists in that respect, and to show that there is always production of sugar in the interior of the animal economy.[51]

The same discovery also fixed the general form which Bernard's pervasive concern with the relation between chemistry and physiology would take for the rest of his life. That problem was, in fact, the principal issue that he believed in October 1848 that he had settled. After summarizing his immediate results briefly near the end of his memoir, he wrote:

> It is evident that in the presence of these facts, that law, that animals do not create any immediate principle, but only destroy those which are fur-

nished to them by plants, must cease to be true, since, in fact, animals in a physiological state can, like plants, create and destroy sugar.

From the fact that the animal organism produces sugar without starch, something which the known chemical means do not permit us to do, I would not conclude that it is necessary to diminish the importance of chemical knowledge in the study of the phenomena of life. I am, on the contrary, among those who most value all of the progress which modern organic chemistry has contributed to physiology. Only I think, as I have already had occasion to say,[52] that in order to avoid error and render all of the service of which it is capable, chemistry must never venture alone in the examination of animal functions; I think that in many cases it alone can resolve the difficulties which block physiology, but it cannot anticipate it, and I think finally that in no case can chemistry believe itself authorized to restrict the resources of nature, which we do not know, to the limits of the facts or the processes which constitute our laboratory knowledge.[53]

Bernard thus refuted both a particular nutritional theory and the assumptions on which it had been formulated. One could not anticipate from the knowledge of chemical properties of organic substances what takes place within the organism. That was the same message which Magendie had tried to impart to the chemists involved in the controversy over animal fat during their debates in the Academy in 1843.[54] Bernard was now able, however, to give that message the force of a demonstration of the falsity of a central deduction derived from their approach. In the context of Bernard's discovery and of all that had gone before it, it is quite plain that he was asserting not that the resources of nature extended beyond chemical phenomena themselves, but beyond what chemists could reproduce of chemical phenomena. One simply could not foretell, from the limited, incomplete knowledge that laboratory reactions provided, what chemical processes were possible in living creatures. Here Bernard directly confronted a basic presumption of the same chemists. As we saw earlier, they considered it almost a prerequisite for supposing a process to occur within the organism that they be able to produce a similar type of reaction outside it.[55]

In 1853 Bernard made it explicit that the lesson of his discovery of the new function of the liver applied particularly to the methods of Liebig and Dumas. He expressed in an eloquent, tactful tone, the same basic point that Alfred Donné had made more harshly a decade before.[56] In a memoir describing all his research on the production of sugar in animals, Bernard wrote:

The rapid progress of organic chemistry and the fertile physiological impulse given to that science by the modern chemists and in particular by the works of MM. Dumas in France, Liebig in Germany, etc., have thrown great light on the diverse questions relating to nutrition in animals. But that luminous torch of chemistry would only have lighted the surface of the phenomena of life, if experimental physiology had not seized it to carry it into the midst of our organs, into the center of our interior functions, of which a great number are still surrounded with so many mysteries.[57]

Donné, writing when the debates of the chemists seemed to overshadow other efforts to deal with nutritional phenomena, had feared that their shallow approach would destroy the opportunity for a sounder application of chemistry to physiology. Ten years later Bernard could take a more confident attitude, because he believed that he had himself forestalled that danger.

In later years Bernard began to explore broader implications of his position. They led him eventually to view the fundamental phenomena of life as common to all organisms, in contrast to the "dualist" view of the followers of Dumas that animal and plant functions are opposite.[58] This and other philosophical ramifications only emerged, however, after Bernard had faced the chemists on the practical ground of whether the operating table or the test tube should take precedence in the investigation of nutritional phenomena.

The outcome of his search for sugar must have given Claude Bernard a gratifying sense of personal fulfillment. Beginning his career in the shadow of physiological theories pronounced by scientific tycoons from another field, the young experimentalist had vowed to find in his own resources and the tradition of his teacher means to prove that these chemists did not represent the true way to deal with animal chemistry. Through years of toil, of personal hardship, modest achievements and setbacks, he never abandoned his goal. Whenever the research he was pursuing offered the slightest opportunity, he returned to that theme. Now after five years he had achieved at once his greatest experimental triumph and the vindication of his belief. He had destroyed the reigning theory of the chemists at the same time that he proved the fertility of his physiological approach to the same problems. This denouement, however, contains one major flaw; for that law which Bernard claimed he was disproving had already ceased to exist in 1845 when its most important supporter, Jean-Baptiste Boussingault, capitulated over the source of animal fat. Moreover, even in its prime it had been fully accepted only within that segment of the scientific community focused on Paris. Why then did Bernard present the issue in 1848 as though the law in its full generality reigned until he challenged it? Would it not have been enough simply to claim that no one had specifically suspected that sugar is formed in animals until his methods disclosed the process?

I believe that this peculiar situation is best explained by the very fact that Bernard had for so long sought issues on which he could reveal the inadequacy of the chemical approach. Now that he had finally come upon a case which demonstrated his argument to perfection, he might understandably be reluctant to dilute the effect by mentioning the inconvenient fact that the chemists themselves, using their own criteria of verification, had already overthrown the "reigning nutritional theory." It was undoubtedly true that Dumas's attractive theoretical doctrines still had a strong residual influence in Paris, as popular ideas often have long after they have been effectively refuted. Bernard was, as we have noted, so closely oriented to his immediate scientific surroundings in Paris that he may not have noticed that this was a provincial influence. Furthermore, it was characteristic of Bernard not to keep himself consistently in touch with the main current of scientific events, not always to distinguish between the latest stage of development of a contemporary problem and arguments which had figured prominently at an earlier point.

Analogous motives can explain, I think, why in his account of his discovery in his *Introduction to the Study of Experimental Medicine* Bernard portrayed himself as having adhered to Dumas's theory until a sudden, unexpected result caused him to see its falsity. For didactic purposes he wished to illustrate simply and forcefully the importance of discarding a theory "in the presence of a well proven new fact in contradiction with it." [59] It was only a small step from representing Dumas's theory in 1848 as still intact, to depicting himself afterward as still guided by it in that period. Then he could concentrate the whole encounter between himself and the chemical theorists in one flash of insight, suitable to drive the lesson home with great impact. If he had tried to relate literally the course of events leading to his position after the discovery of the source of animal sugar, he would have had to describe so many complex situations and small forays that the main argument would have been lost in subtleties. I suspect, in fact, that these few compact events which he constructed mentally came to be for him a symbolic representation of a whole network of thoughts and activities which occupied the first period of his scientific life. It is that complex network which these pages have sought to revive.

XX

Conclusion

The propositions which Claude Bernard expressed concerning the relation between chemistry and the phenomona of life appear justified by his own success. They were, after all, largely abstractions of the issues which he defined by his own discoveries in the area of animal chemistry. They were another manifestation of his habit of drawing the broadest consequences out of particular experiences. Only by focusing exclusively on his successes, however, was Bernard able to support so persuasively his general position. If we consider also his less fortunate ventures, his arguments become less imposing.

We can see the issue most distinctly in the comparison between Bernard and Louis Mialhe. To the end of his life Bernard regarded Mialhe as a prime example of the overly chemical approach. In the unfinished manuscript of his *Principles of Experimental Medicine* Bernard wrote once more of the "great error" of those who thought that the physicochemical phenomena within organisms were identical to those which took place outside them. "It is that error into which certain chemists have fallen, who reason from the laboratory to the organism, whereas it is necessary to reason from the organism to the laboratory (error of Mialhe)." [1] Symbolically, at least, the symmetry of Bernard's statement neatly represents the relation between the two men, for in their respective strengths and limitations they were nearly mirror images. Mialhe was an able and experienced chemist. He had mastered the subtle art of separating and identifying organic substances well enough to apply the methods creatively. Thus he defined albuminose and salivary diastase chemically at the same time that he delineated physiologically significant chemical processes. When he

445

recognized that the physiological aspects of the problem required vivisection experiments, however, he had to ask a friend to help him perform the operations. He was able to borrow for his own needs an experiment created by Bernard's genius, but without extensive personal vivisectional experience he could not himself produce innovative physiological investigations. Claude Bernard was a brilliant operative physiologist. He displayed an ingenuity and dexterity which appeared even beyond his French circle to be *"bewundernswerth."* [2] His knowledge of the techniques of chemical analysis, however, was not outstanding. With the help of Pelouze and Barreswil he learned to use capably a variety of identification tests and extractions essential to his investigations, but he was not able to deploy the full power of the chemical knowledge of biologically important substances available in his time. [3] Whether one or the other of these men was better equipped for investigations in animal chemistry depended on the particular phenomena under study. In the case of gastric digestion Blondlot's fistula method had already solved the principal operative problem. Further definition of the physiological process required chiefly a refinement of knowledge of the chemical properties of the substances undergoing change and of the gastric ferment. Mialhe's approach and experience were better suited to these needs, and he was more successful. When Bernard sought to subordinate the chemical aspects of gastric digestion to the physiological conditions, he contributed observations which, although important in themselves, were peripheral to the understanding of the process itself. When he aimed for the heart of the chemical problem, his narrower chemical background did not prepare him to compete effectively. Either he ran into experimental contradictions he could not resolve or he published general conclusions which could not withstand criticism. The chief prerequisite for attacking pancreatic digestion, however, was a vivisectional procedure for obtaining the fluid in a normal state. Once Bernard had achieved this through his exceptional facility with such methods, he could observe relatively easily the chemical phenomena which interested him. Similarly, the most demanding technical problems in the search for sugar in the animal were operative rather than chemical. Thus each man found areas of investigation for which his own talents and point of view were well adapted. There was no fixed answer to the question of what was the appropriate relation between physiology and chemistry in the study of nutritional phenomena. Bernard's followers admiringly called him a "legislator" of the methods of experimental physiology; [4] but sometimes he tried to prescribe rules which were too restrictive, which equated what would be best for everyone with what had worked best for him.

The issues separating Bernard from Liebig and Dumas were more basic, for the gap between their respective experiences, methods, assumptions, and even their purposes, was much broader. These chemists had so obviously ignored physiological complexities in their initial presentations of the problem of animal nutrition that Bernard was able to dismiss their theories with ease in the areas in which they came into direct conflict. Nevertheless, the limitations of vision were reciprocal. The chemists could not appreciate the necessity for "direct experiments" to follow substances through the organism. Bernard was entirely justified in objecting that "one can determine exactly the two extreme terms of nutrition; but if one then tries to interpret the intermediary which separates them, one finds himself in an unknown, of which the imagination creates the greater part." [5] But he showed that he did not fully comprehend the significance of the interpretations Liebig and Dumas had offered when he wrote:

We can undoubtedly establish a balance between that which a living organism consumes as aliments and that which it renders as excretions; but those will only be pure statistical results, incapable of bringing illumination to the intimate phenomena of nutrition in living creatures. It would be, following the expression of a Dutch chemist [G. J. Mulder], like trying to tell what is taking place inside a house by watching what enters through the door and what leaves by the chimney. [6]

Through their understanding of the nature of chemical conversion processes the chemists could see connections between alimentation, respiratory exchanges, excretions, animal heat, and muscular work which must hold true, no matter how far they might err in their speculations about how these connections were manifested in the internal phenomena of nutrition. By the choice of the analogy he adopted, Bernard revealed that he had not grasped the chemists' meaning, for the measurement of the exchanges between the animal and its environment could provide fundamental insights about processes whose details it could not specify, just as the measurement of the materials entering and leaving a house could provide critical information if one were concerned about the way in which the temperature of the house is maintained rather than about the activities of its human occupants.

Similarly contrasting limitations of view appear in the way each of these men treated specific problems. Liebig had so little feel for the character of vital phenomena that he did not notice the incongruity of believing that the amount of heat and muscular work an animal produces varies directly with the quantities of nitrogenous and respiratory aliments it eats during the same period. Bernard was capable, when his direct measurements seemed to warrant it, of assuming that whatever quantity of sugar passes into the blood is destroyed almost immediately. In terms of the conversion processes which the chemists understood, the consequences would be irreconcilable with the stable production of heat characteristic of the animals Bernard was investigating.[7] Dumas, on the other hand, depended so exclusively on reasoning from his knowledge of the conversion processes that his colleague thought it superfluous to demonstrate that the sugar in the blood which his theory demanded was actually present.[8] Bernard and the chemists saw the same problems in such different ways because they approached them from different directions. Dumas and Liebig, confident in their grasp of the chemical properties of organic substances, had little intimate knowledge of the inner functions of living animals;[9] Bernard, steeped in the observation and manipulation of vital phenomena, had a relatively superficial understanding of chemical processes. Bernard thought that his approach constituted a refutation of that of the chemists. Ultimately, the approaches turned out to be complementary. Each contributed to the further investigation of animal chemistry a crucial element which was beyond the reach of the authors of the other.

Recently, Joseph Schiller has analyzed the differences between Bernard's use of chemistry in physiology and the approach of Liebig and Dumas. The methods of the latter were sterile, according to Schiller, because they proposed an "eminently chemical" solution for an "essentially physiological" problem. Only Bernard closed the gap, subordinating the chemistry to animal experimentation in a synthesis which established a new physiology.[10] Schiller's interpretation is penetrating and valuable, but it depends, I think, on some questionable assumptions. First, he treats Dumas's *Chemical Statics* and Liebig's *Animal Chemistry* as though these represented the final definitive views of the authors and their schools. The French chemists modified both their theories and their standards of judgement, however, during the course of the controversy concerning fat. Liebig also had grown more circumspect by 1847. Had the followers of their views not been able to sift out the fruitful conceptions and methods from the fanciful excesses, the approach they represented could never have had the lasting influence it actually attained. Second, Schiller portrays Liebig and Dumas as the only alternative to Bernard's investigations present in his time. In fact, as we have seen, several other currents of research were flourishing, including the more cautious animal chemistry pioneered by Berzelius, eclectic investigations such as those of Lehmann, and especially the chemistry of digestion pursued on the basis of the pepsin theory. Schiller's most crucial premise is that Bernard was correct in his view that nutrition and its related processes were essentially physiological problems and that chemistry must play an auxiliary role in their treatment. Yet these phenomena were chemical in as real a sense as they were physiological. Bernard insisted that the relation was an unequal one. Chemistry could only supply tools of analysis; the definition of problems and hence direction of investigations must be physiological.[11] In fact the situation could not be so simply defined. New problems were arising on an indistinctly delineated frontier between two older disciplines. Which of these sciences should predominate depended on the nature of the individual questions asked and on conditions peculiar to certain problems which could not always be foreseen. Questions which chemists asked were as legitimate as those physiologists asked, so long as each recognized that the methods of his science alone could not provide complete solutions. Perhaps because he reacted against chemists who had overrated the self-sufficiency of chemical reasoning about biological phenomena, Bernard underrated its role.

Bernard asserted, as we have seen, that chemists produced discordant analyses of the substances comprising animal fluids and tissues because they failed to consider physiological variations affecting the composition of the materials. Only by carefully controlled experiments on living animals could these critical physiological conditions be identified. One should first investigate the chemical processes which actually occur in animals, then explain them through laboratory reactions. Less well known than Bernard's arguments, but equally cogent, were the quite different remarks of Carl Lehmann. Vivisection experiments according to Lehmann often led to confusing, divergent results, because the unknown causes of variation attending them were particularly numerous and unpredictable. So far, such investigations had produced few valuable results concerning the chemical transformation of substances within the organisms, largely because too little was known of the chemical processes themselves. "The chemistry still leaves us in the lurch too often to achieve with these methods the success that they promise." Therefore, the most pressing need was a fuller knowledge of the chemical transformations which particular substances undergo outside of the body. Eventually,

Lehmann conceded, experiments on living animals must form "the capstone of all physiological-chemical investigation," without which "a theory of animal metabolism [*Stoffwechsel*] remains always a very hazardous undertaking." Under present conditions, however, efforts to trace the processes directly within the organism did not necessarily lead to results more conclusive than did efforts to imitate the chemical phenomena outside it.[12] Lehmann and Bernard did not disagree fundamentally in their understanding of the relation of chemical and physiological phenomena, but had quite different perspectives concerning the immediate research priorities.

In the debate which Bernard carried on, questions about the relation between vital phenomena and chemical processes merged with questions of method. Underlying both, however, was a jurisdictional dispute over which of the two existing sciences, organic chemistry or physiology, was best fitted to control the emerging domain of research involving both. In his recent study, *The Scientific Community*, Warren O. Hagstrom has pointed out that often in science "arguments about policies and goals shade into arguments about substantive truth, and in many cases one can make only analytical distinctions between them."[13] Bernard's position involved such a mixed situation. He moved almost insensibly from the issue of whether chemical phenomena within organisms were identical to those outside them, to the issue of whether chemists or physiologists ought to lead the investigation of the phenomena. In one such discussion he ended up simply declaring, "But I repeat, in all of this it is life which is the object and the other sciences are only means of investigation. It is therefore necessary above all to be a physiologist."[14]

Bernard saw the issue in terms of the two sciences as they were constituted in 1840, but neither proved adequate to define the new problems. Instead, the problems defined a new science. The naiveté about biological phenomena which Liebig and Dumas displayed was not due simply to personal blind spots; it revealed the fact that an organic chemist of the period received in his training and research little exposure to such phenomena. By this time chemists obtained highly organized professional education in Liebig's laboratory or others patterned after it. They learned to deal with organic processes, but not organized processes, as Bernard expressed the distinction.[15] Physiological training, on the other hand, did not provide a thorough background in chemistry. Bernard made up for this deficiency as best he could by attending courses and by spending much of his time in Pelouze's laboratory. In this way he acquired essential experience for the solution of problems directly related to his research, but he did not develop the deep familiarity with chemical methods and processes which formal preparation for a career in chemistry could provide. In the early part of the century the interaction between the two sciences was still restricted enough so that those in either needed to pay only nominal attention to the other. Physiologists could append brief chemical discussions to their descriptions of the anatomy and functions of organs. Chemists could speculate loosely on the physiological consequences of the properties of organic materials they had observed. By 1840, however, a deeper interaction was needed. Liebig was able to move hastily into the arena of animal chemistry and yet be influential because he perceived that a vacuum existed. "Physiology took no share in the advancement of chemistry," he wrote with only moderate exaggeration. Physiologists had acquired their own ways of investigation when chemistry could provide little assistance, but the time for a change was now at hand.[16] Liebig and Dumas filled the gap in a makeshift, temporary way. Already, however, the specialty which would occupy this ground more securely was emerging. In 1843 Carl Lehmann became Professor of physiological chemistry at Leipzig,[17] a sign that a new discipline had already taken sufficient form to become institutional.

Lehmann's *Lehrbuch der physiologischen Chemie*, the first edition of which appeared in 1842, and the more influential second edition in 1853, provided an organized view of the nascent science.[18] The final aim of physiological chemistry, in his view, was "to discover precisely and in their causal connections the course of the chemical phenomena which accompany vital processes," and to "derive them from known physical and chemical laws." The first step was to investigate the "organic substrates," the properties and reactions of the chemical substances comprising the animal body. The methods derived from general organic chemistry, but in physiological chemistry the chemical viewpoint must always be amalgamated with the physiological. Chemical properties of individual substances must always be considered in relation to their roles in the organism. The next step would be to determine the "topography" of these substances, that is, their distribution within the fluids, tissues, and organs of the body. On these bases one could finally investigate the processes in which the substances are involved, achieving eventually a *Lehre vom Stoffwechsel*. In the current low state of development of the first two phases, the only rigorous method available for the third was the comparison of materials entering the body with their end products, the "statical" method used by Liebig, Boussingault, and their followers. That could not lead to knowledge of the course of the processes per se, but could at least serve as a general guide for other kinds of investigation, and later as a control on their results. A deeper penetration into the processes could come only from the investigation of the chemical transformations of the substances outside the organism and ultimately from experiments on living animals.[19] Thus Lehmann saw a place for each of the kinds of research which his contemporaries had carried on, and he guarded at the same time against deriving conclusions from each type beyond what it could legitimately offer. His view encompassed the earlier animal chemistry of Berzelius, the more recent version of Liebig, the chemical statics of Dumas and Boussingault, the digestion investigations surrounding the pepsin theory, and vivisection experiments like those of Bernard. He applied these considerations critically in his own investigations as well as in his reviews of the current state of knowledge. An eclectic approach is often a less inspired one, and Lehmann made none of the brilliant thrusts which characterized Bernard's greatest achievements. Yet Lehmann could see, more distinctly than either Bernard or his chemical rivals, the outlines of a future science whose whole program was the investigation of the chemical phenomena of life.

It would hardly be fair to consider Bernard as narrower because he did not embrace as many facets of this particular area of problems. Professional specialization necessarily permits deepened understanding in certain directions at the expense of closer boundaries in other directions. His own accomplishments were not restricted to those physiological phenomena immediately related to chemical processes, but ranged, even in his early years, over such diverse problems as the organization of the nervous system, the effects of poisons, and the mechanics of the circulation. Each involved proficiency with a special set of techniques and acquaintance with a special set of issues. He himself wrote down what amounts to his own best defense: "It is not possible to be an encyclopedist: one cannot demand that a man who is a profound physiologist be at the same time a consummate chemist, physician, and mathematician."[20] As a physiologist he was unexcelled.

Sometimes, very general scientific issues dissolve through further advances of knowledge or the formation of new fields redefining the problems. The question of the relation of vital processes to physical and chemical ones is so basic, however, that it has never disappeared as a source of controversy.[21] Debates resolved in one context reappear in another. The growth of a science especially adapted to the study of the chemical phenomena of life could not exclude biologists in other fields from further concern with the same phenomena. In the areas of overlap, differences of opinion concerning priorities, methods, and conceptions have repeatedly arisen. An example which is particularly interesting because it involved language so reminiscent of Bernard's own position was a complaint which another physiologist, Yandell Henderson, made seventy-five years later. Reviewing the subject of the regulation of the acid-base balance of the blood, Henderson wrote:

> Such facts as these would seem to force recognition of a physiological regulation, a more fundamental mechanism, a superintending nature or physis, determining the particular physicochemical system or interior condition of which the blood should consist at the time . . . Most investigators of the acid-base balance of the blood do not, however, see regulation thus physiologically, but merely chemically. They seem to regard the body as if it were a sort of beaker, or other vessel, containing a standard blood that may be thrown out of normality by the addition of an excess of some constituent.[22]

The particular problems had changed, but the broader issue was the same one that Bernard raised when he objected to treating the stomach as a chemical retort. In both cases the underlying question was more of method and perspective than of ultimate explanatory principles. Powerful new means of analysis had induced people to focus on the question which those techniques could answer, and to neglect other factors less amenable to their own modes of investigation.

Thus the confrontation which we have followed between Claude Bernard and the chemists has a particular interest because of its intimate mixture of timeless issues with events peculiar to a special stage in the development of the sciences involved. Debates over the relation of physiology to chemistry were not new even then, but they took on a new intensity because the question had for the first time become a serious determinant of the direction of major research efforts. In an age in which controversies were carried on in the scientific literature with unusual openness, the issues were posed sharply. Inexperience with the practical limits of their untested disciplines enticed both chemists and physiologists to disclose by their own transgressions what the nature of the problems were. They portrayed in stark, easily recognizable contours, issues which in subtler forms continued to shadow their successors.

I have presented Bernard's view of the relation between chemical and vital phenomena as one growing out of his practical research concerns. Other writers have emphasized the deeper philosophical nature of his position, and it has even been suggested that the "philosophy of the living system adopted by . . . [him] very definitely determined the experimental procedure that . . . [he] used." [23] It is true that one can trace in Bernard's early years a few instances of experiments which may have been directly influenced by such considerations.[24] Even if, as I contend, Bernard addressed himself primarily to the methods for obtaining knowledge of the phenomena involved, rather than to the ultimate status of the explanations, he could conceivably have reached his position from general principles rather than current practices. We have seen that Auguste Comte derived from abstract arguments a general position somewhat like that of Bernard.[25] Yet I think it unrealistic to treat the dynamic factor in Bernard's thought as philosophical in origin. When he worked out his basic position, he was first of all trying to establish himself in a highly competitive profession in which recognition depended on productive, original research. He defined his stand by comparing how he was learning to cope with physiological phenomena experimentally to the methods that chemists of great influence were popularizing. Undoubtedly he absorbed, during his medical training and through less formal communications, attitudes formulated by others from philosophical reasoning. Such influences should be explored. Their effects can only be evaluated meaningfully, however, by defining where they impinged upon the tangible web of research activities which I have attempted to describe.[26]

In later years, when his secure position permitted it, his teaching encouraged it, and his health sometimes forced it, Bernard took more time to read and meditate about the broader implications of his work for physiology, for science in general, and for the definition of life itself. In those years, when August Comte's popularity was at its peak, Comte may well have influenced Bernard's view of the relation between chemistry and physiology. In the *Introduction to the Study of Experimental Medicine* and in some subsequent writings, Bernard developed ideas concerning experimentation, determinism, the limits of knowledge, and other questions, which were so close to the spirit of positivist philosophy that D. G. Charlton has picked him as one of the two thinkers of the period most faithful to positivist tenets.[27] It was also in the *Introduction*, and especially in the passage quoted near the beginning of the present study, that Bernard described the relation of chemistry to physiology in terms most reminiscent of Comte's discussion. Then Bernard spoke of chemists trying to absorb physiology, and emphasized as Comte had done, that chemistry must serve merely as an analytical tool for physiologists. In his later writings Bernard stated repeatedly that the physiological point of view must dominate the chemical point of view.[28] These resemblances suggest that Comte's treatment of the problem may have helped Bernard to generalize thoughts which he had previously expressed in more limited contexts. Even then, it is questionable how deep the similarities ran, for Bernard rejected Comte's "false ideas . . . concerning the supposed progressive complexity of the sciences,"[29] ideas which underlay Comte's view of the connection between chemistry and physiology. Only a close study of the development of Bernard's thought and work between 1850 and 1865 can reveal how much of the later formulation of his ideas on this question is attributable to philosophical influences, and how much must be ascribed to the continuation of his experimental investigations and his interactions with other experimental scientists. Whatever such a study may show, it is nevertheless clear that his basic attitude was already formed by 1848. Underlying all of his later thought were the experiences he had acquired in those years when he struggled to find a place in the tightly structured scientific world of Paris.

Appendices
Abbreviations Used in Bibliography and Notes
Bibliography
Notes
Index

Appendix A

(see Chapter XV, n. 26)

MS C. VIIIe, 7c, pp. 119–120.

Le 4 mars, 1847, sur un tres-gros lapin mâle j'injecte dans la veine jugulaire 3 décigrammes de levure de bière fraiche-puis après j'injecte dans le tissu cellulaire du dos une dissolution concentrée de sucre de canne à laquelle j'ajoute un peu de prussiate pour reconnaître l'absorption ces injections sont faites a midi ½; le lapin n'en paraît pas très-sensiblement incommodé au moment même.

à 2 heures je reviens voir le lapin, il paraît triste et se tient calme d^s un coin. Il a les yeux abattues presque ½ fermés: la respiration est considérablement accélérée, les pulsations très-rapides. Alors je fais pisser le lapin et je compare ces urines ainsi qu'il suit.

1. ...

[The omitted paragraph describes the urine before the operation. It contained no sugar].

2. urines rendues par le lapin à deux heures (1^h½ après l'injection de la levure et du sucre) ..... par réactif bleu *directement* q.q. traces de sucre, mais excessivement peu. par réactif bleu après ébullition avec SO^3—quantités énormes de sucre c.a.d. de précipité. Il y a également du prussiate d'une manière très nette. [Boiling with sulfate was necessary to detect cane sugar with Barreswil's test. The "traces de sucre" was glucose].

...

Le lendemain matin 5 mars je trouve l'animal mort.

The comparable passage in the memoir is in *Archives gén. méd.* 1848, 16: 82–83:

' Sur un gros lapin, j'injectai dan la veine jugulaire 3 décigrammes de levure de bière fraiche délayée dans un peu d'eau; puis, au moyen d'une piqûre faite à la peau du dos, j'introduisis dans le tissu cellulaire un dissolution de sucre de canne …

[The omitted passage is a discussion of the purpose of the experiment].

Les deux injections furent faites à midi et demi, et le lapin ne parut pas influencé immédiatement après cette opération. À deux heures, je revis le lapin: il était triste et se tenait calme dans un coin; il avait les yeux abattus, à demi fermes; la respiration était accélérée, saccadée; les pulsations très-rapides. Un autre lapin, dans les veines duquel j'avais injectés quelques gouttes d'alcool étendues d'eau pour faire la comparaison, se trouvait dans un état assez semblable; cependant le lapin à la levure paraissait plus malade. Le sucre n'était pas arrivé dans l'urine, d'où je conclus que la levure l'avait détruit, et en avait fait de l'alcool. Le lendemain matin, je revis les deux lapins. Celui qui avait eu un peu d'alcool injecté dans la veine vivait et était revenu de son assoupissement; l'autre, qui avait eu la levure dans le sang, était mort.

The descriptions of the autopsy on the animal also support the contention that it is the same experiment. The wording does not correspond so closely, because the memoir summarizes briefly a long description in the notebook; but all of the details of a distinctive set of abnormalities included in the former are also described in the latter. It is puzzling, of course, that the second rabbit is not described in the notebook. But I think it much more improbable that the exact correspondences in the times of day mentioned could have been coincidental.

Appendix B

(See Chapter XV, n. 30)

MS C.VIIIe, 7a No. 2, p.86:

Sur un chien de petite taille, j'ai enlevé l'estomac et j'ai injecté par la veine crurale de cyanure de mercure. Environ ½ minute après l'animal est empoisonné. Il respire difficilement et meurt dans les convulsions, et il exhale par la gueule l'odeur d'acide prussique.

Bernard, *Archives gén. méd.*, 1848, *16*: 220:

Sur un chien de petite taille et bien portant, j'ai enlevé, par une large plaie faite a l'abdomen, 1. l'estomac, 2. les reins, 3. la vessie. Après avoir placé les ligatures convenables, la plaie fut recousie. Au bout de quelques instants, j'injectai par la veine crurale 6 grammes d'une dissolution à 8 pour 100 de cyanure de mercure. Une demi-minute après, l'animal respirait difficilement; bientôt les convulsions survinrent, et il mourut en exhalant fortement l'acide prussique par la gueule. À l'autopsie, tous les tissus étaient imprégnés de l'odeur cyanhydrique, et nulle part cependant je ne trouvai de liquide à réaction acide.

Eight percent mercury of cyanide was also the concentration Bernard was using in other experiments on the day of the above notebook record. There is little doubt that the experiment of injecting the salt into the leg isolated except for its artery and vein, which in both cases above follow the quoted experiment, was the same one.

Appendix C

(See Chapter II at n. 4)

Mais quelles idées on a à Paris sur la nutrition!! Si on avait prouvé que le faeces ou l'urine des personnes nourris de gélatine renfermaient de la gélatine, je ne dirai rien, mais conclure des faits qu'on a observé que la gélatine ne peut servir à quelque chose dans l'organisme c'est une absurdité. Elle ne peut remplacer ou se changer en sang, ni faire engraisser, mais elle peut servir à la reproduction des membranes et de les substances des cellules, et elle sert pour cela. Veuillez dire à Mr. D'arcet que je m'occupe d'un grand travail sur la nutrition, òu je traiterai tout ce qui se rapporte la gélatine; un premier mémoire a paru dans le cahier d'Aout de mes Annales, et tu me rendras dévoué si tu voudrais le faire entrer dans les Annales de chimie. Mr. D'arcet peut faire de ma lettre tout ce qui lui semble bon. C'est une honte pour les physiologistes que des expériences aussi mal fait peuvent avoir de valeur dans leurs vues. Sans avoir une idée nette sur l'assimilation, peut on se fier à de telles expériences. On recommande le chocolat, l'arrowroot, et tant de choses comme nourrissant, qui ne produisent pas une goutte de sang, qui ne peuvent remplacer en aucune manière ce que les organes ont perdu. Fais traduire mon mémoire mon cher Pelouze, et ne crains pas de me compromettre. Chaque mot dans mon mémoire à été dit et redit avec les physiologistes les plus habiles de l'allemagne, et ce n'est qu'après les avoir convaincu de la justesse de mes vues, que je me suis décidé à les imprimer. Il se fait une grande reforme dans la physiologie, et cette reforme se base sur la chimie organique. C'est bien un triomphe sur l'empirisme et sur les théories creuses qu'ils se sont imaginé. Pour moi il est bien indifférent si les physiologistes français adoptent mes vues, mais ils n'oseront pas rejeter mes expériences et mes analyses, et certes en les reconaissant comme vrai, ils seront bien forcés à faire les mêmes conclusions.... Tu concluras mon cher Pelouze que je suis aigri, et que c'est le dépit qui me fait parler ainsi. Tu ne te trompe pas. Les physiologistes français auraient du me prêter quelque attention. Ce n'était pas pour la chimie, mais pour la physiologie et pour l'agriculture, que j'ai sacrifié une année de ma vie, et je n'aime pas qu'on insulte mon enfant, qui a été élevé et avec bien de soins et bien de la peine.

Appendix D

(See Chapter V at n. 8)

Voici, le travail que je vous ai annoncé sur la nourriture aux betteraves et aux P. de terre. Si vous êtes décidé à recommencer la guerre, le présentez à l'académie et dans tous les cas le faire imprimer dans nos annales. Peut-être pourriez vous rendre à l'académie quelques lignes du commencement et surtout quelques lignes de la fin.

J'ai mis au net une première expérience sur les porcs, et les résultats sont tellement en faveur de l'assimilation directe que je ne veux pas la rendre publique, j'en attendrai une seconde, qui se termine en ce moment, puis une troisième. Si cette première expérience eut été contraire à nos idées, j'aurais mis à la publier toute la précipitation que vous avez mis dans l'affaire des abeilles; on est toujours bien venu du public quand on le régale d'un désappointement, même en y mettant toute la componction possible. Pour les vaches aux pommes de terre on peut aller en toute sûreté; je présente d'abord des faits, et je les crois parfaitement constatés. Je n'ai épargné aucune peine, aucune dépense pour bien observer; puis j'explique ces faits a ma manière, ou plutôt à notre manière, peut-être même serait-il bon que dans la conclusion votre nom et celui de Payen se trouvaient engagés: voyez.

Page 2

Voici le résultat de la première expérience sur les porcs. Deux frères jumeaux, âgés de 7 mois ont fait les frais de l'observation. On en a saigné un, le n°1 qui pesait en vie 60.55k. Son frère le n°2 a été mis aux pommes de terre et à l'eau fraiche, on l'a privé de litière, circonstance qu'il ne faut pas négliger, car le porc aux pommes de terre dévore sa litière. Ce porc pesait 9.5k. En 205 jours, depuis la mort de son frère, il a mangé environ 1500 Kil. de pommes de terre; il pesait alors: $\frac{1}{4.5}$k il avait gagné 24k à 25k. Je l'ai fait tuer, et je l'ai fait disséquer par le même artiste qui avait fait l'anatomie de l'autre.

	Porc N° 1 pesant 60.5k		N° 2 pesant 84k	
avec soies et oreille	5.01		7.96	
bouillis et essuyés	3.83		9.00	
des os et de la graisse adherente aux os	0.87 ⎫		0.90 ⎫	
lard (sans la peau)	9.47 ⎪		10.00 ⎪	
saindoux	2.30 ⎬	gras 15.48k	3.50 ⎬	gras 17.39
graisse adhérente à l'intérieur	2.84 ⎭		2.99 ⎭	
viande rouge	23.20		34.25	
sang	2.17		2.60	
intestins	10.86		13.25	
dejections	0.15			
	60.55		84.05	

Dans la pomme de terre jaune, comme dans la pomme de terre rouge, je trouve à l'aide d'un bon procédé, 0.002 de belle graisse.

Page 3

La nourriture a donc apporté 3 kil. de graisse *anhydre,* ce qui ferait plus que le gras trouvé en excès. Mais en faisant réduction pour la graisse du caca qui été très proprement dosé, et analysé, il devient évident que le pore N° 2 ne contient que la graisse qu'il devoit avoir d'après nos idées d'assimilation direct. Vous comprenez qu'on ne peut pas publier un résultat aussi favorable, nos *amis* diraient que c'est un roman. Après tout, l'expérience a été conduite avec un soin tout particulier, et notez que les infractions à la consigne que le porcher pourrait avoir commit se devraient contre nous. Si l'on ne se permet pas de publier ces résultats, on peut en causer avec ses vrais amis. Peut-être même pourriez vous dire à l'académie la chose comme elle est, c'est à dire que le résultat est tellement satisfaisant que nous n'osons pas le publier avant de le voir confirmé par d'autres expériences. Vous causerez toujours, quoiqu'il arrive plus tard, un moment de plaisir à nos *amis.*

Vient maintenant une question qui m'a vivement préoccupé. Le résultat précédent, je l'ai d'abord jugé comme n'étant que d'une très mince valeur; en voici la raison. Le porc N° 2 nourri pendant 205 jours avec des pommes de terre n'a pris qu'une quantité insignifiante de graisse, c'est très bien et cela est concevable; mais ce que l'on conçoit moins, c'est comment le porc N° 1 avant la mort, pouvait [avoir] acquis, dans sept mois, c'était son âge, 15 à 16 kilog. de gras. Il est vrai que dans l'allaitement et pendant les deux mois qui la suivent, la base de la nourriture est du lait, ou du lait caillé; mais ensuite, le porc n'a plus que 5 à 6 k des pommes de terre, délayées dans de l'eau grasse. Alors est venue cette question, qu'est-ce que l'eau grasse et combien un porc en consomme-t-il par jour. Vous comprenez, mon

Page 4

cher ami, que pour un membre de l'académie des sciences qui a été un des brillants officiers de l'état-major du libertador, il est assez humiliant d'analyser de l'eau de vaisselle. J'ai cependant passé par là, et c'est bien pénible je vous assure, j'en ai perdu l'appétit par suite du profond dégout que m'imposai l'odeur de cuisine. N'allez pas trop vous alarmer cependant: je pèse toujours 100 kil. L'eau grasse donnée chaque jour aux porcs a pour origine 1° tout le petit lait, 2° tout le lait de beurre, 3° les débris de table et l'eau de vaisselle qui dérivent des 32 personnes qui sont nourries au Bechelbronn. L'eau de vaisselle (il faut que vous en ayez votre part) ne va pas toute entière à l'eau grasse, on la laisse reposer dans une cuve; et c'est seulement la partie supérieure, le dépôt qui s'y forme, qui va à la porcherie, la couche intermédiaire est jetée. Voici une analyse d'eau grasse: 1 litre d'eau grasse évaporé au bain marie a laissé un résidu brun, cristallin de 47.3 gr. Dans 1/ ... matière, riche en sucre de lait, l'éther a indiqué, en prenant toutes les précautions, 0.091 d'une très belle graisse. Le litre d'eau grasse contient en conséquence 4.34 gr. de graisse.

Deux séries d'expériences m'ont démontré que chaque porc reçoit avec les pommes de terre, par jour, en 2 repas, de 9 à 10 litres d'eau grasse, dans laquelle il entre 36 à 43 gramme de gras *anhydre*. Ce qui, réuni à 12 gr. du gras des pommes de terre, et à celui des débris solides, va certainement à 60 gramme de gras par jour, ce qui augmenté du $1/5$, fait en *graisses humide* 72 à 80 gr. par jour. Vous comprenez qu'il est impossible de donner un nombre exact, mais il est évident pour moi qu'un porc reçoit par les eaux grasses, chaque jour, une dose

Page 5

de graisse beaucoup plus forte qu'on le suppose communément. J'ai préparé mes cages pour les oies de Persoz, mais je ne me sens plus le courage d'entreprendre le travail; j'en ai assez et j'ai besoin de me mettre en jachère; je deviendrai bête si je persiste à m'obstiner dans ces questions je suis bien décidé à leur laisser courir leur chance.

. . . . .

Boussingault

Appendix E

(See Chapter V at n. 12)

J'ai décidément terminé, toutes les expériences que j'avais commencé. Je discuterai tout cela à Paris, j'ai la conscience d'avoir fait un bon travail, mais, il pourra bien prononcer contre nous. Les oies se sont comportées d'une manière indigne. Si l'on fait entrée seulement en ligne de compte l'huile jaune du maïs soluble dans l'ether, (o.o7o) les oies ont fait de la graisse et beaucoup de graisse; si l'on prend tous ce qui, dans le maïs, est soluble dans l'ether et l'alcool et *insoluble dans l'eau*, les oies n'ont pas fait de graisse; car il y a près de o.12 de solubles dans l'ether et dans l'alcool.

Les canards aux pois, se sont bien comportés.

Les canards au riz au Maigne se sont montrés partisans de nos idées, dans la première série. Je viens d'égorger la 2° série, et je trouve bien de la graisse, je ne saurait le résultat final que demain matin, quand les graisses d'ébullition seront figées.

Je crois que la vérité est dans l'ensemble de mes expériences, il s'agit de s'en tirer.

Il pourra bien se faire que l'on soit obligé de faire intervenir un nouvel agent graissogène. Au verso j'exposerai mes résultats très simplement, chacun en tirera les conséquences qu'il lui plaira;

le riz est l'aliment qui doit résoudre la question.

Mes canards au riz non gras, ont fait des prodiges de graisse, il y en a un qui est aussi gras que Rayer. Un autre qui n'a eu que du beurre pour nourriture est aussi gras que Mr. Sylvestre, ainsi que Letellier l'a constaté sur les tourterelles. Il était temps que cela finit, je suis las de tuer, de massacrer, de dépouiller, de faire bouillir, le sang coulait à flots, pendant deux mois Bechelbronn ressemblait à l'espagne moderne.... Quelque soit la conclusion de mon travail vous serez satisfait car j'ai pris toutes les précautions pour être exact, et il en ressortira plusieurs faits intéressants. Nous n'aurons jamais tout à fait tort, car rien n'engraisse ni mieux ni aussi vite que la graisse.

ABBREVIATIONS USED IN THE BIBLIOGRAPHY AND NOTES

AAdSc	Archives of the Académie des Sciences, Paris
AM, P	Library of the Académie de Médecine, Paris
Annalen Chem. Pharm.	*Annalen der Chemie und Pharmacie*
Annalen Pharm.	*Annalen der Pharmacie*
Annales chim. phys.	*Annales de chimie et de physique*
Annales sci. nat.	*Annales des sciences naturelles*
Archiv Anat. Physiol.	*Archiv für Anatomie, Physiologie und Wissenschaftliche Medizin*
Archives gén. méd.	*Archives générales de médecine*
Arch. nat.	Archives nationales, Paris
BM, P	Bibliothèque Mazarine, Paris
BS, M	Bayerische Staatsbibliothek, Munich
C. VIIIe	Manuscripts of Claude Bernard in the archives of the Collège de France
C.r. Acad.	*Comptes rendus hebdomadaires des séances de l'Académie des Sciences*
G-11-5	Archives of the Collège de France, administrative records
Hist. Acad.	*Histoire de l'Académie Royale des Sciences*
J. débats	*Journal des débats*
J. pharm.	*Journal de pharmacie*
J. pharm. chim.	*Journal de pharmacie et de chimie*
J. physiol.	*Journal de physiologie expérimentale*
J. prakt. Chem.	*Journal für praktische Chemie (Erdmann's)*
L-M, G	Liebig-Museum, Giessen
Mem. Soc. Biol.	*Comptes rendus des séances et mémoires de la Société de Biologie*
Phil. Trans Roy. Soc.	*Philosophical Transactions of the Royal Society of London*
Zeit. Physiol.	*Zeitschrift für Physiologie*

All end note references are given in shortened form. For full citations see Bibliography.

Cross-references within the text are given in the form, "see above (or below), chap. —— at n. ——." The passages referred to are usually those preceding the corresponding footnote numbers in the text.

To conform with regulations of the *Académie des Sciences*, passages from manuscript documents belonging to its archives which are directly quoted in English translation in the text are reproduced in the original French transcription in the footnotes.

Bibliography

MANUSCRIPT SOURCES

Arranged according to archival source. Abbreviations used in the footnotes are given in parentheses.

I Collège de France (C. VIIIe.)

A. The descriptions of Claude Bernard's research in the present volume are based on the collection of papers preserved in the archives of the Collège de France. M. D. Grmek's classification divides them into 35 manuscripts, some of these containing multiple documents of related character. I have followed the numbering scheme for these manuscripts used in Grmek, *Catalogue* (1967). Page numbers are sometimes Bernard's original pagination of notebooks, sometimes numbers assigned by Grmek and pencilled on the manuscripts. Grmek grouped many of the loose notes into folios, giving each a separate pagination.

The majority of Bernard's records of his research are contained in eighteen large notebooks, which Grmek has grouped into two series, Manuscripts 7a through 7j, and 8a through 8j (plus 8r). Two notebooks, 7e and 8a, are known to be missing. The notebooks are arranged in part chronologically, in part by general subjects such as experiments on the nervous system, on poisons, and on digestion and nutrition. The investigations treated in this book are contained mostly in Manuscripts 7a n°2, 7b (though a larger portion of this notebook deals with the nervous system), 7c, and the first fifteen pages of 7g. The entries in these notebooks are in a rough chronological order, but Bernard often skipped pages to begin a new experiment while another was still in progress, then filled in the intervening pages at a later time. His dating of experiments was casual, so that one cannot always be certain of their order. The physical form of the notes, as well as the character of their contents, give the strong impression that they comprise the original record of Bernard's experiments, even though it has been suggested that Bernard wrote down his results first on loose pages and copied them into the notebooks at the end of each day. At any rate they appear to be a faithful record of what he did, observed, and thought during the course of his investigations, not reconstructions made after their completion.

In addition to the above notebooks the following manuscripts were especially useful:

Manuscript No. 5, pp 1-86. Contains notes for a book Bernard planned to write on digestion.

Manuscript 9b. Contains records of experiments Bernard carried out for the Gelatin Commission in 1842.

Manuscripts 14c, 14d, and 14e. Small notebooks containing notes of readings and lectures. I have identified some portions of these notebooks as derived from courses by Bérard, Dumas, and de Blainville, which Bernard attended.

Manuscript 26b, folios 1-9 consists of experiments on animal heat performed by Bernard and Magendie in 1842-43.

Manuscript 33a, folios 30-33. Experiments on gelatin, 1841.

Collectively these manuscripts have in the archives of the Collège de France the series number C.VIIIe.

B. A few documents from the administrative records of the Collège de France are used in Chapter XV, (G-11-5).

II   Library of the *Académie de Médecine*, Paris (AM, P, Cote [1426] no. 2)

A. A notebook kept by Bernard of a course he attended as a student.

III   Archives of the *Académie des Sciences*, Paris   (AAd Sc.)

The manuscripts in the archives are classified in "Dossiers," of individual members, of special topics, and of meetings of the Academy. Individual manuscripts within each dossier are not always numbered.

A. Dossier "Gélatine." A collection of letters and other documents concerning the gelatine question (Dos. Gélatine, AAdSc.).

D'Arcet, Joseph. "Objections faites au dernière mémoire publié par M. Donné en juillet 1835."
—— "Note sur l'emploi alimentaire de la gélatine des os." August 10, 1836. No. 61.
—— "Observations relative à la première partie du rapport lue, en mon absence, par Mr. Magendie. No. 87.
Various letters, mostly to or from D'Arcet.

B. Dossier "Dumas." (Dos. Dumas, AAdSc.) A large collection, including letters, reports, research notebooks, and notes for Dumas's lectures. The Archives possesses a mimeographed catalogue of the collection.

Dumas, Jean-Baptiste. "Cours de chimie organique et de pharmacie, 1838, notes." Carton 10. Handwritten notes which Dumas wrote for his lectures at the Faculty of Medicine. The same carton contains also lectures dated 1839.
Letters from Justus Liebig to Jules Pelouze.
Letters from Jean-Baptiste Boussingault to Jean-Baptiste Dumas. (Dates of the letters cited are given in the footnotes.)

C. Dossier "Pelouze." (Dos. Pelouze, AAdSc.)

An anonymous manuscript, probably written by a student of Pelouze, describing his career, in particular his teaching laboratories and his students. The document was probably prepared for Dumas to use in his eulogy of Pelouze.

Dumas, Jean-Baptiste. "Discours prononcé aux funérailles de M. Pelouze."

Letter from Carl Jacob Ettling to Jules Pelouze.

D. Dossier "Payen." (Dos. Payen, AAdSc.)

Two letters from Anselme Payen to Jean-Baptiste Dumas.

E. Dossiers of meetings of the Academy of Science. (Dos. (date), AAdSc.)

(1) [Boussingault] (untitled). Comments on Liebig's article of December 1842 on the formation of fat in animals. Identifiable by its contents as written by Boussingault. Meeting of February 13, 1843.

(2) Dumas, J.-B., Boussingault, J.-B., and Payen, A. "Recherches sur l'origine des matières grasses de l'organisation." Meeting of February 13, 1843.

(3) Guillemin, F. to Payen, December 15, 1842. Meeting of February 13, 1843. (Note: The dossier for February 13, 1843 contains a collection of documents concerning the question of animal fat, some of which were probably not actually presented at that meeting.)

(4) Mialhe, Louis. "Note sur le rôle physiologique des matières sucrées et amiloïdes." Meeting of January 27, 1845.

(5)—— "De la digestion et de l'assimilation des matières sucrées et amiloïdes." Meeting of March 31, 1845.

(6) Persoz, Jean. "Expériences sur l'engrais des oies." Meeting of February 12, 1844.

(7) Lassaigne, Louis. "Nouvelle observation sur l'action que la salive exerce sur les granules de fécule, à la température du corps des animaux mammifères, et sur l'état dans lequel se trouve l'amidon dans les graines céréales après leur mastication." Meeting of June 2, 1845.

IV   Bibliotheque Mazarine (Institut de France), Paris   (BM, P)

Contains several cartons of manuscripts of lecture notes of Jean-Baptiste Dumas. They begin "Cours de chimie professé à l'École de Médecine de Paris en 1842." Each Leçon is dated, from April to June 1842. There are also on some of them dates for 1843, when the same lectures were given again. A few lectures were added in 1843. Marginal comments by H. F. Melsens indicate which Leçons were later published.

A. MS 1943. Leçons 1–10. April, May 1842.

B. MS 1944. Leçons 11–22. May, June 1842.

C. MS 1945. Leçons 23–34. June 1842.

D. MS 1946. Printed page proofs derived from Dumas's Leçons of 1842, edited by H. F. Melsens, and intended for publication as *Leçons de philosophie chimique*. Some of them appeared in 1846 in volume VIII of Dumas's *Traité de chimie appliquée aux arts*.

E. MS 1948, 1950. Leçons for 1843. Some of them are handwritten copies of the Leçons for 1842.

F. MS 1951. Bibliographies collected by Melsens for Dumas's use in the editing of the *Traité*.

V   Archives nationales, Paris   (Arch. Nat.)

Several documents from the archives of the Collège de France, found in MSS F^{17}3849, F^{17}3851, F^{17}3852 and F^{17}13555 of the National Archives, in Paris.

VI   Bayerische Staatsbibliothek, Munich   (BS, M.)

The manuscripts section of this library contains a large collection of documents concerning Justus Liebig, including his correspondence with numerous other scientists. They are classified and identified in an unpublished catalogue available in the manuscript room. Documents used include:

A. Liebigiana 57. Letters from Liebig to Lyon Playfair.

B. Liebigiana 58. Letters to Liebig from J.-B. Dumas, Charles Marignac, Henri Milne Edwards, G. J. Mulder, and Jules Pelouze. Letter from Liebig to Milne Edwards. Dates for letters cited are given in footnotes.

VII   Liebig-Museum, Giessen   (L-M, G.)

The museum has an extensive collection of documents concerning Liebig, and "Inhalts-Verzeichnis" of some of the letters in the Bayerische Staatsbibliothek. Letters used are from Lyon Playfair, Jules Pelouze, and Charles Gerhardt to Liebig, and from Liebig to Dieffenbach.

PUBLISHED SOURCES

The following list of primary and secondary literature contains the sources cited in the footnotes. It is not intended to be a comprehensive list of works related to the topics treated in this book.

Ackernecht, Erwin H. *Medicine at the Paris Hospital.* Baltimore: The Johns Hopkins Press, 1967.

Atlee, Walter Franklin. *Notes of M. Bernard's Lectures on the Blood.* Philadelphia, 1854.

Aulie, Richard P. "Boussingault and the nitrogen cycle." *Proc. American Philosophical Society.* 1970, *114:* 435–479.

Barreswil, Charles. "Faits divers de chimie appliqués à la physiologie." *J. pharm. chim.* 1850, *17:*114–125.

Bates, Donald G. "The background to John Young's thesis on digestion." *Bull. Hist. Med.* 1962, *36:*341–361.

Baumé, Antoine. *A Manual of Chemistry.* Trans. J. Aikin. Warrington, 1778.

Beach, Eliot F. "Beccari of Bologna. The discoverer of vegetable protein." *J. Hist. Med.* 1961, *16:*354–373.

Béclard, Jules. *Traité élémentaire de physiologie humaine.* Paris, 1855.

Bérard, Pierre-Honoré. *Cours de physiologie.* Paris, 1848–1851.

Berman, Alex. "Conflict and anomaly in the scientific orientation of French pharmacy." *Bull. Hist. Med.* 1963, *37:* 440–462.

Bernard, Claude. *Du suc gastrique et de son rôle dans la nutrition: Thèse pour le doctorat en médecine.* Paris, 1843.

—— "De l'influence des nerfs de la huitième paire sur les phénomènes chimiques de la digestion." *C.r. Acad.* 1844, *18*:995–998.

—— "Expériences sur la digestion stomacale, et recherches sur les influences qui peuvent modifier les phénomènes de cette fonction." *Archives d'anatomie générale et de physiologie,* supplement to *Archives gén. méd.* 1846, pp. 1–9.

—— "Remarques sur quelques réactions chimiques qui s'effectuent dans l'estomac." *Archives d'anatomie générale et de physiologie,* supplement to *Archives gén. méd.* 1846, pp. 201–209.

—— "Des différences que présentent les phénomènes de la digestion et de la nutrition chez les animaux herbivores et carnivores." *C.r. Acad.* 1846,*22:* 534–537.

—— "Mémoire sur le rôle de la salive dans les phénomènes de la digestion." *Archives gén. méd.* 1847, *13:*1–29.

—— "Expériences sur les manifestations chimiques diverses des substances introduites dans l'organisme." *Archives gén. méd.* 1848, *16:*62–85, 219–232.

—— "De l'origine du sucre dans l'économie animale." *Archives gén. méd.* 1848,*18:* 303–319.

—— "Sur les usages du suc pancréatique." *Bulletin Société Philomatique de Paris.* 1848, pp. 34–36.

—— "Constitution physiologique de l'urine et de la bile." *Société Philomatique de Paris. Procès-verbaux.* 1848, pp. 14–16.

—— "Du suc pancréatique et de son rôle dans les phénomènes de la digestion." *Mém. Soc. Biol.* 1849, pp. 99–119.

—— *Nouvelle fonction du foie.* Paris, 1853.

—— "Remarques sur la sécrétion du sucre dans le foie, faites dans la même séance, à l'occasion de la communication de M. Lehmann." *Le Moniteur des hôpitaux.* 1855, 3:258.

—— "Mémoire sur le pancréas et sur le rôle du suc pancréatique dans les phénomènes digestifs." *C.r. Acad.* Supplément, I, 1856, pp. 379–563.

—— *Leçons de physiologie expérimentale.* II. Paris, 1856.

—— *Leçons sur les propriétés physiologiques et les altérations pathologiques des liquides de l'organisme.* Paris, 1859.

—— *Introduction à l'étude de la médecine expérimentale.* Paris, 1865. (reprint Culture et Civilisation, 1965)

—— *De la physiologie générale.* Paris, 1872.

—— *Leçons sur les anesthésiques et sur l'asphyxie.* Paris, 1875.

—— *Leçons sur le diabète et la glycogenèse animale.* Paris, 1877.

—— *Leçons de physiologie opératoire.* Paris, 1879.

—— *Leçons sur les phénomènes de la vie communs aux animaux et aux végétaux.* II. Paris, 1879.

—— *Leçons de pathologie.* 2nd. ed. Paris, 1880.

—— *Introduction à l'étude de la médecine expérimentale.* 3rd. ed. Paris: Delagrave, 1912.

—— *Principes de médecine expérimentale.* ed. Léon Delhoume. Paris: Presses Universitaires, 1947.

—— *Lettres beaujolaises.* ed. J. Godart. Villefranche-en-Beaujolais: Cuvier, 1950.

Bernard, Claude. *An Introduction to the Study of Experimental Medicine.* Trans. H. C. Greene. New York: Dover, 1957.

—— *Cahier de notes, 1850–1860.* ed. M. D. Grmek. Paris: Gallimard, 1965.

——, and Barreswil, Charles. "Recherches physiologiques sur les substances alimentaires." *C.r. Acad.* 1844, *28*:783–785.

—— "Sur les phénomènes chimiques de la digestion (Deuxième mémoire)." *C.r. Acad.* 1844, *19*:1284–1289.

—— "Recherches expérimentales sur les phénomènes chimiques de la digestion." *C.r. Acad.* 1845, *21*:88–89.

—— "Sur les voies d'élimination de l'urée après l'extirpation des reins." *Archives gén. méd.* 1847, *13*:449–465.

Bert, Paul. "Claude Bernard," in Claude Bernard, *An Introduction to the Study of Experimental Medicine.* Trans. H. C. Greene. New York, 1957, pp. xii–xix.

—— "Les Travaux de Claude Bernard," in *L'Oeuvre de Claude Bernard.* Paris, 1881.

Berthelot, Marcellin. "Note sur la synthèse des principes immédiats des graisses des animaux." *Mém. Soc. Biol.* 1854, pp. 191–193.

Berthollet, Claude-Louis. "Observations sur la causticité des alkalis et de la chaux." *Hist. Acad.* 1782 (1785), pp. 616–619.

—— "Sur les changements que la respiration produit dans l'air." *Mémoires de la Société d'Arcueil.* 1809, *2*:454–463.

Berzelius, Jöns Jacob. "Mémoire sur la composition des fluides animaux." *Annales de chimie.* 1813, *88*:26–72, 113–141; *89*:20–45.

—— *Jahres-Bericht über die Fortschritte der physischen Wissenschaften.* Trans. F. Wöhler. 1828, *7*:297–331; 1835, *14*:281–286; 1836, *15*:237–244.

—— *Traité de chimie.* Trans. M. Esslinger. V. Paris, 1831.

Bichat, Xavier. *Recherches physiologiques sur la vie et la mort.* 4th ed. Paris, 1822.

Blainville, Henri Ducrotay de. *Cours de physiologie générale et comparée.* I. Paris, 1829.

—— *Histoire des sciences de l'organisation et de leurs progrès, comme base de la philosophie.* ed. F. Maupied. Paris, 1845.

Blondlot, Nicholas. *Traité analytique de la digestion.* Paris, 1843.

Bollman, Jesse L., Mann, Frank C., and Magath, Thomas B. "Effect of total removal of the liver on the formation of urea." *American Journal of Physiology.* 1924, *69*:370–392.

Bostock, John. "Observations and experiments for the purpose of ascertaining the definite characters of the primary animal fluids, and to indicate their presence by accurate chemical tests." *Journal of Natural Philosophy.* (Nicholson's). 1805, *11*:244–254.

Bouchardat, Apollinaire. "Mémoire sur la fermentation saccharine ou glucosique." *C.r. Acad.* 1845, *20*:107–112.

—— "Nouveau mémoire sur la glucosurie ou diabète sucré." *C.r. Acad.* 1845, *20*:1020–1026.

Bouchardat, Apollinaire and Sandras. "Recherches sur la digestion." *Annales sci. nat.* 1842, *18*:225–241.

—— "Recherches sur la digestion et l'assimilation des corps gras, suivies de quelques considérations sur le rôle de la bile et de l'appareil chylifère." *C.r. Acad.* 1843, *17*:296–300.

—— "Réponse à la réclamation de M. Mialhe insérée dans le Compte rendu de la séance précédente." *C.r. Acad.* 1845, *20*:303–304.

—— "Réponse à la nouvelle réclamation de M. Mialhe, insérée dans le Compte rendu de la séance dernière." *C.r. Acad.* 1845, *20*:1026–1027.

—— "Des fonctions du pancréas et de son influence dans la digestion des féculents." *C.r. Acad.* 1845, *20*:1085–1091.

—— "De la digestion des matières féculentes et sucrées, et du rôle que ces substances jouent dans la nutrition." *Annuaire de thérapeutique*, supplement for 1846. pp. 81–138.

Boudet, F. Review of "Cours de chimie générale, par MM. J. Pelouse et E. Frémy." *J. pharm. chim.* 1848, *13*:46.

Boussingault, Jean-Baptiste. "Recherches chimiques sur la végétation, entreprises dans le but d'examiner si les plantes prennent de l'azote à l'atmosphère." *C.r. Acad.* 1838, *6*:102–112; *7*:889–891.

—— "De la discussion de la valeur relative des assolements, par les résultats de l'analyse élémentaire." *Mémoires de l'Académie des Sciences.* 1842, *18*:345–384.

—— *C.r. Acad.* 1843, *16*:668–673.

—— "Considérations sur l'alimentation des animaux." *Annales sci. nat.* 1844, *1*: 229–244.

—— "Recherches sur l'exhalation de l'azote." *Annales sci. nat.* 1844, *2*:216–221.

—— "Expériences sur l'alimentation des vaches avec des betteraves et des pommes de terre." *Annales chim. phys.* 1844, *12*:153–167.

—— "Recherches expérimentales sur le développement de la graisse pendant l'alimentation des animaux." *Annales chim. phys.* 1845, *14*:419–482.

—— "Recherches sur la formation de la graisse chez les animaux." *C.r. Acad.* 1845, *20*:1726.

—— "Recherches expérimentales sur le développement de la graisse pendant l'alimentation des animaux." *Annales chim. phys.* 1845, *14*:419–482.

—— "Expériences statiques sur la digestion." *Annales chim. phys.* 1846, *18*:444–478.

—— "Recherches sur l'influence que certains principes alimentaires peuvent exercer sur la proportion de matières grasses contenue dans le sang." *Annales chim. phys.* 1848, *24*:460–463.

Boussingault, Jean-Baptiste, and Payen, Anselme. "Mémoire sur les engrais et leurs valeurs comparées." *Annales chim. phys.* 1841, *3*:65–108.

Boutron and Frémy, E. "Recherches sur la fermentation lactique." *Annales chim. phys.* 1841, *2*:257–274.

Brock, W. H. "The life and work of William Prout." *Medical History*, 1965, *9*:101–126.

Brodie, B. C. "Observations on the effects produced by the bile in the process of digestion." *Quarterly Journal of Science*, 1823, *14*:341–344.

—— "Expériences sur l'usage de la bile dans la digestion." *J. physiol.* 1823, *3*:93–94.

Burdach, C. F. *Traité de physiologie considérée comme science d'observation.* Trans. A. J. L. Jourdan. Paris, 1837–1841.

Bussy, A. and Lecanu, L.-R. "De la distillation des corps gras." *Annales chim. phys.* 1825, *30*:5–20.

—— "Second mémoire sur la distillation des corps gras." *Annales chim. phys.* 1827, *34*:57–68.

Bylebyl, Jerome J. "William Beaumont, Robley Dunglison, and the " 'Philadelphia physiologists'." *J. Hist. Med.* 1970, *25*:3–21.

Cahours, Auguste. "Éloge historique de Pelouze." *Revue des cours scientifiques.* 1867–1868, 5th year, p. 357.

Canguilhem, Georges. "Preface," in Claude Bernard, *Leçons sur les phénomènes de la vie communs aux animaux et aux végétaux.* Paris: Vrin, 1966, pp. 7–14.

———— *Études d'histoire et de philosophie des sciences.* Paris: Vrin, 1968.

Carrière, J., ed. *Berzelius und Liebig: ihre Briefe von 1831–1845.* 2nd. ed. Wiesbaden: Sändig, 1967.

Charlton, D. G. *Positivist Thought in France During the Second Empire.* Oxford: Clarendon Press, 1959.

Chauveau, Auguste. "Nouvelles recherches sur la question glycogénique." *C.r. Acad.* 1856, *42*:1008–1012.

Chevreul, Michel Eugène. *Recherches chimiques sur les corps gras.* Paris: 1823.

———— "De l'action simultanée de l'oxigène gazeux et des alcalis sur un grand nombre de substances organiques." *Mémoires du Muséum d'Histoire Naturelle.* 1825, *12*:367–383.

———— "Urines." *Dictionnaire des sciences naturelles.* LVI. 1828, p. 354.

———— "Quelques considérations générales et inductions relatives à la matière des êtres vivants." *Journal des savants.* 1837, pp. 664–667.

Chossat, Charles. "Mémoire sur l'analyse des fonctions urinaires." *J. physiol.* 1825, *5*:65–221.

———— "Recherches expérimentales sur l'inanition." *Annales sci. nat.* 1843, *20*:54–81, 182–214, 293–326.

———— "Recherches expérimentales sur les effets du régime de sucre." *C.r. Acad.* 1843, *17*:805–808.

Coleman, William. "Blainville, Henri Marie Ducrotay de." *Dictionary of Scientific Biography.* Ed. C. C. Gillispie. II. New York: Scribner's, 1970, pp. 186–188.

Comte, Auguste. *Cours de philosophie positive.* III. Paris, 1838.

Costa, Albert B. *Michel Eugène Chevreul, Pioneer of Organic Chemistry.* Madison: State Historical Society of Wisconsin, 1962.

Coudraie, Roger de la. "Table alphabétique et analytique des oeuvres complètes de Claude Bernard." in *L'Oeuvre de Claude Bernard.* Paris, 1881.

Crosland, Maurice. *The Society of Arcueil: A View of French Science at the Time of Napoleon I.* Cambridge: Harvard University Press, 1967.

Crosland, Maurice P., and Brooke, John H. "Charles Gerhardt." *Dictionary of Scientific Biography.* ed. C. C. Gillispie. V. New York: Scribner's, 1972, pp. 369–374.

Culotta, Charles A. "Respiration and the Lavoisier Tradition: theory and modification, 1777–1850." *Trans. Am. Phil. Soc.,* 1972, *62*, Pt. *3*:3–41.

D'Arcet, Joseph. "Mémoire sur les os provenant de la viande de boucherie." *J. pharm.* 1829, *15*:236–244.

———— "Mémoire sur les substances alimentaires extraites des os." *Bulletin de la Société d'Encouragement pour l'Industrie Nationale.* 1829, *28*:93–97.

———— "Lettre de M. d'Arcet à l'occasion des expériences faites en Hollande sur les propriétés nutritives de la gélatine." *C.r. Acad.* 1844, *18*:482–483.

Dehérain, P. P. "Edmond Frémy." in *Edmond Frémy (1814–1894).* [L'Association des Élèves de M. Frémy.]

Delaroche, François. "Mémoire sur l'influence que la température de l'air exerce dans les phénomènes chimiques de la respiration." *Journal de physique.* 1813, 77:5–16.

Deschamps, Michel. "De la présure." *J. pharm.* 1840, *26*:412–420.

Despretz, César. "Recherches expérimentales sur les causes de la chaleur animale." *Annales chim. phys.* 1824, *26*:337–364.

Donné, Alfred. *Mémoire sur l'emploi de la gélatine comme substance alimentaire.* Paris, 1835.

—— "Académie des Sciences." *J. débats.* February 22, 1843, March 5, 1843, April 5, 1843, June 13, 1843, September 22, 1843.

Du Bois-Reymond, Emil. "Gedächtnisrede auf Johannes Müller." *Reden von Emil Du Bois-Reymond.* Leipzig: Veit, 1912, I, pp. 135–317.

Du Bois-Reymond, Estelle ed. *Zwei Grosse Naturforscher des 19. Jahrhunderts: ein Briefwechsel zwischen Emil Dubois-Reymond und Karl Ludwig.* Leipzig: Barth, 1927.

Dulong, Pierre Louis. "Mémoire sur la chaleur animal." *Annales chim. phys.* 1841, *1*:440–455.

Dumas, Jean-Baptiste., rapporteur. "Rapport sur un mémoire de M. Boussingault, relatif à l'influence de l'azote atmosphérique dans la végétation." *C.r. Acad.* 1838, *6*:129–131.

——, rapporteur. "Rapport sur un mémoire de M. Boussingault, intitlé: recherches chimiques sur la végétation." *C.r. Acad.* 1839, *8*:54–58.

—— "Mémoire sur la loi des substitutions et la théorie des types." *C.r. Acad.* 1840, *10*:149–178.

—— "Leçon sur la statique chimique des êtres organisés." *Annales sci. nat.* 1841, *16*:33–61.

—— *Essai de statique chimique des êtres organisés.* 2nd. ed. Paris, 1842.

—— "Essai de statique chimique des êtres organisés." *Annales chim. phys.* 1842, *4*:115–126.

—— "Loi de composition des principaux acides gras." *C.r. Acad.* 1842, *15*:935–936.

—— "Rapport sur un mémoire de MM. Sandras and Bouchardat, relatif à la digestion." *C.r. Acad.* 1843, *16*:253–254.

—— *C.r. Acad.* 1843, *16*:558–561, 666–668, 673–675.

—— "Constitution du lait des carnivores." *C.r. Acad.* 1845, *21*:707–717.

—— *Traité de chimie appliquée aux arts.* VIII. Paris, 1846.

—— *Éloge historique de Jules Pélouze.* Paris, 1870.

Dumas, J.-B., and Boussingault, J.-B. "Recherches sur la veritable constitution de l'air atmosphérique." *C.r. Acad.* 1841, *12*:1005–1025.

Dumas, J.-B., Boussingault, J.-B., and Payen, A. "Recherches sur l'engraissement des bestiaux et la formation du lait." *C.r. Acad.* 1843, *16*:345–363.

—— "Recherches sur l'engraissement des bestiaux et la formation du lait." *Annales sci. nat.* 1843, *19*:351–386.

Dumas, J.-B. and Cahours, Auguste. "Mémoire sur les matières azotées neutres de l'organisation." *Annales sci. nat.* 1842, *18*:350–377.

Dumas, J.-B. and Milne-Edwards, Henri. "Note sur la production de la cire des abeilles." *C.r. Acad.* 1843, *17*:531–537.

Dumas, J.-B. (grandson of the chemist). *La Vie de J.-B. Dumas.* MS, AAdSc.

Eberle, Johann N. *Physiologie der Verdauung, nach Versuchen auf natürlichem und künstlichem Wege.* Würzburg, 1834.

[anon.] "Emploi de la gélatine comme aliment," *C.r. Acad.* 1838, 7:1117–1119.

[anon.] "Emploi des bouillons et soupes à la gélatine. Lettres des membres du Bureau de Bienfaisance de Lille." *C.r. Acad.* 1836, 2:655–656.

[anon.] "Extrait du rapport de la première classe de l'Institut royal des Pay-Bas, sur les qualités nutritives de la gélatine." *C.r. Acad.* 1844, 18:423–435.

Faure, Jean Louis. *Claude Bernard.* Paris: G. Cres, 1925.

Florkin, Marcel. *Naissance et déviation de la théorie cellulaire dans l'oeuvre de Théodore Schwann.* Paris: Hermann, 1960.

Flourens, Marie Jean Pierre. *C.r. Acad.* 1843, 17:513–514, 653–654.

Fodéra, Michael. "Recherches expérimentales sur l'absorption et l'exhalation." *J. physiol.* 1823, 3:35–45.

Foster, Michael. *Claude Bernard.* London, 1899.

Fourcroy, Antoine de. "Mémoire sur la nature de la fibre charnue ou musculaire et sur le siège de l'irritabilité." *Hist. Acad.* 1782–1783. (Paris, 1787), pp. 502–513.

Frerichs, Friedrich Theodor. "Verdauung," in Rudolph Wagner, *Handwörterbuch der Physiologie.* III. Braunschweig, 1846, pp. 658–872.

Fruton, Joseph S. *Molecules and Life: Historical Essays on the Interplay of Chemistry and Biology.* New York: Wiley, 1972.

Fulton, John F., ed. *A Textbook of Physiology.* 17th ed. Philadelphia: Saunders, 1955.

Gannal, Jean-Nicholas. *Lettre adressée à M. Le Baron Thenard.* Paris, 1841.

Gautier, Armand. *Chimie appliquée à la physiologie à la pathologie et à l'hygiène.* Paris, 1874.

Genty, Maurice. "Rayer (Pierre-Francois-Olive)," *Les Biographies médicales.* III. Paris: Baillière, 1932–34, pp. 33–48.

Goodman, D. C. "Chemistry and the two organic kingdoms of nature in the nineteenth century." *Medical History.* 1972, 16:113–130.

Grimaux, Édouard, and Gerhardt, Charles. *Charles Gerhardt: Sa vie, son oeuvre, sa correspondance.* Paris: Masson, 1900.

Grmek, Mirko Drazen. "Les Expériences de Claude Bernard sur l'anesthésie des plantes." *Cr. du 89ᵉ Congrès des Sociétès Savants.* (Lyon, 1964). Paris: Gauthier-Vilars, pp. 65–80.

—— *Catalogue des manuscrits de Claude Bernard.* Paris: Masson, 1967.

—— "Examen critique de la genèse d'une grande découverte: 'la piqûre diabétique' de Claude Bernard." *Clio Medica.* 1967, 1:342–350.

—— "La Glycogenèse et le diabète dans l'oeuvre de Claude Bernard," in *Commentaires sur dix grands livres de la médecine française.* Paris: Cercle du livre précieux, 1968, pp. 187–234.

—— "First steps in Claude Bernard's discovery of the glycogenic function of the liver," *J. Hist. Biol.* 1968, 1:141–154.

—— *Raisonnement expérimental et recherches toxicologiques chez Claude Bernard.* "Hautes études médiévales et modernes, no. 18." Paris: Droz, 1973.

Guerlac, Henry. *Lavoisier-the Crucial Year.* Ithaca: Cornell University Press, 1961.

Hagstrom, Warren O. *The Scientific Community.* New York: Basic Books, 1965.

Haller, Albrecht von. *Anfangsgründe der Phisiologie des Menschlichen Körpers.* Trans. J. S. Hallen. II. Berlin, 1762.

Heinrich, F. "Dumas," in Gunther Bugge, ed. *Das Buch der Grossen Chemiker.* Berlin: Verlag Chemie, 1930.

Henderson, Yandell. "Physiological regulation of the acid-base balance of the blood and some related functions." *Physiological Reviews*. 1925, *5*:131–160.

Hirsch, August, ed. *Biographisches Lexikon der Hervorragenden Ärzte*. Berlin: Urban and Schwarzenberg, 1930–32.

Holmes, Frederic L. *Claude Bernard's Concept of the Milieu Intérieur*. unpub. diss. Harvard University, 1962.

—— "Elementary analysis and the origins of physiological chemistry." *Isis*. 1963, *54*:50–81.

—— "Introduction," in Liebig, Justus. *Animal Chemistry*. ("The sources of science, no. 4") New York: Johnson Reprints, 1964.

—— "Analysis by fire and solvent extraction: the metamorphosis of a tradition." *Isis*. 1971, *62*:129–148.

—— "Justus Liebig," *Dictionary of Scientific Biography*. Ed. C. C. Gillispie. VIII. New York: Scribner's, 1973, pp. 329–350.

Hünefeld, Friedrich Ludwig. *Physiologische Chemie des menschlichen Organismus*. Leipzig, 1826.

L'Institut. (dates cited are given in footnotes).

Kapoor, Satish C. "Dumas and organic classification." *Ambix*. 1969, *16*:1–65.

Kirchhoff, Gottlieb. "Formation du sucre dans les graines céréales converties en malt, et dans la farine infusée dans l'eau bouillante." *Journal de pharmacie*. 1816, *2*:250–258.

Kourilsky, Raoul. "La Médecine clinique vue par Claude Bernard," in *Philosophie et méthodologie scientifiques de Claude Bernard*. ("Fondation Singer-Polignac.") Paris: Masson, 1967, pp. 65–83.

Kruta, Vladislav. "J. E. Purkyně—a creative scientist," in *Jan Evangelista Purkyně*. Prague: State Medical Publishing House, 1962.

Kuhn, Thomas S. "Energy conservation as an example of simultaneous discovery," in *Critical Problems in the History of Science*. Ed. M. Clagett. Madison: University of Wisconsin Press, 1969, pp. 321–356.

Lacroix, Alfred. *Notice historique sur Jean-Baptiste Boussingault*. Paris: Gauthier-Villars, 1926.

Lassaigne, Jean-Louis. "Nouvelles recherches chimiques sur le principe qui donne au suc gastrique son acidité." *Journal de chimie médicale*. 1844, *10*:73–77.

—— "Deuxième note sur la recherche du principe qui communique au suc gastrique son acidité." *Journal de chimie médicale*. 1844, *10*:183–189.

—— "Recherches pour déterminer le mode d'action qu'exerce la salive pure sur l'amidon à la température du corps des animaux mammifères et à celle de +75 degrés centigrade." *C.r. Acad.* 1845, *20*:1347–1350.

—— "Recherches sur l'action qu'exerce le tissue pancréatique du cheval sur l'amidon cru ou en grains, et l'amidon cuit dans l'eau ou à l'état d'empois." *C.r. Acad.* 1845, *20*:1350–1351.

—— "Nouvelle observation sur l'action que la salive exerce sur les granules de fécule, à la température du corps des animaux mammifères, et sur l'état dans lequel se trouve l'amidon dans les graines céréales après leur mastication." *C.r. Acad.* 1845, *20*:1640–1641.

—— "Recherches pour déterminer sur le cheval et le mouton, les quantités de fluides salivaire et muqueux que les aliments absorbent dans la bouche pendant la mastication." *C.r. Acad.* 1845, *21*:362–363.

Lehmann, Carl Gotthelf. "Ueber menschlichen Harn in gesunden und krankhaftem Zustande." *J. prakt. Chem.* 1842, *25*:1–29.

—— "Untersuchungen über den menschlichen Harn." *J. prakt. Chem.* 1842, *27*:257–274.

—— "Nachschrift" to Bouchardat and Sandras, "Untersuchungen über die Verdauung." *J. prakt. Chem.* 1842, *27*:480–482.

—— "Den Verdauungsprocess betreffende quantitative Verhältnisse." *Bericht über die Verhandlungen der königlich sächsischen Gesellschaft der Wissenschaften zu Leipzig.* 1849, pp. 8–50.

—— *Lehrbuch der physiologischen Chemie.* 2nd. ed. Leipzig, 1853.

Leroux, Dubois, Pelletan, Duméril and Vauquelin. "Rapport sur un travail de M. d'Arcet, ayant pour objet l'extraction de la gélatiné des os, et son application aux différens usages économiques." *Annales chim.* 1814, *92*:300–310.

Letellier, F. "Observations sur l'action du sucre dans l'alimentation des granivores." *Annales sci. nat.* 1844, *2*:38–45.

Leuchs, Erhard Friedrich. "Ueber die Verzuckerung des Stärkmehls durch Speichel." *Archiv für Chemie und Meteorologie*, bound in *Archiv für die gesammte Naturlehre.* 1831, *3*:105–107.

Leuret, François, and Lassaigne, J.-L. *Recherches physiologiques et chimiques pour servir à l'histoire de la digestion.* Paris, 1825.

Lewy. "Note sur la cire des abeilles." *C.r. Acad.* 1843, *16*:675–678.

Liebig, Justus. "Ueber Verhalten und Zusammensetzung einer Reihe von fetten Körpern." *Annalen Chem. Pharm.* 1840, *35*:44–45.

—— *Organic Chemistry in its Applications to Agriculture and Physiology.* ed. Lyon Playfair. Intro. J. W. Webster. Cambridge, Mass., 1841.

—— "Bemerkungen zu vorstehender Abhandlung." *Annalen Chem. Pharm.* 1841, *38*:202–206.

—— "Ueber die stickstoffhaltigen Nahrungsmittel des Pflanzenreichs." *Annalen Pharm.* 1841, *39*:129–160.

—— "Der Lebensprocess im Thiere, und die Atmosphare." *Annalen Chem. Pharm.* 1842, *41*:189–219.

—— "Die Ernährung, Blut—und Fettbildung im Thierkorper." *Annalen Chem. Pharm.* 1842, *41*:241–285.

—— "Sur les matières alimentaires azotées du règne végétal." *Annales chim. phys.* 1842, *4*:186–211.

—— "Antwort auf Hrn. Dumas's Rechtfertigung wegen eines Plagiats." *Annalen Chem. Pharm.* 1842, *41*:351–357.

—— "Ueber die Fettbildung im Thierkorper." *Annalen Chem. Pharm.* 1842, *45*:112–128.

—— "Die Fettbildung im Thierkorper." *Annalen Chem. Pharm.* 1843, *48*:126–147.

—— "Observations à l'occasion du Mémoire de MM. Dumas, Boussingault et Payen." *C.r. Acad.* 1843, *16*:552–554.

—— "Note sur la formation de la graisse chez les animaux." *C.r. Acad.* 1843, *16*:663–666.

—— *Die Thier-Chemie.* 2nd. ed. unrevised. Braunschweig, 1843.

—— "Ueber die Constitution des Harns der Menschen und der fleischfressenden Thiere." *Annalen Chem. Pharm.* 1844, *50*:161–196.

—— "Ueber die Fettbildung im Thierorganismus." *Annalen Chem. Pharm.* 1845, *54*:376–383.

—— *Animal Chemistry.* ("The sources of science, No. 4"). New York: Johnson Reprint Corp., 1964.

Longet, Francis Achilles. *Traité de physiologie.* 2nd. ed. Paris, 1860–1861.

Magendie, François. "Sur les propriétés nutritives des substances qui ne contiennent pas d'azote." *Ann. chim. phys.* 1816, *3*:66–77.

—— "Mémoire sur le mécanisme de l'absorption chez les animaux à sang rouge et chaud." *Journal de physiologie expérimentale.* 1821, *1*:1–17.

—— "Mémoire sur les organes de l'absorption chez les mammifères." *J. physio.* 1821, *1*:18–31.

—— *Précis élémentaire de physiologie.* 3rd. ed. Paris, 1833.

—— "Rapport fait à l'Académie des Sciences au nom de la Commission dite de la gélatine." *C.r. Acad.* 1841, *13*:237–295.

—— *Phénomènes physiques de la vie.* Paris, 1842.

—— for the Commission on Hygiene. "Étude comparative de la salive parotidienne et de la salive mixte du cheval, sous le rapport de leur composition chimique et de leur action sur les aliments." *C.r. Acad.* 1845, *21*:902–905.

—— "Note sur la présence normale du sucre dans le sang." *C.r. Acad.* 1846, *23*:189–193.

Magendie, F., Milne Edwards, H., and Dumas, J.-B. "Rapport sur un mémoire de M. Bernard, intitulé: Recherches sur les usages du suc pancréatique." *C.r. Acad.* 1849, *28*:283–285.

Maillard, Georges. "Carnet d'un flaneur." *Le Figaro.* July 15, 1868.

Mani, Nikolaus. "Das Werk von Friedrich Tiedemann und Leopold Gmelin: 'Die Verdauung nach Versuchen' und seine Bedeutung für die Entwicklung der Ernährungslehre in der ersten Hälfte des 19. Jahrhunderts." *Gesnerus.* 1956, *13*:200–207.

—— *Die historischen Grundlagen der Leberforschung.* Basel: Schwabe, 1967.

Marchand, Richard Felix. "Fortgesetzte Versuche über die Bildung des Harnstoffs im thierischen Körper." *J. prakt. Chem.* 1838, *14*:490–497.

Marignac, Charles de. "Lettre de M. Marignac, professeur de chemie à Messieurs les rédacteurs des Annales." *Annales chim. phys.* 1842, *4*:460–461.

Melsens, H. F. "Recherches sur l'acidité du suc gastrique." *C.r. Acad.* 1844, *19*:1289–1291.

Mendelsohn, Everett. *Heat and Life.* Cambridge, Mass.: Harvard University Press, 1964.

—— "The biological sciences in the nineteenth century: some problems and sources." *History of Science.* 1964, *3*:39–59.

Mialhe, Louis. "De l'action chimique des sels les uns sur les autres envisagées sous le rapport de l'art de formuler." *C.r. Acad.* 1841, *13*:478–480.

—— *Traité de l'art de formuler, ou notions de pharmacologie appliquée à la médecine.* Paris, 1845.

—— "Sur le rôle physiologique des matières sucrées et amiloides. Note addressée a l'occasion d'une communication récente de MM. Bouchardat et Sandras." *C.r. Acad.* 1845, *20*:247–248.

—— "De la digestion et de l'assimilation des matières sucrées et amiloides." *C.r. Acad.* 1845, *20*:954–959.

Mialhe, Louis. "Note sur le mode d'action qu'exerce la diastase animale sur l'amidon." *C.r. Acad.* 1845, *20*:1485–1488.
—— "De la digestion et de l'assimilation des matières albuminoides." *J. pharm. chim.* 1846, *10*:161–167.
—— *Mémoire sur la digestion et l'assimilation des matières albuminoides.* Paris, 1847.
Milne Edwards, Henri. "Remarques sur la production de la cire." *C.r. Acad.* 1843, *17*:925–931.
—— *C.r. Acad.* 1845, *20*:1726–1728.
—— *Leçons sur la physiologie et l'anatomie comparée de l'homme et des animaux.* VII. Paris, 1862.
Mitscherlich, Eilhard. "Ueber die Aetherbildung." *Annalen der Physik und Chemie (Poggendorff).* 1834, *31*:273–282.
Mitscherlich, E., Gmelin, L., and Tiedemann, F. "Versuche über das Blut." *Zeit. Physiol.* 1833, *5*:1–19.
Moleschott, Jacob. *Physiologie der Nahrungsmittel.* 2nd. ed. Giessen, 1859.
Mulder, Gerardus Johannes. "Zusammensetzung von Fibrin, Albumin, Leimzucker, Leucin u.s.w." *Annalen Pharm.* 1838, *28*:73–82.
Müller, Johannes. *Handbuch der Physiologie des Menschen für Vorlesungen.* 3rd. ed. I. Coblenz, 1838.
Müller, Johannes and Schwann, Theodor. "Versuche über die künstliche Verdauung des geronnenen Eiweisses." *Archiv Anat. Physiol.* 1836, pp. 66–89.
Nash, Leonard K. *Plants and the Atmosphere.* "Harvard Case Histories, No. 5." Cambridge, Mass.: Harvard University Press, 1952.
[anon.] "Note sur l'emploi alimentaire de la gélatine." *Annales chim. phys.* 1831, *47*:220–223.
[anon.] *Notice sur les travaux de chimie agricole de M. Payen.* Paris, 1839.
Olmsted, James M. D. *Claude Bernard, Physiologist.* New York: Harper, 1938.
—— *François Magendie.* New York: Schuman, 1944.
Olmsted, J. M. D. and Olmsted, E. Harris. *Claude Bernard and the Experimental Method in Medicine.* Life of science library, No. 23. New York: Schuman, 1952.
Paolini, Carlo. *Justus von Liebig: Eine Bibliographie sämtlicher Veröffentlichungen.* Heidelberg: Carl Winter, 1968.
Partington, J. R. *A History of Chemistry.* IV. London: Macmillan, 1964.
Payen, Anselme. *C.r. Acad.*, 1843, *16*:555–556, 1271; *17*:540–541; *20*:1726–1728.
—— "Alimentation des chevaux. Documents à l'appui de la réponse verbale à M., Magendie." *C.r. Acad.* 1843, *16*:567–572.
—— "Observations de M. Payen relatives à la lettre de M. Liebig." *Cr. Acad.* 1843, *16*:769–772.
—— "Note sur le principe actif du suc gastrique." *C.r. Acad.* 1843, *17*:655.
—— "Rapport sur un mémoire de M. Mialhe, intitulé: De la digestion et de l'assimilation des matières amyloides et sucrées." *C.r. Acad.* 1846, *22*:522–527.
—— "Influence des substances grasses sécrétées dans les plantes, sur l'engraissement des herbivores." *C.r. Acad.* 1846, *24*:1065–1068.
Payen, A. and Persoz, J. "Mémoire sur la diastase, les principaux produits de ses réactions, et leurs applications aux arts industriels." *Annales chim. phys.* 1833, *53*:73–92.
Pelouze, Théophile Jules. "Mémoire sur l'acide lactique." *J. pharm. chim.* 1845, *7*:5–15.

Pelouze, T. J. and Gelis. "Mémoire sur l'acide butyrique." *C.r. Acad.* 1843, *16*:1262–1271.

Persoz, Jean François. "Expériences sur l'engrais des oies." *C.r. Acad.* 1844, *18*:245–254.

Pickstone, John. *The Origins of general Physiology in France with special emphasis on the work of R. J. H. Dutrochet.* unpub. diss. University of London, 1973.

Playfair, Lyon. "On the changes in composition of the milk of a cow, according to its exercise and food." *Memoirs of the Chemical Society of London.* 1841–1843, *1*:174–190.

Poggendorff, J. C. *Biographisch-literarisches Handwörterbuch zur Geschichte der exacten Wissenschaften.* I. Leipzig, 1863.

Prévost, Jean-Louis and Dumas, J.-B. "Examen du sang et de son action dans les divers phénomènes de la vie." *Annales chim. phys.* 1823, *23*:50–68, 90–102.

Prout, William. "On the nature of the acid and saline matters usually existing in the stomachs of animals." *Phil. Trans. Roy. Soc.* 1824, Part 1, pp. 45–49.

Provençal, Jean Michel and Humboldt, Alexander von. "Recherches sur la respiration des poissons." *Mémoires de la Société d'Arcueil.* 1809, *3*:359–404.

Purkyně, Jan Evangelista and Pappenheim. "Vorläufige Mittheilungen aus einer Untersuchung über künstliche Verdauung." *Archiv Anat. Physiol.* 1838, pp. 1–14.

Puymaurin, A. de. "Mémoire sur les applications dans l'économie domestique de la gélatine extraite des os au moyen de la vapeur." *Bulletin de la Société d'Encouragement pour l'Industrie Nationale.* 1829, *28*:97–127, 158–164.

Rayer, Pierre-François. *Traité des maladies des reins et des altérations de la sécrétion urinaire.* Paris, 1839.

Réaumur, René Antoine Ferchault de. "Sur la digestion des oiseaux. Premier Mémoire. Expériences sur la manière dont se fait la digestion dans les oiseaux qui vivent principalement de grains et d'herbes, et dont l'estomac est un gésier." *Hist. Acad.* 1752 (1756), pp. 266–307.

—— "Sur la digestion des oiseaux. Second Mémoire. De la manière dont elle se fait dans l'estomac des oiseaux de proie." *Hist. Acad.* 1752 (1756), pp. 461–495.

Redtenbacher, Joseph. "Ueber die Zusammensetzung und die Distillations-produkte der Talgsäure." *Annalen Chem. Pharm.* 1840, *35*:46–65.

Reid, Wemyss. *Memoirs and Correspondence of Lyon Playfair.* New York, 1899.

Renan, E. "Claude Bernard." in *L'Oeuvre de Claude Bernard.* Paris, 1881, pp. 3–37.

[anon.] "Report des médecins, chirurgiens et pharmaciens de l'Hôtel-Dieu." *C.r. Acad.* 1841:286–295.

Richerand, Anthelm. *Nouveaux élémens de physiologie.* 10th ed., rev. by Bérard. Paris, 1833.

Robin, Charles. "Sur la direction que se sont proposée en se réunissant les membres fondateurs de la Société de Biologie." *Mem. Soc. Biol. (C.R.).* 1849, *1*:i–xi.

Roger, H. "Notes inédites de Claude Bernard." *La Presse médicale.* 1933, *41*:1785–1789.

Rosen, George. *The Reception of William Beaumont's Discovery in Europe.* New York: Schuman, 1942.

Rouelle, Hilaire Marin. "Expériences." *Journal de médecine.* 1773, *39*:258–265.

—— "Observations sur les fécules ou parties vertes des plantes, et sur la matière glutineuse ou végéto-animale." *Journal de médecine.* 1773, *40*:59–66.

Ruch, Theodore C. and Fulton, John F. eds. *Medical Physiology and Bio-physics*. Philadelphia: Saunders, 1960.

Scheele, Carl Wilhelm. *Sämmtliche Physische und Chemische Werke*. ed. S. F. Hermbstädt. 2nd. ed. Berlin, 1891.

Schiller, Joseph. *Claude Bernard et les problèmes scientifiques de son temps*. Paris: Cedre, 1967.

Schwann, Theodor. "Ueber das Wesen des Verdauungsprocesses." *Archiv Anat. Physiol.* 1836, pp. 90–138.

—— "Ueber das Wesen des Verdauungsprocess." *Annalen Pharm.* 1836, 20:28–34.

Simon, J. Franz. "Beitrag zur Physiologie der Ernährung." *Archiv Anat. Physiol.* 1839, pp. 1–9.

Söderbaum, H. G., ed. *Jac. Berzelius Brev*. Supplement. Uppsala: Almqvist and Wiksells, 1935.

Spallanzani, Lazzaro. *Dissertations Relative to the Natural History of Animals and Vegetables*. Trans. anon. I. London, 1784.

Strahl, Joh. Carl. "Ueber die Zuckerbildung im thierischen Organismus." *Archiv Anat. Physiol.* 1847, pp. 215–220.

[anon.] *Supplément à la notice sur les titres de M. Payen*. Paris, 1840.

Temkin, Owsei. "The philosophical background of Magendie's physiology." *Bull. Hist. Med.* 1946, 20:10–35.

Théodorides, Jean. "Sur deux manuscrits inédits de Magendie." *Clio medica*. 1965, 1:27–32.

Tiedemann, Friedrich. *Traité complet de physiologie de l'homme*. Trans. A. J. L. Jourdan. Paris, 1831.

Tiedemann, Friedrich and Gmelin, Lèopold. *Recherches expérimentales, physiologiques et chimiques, sur la digestion*. Trans. A. J. L. Jourdan. Paris, 1826–1827.

—— *Die Verdauung nach Versuchen*. Heidelberg, 1826–1827.

[anon.] *Titres scientifiques de M. Mialhe, candidat a l'Académie Impériale de Médecine*. Paris, 1856.

Valentin, Gabriel Gustav. "Einige Resultate der im Sommer des gegenwärtigen Jahres zu Breslau über Künstliche Verdauung angestellte Versuche." *Froriep's Notizen aus dem Gebiete der Natur—und Heilkunde*. 1836, 50: cols. 209–212.

Varrentrapp, Franz. "Ueber Margarinsäure." *Annalen Chim. Phys.* 1840, 35:65–86.

Vickery, Hubert B. "The origin of the word protein." *The Yale Journal of Biology and Medicine*. 1950, 22:387–393.

Vogel, ——. "Sur la présence d'une substance grasse dans la bièrre." *J. pharm. chim.* 1843, 14:309–310.

Vogels, fils. "Sur la pepsine, principe présumable de la digestion." *J. pharm. chim.* 1842, 2:273–278.

Vogel, Julius. "Ueber einige Gegenstände der thierischen Chemie." *Annalen der Pharmacie*. 1839, 30:20–44.

Voit, Carl. "Ueber die Entwicklung der Lehre von der Quelle der Muskelkraft und einiger Theile der Ernährung seit 25 Jahren." *Zeitschrift für Biologie*. 1870, 6:303–401.

Wasmann, Adolph. "Ueber die Verdauung." *Neue Notizen aus dem Gebiete der Natur—und Heilkunde* (Froriep). 1839, 10: cols. 113–122.

Watermann, Rembert. *Theodor Schwann: Leben und Werk*. Düsseldorf: L. Schwann, 1960.

Wöhler, Friedrich. "Versuche über den Übergang von Materien in den Harn." *Zeit. Physiol.* 1824, *1*:126–146; 1825, *1*:290–317.

Wollaston, William Hyde. "On cystic oxide, a new species of urinary calculas." *Phil. Trans. Roy. Soc.* 1810, Pt. 4, pp. 229–230.

Wurtz, Charles Adolphe. "Sur la transformation de la fibrine en acide butyrique." *Annales chim. phys.* 1844, *11*:253–255.

Young, Frank G. "Claude Bernard and the theory of the glycogenic function of the liver." *Annals of Science.* 1937, *2*:47–83.

Notes

PREFACE

1. Joseph Schiller has given the most impressive support for this view, in his analysis of Bernard's thesis on gastric digestion of 1843. See Schiller, *Bernard*, pp. 105–110.

2. Faure, *Bernard*, pp. 45–46.

3. Olmsted and Olmsted, *Bernard*, pp. 49–50.

4. Grmek, *Catalogue*. This book gives a summary of the contents of each manuscript item and gives further details about how they were collected at the Collège de France.

5. Grmek, "L'Anesthésie des plantes," pp. 65–80; Grmek, *Clio Medica*, 1967, *1*:341–350; Grmek, "La Glycogenèse," pp. 187–234.

6. Bernard, *Principes*, p. 221.

7. The two most recent and most important of these interpretations are Schiller, *Bernard*, pp. 70–90; and D. C. Goodman, *Medical History*, 1972, *16*:113–130.

CHAPTER I: CHEMISTS, PHYSIOLOGISTS, AND THE PROBLEM OF NUTRITION

1. Bernard, *Introduction*, 3rd ed. pp. 149–150.

2. Bernard, *Leçons sur les anesthésiques*, p. 418.

3. See Crosland, *Arcueil*, for a general description of this group. Among the individual papers on the subject by members of this group are, Berthollet, *Mémoires de la société d'Arcueil*, 1809, *2*:454–463; Provençal and Humboldt, ibid., pp. 359–404; Delaroche, *Journal de physique*, 1813, 77:5–16; Despretz, *Annales chim. phys.*, 1824, *26*:337–364; Dulong, *Annales chim. phys.*, 1841, *1*:440–455.

4. Müller, *Handbuch*, I, 84–90, 326–327. For further assessment of the experiments of Dulong and Despretz and the issues they raised, see Holmes, "Introduction," pp. xxxv–xlii.

5. Mendelsohn, *Heat and Life*, pp. 168–169.

6. Müller, *Handbuch*, I, 86–90. For a detailed study of the physiological difficulties which Lavoisier's chemical theory of respiration encountered during the first half of the nineteenth century, see Culotta, *Trans. Am. Phil. Soc.*, 1972, *62*:3–40.

7. Théodorides, *Clio medica* 1965, *1*:30–31. The incomplete manuscript unfortunately does not reveal in detail what Magendie's objections were.

8. Bernard, MS, AM, P, Cote 554 (1426), no. 2. See also footnote no. 3, Chapter VI.

9. See, for example, Haller, *Anfangsgründe*, II, 237–241.

10. Leroux, et al., *Annales chim.*, 1814, *92*:300–310; Magendie, *C.r. Acad.*, 1841, *13*:240–244.

11. Magendie, *Ann. chim. phys.*, 1816, *3*:66–75.

12. Ibid., p. 70.

13. D'Arcet, "Note," Dos. Gélatine, No. 61, AAdSc.

14. D'Arcet, *Bulletin de la Société d'Encouragement*, 1829, *28*:93; D'Arcet, 1829, *15*:236–244.

15. De Puymaurin, *Bulletin de la Société d'Encouragement*, pp. 97–127, 158–164.

16. Donné, *Mémoire Gélatine*, pp. 5, 8–11.

17. *Ann. chim. phys.*, 1831, *47*:220–223.

18. *C.r. Acad.*, 1841, *13*:286–295. The report was reprinted here as a document for the later report of the Gelatin Commission.

19. Magendie, *C.r. Acad.*, 1841, *13*:248–249; Gannal to M. Blainville, February 14, 1834, Dos. Gélatine, No. 87, AAdSc.

20. D'Arcet to a colleague, August 19, 1834, Dos. Gélatine, No. 86, AAdSc.

21. See, for example, *C.r. Acad.*, 1836, *2*:655–656. Other such letters are collected in Dos. Gélatine, AAdSc.

22. D'Arcet, "Objections," Dos. Gélatine, AAdSc.; D'Arcet, "Observations," Ibid., No. 87, pp. 3–5.

23. D'Arcet to Minister of War, May 30, 1835, ibid., No. 83.

24. Blainville to Gannal, February 15, 1834, ibid., No. 87.

25. Donné, *Gélatine*, p. 3.

26. Gannal to Blainville, February 14, 1834, Dos. Gélatine, No. 87, AAdSc.

27. *C.r. Acad.*, 1837, *4*:183; 1838, *6*:304; 1840, *11*:913; 1841, *12*:354.

28. D'Arcet to colleague, July 18, 1836, Dos. Gélatine, No. 87, AAdSc; D'Arcet, "Objections," Dos. Gélatine, AAdSc., paragraph (c).

29. *C.r. Acad.*, 1838, *7*:1117–1119.

30. *C.r. Acad.*, 1840, *10*:870.

31. Magendie, *C.r. Acad.*, 1841, *13*:253–270.

32. Ibid., pp. 270–275.

33. Fourcroy, *Hist. Acad.*, 1782–1783 [Paris, 1787], pp. 502–513.

34. Magendie, *C.r. Acad.*, 1841, *13*:276–278, 280–281.

35. Ibid., p. 282.

36. Ibid., p. 273.

37. *C.r. Acad.*, 1838, *7*:1131.

38. Magendie, *C.r. Acad.*, 1841, *13*:255–256.

39. D'Arcet, "Observations," July 19, 1841, and covering letter July 21, Dos. Gélatine, No. 87, AAdSc. D'Arcet backed up his complaint with detailed marginal comments. There is little doubt that he was correct in his charge; the bias in Magendie's discussion is quite obvious. See Magendie, *C.r. Acad.*, 1841, *13*:237–252.

40. D'Arcet, "Observations," p. 7.

41. *J. débats*, July 4, 1841; July 7, 1841; July 14, 1841; and July 25, 1841.

42. Ibid., August 6, 1841.

43. Gannal, *Lettre*, pp. 1–13.

44. Grmek, *Catalogue*, pp. 54–56, 203–205.

45. Bernard, MS, C. VIIIe., 33a, f.30–f.33.

46. Magendie, *C.r. Acad.*, 1841, *13*:252–253, 266–269.

47. *C.r. Acad.*, 1841, *13*:315.

48. Bernard, MS, C. VIIIe., 9b, pp. 1–31, 131.

49. D'Arcet to colleague, November 26, 1842, Dos. Gélatine, AAdSc. "ont le moins perdu de leurs poids."

50. Bernard, MS, C. VIIIe., 9b, p. 31.

51. Ibid., 33a, ff.29, 33.

52. Dumas, *C.r. Acad.*, 1840, *10*:149–178.

53. Dumas (grandson of the chemist), *La vie de J.–B. Dumas*, MS, AAdSc., pp. 23–44; Prévost and Le Royer, *Annales sci. nat.*, 1825, *4*:481–487. Dumas later claimed that although not included as an author because he had separated from Prévost and Le Royer by the time they published their observations, he had taken part in the experiments. See Dumas, MS 1943, BM, P, 10ᵉ Leçon, p. 37.

54. Lacroix, *Boussingault*, pp. 14–30, 34, 44; Aulie, *Proc. American Philosophical Society*, 1970, *114*:436–439. Aulie gives a comprehensive account of the experiments on the relation of plants to nitrogen which occupied Boussingault through the rest of his career.

55. Boussingault, *C.r. Acad.*, 1838, *6*:102–112; ibid., 1838, *7*:889–891.

56. Boussingault, *Mémoires de l'Académie des Sciences*, 1842, *18*:345–384.

57. Lacroix, *Boussingault*, p. 35.

58. Dumas, *C.r. Acad.*, 1838, *6*:129–131; Dumas, ibid., 1839, *8*:54–58.

59. *C.r. Acad.*, 1839, *8*:54.

60. Ibid., 1838, *7*:129–130.

61. Ibid., 1839, *8*:57.

62. Dumas, MS, *Cours, 1838*, Dos. Dumas, AAdSc., Carton 10, 1ᵉʳ Cahier, 4ᵉ–7ᵉ, 9ᵉ, 11ᵉ, leçons. "Phénomènes chimiques de la respiration."

63. Mitscherlich, Gmelin, and Tiedemann, *Zeit. Physiol.*, 1833, *5*:1–11.

64. Dumas, *Cours, 1838*, 3ᵉ Cahier, "Acide lactique."

65. Mitscherlich, Gmelin, and Tiedemann, *Zeit. Physiol.*, 1833, *5*:9.

66. Wöhler, *Zeit. Physiol.*, 1824, *1*:143–146, 305.

67. Dumas, *Cours, 1838*, 1ᵉʳ Cahier, 9ᵉ leçon, p. 2.

68. Ibid., p. 3.

69. Dumas, Dos. Dumas, AAdSc., Carton 10, 2ᵐᵉ Cahier 1839, 34th–38th page, following (undated) Cahier, 10th page. (The pages are not numbered.)

70. Dumas, ibid., 1ᵉʳ Cahier 1839, 31ᵐᵉ leçon, 3rd page. "Ce mode d'action est tout a fait inverse de celui que l'on observe chez les animaux: chez les plantes appareils de réduction: chez les animaux appareils de combustion."

71. See Nash, *Plants and the Atmosphere*, pp. 36–44, and Holmes, *Isis*, 1963, *59*:59–60.

72. Dumas, Dos. Dumas, AAdSc., Carton 10, 1ᵉʳ Cahier 1839, 31ᵐᵉ leçon, 4th page. "le problème le plus remarquable que la chimie organique ait à résoudre."

73. I have described some of these developments in "Justus Liebig," and will discuss them more fully in a forthcoming study of Liebig in organic chemistry.

74. Dumas, Dos. Dumas, AAdSc., Carton 10, 1ᵉʳ Cahier 1839, 31ᵐᵉ leçon, 4th page. "Véritable oxidation comparable à l'oxidation du plomb." Dumas wrote the acids in the customary way for the period, as combinations of a hypothetical anhydrous acid and water. Both of these reactions were first described by Liebig.

75. Ibid., 7th page.

76. Ibid., 3rd page. "par une réaction encore mystérieuse que la chimie ne sait pas reproduire."

77. Liebig, *Organic Chemistry*, pp. 64–89, 129–133. This publication was a translation of a somewhat revised version of the introduction to the original French volume, *Traité de chimie organique*, I (Paris, 1840). See Paolini, *Liebig*, p. 74. I have not seen a copy of the French version.

78. Dumas and Boussingault, *C.r. Acad.*, 1841, *12*:1005–1025.

79. Dumas, *Annales sci. nat.*, 1841, *16*:39–40, 61; Dumas, *Annales chim. phys.*, 1842, *4*:126.

80. Dumas, *Annales sci. nat.*, 1841, *16*:34–35. The last statement above should be taken with the caution that it relies on the foreshortened notes of Dumas's lecture of 1838 (see footnote 39 above); it is possible that in fact he made his statement then as strong as he did in the printed lecture of 1841.

81. Ibid., pp. 36–39, 47, 58–59.

82. See Kuhn, "Energy conservation," pp. 321–356.

83. Dumas, *Annales sci. nat.*, 1841, *16*:54–60.

84. The closest to a coherent attempt to bring nutritional exchanges and respiration into a single scheme before this had been the "animalization" theory originated by Fourcroy and Hallé at the end of the eighteenth century. By 1830, however, it had been largely dismissed for lack of evidence. See Holmes, *Isis*, 1963, *54*:61–62.

85. Dumas, *Annales sci. nat.*, 1841, *16*:34.

86. Dumas, *Cours, 1838*, Dos. Dumas, AAdSc., Carton 10, 1ᵉʳ Cahier, 11ᵐᵉ leçon, 2nd page. "Dumas croit que le suc gastrique contient quelque principe particulier capable de produire d. remarquables transformations."

87. Dumas, *Annales sci. nat.*, 1841, *16*:57.

88. See below, Chaps. VII–VIII.

89. Schiller, *Bernard*, pp. 73–75; Goodman, *Medical History*, 1972, *16*:130.

90. Kapoor, *Ambix*, 1969, *16*:2–6.

91. For discussions of some of Dumas's major theoretical efforts see Kapoor, ibid., pp. 32–62, and Holmes, "Justus Liebig," pp. 332–336.

92. Dumas to Justus Liebig, (November 29, 1837), MS. Liebegiana No. 58, BS, M.

93. Cahours, *Revue des cours scientifiques*, 1867–1868, 5th year, p. 357.

94. Dumas, *Annales sci. nat.*, 1841, *16*:36.

95. *J. débats*, August 20, 1841.

96. Dumas, *Annales sci. nat.*, 1841, *16*:33–61.

97. Dumas, *Statique chimique*, 2nd ed., [Preface] (unpaginated).

98. *J. débats*, August 20, 1841.

99. The topics of this paragraph are discussed in Holmes, "Justus Liebig," pp. 330–348.

100. Mulder to Liebig, Rotterdam, July 22, 1838, MS. Liebigiana No. 58, BS, M. See also Mulder, *Annalen Pharm.*, 1838, *28*:73–82.

101. Vickery, *The Yale Journal of Biology and Medicine*, 1950, *22*:387–393.

102. Mulder to Liebig, Rotterdam, October 10, 1838, MS. Liebigiana No. 58, BS, M.

103. Ibid., August 20, 1838, October 29, 1838, December 9, 1838, January 29, 1839, September 23, 1839.

104. Julius Vogel, *Annalen Pharm.*, 1839, *30:*20–37.

105. Liebig, *Annalen Pharm.*, 1841, *39:*129–150.

106. Liebig, *Annalen Chem. Pharm.*, 1842, *41:*351–352. Liebig asserted that he had discussed his propositions at length, lecturing from a manuscript eighteen pages long. I do not know if this manuscript has been preserved, and therefore cannot say what form of argument Liebig used then.

107. Liebig, *Annalen Pharm.*, 1841, *39:*156–160. Joseph Fruton has brought to my attention the basic significance of Liebig's conception of the protective function of respiration. See Fruton, *Molecules*, pp. 271–272.

108. Liebig, *Annalen Pharm.*, 1841, *39:*155–156.

109. Ibid., pp. 156–158.

CHAPTER II: PARIS AND GIESSEN AT ODDS

1. Liebig to Pelouze, October 28, 1841, Dos. Dumas, AAdSc. Liebig did not refer to Boussingault and Payen by name, but it is clear from his description that the article to which he referred was Boussingault and Payen, *Annales chim. phys.*, 1841, *3:*65–108.

2. Pelouze to Liebig, June 7, 1841, MS, Liebigiana No. 58, BS, M.

3. Pelouze to Liebig, October 27, 1841, ibid.

4. Liebig to Pelouze, November 1, 1841, Dos. Dumas, AAdSc. For French text, see Appendix C.

5. Pelouze to Liebig, December 10, 1841, Liebig MSS, L-M, G. The persons mentioned were Nicolas Auguste Eugène Millon (1812–1867), professor of chemistry at the Val-de-Grâce; and Edmond Frémy (1819–1894), a former assistant to Pelouze, then professor at the École Polytechnique. See Partington, *A History of Chemistry*, IV, pp. 395, 427. Frémy was particularly influenced by Liebig's ideas about fermentation. See below, Chap. XIV at n. 45.

6. Playfair to Liebig, November 15, 1841, MS 1762, L-M, G.; Liebig to Playfair, November 6, 1841, MS, Liebigiana No. 57, BS, M.

7. Liebig, *Annalen Chem. Pharm.*, 1842, *41:*189.

8. Dumas, *Annales sci. nat.*, 1841, *16:*50.

9. The nitrogen of the nutrients is excreted in special form in the urine, Liebig pointed out, but in this paper he did not emphasize that aspect of the *Stoffwechsel*.

10. Liebig, *Annalen Chem. Pharm.*, 1842, *41:*189–219. I have discussed the problem of Despretz's experiments in Holmes "Introduction," pp. xxxiii, xxxciii–xl.

11. Liebig, *Annalen Chem. Pharm.*, 1842, *41:*241–285.

12. Ibid., pp. 249–250.

13. Dumas, *Essai de statique chimique*, 2nd ed., p. 57.

14. Ibid., pp. 49–88.

15. Dumas, *Annales chim. phys.*, 1842, *4:*115–126.

16. Ibid., p. 126.

17. Ibid., pp. 124, 126.

18. Liebig, *Annales chim. phys.*, 1842, *4*:187.
19. Ibid., p. 208.
20. Magendie, *C.r. Acad.*, 1841, *13*:278–280, 283.
21. Liebig, *Annalen Chem. Pharm.*, 1842, *45*:116.
22. Boussingault to Dumas, April 1, 1842, Dos. Dumas, AAdSc. "Decidément vous avez mis le doigt dans la gorge de m: Liebig."
23. Ibid.

Il faut maintenant organiser de grands moyens de travail à la faculté, on a fait assez de limonade gazeuse comme ça. Il est vraiment honteux pour la france, et je ne suis jamais aussi bon français que quand je me trouve sur les bords du Rhin, il est vraiment honteux qu'un méchant trou comme Giessen, soit un foyer de science, un point de réunion pour toute l'Europe chimique, et qu'on ne vienne à Paris que pour voir nos savants, comme on y vient voir la ménagerie du jardin des plantes, par un pur sentiment de curiosité.

24. Gerhardt to Liebig, January 26, 1842, Inhalts-Verzeichnis, L-M, G; Grimaux and Gerhardt, *Gerhardt*, pp. 452–453.
25. Liebig, *Annalen Chem, Pharm.*, 1842, *41*:351–357.
26. Dumas to Liebig, April 24, 1842, MS Liebigiana No. 58, BS, M.
27. Marignac, *Annales chim. phys.*, 1842, *4*:460–461.
28. Dumas, MS 1943, BM, P, 10me Leçon.
29. Liebig to Pelouze, April 27, 1842, Dos. Dumas, AAdSc. "j'ai été très irrité."
30. Liebig, *Annalen Chem. Pharm.*, 1842, *45*:115; Pelouze to Liebig, May 19, 1842, MS, Liebigiana No. 58, BS, M.
31. Small wonder. In his "Antwort" Liebig had queried why Dumas had not been able to state his views on nutrition at an earlier time "when he watched on and allowed his colleagues in the Academy to prostitute themselves before the eyes of the world over the question of the nutritional value of animal gelatin." Liebig, *Annalen Chem. Pharm.*, 1842, *41*:354–355.
32. Liebig to Pelouze, July 2, 1842, Dos Dumas, AAdSc.:

dans l'affaire Dumas je viens d'offenser tout le corps de la commission de la gélatine. Si Mr. Dumas veut la guerre il l'aura à s'en repentir, mais quel profit resultera de tous ces discussions pour la science. Je suis sûr aucune, nous dirons des phrases désobligeantes, nous nous faisons avaler de la bile . . . nous nous troublons le répos nécessaire à nos travaux journaliers, tout cela je (l'admets) mais puis je laisser passer en silence des procédés de voleur de grand chemin!?

33. He announced its publication to Pelouze in the same letter.
34. Liebig to Pelouze, April 26, 1840, Dos. Dumas, AAdSc.; Liebig to Berzelius, April 26, 1840, *Berzelius und Liebig: ihre Briefe*, ed. J. Carrière, pp. 210–214.
35. Liebig, *Annalen Chem. Pharm.*, 1841, *38*:202–206.
36. Ibid., 1842, *41*:354. Liebig had written Gerhardt that "everyone knows that Dumas has never occupied himself with plant physiology nor with animal physiology." Grimaux and Gerhardt, *Gerhardt*, p. 453. His statement suggests that Liebig was ignorant even of Dumas's early physiological investigations.
37. See Crosland and Brooke, "Gerhardt," pp. 369–370.
38. In the judgment of A. W. Hofmann, one of Liebig's most eminent students and admireres, there was "no shadow of proof that in the writing of his essay Dumas

used researches which had not yet been published." Quoted in Heinrich, "Dumas," in Bugge, ed., *Grossen Chemiker*, II, 66.

39. For an account of earlier episodes, see Holmes, "Justus Liebig."

40. Pelouze to Liebig, July 4, 1842, Liebigiana No. 58, BS, M.; Liebig to Pelouze, July 7, 1842, Dos. Dumas, AAdSc.

41. Dumas, MS 1943, BM, P, 10me Leçon, pp. 42–43.

il n'y a pas de contestation possible a propos d'antériorité mais ici les opinions de Mr. Liebig sont en désaccord complet et je dirai même que les opinions de Mr Liebig à ce sujet sont dans une telle contradiction avec les principes que nous avons posés et que nous admettons dans toutes leur conséquences que ceci seule semble prouver, que ses opinions différent essentiellement des notres prises au point de vue le plus général.

CHAPTER III: THE DEBATE OVER THE SOURCE OF ANIMAL FAT

1. Dumas, MS 1943, BM, P, 1re Leçon. "faire de l'ammoniaque à bon marché peut se reduire à dire: augmenter la population; en un mot: faire des hommes."

2. Ibid., pp. 12–15.

3. Ibid., pp. 7–10.

4. This conclusion is not incompatible with Dumas's assertion in defense of his original lecture, that there had been enough information available before Liebig's article appeared to account for Dumas's enunciation of the general idea that plants contain all of the animal substances.

5. Liebig, *Annalen Chem. Pharm.*, 1842, *41*:200–201.

6. A slightly revised version of Dumas's lecture was printed four years later, still with no mention of Liebig, in Dumas, *Chimie appliquée*, VIII, 417–431. My interpretation must be tentative, since there are no detailed notes preserved of Dumas's lectures for 1841; the possibility that he had developed these approaches prior to Liebig's publications cannot be ruled out.

7. Dumas, MS 1943, BM, P, 2me, 3me, 4me Leçon.

8. Ibid., 5me Leçon, April 20, 1842, pp. 1–8. Reproduced in Dumas, *Chimie appliquée*, VIII, 446–452.

9. Dumas, *Cours*, 4me Leçon, p. 21.

10. Chevreul, *Corps gras, passim*; Berzelius, *Traité*, p. 326; Varrentrapp, *Annalen Chem. Pharm.*, 1840, *35*:65–67; Costa, *Chevreul*, pp. 46–70.

11. Chevreul, *Corps gras*, pp. 25–26, 28–31.

12. Ibid., pp. 71–74; Bussy and Lecanu, *Annales chim. phys.*, 1825, *30*:5–20; 1827, *34*:57–68.

13. Chevreul, *Corps gras*, pp. 23, 61; Berzelius, *Traité*, V, 351–352. Berzelius considered the C_{34} in Chevreul's formula for margaric acid to be a typographical error, and he thought there might have been small errors in the numbers of hydrogen atoms because it was impossible to eliminate all of the oleic acid mixed with margaric acid. Chevreul's margaric acid was later shown to be a mixture of stearic and palmitic acid. See Costa, *Chevreul*, pp. 74–76.

14. Liebig, *Annalen Chem. Pharm.*, 1840, *35*:44–45.

15. Varrentrapp, ibid., pp. 65–86; Redtenbacher, ibid., pp. 46–65.

16. Dumas, MS 1946, BM, P, 23ᶜ and 24ᶜ Leçon, pp. 20, 24–26.

"elle nous conduira à l'exposition des transformations que les corps gras éprouvent dans les animaux."

"elles subissent un commencement de combustion, et, en s'oxydant, l'acide stéarique se dédouble et donne de l'acide margarique."

The manuscript is a page proof for a volume which was not published, based on Dumas's lecture notes. The numbers referred to are on the backs of the sheets.

17. Ibid., pp. 21–22. In November Dumas published the series in a short note: Dumas, *C.r. Acad.*, 1842, *15:*935–936. There he doubled the numbers of carbon and hydrogen atoms in the above formulas. I have corrected two obvious typographical errors in the formulas for caproic and enanthic acid.

18. Costa, Chevreul, p. 69.

19. Dumas, MS 1946, BM, P, pp. 22, 32–33. "la plus grande simplicité." Liebig made similar calculations of the heat produced in the formation of a given amount of carbonic acid. For a critique of the assumptions on which they were based, see Holmes, "Introduction," pp. lxxv–lxxxvi.

20. Dumas, MS 1946, BM, P, 23ᶜ and 24ᶜ Leçon, pp. 26, 33.

21. Dumas and Cahours, *Annales sci. nat.*, 1842, *18:*351.

22. Ibid., pp. 356–363.

23. Ibid., pp. 357–358, 362–372.

24. Ibid., pp. 350–351.

25. Ibid., pp. 353–354.

26. Ibid., pp. 375–376.

27. Liebig, *Animal Chemistry*, pp. 71–75. See above, Chap. II at n. 11.

28. See above, Chap. I at n. 109, Chap. II at n. 11.

29. Liebig, *Animal Chemistry*, pp. 290–296.

30. Ibid., p. xxxi.

31. Liebig, *Annalen Chem. Pharm.*, 1842, *45:*125–126.

32. *C.r. Acad.*, 1842, *15:*792–793.

33. See Holmes, *Isis*, 1963, *54:*71–72.

34. Liebig, *Annalen Chem. Pharm.*, 1842, *45:*113–128.

35. Ibid., pp. 123–124, 128.

36. Dumas, Boussingault, and Payen, *C.r. Acad.*, 1843, *16:*348; Boussingault, ibid., p. 668.

37. *Travaux ... de Payen*, pp. 3–24; *Supplement ... sur ... Payen*, pp. 1–8.

38. *Travaux ... de Payen*, p. 19; Payen to Dumas, December 4, 1839 and May 7, 1840. MS, Dos. Payen, AAdSc. I have inferred their state of friendship from the tone of these and other letters of Payen to Dumas, and evidence such as that in the second letter, that the Payen's and Dumas's sometimes dined together.

39. *Supplement ... sur ... Payen*, pp. 1–2; *C.r. Acad.*, 1842, *14:*59.

40. Dumas, Boussingault and Payen, "Recherches sur l'origine des matières grasses de l'organisation," MS, Dossier of the meeting of the Academy of February 13, 1843, AAdSc. "je me fais un véritable honneur de me rallier le premier à des vues dont personne n'apprécie mieux que moi la haute valeur." The document is mostly comprised of Payen's explanation of his own position. There is also a rough draft of the statement. There is no indication of whether or not Payen ever read it to the Academy.

41. *Supplement ... sur ... Payen*, pp. 3–4.

42. Dumas, Boussingault and Payen, "L'origine des matières grasses." "les

méthodes de la chimie pratique et les lumières de la physiologie animal ou végétale, deux sciences si dignement représentées dans le sein de l'Académie."

43. Payen to Dumas (two undated letters), Payen to Dumas, December 22, 1842, Douz (?) to Payen, December 17, 1842, Guillemin to Payen, December 15, 1842, MS, Dossier of the meeting of the Academy of February 13, 1843, AAdSc. "elle s'accorde avec nos idées et nos résultats."

44. *L'Institut*, No. 474, January 26, 1843, p. 27, and No. 477, February 16, 1843, p. 52. The memoir was probably read at some subsequent meeting. See ibid., No. 480, March 9, 1843, p. 80.

45. Dumas, Boussingault and Payen, *C.r. Acad.*, 1843, *16*:352–353.

46. Ibid., pp. 350–352. Deliberately Payen made no mention at all that it was the recent investigation of Gundlach, not the older ones of Huber upon which Liebig had based his arguments. When Liebig complained about this, Payen condescendingly lectured Liebig on using self-proclaimed novel results in place of the same results obtained long before.

47. Ibid., pp. 347, 354.

48. Ibid., p. 352.

49. Ibid., p. 362.

50. Dumas, Boussingault, and Payen, ibid., pp. 348–349. Dumas later asserted that he had already been teaching these ideas in the spring of 1842. Dumas, *C.r. Acad.*, 1843, *16*:667.

51. Payen, *C.r. Acad.*, 1843, *16*:555.

52. Liebig, *C.r. Acad.*, 1843, *16*:552–554.

53. Payen, *C.r. Acad.*, 1843, *16*:555–556.

54. *L'Institut*, No. 480, March 9, 1843, p. 81, No. 481, March 16, 1843, p. 86.

55. Dumas, *C.r. Acad.*, 1843, *16*:559–560.

56. Ibid., pp. 558–559.

57. Donné, *J. débats*, April 5, 1843.

58. Liebig, *C.r. Acad.*, 1843, *16*:664–665.

59. Dumas, *C.r. Acad.*, 1843, *16*:673–675.

60. Liebig, *C.r. Acad.*, 1843, *16*:664.

61. *C.r. Acad.*, 1843, *16*:666–668; Lewy, ibid., 675–678.

62. Boussingault, *C.r. Acad.*, 1843, *16*:668–673.

63. Dumas, *C.r. Acad.*, 1843, *16*:668.

64. Liebig, *C.r. Acad.*, 1843, *16*:663.

65. Payen, *C.r. Acad.*, 1843, *16*:770.

66. Ibid.

67. Dumas, Boussingault, and Payen, *C.r. Acad.*, 1843, *16*:349. They presented a more elaborate discussion of a possible chemical basis for such reactions in an expanded version of their memoir which appeared later in the year in *Annales chim. phys.*, 1843, *8*:63–114 (see esp. pp. 70–75).

68. Dumas, *C.r. Acad.*, 1843, *16*:561.

69. [Boussingault] MS, Dossier of the meeting of February 13, 1843, AAdSc.

"Si l'expérience de Huber est vrai, il est évident que notre opinion n'est pas fondée."

"Néanmoins en discutant mon expérience sur la vache ... je reconnais qu'elle n'est pas favorable à l'opinion que nous soutenons."

The loose page has no title. It lists points (2) to (8).

70. Dumas, Boussingault, and Payen, *C.r. Acad.*, 1843, *16*:352. See also Dumas, *C.r. Acad.*, 1843, *16*:667.

71. Dumas, Boussingault, and Payen, *C.r. Acad.*, 1843, *16*:353.

72. Lewy, *C.r. Acad.*, 1843, *16*:678.

73. Liebig, *Annalen Chem. Pharm.*, 1842, *45*:123, 128.

74. Dumas, Boussingault, and Payen, *Annales sci. nat.*, 1843, *19*:385; see also *Annales chim. phys.*, 1843, *8*:114.

75. *Annales sci. nat.*, 1843, *19*:386.

76. Payen, *C.r. Acad.*, 1843, *16*:568.

77. Magendie, Payen, ibid., pp. 554–555.

78. Payen, ibid., pp. 567–572.

79. Magendie, *C.r. Acad.*, 1843, *16*:601.

80. Magendie, *C.r. Acad.*, 1843, *16*:557; see also p. 571.

81. Dumas, *C.r. Acad.*, 1843, *16*:557–558.

82. Payen, *C.r. Acad.*, 1843, *16*:571, 572.

83. For illustrations of Donné's attitude see his comments on a paper by Poiseuille, *J. débats*, March 5, 1843, and his comparison of the merits of Andral and Poiseuille, ibid., February 22, 1843.

84. "Donné," *Biographisches Lexikon*, ed. Hirsch, II, pp. 294–295; Magendie, *C.r. Acad.*, 1841, *13*:248.

85. Donné, *J. débats*, October 26, 1842.

86. Ibid., April 5, 1843.

87. Ibid.

88. Ibid.

89. Dumas, MS 1946, BM, P, 23ᶜ and 24ᶜ Leçon, pp. 33–40 (See fn. 16). The conclusion that this section was added in 1843 to the original lecture is partly based on internal evidence, partly on a notation by the editor Melsens (p. 6), that it was not included in the portion he had originally edited, and partly on the fact that the printed dates of the lecture are May 13 and 16, 1843, whereas a pencilled notation gives June 1 and 3, 1842.

90. Ibid., "Leçon de 10 Juin, 1843—Glucose," pp. 8–10, 18–22. "la présence ... de soude ... dans le sang modifie les procédés de combustion d'une façon très notable." "l'acide gallique respire."

91. Ibid., "Leçon de 10 Juin, 1843—Glucose," pp. 8–10, 18–22.

CHAPTER IV: THE FRENCH CHEMISTS ON THE DEFENSIVE

1. Donné, *J. débats*, June 13, 1843.

2. Cahours, *Revue des cours scientifiques*, 1867–68, *5*:357–358; Dumas, "Discours," Dos. Pelouze, AAdSc., p. 2.

3. See Pelouze to Berzelius, March 28, 1838, May 12, 1838, September 11, 1838, *Berzelius Brev*, ed. Söderbaum, pp. 29–39. I have treated this situation in "Justus Liebig."

4. Pelouze to Berzelius, February 27, 1840, August 26, 1840, *Berzelius Brev*, ed. Söderbaum, pp. 58–69; Pelouze to Liebig, March 12, 1840, MS, Liebigiana No. 58, BS, M.

5. Pelouze to Berzelius, May 19, 1842, *Berzelius Brev*, ed. Söderbaum, p. 101.

6. Pelouze to Liebig, May 19, 1842, MS, Liebigiana No. 58, BS, M.

7. ("Voilà donc l'oie de Mr. D.enfoncée!!") Pelouze to Liebig, December 30, 1842. ibid.

8. Pelouze to Liebig, April 22, 1843, ibid.

9. Pelouze to Liebig, December 30, 1842, ibid.

10. Dumas, *Éloge de Pelouze*, p. 50; Dehérain, "Frémy," p. 23.

11. Boutron and Frémy, *Annales chim. phys.*, 1841, *2*:257–274.

12. Pelouze and Gelis, *C.r. Acad.*, 1843, *16*:1262–1271.

13. Berthelot, *Mém. Soc. Biol.*, 1854, pp. 191–193.

14. Pelouze and Gelis, *C.r. Acad.*, 1843, *16*:1263–1264.

15. My account must be qualified to the extent that it is based on the printed memoir. Donné noted, however, that because of lack of time at the session Pelouze was unable to read the paper, but could only "give the substance of it" and show samples of the butyric acid. "They have," he related, "exhibited their curious products under the eyes, we should say under the nose of the Academy: for the hall of the Institute was filled throughout the session with the odor of butter." The perfume affected the members disagreeably. Donné, *J. débats*, June 13, 1843.

16. Ibid.

17. Payen, *C.r. Acad.*, 1843, *16*:1271.

18. Dumas, *C.r. Acad.*, 1842, *15*:935–936.

19. Donné, *J. débats*, June 13, 1843.

20. Ibid.

21. Liebig to Dieffenbach, August 6, 1843, MS 1363, L-M, G.

22. Dumas (grandson), *La vie de J.-B. Dumas*, MS, Dos. Dumas, AAdSc., p. 44.

23. Dumas, Payen, and Boussingault, *C.r. Acad.*, 1843, *16*:350.

24. Dumas and Edwards, *C.r. Acad.*, 1843, *17*:531–537.

25. Ibid.

26. Ibid., p. 537.

27. Payen, *C.r. Acad.*, 1843, *17*:537–539.

28. Ibid., p. 538.

29. Dumas, Payen, and Boussingault, *Annales sci. nat.*, 1843, *19*:385.

30. Payen, *C.r. Acad.*, 1843, *17*:540–541.

31. *C.r. Acad.*, 1843, *17*:541–542, 545.

32. Ibid., pp. 542–544.

33. Ibid., pp. 545–546.

34. Donné, *J. débats*, September 22, 1843.

35. Ibid.

36. Chossat, *C.r. Acad.*, 1843, *17*:805–808.

37. Vogel, *J. pharm. chim.* 1843, *14*:309–310.

38. Milne Edwards, *C.r. Acad.*, 1843, *17*:925–931; Liebig, *Annalen Chem. Pharm.*, 1843, *48*:130–138; Liebig to Milne Edwards, October 17, 1843; Milne Edwards to Liebig, October 27, 1843, MS, Liebigiana No. 58, BS, M; Liebig, *Die Thier-Chemie*, 2nd. ed., pp. 79–80, 86–87, 141–142. The pagination in the second edition differs from that in the first edition cited by Liebig, but the statements are nearly identical.

39. Liebig, *Annalen*, 1843, *48*:139–140, 144–147.

40. Ibid., p. 136.

41. Wurtz, *Annales chim. phys.*, 1844, *11*:253–255.

42. Playfair, *Memoirs of the Chemical Society*, 1841–1843, *1*:174–190.
43. Ibid., pp. 174–181.
44. Reid, *Playfair*, p. 43. See also pp. 45–52, 88–90; Playfair to Liebig, November 1, 1841, MS 1763, L-M, G.
45. Playfair, *Memoirs of the Chemical Society*, 1841–1843, *1*:177.
46. Ibid., p. 184.
47. Dumas to Liebig, November 29, 1837, MS Liebigiana No. 58, BS, M.
48. Carl Jacob Ettling to Pelouze, April 4, 1837, MS, Dos. Pelouze, AAdSc. Ettling had visited Persoz on the way from Paris to Giessen.
49. Persoz, "Expériences," MS, Dossier of the meeting of February 12, 1844, AAdSc., 2nd page.
50. Persoz, *C.r. Acad.*, 1844, *18*:245–254. The published extract omits the introduction contained in the manuscript.

CHAPTER V: THE PERSISTENCE OF JEAN-BAPTISTE BOUSSINGAULT

1. Boussingault, *Annales chim. phys.*, 1845, *14*:421.
2. Boussingault to Dumas, May 26, 1844; Dos. Dumas, AAdSc.
3. Ibid.

Vous aurez bientôt des nouvelles de mes porcs, mais j'ai si peu de curiosité que bien que j'ai toutes les données je ne sais pas encore si le résultat est pour ou contre nous. Sous le rapport pratique la question est jugée en notre faveur; reste la question physiologique.

4. Boussingault, *Annales sci. nat.*, 1844, *1*:234.
5. *L'Institute*, No. 550, July 10, 1844, p. 240.
6. Letellier, *Annales sci. nat.*, 1844, *2*:38–45; for evidence of the close relation of Letellier's work to other investigations by Boussingault, see Boussingault, ibid., pp. 216–221. The letter of Boussingault to Dumas of May 26, 1844 implies that Letellier was a trusted friend of the former. Letellier apparently did very little other experimental research.
7. Boussingault, *Annales sci. nat.*, 1844, *2*:218.
8. Boussingault to Dumas, August 14, 1844, Dos. Dumas, AAdSc. For French text, see Appendix D.
9. Boussingault, *Annales chim. phys.*, 1844, *12*:153–164.
10. Ibid., pp. 164–167. Even in his own terms there was a lapse in Boussingault's reasoning. If he assumed that the sole cause of the loss of weight in the cows was the missing fat in their diets, then the deficit should equal the decrease in weight. Conversely the excess of dietary fat over the fat lost in the excrements and milk when the animals were gaining weight should have equalled the increase of weight. These requirements were not even approximately met in his data. His data were, however, compatible with his conclusion that the butterfat could have been produced from the loss of weight in the cows.
11. Pierre Rayer, professor of comparative medicine at the Faculty of Medicine in Paris, and a member elected to the Academy of Sciences in rural economy in 1843.

12. Boussingault to Dumas, January 13, 1845, Dos. Dumas, AAdSc. For French text, see Appendix E.

13. Boussingault, *C.r. Acad.*, 1845, *20:*1726.

14. Milne Edwards, Payen, *C.r. Acad.*, 1845, *20:*1726–1728.

15. Payen, *C.r. Acad.*, 1845, *20:*1728.

16. Liebig, *Annalen Chem. Pharm.*, 1845, *54:*376.

17. Ibid., pp. 376–383.

18. Boussingault, *Annales chim. phys.*, 1845, *14:*419–482.

19. Carbon was Boussingault's principal concern here, but he also believed that some nitrogen is exhaled in respiration. See Boussingault, *Annales sci. nat.*, 1844, *2:*211–221.

20. Boussingault, *Annales chim. phys.*, 1845, *14:*436–447, 477–478.

21. Boussingault's use of the term protein here reflected undoubtedly the influence of the protein theory of Mulder. Elsewhere in the article he used the older terms "nitrogenous substances," or "nitrogenous principles."

22. Boussingault, *Annales chim. phys.*, 1845, *14:*454, 481–482.

23. Ibid., pp. 419–422.

24. Boussingault to Dumas, December 27, 1845, Dos. Dumas, AAdSc.

> Samedi 27 décembre 1845
>
> Mon cher ami. Venez donc dîner rue du pas de la mule 8, mardi 30. Vous aurez à prononcer sur la valeur d'un pâté de foie gras, préparé avec des foies engraissés par une nouvelle méthode, nécessairement contraire à nos idées théoriques.
>
> > tout à vous
> > Boussingault
> > r.s.p.

25. See Voit, *Zeit. Biologie*, 1870, *6:*371.

26. Other factors besides the fat controversy were also contributing to this lesson. For an account of Liebig's growing caution, and even skepticism over these years, see Holmes, "Introduction," pp. lxxix-xc.

27. Boussingault, *Annales chim. phys.*, 1845, *14:*479.

28. See above, Chap. V at n. 20.

29. See above, Chap. IV at n.33.

30. Milne Edwards, *C.r. Acad.*, 1845, *20:*1727.

31. Magendie, *C.r. Acad.*, 1846, *23:*189. As Chap. VIII will show, such a view was not new in 1846, but it was becoming more prominent.

32. Payen, *C.r. Acad.*, 1846, *24:*1065–1068.

33. Dumas, *C.r. Acad.*, 1845, *21:*707–717.

34. See above, Chap. III at nn. 74, 75.

35. Boussingault, *Annales chim. phys.*, 1845, *14:*420.

36. See above, Chap. I at n. 87.

37. See above, Chap. III at n. 87.

38. Boussingault, *Annales chim. phys.*, 1846, *18:*444–478.

39. Ibid.

40. Ibid., pp. 469–472.

41. Another term commonly used at the time to refer to albumin, fibrin, casein, and other analogous nitrogenous substances.

42. Boussingault to Dumas, August 29, 1846, Dos. Dumas, AAdSc. "je vous prie d'insister sur la partie qui concerne les expériences faites avec cette substance."

Je fais un acte de justice, plutôt qu'un acte d'amitie en faisant ressortir la grandeur des vues que vous avez émisé sur la digestion. Le principal mérite de mon travail est de justifier complètement vos idées sur les aliments que vous avez nommé respiratoires. Un animal qui ne reçoit qu'un albuminoïde pur, brûle de sa propre substance et finit par mourir d'inanitié, parce que cet albuminoïde, ne sut donne pas assez de carbone. Ne m'en voulez pas si j'ai rappelé vos conceptions avec un peu de chaleur; c'est que je suis agacé par tous ces menus travaux des physiologistes qui viennent nous dire en 1846 que le sucre passe dans le sang pour être brûlé.

43. Magendie, *C.r. Acad.*, 1846, *23*:189–193.
44. Olmsted, *Claude Bernard, Physiologist*, p. 158.
45. See above, Chap. III at n. 47.
46. Boussingault, *Annales chim. phys.*, 1848, *24*:460–463.
47. Another reason that Boussingault's investigation made less impact, is that its result was soon afterward contradicted by researches of others, such as Herman Nasse. See Moleschott, *Nahrungsmittel*, p. 499.

CHAPTER VI: ORIGINS OF CLAUDE BERNARD'S RESEARCH IN ANIMAL CHEMISTRY

1. Bernard, *Introduction* (rep., 1965), p. 228.
2. Bernard did not name the chemists he had in mind, but his description and reference to the "very eminent chemists" who wished to establish "the laws of a chemical statics of animals" make quite clear whom he meant. *Introduction* (rep., 1965), p. 228.
3. Bernard, MS, AM, P, Cote 554 (1426), no. 2. The notebook is unpaginated. It was begun in 1839, but some entries are as late as December 1843. See Roger, *La presse médicale*, 1933, *41*:1785–1789, in which extensive extracts from the notebook are printed. The notes on Liebig were probably not written earlier than the fall of 1842, when the French edition of his *Animal Chemistry* appeared. The discussion of Liebig's ideas is contained on consecutive left-hand pages of the notebook, opposite discussions of similar topics referring to earlier authors. It is possible, therefore, that the notes on the right-hand pages do date from 1839, and that Bernard added the notes on Liebig later when his book was published. If such were the case it would suggest even more strongly the impact of Liebig's thought on what Bernard had previously learned as a student. The quotation in Chap. I at n. 8 is from the discussion on the right-hand page, following a summary of the debate between followers of the Lavoisier view that combustion occurs in the lungs and the Lagrange view that it takes place in the general circulation. I have assumed therefore that the skeptical response implied in that passage relates to the situation prior to the appearance of the ideas of Liebig and Dumas. The discussions of Liebig to which Bernard's notes refer are found in Liebig, *Animal Chemistry*, pp. 13–14, 253–263. The paraphrased sentences are on p. 12. If the notes are lecture notes certain references in it suggest that the lecturer may have been Pierre-Honoré Bérard (see also below n. 9).
4. Bernard, MS C. VIIIe, 14d, 25 pages beginning from back of notebook; MS C. VIIIe, 14c, 79 pages beginning from back. These notebooks do not state that they

consist of notes from Dumas's lectures, but the subject matter and some of the language follow so closely that of the lecture notes of Dumas in MS 1943 and MS 1945, BM, P, that there can be little doubt about their source. Particularly close correspondences can be seen between Bernard MS C. VIIIe, 14d, pp. 12–13 and Dumas MS 1943, BM, P, 5me Leçon, p. 21. There are several references suggesting Dumas was the speaker, such as "-exp. excessivement concluantes dit Dumas-," MS C. VIIIe, 14d, p. 25 verso. Most of Bernard's notes are undated, but two of them on digestion, July 13, 1843 (14d, p. 20 verso), and July 15, 1843 (14c, 53rd page), coincide with lectures on the same topics by Dumas (MS 1945, 28me Leçon and 29me Leçon). Bernard's notes on digestion clearly follow the same sequence of topics as do Dumas's notes. Grmek, *Catalogue*, pp. 236–37, describes the contents in question from 14c as derived from Bernard's reading, and gives no source for 14d. Dr. Grmek also now considers these notebooks, however, to contain notes from Dumas's course (Personal communication, July 18, 1972).

5. Bernard, *Leçons sur le diabète*, p. 167.

6. Magendie, *J. physiol.*, 1821, *1*:28.

7. Théodorides, *Clio medica*, 1965, *1*:31.

8. Schiller has gathered together the fragmentary evidence available from published and manuscript sources to demonstrate how extensive and important Bernard's association with Pelouze's laboratory was. See Schiller, *Bernard*, pp. 63–66.

9. Bernard, MS C. VIIIe No. 14d, pp. 1–27 (from front of notebook). The identification of these notes with Bérard's lectures is based on internal similarities to sections of Bérard, *Cours*. Although published later, this work was, according to Bérard, based on his teaching over the preceding sixteen years (ibid., p. vii). The following comparisons are especially close; Bérard, I, pp. 501–511 and 14d, pp. 8–9; Bérard, I, pp. 535–539 and 14d, p. 11; Bérard, I, pp. 546–552, and 14d, p. 11 verso. Bérard's name is mentioned three times, 14d, pp. 13 verso, 16, 18.

10. Kourilsky, "La médecine clinique," pp. 66–70; Olmsted, *Bernard*, p. 19.

11. See Rayer, *Traité des maladies des reins*.

12. Kourilsky, "La médecine clinique," p. 66; Olmsted, *Bernard*, pp. 18–19.

13. Bernard MS C. VIIIe, No. 14e, pp. 1–68, 104–124. The places and dates of lectures are given, but not the lecturer. The ideas are easily identifiable as those of de Blainville. See Blainville, *Histoire des sciences*, and Coleman, "Blainville," p. 187. De Blainville is mentioned frequently in Bernard's notes. Pages 69–103 are on an unrelated topic in physiological chemistry. They also date from 1840, but are probably not by de Blainville.

14. See, for example, Bernard, *Introduction*, p. 109.

15. Bernard, MS C. VIIIe, No. 14e, pp. 10, 42, 43. There were, of course, other sources of these general ideas. The pursuit of the first idea was generally associated with de Blainville. See Robin, *Mém. Soc. Biol.*, 1849, *1*:iv.

16. Bernard, MS C. VIIIe, No. 26b, f. 1, p. 1.

17. Bernard, *Liquides de l'organisme*, I, 62–162.

18. Bernard, MS C. VIIIe, No. 26b, f. 1, p. 2.

19. Ibid., ff. 2–4, pp. 3–7; ff. 5–7, pp. 3–6.

20. Ibid., f. 5, pp. 1–2; f. 8, p. 7. As will be seen below, however, Magendie had already reasoned in earlier experiments that no combustion of these substances occurs in the blood.

21. Ibid., ff. 8–9, pp. 7–10.

22. Magendie, *J. physiol.*, 1821, *1*:1–17; Magendie, ibid., pp. 18–31; Magendie, *Phénomènes*, I, 18–53, 79–164.

23. Ibid., p. 121

24. Ibid., p. 89.

25. Schiller has noted that the reaction was known in the eighteenth century. He considered Bernard to have been original in applying the "chemical method to physiological purposes," Schiller, *Bernard*, p. 67, although he mentions also its prior use by Fodéra and Magendie. Magendie, *Phénomènes*, pp. 67, 108.

26. Fodéra, *J. physiol.*, 1823, *3*:35–45. For a fuller discussion of the evolution of Magendie and Fodéra's experiments and ideas concerning absorption, see Pickstone, *Origins*, chap. IV.

27. See n. 22.

28. See Grmek, *Catalogue*, p. 386, and the manuscript entries listed there for 1841 and 1842.

29. Bernard, C. VIIIe, 7a No. 2, pp. 1–4.

30. Bernard, MS C. VIIIe, 7a No. 2, pp. 4–5.

31. I owe the information concerning M. Coze and his theories to M. D. Grmek, *Raisonnement expérimental*, p. 407. This excellent and detailed study of Bernard's researches on poisons and drugs appeared at the time my own book was going to press. Grmek's book illuminates some of the same general characteristics of Bernard's experimentation and thought that emerge in the present account of his early work in the areas of digestion and nutrition.

32. Bernard, MS C. VIIIe, 7a No. 2, pp. 6–8, 38–40, 43–47, 51–60.

33. Ibid., p. 8.

34. Ibid., pp. 53–54.

35. Ibid., p. 11.

36. Bernard was thinking of using lactate of iron to react with the prussiate of potassium.

37. Bernard, MS C. VIIIe, 7a No. 2, pp. 11–12.

38. See, for example, Béclard, *Traité*, pp. 296–298; Bérard, *Cours*, III, 190; Longet, *Traité*, I, 2–3. These treatises date from a few years later, of course, but it is reasonable to assume that such general textbooks were relatively conservative.

39. This reconstruction of the development of Bernard's thought must remain tentative, for the passages cited above are not dated, and since the notebook is not written strictly in chronological order, they may not have been written at the time their general position with respect to the dated experimental protocols seems to suggest.

40. Bernard, MS C. VIIIe, 7a No. 2, pp. 15, 19.

41. Ibid., p. 20.

42. I have discussed both these analyses and Bernard's later critical opinions of them in Holmes, "Claude Bernard's concept of the milieu intérieur," 1962, pp. 86–90. Paradoxically, Dumas was also one of the principal founders of this endeavor, but it was work of the early, physiological phase of his career, related only indirectly to his nutritional theories.

43. Mialhe, *C.r. Acad.*, 1841, *13*:478–480. See also, Mialhe, *Traité*, pp. 1–105.

44. Chevreul, *Journal des savants*, 1837, pp. 664–667.

45. Bernard, MS C. VIIIe, 7a No. 2, pp. 61–62, 64–65.

46. Ibid., pp. 85–87.

47. Ibid., p. 100.

48. Ibid., pp. 63–64.

49. Bernard later wrote that he had settled on the use of lactate of iron because other iron salts, such as the chlorate and the sulfate caused the animals to become sick or die. He next made a salt of iron filings and gastric juice, but the preparation was not stable. Then, "knowing otherwise that lactic acid exists free in the gastric juice," he thought that lactate of iron would not be harmful, and used it successfully. Bernard, *Archives gén. méd.*, 1848, *16*:64–65. The account as he gave it, however, is chronologically impossible. As the basis for his knowledge of lactic acid in gastric juice he referred to a paper which he actually did not publish until over a year after he began using lactate of iron for his injection experiments. (See also Chap. XV at n. 19.)

50. Bernard, MS C. VIIIe, 7a No. 2, pp. 65–67.

51. Ibid., pp. 69–70.

52. Ibid., p.73.

53. Ibid., pp. 92–94.

54. Ibid., pp. 68–69.

55. Ibid., p. 71.

56. Ibid., p. 72.

57. Ibid., pp. 75–76.

58. Ibid., pp. 76–77.

59. Ibid., p. 78.

60. With the exception, of course, of his assistance with the work of the gelatin commission. Those experiments, however, did not delve into what happens to the nutrient substances after they enter the body.

61. Bernard, MS C. VIIIe, 7a No. 2, p. 79.

62. Ibid., p. 92.

63. Ibid., pp. 80, 82.

64. Ibid., pp. 89–92.

65. He was aware, however, of the alternative explanation that the substance could have reached the chyle through the general lymphatic vessels. The question caused him to ponder what the relation was between chyle and lymph. Bernard, MS C. VIIIe, 7a No. 2, pp. 101–102.

66. Ibid., pp. 101–104.

CHAPTER VII: THE INVESTIGATION OF DIGESTION,
1750–1830

1. Réaumur, "Sur la digestion des oiseaux. Premier Mémoire," *Hist. Acad.*, 1752 [1756], pp. 266–307; Réaumur, "Sur la digestion des oiseaux. Second Mémoire," ibid., pp. 461–495.

2. Réaumur, "Second Mémoire," p. 471.

3. Ibid., pp. 473, 480–487.

4. Ibid., p. 473. The analogy itself was not new, but had previously been used by partisans of the solvent theory of digestion. See Blondlot, *Traité*, p. 7.

5. Ibid., pp. 481, 486–487.

6. Spallanzani, *Dissertations*, I, 7–293.

7. Ibid., pp. 261–272. Marine acid was the traditional name for what became after

the chemical revolution muriatic acid and, after the first decades of the nineteenth century, hydrochloric acid. Scopoli's conclusion was therefore not unfounded.

8. Ibid., pp. 48, 76–77.

9. This paragraph follows the discussion of those topics in Bates, *Bull. Hist. Med.*, 1962, *36*:341–361; and in Bylebyl, *J. Hist. Med.*, 1970, *25*:3–21. The latter treats especially the effects of Montegre's work.

10. Holmes, *Isis.*, 1971, *62*:141–148.

11. Baumé, *Manual*, p. 306.

12. Beach, *J. Hist. Med.*, 1961, *16*:361–363.

13. Rouelle, *Journal de médecine*, 1773, *39*:258–265; Rouelle, ibid., 1773, *40*:59–66.

14. Scheele, *Werke*, II, 249–254; Berthollet, *Hist. Acad.*, 1782 [1785], pp. 616–619.

15. Fourcroy, *Hist. Acad.*, 1782–1783 [Paris, 1787], pp. 502–509.

16. Bostock, *Journal of Natural Philosophy* (Nicholson's), 1805, *11*:244–254.

17. Berzelius, *Annales de chimie*, 1813, *88*:26–72, 113–141; *89*:20–45.

18. Ibid., pp. 26–72, quotations pp. 44, 59, 71.

19. Ibid., pp. 113–141.

20. Tiedemann and Gmelin, *Sur la digestion*, I, v–vii.

21. Tiedemann and Gmelin, *Verdauung*, I, 306. Tiedemann and Gmelin, *Sur la digestion*, pp. 227–229, 344. References to both the German and French editions of this book are given because I have translated from the German and followed it when they differ in emphasis, but the French edition was most likely that with which Bernard and other French scientists were familiar. The pages in the French edition will in the following references be given in parentheses following the reference to the German.

22. Tiedemann and Gmelin, *Verdauung*, I, 2 (Fr. pp. ix–x, 2).

23. Ibid., "Introduction" (paginated separately), p. 3, pp. 143–149 (Fr. pp. viii, 160–165).

24. Müller, *Handbuch*, I, 511.

25. Tiedemann and Gmelin, *Verdauung*, I, 156 (This paragraph is not present in the French edition. See Fr., p. 171).

26. Tiedemann and Gmelin, *Verdauung*, I, 7–14, 20–22, 31–35 *et passim* (Fr., 7–14, 20–21, 29–33 *et passim*).

27. Ibid., pp. 97–100, 137–138, 151–153 (Fr., pp. 96–99, 151, 166–168).

28. Prout, *Phil. Trans. Roy. Soc.*, 1824, Pt. 1, pp. 45–49. See also Brock, *Medical History*, 1965, *9*:114–115.

29. Tiedemann and Gmelin, *Verdauung*, I, 162–286. (Fr., pp. 176–325).

30. Ibid., "Intro.," p. 5 (Fr., p. x).

31. The French translation says erroneously, "semblable à l'amidon." (Fr. p. 340).

32. Ibid., pp. 300–302, 345, 354 (Fr., pp. 338–340, 377–378, 387).

33. Ibid., pp. 180–183 (Fr., pp. 199–201).

34. Kirchhoff, *J. pharm.*, 1816, *2*:250–258.

35. Tiedemann and Gmelin, *Verdauung*, I, 183 (Fr., p. 201). Kirchhoff had found in addition to sugar a residue insoluble in alcohol but soluble in water, which he considered to be "modified starch which has not yet completely changed to sugar." Kirchhoff, *J. pharm.*, 1816, *2*:253. Tiedemann and Gmelin also found besides sugar a substance soluble in water which they regarded as "a starch approaching gum" and which no longer reacted with iodine as starch does. Their substance was not the same

as that of Kirchhoff, however, for that found by the latter did not form a precipitate with infusion of gall-nuts, while theirs did. Tiedemann and Gmelin, *Verdauung*, pp. 185–186. The nature of these intermediary products, named dextrin shortly afterward by Biot, because they rotated polarized light strongly to the right, was partially clarified in 1833 by Payen and Persoz. See below, Chap. VIII at n. 14.

36. Tiedemann and Gmelin, *Verdauung*, I, 185 (Fr., p.202).

37. Ibid., p. 305 (Fr., p. 343). See also p. 327 (Fr., p. 363).

38. Ibid., pp. 330–333 (Fr., pp. 366–368).

39. Müller, *Handbuch*, I, 543–544.

40. Tiedemann and Gmelin, *Verdauung*,I, 333 (Fr., pp. 368–369).

41. Ibid., I, 175–178; II, 1–178; II, 1–65, esp. 49–50; (Fr., I, 192–195; II, 1–72, esp. 57–58).

42. Ibid., I, 336–341 (Fr., I, 371–375).

43. Tiedemann, *Traité*, I, 131–136; II, 415–416, 420–422.

44. Bylebyl,*J. Hist. Med.*, 1970, *25*:3–21.

45. Nicholas Mani has pointed out, however, that the analysis of bile which Gmelin performed was a major contribution toward the identification of the constituents of that complex fluid. Mani also emphasizes the importance of their model experimental method of blocking the bile duct in order to investigate the role of the bile in digestion. They inferred from the result that "without the entrance of bile less fat is absorbed." Mani, *Gesnerus*, 1956, *13*:200–207.

46. Bernard, *Principes*, pp. 91–92. See also, Bernard, *Leçons de physiologie opératoire*, p. 6; Bernard, *Cahier*, p. 145.

47. Mani has discussed the elements of Bernard's general methods, and some of the specific procedures which derived from Tiedemann and Gmelin's investigations. Mani, *Gesnerus*, 1956, *13*:208, 212–214.

48. Bernard, *Principes*, p. 245.

49. Leuret and Lassaigne, *Recherches*, *passim.*, esp. pp. 102–105, 112–123, 144–146, 158–160, 167–173, 187–188, and facing p. 220.

50. Tiedemann and Gmelin, *Verdauung*,I, 14–20.

51. Berzelius,*Jahres-Bericht*, 1828, 7:297–331.

CHAPTER VIII: THE PEPSIN THEORY

1. Leuchs, *Archiv für die gesammte Naturlehre*, 1831, *3*:105–107.

2. Eberle, *Verdauung*, p. 1.

3. Ibid., pp. 49–51, 67–74. Eberle did not state what methods he used to determine these acids.

4. Ibid., pp. 74–80.

5. Ibid., pp. 81–122.

6. Ibid., pp. 122–136.

7. Ibid., pp. 65, 91–96, 148, 159–160, 164–168.

8. Ibid., p. ix.

9. Ibid., p. xiv.

10. Kruta, *Purkyně*, p. 96.

11. Müller and Schwann, *Archiv Anat. Physiol.*, 1836, pp. 68–69.

12. Ibid., pp. 67, 76; Müller regarded William Beaumont's contribution to digestive physiology as extremely important also. See Rosen, *Reception*, pp. 33–40.

13. Müller and Schwann, *Archiv Anat. Physiol.*, 1836, p. 77.

14. Payen and Persoz, *Annales chim. phys.*, 1833, *53*:73–92. See also Berzelius's summary of their results, his criticism of their characterization of dextrin, and his reasons
for believing that the diastase was not a pure substance, in Berzelius, *Jahres-Bericht*,
1835, *14*:281–286.

15. Berzelius, *Jahres-Bericht*, 1836, *15*:237–241.

16. Mitscherlich, *Annalen der Physik und Chemie*, 1834, *31*:273–282. The article was
a reprint of a section from Mitscherlich's *Lehrbuch* published the previous year.

17. Berzelius, *Jahres-Bericht*, 1836, *15*:241–244.

18. Ibid., pp. 244–245.

19. Müller, *Handbuch*, I, 544; Müller and Schwann, *Archiv Anat. Physiol.*, 1836, p.
66.

20. Berzelius's *Jahres-Bericht* was published in German in 1836, probably not much,
if any, earlier than Müller and Schwann's article. The original Swedish version, however, appeared in March 1835. Mitscherlich was a student of Berzelius, and through
this or other channels, Müller and Schwann might have heard of his ideas sooner.

21. Müller and Schwann, *Archiv Anat. Physiol.*, 1836, p. 67.

22. Ibid., pp. 68–70, 81, 88; Müller, *Handbuch*, I, 544.

23. Müller and Schwann, *Archiv Anat. Physiol.*, 1836, pp. 86–89.

24. Schwann's work on digestion is summarized in Florkin, *Naissance*, pp. 41–46;
and discussed more fully in Watermann, *Theodor Schwann*, pp. 59–70.

25. Schwann, *Archiv Anat. Physiol.*, 1836, pp. 93–98.

26. Ibid., pp. 98–104.

27. Ibid., pp. 104–110.

28. Ibid., pp. 111–113.

29. Ibid., pp. 113–114.

30. Ibid., pp. 111–126.

31. Ibid., pp. 131–137.

32. Ibid., p. 138.

33. Kruta, *Purkyně*, pp. 96–99; Valentin, *Froriep's Notizen*, 1836, *50:* cols. 209–212;
Burdach, *Traité*, IX, 316; Purkinje and Pappenheim, *Archiv Anat. Physiol.*, 1838, pp.
1–14.

34. Simon, *Archiv Anat. Physiol.*, 1839, pp. 1–9.

35. Schwann had recently published his epochal study of cell formation, a work
which evidently influenced Wasmann's research as strongly as did Schwann's work
on pepsin.

36. Wasmann, *Neue Notizen* (Froriep), 1839, *10:* cols. 113–122.

37. Liebig was at this time attacking the whole idea of a *catalytic force* as Berzelius
had defined it.

38. Schwann, *Annalen Pharm.*, 1836, *20*:33–34, f.n. signed "J.L." The extract had
appeared previously in *Poggendorff's Annalen*.

39. See above, Chap. I.

40. Julius Vogel, *Annalen Pharm.*, 1839, pp. 37–44.

41. Liebig, *Animal Chemistry*, pp. 104–105, 114.

42. Ibid., pp. 104–107.

43. Payen described the discovery of pepsin by Schwann as having "fixed the attention of scientists in Germany." Payen, *C.r. Acad.*, 1843, *17*:655.

44. Burdach, *Traité*, IX, 293–320, 380–424, esp. pp. 308, 419.
45. Ibid, IX, 417–418.
46. Ibid., IX, 311.
47. Ibid., pp. 383–388, 422.
48. See, for example, Bouchardat and Sandras, *C.r. Acad.*, 1845, *20*: 1086; Mialhe, ibid., p. 1486.
49. There are, for example, three references to Burdach in the previously mentioned student notebook of Bernard, one of them a specific page reference to volume IX of Burdach's treatise, and including notes obviously copied from that page. See Bernard MS, AM, P, Cote 554 (1426), no. 2, pp. 2 left side, 9 right side, 1 left side (compare the last with Burdach, *Traité*, IX, 488).

CHAPTER IX: FRENCH INVESTIGATIONS OF DIGESTION

1. Bouchardat and Sandras, *Annales sci. nat.*, 1842, *18*: 225–226.
2. Blondlot, *Traité*, p. 370.
3. Payen, *C.r. Acad.*, 1843, *17*: 655.
4. Another striking example of such a situation is suggested in the letters of Emil du Bois-Reymond to Carl Ludwig. In 1850 du Bois-Reymond visited Paris to demonstrate his discoveries of the electrical phenomena accompanying the actions of nerves and muscles, which had attracted considerable debate there. While in Paris he wrote Ludwig, who was already a very accomplished experimental physiologist, that Ludwig, as well as their colleague Ernst Brücke, was "absolutely unknown" in Paris. Helmholtz, the fourth member of this well-known German physiological school was, according to du Bois-Reymond, considered by Parisian scientists to be "mad" [*einen Verrückten*]. *Zwei Grosse Naturforscher*, ed. Estelle du Bois-Reymond, pp. 88–89, 93.
5. The necessity of taking into account the differences in awareness of the state of a particular scientific field in separate scientific centers, and the way in which information filters across the partial barriers between them, are very well displayed in Henry Guerlac's study of the belated recognition of the work of Joseph Black in Paris. See *Lavoisier—the Crucial Year*, esp. pp. 11–24, 36–75. The present case is less dramatic. Yet international scientific and personal communications had become so much more rapid and regular by the mid-nineteenth century that it is interesting to see similar lags persist. See also Hagstrom, *The Scientific Community*, pp. 182–183.
6. For a characterization of French science in the nineteenth century as extraordinarily biased in this way, see Crosland, *Arcueil*, p. 474.
7. Dumas, *Annales sci. nat.*, 1841, 2d. ser. *16*: 57.
8. Ackerknecht, *Paris Hospital*, pp. 124–125; Berman, *Bull. Hist. Med.*, 1963, *37*: 450–452.
9. Bouchardat and Sandras, *Annales sci. nat.*, 1842, *18*: 225–232.
10. Ibid., pp. 232–236, 238.
11. Ibid., pp. 229–230, 236–237, 239–240.
12. Ibid., p. 230, 232.
13. Dumas, *C.r. Acad.*, 1843, *16*: 253–254.
14. Dumas, like the authors, mentioned as a specific observation the conversion of starch to lactic acid, without modifying the general description of digestion to reflect such processes. He would probably have been able to accommodate the discovery to

his scheme without giving up his general point of view, for he had already considered lactic acid one of the steps in the oxidation of the respiratory aliments, but he had believed it to occur in the blood. See above, Chap. I at nn. 62–66.

15. Dumas, *C.r. Acad.*, 1843, *16*:254.

16. Deschamps, *J. pharm.*, 1840, *26*:412–420.

17. Dumas, *C.r. Acad.*, 1843, *16*:254–255.

18. Lehmann, *J. prakt. Chem.*, 1842, *27*:480–482.

19. Bernard's experiments seemed to take this turn on January 20, 1843 (see above Chap. VI at n. 40). The commission read its report on January 30.

20. See above Chap. VI at n. 64.

21. Bernard, MS 14d, pp. 20 verso-25 (numbered from back). For the evidence that these were Bernard's notes of Dumas's lectures see above, Chap. VI, n. 4 . In Dumas's own lecture notes he expressed "strong doubt" that pepsin actually existed. See Dumas, MS 1945, BM, P, 28me, 29me Leçon. It is tempting to see in this skepticism one reason that Bernard gave so little attention to pepsin in his experiments of the following autumn, and in his M.D. thesis on digestion (see below, Chap. X). Bernard's notes, however, do not record such an attitude, but rather suggest that Dumas regarded pepsin as essential. Since Dumas used the same notes for his lecture on the topic in 1842 and in 1843, it may well be that he had changed his opinion in the meantime and did not express this doubt when Bernard heard him.

22. Bernard, MS C. VIIIe 14c, 77th page. See below, Chap. X at nn. 7 and 15.

23. Ibid., 69th page. See below, Chap. XV at n. 37.

24. Ibid., 26th page.

25. For an account of Beaumont's influence on Blondlot and other European scientists and physicians, see Rosen, *Reception*.

26. Blondlot, *Traité*, pp. 201–206.

27. Ibid., pp. 206–220.

28. Ibid., pp. 235–237.

29. Tiedemann and Gmelin, *Verdauung*, I,138–150. On the last point translation problems may have contributed to a misunderstanding. The German gives the two explanations as alternatives, using the conjunction "oder." The French (p. 166) translates this word "et," making the small quantity of acid and the retention by animal matter appear more like a single explanation.

30. Blondlot, *Traité*, pp. 243–250.

31. Ibid., pp. 258–299.

32. Ibid., pp. 300–302.

33. Ibid., pp. 335–341. He also ascribed to gastric juice the special property of preventing putrefaction, a property Spallanzani had noticed and which Blondlot confirmed by studies of his own.

34. Ibid., pp. 27–28.

35. Ibid., p. 236.

36. Ibid., pp. 211, 215.

37. Ibid., p. 374.

38. See above, Chap. VIII at n. 22.

39. Blondlot, *Traité*, pp. 367–370.

40. Ibid., pp. 365–379. Henri Milne Edwards later pointed out that Blondlot had misrepresented some of Schwann's statements, and suggested that the reason was that Blondlot had relied on Burdach's summary of Schwann's work without reading the

original memoir. If this is true, and Blondlot was representative, perhaps the generally inadequate appreciation of Schwann's significance by French physiologists, including Bernard, could be explained in the same way. Milne Edwards, *Leçons*, VII, 35.

41. Blondlot, *Traité*, p. 380.
42. Ibid., p. 275.
43. Ibid., pp. 38–41.
44. Ibid., p. 221.
45. Ibid., p. 224.
46. Ibid., p. 254.
47. Ibid., p. 352.
48. Ibid., p. 205.
49. Flourens, *C.r. Acad.*, 1843, *17*:513–514.
50. Flourens, Payen, *C.r. Acad.*, 1843, *17*:653–656.

CHAPTER X: BERNARD'S FIRST THEORY OF GASTRIC DIGESTION

1. Olmsted and Olmsted, *Bernard*, p. 37.
2. Bernard, MS C. VIIIe, 7a No. 2, pp. 110, 111.
3. Bernard, *Du suc gastrique*, p. 13.
4. Bernard, MS C. VIIIe, 7a No. 2, pp. 114–118, 184. That Bernard utilized Blondlot's technique is well known, there being more direct statements than these. See, for example, Olmsted and Olmsted, *Bernard*, p. 41. "I was doing experiments on digestion with the help of the stomach fistula which Blondlot had devised, in a laboratory which my friend Pelouze had in the rue Dauphine." The statements I have used are significant, therefore, only for helping to determine when he first used the method.
5. Bernard, *Du suc gastrique*, p. 10.
6. Some aspects of the following account remain tentative for the same reason as given previously. See Chap. VI, n. 25.
7. Bernard, MS C. VIIIe, 7a No. 2, p. 110.
8. Ibid., p. 112.
9. Ibid., p. 113.
10. Ibid., pp. 114–115, 117–119.
11. Ibid., p. 122.
12. Ibid., pp. 123–124.
13. Ibid., pp. 126–135.
14. Ibid., p. 135.
15. Ibid., pp. 125, 135.
16. See above, Chap. VI at nn. 57, 58.
17. Bernard, MS C. VIIIe, 7a No. 2, p. 111.
18. Ibid., p. 143.
19. Schiller, *Bernard*, p. 64.
20. Bernard, MS C. VIIIe, 7a No. 2, p. 146.
21. Ibid., pp. 151–152.
22. Ibid., p. 152.
23. Bernard, *Du suc gastrique*, p. 32.

24. Olmsted and Olmsted, *Bernard*, p. 36.
25. Bernard, *Du suc gastrique*, pp. 8–9.
26. Ibid., pp. 14–22.
27. Bernard, MS C. VIIIe, 7a No. 2, pp. 138–139.
28. Bernard, *Du suc gastrique*, pp. 23–24.
29. Ibid., pp. 24–25.
30. Ibid., pp. 7–8.
31. Ibid., p. 14.
32. See above, Chap. VIII at n. 33, n. 35.
33. Ackerknecht, *Paris Hospital*, pp. 125–126.
34. Bernard, *Lettres beaujolaises*, p. 7.
35. Ibid.
36. Ibid., pp. 26–27, 30. Bernard's comments in this case add a late example to the early ones in his M.D. thesis of not following closely the physiological results in Germany. The work in question was an article by Carl Voit. Bernard acknowledged, in 1870, that he had not read Voit's numerous articles and was not familiar in detail with Voit's nutritional views. This was after Voit's work had been considered important in Germany for over ten years. It is true that Bernard was so out of sympathy with Voit's approach that after he read the translation he apologized to Madame Raffalovich for having asked her to translate it, but that does not alter the fact that he was also apparently quite out of touch with some major developments in areas of physiology related to his own concerns.
37. See Grmek, *Catalogue*, pp. 214, 235, 241–242.
38. Bernard, *Du suc gastrique*, pp. 27–28.
39. Ibid., pp. 29–31.
40. Ibid., p. 26.
41. See above, Chap. VI at n. 37.
42. Bernard, *Du suc gastrique*, p. 5.
43. See above, Chap. VIII at nn. 45, 46.
44. *Gazette médicale de Paris*, 1844, *12*:165–172; *J. pharm.* 1844, *5*:428–433.
45. Bernard, *Du suc gastrique*, p. 31.
46. Olmsted, *Bernard*, p. 36: Schiller, *Bernard*, p. 105.
47. Guerlac, *Lavoisier–the Crucial Year*, passim.

CHAPTER XI: BERNARD AND BARRESWIL IN A BUSY FIELD

1. Bernard, *Du suc gastrique*, p. 31. The thesis was presented on December 7, 1843. The tenth experiment of the new series was dated December 2, 1843. Bernard, MS C. VIIIe 7a No. 2, p. 157.
2. Bernard, MS C. VIIIe, 7a No. 2, pp. 153–159.
3. Ibid., p. 160.
4. *C.r. Acad.*, 1844, *18*:423–435; ibid., pp. 482–483; ibid., p. 532.
5. *J. débats*, April 10, 1844.
6. Ibid.; *L'Institut*, No. 536, April 3, 1844; *C.r. Acad.*, 1844, *18*:564–565.
7. Bernard, MS C. VIIIe, 7a No. 2, pp. 160–162.
8. Anonymous MS, Dos. Pelouze, AAdSc, pp. 5–7. The document describes

Pelouze's laboratories and students, and was probably prepared by a student of Pelouze for Dumas's eulogy of him. Schiller, *Bernard*, p. 65, has also cited this document to show that Bernard used Pelouze's laboratory throughout his early career.

9. Bernard and Barreswil, *C.r. Acad.*, 1844, *28*:783–785. See also *L'Institut*, No. 539, April 24, 1844, p. 144.

10. Ibid., p. 783.

11. See above, Chap. II at n. 4.

12. Bernard, MS C. VIIIe, 7a No. 2, pp. 181–199.

13. Bernard, *C.r. Acad.*, 1844, *18*:995–998; *L'Institut*, No. 544, May 29, 1844, p. 186.

14. See above, Chap. VII, at n. 42.

15. Bernard, *C.r. Acad.*, 1844, *18*:998.

16. See the references cited for June and September, 1844, in Grmek, *Catalogue*, p. 387. If Bernard returned to St. Julien in this year, it must have been in July or August, since there are experiments recorded through his usual vacation period of September and early October.

17. Bernard and Barreswil, *C.r. Acad.*, 1844, *19*:1285.

18. The Royal Society of London, *Catalogue of Scientific Papers (1800-1863)* (London, 1869), III, 859–863.

19. Lassaigne, *Journal de chimie médicale*, 1844, *10*:73–77.

20. Ibid., pp. 183–189.

21. Melsens, *C.r. Acad.*, 1844, *19*:1289–1291.

22. Bernard, MS C. VIIIe, 7a No. 2, facing p. 166.

23. Bernard and Barreswil, *C.r. Acad.*, 1844, *19*:1285.

24. Bernard, MS C. VIIIe, 7a No. 2, facing pp. 166, 167.

25. Ibid., pp. 166, 171–173, 175, 177; Bernard and Barreswil, *C.r. Acad.*, 1844, *19*:1286–1287.

26. Bernard and Barreswil, *C.r. Acad.*, 1844, *19*:1286–1287.

27. Bernard, MS C. VIIIe, 7a No. 2, p. 209.

28. Ibid., p. 208.

29. Ibid., p. 209.

30. Ibid., pp. 211–212.

31. Bernard and Barreswil, *C.r. Acad.*, 1844, *19*:1284.

32. This account of the change in Bernard's viewpoint is the most reasonable reconstruction I can make from the remaining record and the assumption that there was an identifiable time associated with some particular observations or experiences which stimulated the change. It is, of course, quite possible that Bernard dropped his earlier theory of gastric digestion because of some event which has left no trace in his notes or publications, or that those ideas simply faded out of his mind gradually without any clearly definable cause.

33. *L'Institut*, No. 572, December 11, 1844, p. 414.

34. Bernard and Barreswil, *C.r. Acad.*, 1844, *19*:1285–1287.

35. Ibid., pp. 1287–1288; Pelouze, *J. pharm. chim.*, 1845, 7:5–15. According to Olmsted, the explanation of their result arises "from the continued presence of wood in the stomachs of fasting animals from which gastric juice was collected." Olmsted and Olmsted, *Bernard*, p. 51.

36. Bernard and Barreswil, *C.r. Acad.*, 1844, *19*:1289.

37. Bouchardat, *C.r. Acad.*, 1845, *20*:107–112.

38. Bouchardat and Sandras, *C.r. Acad.*, 1843, *17*:296–300.

39. Bouchardat and Sandras, *Annuaire de thérapeutique*, supplement for 1846, pp. 82–83. This article was the complete memoir which they had presented to the Academy, and of which an extract appeared in *C.r. Acad.*, 1845, *20*:143–148.

40. Bouchardat and Sandras, *C.r. Acad.*, 1845, *20*:145–147; *Annuaire*, 1846, pp. 107–132. Bernard credited Magendie with being the first to discover sugar in the blood of normal animals digesting starch. Bernard, *Leçons sur le diabète*, p. 159 (see above, Chap. V at n. 43). He described Bouchardat as having detected sugar in the blood of diabetics in 1839, but for some reason did not point out that Bouchardat had anticipated Magendie's observation also by a year, and that even earlier Tiedemann and Gmelin had found a fermentable sugar in the blood of an animal fed starch. Nikolaus Mani regards Magendie's investigation as a confirmation of that of Tiedemann and Gmelin. See Mani, *Gesnerus*, 1956, *13*:213. J.M.D. Olmsted apparently took Bernard's word for the fact that Magendie's result was the first demonstration of sugar in the blood of normal animals. See Olmsted, *Magendie*, p. 238; and Olmsted, *Bernard*, p. 158.

41. A. P. Dubrunfaut showed one year later (1846), that invert sugar actually is composed of two fermentable sugars, one of which is glucose. See Partington, *A History of Chemistry*, IV, 821.

42. Bouchardat and Sandras, *Annuaire*, 1846, pp. 85–96.

43. Bouchardat and Sandras, *C.r. Acad.*, 1845, *20*:144.

44. Bouchardat and Sandras, *Annuaire*, 1846, p. 96. Like Bernard, Bouchardat and Sandras had to manage the conditions of the experiments carefully in order to obtain the distinction they sought. First they injected a solution containing 10 grams of inverted sugar or of glucose and found it in the urine. When they reduced the dose to 5 grams it no longer appeared, whereas cane sugar injected in that quantity did. Ibid., pp. 98–99.

45. Ibid., pp. 98–99.

46. Ibid., pp. 97–98.

47. See below, Chap. XII at nn. 3–10, n. 45; Chap. XIII at n. 21, n. 32; Chap. XVI at nn. 39–40; Chap. XVIII at nn. 48–51.

48. Chevreul, *Mémoires du Muséum d'Histoire Naturelle*, 1825, *12*:367–383.

49. Dumas, *Essai de statique chimique*, p. 44.

50. Bouchardat and Sandras, *Annuaire*, 1846, pp. 99–100.

51. Ibid., pp. 94–96.

52. Ibid., p. 103.

53. Ibid., pp. 101, 137.

54. Ibid., pp. 86–90, etc.

55. Mialhe, *C.r. Acad.*, 1845, *20*:247–248; Mialhe, "Note sur le rôle physiologique," MS Dossier meeting of January 27, 1845, AAdSc, pp. 1–7. The manuscript contains several paragraphs deleted from the published version.

56. Bouchardat and Sandras, *C.r. Acad.*, 1845, *20*:303–304. See also ibid., pp. 1026–1027.

57. Mialhe, *C.r. Acad.*, 1845, *20*:954–955; Mialhe (same title), MS Dossier meeting of March 31, 1845, AAdSc., pp. 5–8, 20–24. Only a brief summary of these lengthy discussions is given in the published version.

58. Mialhe, MS Dossier March 31, pp. 9–13. The published version, *C.r. Acad.*, 1845, *20*:955, reduces this discussion to a single sentence.

59. See above, Chap. III at n. 91.

60. See below, Chap. XII at n. 63.

61. Mialhe, *C.r. Acad.*, 1845, 20:955–959. The published text presents this section in full.

62. Bouchardat, *C.r. Acad.*, 1845, 20:1020–1026.

63. Bouchardat and Sandras, *C.r. Acad.*, 1845, 20:1085–1091. Gabriel Valentin had already observed the action of pancreatic juice on starch somewhat earlier, and reported it in his *Lehrbuch der Physiologie des Menschen* in 1844. See Milne Edwards, *Leçons*, VII, 67. Bouchardat and Sandras apparently made their discovery independently. Their demonstration was more extensive. See Frerichs, "Verdauung," p. 847.

64. Lassaigne, *C.r. Acad.*, 1845, 20:1347–1350; ibid., pp. 1350–1351.

65. Mialhe, *C.r. Acad.*, 1845, 20:1485–1488. In his use of the term "abdominal salivary gland," Mialhe was engaged in a ploy; the term was in fact used for the pancreas, and it enabled him to appear to be maintaining his original position that saliva alone causes the reaction. Yet he undoubtedly had meant earlier only the usual saliva secreted into the mouth. In this way also he avoided acknowledging that he was adopting a view closer to that of Bouchardat and Sandras.

66. Lassaigne, *C.r. Acad.*, 1845, 20:1640–1641; Lassaigne (same title as publ. mem.), MS, Dossier of the meeting of June 2, 1845, AAdSc, pp. 1–5. The published extract gives only the conclusions from the manuscript memoir.

67. Bouchardat and Sandras, *C.r. Acad.*, 1845, 20:147; Bernard, MS C. VIIIe, 7a No. 2, pp. 168–169.

68. Foster, *Bernard*, pp. 52–54.

69. Bernard, MS C. VIIIe, 7a No. 2, pp. 233–234.

70. Ibid., pp. 235–279.

71. Ibid., p. 236.

72. Ibid., pp. 263–264.

73. Ibid., p. 234. "N'y a t-il pas là un mémoire."

74. Ibid., pp. 283–287. The fact that these experiments took place at the Collège de France, although Bernard was no longer Magendie's préparateur there, suggests that he was in this case possibly assisting in some of Magendie's experiments on absorption.

75. Olmsted and Olmsted, *Bernard*, pp. 52–56.

76. Bernard, MS C. VIIIe, 7a No. 2, pp. 218–219.

77. Ibid., p. 220. Compare with Bouchardat and Sandras, *C.r. Acad.*, 1845, 20:1089–1090, and Lassaigne, *C.r. Acad.*, 1845, 20:1351.

78. Bernard, MS C. VIIIe, 7a No. 2, p. 224. The lower part of the page, presumably containing the results of this experiment, has been removed.

79. Ibid., pp. 220–228, 289. I have throughout described these as joint experiments, since both names appeared on the memoir which came from them. The laboratory notes, however, do not indicate what part Barreswil played, and in some places by use of the first person singular, suggest that Bernard was working alone.

80. Ibid., p. 296.

81. Ibid., p. 300, 306.

82. Ibid., pp. 291–302, 309.

83. Bernard and Barreswil, *C.r. Acad.*, 1845, 21:88–89; *L'Institut*, No. 602, July 9, 1845, pp. 245–246.

84. Bernard and Barreswil, *C.r. Acad.*, 1845, 21:89; Bernard, MS C. VIIIe, 7a No.

2, pp. 293, 295, 300, 301, 306–308. From the five recorded experiments involving acidified saliva on meat the only change observed was one case in which after two days there was "a little dissolution (défibrillation), but no obvious dissolution."

85. Bernard, MS C. VIIIe, 7aˑNo. 2, pp. 303–309.

86. See above, Chap. III at n. 76.

87. Magendie, *C.r. Acad.*, 1845, *21*:902–905.

88. Bernard, MS C. VIIIe, 7a No. 2, p. 280.

89. See above, this chap. at n. 64.

90. Lassaigne, *C.r. Acad.*, 1845, *21*:362–363.

91. Bernard, MS C. VIIIe, 7a No. 2, pp. 279–282.

92. Magendie, *C.r. Acad.*, 1845, *21*:902–905.

93. Bernard, MS C. VIIIe, 7a No. 2, pp. 288–290.

94. Magendie, *C.r. Acad.*, 1845, *21*:903–904. J. M. D. Olmsted explains their result as due to the fact that the enzyme in parotid saliva is inactive until it comes into contact with the air. Their method of collecting it from the duct prevented it from mixing with air. See Olmsted, *Magendie*, p. 326.

95. See above, Chap. VI at n. 41.

96. See above, Chap. V at n. 13.

97. The time at which this passage was written is uncertain. It comes immediately after experiments on the pancreatic digestion of July 1845, but at least the experiment on blood probably preceded the former, because they break off and continue two pages beyond. Next comes another page of undetermined date and then experiments performed in October 1844. The penciled statement, however, might have been later than the experiments on blood. The earlier the passage is, of course, the less forceful is my use of it as evidence of the persistence of Bernard's aim, but it even then provides valuable insight into the nature of his aim. There is further uncertainty due to the number of words which are doubtful, but even if several of my choices are wrong I think that the general sense of the passage must be near to this translation.

98. For a discussion of these ideas in the first half of the century see Holmes, "Claude Bernard's concept of the milieu intérieur," pp. 92–98.

99. See Bernard's discussion of the subject in 1854 in Atlee, *Notes of M. Bernard's Lectures*, pp. 87–142.

100. See especially Bernard, *Cahier*, pp. 146, 189, 196, and *Liquides de l'organisme*, I, 288–331.

CHAPTER XII: SCIENTIFIC IMAGINATION CONFRONTED BY EXPERIMENTAL COMPLEXITY

1. Bernard, MS C. VIIIe, 7b, p. 44.

2. Ibid., 7a No. 2, p. 302.

3. Ibid., 7b, pp. 99–100.

4. Ibid., pp. 103–105. Bernard did not quantitatively measure the sugar which appeared in the urine. By the strength of the reaction with cupric tartrate he classified the amount of sugar in any given sample as "large," "small," or "trace." The elimination was complete, then, not because the original amount was recovered, but when sugar ceased to appear.

5. Ibid., pp. 106–107, 109.

6. Ibid., p. 100.

7. In the extract published at the time, Bouchardat and Sandras did not mention that they too had to choose the quantities carefully in order to demonstrate the difference.

8. Bernard, MS C. VIIIe, 7b, pp. 185–188.

9. Ibid., p. 190.

10. Ibid., pp. 190–191, 194.

11. Ibid., pp. 198, 199, 205, 210.

12. Ibid., p. 217. The situation was made still less satisfactory by the fact that boiled gastric juice also could cause this transformation. It would not, therefore, have appeared to be a specific action of gastric juice.

13. Ibid., pp. 178–179.

14. Ibid., p. 180.

15. Ibid., pp. 180–181.

16. Ibid., pp. 183–189, 193–194.

17. Ibid., pp. 195–199, 205.

18. Ibid., pp. 200–202.

19. See above, Chap. XI at n. 83.

20. Bernard, MS C. VIIIe, 7b, pp. 205–207, 211.

21. Ibid., pp. 208–210, 212–213.

22. Ibid., pp. 214, 216–217, 219.

23. Ibid., p. 215.

24. Ibid., p. 218.

25. Bernard, *Introduction* (rep., 1965), p. 57.

26. Ibid., p. 64. See also p. 71.

27. Bernard, MS C. VIIIe, 7b, p. 218.

28. Renan, "Bernard," pp. 24–25; Bert, "Bernard," pp. 64–65; Foster, *Bernard*, p. 80; Olmsted and Olmsted, *Bernard*, p. 64.

29. Bernard, *Introduction* (rep., 1965), p. 68.

30. Ibid., p. 287.

31. Bernard, MS C. VIIIe, 7b, pp. 221–222.

32. Bernard, *Introduction* (rep., 1965), pp. 267–268.

33. Bernard, MS C. VIIIe, 7b. pp. 117–120.

34. Ibid., pp. 121–124.

35. Ibid., p. 61.

36. Olmsted, *Magendie*, pp. 85, 205–208.

37. Bernard, MS C. VIIIe, 7b, pp. 61–87, 94–98, 148–154.

38. Ibid., p. 46.

39. Sometimes he wrote one of these three locations at the top of his laboratory entry, but more often the place was unspecified. My evidence that *13 rue Suger* was the quarters where he gave his course comes from the experiment of December 13, which is described as "à mon cours—13 rue Suger." Ibid.

40. Ibid., pp. 129–130.

41. Ibid., p. 130.

42. Ibid., p. 131.

43. Ibid., p. 132.

44. Ibid., p. 133.

45. Ibid., pp. 132–133. The last point is not explicitly made, but is clearly implied in the other statements considered in the light of his preceding research.

46. Ibid., p. 133.

47. Remembering, of course, that throughout this period he also carried out researches on the functions of the nervous system more closely allied with Magendie's interests.

48. See Holmes, "Claude Bernard's concept of the milieu intérieur," pp. 93–97; Schiller, *Bernard*, p. 97.

49. Bernard, *Introduction* (rep., 1965), p. 84.

50. Bernard, MS C. VIIIe, 7b, pp. 134–136.

51. Ibid., pp. 136–139.

52. Ibid., pp. 139–141.

53. Ibid., pp. 141–143.

54. Ibid., pp. 144–145.

55. This was not an unprecedented application of the term digestion. See Chossat, *J. physiol.*, 1825, *5:* 148.

56. Bernard, *Introduction* (rep., 1965), p. 287.

57. Bernard, MS C. VIIIe, 7b, p. 130.

58. Ibid., p. 139.

59. See above, Chap. VI at n. 43.

60. See above, Chap. VI at n. 44.

61. Miahle, *Traité*, pp. ii–v.

62. Ibid., pp. xvi–xvii.

63. Ibid., p. I. (This section of Mialhe's treatise is paginated separately from the portion referred to in the preceding and following footnotes); *Titres scientifiques de M. Mialhe*, pp. 3–25. There seems to be little biographical information available concerning Mialhe.

64. Mialhe, *Traité*, p. vi.

65. See above, Chap. X at n. 41; Chap. XI at n. 9.

66. Mialhe, *Traité*, pp. viii–x.

67. Bernard, *C.r. Acad.*, 1844, *18:*995. See above, Chap. XI at n. 15.

68. Mialhe, *Traité*, pp. x–xv.

69. Ibid., pp. xvii–xviii.

70. Ibid., pp. CCLVI–CCLVII.

71. See, for example, Müller, *Handbuch*, I, p. 2; Magendie, *Précis*, pp. 18–19.

72. Bernard, *Archives d'anatomie générale et de physiologie*, supplement to *Archives gén. méd.*, 1846, p. 201.

73. The date is uncertain. The supplement is not subdivided. Bernard, however, referred in his second article to the first one's having appeared in "*Archives d'anatomie générale et de physiologie*, Janvier 1846" (ibid., p. 208).

74. Bernard, *Archives gén. méd.*, 1846, suppl. pp. 1–2.

75. Ibid., pp. 2–9.

76. Bernard, *Archives gén. méd.*, 1846, suppl., pp. 201–202.

77. Ibid., pp. 204–205; Mialhe, *Traité*, p. CCLII.

78. Bernard, *Archives gén. méd.*, 1846, suppl., pp. 206–207.

79. Ibid., p. 209.

CHAPTER XIII: HERBIVOROUS AND CARNIVOROUS NUTRITION

1. Bernard, MS C. VIIIe, 7c, pp. 1–9.

2. Ibid., pp. 10–13.

3. Ibid., pp. 15–17.

4. Ibid., p. 18.

5. Ibid., p. 19.

6. Ibid., pp. 20–23.

7. Ibid., p. 23.

8. Ibid., p. 24. Bernard's proposed method for separating mucus relied on solubility properties commonly used in contemporary descriptions of the material. See Berzelius, *Annales de chimie*, 1813, *88*:132–133; Marchand, *Lehrbuch*, p. 404.

9. Ibid., pp. 20–21.

10. Ibid., pp. 26–28, 30–31.

11. Ibid., pp. 28–29, 33–35.

12. Ibid., pp. 36–38, 43–44.

13. Ibid., p. 36.

14. Ibid., pp. 47–48.

15. Ibid., pp. 51–52. Mialhe had already adopted this standard in 1844, so Bernard was once again only catching up with his colleagues.

16. Bernard, MS C. VIIIe, 7b, pp. 225–226.

17. *Biographiches Lexikon*, ed. Hirsch, IV, 736–737; Rayer, *Traité*.

18. Olmsted and Olmsted, *Bernard*, pp. 29, 30, 39–40, 58. See also Genty, "Rayer," p. 44.

19. Bernard, MS C. VIIIe, 7b, p. 226.

20. Bernard, MS C. VIIIe, 7c, p. 6.

21. Ibid., p. 14.

22. Ibid., pp. 41–42.

23. Ibid., pp. 93–94.

24. Ibid., pp. 95–96.

25. Ibid., pp. 96–98.

26. Ibid., pp. 101–102. There were some additional complications at the end of the experiment. At the autopsy he found in the animal's bladder some acidic but turbid urine, suggesting that possibly there had been some digestion after all. He noted that he should study the question further, but there is no record that he did at this time.

27. Ibid., pp. 102–104.

28. Bernard, *C.r. Acad.*, 1846, *22*:534–537.

29. Ibid., p. 534.

30. Ibid., p. 535.

31. Ibid., pp. 535–536.

32. Ibid., pp. 536–537.

33. Ibid., p. 537.

34. See, for example, Müller, *Handbuch*, I, 583; Burdach, *Traité*, VII, 462.

35. Magendie, *Annales chim. phys.*, 1816, *3*:71–72.

36. Magendie, *Précis*, II, 500; Hünefeld, *Physiologische Chemie*, I, 150; Müller, *Handbuch*, I, 477, 589; Rayer, *Traité*, I, 110.

37. Wollaston, *Phil. Trans. Roy. Soc.*, 1810, Pt. 1, pp. 229–230; Chevreul, "Urines," p. 354.

38. Chossat, *J. physiol.*, 1825, *5*:65–221, especially pp. 148–151, 199–200.

39. *Biographisches Lexikon*, ed. Hirsch, III, 727.

40. Lehmann has already appeared as the critic of Bouchardat and Sandras's first memoir on digestion. See above, Chap. IX at n. 18.

41. Lehmann, *J. prakt. Chem.*, 1842, *25*:1–29; 1842, *27*:257–274.

42. Liebig, *Annalen Chem. Pharm.*, 1844, *50:*190–191.
43. See above, Chap. X at nn. 36, 37.
44. Bernard *C.r. Acad.*, 1846, *22:*536.
45. Lehmann, *Lehrbuch*, II, 403.
46. See above, Chap. V at n. 43.
47. The fact that Magendie attributed to Bernard and Barreswil a discovery which was reported in a paper by Bernard alone, is another instance of the difficulty of sorting out the relative roles of Bernard and that of his "friend and collaborator."
48. Magendie, *C.r. Acad.*, 1846, *23:*189–193.
49. Ibid., p. 193. See above, Chap. XII at n. 34, for Bernard's contemplated experiment.
50. See Holmes, "Introduction," p. lvii.
51. Bernard, *Archives gén. méd.*, 1846, suppl., p. 201. See also Bernard, ibid., p. 1; ibid., 1847 *13:*1.
52. Bernard, MS C. VIIIe, 7c, pp. 105–108.
53. Ibid., p. 108.
54. Ibid., pp. 109–111.
55. Ibid., pp. 57–64.
56. Ibid., pp. 111–115.
57. Grmek, *Catalogue*, pp. 387–388.

CHAPTER XIV: CLAUDE BERNARD AND LOUIS MIALHE

1. Payen, *C.r. Acad.*, 1846, *22:*524.
2. Mialhe, *Matières albuminoides.*
3. See Vogel fils, *J. pharm. chim.*, 1842, *2:*274–275.
4. See above, Chap. IX at n. 16.
5. See above, Chap. IX at n. 50.
6. Mialhe, *Matières albuminoides*, pp. 11–17; Mialhe, *J. pharm. chim.*, 1846, *10:*162.
7. Mialhe, *Matières albuminoides*, pp. 18–22.
8. Strahl, *Archiv Anat. Physiol.*, 1847, p. 216.
9. Lehmann, *Lehrbuch*, II, 33. Lehmann commented further on that Bernard's view "has been disproven by Mialhe and by Jacubowitsch through positive experiments" (ibid., p. 50); Bérard, *Cours*, II, 149.
10. Mialhe, *Matières albuminoides*, pp. 39–40.
11. See above, Chap. IX at n.9.
12. Mialhe, *Matières albuminoides*, pp. 24–28.
13. Ibid., pp. 28–33.
14. Ibid., pp. 32–33.
15. Ibid., pp. 33–34.
16. Ibid., p. 34n.
17. Ibid., pp. 36–38. See the similar comment by Burdach, above, Chap. VIII at n. 46.
18. Frerichs, "Verdauung," p. 810.
19. Lehmann, *Lehrbuch*, II, 317.
20. Ibid., p. 318.
21. Milne Edwards, *Leçons*, VII, 49.

22. Mialhe, *Matières albuminoïdes*, p. 11.
23. Ibid., frontispiece.
24. Ibid., pp. 8, 14, 26.
25. Ibid., p. 9.
26. See above, Chap. X at n. 25. Other aspects of Bernard's thesis, such as his view of the role of the gastric acid at that time, could not have been reconciled with Mialhe's views.
27. Mialhe, *J. pharm. chim.*, 1846, *10*:163.
28. Bernard, MS C. VIIIe, 7c, pp. 52–55, 50.
29. Ibid., p. 50.
30. Ibid., p. 2. [sic: the discussion was continued from p. 50 to a leftover space on p. 2].
31. See above, Chap. XI at nn. 85–94.
32. See above, Chap. XIII at n. 47.
33. Bernard, *Cahier*, p. 89.
34. Ibid.
35. Bernard, MS C. VIIIe, 7c, pp. 2, 5, 64–65.
36. Ibid., pp. 65–66.
37. Ibid., p. 67.
38. Ibid., pp. 68–69, 68bis–69bis.
39. Ibid., p. 151.
40. Ibid., pp. 151–152.
41. Ibid., p. 153.
42. Grmek's chronological index places the appearance of the memoir in February. See *Catalogue*, p. 388. This would have enabled him to write it after the experiments on gastric juice of January 10. That order is made more probable by the opinion he expressed in the memoir concerning the action of alkaline gastric juice (below, this chap. at n. 64). If the memoir was written earlier, then Bernard changed his mind more often concerning his gastric theory—a less likely, but not altogether implausible situation.
43. Bernard, *Archives gén. méd.*, 1847, *13*:5–8 See above, Chap. XI at nn. 85–94.
44. Ibid., pp. 8–10. Evidently Bernard had discarded the observation, puzzling to him in September, that saliva collected in small tubes just as it issued from the ducts behaved like mixed saliva. See above, this chap. at n. 30.
45. See above, Chap. IV at n. 11.
46. Boutron and Frémy, *Ann. chim. phys.*, 1841, *2*:257–274.
47. See above, Chap. IV at n. 13.
48. Bernard, *Archives gén. méd.*, 1847, *13*:10–17.
49. Boutron and Frémy, *Ann. chim. phys.*, 1841, *2*:258.
50. Ibid., pp. 266–267.
51. Bernard, *Archives gén. méd.*, 1847, *13*:17–20.
52. Ibid., pp. 21–28.
53. Ibid., p. 28.
54. See above, Chap. XIII at nn. 1–6.
55. See above, Chap. XI at n. 63.
56. Bernard, *Archives gén. méd.*, 1847, *13*:19–20.
57. Ibid., p. 1.
58. Ibid., p. 20.

59. Ibid., p. 18.
60. Lehmann, *Lehrbuch*, II, 32.
61. Bernard, *Archives gén. méd.*, 1847, *13*:2, 4, 11, 15.
62. Ibid., pp. 1–4.
63. Payen, *C.r. Acad.*, 1846, *22*:524, 526. Payen, who wrote the report, was the person who had defined diastase itself. Perhaps as a fellow follower of the Dumas school he was somewhat biased in favor of Mialhe. But the presence of Magendie, Flourens, and Milne Edwards on the committee must have meant that they shared in general the favorable opinion of Mialhe's contribution.
64. Bernard, *Archives gén. méd.*, 1847, *13*:19. My italics.
65. Lehmann gave an excellent review of these experimental problems. See *Lehrbuch*, II, 25–35.
66. Ibid., pp. 26–27.
67. See, for example, Milne Edwards, *Leçons*, VII, 54–67; and Gautier, *Chimie*, I, 377–386.

CHAPTER XV: A NEW LOOK AT OLD PROJECTS

1. Bernard, MS C. VIIIe, 7c, pp. 77–78.
2. See above, Chap. VI at nn. 40, 48–53.
3. Bernard, MS C. VIIIe, p. 78. The experiment is undated, but is placed between the preceding experiment and the one described in the following paragraph. See Olmsted, *Magendie*, pp. 244–246.
4. Bernard, MS C. VIIIe, 7c, pp. 79–80.
5. Ibid., p. 80. The words I have placed in parentheses were added above the preceding phrase.
6. Bernard, MS C. VIIIe, 7a, No. 2, pp. 85–87.
7. Ibid., 7c, p. 80.
8. See above, Chap. VI at n. 48.
9. Bernard, MS C. VIIIe, 7c, pp. 81–82. These experiments are dated "1er fevrier 1845," but it is evident from their contents, especially the note at the bottom of p. 81, that the correct year must be 1847.
10. Ibid., pp. 83–86.
11. Ibid., p. 85.
12. Ibid., p. 87. Several other reflections dealt with particular situations such as the reactions in the urine.
13. See above, Chap. VI at n. 37.
14. Bernard, MS C. VIIIe, 7c, pp. 115–117.
15. Ibid., pp. 118–122,124–125.
16. One such involving the injection of cane sugar and yeast was dated January 18, 1848. It did not appear to add much to the previous experiments (ibid., p. 263).
17. Bernard, *Archives gén. méd.*, 1848, *16*:62.
18. See above, Chap. VI at n. 41.
19. Bernard, *Archives gén. méd.*, 1848, *16*:62–70. He did not give the dates of his experiments in the memoirs. I have identified those in which the similarity of language is persuasive enough to indicate that an experiment in his notebook is the same one as in his memoir. Compare, for example, p. 64 with MS C. VIIIe, 7a No. 2, pp. 13–15;

p. 66 with 7a No. 2, p. 63; p. 69 with 7c, p. 77. The memoir illustrates how Bernard sometimes reconstructed his course of research according to logic rather than the true chronology of his experiments. He said, for example, (pp. 64–65) that he tried to prepare an iron salt with gastric acid, but that the liquid was too easily alterable. Then "knowing besides that lactic acid exists free in the gastric juice," he thought of employing lactate of iron. As the source of the knowledge in the cited passage, he referred to his paper with Barreswil on gastric juice of 1844. Yet the laboratory notebook shows that he used lactate of iron during the spring of 1843.

20. Bernard, *Archives gén. méd.*, 1848, *16*:70–76.

21. Ibid., pp. 76–78.

22. Ibid., p.72.

23. Ibid., p 79.

24. Ibid., p. 85.

25. See above, this chapter at n. 15.

26. Bernard, *Archives gén. méd.*, 1848, *16*:83. The evidence for this conclusion should be presented. Since Bernard did not date the experiment in his memoir one might at first think that he was referring to a similar but different experiment which yielded the outcome he sought. The descriptions are so similar, however, that it is hard not to believe that they represent the same events. The relevant portions are given in Appendix A.

27. Bernard, *Cahier*, p.154.

28. Bernard, *Archives gén. méd.*, 1848, *16*:85.

29. See above, this chapter at n. 6.

30. Bernard, *Archives gén. méd.*, 1848, *16*:220. The reader can best judge whether in this case the parallels are strong enough to conclude that both descriptions are of the same experiment. See Appendix B.

31. Bernard, *Archives gén. méd.*, 1848, *16*:222–223.

32. Ibid., p. 223.

33. Ibid., pp. 224–228.

34. Ibid., pp. 230–231.

35. Ibid., pp. 231–232.

36. See above, Chap. XI at nn. 70–73.

37. Bernard and Barreswil, *Archives gén. méd.*, 1847, *13*:451.

38. Bernard, MS C. VIIIe, 7a No. 2, pp. 255, 259, 261, 262, 269–271, 274–278.

39. Ibid., pp. 275–276.

40. Prévost and Dumas, *Annales chim. phys.*, 1823, *23*:93–94, 103.

41. Bernard, MS C. VIIIe, 7a No.2, p. 265, "ablation des reins à la fois." In most of the other experiments he simply stated that he removed both kidneys, but there was never any indication of a long delay between the first and the second.

42. Prévost and Dumas, *Annales chim. phys.*, 1823, *23*:94.

43. The experiments in the memoir which I have been able to identify with those in the notebook are as follows: Bernard and Barreswil, *Archives gén. méd.*, 1847, *13*:454 (exp. No. 2), with MS C. VIIIe, 7a No. 2, pp. 257–259 (January 28, 1845); p. 455 with 7a No. 2, pp. 265–270 (January 31, 1845); and p. 456 (exp. No. 2) with 7a No. 2, pp. 277–278 (March 13, 1845).

44. Bernard and Barreswil, *Archives gén. méd.*, 1847, *13*:450, 457–462.

45. Prévost and Dumas, *Annales chim. phys.*, 1823, *23*:92.

46. Richerand, *Nouveaux élémens*, 10th ed., II, 144. I have not seen the edition

which Prévost and Dumas were citing (they do not specify it). Although the 10th edition appeared after Prévost and Dumas's experiment, and cited them in confirmation, it appears from Prévost and Dumas's summary that an earlier edition of Richerand contained the same statements that I have quoted here.

47. Wöhler, *Zeit. Physiol.*, 1824, *1*:311–312.

48. Mitscherlich, Gmelin, and Tiedemann, *Zeit. Physiol.*, 1833, *5*:12–15.

49. Joseph Schiller has used Bernard's research on the excretion of urea after extirpation of the kidneys as an example of the research which led Bernard to a further development of Magendie's important conception of a physiological function as "the common goal of the action of a certain number of organs." This view was a crucial advance, Schiller contends, over the common contemporary view that each function must be identified with one organ. This example of urea excretion, however, is not as good support for the distinctiveness or novelty of the approach of Magendie and his student as it seems at first, because, as suggested here, others before Bernard had already expected for this situation that "the presence of an organ is not indispensable to the accomplishment of a function since in its absence compensatory mechanisms enter into play." See Schiller, *Bernard*, pp. 47, 52. Schiller's interpretation, therefore, may need some qualification, although on the whole it is an important insight. Georges Canguilhem has discussed the same general issue, taking a more qualified position, in *Études*, pp. 227–230.

50. Their recognition of the equivalence of urea and ammonia may have been aided by the fact that Dumas had very much emphasized that equivalence in his *Essai de statique chimique* (see pp. 37–39). The explanation Bernard and Barreswil gave, that urea is converted by a kind of fermentation in the stomach, resembled Dumas's description.

51. See above, Chap. XI at n. 72.

52. Bernard and Barreswil, *Archives gén. méd.*, 1847, 13:464–465.

53. Magendie, *Précis*, II, 489; see also Müller, *Handbuch*, I, 585.

54. Mitscherlich, Gmelin, and Tiedemann, *Zeit. Physiol.*, 1833, *5*:12.

55. Magendie, *Précis*, II, 489.

56. Mitscherlich, Gmelin, and Tiedemann, *Zeit. Physiol.*, 1833, *5*:15–18. For further discussion of the influence of Prévost and Dumas's experiment on the general question of secretion, see Mani, *Leberforschung*, II, 302–306.

57. Müller, *Handbuch*, I, 585–586.

58. "Procès verbal de l'assemblée, le 28 Mars 1847," and "Assemblée du Dimanche 14, 1847." MS F^{17}3849, Arch. Nat. See also "Procès verbal de l'assemblée des professeurs," MS, G-11-5, p. 42. During the previous academic year Magendie had a different substitute, apparently Dahremberg (ibid., p. 34).

59. Olmsted, *Magendie*, p. 243.

60. MS G-11-5, pp. 107, 113, 134. The figures are:

Years	Magendie	Bernard
1850–1851	22	21
1851–1852	23	20
1852–1853	10	24

The last year reflects Magendie's lessening activity as his health declined near the end of his life. See Olmsted, *Magendie*, pp. 258–260. According to Olmsted, the 1851–52 course was Magendie's last, but this record suggests that it was only his last *complete* course at the Collège de France.

61. MS F^{17}3849, *Arch. Nat.* This course title is from the description for the second semester of 1848, but it is called a continuation. Bernard, MS C. VIIIe, No. 6, p. 3.

62. MS F^{17}3849, *Arch. Nat.*

63. Olmstead, *Magendie*, p. 250.

64. See above, n. 58.

65. Collège Royal de France. Procès Verbal November 18, 1838, 1843–44, April 5, 1846, MS F^{17}3849, *Arch. Nat.;* Boudet, *J. pharm. chim.*, 1848, *13*:46.

66. Olmsted, *Magendie*, pp. 243, 250.

67. Not the certainty, however. Although Magendie asked and obtained the consent of the assembly of professors in 1853 that "he be eventually replaced by M. Bernard," Bernard still had to go through the formality of a competitive election in 1855. MS G-11-5, pp. 136, 161, 163; "Ministère de l'Instruction Publique, Paris le 16 9bre 1855," MS F^{17} 13555, *Arch. Nat.*

68. "Paris, le 184_, Collège de France"; "Collège Royal de France, Budget de 1846," MS F^{17}3851, *Arch. Nat.;* "Comptes définitifs 1860–1878," (see budgets of Collège de France for 1859, 1860, 1861.) MS F^{17}3852, *Arch. Nat.*

69. "Collège de France, 28 Nov. 1853," letter of the administrator to the minister of public instruction, and reply; "Collège Impérial de France, le 24 Nov. 1854," MS F^{17}3852, *Arch. Nat.;* Olmsted, *Magendie,* p. 261.

70. Olmsted, *Magendie*, p. 231; Bernard, *Physiologie générale*, p. 203.

71. "Collège Royal de France, 14 novembre 1844," and "7 novembre 1845," Letters of the administrator to the minister, MS F^{17}3851, *Arch. Nat.*

72. Bernard, *Physiologie générale*, p. 203.

73. The amusing incident by which this happened is too well-known to bear repeating here. For a detailed account see ibid., pp. 204–206.

74. Ibid., p. 206.

75. Ibid., p. 209.

76. Ibid., p. 206: "... pendant plusieurs années, je pus continuer mes cours privés de physiologie expérimentale dans le quartier .... jusqu' à l'époque où enfin je fus nommé suppléant de Magendie au Collège de France."

CHAPTER XVI: THE PERSISTENCE OF CLAUDE BERNARD

1. See above, Chap. XII at n. 1.

2. Bernard, MS C. VIIIe, 7c, p. 88.

3. Ibid., p. 122.

4. Ibid., pp. 123–147.

5. Olmsted, *Magendie*, p. 250; Grmek, *Catalogue*, pp. 115–122.

6. Bernard, MS C. VIIIe, 7e, pp. 148–150, 156, 162.

7. Ibid., pp. 163–164.

8. Ibid., pp. 164–166.

9. Bernard, MS C. VIIIe, 17e, p.9.

10. Temkin, *Bull. Hist. Med.*, 1946, *20*:10–35; Schiller, *Bernard*, pp. 47–49.

11. Bernard, MS C. VIIIe, 7c, p. 166.

12. See Liebig, *Animal Chemistry*, pp. 12–15; Dumas and Cahours, *Annales sci. nat.*, 1842, *18:*376.

13. Bernard, MS C. VIIIe, 7c, pp.167–169.

14. Ibid., pp. 158–160.

15. Ibid., pp. 182–187.

16. Ibid., p. 186.

17. Ibid., p. 184. The most extensive investigation of the effects upon animals of death by starvation was that submitted to the Academy of Sciences in 1838 by Charles Chossat, awarded the prize in experimental physiology in 1841, and published in 1843. Chossat did not specifically state that the flow of lymph diminishes in the last days of abstinence, but he did present evidence that the volume of blood, the circulation, respiration, the production of animal heat all decrease, leading Chossat to the general inference that the vital processes dependent on the consumption of alimentary materials, including secretions, diminish. See Chossat, *Annales sci. nat.*, 1843, *20:*54–81, 182–214, 293–326, esp. pp. 304–318. His conclusions might easily suggest that the flow of lymph would be included among the diminishing processes.

18. Bernard, MS C. VIIIe, 7c, pp. 172–177.

19. Ibid., pp. 178–181.

20. Ibid., p. 188.

21. Ibid., pp.190–192.

22. Ibid., p. 191.

23. Ibid., p. 197.

24. On October 20 Bernard again observed no urea in the urine of an animal produced during a major operation, and concluded more definitely that the suffering caused the absence (ibid., pp. 196–197). On October 23 he found little urea and much uric acid in a patient recently dead of consumption (ibid., p. 235). The investigation apparently did not go beyond this.

25. For an overview of the development of the problem from Prévost and Dumas to 1924, when it became established that the liver is the source of urea, see Bollman, et al., *American Journal of Physiology*, 1924, *69:*370–392.

26. Holmes, *Isis.*, 1963, *54:*64.

27. Marchand, *J. prakt. Chem.*, 1838, *14:*494–496. Marchand was "personally nearly convinced" that no urea derived from unassimilated nutritive material. Yet the fact that there was a noticeable decrease of urea during the experiment would seem to have left that part of the question open. It could be explained either as due to the subtraction of that part of the urea formed from the aliments, or as due to a lessened vital activity in the tissues and consequently diminished decomposition of their constituents. Perhaps Marchand reached his conclusion because the question had been posed as one of alternative choices rather than with the possibility that both factors might contribute.

28. Liebig, *Animal Chemistry*, pp. 55–58, 60. In my "Introduction" to Liebig's book I oversimplified the basis for Liebig's conclusion by not recognizing the use he made of Marchand's investigation. It is, however, characteristic of the way Liebig slanted such sources in his favor that he wrote, "we know that the urine of dogs, fed for three weeks exclusively on pure sugar, contains as much of the most highly nitrogenized constituent, urea, as in the normal condition. (Marchaud [sic] *J. prakt. Chem.*, XIV, p. 495.)"

29. Bernard, MS C. VIIIe, 7c, pp. 192–193.

30. Bernard, *Introduction* (rep. 1965), p. 64.

31. Bernard, *Société philomatique*, 1848, p. 15; Bernard, MS C. VIIIe, 7c, p. 236. Even these last results were not quite as consistent as he represented the situation in his published note, for he found in another dog neutral bile.

32. See above, Chap. XIII at n. 56.

33. Bernard, *Société philomatique*, 1848, pp. 14–15.

34. It is instructive to compare Bernard's position with that of Lehmann. Lehmann, too, recognized the importance of physiological variations, but he ascribed the difficulties with contemporary analyses of animal fluids and tissues chiefly to the "still too deficient analytical foundations," which were not yet fully adequate to cope with the complex chemical constitution of these biological entities (Lehmann, *Lehrbuch*, I, 7–12).

35. Bernard, *Société philomatique*, 1848, pp. 15–16.

36. Bernard, MS C. VIIIe, 7c, pp. 156–158.

37. The experiments are described above, this chap. at n. 19.

38. Ibid., p. 180.

39. See above, Chap. XI at n. 40.

40. Bernard, MS C. VIIIe, 7c, pp. 193–194.

41. Ibid., pp. 197–199.

42. Ibid., pp. 199–207.

43. Ibid., p. 209.

44. Ibid., p. 208.

45. See above, this chap. at n. 3.

46. See above, Chap. IX at n. 11.

47. In December 1846 he fed large quantities of fat to a dog and then sacrificed it to examine its stomach and intestines. He found emulsified fat in the stomach, both the stomach and intestines acidic, the gall bladder full of bile, and "the lacteal vessels gorged with perfectly white and very abundant chyle." His principal conclusion was that "the exclusive digestion of fat (pig lard) coincides with an excessively acidic intestinal reaction." On January 17, 1847, he performed a similar experiment on a cat. Bernard MS C. VIIIe, 7c, pp. 74–76. (The first experiment is dated 1845, but this is evidently a mistake. Grmek, *Catalogue*, p. 99, reads "December, 1846.")

48. See Grmek, *Catalogue*, p. 120.

49. Bernard, MS C. VIIIe, pp. 212–214.

50. Ibid., pp. 214–215.

51. Ibid., p. 215.

52. Ibid., pp. 216–217.

53. Ibid., p. 218.

54. Ibid., pp. 218–219.

55. Ibid., pp. 219–221.

56. Ibid., pp. 222–223.

57. Ibid., p. 223.

58. Ibid., p. 209.

59. Ibid., pp. 224–225.

60. Ibid., p. 224.

61. Ibid., p. 225.

62. Ibid., 225–227.

63. Ibid., p. 228.

64. Ibid., pp. 228–229.
65. Ibid., p. 229.
66. November 31 according to his notebook! (ibid., p. 210).
67. Ibid., pp. 210–212.
68. Ibid., pp. 231–232.
69. Ibid., p. 232.
70. See above, Chap. IX at n. 9.
71. Bernard, MS C. VIIIe, 7c, pp. 232–233.
72. Bernard, *Cahier*, pp. 138–139.
73. Bernard, MS C. VIIIe, 7c, p. 234.
74. Ibid., p. 239.
75. Ibid., p. 226.
76. Lehmann, *Bericht*, 1849, pp. 8–50.
77. See above, Chap. XIV at n. 51.
78. Bernard, MS C. VIIIe, 24b, feuille 231. Compare also Bernard's statement quoted above in the present "Introduction," at n. 6.
79. Bernard, MS C. VIIIe, No. 5, pp. 41–86. The second section is headed "Leçons sur la digestion. 1ere Leçon. 1848" (ibid., p. 49), and must have been written during the first three months of that year, because the portion on pancreatic juice (pp. 76–77) does not reflect the striking discoveries concerning it that Bernard made at the end of March (see below, Chap. XVII), even though he wrote "My procedures and my apparatus for obtaining pancreatic juice." The first section is undated, so it is not possible to be certain how much earlier Bernard may have begun it.
80. He began a "second plan" for a general work in May 1849, on the following pages (ibid., pp. 87–133). By then his ideas had been modified by the momentous results of his investigations during the intervening year.
81. Ibid., pp. 41–43.
82. Ibid., p. 59.
83. Ibid., pp. 59, 63–72.
84. Ibid., pp. 72–76, 77–80.
85. Ibid., p. 81.
86. Ibid., pp. 83–84.
87. Ibid., p. 85.
88. Ibid., p. 50.
89. Bernard, *An Introduction* (1957), p. 3.
90. Bernard, MS C. VIIIe, No. 5, p. 53.
91. Ibid., p. 86.
92. Canguilhem, *Études*, pp. 152–153.
93. Ibid., pp. 52–53.
94. Bernard, *An Introduction* (1957), p. 22.
95. Réaumur, *Hist. Acad.*, 1752 [Paris, 1754], p. 466.

CHAPTER XVII: THE PANCREATIC JUICE

1. See above, Chap. XVI at n. 2.
2. See below, this chapter at n. 42.
3. Bernard, *C.r. Acad.*, *Supplément*, I, 1856, pp. 413–414. See above, Chap. VII at

nn. 23–25, Chap. XI at n. 63. The first experiment to collect pancreatic juice is supposed to have been that of Regnier de Graaf, in 1662. Bernard believed, however, from de Graaf's procedure and description of the juice, that he probably had never really observed the pancreatic fluid. See Bernard, *Leçons de physiologie expérimentale*, II, 176.

4. The fullest description of the operation is in Bernard, *C.r. Acad., Supplément*, I, 1856, pp. 414–417.

5. Bernard, MS C. VIIIe, 7c, pp. 240–242.

6. Ibid., pp. 242a–242c.

7. Ibid., pp. 242c–242d, 243.

8. Ibid., p. 244.

9. Ibid., p. 245.

10. Ibid., p. 242.

11. Ibid., pp. 246a–246b.

12. Ibid., p. 247.

13. Ibid., p. 249.

14. Ibid., pp. 249–250.

15. Ibid., pp. 250–253.

16. Ibid., pp. 254–255.

17. Ibid., pp. 256–259.

18. Ibid., pp. 259–261.

19. Ibid., pp. 262, 264.

20. See above, Chap. XVI at n. 3.

21. Bernard, MS C. VIIIe, 7c, p. 264.

22. Ibid., p. 265.

23. Ibid., pp. 274–278, 304.

24. Ibid., pp. 279–280.

25. Ibid., pp. 281–283.

26. Brodie, *Quarterly Journal of Science*, 1823, *14*:341–344; Brodie, *J. physiol.*, 1823, *3*:93–94. Bernard lists the letter as containing Magendie's result, but it does not. Magendie merely reports "Je me propose de répéter les expériences de M. Brodie." I have not found a statement of his own result by Magendie.

27. Bernard, MS C. VIIIe, 7c, pp. 283–284.

28. Bernard, *Mém. Soc. Biol.*, 1849, pp. 113–114.

29. Bernard, *Introduction* (rep. 1965), p. 323.

30. Bernard, *C.r. Acad., Supplément*, I, 1856, p. 466, n. 1. "J'avais même cru pouvoir expliquer par cette union d'un conduit pancréatique unique avec le canal cholédoque, chez le chat, les dissidences qui existent entre les expériences de MM. Magendie et Brodie. Mais dupuis j'ai voulu vérifier par moi-même l'anatomie du pancréas chez le chat, et j'ai toujours trouvé deux conduits...." Olmsted remarks that Bernard "was able to clear up the difference," but does not take note of this complication. See Olmsted, *Magendie*, p. 236, and Olmsted and Olmsted, *Bernard*, p. 50.

31. Bernard, MS C. VIIIe, 7c, pp. 285–286.

32. Bernard, *Bulletin Société Philomatique*, 1848, pp. 34–36.

33. Ibid., p. 36.

34. Bernard, *Physiologie expérimentale*, II, 1–21, 173–175, 377.

35. See above, Chap. XI at n. 65.

36. See above, Chap. XIV at n. 10.

37. Bernard, *Mém. Soc. Biol.*, 1849, p. 115; Bernard, *Physiologie expérimentale*, II, 372–377.

38. Following his first presentation Bernard was able to separate organic matter sufficiently to characterize it as a coagulable substance possessing properties common to albumin and casein but not identical to either. On this basis he called it a substance "which plays the role of a true ferment" (Bernard, *Physiologie expérimentale*, II, 238–241). See also, Bernard, *Introduction*, (rep. 1965), pp. 270–271. "In fact pancreatic juice obtained in suitable conditions . . . mixed with oil or melted fat instantly emulsified in a consistent manner, and later acidified these fatty bodies, decomposing them into fatty acids, glycerine, etc., etc., with the help of a specific ferment."

39. Olmsted and Olmsted, *Bernard*, pp. 49–60.

40. Bert, "Claude Bernard," 1957, p. xvi.

41. Bernard, *Mém. Soc. Biol.*, 1849, p. 113.

42. Bernard, *C.r. Acad.*, *Supplément*, I, 1856, pp. 380–381.

43. Bernard, *Physiologie expérimentale*, II, 178.

44. Bernard, *Introduction* (rep. 1965), pp. 153–154.

45. Olmsted and Olmsted base their account on Bernard's later statements when they say, "Bernard worked at his experiments for more than two years before he published his results in a preliminary form in April, 1848" (Olmsted and Olmsted, *Bernard*, p. 54).

46. Eberle, *Verdauung*, pp. 251–253.

47. Longet, *Traité*, I, 260–261. The first edition, which I have not seen, but which probably contained essentially the same account, was published in 1850. See also Frerichs, "Verdauung," p. 847. (Despite the publication date, the article was written sometime after the beginning of 1849. See note on p. 871).

48. Bernard, *C.r. Acad.*, *Supplément*, , I, 1856, p. 445.

49. Bernard, *Physiologie expérimentale*, II, 268.

50. Frerichs, "Verdauung," p. 847.

51. Ibid., p. 846; Lehmann, *Lehrbuch*, II, 94.

52. Magendie, Milne Edwards, Dumas, *C.r. Acad.*, 1849, 28:283–285.

53. Frerichs, "Verdauung," pp. 846–850, 871; Poggendorff, *Biographisch-literarisches Handwörterbuch*, I, 798–799.

54. Lehmann, *Lehrbuch*, II, 93–95.

55. Bernard listed some of them in *C.r. Acad.*, *Supplément*, I, 1856, p. 381.

56. Ibid., pp. 428, 447–450, 458–460, 462–465.

57. See particularly his discussion in ibid., pp. 469–470. For an illustration of recent shifts in the answer to the question compare the discussion in Fulton, ed., *A Textbook of Physiology*, pp. 1023–1024, with that in its successor, Ruch and Fulton, eds., *Medical Physiology and Biophysics*, pp. 944–945.

58. Bernard, *Mém. Soc. Biol.*, 1849, p. 115.

59. Bernard, *Physiologie expérimentale*, II, 178.

60. Ibid., *passim*. The discussion of pepsin is on pp. 399–401.

61. Ibid., pp. 401, 417–419, 422, 424, 425.

62. Albuminose did not turn out to be a single species, of course. Already Lehmann had found differences among the materials derived from different foods, and named the products peptones. Bernard also claimed to have found a material answering to the character of albuminose in pure gastric juice (ibid., p. 421). Clearly there was vagueness concerning the substance, but my point is that by the tests and infor-

mation available at the time, Mialhe's identification of a substance was reasonable enough to deserve more serious consideration than Bernard seemed to give it.

63. In later years when he taught the same subject his treatment had considerably moderated, and he had accepted more of the by-then conventional description of gastric digestion. Even then traces of his earlier biases still remained. See Bernard, *Leçons sur les phénomènes*, II, 283–310.

64. Bernard so completely identified the progress of physiology with his own efforts that he wrote in his *Cahier rouge*, "I am the director of the present physiological movement." Bernard, *Cahier*, p. 188.

65. Maillard, *Le Figaro*, July 15, 1868.

66. Frerichs, "Verdauung," pp. 756 n. 1, 758 n. 1, 769–771, 733, 782, 795, 796–798, 800, 808, 824.

67. Lehmann, *Lehrbuch*, II, 42.

68. See especially Frerichs, "Verdauung," pp. 737–738.

69. Ibid., p. 810, 847. He criticized, however, Mialhe's theory of salivary diastase (ibid., pp. 763, 772).

70. "Bernard ist ein grosses Talent, aber sehr voreilig." *Zwei grosse Naturforscher*, ed. Estelle Du Bois-Reymond, p. 65.

71. Du Bois-Reymond, "Müller," p. 186.

CHAPTER XVIII: THE SEARCH FOR SUGAR

1. *C.r. Soc. Biol.*, 1849, *1*:1–2.

2. Mendelsohn, *History of Science*, 1964, *3*:40.

3. Blainville, *Cours*, I, 18–19.

4. Comte, *Cours*, III, 269 n. 1, 279–288, 305–312.

5. Robin, *Mém. Soc. Biol.*, 1849, *1*:i–xi; Canguilhem, *Etudes*, 1968, pp. 71–72.

6. See, for example, Bernard, *Leçons de pathologie*, pp. 9, 428–429, 430, 461–462, etc.

7. Comte, *Cours*, III, 228–234.

8. Ibid., pp. 241–251.

9. Canguilhem, *Études*, p. 71.

10. See above, Chap. XVI at nn. 34–35. Compare Bernard, *Société philomatique*, 1848, pp. 14–16, first and last paragraphs of the note, with Comte, *Cours*, III, 237–239.

11. Charlton, *Positivist Thought*, pp. 19–21.

12. Comte, *Cours*, III, 227–228, 252–267, 312–341.

13. Bernard, MS C. VIIIe,7c, pp. 289–292.

14. Ibid., p. 293.

15. See above, Chap. XII at nn. 40–44.

16. Bernard, MS C. VIIIe, 7c, p. 295.

17. Bichat, *Recherches*, p. 105.

18. Comte, *Cours*, III, 288.

19. For the difficulty one contemporary had in freeing himself from ideas of Bichat on which he had been brought up, see Bérard, *Cours*, I, 131–132.

20. Bichat, *Recherches*, p. 10.

21. Comte, *Cours*, III, 295; Blainville, *Histoire des sciences*, III, 201–202; Bernard, MS C. VIIIe, No. 14e, p. 43.

22. See below, Chap. XIX at nn. 53–55.

23. Bernard, MS C. VIIIe, 7c, p. 293.

24. Müller, *Handbuch*, I, 153, 476, 563.

25. See above, Chap. III at n. 87.

26. Bichat, *Recherches*, p. 8.

27. Ibid., p. 11. Here Bichat used the terms "assimilation" and "désassimilation," in keeping with his less chemical conception of the process. He used these more often than "composition" and "décomposition," although he seemed to regard them as synonymous. Georges Canguilhem's perceptive essay "Claude Bernard et Bichat," *Études*, 1968, pp. 156–162, discusses the special affinity between the ideas of Bichat and those of Bernard's later writings.

28. Bernard, MS C. VIIIe,7c, pp. 316–319.

29. Ibid., pp. 305–306.

30. Ibid., p. 307.

31. Ibid., pp. 339–349.

32. See above, Chap. VIII at n. 41, Chap. XII at n. 40.

33. Bernard, MS C. VIIIe, 7c, p. 308.

34. Everett Mendelsohn has assumed that such a relation held generally for Bernard's work. For a general discussion of this issue, see below, Chap. XX at nn. 23–29.

35. Bernard, MS C. VIIIe, 7c, p. 308.

36. Ibid., pp. 308–309.

37. Ibid., pp. 309–310.

38. Ibid., p. 311. The remainder of the material in this chapter and most of the following chapter has been treated in Grmek, "La glycogenèse," pp. 200–209. It is necessary to repeat the story which Professor Grmek has already told well, in order to fill out the overall plan of the present volume. We differ also in the interpretation of one crucial event, as will be seen below.

39. Bernard, MS C. VIIIe, 10b, p. 105. This note was written in 1857. It was Berzelius who first designated the nutritional theories of Liebig and Dumas the physiology of "probabilities." See Holmes, "Introduction," p. lx.

40. Bernard, *Introduction* (rep. 1965), pp. 228–229.

41. See above, Chap. VI at n. 41.

42. Bernard, MS C. VIIIe,7c, p. 311.

43. Ibid., pp. 320–322.

44. Ibid., pp. 313–314.

45. Ibid., pp. 332bis, 328bis and verso.

46. This assumes that he no longer held, as he did in 1845, that the absorption is through the lymphatic system. See above, Chap. XII at n. 46.

47. Bernard, MS C. VIIIe,7c, unnumbered pages inserted following p. 330. Bernard may also have been influenced by the pattern of Magendie's earlier and similar experiments. See above, Chap. V at n. 43.

48. It is possible that he saw that the substitution of one type of nutrient for another in respiratory combustion could compensate for such fluctuations in the consumption of any one of them. If he had thought out his position so far, however, one would expect to find some trace of it in his reflections at the time. Moreover, a little further on he indicated that he expected that when sugar is exhausted within an animal its respiration of CO_2 might cease. By that time his discovery of a new source of sugar had

changed the particular nature of his problem, but the expectation then still helps elucidate his approach at this time. See below, Chap. XIX at nn. 21–23. The experiments on animal heat undertaken with Magendie in 1843 (see Chap. VI at nn. 16–21) might have left Bernard with lingering doubts about the general chemical theory. Later on, Bernard explicitly formulated grounds for skepticism concerning the equation of animal heat with the combustion of food, basing his criticisms on the experiments of Regnault and Reiset, which showed that the whole problem was more complicated than hitherto assumed. See Bernard, *Introduction* (rep. 1965), pp. 233–234.

49. See above, Chap. XII at nn. 2–10.

50. Bernard, MS C. VIIIe, 7c, p. 312.

51. Ibid., p. 327.

52. Ibid., pp. 331–332.

53. Ibid., pp. 328–329, 355–336.

54. Ibid., pp. 337, 333–334.

55. Ibid., p. 323.

56. Grmek, *Catalogue*, p. 121. The experiment concerned the nervous system.

57. Bernard, MS C. VIIIe, 7c, pp. 324, 368.

58. Pelouze to Liebig, November 1, 1848, MS, Liebigiana 58, No. 75, BS, M.

59. Ibid., pp. 357–358.

60. Ibid., pp. 332bis, 333, 336–338.

61. Ibid., pp. 359–361.

62. Bernard, *Introduction* (rep. 1965), pp. 318–319.

63. See above, Chap. XII at nn. 57–58. In 1853 Bernard maintained that since 1843 he had suspected that the animal organism is "capable of giving rise to sugar with something other than amylaceous substances," because diabetics excrete much more sugar than they are furnished by sugar or starch (Bernard, *Nouvelle fonction du foie*, pp. 8–9). Therefore Bernard himself afterward gave two contradictory accounts of his opinion prior to August 1848. This second account, however, is also suspect, for he added that ". . . from 1843, these facts became for me a motive for physiological investigation." The record does not sustain his recollection that between 1843 and 1848 the search for a non-starch source of sugar in animals was a major theme of his research.

64. Bernard, MS C. VIIIe, 7c, pp. 368–378; Bernard, *Mém. Soc. Biol.*, 1849, *1:*105; Bernard, *C.r. Acad., Supplément*, I, 1856, p. 419.

65. Bernard, MS C. VIIIe, 7c, p. 379. The fact that the "extremely small amount" was 15 grams shows how difficult such tests were at the time.

66. Ibid., pp. 379–381.

67. Ibid., pp. 381–382.

68. Bernard, *Introduction* (rep. 1965), pp. 286–287.

69. Ibid., pp. 318–319.

70. Ibid., p. 287; Grmek, *J. Hist. Biol.*, 1968, *1:*153. Grmek quotes Bernard's laboratory notebook of this experiment in full in his longer treatment of the same subject, in "La glycogenèse," pp. 203–204. There he does not state the above interpretation so directly, but his overall account implies it.

71. Grmek, *J. Hist. Biol.*, 1968, *1:*150–151. Owing to a translator's error, the last word of this sentence is given incorrectly as "reactive" in the original.

72. Bernard, *Introduction* (rep. 1965), p. 288.

CHAPTER XIX: THE SOURCE OF SUGAR
IN ANIMALS

1. Bernard, MS C. VIIIe, 7c, pp. 382–384.
2. Ibid., pp. 355–356.
3. Ibid., pp. 248, 360bis.
4. Ibid., p. 385.
5. Ibid., pp. 387–389.
6. Bernard, *Archives gén. méd.*, 1848, *18*:308.
7. Bernard, MS C. VIIIe, 7c, pp. 388–391.
8. Ibid., p. 392.
9. Ibid., p. 396.
10. Ibid., p. 398.
11. Ibid., pp. 392, 397–398.
12. MS, Dossier of the meeting of August 28, 1848, AAdSc.; *C.r. Acad.*, 1848, 27:247. Two of the most comprehensive recent descriptions of Bernard's investigation say that Bernard and Barreswil submitted on this date their note "De la presence du sucre dans le foie," *C.r. Acad.*, 1848, 27:514–515, which was actually communicated to the meeting of November 13, 1848 (see Olmsted and Olmsted, *Bernard*, pp. 64–65; Grmek, "La glycogenèse, pp. 205–206). The first comprehensive bibliography of Bernard's publications, Coudraie, "Table alphabétique," p. 342, also gives the errone-ous date of August 28 for the joint communication. Professor Grmek, who now agrees that the published note was read on November 13, gives the following explanation for the origin of the mistake: "Claude Bernard himself attributed the date of August 28, 1848, to his communication of November 13. The error was repeated by Roger de la Coudraie, then by Olmsted and Grmek. The sealed note was not opened, and in Ber-nard's mind it already contained the essential features of his note of November 13. Even while giving the incorrect date, Grmek noticed a chronological difficulty be-cause Bernard expressed in that note ideas which he had not yet confirmed in August 1848." M. D. Grmek, personal communication, August 1971 (my translation). Since the sealed note has not been found, its contents cannot be directly confirmed, but the circumstantial evidence of its general character seems very strong. The published note was not, therefore, the initial announcement of Bernard's discovery of sugar in the liver, but a follow-up of his more comprehensive memoir read on October 21.
13. Bernard, MS C. VIIIe, 7c, pp. 393–394, 403.
14. See above, Chap. VI at n. 1. See also Bernard, *Nouvelle fonction du foie*, pp. 10–11.
15. Bernard, MS C. VIIIe, 7c, p. 401.
16. Ibid., p. 402.
17. Ibid., pp. 404–407.
18. Ibid., pp. 410, two pages inserted following 410.
19. Bernard, MS C. VIIIe, 7g, p. 4.
20. Ibid., pp. 4–5.
21. Ibid., pp. 6–7.
22. Ibid., p. 8.
23. Ibid., p. 11.
24. Ibid.
25. Ibid.

26. Ibid., pp. 1–2.

27. Ibid., pp. 13–14.

28. Bernard, *Archives gén. méd.*, 1848, *18*:315.

29. In his later researches Bernard was able to eliminate the ambiguity which this early formulation covered. After refining his analytical methods, he eventually could show that the blood contained sugar under all conditions. A prolonged abstinence did not cause it to disappear, and even at the moment of death of an animal by starvation he could still detect sugar, "only in more and more feeble proportion." Bernard, *Leçons sur le diabète*, pp. 130–131. By then his phrase "independent of aliments" could be taken to mean that the animal can form sugar without an alimentary source so long as it can survive at all. Obviously, the phrase still cannot be taken literally, for such animals are utilizing materials which once were aliments.

30. We have seen repeatedly that the definitive results which Bernard used in his published records are often those which are missing in the laboratory notebooks.

31. Bernard, MS C. VIIIe, 7g, p. 12.

32. An argument against regarding this observation as the initial one is that Bernard made no comment about it and went immediately on to a remark about another property of portal vein blood. That would suggest either that he did not immediately see the significance of the result or that he was confirming a previous observation of the same phenomenon. His published accounts describe his definitive demonstration, but provide little additional insight on how he first discovered the clue.

33. Bernard, *Archives gén. méd.*, 1848, *18*:303.

34. Ibid., p. 304.

35. Ibid., p. 318. Grmek has also noted discrepancies between the order of experiments presented in Bernard's memoir and the chronological record in his notebook. Grmek, "La glycogenése," p. 207.

36. For example, the "1re expérience" (ibid., pp. 304–305) is evidently that of June 11, described in MS C. VIIIe, 7c, pp. 333–334. The original, however, describes the analysis for sugar of blood from four different places, whereas the memoir says only that Bernard ascertained that sugar was present in the blood.

37. Bernard, *Archives gén. méd.*, 1848, *18*:307.

38. Nikolaus Mani, in his careful study of Bernard's investigations of the liver, has treated Bernard's memoir as an accurate representation of the course of the investigation (*Leberforschung*, pp. 350–353).

39. Bernard, *Archives gén. méd.*, 1848, *18*:304–308.

40. Ibid., p. 309.

41. Ibid., p. 310. He did not intend to imply that this is true even if the animal is digesting starch or sugar.

42. Bernard, *Le Moniteur des hôpitaux*, 1855, *3*:258.

43. Olmsted, *Bernard*, pp. 169–170. Documents and editorials relative to the debate were printed in *Le Moniteur des hôpitaux*, 1855, *3*:129–130, 133–135, 144–146, 150–156, 192, 257–259, 313–314, 317–319, etc.

44. Bernard, *Archives gén. méd.*, 1848, *18*:314–316.

45. Ibid., pp. 313, 316.

46. Bernard, MS C. VIIIe, 7g, p. 3.

47. Olmsted, *Bernard*, pp. 170–172. Using a quantitative adaptation of Barreswil's test, Chauveau was able to show in 1856 that there is regularly a slightly lower concentration of sugar in the blood of a given vein than in the collateral artery. He

concluded that "a certain quantity of glucose of the arterial blood disappeared during the passage of this fluid through the capillaries of the general circulation." He found no evidence of sugar disappearing in the passage through the lungs. Chauveau, *C.r. Acad.*, 1856, *42*:1008–1012. Later Bernard also adopted quantitative measurements and reached a similar conclusion. See Bernard, *Leçons sur le diabète*, pp. 228–236.

48. The simplicity was deceptive, of course, for, as the preceding note suggests, the problem of determining blood sugars became the issue on which Bernard's theory turned. This difficulty only entered at a later stage of the problem, however.

49. Bernard, *Archives gén. méd.*, 1848, *18*:312. These remarks leave a question concerning how active Bernard's coauthor Barreswil was in the investigation. Clearly Bernard wrote the memoir from his own point of view alone, for Barreswil as a chemist would not be likely to have collaborated on the statement: "Il serait peut-être d'un grand intérêt pour les chimistes de pouvoir séparer et analyser le sucre du foie; mais, à mon point de vue, la chose ne me semble pas indispensable." The part which Barreswil played in the experiments themselves is not visible either in the notebooks or the memoir. In 1853, however, Bernard wrote, referring to the experiments reported there, "Beaucoup de ces expériences chimiques ont été faites dans le laboratoire de M. Pelouze, de concert avec mon ami M. Barreswil" (Bernard, *Nouvelle fonction*, p. 16). Barreswil himself felt that he had been a true partner with Bernard in this as in their earlier collaborations. In a paper which touched on several of those investigations he wrote, "les expériences communes à M. Bernard et à moi prouvent que le sang des animaux ... renferme constamment du sucre lors même qu'il n'a reçu aucune matière végétale, ..." He described other investigations similarly: for example, of the lactic acid in gastric juice he wrote, "à celui que nous avons avancé, M. Bernard et moi, sur le suc gastrique" (Barreswil, *J. pharm. chim.*, 1850, *17*:119).

50. The later phases of the story are described in Olmsted, *Bernard*, pp. 162–174; Young, *Annals of Science*, 1937, *2*:47–83; Mani, *Leberforschung*, pp. 353–364.

51. Milne Edwards, *Leçons*, VII, 560–561.

52. He referred to his articles on "experiments on the diverse chemical manifestations of substances introduced into the organism." See above, Chap. XV at n. 35.

53. Bernard, *Archives gén. méd.*, 1848, *18*:316–317.

54. See above, Chap. III at n. 80.

55. See above, Chap. III at nn. 72–73.

56. See above, Chap. III at n. 87.

57. Bernard, *Nouvelle fonction*, pp. 7–8.

58. See Canguilhem, "Preface," pp. 9–10.

59. Bernard, *Introduction* (rep. 1965), p. 287.

CHAPTER XX: CONCLUSION

1. Bernard, *Principes*, p. 242.

2. Lehmann, *Lehrbuch*, II, 31.

3. This generalization is based chiefly on the evidence from the time period covered by this study. Clearly, such limitations did not prevent him from producing later on a model chemical investigation in the isolation of glycogen and demonstration of its conversion to glucose. A careful study of his later career would, I suspect, show that Bernard did devote more attention to chemical methods during the next decade, but

still only within the somewhat narrow scope of the methods which he directly needed for his own physiological investigations.

4. Bert, "Les Travaux de Claude Bernard," p. 75.

5. Bernard, *Introduction* (rep. 1965), p. 228.

6. Ibid.

7. That was a temporary result of Bernard's thought, for the difficulty disappeared *after* he discovered the source of sugar in the liver. It was only while he still regarded alimentation as the source of the sugar that the absurd consequence would arise. The point is simply that he apparently did not see the incongruity while it was present.

8. See above, Chap. V at nn. 42–45.

9. Despite the paradox that Dumas had once participated in a classic vivisection experiment; but that was nearly twenty years earlier.

10. Schiller, *Bernard*, pp. 59–90.

11. Bernard, *Principes*, p. 245.

12. Lehmann, *Lehrbuch*, I, pp. 15–16; II, pp. 31–32. Lehmann nevertheless fully appreciated the importance of Bernard's discovery of the production of sugar in the liver, and became one of Bernard's principal supporters in the ensuing controversy.

13. Hagstrom, *The Scientific Community*, p. 194.

14. Bernard, *Principes*, p. 247.

15. See Schiller, *Bernard*, p. 86.

16. Liebig, *Animal Chemistry*, p. xxvii.

17. "Lehmann," *Biographisches Lexicon*, ed. Gurlt, Wernich, and Hirsch, 2nd ed. (Berlin: Urban and Schwarzenberg, 1931), III, p. 727.

18. Lehmann's was not the first attempt at such a view. See Hünefeld, *Physiologische Chemie*.

19. Lehmann, *Lehrbuch*, I, pp. 9–16.

20. Bernard, *Principes*, p. 245.

21. This recurring question is one of the main themes of an important new book by Joseph S. Fruton, *Molecules and Life*.

22. Henderson, *Physiological Reviews*, 1925, 5:132.

23. Mendelsohn, *History of Science*, 1964, 3:45. From personal conversations with Professor Mendelsohn I believe that he has since modified his opinion.

24. See above, Chap. XVIII at n. 33.

25. See above, Chap. XVIII at nn. 7–8.

26. One might reply that Bernard's choice of a research career itself, and his decision to begin it as assistant to Magendie, already reflected underlying philosophical considerations. The general accounts of Bernard's entry into his field suggest more fortuitous circumstances, but these are so far only treated at the anecdotal level. A more profound study of the intellectual influences Bernard probably encountered between 1834 and 1840 is badly needed.

27. Charlton, *Positivist Thought*, pp. 51–81.

28. See above, Chap. I at n. 1; Bernard, *Introduction*, 3rd. ed., pp. 147–151; and Bernard, *Principes*, pp. 244–247.

29. Bernard, *Principes*, p. 247.

Index

Absorption, 126-128, 183-184, 236, 239, 263
Albuminose, 301-303, 397-398, 408, 445, 526 n.62
Albuminous matters, 148-149; *see also* "Animal" matters
Anatomy and physiology, 390
Andral, Gabriel, 284
Animal heat, 3-5, 37-38, 114-115, 404; experiments of Magendie and Bernard on, 123-125; Bernard and, 448, 529 n.48
"Animal" matters: composition of, 20, 30-31, 54-55; classification of, 24, 146-149; chemical tests for, 146-148, 151, 170-171, 174, 216; *see also* Nitrogenous nutrients
Arago, François, 10, 103

Barreswil, Charles-Louis: test for sugar, 187, 203; collaboration with Claude Bernard, 203, 213, 419, 511 n.79, 516 n.47, 532 n.49; joint research with Bernard, 215-219, 222-228, 237-243, 295, 332-335; Bernard and, theory of digestion, 242, 298-300; analyses for Bernard, 296, 384, 387
Baumé, Antoine, 145-146
Beaumont, William, 121, 166, 274, 370, 504 n.12; and gastric juice theory of digestion, 157; and Blondlot, 187
Beccari, Iacopo Bartolomea, 146
Bérard, Pierre Honoré, 121, 300
Bernard, Claude: experiments with gelatin, 13-15, 215-219; experiments on sites of chemical reactions in animals, 129-131, 134-136, 321-330, 501 n.49, 501 n.65; experi-

ments with gastric juice, 198-202, 220, 223-226, 249-253, 254-255, 305-312, 357-366, 381, 385, 416-417; experiments on injection of aliments, 199-200, 203, 210, 215, 217, 225-226, 248-250, 259-260, 285-286, 302, 410, 412-415, 418, 426-427, 429-430, 512 n.4; experiments on influence of nerves on digestion, 219-220, 260-261, 271, 285-286, 289; experiments on pancreatic digestion, 238, 240-243, 358, 362, 377-396, 418; experiments on excretion of urea, 238-239, 332-335, 345-351; experiments on action of saliva, 240-244, 254, 257, 278-283, 305-316; experiments on effects of diet on urine, 258-261, 283-289, 295-297, 341-354; experiments on destruction of sugar in animals, 410-420; experiments on source of sugar in animals, 420-437
  and respiration, 5-6, 123-125; and fermentation, 176, 275-276, 312-315, 324-326, 329, 361-362; theory of digestion, 209-210, 242-243, 252, 255-256, 262-263, 299-300, 311, 361; definition of aliment, 210, 218, 270-271; theory of nutrition, 261-267, 406-408; on experiment and observation, 372-373; and relation between chemistry and physiology, *see* Chemistry and physiology
  and Liebig, 119, 133, 158, 176, 264, 344, 447-448; and Dumas, 119-121, 133, 138, 158, 187, 245, 264, 267-268, 275, 284, 335-336, 344, 394, 408, 423-425, 437, 442-444, 447-448; and Magendie,